JOHN DONNE: THE CRITICAL HERITAGE

Volume II

THE CRITICAL HERITAGE SERIES

GENERAL EDITOR: B. C. SOUTHAM, M.A., B.LITT. (OXON.)
Formerly Department of English, Westfield College,
University of London

The Critical Heritage series collects together a large body of criticism on major figures in literature. Each volume presents the contemporary responses to a particular writer, enabling the student to follow the formation of critical attitudes to the writer's work and its place within a literary tradition.

The carefully selected sources range from landmark essays in the history of criticism to fragments of contemporary opinion and little-published documentary material, such as letters and diaries.

Significant pieces of criticism from later periods are also included in order to demonstrate fluctuations in reputation following the writer's death.

For a list of volumes in the series, see the end of the book.

JOHN DONNE

THE CRITICAL HERITAGE

Volume II

Edited by
PROFESSOR A. J. SMITH

Completed with introductory and
editorial material by
CATHERINE PHILLIPS

London and New York

First published 1996
by Routledge
2 Park Square, Milton Park, Abingdon, Oxfordshire OX14 4RN

Simultaneously published in the USA and Canada by
Routledge
711 Third Avenue, New York, NY 10017

First issued in paperback 2014

Routledge is an imprint of the Taylor and Francis Group, an informa business

Transferred to Digital Printing 2008

Typeset in Baskerville by
Ponting–Green Publishing Services, Chesham, Bucks

British Library Cataloguing in Publication Data
A catalogue record for this book is available from
the British Library

Library of Congress Cataloguing in Publication Data
John Donne: the critical heritage / edited by A. J. Smith;
completed with introductory and editorial material
by Catherine Phillips.
    p.   cm. – (The critical heritage series)
Includes bibliographical references and index.
ISBN 978-0-415-07445-2 (hbk)
ISBN 978-0-415-75590-0 (pbk)
1. Donne, John, 1572–1631–Criticism and interpretation.
I. Smith, A. J. (Albert James)
II. Phillips, Catherine.   III. Series.
        PR2248.J63   1996
        821'.3–dc20   96–1910
                    CIP

Publisher's Note
The publisher has gone to great lengths to ensure the quality
of this reprint but points out that some imperfections in the
original may be apparent

General Editor's Preface

This second Donne volume covers a key period of fifty years – from the remarks of Henry Morley in 1873 to Eliot's review of the *Love Poems* in 1923 – a half-century which saw the full emergence of Donne as a widely-known poet and, moreover, a powerful influence upon the development of modern poetry.

What enabled this process was Grosart's great edition of 1872–3. This firmly established Donne's standing among the great English poets, a place in the canon consolidated by the editors and critics of the time, including the notable and revealing contributions by Gosse, Chambers, Saintsbury, Dowden, Symons, Grierson, Edward Thomas, Bridges, Yeats and Pound. Beyond their focus upon Donne are the wider implications of the way in which literary tastes and canons change. As the late Professor Smith commented in his Preface to the earlier Donne volume (1975), 'Donne has challenged his critics from the first, so that the successive revaluations of him tend to mirror changing critical assumptions' (p. xv). Of such challenge and change, this second volume provides the documentation we need to trace and analyse these literary and cultural processes.

B. C. S.

Contents

CONTENTS

Preface

This second volume of the reception of Donne was titled by the late Professor A. J. Smith, 'The Critical Rehabilitation of John Donne'. When his typescript was given to me to complete it contained a plan of the book, most of the excerpts from commentaries on Donne's poems, and seven pages out of a projected total of twenty-five pages allocated to an Introduction. Not having had the opportunity of knowing Professor Smith and discussing the project with him, I decided against trying to expand his Introduction and instead have made a summary of the material he gathered. It is deeply regrettable that he was unable to complete his contribution to our understanding of Donne. The excerpts he left make a fascinating tale of changing ideas about the nature of poetry, about the effect of social mores on a writer's reputation, and I have appreciated the privilege of working on it. I have expanded over half the headnotes, trying not to alter the judgements that were explicit or implicit in Professor Smith's wording. The selections by Gosse (1891, 1921), Anon. *The Academy* (1897 and 1900), Anon. *The Dial* (1905), H. J. C. Grierson (1909), J. L. Lowes (1919) and Louise I. Guiney (1920) are mine. I am also responsible for the appendices and apologize for omissions and errors in what was a lengthy treasure-hunt for bibliographical detail.

Catherine Phillips
Downing College
Cambridge

Acknowledgements

It has unfortunately not been possible to identify individuals whose assistance the late Professor A. J. Smith would have wished to acknowledge. I am grateful to Professor Howard Erskine-Hill for suggesting that I undertake the completion of the book and to Dr Richard Luckett, Sandra Dawe of the Pendlebury Music Library, and Julie Crawley, Music Librarian of the University of Exeter Library, for help with the compilation of settings of Donne's poems to music. I am much obliged to the Oxford University Press for permission to reprint excerpts from: (i) vol. ii of *The Poems of John Donne* edited by Herbert John Clifford Grierson, Oxford University Press, 1912; (ii) *Donne's Sermons: Selected Passages, with an Essay* by Logan Pearsall Smith, Oxford University Press, 1919; (iii) a letter by W. B. Yeats, edited by John Kelly et al., Oxford University Press, W. B. Yeat's poem, 'To a Young Beauty' is reprinted with permission of A. P. Watt Ltd from *The Wild Swans at Coole* and Simon & Schuster *from The Poems of W. B. Yeats: A New Edition*, edited by Richard J. Finneran, copyright 1919 by Macmillan Publishing company, renewed 1945 by Bertha Georgie Yeats. Thanks are given to A. P. Watt Ltd for permission to include an extract from W. B. Yeat's 'The Tragic Generation' out of *The Trembling of the Veil* (1922), reprinted in *Autobiographies*, Macmillan Press, 1961. Cambridge University Press kindly gave permission for the inclusion of 'John Donne, Poetry and Prose' by Herbert John Clifford Grierson in vol. iv of *The Cambridge History of English Literature*, Cambridge University Press, 1909. Excerpts from *Selected Essays* by T. S. Eliot, copyright 1950 by Harcourt Brace & Company and renewed 1978 by Esmé Valerie Eliot, are reprinted by permission of the publisher. The excerpt from *The Letters of T. S. Eliot, 1898–1922* by T. S. Eliot, copyright 1989 by SET Copyrights Limited is reprinted by permission of Harcourt, Brace & Company. Grateful acknowledgement is also made to Faber and Faber and the Estate of T. S. Eliot for permission to include extracts by T. S. Eliot from *Selected Essays, The Letters of T. S. Eliot: vol. I 1898–1922* edited by Valerie Eliot, and from his articles in the *Athenaeum, The Nation and Athenaeum* and *A*

ACKNOWLEDGEMENTS

Garland for John Donne. We are grateful to *The Sewanee Review* for permission to reprint Arthur H. Nethercot's article, 'The Reputation of John Donne as Metrist', which was first published in the *Sewanee Review* vol. 30 no.4 Fall, 1922. Thanks are also owed to Yale University Press, who published Edward Bliss Reed's *English Lyrical Poetry* in 1912. Considerable efforts were made to contact possible copyright holders affected by the newly extended copyright law. The publishers would welcome correspondence from any copyright holders they were unable to trace.

Catherine Phillips
Downing College
Cambridge

Note on the text

Documents follow the form of the original texts. Extracts are shown as such and excisions noted. Quotations from Donne's poems have sometimes been omitted, and line-references supplied. Titles and lines of poems are given as they were quoted, and regularized by the standard modern editions only in the editor's commentary. The editions of Donne used for this purpose are the following:

The Poems of John Donne, ed. H. J. C. Grierson, Oxford, 1912.

John Donne: The Divine Poems, ed. Helen Gardner, Oxford, 1952.

John Donne: The Elegies and the Songs and Sonnets, ed. Helen Gardner, Oxford, 1965.

John Donne: The Satires, Epigrams and Verse Letters, ed. W. Milgate, Oxford, 1967.

John Donne: The Complete English Poems, ed. A. J. Smith, Harmondsworth, 1971.

Introduction

Asked to name the most important person in the rehabilitation of John Donne's reputation, most people, would say, 'T. S. Eliot'; a few would probably recall H. J. C. Grierson's work. This volume shows how changes in literary and social values led symbiotically to the rediscovery of Donne and the preparation of public taste to admire Modernist writers such as Eliot. Appreciation of Donne in the eighteenth century was so slight that during the whole of it only three editions of his verse were produced. The nineteenth century saw eight fairly substantial collections and by 1872-3 – the point at which this book opens – there was sufficient interest to support annotated editions that filled two volumes. Writers, such as Edmund Gosse and George Saintsbury, attempted to construct from these collections biographical and stylistic analyses until, early in the twentieth century, glaring anomalies in interpretation led to realization that little more could be achieved without thorough re-examination of the text of the poems. Grierson's two-volume edition of 1912 was timely and immediately hailed for its careful collation of the manuscripts and early printings. It laid the foundations for other scholars, among them John Hayward, Helen Gardner, Theodore Redpath, W. Milgate and A. J. Smith.[1] Donne's poetry attracted one of early facsimile editions with a copy in 1969 of the first edition of 1633 (which Grierson had used as his copy-text), followed in 1988 by facsimiles of the First and Second Dalhousie Manuscripts. In the variorum format, however, only the first volume of the projected University of Missouri Variorum Edition was available by 1992.

Opinion of Donne has depended heavily on which and how many of his works have been well known at any period. The popularity of the *Songs and Sonnets* and a few of the *Divine Poems* has risen, until most people now base their view of Donne almost exclusively on these, with a consequent skewing of understanding that has been criticized with asperity by John Roberts.[2] Musical settings of Donne have followed a similar trajectory in popularity, and again the range of poems favoured is narrow, though this is commonly the case in composers' choice of literary texts. Appendix B shows that about a hundred musical settings of Donne's poetry have been made since 1872, rather fewer than of Blake's *Songs of Innocence and Experience* or of Walt Whitman's verse.[3]

Plotting the upward curve of Donne's reputation during this period also makes clear how close the literary worlds of the United States and Britain have become. Although, as Professor Smith showed in volume I, appreciation of Donne had led to keen and approving analyses in the States early in the nineteenth century. And since 1850 the production of editions as well as commentary has proceeded in a strikingly even way on both sides of the Atlantic.

In 1880 Professor William Minto of the University of Aberdeen produced an essay representative of the approach of many of the more modern critics in the period. The product of the wider availability of Donne's poems as a result of the popular 1855 Boston edition and Grosart's *Complete Poems* of 1872–3, it investigates why so good a poet as Donne should have been so neglected. Blaming the continuing disapproval of Donne on Samuel Johnson's criticism, of which he gives a fair account, Minto remarks that although 'a very different opinion was formed by the great critics at the beginning of this century ... unhappily for Donne's general reputation, for one person that reads De Quincey's essay on Rhetoric or Coleridge's priceless fragments of criticism, twenty read Johnson's *Lives of the Poets*'. The problem, he argues, has been compounded by M. Taine, who, 'in his rapid [and well-known] survey of English literature, has unhesitatingly adopted Johnson's condemnation', and developed it into an historical theory based on the classical scheme inflicted on English literature by Hume in the eighteenth century.[4] The poetry of Donne and his imitators Taine seized on as 'a sign of the decadence of the grand inspiration that produced the literature of the Elizabethan period'. But, Minto protests, 'Literature must always be conditioned by its readers, and if we take prettiness and affectation [Taine's terms] as marks of decadence, we must be driven to the conclusion that the grand style of the Elizabethan period decayed before it came into existence.' He points out that the 'metaphysical' characteristic of 'far-fetched' conceits saturated 'the most earnest of the love poets before Shakespeare reached his meridian' and there 'was plenty of three-piled hyperbole and pedantical figures in [Shakespeare's] sugared sonnets among his private friends.' In fact, 'without the fantastic love poetry of the Elizabethan period, the dramatic literature might have remained what it was before Marlowe descended to rescue it from clownish horseplay, bustling spectacle, and the crude representation of sensational incidents'.

The chronology of Donne's poems is still largely based on a few dated poems and the assignation of many to periods when such work would be appropriate to what is known of Donne's life. Views of the man have often become the gist of poetical interpretation, and a litmus test of the critic's moral attitudes, yet getting an enriching balance between biographical context and close reading is not only difficult but necessary with poetry as complex and obscure as Donne's. The satires, for example, condemned out of hand by writers such as Taine for 'terrible crudeness and power', Minto sympathetically sees as the product of

the boisterous extravagance of youth, the delight of a fresh untamed intellect in its own strength. . . . He questioned and canvassed everything with all the daring of an intellectual athlete, till he was ready to believe nothing, ready at least to maintain with brilliant rhetoric the converse of any proposition that was generally accepted in the world.

Similarly, citing 'The Funeral' as an example of the 'brilliant and profane uses' to which Donne later put his investigation into medieval ideas of the relation between body and soul, he comments that he

has suffered not a little from the perversity of critics who have insisted upon giving too serious a meaning to his fantasies. This misfortune is perhaps partly the fault of his imitators, who have copied his extravagant fancies without being able to master the quick shifting between jest and earnest which is as it were the salt with which they are seasoned.

Although Johnson directed his complaints against Donne's successors, writing of Donne primarily as a pernicious influence, he wrenched many lines from Donne's poems as examples of the characteristics he detested. Coleridge had countered the resulting unfairness by stressing the organic unity of Donne's poems, and Minto, with similar appreciation, makes a general criticism of testing Donne's lines out of context, though he is careful not to blame Johnson directly for having done this:

There is no poet who can be more easily misrepresented than Donne by fragments torn from their context, because there is no poet whose images are more closely interwoven with some central thought. They cannot be understood without some knowlege of this thought, and some sympathy with it. . . . The very fact that these images are charged with intense feeling makes them appear forced and unnatural to readers who approach them in a different mood, and are left without a clue to the mood in which they shaped themselves to the poet's fancy.

Johnson, he notes, 'had no sympathy with impassioned mysticism and the subtle fancies born of it'. Minto takes seriously Donne's accounts of mystical experience:

A man of warm affections, Donne loved to think that his soul could hold communion with distant friends in a rapt trance such as that in which the solitary mystic, striving to shut out every impression of sense, sought to transport his soul into direct communion with the great soul of the universe. It may have been but a half-belief, a pleasing self-imposture, but that it was earnest, we cannot doubt.

He describes the 'Metempsychosis' as a fragment that represents Donne 'perfectly in the extent as well as in the limitation of his powers. It breaks off abruptly and unworthily, with a commonplace scoff at the wickedness of women', but

If Donne had completed the original design of this great poem, and traced the fortunes of the soul – the hero of the epic – through all the great political and religious epochs of Roman history, it would have been an achievement worthy of his extraordinary powers. But to have realised this *if*, he would have needed the addition to his many splendid gifts of still another, the gift of perseverance.

His rather disappointing conclusion is one reached by a number of critics in the period: Donne belongs to 'the class of failures in literature – failures, that is to say, for the purpose of making an enduring mark, of accomplishing work which should be a per- petual possession to humanity. He was a failure, not from lack of power, but from superabundance.' His fault was that no one mood or faculty dominated, bending all his other powers into its service. He was also hampered by the conditions under which he wrote, satisfying a discrete circle whose 'ideas of refinement and culture', Minto warned, were not totally in accord with those of the 1880s, and who shunned the commonplace. In satisfying them, Donne failed to contribute to that very commonplace of the period which, according to Minto, is what is passed down to all but the 'curious explorers of the past' in subsequent ages.

But not all commentators were as independent in their assessment or tolerant in their taste. The following year David Masson's
biography of Milton appeared. Masson's influence as a result of
having founded *Macmillan's Magazine* and edited it until 1867 was
considerable. He had been an active participant in discussion of
theories of the nature of poetry in the middle of the century, and
in tackling Donne he sustained the position he had taken in the
earlier controversies. His comments repeat two of the well-
established strains of complaint against Donne: over-intellectuality
and moral impropriety. Masson's working assumption is apparent
in the sentence: 'The peculiarity by which they [the 'Metaphysicals']
are associated is that they seemed to regard verse less as a vehicle
for pure matter of imagination, or for social allusion and invective,
than as a means of doctrinal exposition or abstruse and quaint
discourse on any topic whatsoever'. Added to his conviction that
Donne and his followers were not doing what he conceived of as the
purposes of poetry, he found in the school 'an inordinately particular recognition of the fact of sex'. He distinguishes this from 'the
perception of love as an influence in all human affairs':

Quite different was the mental habit of which we speak. It was rather a
fascination of the mind round the radical fact of sex, a limitation of the
mental activity within the range of the immediate suggestions of that fact,
a diffusion of it and of deductions from it through all kinds of considerations. . . . Even the saintly Herbert is not free from this narrowness.

And as for Donne,

whose grasp of the fact was bold to audacity, and in whose earlier poems
there is an absolute contempt of all distinction between licit and illicit, it
is as a text susceptible of endless metaphysical interpretations, in addition
to the literal one, that the fact continually figures.

He concludes that *The Second Anniversary* is

Donne at about his best. Throughout the rest of his poetry, with not a few
passages of the same order, and with frequent feats of intellectual agility
that make the reader start, the most tolerant modern taste is apt to be
offended by the grossly physical cast of the images.

Another of the threads of discussion of Donne to run through
criticism is of his relationship to his age. John Churton Collins, the
moving force behind the establishment of the Chair of English at

the University of Oxford, and himself later professor of English at Birmingham, tackled the subject in the introduction to an edition of the poems of Lord Herbert, generalizing that

In all eras of great creative energy poetry passes necessarily through two stages: in the first stage, imagination predominates; in the second, reflection. . . . If a literature run its natural course, we may predict with absolute certainty that mere rhetoric will usurp the place of the eloquent language of the passions, that fancy will be substituted for imagination, and that there will cease to be any necessary correspondence between the emotions and the intellect. This stage was not completely attained till the age of Cowley. In the poetry of Donne we find the transition between the two stages marked with singular precision. Some of his poems remind us of the richest and freshest work of the Elizabethan age; in many of them he out-Cowleys Cowley himself.

This is a simplistic form of the simplified distinction so frequently made between the literature of the Elizabethan and Jacobean periods. Collins offers an advance over many of his predecessors who had pinned Donne firmly to one or other of the styles, but then uses his perception to double his complaints against him. Denying that Donne contributed new elements to thought or diction, he says,

What he did was to unite the vicious peculiarities of others, to indulge habitually in what they indulged in only occasionally. He was not, for example, the first to substitute philosophical reflection for poetic feeling, as his contemporaries, Samuel Daniel, Sir John Davies, and Fulke Greville, were simultaneously engaged in doing the same thing. He was not the first to indulge in abuse of wit, in fanciful speculations, in extravagant imagery, or in grotesque eccentricities of expression. But, in addition to uniting these vices, he carried them further than any of his predecessors or contemporaries had done, and, aided by the spirit of the age, he succeeded in making them popular.

The poetical taste that lies behind Collins's disdain of Donne was more clearly stated by other critics such as A. H. Welsh (1882) and T. J. Backus (1884). Welsh, an American, followed Taine and Johnson in assailing the Metaphysicals for 'their involved obscurity of style, their ingenious absurdities, their conceits. They desire to display their skill and wit in yoking together heterogeneous ideas, in justifying the unnatural, in converting life into a puzzle and dream.' Quoting lines from Donne's 'The Storm' and 'The Flea', he lamented,

We find little to admire and nothing to love. We see that far-fetched similes, extravagant metaphors, are not here occasional blemishes but the substance. He should have given us simple images, simply expressed; for he loved and suffered much: but fashion was stronger than nature.

T. J. Backus, like Collins, saw the seventeenth century as producing a style of writing

in which intellect and fancy played a greater part than imagination or passion ... that tendency to intellectual subtilty which appears in the prose and verse of the Elizabethan writers, and occasionally extends its contagion to Shakespeare himself, became with [the Metaphysicals] a controlling principle. As a natural consequence, they allowed ingenuity to gain undue predominance over feeling.

Of Donne he remarked:

His ideal of poetical composition was fulfilled by clothing every thought in a series of analogies, always remote, often repulsive and inappropriate. His versification is singularly harsh and tuneless, and the crudeness of his expression is in unpleasant contrast with the ingenuity of his thinking.

Although Backus acknowledges that 'the criticism of our day . . . discovers much genuine poetical sentiment beneath his faults of taste [and] his writings certainly give evidence of rich, profound, and varied learning', it is clear that his own view is summed up by quoting Dryden's comment that 'Donne was the greatest of English wits', by which critics generally meant 'Donne was far from being the greatest of poets'. Conservative too in his choice of pantheon, Backus was anxious to keep Milton free of the taint of having lived in the seventeenth century. He commented that 'towards the close of the period Milton is a grand and solitary representative of poets of the first order. He owed little to his contemporaries.'

In the late 1880s and the 1890s two doughty champions of considerable stature turned their attention to Donne: George Saintsbury and Edmund Gosse. Saintsbury's first long account of Donne occurs in his book on *Elizabethan Literature* (1887). He starts by accepting Ben Jonson's comment that Donne was 'the first poet of the world in some things'. With the rider 'possibly Ben might not have meant the same things that I mean', he says:

It is sufficient for me that in one special point of the poetic charm – the faculty of suddenly transfiguring common things by a flood of light, and opening up strange visions to the capable imagination – Donne is surpassed

xxi

by no poet of any language, and equalled by few.

In one long sentence he catalogues the main complaints that have been made against him and sets them aside:

That he has obvious and great defects, that he is wholly and in all probability deliberately careless of formal smoothness, that he adopted the fancy of his time for quaint and recondite expression with an almost perverse vigour, and set the example of the topsy-turvified conceits which came to a climax in Crashaw and Cleveland, that he is almost impudently licentious in thought and imagery at times, that he alternates the highest poetry with the lowest doggerel, the noblest thought with the most trivial crotchet – all this is true, and all this must be allowed for; but it only chequers, it does not obliterate, the record of his poetic gifts and graces.

Saintsbury's choice of diction does much to reduce literary and moral 'sins' to peccadilloes.

Sketching Donne's life in a paragraph, Saintsbury assigns most of his poems to the earlier part of it, especially the amatory ones. He singles out for comment 'that mixture of voluptuous and melancholy meditation, that swift transition of thought from the marriage sheet to the shroud, which is characteristic of French Renaissance poets, but less fully, until he set the example, of English'. He cites as examples lines from 'The Relic' and 'Love's Deity'. Where Masson had berated Donne for pervasive allusion to sex, Saintsbury shifts the emphasis:

In some of his poems, as the *Anatomy of the World*, occasioned by the death of Mrs Elizabeth Drury, this melancholy imagery mixed with touches (only touches here) of the passion which had distinguished the author earlier (for the *Anatomy* is not an early work), and with religious and philosophical meditation, makes the strangest amalgam – shot through, however, as always, with the golden veins of Donne's incomparable poetry.

Evidently feeling vulnerable, Saintsbury continues: 'expressions so strong as this last may seem in want of justification', and he quotes 'The Dream' and parts of *Satire 5* and *The Second Anniversary*. His apparent turn to consideration of the satires contains a defence against being accused of too lax an attitude to Donne's 'sexual immorality'. Admitting that Donne has 'glaring faults', he comments:

Those faults are not least seen in his Satires, though neither the unbridled voluptuousness which makes his Elegies shocking to modern propriety, nor the far-off conceit which appears in his meditative and miscellaneous poems, is very strongly or specially represented here. Nor, naturally enough, is the extreme beauty of thought and allusion distinctly noteworthy in a class of verse which does not easily admit it. On the other hand, the force and originality of Donne's intellect are nowhere better shown.

Lack of beauty in the verse most widely known – Donne's *Satires* – thus becomes not a stylistic characteristic of Donne but a feature of a genre:

It is now agreed by all the best authorities that it would be a mistake to consider this roughness unintentional or merely clumsy, and that it sprung, at any rate in great degree, from an idea that the ancients intended the *Satura* to be written in somewhat unpolished verse, as well as from a following of the style of Persius, the most deliberately obscure of all Latin if not of all classical poets.

Analysing the versification, which, Saintsbury says, 'leaves much to desire', he comments that

At one moment the ten syllables are only to be made out by a Chaucerian lengthening of the mute *e*; at another the writer seems to be emulating Wyatt in altering the accent of syllables, and coolly making the final iambus of a line out of such a word as 'answer'. It is no wonder that poets of the 'correct' age thought him in need of rewriting.

Along with Ben Jonson, Saintsbury concludes, Donne 'determined much of the course of English poetry for many years'; his 'union of spiritual and sensual fire influenced the idiosyncrasies of each [of his followers] as hardly any other writer's influence has done in other times; while his technical shortcomings had unquestionably a fatal effect on the weaker members of the school'.

In 1890 Edward Dowden published a paper on Donne's poetry in the *Fortnightly Review*. It was one of several appearances the paper made. In it Dowden followed cautious tactics in winning over his audience. He begins not with the notorious elegies but with 'The Litanie', displaying Donne the penitent. He then turns to some of the verse letters; the letter to Sir Henry Wotton, with its sage advice to cultivate the 'tranquillity of a self-sufficing soul', and that to Sir Edward Herbert on the development of personality which allows him to draw parallels with *In Memoriam*, Matthew Arnold's poems and Marcus Aurelius.

The love poetry he approaches by first considering those poems thought to have been addressed to Donne's wife, such as 'On his Mistress', 'Sweetest Love, I Do Not Go' and 'A Valediction: Forbidding Mourning'; the section concludes with a description of Donne's grief on Ann's death. Dowden's account of the other love poems is in two parts, the first prefaced by the statement: 'we cannot doubt that Donne himself had followed false fires of passion before he found his true home of love. But it were rash to take all his poems of intrigue as passages of autobiography.' The poems he then describes are discreetly chosen: 'The Perfume' and 'The Picture'. The latter leads naturally to description of 'The Storm' and 'The Calm', poems whose origin reveals Donne's military service. After describing the principal subjects of the satires, Dowden turns to the *Songs and Sonnets*, saying: 'when Donne writes in his licentious vein he is not light and gay but studiously sensual; he makes voluptuousness a doctrine and argues out his thesis with scholastic diligence'. The descriptions of individual poems begin with one belonging to the 'other extreme': the celebration of platonic love, 'I Have Done One Braver Thing'. Dowden's quotations are unexceptionable and allow him to make comparison with Patmore's *Angel in the House* and *Preludes*.

The article draws to a close with descriptions of the two *Anniversaries* written for Elizabeth Drury's parents, and the *Metempsychosis*. Of the *Anniversaries* Dowden says: 'on each anniversary of the day of death [Donne] purposed to present his friend with a memorial poem; but not more than two of these were written, nor can we regret that this funereal Eiffel tower was carried no higher than the second stage' though he discerns their abstract themes and credits them with admirable lines. The description of the *Metempsychosis*, with which Dowden ends abruptly, abandons the reader among Donne's stranger fancies. Despite the disconcerting end of the article, Dowden did assist Donne's reputation by presenting an account more in keeping with emphasis earlier in the century on the religious and domestic poems and by moderating the picture given by David Masson of a monomaniacal interest in sex.

Edmund Gosse's first contribution to criticism of Donne was made in 1883 and suggests that he did not yet feel that he had come to terms with his writing. He had at this point been working on his biography of Donne for five of the twenty years it took him. Declining to include him in his *Seventeenth Century Studies*, he explained wearily:

to write fully of his work would be to write the history of the decline of English poetry, to account for the Augustan renaissance, to trace the history of the national mind for a period of at least a century. I felt Donne to be as far beyond the scope of my work as Ben Jonson would have been.

Ten years later he contributed an article to *The New Revue* in which he accepted the charge against Donne of writing obscurely and compared him with Browning – not exactly an innovative comparison at the time. But he did try to revise opinion of Donne in two respects. First, he suggested a more flexible reading of Donne's rhythm, something that Robert Bridges had recently been attempting to do for Milton.[5] Donne, according to Gosse, was in rebellion against the flaccid iambic line of his time and wrote 'five-foot verse not as a fixed and unalterable sequence of cadences, but as a norm around which a musician weaves his variations'. As Coleridge had asserted, the rhythm thus must be taken from the sense. Donne is capable in such a poem as 'The Dream' of realizing 'the very paroxysm of amatory song'.

More importantly, he revalued Donne's individual style, asserting that

Donne was . . . by far the most modern and contemporaneous of the writers of his time. He rejected all the classical tags and imagery of the Elizabethans, he borrowed nothing from French or Italian tradition. He arrived at an excessive actuality of style, and it was because he struck them as so novel and so completely in touch with his own age that his immediate coevals were so much fascinated with him.

For Gosse, seeking to explain why Donne had been so neglected,

This extreme modernity . . . is one potent source of our lack of sympathy with the poetry so inspired. In the long run, it is the broader suggestion, the wider if more conventional range of classic imagery, which may hope to hold without fatigue the interest of successive generations.

The following year Gosse included a chapter on Donne in a study of the Jacobean poets. His historical placing of Donne contained nothing new though, like Saintsbury's account ten years earlier, it helped to free Donne from being damned for his followers' weaknesses. Gosse concludes:

The empassioned sincerity, the intuitions, the clarion note of Donne were individual to himself and could not be transmitted. It was far otherwise with the jargon of 'metaphysical' wit, the trick of strained and inappropriate imagery. These could be adopted by almost any clever person, and were, in fact, employed with fluent effect by people in whom the poetical quality was of the slightest.

Gosse's chapter shows his interest in the textual history of Donne's work. He includes the previously unprinted sonnet 'Since She Whom I Loved', usually thought to have been written about Donne's wife, and speculates that a sonnet on the Blessed Virgin had falsely been attributed to him.

Charles Eliot Norton joined the contemporary effort to place Donne in literary history in the introduction to his edition of Donne's poetry. Norton described Donne as 'essentially a product of the Elizabethan age'. As such he was susceptible to the influence of the Italian Renaissance, which 'refined manners', 'corrupted the moral sense', 'quickened life' and 'spread mortal contagion'. He gives his own, rather muted version of what was, by 1895, the established view of Donne, redolent of the influence of Saintsbury:

The mingling of good and bad is often intricate. The sensualism of the verses of his youth is now and then lifted by a stroke of the wing of imagination out of the lower into the higher regions of life. The dreariness of a long stretch of labored and intricate conceits is not seldom lighted up by a flash of wit, or the illumination of an original and impressive thought.

One of Norton's contributions to the revitalization of Donne's reputation was his outspoken dislike of Pope's and Parnell's rewritten versions of Donne's satires: Pope vulgarized the second, and Parnell took the third satire – 'one of the most direct, serious, and masculine of Donne's poems, full of real emotion and the expression of sincere conviction' and made it 'a piece of artificial diction, feeble in substance and poor in form'. Howard Erskine-Hill has since suggested that Pope was using his translation for political purposes of his own and not simply trying to correct Donne.[6]

The Introduction to E. K. Chambers's two volumes of Donne's poetry, published in 1896 for the Muses' Library, provided a prominent dais from which Saintsbury made his next attempt to establish Donne's reputation. Turning David Masson's criticism on its head, Saintsbury claimed that Donne has 'at once the transcendentalism which saves sensuality and the passion which saves mysticism'. He asserts that 'Donne was "of the first order of poets"; but he was not of the first amongst the first'. His discussion is strewn with positive tags: lines of Donne have 'been constantly quoted, praised, and imitated'; there are lines that 'everybody knows'. Saintsbury brackets his argument by suggesting that reactions to Donne must be extreme but he loads his conclusion by saying that for those who

have experienced, or at least understand, the ups-and-downs, the ins-and-outs of human temperament, the alternations not merely of passion and satiety, but of passion and laughter, of passion and melancholy reflection, of passion earthly enough and spiritual rapture almost heavenly, there is no poet and hardly any writer like Donne.

The imperfections of metre and form so often commented on he excuses by saying that Donne is like Dante in the richness of the material he wishes to shape into verse but, 'being of course a lesser poet than Dante', the effort to forge his work is more visible. He also wrote for a private audience and so did not give his poetry the final polish that precedes publication.

All Saintsbury's criticism of Donne relies on a division of his work into an early phase given to amatory adventure that may be forgiven because of Donne's youth, a period of connubial bliss and faithfulness, and a devout old age, a pattern followed contemporaneously by the American C. B. Furst in a long essay in the *Citizen*. But Saintsbury's later articles show less fear of condemnation for praising Donne's love poetry, less bending of his critical acumen by fear of social propriety. His passages on Donne in his *Short History of English Literature* (1898) single out the *Songs* and the *Anniversaries* for praise. The former

exhibit Donne's quintessential, melancholy, passionate imagination as applied, chiefly in youth, to Love; the *Anniversaries*, the same imagination as applied later to Death, the ostensible text being the untimely death of mistress Elizabeth Drury, but the real subject being the riddle of the painful earth as embodied in the death of the body.

Critical assessment of Donne's prose lagged behind comment on his poetry. Saintsbury was one of the first to give much space to it in a later chapter of his *Short History*. Remarking that 'few [writers] are more of a piece in poetry and prose than Donne', he says of his tracts, letters and sermons that Donne

has the three great characteristics of Jacobean writing – the learning, the profundity, and the fantastic imagination. And the profundity is here not merely real, but of a depth rarely surpassed in English, while the fantastic imagination becomes something more than merely fantastic . . . . It may be questioned whether Donne's very best passages are exceeded, whether they are equalled, by any English prose-writer in the combination of fulness and rarity of meaning with exquisite perfection of sound and charm of style.

He ends by furthering his separation of Donne from his followers, this time by re-examining the meaning of the term 'metaphysical'. The term, he says, is applicable to Elizabethan writers and to almost all the poets writing between 1630 and 1660, when it is taken to mean 'the habit . . . of always seeming to express something after, something behind, the simple, obvious first sense and suggestion of a subject'. In this sense, Cowley is 'only half a metaphysical', and Donne is metaphysical

in the greatest and widest sense. His thoughts, even his conceits, are never far-fetched, because his immense and brooding imagination reaches to them all without the trouble of fetching. The others have to fetch them; they could in some cases hardly go farther, they could in many hardly fare worse.

In 1899 Gosse's biography of Donne was published. It was enormously influential, the standard life, despite its improbable conjectures and errors, until R. C. Bald's biography of 1970. Its strengths are Gosse's imaginative and vivid style and his provocatively bold construction of a literary context for Donne's work. For example:

The Satires of Donne are not general invectives as those of Hall are, nor fantastic libels against individuals like those of Marston, but a series of humorous and sardonic portraits of types. The edition of Theophrastus, which Casaubon was to revolutionise European *belles-lettres* by publishing in 1598, was still unknown, but Scaliger had more vaguely drawn attention to this class of ironic portraiture.

Donne's verse letters, says Gosse, show similarities in style to the satires 'and are written in the same harshly cadenced heroic measure'. He quotes from 'The Storm' and 'The Calm' and explains his comment of 1883 regarding Donne's historical importance:

Here [in 'The Storm' and 'The Calm'] we find ourselves at the very start-point of a new spirit in literature, the love of precise notation of prosaic fact in the forms and languages of poetry. The exquisite Elizabethan idealism was undermined at last; here was the beginning of decadence.

In compiling his record of Donne's life, Gosse made heavy use of Donne's letters and interpreted many of the poems in a straightforwardly biographical manner. He was most criticized (see No. 48) for the speculative account of a love affair with a married woman, which he constructed from some of the *Songs* and *Elegies*. Gosse uses it to explain many of the poems 'of hatred and enforced resignation'. The dramatic visualizing that this enabled him to bring to his speculative interpretation can be seen in the following example:

But all these poems of hatred . . . pale before 'The Apparition', in which, as he tosses between sleep and waking, the horror of his situation, the vileness of the woman he has loved, and the whole squalor of the outworn liaison come upon him and overwhelm him.

To the debate on the critical estimate of the *Anniversaries* Gosse contributed a sensitive but purely practical explanation:

In return for house and home, for comforts to Donne's wife and food to his children, Sir Robert Drury asked a small expenditure of extravagantly laudatory verse, and Donne, no doubt, saw no shame in supplying what was asked for. He would probably have seemed to himself niggardly and ungrateful if he had refused to give it. But poetry composed under such conditions must needs be void and frigid, and if Donne thought to escape these faults by a strenuous exercise of intellect and fancy, he was disappointed. The expressions in his letters show that he was conscious of failure, and vexed at the sacrifice of his own dignity.

Gosse sums up Donne's personality as one of 'extreme versatility and passion', and admires 'the profundity, the saintliness, the mystery of his inscrutable character'. And he concludes his biographical account with the statement: 'We are tempted to declare that of all great men he is the one of whom least is essentially known. Is not this, perhaps, the secret of his perennial fascination?' The book ends with an appraisal of reasons why Donne had so large an influence on his age, and an assessment of what he contributed to literature. Gosse picks first the density of Donne's verse. 'The Elizabethan poet had held a mirror up to nature; Donne . . . shivered the glass, and preserved a reflection from every several fragment. This redundancy of intellectual suggestion was one of Donne's principal innovations.' He avoided most conventional and historical ornaments: 'he was, in a totally new and unprecedented sense, a realist [and] the forerunner of modern Naturalism in English poetry'. Donne the stylistic contemporary of Browning, Tennyson and Arnold for earlier critics thus becomes the psychological companion of the *fin de siècle* and the transition to Modernism. Donne 'neither translates nor paraphrases the poets of antiquity and draws almost no imagery from mythology or romantic history'. Instead 'he draws his illustrations . . . from the humdrum professional employments of his own age'. Gosse points out that many of the 'phrases which now call for a commentary, and disturb our appreciation of the poet's fancy, were references to the science or half-science of the Jacobean age as modern and "topical" as allusions to the Röntgen rays would be today.' Furthermore, this appetite for novelty of reference which Donne satisfied in England was matched 'in all parts of Europe at the same moment, and in a manner so simultaneous as to baffle the critical historian'; the characteristics of Donne can also be found in Marini and Góngora at the same period, and it is 'very difficult to say whether either of the three was affected by the practices of the others', and extremely unlikely that Donne knew the work of the others.

'The intensity of Donne's style at its best, and the mental concentration which he had taught, lent themselves peculiarly well to the expression of transcendental spiritual emotion. Indeed, in England, mysticism has always since the reign of Elizabeth spoken in the voice of Donne'; Donne's legacy can be seen in Crashaw's spiritual verse. In his concluding statements Gosse retreated, returning the poet to the stream of influences that critics had commented upon for decades – his influence on Dryden's and Pope's satires, Young's *Night Thoughts* and Browning's 'famous "obscurity"'.

Gosse's provision of a context for Donne's writing provoked in reviews of his book a flurry of historical comments, such as Richard Garnett's of 1899, contending that Donne's conceits, especially at the beginning of poems, were a transference to poetry of what was customary in the letter-writing of the day. Leslie Stephen similarly explained that Donne's thinking was filled with the scholastic controversies of the time and that as the preachers of the next generation, such as Tillotson and South, 'condescended to drop their doctoral robes', so Donne's style became obsolete, and so his reputation waned. An anonymous writer in the *Quarterly Review* (1900) asserted, as Minto had, that Donne's contorted style was the court style of the day, and his display of learning to be found 'in Burton . . . in ceremonial and Parliamentary speeches, in the diaries of Sir Symonds D'Ewes, and in pamphlets, letters, and sermons by the dozen. It was neither invented nor brought into currency by Donne or any other single authority.' J. W. Chadwick gave further credence to the idea that Donne was imitating Persius' style in his *Satires* by recording in his review of Gosse's biography the 'vigorous outburst in this kind' of Latin satire in England from 1593 to 1599, 'Donne's contribution being more than all the rest'.

In 1903 W. J. Courthope started a train of criticism of Donne that has been far more prominent in the last few decades, particularly in the work of William Empson and John Carey.[7] Courthope in *A History of English Poetry* said of Donne: 'No more lively or characteristic representative can be found of the thought of an age when the traditions of the ancient faith met in full encounter with the forces of the new philosophy'. Empson has argued that Donne was fully conversant with the dangerous implications for religion of contemporary astronomical discoveries and used traditional love-poetry to proclaim freedom from the rigid constraints imposed by the Church. Carey has seen the same poems as in part Donne's fantasies, allowing him escape from the position forced on him by his Catholicism, or as vicarious self-criticism in which women are used as scapegoats for his religious infidelity in abandoning Catholicism. Courthope placed Donne among those imbued with the beliefs of the Schoolmen. Picking up an idea poems of Donne'. Probably with Saintsbury in mind he concluded: 'there is perhaps in our own day a tendency to exaggerate his merits'.

H. J. C. Grierson, who was to become one of the most important contributors to the revival of interest in Donne, entered the arena in 1906 in a book on *The First Half of the Seventeenth Century*. He, like Courthope, stressed Donne's use of 'all that was most subtle and metaphysical in the thought and fancy of the Middle Ages'. He contrasted him with Ben Jonson, who shows classical characteristics, the elegance and extravagance of Petrarch yielding to the simpler and dignified common sense later to be found in 'Dryden's ideal of wit'. The movement in which both Donne and Jonson were caught up he described as

a reaction against the diffuse, flamboyant, Italianate poetry which Spenser, Sidney, and Lodge had made fashionable, – a reaction which showed itself in the satires of Hall and Marston, but found its fullest expression in the poetry – much of which is satirical – of Donne and of Jonson.

Donne's *Elegies*, he said, might be autobiographical (referring to the dispute raised by Gosse's biography) but are certainly his 'very characteristic contribution to the frankly pagan and sensuous poetry of the Nineties, represented otherwise by *Hero and Leander* and *Venus and Adonis*.' Grierson was clearly beginning to be very interested in establishing a more precise chronology of Donne's poems; he notes, for example, that Donne's *Satires* 'may date from 1593, but the earliest unmistakable reference is to 1597. . . . The satirical *Progress of the Soul* dates from 1601.' Reiterating well-established ideas, he also seeks to place the poetry in the cultural currents of the time:

The temper of Donne's poetry is that of Marlowe's and Shakespeare's. . . . To the imaginative temper of Marlowe Donne superadded the subtlety and erudition of a schoolman, and brought to the expression of his intense, audacious passions imagery drawn from an intimate knowledge of mediaeval theology and of the science mediaeval, but beginning to grow modern, of the seventeenth century.

He places Donne's love-lyrics in a tradition that includes Dante and Petrarch for their intensity and erudition, but then comments on the vast difference between Donne and Dante brought about by Donne's 'lack of a consistent metaphysic of love and its place in the upward movement of the soul to God'. Instead, he has in the *Songs and Sonnets*

two radically inconsistent ideas, one the inherent fickleness of woman, the other the mystical identity of the souls of lovers. But often he simply ransacks his multifarious knowledge to discover new and startling conceits in which to express his bizarre and subtle moods.

However, despite the erudition, 'no love-poetry of the closing sixteenth century has more of the sting of real feeling in it except Shakespeare's'. He suggests that Donne's love-poetry most closely resembles that of Browning because passion seems not to evoke the 'usual images voluptuous and tender' but 'quickens the intellect to intense and rapid trains of thought', producing images that are bizarre, sometimes repellent, often penetratingly vivid and powerful. He sees the devout Anglican poets as Donne's closest followers. It is apparent that not only was Browning's interest in Donne important in revitalizing the Renaissance poet's reputation, but, through the similarities seen in their style, his own reputation increased with that of Donne, a re-ordering of the pantheon of English poets that, like the attention paid to contemporary French writers, prepared the ground in which Modernist poetry could take root.

Saintsbury's last contribution to the revival of Donne in this period occurred in his *History of English Prosody* (1908), though the republishing of his many books, such as his *History of English Literature*, brought his arguments and warm support of Donne before the public repeatedly. The puzzle about Donne that Saintsbury broods over in his *History of English Prosody* is of the contrast between the metrical *finesse* of the *Songs* and the 'roughness' of the *Satires*. He aggravates the problem by taking a still rougher poem, 'Sleep, Next Society', as Donne's, although modern commentators no longer include it in the canon. His tentative explanation of the discrepancy in technical proficiency is that Donne experimented unsuccessfully in his *Satires* with classical conventions of equivalence and substitution. Saintsbury's quandary shows that before more detailed work could be carried out profitably on Donne someone had to establish a more authoritative text.

By 1909 there was some enthusiasm for publishing an edition of the poetry of another 'difficult' religious poet, Gerard Manley Hopkins,[8] an appreciation that suggests the shift in literary taste that was to become more marked in the following decade. There was also a feeling, expressed by Janet Spens, that poetry of disillusion such as she found in Donne spoke to a similar contemporary mood. In her book, *Two Periods of Disillusion*, she wrote:

the early seventeenth century resembles our own time in that it was a period of disillusion. The men of that day, like ourselves, had a despairing sense of their own littleness, of their incapacity for great passions. Sometimes the expression is gay and cynical, sometimes desperate with the darkness of personal experience, sometimes overwhelming as with the sense of being the only creed found possible after prolonged search.

Such 'Modern' feelings were to become more frequently expressed and important in the valuing of Donne in the next few years.

Grierson's edition of 1912, unquestionably the best modern text to have been produced till then, was accompanied by a second volume of commentary. The appearance of the edition coincided with the first of the Georgian anthologies, and the tone of Grierson's commentary on Donne's work shows similar traits to Edward Marsh's selected poets in its slightly guarded attitude to sexuality, and in its welcoming of freer rhythm, in conjunction with an emphasis on expressing personal experience. Grierson's definition of poetry 'in the full and generally accepted sense of the word' is suggestive: it 'quickens the imagination and touches the heart', 'satisfies and delights', 'is the verbal and rhythmical medium whereby a gifted soul communicates to those who have ears to hear the content of impassioned moments'. He contrasts the early poem 'Awake, My Heart, To Be Loved' by Robert Bridges, with its evident aesthetic aims, with the 'sacrifice of beauty to dramatic vividness' in some of Donne's poems such as 'The Extasie'. It is clear that the ideas of what constituted poetry were changing away from those held by Collins and Welsh or even Arthur Symons (see No. 43). It is also clear that the relationship of feeling and thought, an issue often mentioned as a way of criticizing Donne for being over-intellectual, was open for further discussion. Grierson still turns to Tennyson as a touchstone, comparing Donne's religious questioning to Tennyson's, but suggests that the passion of 'Crossing the Bar' grows 'a little pale' in comparison with 'A Hymn to God the Father'.

An anonymous reviewer of Grierson's edition in the *Nation* wrote in a way suggestive of slightly more liberal social attitudes to sexuality. While praising Grierson's editorial and scholarly achievement, he criticized him for being insufficiently sympathetic to Donne's love-poetry: 'it is so easy to distinguish between obscenity and non-obscenity; so hard and so much more important to distinguish between cleanness and dirtiness'. For

Donne's glory is ever increasing. He was the one English love-poet who was not afraid to acknowledge that he was composed of body, soul, and mind; and who faithfully recorded all the pitched battles, alarms, treaties, sieges, and fanfares of that extraordinary triangular warfare.

Grierson's edition was also reviewed, somewhat hurriedly, by Rupert Brooke, whose principal contribution to assessment of Donne is an appreciation of the sense of humour in his verse:

There is no true lover but has sometimes laughed at his mistress, and often at himself. But you would not guess that from the love-songs of many poets. Their poems run the risk of looking a little flat. They are unreal by the side of Donne. For while his passion enabled him to see the face of love, his humour allowed him to look at it from the other side. So we behold his affairs in the round.

Brooke makes the curious claim that Donne 'never visualises, or suggests that he has any pleasure in looking at things . . . . The mediation of the senses is spurned. Brain does all.' Brooke makes the comment in the course of his tussle with the question of the balance in Donne between passion and intellect. Donne was, he concludes, a 'composition of brain, soul, and heart in a different proportion from the ordinary prescription' with the result that 'when passion shook him, and his being ached for utterance, to relieve the stress, expression came through the intellect'.

The Oxford don George Stuart Gordon remarked on Donne's sudden widespread popularity in an anonymous review of Grierson's edition in the *Times Literary Supplement* (30 January 1913). He evidently did not share the enthusiasm. Seeing in Donne a barometer of changing taste, Gordon conceded that the rediscovery of a poet of a former age may be as significant as the appearance of a new one and that the newfound admiration of Donne seemed to confirm a contemporary turning-away from nature poetry to the 'turbulent mystery of man and woman'; 'spirit and flesh contending nakedly . . . in the eternal battle of sex how two shall be two and yet be one'. For Gordon, the poets to compare with Donne are not Browning or Tennyson, but Villon and Baudelaire – a comparison he makes on the ground that all are 'voluptuaries'. Criticizing Grierson's essay for a basic misunderstanding of Donne, he sees him instead as 'martyr to the nausea' which follows passion; even his most spiritual poems are permeated by disgust. For Gordon, no man can suggest like Donne 'the universal desolation' and the '"dead low tide of the world"', and he clearly felt at odds with the growing absorption in the interrelation of sexuality, *ennui* and death in Decadent and Modernist writing.

The most important Modernist to assist a revival of interest in Donne was T. S. Eliot, who recalled that he had been attracted to 'private reading of Donne' by verses Professor Le Baron Russell Briggs had read to freshmen taking English at Harvard.[9] When Eliot came to England, he said, he 'heard more of Donne, in social conversation, than I had heard before'. His engagement with Donne appears first in his essay on Swinburne as 'imperfect critic', published in the *Athenaeum*, 19 September 1919. In an essay on Chapman, Swinburne had compared him to Jonson. Eliot remarks that the similarity holds only superficially, whereas comparison of Chapman with Donne might have prompted Swinburne to consider what Eliot sees as a far wider issue, the possession by many

Elizabethan and Jacobean writers of 'a quality of sensuous thought, or of thinking through the senses, or of the senses thinking, of which the exact formula remains to be defined'. The investigation of the loss of this united sensibility, which he later called its 'dissociation', would, he remarks, have improved Swinburne's essay.[10] Eliot pursued a similar line of thought in an article on Philip Massinger published in the *Times Literary Supplement* on 27 May 1920, giving examples of a resultant fusion of two or more diverse impressions in a single phrase such as Shakespeare's 'in her strong toil of grace'.

Eliot's essay on Ben Jonson of 13 November 1919 made the distinction between Jonson's 'poetry of the surface' of life, and the work of Donne, Webster, Tourneur (and sometimes Middleton), in which 'words have often a network of tentacular roots reaching down to the deepest terrors and desires'. The observation shows the influence of Freudian psychology in its sharpening of Saintsbury's definition of metaphysical as suggesting 'something behind and beneath the surface'. Eliot included the essays on Swinburne, Jonson and Massinger in *The Sacred Wood* where, with ambiguous intention, he ended the Introduction with Johnson's passage on the Metaphysicals from the 'Essay on Cowley' as a touchstone of good criticism.

At the end of November 1919, Eliot reviewed for the *Athenaeum* Logan Pearsall Smith's selection from Donne's sermons. Eliot did not reprint this essay in which he compared Donne's sermons with those of Andrewes and Latimer: 'as a writer of sermons, Donne is superior to Latimer, and more mature in style, if not more original or more important, than Andrewes'. These opinions, which he was to reverse in 1931, but which were forerunners of the enthusiasm showered on Donne's sermons during the 1920s.

Discussion of the relation of thought and emotion in Donne, a perennial topic for Donne's critics, was given a new slant in 1921, when Grierson brought out an anthology of *Metaphysical Lyrics and Poems of the Seventeenth Century: Donne to Butler.* In his introductory essay he isolated 'passionate thinking' as the group's 'greatest achievement'. Grierson says of Donne:

the thought in his poetry is not his primary concern but the feeling. No scheme of thought, no interpretation of life became for him a complete and illuminating experience. The central theme of his poetry is ever his own intense personal moods, as a lover, a friend, an analyst of his own experiences worldly and religious. His philosophy cannot unify these experiences. It represents the reaction of his restless and acute mind on the intense experience of the moment, a reading of it in the light now of one, now of another philosophical or theological dogma or thesis caught from his multifarious reading, developed with audacious paradox or more serious intention, as an expression, an illumination of that mood to himself and to his reader.

The anthology was reviewed anonymously in the *Times Literary Supplement* (1921) by Eliot, in an essay later republished in his *Selected Essays* as 'The Metaphysical Poets'. In it Eliot brought together observations he had made in the earlier essays on Swinburne, Jonson and Massinger. Grierson had pointed out that 'metaphysical' conceits could be found in mediaeval love-poetry. Eliot goes on to show that 'a degree of heterogeneity of material compelled into unity by the operation of the poet's mind is omnipresent in poetry', and he quotes an example from Johnson's 'Vanity of Human Wishes'. He traces a dissociation between refined sensibility and the development of the English language prompted by the linguistic success of Milton and Dryden. The 'Metaphysicals' were,

at best, engaged in the task of trying to find the verbal equivalent for states of mind and feeling. And this means both that they are more mature, and that they wear better, than later poets of certainly not less literary ability.

Modern civilization with its complexity produces in the refined sensibility of certain modern poets a method that is 'curiously similar' to that of the 'Metaphysicals'.

May we not conclude, then, that Donne, Crashaw, Vaughan, Herbert and Lord Herbert, Marvell, King, Cowley at his best, are in the direct current of English poetry, and that their faults should be reprimanded by this standard rather than ... praised in terms which are implicit limitations.

He ends by calling for a substantial study to 'break up the classification of Johnson ... and exhibit these poets in all their difference of kind and of degree'.

The final selection in this volume is Eliot's review of the Nonesuch *Love Poems of John Donne* (1923). In it Eliot pays tribute to the importance not only of Grierson's edition but of the criticism of Gosse and Saintsbury in the re-establishing of Donne's popularity.

One of his principal interests in the article is the question of why Donne should be felt to be so sympathetic to modern consciousness. 'The age', he says,

objects to the heroic and sublime, and it objects to the simplification and separation of the mental faculties. The objections are largely well grounded, and react against the nineteenth century; they are partly . . . a product of the popularization of the study of mental phenomena. Ethics having been eclipsed by psychology, we accept the belief that any state of mind is extremely complex, and chiefly composed of odds and ends in constant flux manipulated by desire and fear. When, therefore, we find a poet who neither suppresses nor falsifies, and who expresses complicated states of mind, we give him welcome.

For Gosse's conviction that Donne was recording his experiences in a straightforward manner Eliot substitutes the belief that Donne's apparent sincerity is faithfulness to felt emotion, whether arising from actual or from imagined events.

In 1926 Eliot gave a series of lectures on Donne. In 'Donne in Our Time' (1931) he stated:

I know that by 1931 the subject has been so fully treated that there appears to me no possible justification of turning my lectures into a book. . . . It is not exactly that anyone has actually written a definitive book . . . there might still be place for another book on Donne: except that, as I believe, Donne's poetry is a concern of the present and the recent past, rather than of the future.[11]

The essay becomes a farewell to his interest in Donne in which he attempts to analyse Donne's strengths and weaknesses and those aspects that had influenced him. In it Eliot clearly turns away from his earlier advocacy:

In Donne there is a manifest fissure between thought and sensibility . . . his learning is just information suffused with emotion, or combined with emotion not essentially relevant to it . . . perhaps one reason why Donne has appealed so powerfully to the recent time is that there is in his poetry hardly any attempt at organisation; rather a puzzled and humorous shuffling of the pieces; and we are inclined to read our own more conscious awareness of the apparent irrelevance and unrelatedness of things into the mind of Donne.

Donne's sermons, which were receiving critical attention at the time, Eliot suggested were likely 'to disappear as suddenly as they have appeared', since Donne was not as good a prose stylist as

Cranmer and Latimer and Andrewes and not as good a theologian as Bramhall and Thorndike. However, his place in history is safe because he 'first made it possible to think in lyric verse, and in a variety of rhythms and stanza schemes' while retaining 'a quality of song and the suggestion of instrumental accompaniment of the earlier lyric. No poet has excelled him in this peculiar combination of qualities.'

The question of the relationship between Donne's life and his work has remained an important strand in criticism. The New Critics, who followed Eliot in his declaration that 'biographical data' are irrelevant to literary value, made it possible to concentrate on the thought and emotion in poems without moral censure of Donne the man. Eliot's insistence on the usefulness of Donne to modern poets was also a powerful factor in criticism of Donne, whose reputation became linked with that of Modernist poetry and most especially with Eliot. While the revitalization of Donne as a contemporary led to admiration of the obscurity and sensuality that had been disparaged by earlier critics, it also made Donne's reputation a hostage to that of Modernist practitioners, so that attacks on Eliot as a poet or as a critic frequently spilled over into criticism of Donne. The most intransigent opposition to Donne often came from admirers of Milton, who, in reaction to Eliot's arguments, resentfully attacked Donne.

The types of approach seen in this volume, and the critical arguments, have continued in the later twentieth century, with studies of Donne's inheritance or breach of literary convention, with questions of the relationship of his work to his life. John R. Roberts, who has prepared two annotated bibliographies of criticism of Donne (see Appendix C) remarks on the explosion of interest. The first of his bibliographies covered the period 1912–67 and contained 1300 items, the second covered only the ten years 1968–78 and had just over 1000 items. By 1982, he records,

even a cursory glance at the seventeenth-century section of the annual MLA bibliography, which is, of course, far from comprehensive, will reveal that only Milton exceeds Donne in the number of yearly entries; that typically more items on Donne appear each year than on Herbert, Crashaw, and Vaughan combined; and that Donne entries far exceed those for Dryden and are roughly twice in number those listed in the Renaissance section for Sidney.[12]

Roberts laments two trends that he noticed in reading the more than 2000 items he annotated: first, that modern criticism 'concerns itself primarily with less than half of Donne's canon, confining itself narrowly to his secular love poems (a dozen or less of the poems in the *Songs and Sonnets* and to a much lesser extent the *Elegies*), to his specifically religious poems (almost exclusively the *Holy Sonnets*, "Goodfriday, 1613", and the hymns), and more recently, to the *Anniversaries*' (p. 357). Intimately connected to this problem is his second complaint: that Donne's critics fall too readily into two antagonistic camps: the 're-coverers', who too often have tended to discover increasingly exotic and arcane influences for Donne's thought, and the 'dis-coverers', those disciples of the New Critics, who use a selection of Donne's poems to teach analytical techniques and pass on a sense of these poems as the most characteristic of Donne. While evidence for such criticism is easy to provide, it would be the wrong note on which to end a survey of the 're-habilitation' of Donne, for there have also been exciting pieces of research that question various long-held assumptions. For example, John Shaw-cross has emphasized the importance for interpretation of how the poems were originally grouped, with associated implications for their biographical relevance.[13] Ilona Bell has suggested that three letters in the Burley manuscript are not Petrarchan compliments addressed to Donne's patronesses but were written to Ann More.[14] And, third example, Mrs E. E. Duncan-Jones has argued convincingly that the 'Anniversary' 'All Kings, and All Their Favorites', was written to Donne's friend Henry King rather than to his wife.[15] Such work, all of it stirring discussion, testifies to the richness of Donne's writing and to our continuing fascination with the riddles of its intimate relation to his life and his time.

Catherine Phillips
Downing College
Cambridge

NOTES

1 See Appendix A.
2 'The most unfortunate result of centering attention almost exclusively on less than half of Donne's canon is that we have developed over the

years what might be called a synecdochical understanding of and appreciation for Donne's total achievement as a poet: we have, in other words, substituted the part for the whole and then proceeded as if the part were, in fact, the whole. As a result, literary historians, critics, and teachers continue to repeat generalizations about Donne's poetry that although incomplete, partial, misleading, and sometimes incorrect, have about them almost the strength of established fact and the sacredness of a hallowed tradition' ('John Donne's Poetry: An Assessment of Modern Criticism', *John Donne Journal*, 1 (1982), 55–67, rep. in *John Donne's Poetry*, sel. and ed. Arthur L. Clements, 2nd edn, (London: Norton, 1992), pp. 357–8).

3 See Appendix B.

4 '[David] Hume had a particular view of historical change in mind which he brings out by a model from antiquity, the degeneration of oratory between Greek times and Roman. He contrasts the admirable simplicity of Greek oratory with the false ornaments and conceits of the later Roman rhetoric. The Greeks, he argued, had a language which permitted an easy unforced strain of sentiment and was fit to express genuine movements of nature and passion; but in Roman times the neglect of nature and good sense brought about a total degeneracy of style and language which opened the way to ignorant barbarism. These are the common terms and antitheses of attacks on Donne for a century and a half' (Introduction to *John Donne: The Critical Heritage*, vol. I, ed. A. J. Smith (London: Routledge and Kegan Paul, 1975), p. 15).

5 Robert Bridges, *Milton's Prosody*, first published in 1887 as an introduction to Henry Beeching's school edition of the first book of *Paradise Lost*. Bridges' essay was published separately with additional analysis of Milton's later work in 1893, and in 1901 he appended W. J. Stone's posthumous 'Classical Metres in English Verse'. The final edition appeared in 1921.

6 Howard H. Erskine-Hill, 'Courtiers out of Horace: Donne's Satyre IV; and Pope's Fourth Satire of Dr John Donne, Dean of St Paul's Versifyed', in *John Donne: Essays in Celebration*, ed. A. J. Smith (London: Methuen, 1972), pp. 273–307.

7 See, for example, William Empson, *Essays on Renaissance Literature*, vol. I: *Donne and the New Philosophy*, ed. John Haffenden (Cambridge: Cambridge University Press, 1993), and John Carey, *John Donne: Life, Mind and Art* (London: Faber, 1981).

8 Early in 1909 Elkin Matthews asked Edmund Gosse to edit an edition of Hopkins' poems, a project about which Gosse was initially enthusiastic but which he then declined, perhaps on being told that another literary man, Robert Bridges, was effectively Hopkins' literary executor (Catherine Phillips, *Robert Bridges: A Biography* (Oxford: Oxford University Press, 1992), p. 215).

9 T. S. Eliot, 'Donne in Our Time', in *A Garland for John Donne*, ed. Theodore Spencer (Cambridge, Mass.: Harvard University Press, 1931), p. 3.

10 Swinburne was familiar with Donne's verse and compared it favourably with Jonson's (see *John Donne: The Critical Heritage*, vol. I, ed. A. J. Smith (London: Routledge and Kegan Paul, 1975), No. 215.

11 Eliot, 'Donne in Our Time', p. 4.

12 John R. Roberts, 'John Donne's Poetry: An Assessment of Modern Criticism', *John Donne Journal* (1982), 55–67, reprinted in *John Donne's Poetry*, sel. and ed. Arthur L. Clements, 2nd edn (London: Norton, 1992), p. 353.

13 John Shawcross, 'The Argument and Order of Donne's Poems', in *Poems in Their Place: The Intertextuality and Order of Poetic Collections*, ed. Neil Freistat (Chapel Hill: University of North Carolina Press, 1986), pp. 119–63; cited in Deborah A. Larson, *John Donne and Twentieth-Century Criticism* (London: Associated University Presses, 1989), p. 163.

14 Ilona Bell, '"Under Ye Rage of a Hott Sonn & Yr Eyes": John Donne's Love Letters to Ann More', in *The Eagle and the Dove*, ed. Claude J. Summers and Ted-Larry Pebworth (Columbia: University of Missouri Press, 1986); cited in Larson, *John Donne and Twentieth-Century Criticism*, p. 163.

15 E. E. Duncan-Jones, 'Marriage of Souls', *London Review of Books*, 7 Oct. 1993, p. 4.

1. Henry Morley
1873

Professor Henry Morley (1822–94), of University College London, gave a brief account of Donne in a general outline of English literature (*A First Sketch of English Literature* (1873), 1896, pp. 527–9).

[Most of Morley's sketch inaccurately summarizes Donne's life and career. His few critical observations are perfunctorily patronizing. *An Anatomy of the World* (first published in 1625, he says) generally offers a specimen of artificial diction, though it also]

contains by rare chance one conceit rising in thought and expression to the higher level of Elizabethan poetry.

[He quotes lines 226–47 of *The Second Anniversary*.]
[Donne's 'lighter poems' display the 'unreality of a style that sacrifices sense to ingenuity', 'The Flea' is]

an ingenious piece, of which the sense is, so far as it has any, that a woman's honour is not worth a flea.

[Donne himself]
was unquestionably a man with much religious earnestness, but he was also a poet who delighted men of fashion.

2. Rosaline Orme Masson
1876

Rosaline Orme, wife of David Masson, shared her husband's interest in Scottish history, publishing a *Short History of Scotland* as well as a book on Edinburgh, and biographical sketches of eminent Scots. They also both published books on English

1

literature. In an anthology of poetic *Selections from Chaucer to Herrick,* Mrs Masson allotted some eight pages to Donne, introducing a set of extracts from poems with a brief general account of the poet (*Three Centuries of English Poetry,* 1876, pp. 338–46).

[Mrs Masson acknowledges Grosart's edition of Donne's poems (which Professor David Masson fulsomely lauds in his General Preface to her anthology) but displays a somewhat fanciful notion of the circumstances of the poems themselves. Thus she discerningly singles out Donne's three longest poems but then writes of them as if they constitute a single series which presents a spiritual progress. The easy irreverence of the *Metempsychosis,* a poem 'so marvellously clever and so completely anti-Christian in its doctrine and mood', gives way under the pressure of personal grief to the piously reflective mood of *The First Anniversary,* Donne's 'song of sorrow'; then *The Second Anniversary* records the poet's painful emergence from 'fresh and poignant sorrow' into 'the joy of religious faith'. She judges that]

The Second *Progress* is the most sustained and elevated of all Donne's poems, as the first *Progress* is the most bright and subtle.

[She is evidently in two minds about Donne. She quotes De Quincey on Donne's extraordinary combination of sublime dialectical subtlety with impassioned majesty, only to draw back at once from De Quincey's judgement.]

The epithets 'majesty' and 'sublimity' appear to us altogether out of place in a criticism of Donne. On any level below these no praise can be too extensive to be true; but in naming these qualities De Quincey has only reminded us of exactly what is wanting in Donne's poetry and in the man.

[Her selection of Donne's verse is idiosyncratic. She gives two extracts from *Satire* 3 (lines 5–32 and 72–84); a series of extracts from *Satire* 4 (lines 1–8, 17–44, 49–51, 61–70a, 71–80), which she chooses to make up a picture of *The Court Toady*; *Holy Sonnet* 10, 'Death, Be Not Proud'; 'Woman's Constancy' (interestingly retitled 'A Woman's Constancy'); a series of extracts from the *Metempsychosis* (lines 171–90, 301–40, 451–68); and lines 173–213 of *The Second Anniversary.*]

3. William Minto

1880

Professor W. Minto (1845–93) of the University of Aberdeen contributed a substantial appraisal of Donne to a leading review. He had formerly published a book on *Characteristics of English Poets from Chaucer to Shirley* (1874; second edition 1885), with the aim of setting out 'the characters, personal and artistic, of the poets dealt with', but, although he included Ben Jonson, he made no mention of Donne. ('John Donne', *Nineteenth Century*, 7 (1880), 846–63.)

[Minto ponders the continuing neglect of Donne's poetry:]

it is strange that a man who in such an age was numbered among the masters of literature should have received so little honour from posterity.

Neglect, indeed, is not the only indignity that the poetry of Dr Donne has suffered. It was stamped with emphatic condemnation by the great critical authority of the eighteenth century. Dr Johnson recognised Donne as a master and the founder of a school, but it was a school with which he had no sympathy. He nicknamed Donne and his followers 'the metaphysical poets', and he culled from their works a variety of specimens to prove that the characteristics of the school were unnatural and far-fetched conceits, 'enormous and disgusting hyperboles', 'violent and unnatural fictions', 'slight and trifling sentiments'. At the same time he did not deny that there was something to be said in their favour.

Great labour, directed by great ability, is never wholly lost; if they frequently threw away their wit upon false conceits, they likewise sometimes struck out unexpected truth; if their conceits were far-fetched, they were often worth the carriage.... If their greatness seldom elevates, their acuteness often surprises; if the imagination is not always gratified, at least the powers of reflection and comparison are employed; and in the mass of materials which ingenious absurdity has thrown together, genuine wit and useful knowledge may be sometimes found buried perhaps in grossness of expression, but useful to those who know their value; and such as, when they are expanded to perspicuity and polished to elegance, may give lustre to works which have more propriety, though less copiousness, of sentiment.

3

Such was Dr Johnson's opinion of the works which his great namesake in the Elizabethan time pronounced to be 'examples,' and did his best to rival; they were worth digging into as mines, but their art was detestable. A very different opinion was formed by the great critics at the beginning of this century: but, unhappily for Donne's general reputation, for one person that reads De Quincey's essay on Rhetoric or Coleridge's priceless fragments of criticism, twenty read Johnson's *Lives of the Poets*. M. Taine, in his rapid survey of English literature, has unhesitatingly adopted Johnson's condemnation, and developed it into an historical theory. The poetry of Donne and his imitators M. Taine marks as a sign of the decadence of the grand inspiration that produced the literature of the Elizabethan period. The flood of great thoughts and great passions had spent itself; the mighty men of genius, through whom the heroic spirit had spoken, were succeeded by a feebler race, who, instead of giving free vent to fire that was burning in their hearts, strained and tortured their intellects in the devising of pretty compliments, and sought to outdo the natural language of overpowering passion by cold and artificial hyperbole. M. Taine admits that there is something of the energy and thrill of the original inspiration in Donne, but he does not admit that there is enough to exempt him from the sweeping censure passed by Johnson upon the school which he founded.

Critics, like travellers, too often see only what they look for. The truth is that the prettiness and pedantic affectation which M. Taine assumed to be marks of decadence were as common in Elizabethan literature before it reached its grand period as they were after. The poetry of the Elizabethan time may be divided roughly into two kinds, the poetry of the Court and the poetry of the stage. The poets cannot be so classified, because most of them attempted both kinds; but there were two classes of audience who had to be moved and delighted by essentially different means. It is in the poetry of the stage that we find the rushing abundance of impassioned feeling and sublime thought, divine and demoniac emotion, simple freshness of sentiment. The poetry of the Court demanded more veiled and intricate forms of utterance. But it is a mistake to represent the one style as a degradation of the other, the prettiness and affectation of the courtly poetry as a sign of the exhaustion of the inspiration which produced the grand style of the stage. Literature must always be conditioned by its readers, and if we take prettiness

4

and affectation as marks of decadence, we must be driven to the conclusion that the grand style of the Elizabethan period decayed before it came into existence. The works of the most earnest of the love poets before Shakespeare reached his meridian were saturated with violent and unnatural fictions, trifling and far-fetched conceits. Sir Philip Sidney, in common with the more robust intellects of the time, rebelled against the prevailing foppery, and exhorted himself to 'look in his heart and write'. But he could not escape the infection of what he despised, and to a later generation his sonnets bear as much evidence of ambition to show his wit as of urgent necessity to pour out the feelings of his heart. We know from *Love's Labour Lost* [*sic*] what Shakespeare thought of the reigning mode. The King of Navarre and his lords make love at first in the very height of the fashion, and bandy wit with their mistresses; but when they get the worst of the gay encounter, they abjure –

> Taffeta phrases, silken terms precise,
> Three-piled hyperboles, spruce affectation,
> Figures pedantical,

and vow henceforth to conduct their wooing 'in russet yeas and honest kersey noes'. But Shakespeare, the universal, was not entirely wrapt up in the grand passions; and there was plenty of three-piled hyperbole and pedantical figures in his 'sugared sonnets among his private friends'.

In love, as in religion, there are three Churches, the High Church, the Low Church, and the Broad Church. Love was worshipped in the Elizabethan age with elaborate rites and ceremonies. The poets were all extreme Ritualists. Here and there we come across notes of impatience under the burden of minute formalities, vows to have done with them as tedious fopperies, and to revert to 'the russet yeas and honest kersey noes'. But the tide of fashion was too strong, and the rebels who had solemnly repudiated one ritual, soon found themselves racking their brains to devise another. There was no keener satirist of the erotic commonplaces of his youth than John Donne; but his indignation was not against the style, but against the commonplace abuse of it, against the barren versifier

> who beggarly doth chaw
> Others' wits' fruits, and in his ravenous maw
> Rankly digested, doth those things outspue
> As his own things.

5

Donne's own love poems were written in a fashionable style. He threw, however, so much wit and learning and ingenuity into them that he was looked up to in his own age and held up to ridicule in a succeeding age as the founder of a new school. His poetry was not a sign of the decadence of the grand style, the exhaustion of the grand inspiration. The simple fact that he began to write, as he continued to write, before the dramatic masterpieces of Shakespeare were produced is sufficient to refute this notion. His poetry was really a sort of new departure in the trifling style. And before we condemn the style of the Court, with its absurd ingenuities, its far-fetched conceits, its passion for saying only what had never been said before, as mere trifling and waste of brains, we must remember what the great poetry of the stage owed to it. The ransacking of heaven and earth for occult images, the elaborate torture with which those images were twisted and turned and broken into fragments, the indefatigable manipulation of words and ideas – all this belonged to the intense occupation of the best intellect of the time with the materials of poetry. The labour was not thrown away. The great masters of the dramatic art were gainers by it. Dr Johnson admits that the rubbish heaps of the metaphysical poets contained many things that 'might be useful to those who know their value'. But they were useful also in their own generation to poets who possibly did not know their value, but owed to them unconsciously much stimulation and suggestion. The fantastic love poetry of the Elizabethan period was the soil from which the great works drew their sap, the atmosphere in which they put forth leaf and branch. The dramatic literature might have been still nobler without it; but without it this literature might never have existed, and the stage might have remained what it was before Marlowe descended to rescue it from clownish horseplay, bustling spectacle, and the crude representation of sensational incidents.

The admiration which Donne's contemporaries expressed for him as a writer was doubtless largely influenced by the impression which he made upon them as a man. A writer's personality cannot be separated from his works in his own time. Posterity judges him by what he has done, what he has finished and left behind him; the judgment of contemporaries is insensibly influenced by what they believe him to be capable of doing. The knowledge of Donne's immense learning, the subtlety and capacity of his intellect, the intense depth and wide scope of his thought, the charm of his conversation, the sadness of his life, gave a vivid meaning and interest to his poems – not published, it must be remembered, but circulated among his acquaintances – which at this distance of time we cannot reach without a certain effort of imagination. The effort is quite worth making. Dr Donne is one of the most interesting personalities among our men of letters. The superficial facts of his life are so incongruous as to be an irresistible provocation to inquiry. What are we to make of the fact that the founder of a licentious school of erotic poetry, a man acknowledged to be the greatest wit in a licentious Court, with an early bias in matters of religion towards Roman Catholicism, entered the Church of England when he was past middle age and is now numbered among its greatest divines? Was he a convert like St Augustine, or an indifferent worldling like Talleyrand? Superficial appearances are rather in favour of the latter supposition. He took holy orders at the command of King James, after long waiting in vain for a political appointment.

[He remarks that nineteenth-century students who projected their inner consciousness upon the Elizabethan age, and mistakenly discovered in Hamlet a type of gentle and irresolute humanity, might have 'found in Donne in real life the type that they sought in the hero of Shakespeare's tragedy'; and he goes on to discuss the writings of the young Donne.]

The first poems that Donne wrote were satires, very different productions from the dashing, smirking, fluent imitations of the ancients which Joseph Hall put forth with a claim to be the first of English satirists. They are not scholarly exercises or artistic displays; they have their root in the individual feelings and thoughts of the writer; they reveal the genuine workings of his mind upon the facts that life presented to it. The high spirits and unworldly mind of generous youth shine through them.

[He gives an account of *Satire* 3.]

That so earnest and thoughtful a boy – Donne was not twenty when he wrote this – an ardent bookworm, with 'an hydroptic immoderate desire for human learning and languages', should have entered the lists with the erotic poets of the Court, and by the ascendancy of his wit have founded a new school, is a greater paradox than that in the evening of his life he should have become or rather been made one of the pillars of the English Church. His companions of his own age would seem to have had almost as much difficulty in dragging the boy from his study, as King James in persuading the mature man to take holy orders. Not that he was a gloomy youth, a precociously sour and rabid satirist. The terrible crudeness and power which some critics have seen in his satires is not a churlish crudeness; it is nothing but the boisterous extravagance of youth, the delight of a fresh untamed intellect in its own strength. He loved his books and exulted with buoyant pride in the con-sciousness of power which communion with great minds gave him.

[He gives the opening of *Satire* 1, and then some passages from *Satire* 4, asking why Donne 'joined the gay throng at Court' at all.]

He may have said to himself that he would have to tell fewer lies as a courtier than as a barrister. It is more than probable, too, that the uncompromising ardour of his youthful worship of truth was considerably shaken by his speculative inquiries into the founda-tions of morality. He questioned and canvassed everything with all the daring of an intellectual athlete, till he was ready to believe nothing, ready at least to maintain with brilliant rhetoric the converse of any proposition that was generally accepted in the world.

[He speaks of Donne's *Paradoxes and Problems*, and of the para-doxical spirit in Donne's work altogether:]

The virtue of inconstancy in women was the burden of many of his verses. 'Everything as it is one thing better than another, so is it fuller of change', he said in prose. Constancy is a 'sluttish virtue'. And he embodied this notion with equal spirit in verse.

> I can love both fair and brown;
> Her whom abundance melts and her whom want betrays;

and so forth –

> I can love her, and her, and you, and you,
> I can love any, so she be not true.

His reading in the casuists furnished him with admirable fuel for his graceless wit.

[He gives the whole of 'Woman's Constancy'.]

Dr Johnson admits that 'no man could be born a metaphysical poet,' and that 'to write on their plan it was at least necessary to read and think'. It certainly required learning as well as wit to embody as in the above poem the quintessence of the casuistical sophistry which Pascal ridiculed. Donne also turned to great account in these humorous sallies his intimate knowledge of the speculations with which the mind of 'Nature's Secretary, the philosopher', was busied in the middle ages. He had been fascinated in real earnest by the ingenious philosophy which tortured itself in hunting through never-ending mazes the mysterious problems of being. What was the connexion between soul and body? Why was it that the bodily fabric ceased to perform its functions and decayed when the soul was removed from it? Could any principle be discovered which would bind the soul to perpetual tenancy of its house of clay? Where did the soul reside? Donne had been an earnest student of the theories of the learned on these knotty problems, but in the flush of youthful spirits he did not scruple to turn his learning to brilliant and profane uses. For example in *The Funeral* he plays ingeniously with the fantastic notion that a lock of his mistress's hair tied round his arm might keep his body from decay, binding its members together as the nerves do which are let fall from the seat of the soul in the brain. If the threads that are let fall from his brain can perform this office, the hairs which are sent upwards from a better brain must be much more efficacious.

[He quotes the entire poem, and comments on it.]

[Donne] was still in his mocking vein when he wrote these stanzas. They are a sort of trap for the object of his addresses; he begins all seriousness, sweet fantastic seriousness, but he turns round at the end and laughs at his own sentiment. Yet the sentiment, with all the far-fetched ingenuity of its clothing, is so deep and tender that his mistress might have been pardoned if she did not know what to make of it. Donne has suffered not a little from the perversity of critics who have insisted upon giving too serious a meaning to his fantasies. This misfortune is perhaps partly the fault of his imitators, who have copied his extravagant fancies without being able to master the quick shifting between jest and earnest which is as it were the salt with which they are seasoned. There is all the difference in the world, it need hardly be said, between absurdity

9

that is deliberate and playful, and absurdity that is unconscious and sincere.

But Donne's love-poetry is not all playful and humorous in intention. The brilliant scoffer at constancy, the gay advocate of licentious paradoxes, underwent a change when he fell seriously in love himself. The distinction which he drew between 'Jack' Donne and 'Dr' Donne is not more marked than the difference between Jack Donne the sprightly 'indifferent', and John Donne the married man. There is, no doubt, much in the serious poetry of his mature life which must appear as grossly absurd and unnatural to those who have no sympathy with it as anything that is to be found in the productions of his early wit. It is, in fact, from the later poems that Dr Johnson draws most of his examples of what he condemns in Donne and his school. Johnson had no sympathy with impassioned mysticism and the subtle fancies born of it. There is no poet who can be more easily misrepresented than Donne by fragments torn from their context, because there is no poet whose images are more closely interwoven with some central thought. They cannot be understood without some knowledge of this thought, and some sympathy with it. They are meaningless when divorced from it. The very fact that these images are charged with intense feeling makes them appear forced and unnatural to readers who approach them in a different mood, and are left without a clue to the mood in which they shaped themselves to the poet's fancy.

However much Donne might toy and trifle with some of the mediaeval fancies about the soul and the principles of life, there were others which had taken a deep hold of him, and installed themselves as the organs of his innermost feelings. 'I make account', he says, in writing to one of his friends, 'that this writing of letters, when it is with any seriousness, is a kind of ecstasy and a departure and secession and suspension of the soul, which doth then communicate itself to two bodies.' A man of warm affections, Donne loved to think that his soul could hold communion with distant friends in a rapt trance such as that in which the solitary mystic, striving to shut out every impression of sense, sought to transport his soul into direct communion with the great soul of the universe. It may have been but a half-belief, a pleasing self-imposture, but that it was earnest, we cannot doubt. We may call it fantastic, if we please, and even artificial, but we cannot call it forced or cold. No more can we fairly apply these epithets to the sweet fancies which it inspired, and which appear, it must be admitted, strained and exaggerated enough if we have no regard to the feeling in which they had their root. Dr Johnson quotes some stanzas from Donne's beautiful leave-taking of his wife before setting out on a journey, with the savage remark – 'To the following comparison of a man that travels and his wife that stays at home, with a pair of compasses, it may be doubted whether ingenuity or absurdity has the better claim.' But in a generation when Donne's doctrine of ecstatic communion, whether as a belief or as a sentimental fiction, would have obtained a more indulgent reception than Dr Johnson would have given it, Izaak Walton records that he had heard many good judges say that the Greek and Latin writers had never surpassed this poem.

[He quotes the whole of 'A Valediction: Forbidding Mourning'.]

'Their sentiments were trifling and affected.' M. Taine marks for peculiar reprobation the extravagance of Donne's adjuration to his mistress when she lay sick of a fever.

> Oh, do not die, for I shall hate
> All women so when thou art gone,
> That thee I shall not celebrate
> When I remember thou wast one.

He can see no motive for so strained an hyperbole except literary foppery – it was a lovers' commonplace to say that they would hate all women if their mistress were no more, and Donne was bound to outdo the commonplace extravagance. There is no arguing about lovers' hyperboles.

[He gives stanzas 2–4 of 'A Fever', and comments:]

Such sallies into the pure empyrean of hyperbole must always appear incomprehensible and heartless absurdity to certain temperaments. The heat of flames so thin and fantastic has no warmth for them. They need a more gross and material blaze to lift them out of coldness and discomfort.

> O Love, Love, Love, O withering might,
> O Sun, that at thy noonday height
> Shudderest when I strain my sight
> Throbbing through all thy heat and light!

11

Such utterances as this of our present Poet Laureate's youth move them. They recognise in this the voice of true passion, but they will not admit that any sincerity of feeling whatever can lie at the heart of the more insubstantial extravagances of Donne. There must always be Low Churchmen as well as Ritualists in impassioned poetry, temperaments that cannot be stirred except by raw brandy, and temperaments that acknowledge the influence of milder stimulants.

The bulk of Donne's poems – a very small bulk compared with his reputation in his own time – consists of short pieces elaborately finished. His want of self-determining impulses, his discursive and dilatory habits, and his difficulty in satisfying himself with his work, were not favourable to copious composition. He had difficulty in making up his mind, he tells us, about the writings of other people, and still greater difficulty in making up his mind about his own. 'I doubt and stick, and do not quickly say "good". I censure much and tax.' His longest work, 'The Progress of the Soul', which might have been a monument worthy of his genius, remains an unfinished fragment. . . .

Donne inscribes his work 'poema satyricon,' and many touches in the completed section justify the title, but it was not intended to be a satire of fugitive fashions and customs. No other satirist ever expounded his design in such a strain of impassioned sublimity.

[He gives an account of the *Metempsychosis,* quoting freely from it. Quoting lines 327–30, he says:]

Touches of satire like the above hit at the abuses of the courts of law are intermingled with the main flow of the descriptive story. Every stage in the soul's progress is made to yield some sarcastic lesson for the times, some political or social maxim.

If Donne had completed the original design of this great poem, and traced the fortunes of the soul – the hero of the epic – through all the great political and religious epochs of Roman history, it would have been an achievement worthy of his extraordinary powers. But to have realised this *if,* he would have needed the addition to his many splendid gifts of still another, the gift of perseverance. 'The Progresss of the Soul' completed in the same high strain with which it begins would have been a great monument, but it would have been a monument of a different type of man from Donne. The fragment, as it stands, represents him perfectly in the extent as well as in the limitation of his powers. It breaks off abruptly and unworthily, with a commonplace scoff at the wickedness of women.

> She knew treachery
> Rapine, deceit, and lust and ills enough
> To be a woman; Themech she is now,
> Sister and wife to Cain, Cain that first did plow.

He takes leave of his Soul when it has reached this halting-place as if he were tired of pursuing its history.

It must be admitted that Donne belongs to the class of failures in literature – failures, that is to say, for the purpose of making an enduring mark, of accomplishing work which should be a perpetual possession to humanity. He was a failure, not from lack of power, but from superabundance. No single faculty had the lead in his richly endowed organisation. No one mood had sufficient strength to overbear all others, and compel all his powers into its service. It may be thought that this is only another way of saying that Donne was a man of amazing talents without being a man of genius. Yet there is no poet of the Shakespearian age to whom it would be more inappropriate to deny the rank of genius, in any conceivable acceptation of the term. If we take talent to be the power of adroitly manipulating common material into common forms, no man had less of it than Donne. He had an invincible repugnance to the commonplace. Everything is his own, alike the thought and the instrument by which it is expressed. He is no man's debtor. He digs his own ore, and uses it according to his own fancies.

For the widest and most enduring kind of reputation, talent is as necessary as genius. He who writes for the greatest number must have both. Donne was confirmed in the exclusive cultivation of his genius by the conditions under which he wrote. His poems were not intended for wide publicity; they were intended for the delight and amusement of a small circle among whom they were circulated in manuscript. There is much in them that does not accord with our ideas of refinement and culture; but we must make allowance for changes of taste, and the circle for which Donne wrote had at least this much of the characteristics of refinement and culture that it was weary and impatient of commonplace. There is always the danger with such select circles, that they put themselves in antagonism to the dominant spirit of their time. We may almost say in fact that this antagonism is an inevitable element in the atmosphere of sentiments and ideas that gathers round a group who have separated themselves from the crowd and organised any sort of intellectual or artistic aristocracy. Their shibboleths are coloured by it, and much of their work is inspired by it. The men who write for such an aristocracy must be content with a limited popularity in their own time, and must be prepared for a very rapid diminution in the numbers of their audience as time rolls on and generation after generation forms for itself its own watchwords of culture. A generation is represented to posterity by its best commonplace, and those who do not enter the main stream but stand critically on the banks or disport themselves in retired eddies soon pass from the notice of all but the curious explorers of the past.

4. John Henry Shorthouse

1881

In a novel which had a considerable vogue in its day J. H. Shorthouse (1834–1903) evoked the intellectual milieu of a seventeenth-century Anglo-Catholic churchgoer (*John Inglesant: A Romance*, pp. 82–3).

He had several friends whose society he much valued among the Papists, and he frequently attended mass when not obliged to by his attendance upon the queen; but he was rather more inclined to attach himself to the members of the Laudian and High Church party, who presented many qualities which interested and attracted him. He read with delight the books of this party, Dr Donne's and Herbert's Poems, and the writings of Andrews [*sic*] and Bishop Cosin's Devotions.

5. Alice King

1881

Alice King (1839–94) was the daughter of a clergyman. She became blind at the age of 7 and was educated by her mother. She learned by ear seven languages and contributed to the *Argosy* and the *Quiver*, both journals largely devoted to fiction and associated with Mrs Henry Wood. She also wrote eleven three-decker novels, published between 1861 and 1887. Her account of Donne in a journal article was sentimental and showed little awareness of the facts of his life, but conveyed enthusiasm for his poetry ('John Donne', *Argosy*, 32 (1881), 300 and 304–5).

Before he was twenty he published a volume of poems, which got quickly into brisk circulation, and were greatly admired in his day, though they are too full of over-strained conceits and too stiff to suit our modern taste. There is, however, so much of the fire and melody of true poetry in Donne's verse, that every age must grant him the title of a poet. . . .

His genius as a poet no doubt had much to do with his success as a preacher; it bore him aloft into heights of inspired fancy, and clothed his thoughts in language of glowing splendour. . . .

Donne wrote some beautiful and touching sacred poetry after he was a clergyman. . . . His poetry before he entered the Church is occasionally stained by some degree of licence, but all that vanishes in his later verse.

6. David Masson

1881

David Masson (1822–1907) married Rosaline Orme (see No. 2) in 1853, the year in which he became Professor of English

Literature at University College London. He was the founder of *Macmillan's Magazine* and later Historiographer Royal for Scotland, and Regius Professor at Edinburgh. He spoke of Donne in his standard biography of Milton, written 1859–80, in the course of surveying English poetry before Milton (*The Life of Milton*, 1881, pp. 484–98).

Distinct from both the SPENSERIANS and the SOCIAL POETS was a group of metrical writers whom it is easier to enumerate than to describe by a common name. The peculiarity by which they are associated is that they seemed to regard verse less as a vehicle for pure matter of imagination, or for social allusion and invective, than as a means of doctrinal exposition or abstruse and quaint discourse on any topic whatsoever. According to the nature of the topics on which they wrote, they might be distributed into sub-varieties. Collectively they may be described as THE POETS OF METRICAL EXPOSITION AND METRICAL INTELLECTION. The double form of the name is useful. There is such a thing as *exposition* in metre, – *i.e.* Verse, on account of its own charms, or because it impresses matter on the memory more surely than prose, may be used as a vehicle for ideas already thought out or acquired by the writer in any department of science or speculation. Different from this, though likely to run into it, is *intellection* in metre, – *i.e.* the use of the stimulus of verse, its nimble and subtle action upon the thought, to generate ideas or supplementary ideas that were not in the mind before, lead to ingenious trains of thinking, and suggest odd analogies and combinations. It was mainly for poets practising this process of metrical intellection, though with some inclusion also of poets of metrical exposition, that Dr Johnson invented, or adopted from Dryden, the designation METAPHYSICAL POETS. That, however, was a singularly unhappy choice of a name, vitiating as it did the true and specific meaning of the word 'metaphysical', and pandering to the vulgar Georgian use of the word, which made it an adjective for anything whatever that seemed hard, abstract, or bewildering.

A good deal of the English Poetry of the Elizabethan age consisted of what might be called, properly enough, metrical exposition. . . .

[He goes on to discuss Donne's followers; and in speaking of

16

Habington he notes 'a characteristic which ... exists in almost all the poets whom we have associated with him':]

It may be described as an inordinately particular recognition of the fact of sex. These words are used to distinguish between what they are here meant to signify and that apparently identical, but really different, perception which pervades the poetry of all ages, and without which history would be full of fallacy and philosophy itself imperfect, – the perception of love as an influence in all human affairs. Quite different was the mental habit of which we speak. It was rather a fascination of the mind round the radical fact of sex, a limitation of the mental activity within the range of the immediate suggestions of that fact, a diffusion of it and of deductions from it through all kinds of considerations. There may be noted, for example, in most of the writers under view, a strained attention to the fact, as if all morality depended on continual reference to it, a vigilance of it as of the only tree of the knowledge of good and evil within the whole circle of the garden wherein men now walk. The word *sin* in their language almost invariably means but one class of those actions which are included in a larger and manlier definition. Hence, in some of them, a view of human duty negative and special rather than positive or broad. Even the saintly Herbert is not free from this narrowness, and Ferrar's very notion of the best means towards a blessed life may be referred to some such cause. But it is worse when, as is the case with some of them, they will not, with all their alarm over the fact, take the obvious precaution of getting out of its way. With some of them it is as if, in walking round and round this one charmed tree, and avoiding every other part of the garden, they divided their business between warnings not to eat of the fruit and praises of its deliciousness when licit.

But this is not all. The same fact by which, in its primary aspect, some were alternately repelled and attracted, was transformed and allegorized and sublimed in the minds of others, till it passed into a permanent mode of their thought and affected all their rhetoric. In Donne, indeed, whose grasp of the fact was bold to audacity, and in whose earlier poems there is an absolute contempt of all distinction between licit and illicit, it is as a text susceptible of endless metaphysical interpretations, in addition to the literal one, that the fact continually figures. In others, however, the fact, in proportion as it is shunned by the hard intellect, seems to take out its influence in a certain enervation and languor of sentiment, a

17

kind of introversion of the sensual into the spiritual. In some of the devotional poets under notice it is as if the allegory of Solomon's Song had taken exclusive possession of their imagination, and had there melted and inhered till all their language was tinged by the deliquescence.

[He instances Crashaw.]

But metrical intellection was also common enough among the Elizabethans, perhaps more common among them than it has ever been in our Islands since. That fondness for 'conceits', or the pursuit of quaint analogies and jingling word-play, with which the Elizabethan poets have been charged, Shakespeare himself not excepted, was one of the results of the wide diffusion among them of the habit of using verse merely to quicken wit and dialectic. In one Elizabethan the habit attained proportions that were enormous. If there has been any single poet in the world who may stand to all time as an example of the genius of metrical intellection at its utmost, it is John Donne. No wonder that Dr Johnson selected Donne as the father of all his so-called English Metaphysical Poets. In him were gathered into one, as it were, all the tips and clippings of intellectual super-subtlety among the Elizabethans.

[He speaks of the publication of Donne's poems in 1633:]

the first collective edition of his Poems, giving to the world those earlier productions of his pen in one medley with the more sacred metrical effusions of his later years. Without much regard to the chronology of the pieces, readers look at them all now indiscriminately as Donne's poetical remains. Nor are they wrong. The pious Dean Donne, whom Herbert admired and Izaak Walton all but worshiped, was essentially the same man who had gone about with bricklayer Ben in his early dramatic days; and in all his poetical remains – his *Satires* of 1593–4, his *Metempsychosis* or *Progress of the Soul*, written in 1601, his *Elegies, Epithalamia, Epigrams, Epistles*, and *Lyrics*, of the same or later dates, including the *Divine Poems* which may represent him clerically and theologically – there is the same intellectual manner. What a reputation he had gained by this manner among his contemporaries may be inferred from the fact that on Jonson's visit to Hawthornden in 1619–20 there was no poet besides himself of whom he talked so much as of Donne. . . .

With much of the true poet in him, Donne was, most essentially, a wit, a subtle thinker and dialectician, using verse to assist him in his favourite mental exercise – the stanza, let us say, as a wheel by which to spin out his thought into ingenious threads, the couplet as a shuttle by which to lay the threads together. His very notion of verse seems to be revealed in these lines in one of his love poems: –

> Then, as th' Earth's inward, narrow, crooked lanes
> Do purge sea-water's fretful salt away,
> I thought, if I could draw my pains
> Through rhyme's vexation, I should them allay.
> Grief, brought to number, cannot be so fierce;
> For he tames it that fetters it in verse.

Unfortunately, it was not only his love pains that he drew through 'rhyme's vexation', but his feelings and thoughts on all subjects whatsoever. Thus it is, that, notwithstanding his great celebrity in his life, posterity in general has become utterly impatient of his poetry. Yet, in reading him, one can see on what it was the vast admiration of his contemporaries, and also of such recent critics as Coleridge and De Quincey, was founded. His poetry serves as an intellectual gymnastic, even where, as poetry, it can give but little pleasure.

[He misdates *The Second Anniversary* by some thirteen years, assigning it to 1625; and he gives lines 81–95 and 179–213 as characteristic passages, 'representing Donne's later style and tone'.]

This is Donne at about his best. Throughout the rest of his poetry, with not a few passages of the same order, and with frequent feats of intellectual agility that make the reader start, the most tolerant modern taste is apt to be offended by the grossly physical cast of the images. Love in Donne's poetry is a physiological fact, susceptible of all kinds of metaphysical interpretations; his love verses are abstruse alternations between the fact and its metaphysical renderings; and that element in which most love poets dwell, the exquisite intermediate psychology, is all but wholly omitted. One of his short poems is entitled *The Flea*, and is an argument to his mistress in favour of their speedy marriage, deduced from the fact that, as the insect has skipped from the one to the other, and exercised its functions on both, their beings are already one within its jetty cover. In other poems facts of the most putrid order are jumbled together with others of the most sacred

19

associations, as equally holy to the eye of practiced intellect, and equally rich in symbolisms and analogies. In short, though we must regard Donne personally as an interesting study, and though we may admit also that in his hands the art of metrical cogitation with a view to novel combinations of ideas was exercised so superbly as almost to become the legitimate principle of a new variety of literature, we cannot but be glad that the avatar of Donne, as an intermediate power in English Poetry between Spenser and Milton, was so brief and partial.

7. John Churton Collins

1881

Introducing his edition of the poems of Lord Edward Herbert of Cherbury, J. C. Collins (1848–1908), then an extension lecturer in London, discussed the relationship between Donne's style and Lord Herbert's. Collins later became Professor of English at the University of Birmingham and campaigned successfully to have English literature recognized as a discipline at Oxford (*The Poems of Lord Herbert of Cherbury*, 1881, pp. xxii–xxvi and xxxiii).

The reader will at once discover that Herbert belongs, like his brother, to that school of poets whose characteristics have been so admirably analysed by Johnson – the Metaphysical or Phantastic School. This singular sect first appeared during the latter years of Elizabeth's reign. Their origin is popularly ascribed to Dr Donne, though it would in truth be more correct to say that in the poetry of Donne their peculiarities of sentiment and expression are most conspicuously illustrated. They owed their origin, indeed, not to the influence of Donne, but to the spirit of the age. In all eras of great creative energy poetry passes necessarily through two stages: in the first stage, imagination predominates; in the second, reflection. In the first stage, men feel more than they think; in the second, they think more than they feel. If a literature runs its natural course, we may predict with absolute certainty that mere rhetoric will usurp the place of the eloquent language of the passions, that fancy will be substituted for imagination, and that there will cease to be any necessary correspondence between the emotions and the intellect. This stage was not completely attained till the age of Cowley. In the poetry of Donne we find the transition between the two stages marked with singular precision. Some of his poems remind us of the richest and freshest work of the Elizabethan age; in many of them he out-Cowleys Cowley himself. But his work was not the work, in any sense, of a creator. He contributed no new elements, either to thought or to diction. What he did was unite the vicious peculiarities of others, to indulge habitually in what they indulged in only occasionally. He was not, for example, the first to substitute philosophical reflection for poetic feeling, as his contemporaries, Samuel Daniel, Sir John Davies, and Fulke Greville, were simultaneously engaged in doing the same thing. He was not the first to indulge in abuse of wit, in fanciful speculations, in extravagant imagery, or in grotesque eccentricities of expression. But, in addition to uniting these vices, he carried them further than any of his predecessors or contemporaries had done, and, aided by the spirit of the age, he succeeded in making them popular. It would not, perhaps, be saying too much to say that no single author contributed more to the foundation of the Metaphysical School than Joshua Sylvester, whose translation of Du Bartas preceded the 'metaphysical' poems of Donne, and was probably as favourite a work with Donne as it certainly was with most of the young poets of that age. The style of Donne is, however, marked by certain distinctive peculiarities which no intelligent critic would be likely to mistake, and his influence on contemporary poetry was unquestionably considerable. Lord Herbert appears to have been the earliest of his disciples. . . .

Where Herbert most reminds us of Donne is not so much in his lyrics as in his poems written in the heroic measures; in the two satires, for example, in the verses 'To his Mistress for her True Picture', in the elegy on Donne himself. The poem also entitled 'The Idea' is very much in his friend's vein, as well as written in a measure which Donne perhaps invented, and which was certainly a favourite with him. The numerous poems dedicated to the praise of dark beauty were perhaps suggested by Donne's verses *To a Lady*

21

of Dark Complexion. In the two poems on Platonic Love we may also discern the presence of the master. It would, of course, be absurd to assert that the lyric poetry of Donne had no influence on that of Herbert, but its influence was far less considerable than it would at first appear to be. Herbert's rhythm is his own. Where it is musical its music is not the music of the older poet, where its note is harsh and dissonant it is no echo of the discords of that unequal and most capricious singer. Many of Donne's favourite measures he has not employed; some of his own measures, the measures in which he has been most successful, have no prototype in Donne's poems. What he owes in lyric poetry to the leader of the Metaphysical School is to be found, so far as form is concerned, rather in what Donne suggested than in what he directly taught. In spirit he owed, it must be allowed, much. From Donne he learned to sport with extravagant fancies, to substitute the language of the schools for the language of the heart, to think like the author of the *Enneads* and to write like the author of *Euphues.* He has, however, had the good taste to avoid the grosser faults of his master. He never indulges in preposterous absurdities; he never, if we except one couplet, clothes mysticism in motley.

Herbert's most conspicuous defects, both in these and in his other poems, are want of finish and excessive obscurity. He seldom does justice to his conceptions. He had evidently no love for the labour of the file, and he has paid, like Donne and Fulke Greville, the just penalty for his carelessness.

8. A. H. Welsh

1882

An American literary historian followed Taine's view of the Jacobean and Caroline poets[1] (*The Development of English Literature and Language,* vol. I, 1882, pp. 412–13).

[Welsh cites the poetry of Vither, Carew, Herrick and Suckling as evidence of a prevailing decadence in seventeenth-century writing, then turns to Donne to show how this decadence corrupts the writing.]

A second mark of decadence is the affectation of poets, their involved obscurity of style, their ingenious absurdities, their conceits. They desire to display their skill and wit in yoking together heterogeneous ideas, in justifying the unnatural, in converting life into a puzzle, and dream. They are characterized by the philosophizing spirit, the activity of the intellect rather than that of the emotions. The prevalent taste to trace resemblances that are fantastic, to strain after novelty and surprize. Thus Donne, earliest of the school, says of a sea-voyage:

> There note they the ships sicknesses, the Mast
> Shak'd with this ague, and the Hold and Wast
> With a salt dropsie clog'd, . . .

When a flea bites him and his mistress, he says:

> This flea is you and I, and this
> Our mariage bed, and mariage temple is . . .

[He quotes the rest of the stanza.]

We find little to admire and nothing to love! We see that far-fetched similes, extravagant metaphors, are not here occasional blemishes but the substance. He should have given us simple images, simply expressed; for he loved and suffered much: but fashion was stronger than nature.

NOTE

1 See *The Critical Heritage: John Donne*, vol. I, ed. A. J. Smith (London: Routledge and Kegan Paul, 1975), pp. 450–2.

9. Edmund Gosse

1883

Gosse (1848–1929) prepared his long embroilment with Donne by explaining in a preface why he had omitted Donne from a set of essays on seventeenth-century topics (*Seventeenth Century Studies*, 1883, pp. viii–ix).

[Gosse claims that Donne is too big a subject, as Randolph is too small, to be dealt with at essay-length.]

That extraordinary writer casts his shadow over the vault of the century from its beginning to its close.... Donne is himself the paradox of which he sings; he is a seeming absurdity in literature. To be so great and yet so mean, to have phrases like Shakespeare and tricks like Góngora, to combine within one brain all the virtues and all the vices of the imaginative intellect, this has been given to only one man, and that the inscrutable Dean of St Paul's. To write fully of his work would be to write the history of the decline of English poetry, to account for the Augustan renaissance, to trace the history of the national mind for a period of at least a century. I felt Donne to be as far beyond the scope of my work as Ben Jonson would have been.

10. T. J. Backus

1884

A literary historian briefly surveyed 'The So-Called Metaphysical Poets', then gave an account of Donne (*Shaw's New History of English Literature*, rev. edn, 1884, pp. 143–4).

Although the literature of the seventeenth century indicates no marvelous outburst of creative power, it has yet left deep and enduring traces upon English thought and upon the English language. The influences of the time produced a style of writing in which intellect and fancy played a greater part than imagination or passion. Samuel Johnson styled the poets of that century the metaphysical school; that tendency to intellectual subtilty which appears in the prose and verse of the Elizabethan writers, and occasionally extends its contagion to Shakespeare himself, became with them a controlling principle. As a natural consequence, they allowed ingenuity to gain undue predominance over feeling; and in their search for odd, recondite, and striking illustrations they were guilty of frequent and flagrant violations of sense. Towards the close of the period Milton is a grand and solitary representative of poets of the first order. He owed little to his contemporaries. They were chiefly instrumental in developing the artificial manner which characterizes the classical writers of the early part of the eighteenth century.

John Donne ... was declared by Dryden to be the greatest of English wits. He was a representative of the highest type of the extravagances of his age. His ideal of poetical composition was fulfilled by clothing every thought in a series of analogies, always remote, often repulsive and inappropriate. His versification is singularly harsh and tuneless, and the crudeness of his expression is in unpleasant contrast with the ingenuity of his thinking. In his own day his reputation was very high. 'Rare Ben' pronounced him 'the first poet of the world in some things', but declared that 'for not being understood he would perish'. This prophecy was confirmed by public opinion in the eighteenth century, but has been somewhat modified by the criticism of our day, which dis-covers much genuine poetical sentiment beneath his faults of taste. His writings certainly give evidence of rich, profound, and varied learning.

Donne's early manhood was passed in company with the famous wits of the Mermaid Tavern. The chief productions of his youthful muse were his *Satires*, the *Metempsychosis*, and a series of amatory poems. When forty-two years old, he was ordained as a priest in the Church of England. He soon became a famous preacher, and was appointed Dean of St Paul's.

11. George Edward Bateman Saintsbury

1887

George Saintsbury (1845–1933), Regius Professor at Edinburgh, proved to be one of Donne's most steadfast champions. He sustained his qualified admiration for Donne's
writings in published commentaries over some three decades.
His first substantial account of Donne started in a discussion
of the development of English satire (*Elizabethan Literature*
(1887), 1910, pp. 145–51, 177 and 387).

... the Satires of Donne ... were indeed, like the other poetical
works of their marvellously gifted writer, not published till many
years after; but universal tradition ascribes the whole of Donne's
profane poems to his early youth. ...

At any rate after the work (in so many ways remarkable) of
Donne, Hall, and Marston, there could hardly be any more doubt
about the matter, though part of the method which these writers,
especially Donne and Marston, took to give individuality and 'bite'
to their work was as faulty as it now seems to us peculiar.

Ben Jonson, the least gushing of critics to his contemporaries,
said of John Donne that he was 'the first poet of the world in some
things', and I own that without going through the long catalogue
of singularly contradictory criticisms which have been passed on
Donne, I feel disposed to fall back on and adopt this earliest,
simplest, and highest encomium. Possibly Ben might not have
meant the same things that I mean, but that does not matter. It is
sufficient for me that in one special point of the poetic charm – the
faculty of suddenly transfiguring common things by a flood of light,
and opening up strange visions to the capable imagination – Donne
is surpassed by no poet of any language, and equalled by few. That
he has obvious and great defects, that he is wholly and in all
probability deliberately careless of formal smoothness, that he
adopted the fancy of his time for quaint and recondite expression
with an almost perverse vigour, and set the example of the topsy-
turvified conceits which came to a climax in Crashaw and Cleveland, that he is almost impudently licentious in thought and
imagery at times, that he alternates the highest poetry with the

lowest doggerel, the noblest thought with the most trivial crotchet – all this is true, and all this must be allowed for; but it only chequers, it does not obliterate, the record of his poetic gifts and graces. He is, moreover, one of the most historically important of poets, although by a strange chance there is no known edition of his poems earlier than 1633, some partial and privately printed issues having disappeared wholly if they ever existed. His influence was second to the influence of no poet of his generation, and completely overshadowed all others, towards his own latter days and the decades immediately following his death, except that of Jonson. Thomas Carew's famous description of him as

> A king who ruled as he thought fit
> The universal monarchy of wit,

expresses the general opinion of the time; and even after the revolt headed by Waller had dethroned him from the position, Dryden, his successor in the same monarchy, while declining to allow him the praise of 'the best poet' (that is, the most exact follower of the rules and system of versifying which Dryden himself preferred), allowed him to be 'the greatest wit of the nation'.

His life concerns us little, and its events are not disputed, or rather, in the earlier part, are still rather obscure. Born in 1573, educated at both universities and at Lincoln's Inn, a traveller, a man of pleasure, a law-student, a soldier, and probably for a time a member of the Roman Church, he seems just before reaching middle life to have experienced some religious change, took orders, became a famous preacher, was made Dean of St Paul's, and died in 1631.

It has been said that tradition and probability point to the composition of most, and that all but certain documentary evidence points to the composition of some, of his poems in the earlier part of his life. Unless the date of the Harleian MS is a forgery, some of his satires were written in or before 1593, when he was but twenty years old. The boiling passion, without a thought of satiety, which marks many of his elegies would also incline us to assign them to youth, and though some of his epistles, and many of his miscellaneous poems, are penetrated with a quieter and more reflective spirit, the richness of fancy in them, as well as the amatory character of many, perhaps the majority, favour a similar attribution. All alike display Donne's peculiar poetical quality – the fiery imagination shining in dark places, the magical illumination

27

of obscure and shadowy thoughts with the lightning of fancy. In one remarkable respect Donne has a peculiar cast of thought as well as of manner, displaying that mixture of voluptuous and melancholy meditation, that swift transition of thought from the marriage sheet to the shroud, which is characteristic of French Renaissance poets, but less fully, until he set the example, of English. The best known and most exquisite of his fanciful flights, the idea of the discovery of

> A bracelet of bright hair about the bone

of his own long interred skeleton: the wish –

> I long to talk with some old lover's ghost
> Who died before the god of love was born,

and others, show this peculiarity. And it recurs in the most unexpected places, as, for the matter of that, does his strong satirical faculty. In some of his poems, as the *Anatomy of the World*, occasioned by the death of Mrs Elizabeth Drury, this melancholy imagery mixed with touches (only touches here) of the passion which had distinguished the author earlier (for the *Anatomy* is not an early work), and with religious and philosophical meditation, makes the strangest amalgam – shot through, however, as always, with the golden veins of Donne's incomparable poetry. Expressions so strong as this last may seem in want of justification. And the three following pieces, the 'Dream', a fragment of satire, and an extract from the Anatomy, may or may not, according to taste, supply it. . . .

[He quotes the whole of 'The Dream', lines 35–55 of *Satire* 5, and lines 221–50 of *The Second Anniversary*, and apologizes for representing Donne's poetry by so few examples of it.]

But no short extracts will show Donne, and there is no room for a full anthology. He must be read, and by every catholic student of English literature should be regarded with a respect only 'this side of idolatry', though the respect need not carry with it blindness to his undoubtedly glaring faults.

Those faults are not least seen in his Satires, though neither the unbridled voluptuousness which makes his Elegies shocking to modern propriety, nor the far-off conceit which appears in his meditative and miscellaneous poems, is very strongly or specially represented here. Nor, naturally enough, is the extreme beauty of thought and allusion distinctly noteworthy in a class of verse which does not easily admit it. On the other hand, the force and originality of Donne's intellect are nowhere better shown. It is a constant fault of modern satirists that in their just admiration for Horace and Juvenal they merely paraphrase them, and, instead of going to the fountainhead and taking their matter from human nature, merely give us fresh studies of *Ibam forte via sacra*[1] or the Tenth of Juvenal, adjusted to the meridians of Paris or London. Although Donne is not quite free from this fault, he is much freer than either of his contemporaries, Regnier or Hall. And the rough vigour of his sketches and single lines is admirable. Yet it is as rough as it is vigorous; and the breakneck versification and contorted phrase of his satires, softened a little in Hall, roughened again and to a much greater degree in Marston, and reaching, as far as phrase goes, a rare extreme in the *Transformed Metamorphosis* of Cyril Tourneur, have been the subject of a great deal of discussion. It is now agreed by all the best authorities that it would be a mistake to consider this roughness unintentional or merely clumsy, and that it sprung, at any rate in great degree, from an idea that the ancients intended the *Satura* to be written in somewhat unpolished verse, as well as from a following of the style of Persius, the most deliberately obscure of all Latin if not of all classical poets. In language Donne is not (as far as his Satires are concerned) a very great sinner; but his versification, whether by his own intention or not, leaves much to desire. At one moment the ten syllables are only to be made out by a Chaucerian lengthening of the mute *e*; at another the writer seems to be emulating Wyatt in altering the accent of syllables, and coolly making the final iambus of a line out of such a word as 'answer'. It is no wonder that poets of the 'correct' age thought him in need of rewriting; though even they could not mistake the force of observation and expression which characterises his Satires, and which very frequently reappears even in his dreamiest metaphysics, his most recondite love fancies, and his warmest and most passionate hymns to Aphrodite Pandemos.

[He remarks that Donne, with Ben Jonson, 'determined much of the course of English poetry for many years', and describes Donne's effect upon his followers.]

That great writer's burning passion, his strange and labyrinthine conceits, the union in him of spiritual and sensual fire, influenced the idosyncrasies of each as hardly any other writer's influence has done in other times; while his technical shortcomings had unquestionably a fatal effect on the weaker members of the school.

NOTE

1 'I was strolling by chance along the Sacred Way' (Horace, *Satires*, I.ix.1, Loeb translation).

12. Jakob von Schipper

1888/95

Professor J. von Schipper of the University of Vienna made free use of Donne in his illustration of English rhythms (*Englische Metrik*, vol. II, 1888, p. 204 and passim; *Grundriss der englischen Metrik*, 1895, translated by the author as *A History of English Versification*, 1910, pp. 353–67).

[Schipper notes a number of metrical characteristics of Donne's verse, and some innovations in it. Nonetheless he takes an orthodox view of Donne's metrical idiosyncrasies, noting that the rhymed pentameter verse of Shakespeare and other sixteenth-century poets]

is on the whole as excellently correct and euphonic as John Donne's is full of faults and jerky; yet he achieves a flowing rhythm in most of his poems written in stanza form, for some of which he uses shorter metres.

13. Margaret Woods
1889

The headmistress of the Clifton High School for Girls, Bristol, compiled a third collection of poetry 'primarily for the Upper Forms of High Schools' (*A Third Poetry Book*, 1889, pp. 127, 211–12 and 273–6).

[The volume gives some 196 poems or bits of poems, from Chaucer to J. R. Lowell, and includes three items by Donne. A fragment of 'Love's Growth' (lines 1–6 and 15–20) appears as a whole conception. *The First Anniversary* is given entire. Some three pages of highlights from *The Second Anniversary*, not always indicating cuts, string together lines 1–6, 67–81, 221–30, 241–50, 435–67, 516–28. No comments are offered on the poems, but unfamiliar uses are sensibly glossed.]

14. Edward Dowden
1890

Professor Dowden (1842–1913), of Trinity College Dublin, read an appreciative paper on Donne's poetry to the Elizabethan and Literary Society in May 1990. Dowden promptly published the paper in a periodical, and evidently judged it to have still wider interest ('The Poetry of John Donne', *Fortnightly Review*, n.s. 232 (1890), 791–808). The paper was reprinted three times in journals in 1890, and Dowden also included it in his *New Studies in Literature*, 1895, pp. 90–120).

The study of a great writer acquires its highest interest only when we view his work as a whole; when we perceive the relation of the parts to one another, and to their centre; when nothing remains isolated or fragmentary; when we trace out unity in variety; when we feel the pulse and the rhythm of life. I had hoped to speak of Donne the famous preacher as well as Donne the poet, and to show how the same intellect and the same heart lived under the doublet of the poet, courtier, scholar, and the gown of the grave, yet passionate divine. But the task has proved too much for the limited time at my disposal. I must reserve for some other occasion what I have to say of the eloquent Dean of St Paul's. In presenting to Sir Robert Carr, afterwards Earl of Somerset, the unworthy favourite of James I, one of his early works, the author begs him to remember that 'Jack Donne', not 'Dr Donne', was the writer. It is of Jack Donne that I propose to speak this evening. After he had taken holy orders Donne seldom threw his passions into verse; even his 'Divine Poems' are, with few exceptions, of early date; the poet in Donne did not cease to exist, but his ardour, his imagination, his delight in what is strange and wonderful, his tenderness, his tears, his smiles, his erudition, his intellectual ingenuities, were all placed at the service of one whose desire was that he might die in the pulpit, or if not die, that he might take his death in the pulpit, a desire which was in fact fulfilled.

The latest historian of Elizabethan literature, Mr Saintsbury, has said that Donne the poet should be regarded with a respect only 'this side idolatry'. There is indeed a large expense of spirit in the poems of Donne, an expense of spirit not always judicious or profitable, and the reader who comes with reasonable expectations will get a sufficient reward. When prospecting for gold the miner considers himself fortunate if he can reckon on finding some twenty pennyweights of the precious metal in a ton of quartz and wash-dirt. The prospector in the lesser poetry of any former age must be content to crush a good deal of quartz and wash a good deal of sand in the expectation of an ounce of pure gold. But by vigour and perseverance in the pursuit large fortunes may be amassed.

Donne as a poet is certainly difficult of access. How shall we approach him, how effect an entrance? With different authors we need different methods of approach, different kinds of cunning to become free of their domain. Some must be taken by storm, some must be entreated, caressed, wheedled into acquiescence. There are poets who in a single lyric give us, as it were, a key which admits us to the mastery of all their wealth. Towards others we must make an indirect advance, we must reach them through the age which they represent, or the school in which they have been teachers or pupils. It is as the founder of a school of English poetry that Donne is ordinarily set before us. We are told that in the decline of the greater poetry of the Elizabethan period a 'metaphysical school' arose, and that Donne was the founder or the first eminent member of this school. I do not believe in the existence of this so-called 'metaphysical school'. Much of the most characteristic poetry of Donne belongs to the flood-tide hour of Elizabethan literature; to the time when Spenser was at work on the later books of the *Faerie Queene* and Shakespeare was producing his early histories and comedies. The delight in subtleties of thought, in over-ingenious fantasies, in far-fetched imagery, in curiosity, and not always felicitous curiosity, of expression was common to almost all the writers of the period. The dramatists were to some extent preserved from the abuse of fantastic ingenuity by the fact that they wrote for a popular audience, and must have failed unless they were at once intelligible. But authors of prose as well as authors in verse were fascinated by subtilties of the fancy; the theologian and the philosopher, as well as the poet, swung in the centre of a spider's web of fantasies.

> All the waving mesh
> Laughing with lucid dew-drops rainbow-edged.

There was no special coterie or school of 'metaphysical poets', but this writer or that yielded with more abandon than the rest to a tendency of the time.

It is not then by studying Donne as the leader of a school that we shall come to understand him. We get access to his writings, I believe, most readily through his life, and through an interest in his character as an individual. And fortunately he is the subject of a contemporary biography which is one of the most delightful biographies in the language.[1] We possess a large number of his letters, and for Donne friendship was almost a second religion, and to write a letter was often to give himself up to an ecstasy. The story of his life is an Elizabethan romance, made the more impressive by the fact that the romance is a piece of reality. . . .

[He gives an account of some episodes in Donne's life, showing how they bear upon the poetry.]

. . . he became a student of Lincoln's Inn, but he was more interested in poetry and theology than in the law. When he was twenty he was already known as a writer of high-conceited love lyrics, and led the way in another department of poetry as the first English satirist. He was the friend of wits and ladies and men of letters; he probably had known some of the bitter-sweets of forbidden pleasure.

'I be in such a planetary and erratique fortune', he writes, 'that I can do nothing constantly.' Papist and Protestant; doubter and believer; a seeker for faith and one who amused himself with sceptical paradoxes; a solitary thinker on obscurest problems and 'a great visitor of ladies', as Sir Richard Baker describes him, 'a great frequenter of plays'; a passionate student longing for action; a reader of the law; a toiler among folios of theology; a poet and a soldier; one who communed with lust and with death; a courtier and a satirist of the court; a wanderer over Europe and one who lay inactive in a sullen weedy lake without space for stroke of arms or legs – such was Donne up to his fortieth year.

About the time when Donne wrote the melancholy letter to Sir Henry Goodere from which I have quoted, he wrote also the poem entitled *The Litanie*, and sent the manuscript to the same friend. Through this poem we can obtain, perhaps, a clearer insight into Donne's character than through any other that he has written. In a series of stanzas, full of spiritual ardour, he invokes the persons of the Trinity, the Virgin Mary, the Angels, Patriarchs, Prophets, Apostles, Martyrs, Confessors, Virgins, and Doctors. He laments that he has fallen into ruin, that his heart by its dejection has turned to clay, that he who had been wasted by 'youth's fires of pride and lust' is now weather-beaten by new storms; he prays that his perpetual inquisition of truth may not darken the spiritual wisdom within him: –

> Let not my mind be blinder by more light.

He implores the 'eagle-sighted Prophets' to petition on his behalf that he may not by their example excuse his excess

> In seeking secrets or poetiqueness.

He hopes to win, through the blood of the martyrs, 'a discreet patience', which may endure death, or life, and, if life, then without too passionate a longing for the grave: –

> For oh, to some
> Not to be martyrs is a martyrdom!

34

And then in his litany he passes on to a series of petitions, which seem to be veritable sighs of desire from his inmost heart. The general purport of these may be expressed by saying that they are prayers for temperance of mind, for a *via media* between the extremes and excesses natural to a temperament at once ardently sensual and ardently spiritual. Donne feels that in either extreme of passion he must lose himself. He fears that the world may be too much to him, and fears equally that it may be too little; he would not think that all happiness is centred in earth's brightest places, nor yet that this earth is only framed for our prison; he prays that we may be preserved from the danger 'of thinking us all soul', and in consequence neglecting our mutual duties; from the danger of indiscreet humility; from thirst of fame, and no less from an unjust scorn of fame; from contempt of poverty, and from contempt of riches. The bodily senses, he maintains, though often fighting for sin, are in truth, not opposed to righteousness, but rather the 'soldiers of God'; learning, which sometimes tempts us from our allegiance, is, in truth, God's ambassador; beauty, though it may be poisoned, is, in truth, a flower of Paradise made for precious uses. The whole poem is directed against the temptations to which a man liable to the opposite violences of the flesh warring against the spirit, and the spirit warring against the flesh, is exposed. He fears a barren asceticism or the sweet blindness of mystical devotion almost as much as he fears the world and the flesh. With both extremes he has been acquainted, and now would win, if possible, an 'evenness' instead of his 'intermitting aguish piety'. He would especially seek deliverance from temptations of the intellect; from dwelling with an endless idle curiosity on nature, and so ceasing to bear his part in the life of the world, from a dilettante interest in religion, which uses it only as a mode of deploying a shallow intellectuality. The poem is the litany of the scholar, the courtier, the poet; it admits us to the secrets of its writer's troubled spirit.

Something of the same feeling appears in poems which are rather ethical than religious. Donne commends what he does not himself possess – a philosophical equanimity. In one of his letters in verse addressed to Sir Henry Wotton, he speaks of the various ways in which men lose themselves in cities, in courts, and in the solitude of the country, how the ideals of early life are corrupted and destroyed, so that if one of these men were to meet his true self there would scarcely be a recognition between the pair: –

> They would like strangers greet themselves, being then
> Utopian youth grown old Italian.

And then Donne proceeds to exhort his friend to seek for the tranquillity of a self-sufficing soul: –

> Be then thine own home, and in thyself dwell;
> Inn anywhere; continuance maketh hell.
> And seeing the snail, which everywhere doth roam,
> Carrying his own house still, is still at home,
> Follow – for he is easy-paced – this snail:
> Be thine own palace, or the world's thy jail.

But it is not a barren quietism that Donne commends. Man's nature is at first a wilderness, which must by degrees be reclaimed, and then actively tilled, that it may bear the noblest fruits. We are familiar with Tennyson's exhortation in *In Memoriam*: –

> Work out the beast,
> And let the ape and tiger die.

The same image is to be found in Donne's letter to Sir Edward Herbert, afterwards Lord Herbert of Cherbury: –

> How happy's he which hath due place assigned
> To his beasts, and disafforested his mind.

Donne would have these beasts tamed and put to the uses for which they are best fitted. How happy, the poet goes on, is he who has

> Empal'd himself to keep them out, not in:
> Can sow, and dares trust corn where they have bin,
> Can use his horse, goat, wolf, and every beast.

When the wilderness is reclaimed, then begins the vigorous tillage of the soil; as Donne elsewhere puts it: –

> We are but farmers of ourselves, yet may,
> If we can stock ourselves and thrive, uplay
> Much, much good treasure for the great rent day.

The vital centre of some of Matthew Arnold's poems, in which he tells of the pains of outward distraction and inward division, may be found in his exhortation to us to 'rally the good in the depths of ourselves', or in such a line as that which concludes the remarkable sonnet suggested by words of Marcus Aurelius: –

36

The aids to noble life are all within.

Donne preaches no such stoical gospel constantly; but he, too, can at times take a stoical text for his discourse: –

> Seek we then ourselves in ourselves; for as
> Men force the sun with much more force to pass
> By gathering his beams with a chrystal glass,
>
> So we, if we into ourselves will turn,
> Blowing our spark of virtue, may out-burn
> The straw which doth about our hearts sojourn.

There is some danger in the pride of stoicism; in the notion that one has attained; in the tendency to look down as from a pinnacle, rather than up towards the endless height yet to be climbed. In our own day no poet has expressed so nobly as Robert Browning the unsatisfied aspiration of the soul after perpetual progress. What though the body stand still or decline, the soul only rises from the body's decay and spreads wings for a farther flight. We remember the exultant spiritual advance of Rabbi ben Ezra amid the growing infirmities and sadnesses of old age. Browning hardly expressed this prerogative of the soul with more imaginative energy than Donne in his letter to Sir Henry Goodere: –

> A palace, when 'tis that which it should be,
>   Leaves growing, and stands such, or else decays;
> But he which dwells there is not so; for he
>   Strives to urge upward, and his fortune raise:
>
> So had your body her morning, hath her noon,
>   And shall not better; her next change is night:
> But her fair larger Guest, to whom sun and moon
>   Are sparks and short-liv'd, claims another right.

Donne apologises in this poem for his moralisings, which might as well be found, he says, at the end of fables or in the mottoes inscribed on fruit-trenchers. Even if this were true, we might read what he has written in this kind with interest. Much of a man's character and inmost experience is revealed by the selection which he makes from among the commonplaces of morality. When a truism strikes us as eminently true, it must have been vivified for us by some passage of the inner life, some moral victory or moral failure.

Several of Donne's most interesting poems are connected with incidents of his personal history, and gain an added interest from the fact that they are autobiographical. Few lovers of poetry are unacquainted with the Elegy addressed perhaps to his young wife when he thought of quitting his native land, and the ardent girl – a Shakespearean Viola in real life – proposed to accompany him in the disguise of a page. There is a vigour of movement, a strong coherence, a freedom from conceits in these lines which is not always, or perhaps very often, to be found in a like degree in Donne, and which we may ascribe to the fervour and directness of his feeling. . . .

[He quotes the first fourteen lines of *Elegy* 16, 'On his Mistress'.]

Touches of dramatic power are rare in Donne, whose genius was lyrical and meditative, not that of a dramatist; but in this Elegy there is one touch which might seem of triumphant power even if it had occurred in a tragedy by Webster. Having pictured the dangers to which his lady would be exposed in foreign lands, where, in spite of her garb of a boy, all would spy in her

> A blushing womanly discovering grace.

Donne goes on to exhort her, for his sake, to be of good cheer, and to dream no ill dreams during his absence: –

> Nor in bed fright thy nurse
> With midnight startings, crying out, 'Oh! Oh!
> Nurse, oh! My love is slain! I saw him go
> O'er the white Alps alone; I saw him, I,
> Assail'd, fight, taken, stabb'd, bleed, fall, and die.

All the greatness and terror of external nature are here made subservient to the passion of a girl's heart in that midnight cry – 'I saw him go o'er the white Alps alone.'

There are other poems of parting which probably refer to later seasons of their writer's life.

[He gives Walton's account of Donne's visit to France with Sir Robert Drury in 1612, and quotes the first stanza of 'the exquisite lyric of parting', the *Song*, 'Sweetest Love, I Do Not Go'.]

Walton refers to the same occasion of parting, Donne's 'Valediction, forbidding to mourn', in which occurs the quaint image of the two feet of the compass, one fixed, the other moving, and each inseparably united to the other.

[He describes the opening of 'A Valediction: Forbidding Mourning', and quotes lines 5–8.]

It will be for some close investigator of the facts of Donne's life – for Dr Jessop, let us hope – to attempt to ascertain the precise occasions of several of his poems. I like to think that it is of his young bride and the new glad morning of life which he found in her love that he speaks in his 'Good-morrow'. . . .

[He quotes the first stanza of 'The Good Morrow'.]

And I suppose there can be little doubt that it is the first annual return of the day of his meeting with her which is celebrated in another poem, written before marriage, and entitled *The Anniversary*. The two lovers are a king and queen, and what king and queen so safe as they, whom no treason can assail?

> True and false fears let us refrain
> Let us love nobly, and live, and add again
> Years and years unto years, till we attain
> To write three-score: this is the second of our reign.

A Lecture upon the Shadow, one of the most admirable of Donne's shorter poems, has in it a touch of fear lest love may, indeed, pass its meridian and decline towards the west. The poet undertakes to read his mistress a lecture in love's natural philosophy; as they walked side by side in the morning hours, the eastern sun threw their shadows behind them on the ground; so it was in the early days of secret love, when they practised disguises and concealment upon others; but now it is love's full noon, and they tread all shadows under foot: –

> That love hath not attain'd the highest degree,
> Which is still diligent lest others see.

Ah! What if the sun of love decline westerly? Then the shadows will work upon themselves and darken their path; each of them will practise disguisings upon the other: –

> The morning shadows wear away,
> But these grow longer all the day,
> But oh, love's day is short, if love decay.

39

Unfaith in aught, sings Vivien, is want of faith in all, and Donne's *Lecture upon the Shadow* closes with the same truth – or shall we say sophism? – of an ardent heart: –

> Love is a growing, or full constant light:
> And his short minute after noon is night.

The love of Donne and his wife may, perhaps, have known some of the cloudy vicissitudes incident to all things on earth, but it never waned. After her death, which took place before the days of his worldly prosperity as Dean of St Paul's, 'his first motion from his desolated house was,' says Walton, 'to preach where his beloved wife lay buried, in St Clement's Church, near Temple Bar, London; and his text was a part of the Prophet Jeremiah's Lamentation: "Lo I am the man that have seen affliction."'

In several of his early poems Donne, with his delight in paradox and dialectical ingenuity, maintains that love must needs range and change with boundless inconstancy: –

> Change is the nursery
> Of music, joy, life, and eternity.

It is, he declares, the very law of man's nature; and as for woman, a fair woman and a true may be found when we can catch a falling star, or translate the mermaid's song, or tell who cleft the devil's foot. We cannot doubt that Donne himself had followed false fires of passion before he found his true home of love. But it were rash to take all his poems of intrigue as passages of autobiography. He sometimes wrote best, or thought he wrote best, when his themes were wholly of the imagination. Still it is evident that Donne, the student, the recluse, the speculator on recondite problems, was also a man who adventured in pursuit of violent delights which had violent ends. I cannot think that the Elegy entitled *The Perfume*, has reference to an incident in his secret wooing of Ann More, his wife to be; if there be any autobiographical truth in the poem, it must be connected with some earlier passion. Once and only once, the Elegy tells us, was the lover betrayed in his private interviews with his mistress; her little brothers had often skipped like fairy sprites into the chamber, but had seen nothing; the giant porter at the gate, a Rhodian colossus –

> The grim eight-foot-high iron-bound serving-man,

for all his hire could never bear witness of any touch or kiss. Who then was the traitor? Not silks that rustled nor shoes that creaked. It was the courtier's perfume, scenting the air, as he crept to the chamber of his beloved, which betrayed his presence; whereupon the narrator breaks forth into reproaches against the effeminacy of perfumes, of which the one happy use were to embalm the corpse of the father who had interrupted their delights: –

> All my perfumes I give most willingly
> To embalm thy father's corpse. What, will he die?

We can well believe that in this poem Donne has set his fancy to work and created what he thought a piquant incident out of the stuff of dreams.

The Picture seems clearly to have been written on the occasion of his voyage as a volunteer with the Earl of Essex, or to have been suggested to his imagination by some such soldierly adventure. As he starts on his seafaring he bids farewell to his beloved, and places his picture in her hands. Thoughts of death fly like shadows across his mind; even if he should ever return, he will come back changed, with rough and weather-beaten face, his hand, perhaps, grown coarse, from labour at the oar, and tanned by the sun, his skin speckled with blue marks of the powder-grains: –

> If rival fools tax thee to have loved a man
> So foul and coarse as, oh, I may seem then,
> This [his picture] shall say what I was.

His lady will have the greater joy in knowing that she still owns her full beauty to bestow on one so worn, and will feel that the loss of what was fair and delicate in him is more than compensated by the manlier complexion of his love. There is no doubt that two descriptive poems, *The Storm* and *The Calm*, record some of Donne's experience on the Spanish expedition. In the former of these poems the terrors and miseries of a tempest at sea are set forth as they might be by one who had himself endured them. The writer does not paint from fancy, but had surely seen with his bodily eyes the pale landsmen creeping up on deck to ask for news, and finding no comfort in the sailors' rough replies: –

> And as sin-burden'd souls from graves will creep
> At the last day, some forth their cabins peep,
> And trembling ask, What news? And do hear so
> As jealous husbands what they would not know.

The Calm was a favourite with Ben Jonson, who could repeat by heart some of Donne's poems. It describes such a weary, torrid stillness of the elements as that suffered by the ancient mariner of Coleridge's poem; the men lying helpless on the hatches, the tackling hung with idle garments, the air all fire, the sea 'a brimstone-bath', the deck as hot to the feet as if an oven: –

> And in one place lay
> Feathers and dust to-day and yesterday.

The descriptions in these companion poems are unique in Elizabethan literature by virtue of Donne's choice of unusual subjects and his realistic manner of treatment.

Donne's *Satires* are also among the poems which were not spun out of his brain, but were written, to use Wordsworth's expression, with his eye upon the object. In one he tells how he was tempted away from the companionship of his beloved books, into the London streets, by a coxcomb, who, says Donne, though superstitiously devoted to all the rites and ceremonies of good manners, might be called for the precision of his fine breeding a very Puritan. There is something of majesty in the lines contrasting the poet's own condition with the elegance of this spruce master of ceremonies: –

> And in this coarse attire which now I wear
> With God and with the Muses I confer.

In another satire the object of Donne's ridicule is a small poet of the day who has turned lawyer, and who interlards his ordinary conversation with legal term and phrase, nay, who wooes in language of the pleas and bench: –

> Words, words, which would tear
> The tender labyrinth of a maid's soft ear
> More, more than ten Sclavonians' scoldings, more
> Than when winds in our ruin'd Abbeys roar.

In yet another there is a lively picture of the needy court suitor assuming courtier's airs, and in the end thankful to be dismissed with the gift of a crown-piece, a figure half-piteous, half-grotesque: –

> A thing more strange than on Nile's slime the sun
> E'er bred.

But of the *Satires* the most remarkable is one which hardly deserves that name; it is rather a hortatory poem addressed to those who fail as Christians to stand with their loins girt and their lamps burning. How is it, asks Donne, that the Stoic philosopher of Greece or Rome should be more zealous in the pursuit of the true ends of life than the Christian of to-day?

> Is not our mistress, fair Religion,
> As worthy of all our soul's devotion
> As Virtue was to the first blinded age?

How is it that a man will dare the frozen North and burning South, and undertake forbidden wars and give rash challenges for idle words, and yet will not be bold against his true foes and the foes of God, 'who made thee to stand sentinel in this world's garrison'? Donne glances at the various creeds and churches – Rome where the rags of religion are loved: –

> As we here obey
> The state-cloth where the Prince sate yesterday;

Geneva where religion is 'plain, simple, sullen, young, contemptuous, yet unhandsome'; and having spoken of the man who cares nothing for any form of faith, and the amateur in creeds who cares a little for all, he justifies the earnest seeker for truth, even though he still remain a doubter. We are reminded of an often-quoted stanza of *In Memoriam* by the words of Donne: –

> Doubt wisely; in strange ways
> To stand inquiring right is not to stray;
> To sleep, or run wrong, is.

But Donne would have the doubter attain, if possible, before old age comes, which he names the twilight of death, for that is the season to which rest in the possession of truth is due, and soon follows the night when no man can work. In this passage we have unquestionably a personal confession, a vindication of Donne's own attitude of inquiry and doubt, addressed by himself to himself.[2]

The section of Donne's poems entitled *Songs and Sonnets* is almost wholly devoted to love, and the metaphysics and casuistry of love. On occasions he can write, at least for a line or two, with a directness like that of Burns: –

> Yet I had rather owner be
> Of thee one hour than all else ever.

What words can be simpler than those, which sound almost as if they had come out of a song to Mary Morison or Jean Armour? More often he is ingeniously subtle. Mr Ruskin, if I remember right, has somewhere praised and overpraised the delicacy of a quatrain in Mr Coventry Patmore's *Angel in the House*, which is indeed a pretty Chinese puzzle in verse: the lady who has taken her lover's kiss maintains that her modesty is still inviolate: –

> He thought me asleep; at least, I knew
> He thought I thought he thought I slept.

A parallel may be found in Donne's poem *Love's Exchange*: –

> Let me not know that others know
> That she knows my pains, lest that so
> A tender shame make me mine own woe.

For the most part Donne in his love poems is high-fantastical, but this does not imply any coldness or insincerity. 'True love', he says, 'finds wit', but he whose wit moves him to love confesses that he does not know genuine passion. In a poem in which he makes various imaginary legacies, he leaves all that he has written in rhyme to Nature, in doing which, as he tells us, he does not *give* but *restore*; and it is undoubtedly a fact that there have been periods of literature when it was natural to seek out ingenuities of fancy and curiosities of expression. When Donne writes in his licentious vein he is not light and gay but studiously sensual; he makes voluptuousness a doctrine and argues out his thesis with scholastic diligence. To the other extreme belongs such a poem as that admirable lyric beginning with the lines: –

> I have done one braver thing
> Than all the Worthies did;
> And yet a braver thence doth spring,
> Which is – to keep that hid.

This rare achievement is to love a woman without a single thought of the difference of 'he and she'; but profane men would deride such love as this, and hence the braver thing is called for – to keep this spiritual friendship a secret from the unbelieving world. In this book of his, Donne declares –

Love's divines – since all divinity
  Is love or wonder – may find all they seek,
  Whether abstracted spiritual love they like,
Their souls exhaled with what they do not see,
    Or, loth so to amuse
    Faith's infirmities, they choose
  Something which they may see and use;

for though Mind be the heaven of love, Beauty is a type which represents that heaven to our mortal senses. Or, to cite another of Donne's similitudes, if love be an angel, yet an angel takes to himself a face and wings of air, else he were invisible; and in like manner love materialises itself through beauty while yet it remains a spirit. In *The Extasie* the same doctrine of amorous metaphysics is up-held; two lovers seated upon a flowery bank hold commune in the spirit, and time seems almost suspended: –

    And whilst our souls negotiate there
      We like sepulchral statues lay;
    All day the same our postures were,
      And we said nothing all the day.

But why should not hand meet hand and lip touch lip? There is an ascent and a descent in this complex nature of ours; the blood rarifies itself into the animal spirits,

      Because such fingers need to knit
      The subtle knot which makes us man;

and in like manner the soul must descend into the affections and the lower faculties,

    Else a great Prince [the soul] in prison lies.

The metre of *The Extasie* is the same as that of the *Angel in the House*, and the manner in which meaning and metre move together closely resembles that of Mr Patmore's *Preludes*.

The piece best known of all that Donne has written is that in which he imagines the exposure of his own skeleton, when his grave shall be reopened to receive a second guest, and the discovery of the secret love-token, 'a bracelet of bright hair about the bone'. It is sometimes forgotten that in this romantic piece of fantasy Donne heightens the effect by representing the lovers as during all their lives no other than ideal friends to whom such a pledge as this golden tress was the highest symbol granted of their perfect union: –

> Differences of sex we never knew,
> No more than guardian angels do.

The Funeral is a companion piece:

> Whoever comes to shroud me do not harm,
>   Nor question much,
> That subtle wreath of hair about mine arm;
> The mystery, the sign you must not touch,
>   For 'tis my outward soul.

But here it is evident that there was a time when the speaker 'knew difference of sex', had offered a man's love to the woman of his choice, had been rejected, and had received this gift as a token of friendship from which all thought of wedded union must be banished. Cartwright names one of his lyrics, *No Platonique Love*, and tells with what result he had once tried 'to practise this thin love': –

> I climb'd from sex to soul, from soul to thought;
>   But, thinking there to move,
> Headlong I roll'd from thought to soul, and then
> From soul I lighted at the sex again.

It may be conjectured that Donne sometimes toppled from his heights (if indeed it is a fall); but there is one poem in which, with evident sincerity and with rare grace, he sings the praises of autumnal beauty like that so gracefully pictured in Mr Alfred Austin's *Love's Widowhood*, and Donne finds in this loveliness, which is almost spiritual, a charm found nowhere else: –

> No Spring nor Summer's beauty hath such grace
> As I have found in one Autumnal face.

Here is Love's abiding-place: –

> Here dwells he, though he sojourn everywhere
> In Progress, yet his standing house is here.
> Here where still evening is, nor noon nor night,
> Where no voluptuousness, yet all delight.

The range is indeed wide between the feeling expressed in this poem and in others of the same group of Elegies.

In several of the passages from which I have quoted examples occur of the juxtaposition, so frequent in Donne, of thoughts of love and thoughts of the grave:

A fancy shared party per pale between
Death's heads and skeletons and Aretine.

When he gazes at womanly beauty he reflects that one day it will
be as useless as 'a sun-dial in a grave'; when at parting from his
mistress he scratches his name with his diamond upon her window-
pane, he leaves the ragged signature with her, he says, as a death's
head to preach the mortality of lovers; when he would learn the
ancient lore of passion in happier days before the Lord of Love
grew tyrannous, he desires to hear the tradition from a phantom: –

I long to talk with some old lover's ghost
Who died before the god of love was born.

His own brief love-lyrics are likened by him to 'well-wrought urns',
which will preserve the ashes confided to them as becomingly as
'half-acre tombs'. Even from an epithalamion he cannot banish a
thought of death; when the bride rises on the wedding morning
from her downy bed, the impression left by her body reminds him
of the grave: –

Your body's print
Like to a grave the yielding down doth dint.

In whatever sunny garden and at whatever banquet Donne sits,
he discerns in air the dark scythesman of that great picture
attributed to Orcagna. An entire section of his poetry is assigned
to death. In one of the funeral elegies he compares death to the
sea that environs all, and though God has set marks and bounds to
it, yet we can for ever hear it roar and gnaw upon our shores. In
another the similitude is hardly less majestic: Death is a 'mighty bird
of prey', but 'reclaimed by God', and taught to lay all that he kills
at his Master's feet.

Donne's most ambitious efforts as a poet are not the most
successful. One of these is the sequence of elegiac poems suggested
by the death of Mistress Elizabeth Drury, his friend Sir Robert
Drury's daughter, who died in her fifteenth year. Donne had had
no personal knowledge of her; he was, as it were, the poetical tomb-
maker, and he determined to erect a pompous monument in verse.
On each anniversary of the day of death he purposed to present his
friend with a memorial poem; but not more than two of these were
written, nor can we regret that this funereal Eiffel tower was carried

47

no higher than the second stage. Donne expatiates on a general theme rather than laments an individual; true sorrow is discreet, and sets a bound to extravagance; but here the poet, taking for his subject the loss of ideal womanhood, does not write under the controlling power of deep personal grief, and pushes to an extreme his fantastic exaggerations. In the poem of the first anniversary Donne enlarges on the frailty and decay of the whole world; in the second elegy he traces the progress of the soul. Thus they form a contrasted pair. The lines in the second poem, which picture the face of the dead maiden as it was in life, sensitive to every motion of her spirit, are well known: –

> Her pure and eloquent blood
> Spoke in her cheeks, and so distinctly wrought
> That one might almost say her body thought.

But in the earlier elegy there are lines perhaps more admirable which have been forgotten. Donne is maintaining that while the doers and workers of the world may be named the active organs of society, the very life of its life and soul of its soul resides in rare spirits, like that of the dead girl, which awaken in us what he elsewhere calls 'the whole of divinity' – wonder and love: –

> The world contains
> Princes for arms, and Counsellors for brains,
> Lawyers for tongues, Divines for hearts and more,
> The rich for stomachs, and for backs the poor;
> The officers for hands, merchants for feet
> By which remote and distant countries meet:
> But those fine spirits which do tune and set
> This organ are those pieces which beget
> Wonder and love.

It will be remembered that the word 'piece' is used by Elizabethan writers in the sense of perfect specimen or masterpiece, as where Prospero describes her mother to Miranda as 'a piece of virtue'.

Donne's other ambitious effort in verse is also a fragment. It is that singular poem, written in an elaborate stanza of his own, and embodying the doctrine of metempsychosis, which bears the same title as the later written elegy on the death of Mistress Elizabeth Drury – *The Progress of the Soul.* 'Now when I begin this book', Donne writes – and at this time he was in his twenty-eighth year – 'I have no purpose to come into any man's debt; how my stock will hold out I know not.' We may lament that he did not carry out his complete design, for though the poem could never have been popular, it would have afforded, like the Scotchman's haggis, 'a hantle of miscellawneous feeding' for those with an appetite for the strange dishes set before them by Donne. Professor Minto, in an excellent study of Donne, contributed to *The Nineteenth Century*, has said of this poem that, if finished, it might have been a monument worthy of its author's genius. The soul whose progress the poet traces was once the apple of temptation in the garden of Eden:

> Prince of the orchard, fair as dawning morn.

Thence it passed into the dark and mysterious life of the mandrake, and ascending through antediluvian fish and bird and beast, became in the course of time the ape which toyed wantonly with Adam's fifth daughter, Siphatecia. In the last transformation recorded by the poet the soul is incarnated in Themech, the sister and the wife of Cain; but its brave adventures have only just begun. There was scope in Donne's design for a history of the world; the deathless soul would have been a kind of Wandering Jew, with this advantage over Ahasuerus, that it would have been no mere spectator of the changes of society, but itself a part and portion of the ever-shifting, ever-progressing world of men.

NOTES

1 Izaak Walton's *Life*.
2 Another parallel with a passage of *In Memoriam* may be noted –

> I thought if I could draw my pains
> Through rhyme's vexation, I should them allay.
> Grief brought to number cannot be so fierce,
> For he tames it that fetters it in verse.

So Donne. And Tennyson similarly in the well-known stanza –

> But, for the unquiet heart and brain,
>   A use in measured language lies;
>   The sad mechanic exercise
> Like dull narcotics lulling pain.

[Dowden's note.]

15. W. F. Collier

1891

W. F. Collier was a prolific writer of history texts for schools. His popular *History of English Literature in a Series of Biographical Sketches* (1861; reprinted a number of times, and extended to include a section on American literature) showed that a warmer response to Donne was becoming orthodox (*A History of English Literature in a Series of Biographical Sketches* (1861), 1891, p. 168).

[Collier delivers summary judgement upon Donne.]

He deserves remembrance as a very learned man, who began the list of what critics call the Metaphysical poets. Beneath the artificial incrustations which characterise this school, Donne displays a fine vein of poetic feeling.

16. Edmund Gosse

1891

In *Gossip in a Library*, Gosse reprinted a series of articles originally published in the *Saturday Review, St James's Gazette, Black and White*, and the *Independent* (New York). The articles were either 'retrospective reviews' of books Gosse possessed 'which seem less known in detail to modern readers than they should be', or cases 'where personal history of a well-known book seems worth detaching from our critical estimate of it'. His article on Donne, titled 'Death's Duel', is an account of Donne's last days and his final sermon before James I, on the text of the words from the sixty-eighth psalm: 'And unto God the Lord belong the issues of death.' This was subsequently published as *Death's Duel*, with a reproduction of the upper part of the painting of Donne wrapped in a winding sheet as frontispiece (*Gossip in a Library*, 1891, pp. 55–64).

[The article opens with an arresting account of the painting of the famous picture. In early March 1630 (1631) Donne 'being desperately ill, and not likely to recover', ordered a wooden urn 'just large enough to hold his feet, and a board as long as his body, to be produced'. When they were brought to his warmed study]

the old man stripped off his clothes, wrapped himself in a winding-sheet which was open only so far as to reveal the face and beard, and then stood upright in the little wooden urn, supported by leaning against the board. His limbs were arranged like those of dead persons, and when his eyes had been closed, a painter was introduced into the room, and desired to make a full-size picture of this terrific object, this solemn theatrical presentment of life in death.

[Donne had the portrait placed beside his bed during his final two weeks, the '"hourly object" of his attention'.

The sermon, which was preached in the first Friday in Lent, is written in 'long, stern sentences of sonourous magnificence, adorned with fine similes and gorgeous words'.]

[The] dying poet shrinks from no physical horror and no ghostly terror of the great crisis which he was himself to be the first to pass through.... The most ingenious of poets, the most subtle of divines, whose life had been spent in examining Man in the crucible of his own alchemist fancy, seems anxious to preserve to the very last his powers of unflinching spiritual observation.

[The book also contains the funeral verses on Donne by Dr Henry King, Bishop of Chichester, and Edward Hyde, later to become the Earl of Clarendon. Gosse concludes:]

the materials for a Life of Dr Donne are fairly copious, but no good memoir of him exists, none better than the garrulous and amiable narrative of Izaak Walton.... Donne is one of the most fascinating, in some ways one of the most inscrutable, figures in our literature, and we would fain see his portrait drawn from his first wild escapade into the Azores down to his voluntary penitence in the pulpit and the winding-sheet.

17. Gamaliel Bradford

1892

In a substantial commendation of Donne's poetry, the American psycho-biographer Gamaliel Bradford (1863–1932) set out to bridge the gap between 'those who know', to whom Donne's poetry is 'an object of enthusiasm', and the general reading public, which ignores Donne altogether ('The Poetry of Donne', *Andover Review,* 106 (1892), 350–67; reprinted in *A Naturalist of Souls,* 1917).

[Bradford quoted J. R. Lowell's and Swinburne's high praise of Donne,[1] threw in Ben Jonson's and Carew's tributes to Donne, and then staked his own claim.]

We shall find, I think, that the study of his poems fully justifies this high estimate of him, though his unpopularity with those who read to pass an idle hour is perfectly explicable.

[Bradford uses the circumstances of Donne's life and career to throw light on the character of the work. He finds that Donne's early canvassing of theological controversy reveals a nature which is marked by its intensity.]

... that restless, hungry energy of mind, which will not let a man shut his eyes while there is a corner of thought unprobed, unlightened. Vigor of intellect, fervor of emotion, – these are what give Donne his high position as a man and as a poet.

[Bradford disparages Pope's rewriting of *Satires* 2 and 4, and reprehends Johnson's use of Donne 'as a sort of scapegoat for Cowley ... two writers who have as little as possible in common'. He derides the idea that Pope mirrored nature more searchingly than Donne.]

The most obscure and elaborate poem of Donne strikes more deeply into the truths of nature and the heart of man than the most brilliant production of the clever rhymer of Twickenham.

[Donne's coarseness and needless difficulty must be allowed; nonetheless, his ruggedness is often the condition of his success.]

there is a strangeness, an appearance of labor, resulting from the intense, crowding energy of the poet's thought, an energy that cannot stop to arrange its expressions, to choose its figures, that strikes the iron at a white heat, moulds it, often awkwardly, but always leaves it with a stamp of power: I cannot propose a better instance of this than some parts – only some parts – of Shakespeare and almost the whole of Donne. Of course, these are all forms of one tendency manifesting itself in different temperaments; but Donne's was a different temperament from that of Sidney on the one hand and that of Cowley on the other. The essence of his poetical gift, the essence of his moral character, was effort, struggle. No one could be further removed than he from such simple sweetness as that of Spenser. Donne was always at war with the elements of style, bending them, rending them, straining them to match the sweeping tide of his thoughts and passions. Sometimes he conquered, and soared into the highest heaven of poetry; sometimes he was worsted and sank to depths lower than the lowest of prose. The effort he makes in the latter case, the distortions he produces, are painful, like the scratching of a pin on glass, as in the hideous exaggeration so often quoted.

[Bradford quotes stanza 1 of 'A Fever'. He dwells on Donne's versification, admitting the harshness of the *Satires*, demonstrating Donne's formal idiosyncrasies, yet urging that Donne had an artistic aim throughout and a profound metrical skill. He points out the vigour of movement in the *Satires*, the 'lines of extraordinary rhythmic power' in the *Holy Sonnets*, the 'exquisite subtlety of delicate music' in some of the *Songs and Sonnets*. All these felicities suggest that Donne's fault was carelessness rather than lack of ear; and even then his irregularities have been compounded by corrupt texts, now happily amended in Grosart's edition. Nonetheless, Bradford finds a positive value in Donne's roughness.]

The ruggedness, the force that stamps his verse is far more characteristic of his thought. He ransacks all nature for an image that will not dull the intensity of his feelings, and he thus falls into the vagaries that horrified Dr Johnson. But the originality and startling effectiveness of his figures have never been surpassed. He darts a flash of lightning on his object, strips it of all conventional trappings, with a grasp recalling Dante in power, if not in simplicity.

Here is a most Dantesque and terrible simile from the *Second Anniversary*.

[Bradford gives lines 9–22 of the poem. He quotes copiously from a wide range of Donne's poetry to demonstrate Donne's satires as masterly in their kind, with a power such as even Dryden cannot approach and which 'makes Pope seem dry and tame'. Hall's satires are more conventional, Wither's are thinner, Marston's have force but are difficult from affectation.]

Donne's, like all his work, are molded directly and naturally by the stern and tumultuous cast of his thought. He plows his way along, regardless of obstacles, tearing up language and metre by the roots; but his result is unequaled. Obscurity and coarseness will keep his satires from ever becoming popular, but no one has studied them carefully without being repaid. How the characters stand out! With what energy he lashes the vices and follies around him!

[He gives lines 93–105 and 107–8 of *Satire* 4, commenting on the 'keen wit' which lightens and enlivens it, then adds lines 83–7 of *Satire* 1 to show how divertingly Donne writes dialogue.]

This admirable comic gift is shown not only in Donne's satires, but in almost all his poems, and atones for many of his extravagances. Often, if you look carefully, you can see him with a half smile on his face that you should take him seriously. The richness and variety of his humor appear in such poems as *Woman's Constancy, The Triple Fool, . . . Love's Legacy*, and in flashes everywhere. Something in this mingling of mirth with passion, this swift interchange of grief and laughter, recalls Heine; but Donne had nothing of the cynic about him. The thing above all others that makes him beautiful and lovable is his tenderness, which separates him absolutely from the mockery of Heine, and still more from the savage invective of satirists like Marston.

[Bradford finds that a breadth of human sympathy dignifies Donne's artistic vision, as all his intellectual endeavours.]

As a poet and as a man Donne does, indeed, rise far above mere railers at humanity and life. His smile is that of sympathy, not that of scorn. His philosophy was too deep, his nature too serious, to allow him ever to be a trifler, jester, scoffer. His high intellectual earnestness never leaves him even in matters that seem light and trifling. He never shuns the struggle with great problems. One does not go to poets nor to Elizabethans for consistent philosophical reasoning; but in acute, thoughtful, and far-reaching comment on human life Donne is unsurpassed. Instances of this are best taken from his *Verse Letters*, where the dignity of tone is least often marred by conceits and strangeness.

[He quotes lines 47–52 of the verse letter 'To Sir Henry Wotton', 'Sir, more than kisses'; lines 19–24 of the verse letter 'To Mr Roland Woodward', 'Like one who in her third widowhood'; and lines 1–4 of 'the noble letter "To Sir Henry Goodyere", "Who makes the past, a pattern for next year".' He concludes that the dominant feature of Donne's work is intellect. Thought predominates to the point of pedantry, as in all Elizabethan poetry.]

But intellectual as they are, they all have imagination, passion. Compare Donne with Emerson and this point becomes clear. Emerson has no greater fancy for epigram, for cleverness, than the older poet, but he is always cold, never touched, fired, carried away. Donne at his strangest is stung with intense feeling, he blends beauty and grace with his harshest rhythms, with the subtlest refinements of his thought. This is his supreme excellence, the merit that makes one overlook all his faults, if it does not outweigh them. This lifts him a whole heaven above the ease of Waller and the sweetness of Cowley. He is real, he is alive. In satire, in elegy, in love lyric, in hymn, his words burn, and the reader who feels cannot but be kindled by them.

[Bradford allows that Donne's output is capriciously uneven, and particularly censures *The First Anniversary* as 'general and full of expressions that are exceedingly repulsive'. He finds only occasional effects to commend in *The Second Anniversary* and the *Metempsychosis*. Then he turns with evident relief to 'Donne's most satisfactory productions', the *Elegies*, 'and, above all, the *Lyrics*'.]

But, I confess, of all Donne's works his lyrics are to me the most delightful in their wisdom, their humor, their passion, their varying play of sense and sound. Has any one ever flashed the light of imagination so vividly upon the depths of feeling? Now he does this by a simple, almost careless touch, as in that line of the *Relic* so much praised by Lowell, which describes the openers of the poet's grave as finding 'A bracelet of bright hair about the bone' – just that one word 'bright' gleams like a star; or as in *Love's Legacy*.

[He quotes lines 50–1 of 'The Will'.]

Now he twists a wreath of faint, sweet, strange thoughts about a subject almost grotesque, which yet under his hands becomes intensely real, as in 'Air and Angels'.

[He quotes lines 19–28 of the poem.]

now he inserts in a poem made up of curious subtleties a few lines of the most solemn and touching dignity, like the conclusion of the lyrical *Anniversary*.

[He quotes lines 28–30 of the poem.]

In his lyrics the necessity of passion often saves Donne from using conceits, makes the conceits tolerable or even impressive when they come. This is illustrated by the whole poem called *A Valediction: of Tears*, also by the one 'Upon the Parting of His Mistress' which contains in a stanza condemned by Johnson, but praised by most critics, the comparison of himself and her to a pair of compasses.

[He quotes lines 27–32 of 'A Valediction: Forbidding Mourning'. Bradford notes Donne's preoccupation with death and the grave, and relates it to his Christian conviction, citing the 'Devotions', the 'Autumnal', the 'Nocturnal upon S. Lucy's Day', and the 'Hymn to Christ, at the Author's Last Going into Germany'. He quotes the first stanza of this hymn, 'with its movement swift and overwhelming as the mystical devotion it illustrates', and then attempts a balanced appraisal of Donne's poetry and of Donne.]

But the intensity and profound earnestness of Christian thought belong to Donne's secular poems also. This separates him not only from modern pessimists, but from his literary contemporaries, from the serene naturalism of Shakespeare, from the stern stoicism of Milton and Marvell. At any rate his Christianity was of another type than theirs. To him the essence of our life here was struggle and war. He never lost sight of the goal, the star of faith was never over-clouded for him; but the flesh was unequal to the spirit. He loved no eremitical solitude. He moved amid the bustle and confusion of cities and courts. He knew all the temptations and was led astray by them. But he always hated them, he never yielded, never despaired.

Through sin and wretchedness he fought his way upward, and the stamp of strife is left on all he ever wrote, not only on his sermons, but on the freest of his verses; all alike are the passionate expression of one of the noblest, tenderest, broadest, and deepest natures that ever received the subtle gift of genius. It is for this that Donne must remain preeminently great to those who will labor with him, not for his wit, nor his learning, nor his eccentricity. He has not the ingenious sanctity of Herbert, nor the lark-like loveliness and bright simplicity of Vaughan, nor the serene elevation of Giles Fletcher; but he has the moral dignity and grandeur of a soul which, not ignorant of the wretchedness of this world, is yet forever ravished with the love and worship of the eternal.

NOTE

1 'See *John Donne: The Critical Heritage*, vol. I, ed. A. J. Smith (London: Routledge and Kegan Paul, 1975), pp. 402 and 483.

18. Rudyard Kipling

1893

While snowed up in Vermont in December 1893, Kipling seems to have got down to some attentive reading of Donne, which he was eager to urge upon his friends (*The Letters of Rudyard Kipling*, ed. T. Pinney, vol. II: *1890–99*, 1990, pp. 111 and 115).

[Kipling wrote to W. E. Henley early in the month, exulting in his discovery of a cheap copy of the 1719 edition – 'I have found Tonson's 1719 Donne with the portrait in crushed levant and . . . the ass that sold it knew not its worth.' Then a fortnight later some remarks in a letter to Edward Lucas White indicate that Donne had stirred a lively response in him.]

I've been scandalously neglecting my duties to follow – Euterpe, I think, but it is one anyway of the nine harlots – these few weeks past experimenting with divers metres and various rhymes. The results serve excellent well to light fires and the work amuses one while it goes on. There's a heap in verse though apt to get out of hand – some of it – very. Do you know to the extent you ought the poems of Donne who was Browning's great-great grandfather? I've been reading him again for the health of my spirit and – he is no small singer. Must have been a haughty and proud stomached individual in his life – with R. B.'s temperament for turning his mind clean upside down as it were a full bottle and letting the ideas get out as they best could. He is not very accessible – all of him – by reason of his statements which are occasionally free. There were giants in those days and it is profitable to read 'em [he instances Fletcher, Drayton, and Drummond]. These are not of the first ranks you say? No but they worked largely and gave all they had to their verses. Read 'em again and yet again.

19. Edmund Gosse

1893

In a short study in a literary journal Gosse sought a better understanding of Donne's foibles ('The Poetry of John Donne', *New Revue*, 9 (1893), 244–7).

. . . first of all, it is necessary to make some remarks with regard to Donne's whole system of prosody. The terms 'irregular', 'unintelligible', and 'viciously rugged' are commonly used in describing it, and it seems even to be supposed by some critics that Donne did not know how to scan. This last supposition may be rejected at once; what there was to know about poetry was known to Donne. But it seems certain that he intentionally introduced a revolution into English versification. It was doubtless as a rebellion against the smooth and somewhat nerveless iambic flow of Spenser and the earliest contemporaries of Shakespeare that Donne invented his violent mode of breaking up the lines into quick and slow beats. The best critic of his own generation, Ben Jonson, hated the innovation, and told Drummond 'that Donne, for not keeping of accent, deserved hanging'. It is difficult to stem a current of censure which has set without intermission since the very days of Donne himself, but I may be permitted to point out what I imagine was the poet's own view of the matter.

He found, as I have said, the verse of his youth, say of 1590, exceedingly mellifluous, sinuous, and inclining to flaccidity. A five-syllabled iambic line of Spenser or of Daniel trots along with the gentlest amble of inevitable shorts and longs. It seems to have vexed the ear of Donne by its tendency to feebleness, and it doubtless appeared to him that the very gifted writers who immediately preceded him had carried the softness of it as far as it would go. He desired new and more varied effects. To see what he aimed at doing, we have, I believe, to turn to what has been attempted in our own time by Mr Robert Bridges, in some of his early experiments, and by the Symbolists in France. The iambic rhymed line of Donne has audacities such as are permitted to his blank verse by Milton . . . and although the felicities are rare in the older poet, instead of being almost incessant, as in the later, Donne at his best is not less melodious than Milton. When he writes –

> Blasted with sighs and surrounded with tears,

we must not dismiss this as not being iambic verse at all, nor – much less – attempt to read it –

> Blastéd with síghs, and surroundéd with teárs,

but recognise in it the poet's attempt to identify the beat of his verse with his bewildered and dejected condition, reading it somewhat in this notation –

> Blasted | with sighs | and surrounded | with tears.

The violence of Donne's transposition of accent is most curiously to be observed in his earliest satires, and in some of his later poems is almost entirely absent. Doubtless his theory became modified with advancing years. No poet is more difficult to read aloud. Such a passage as the following may excusably defy a novice: –

No token of worth but Queen's man and fine
Living barrels of beef and flagons of wine.
I shook like a spied spy. Preachers which are
Seas of wit and arts, you can then dare
Drown the sins of this place, for, for me,
Which am but a scant brook, it enough shall be
To wash the stains away.

But treat the five-foot verse not as a fixed and unalterable sequence of cadences, but as a norm around which a musician weaves his variations, and the riddle is soon read –

No token | of worth | but Queen's | man | and fine
Living | barrels of | beef and | flagons of | wine.
I shook | like a spied | spy. Preachers | which are
Seas | of wit | and arts, | you can then | dare
Drown | the sins | of this place, | for, | for me,
Which am | but a scant | brook, | it enough | shall be
To wash | the stains | away.

The poetry of Donne possesses in no small degree that 'unusual and indefinable witchery' which Dr Jessopp has noted as characteristic of the man himself. But our enjoyment of it is marred by the violence of the writer, by his want of what seems to us to be good taste, and by a quality which has been overlooked by those who have written about him, but which seems to provide the key to the mystery of his position. Donne was, I would venture to suggest, by far the most modern and contemporaneous of the writers of his time. He rejected all the classical tags and imagery of the Elizabethans, he borrowed nothing from French or Italian tradition. He arrived at an excessive actuality of style, and it was because he struck them as so novel and so completely in touch with his own age that his immediate coevals were so much fascinated with him. His poems are full of images taken from the life and habits of the time. Where earlier poets had summoned the myths of Greece to adorn their verse, Donne weaves in, instead, the false zoology, the crude physics and philosophy, of his own fermenting epoch. The poem called 'Love's Exchange' is worthy of careful examination in this respect. Each stanza is crowded with conceits, each one of which is taken from the practical or professional life of the moment in which the poet wrote. This extreme modernity, however, is one potent source of our lack of sympathy with the poetry so inspired. In the long run, it is the broader suggestion, the wider if more conventional range of classic imagery, which may hope to hold without fatigue the interest of successive generations.

For us the charm of Donne continues to rest in his occasional felicities, his bursts of melodious passion. If his song were not so tantalisingly fragmentary, we should call him the unquestioned nightingale of the Jacobean choir. No other poet of that time, few poets of any time, have equalled the concentrated passion, the delicate, long-drawn musical effects, the bold and ecstatic rapture of Donne at his best. In such a poem as 'The Dream' he realises the very paroxysm of amatory song. In his own generation no one approached the purity of his cascades of ringing monosyllables, his

> For God's sake, hold your tongue and let me love,

or,

> I long to talk with some old lover's ghost,
> Who died before the God of Love was born,

or,

> O more than moon,
> Draw not thy seas to drown me in thy sphere.

In these and similar passages, of which not a very slender florilegium might be gathered from his voluminous productions, Donne reminds us that Ben Jonson esteemed him 'the first poet in the world in some things'. But this quality of passionate music is not the only one discernible, nor often to be discerned. The more obvious characteristic was summed up by Coleridge in a droll quatrain: –

> With Donne, whose Muse on dromedary trots,
> Wreathe iron pokers into true-love-knots;
> Rhyme's sturdy cripple, Fancy's maze and clue,
> Wit's forge and fire-blast, Meaning's press and screw.

In the use of those ingenuities which it was once the fashion to call 'metaphysical' Donne shows an amazing pertinacity. He is never daunted by the feeling that his wit is exercised 'on subjects where we have no right to expect it', and where it is impossible for us to relish it. He pushes on with relentless logic – sometimes, indeed, past chains of images that are lovely and appropriate, but oftener through briars and lianas that rend his garments and trip up his feet. He is not affected by the ruggedness of his road, nor by our unwillingness to follow him. He stumbles doggedly on until he has reached his singular goal. In all this intellectual doggedness he has a certain kinship to Browning, but his obscurity is more dense. It is to be hoped that the contemporary maligned him who reported Donne to have written one of his elegies in an intentional obscureness, but that he delighted in putting his readers out of their depth can scarcely be doubted. It is against this lurid background, which in itself and unrelieved would possess a very slight attraction to modern readers, that the electrical flashes of Donne's lyrical genius make their appearance, almost blinding us by their brilliancy, and fading into the dark tissue of conceits before we have time to appreciate them.

20. Edmund Gosse

1894

Gosse devoted the third chapter of a book on the Jacobean poets to an account of Donne's poetry. Gosse's uncertainty about the canon, and his many errors of fact, suggest that Donne had not yet become the subject of accurate scholarship. Yet Gosse did give a *Holy Sonnet* from the Westmoreland Manuscript, no. 17, 'Since She Whom I Loved', which had never before appeared in print ('John Donne', in *Jacobean Poets*, 1894, pp. 47–67).

Among the non-dramatic poets who flourished under James I, incomparably the most singular and influential was the Roman Catholic scholar who became Dean of St Paul's. John Donne was thirty years of age when Elizabeth died, and no small portion of his most characteristic work must have been written in her reign. But Donne belongs, essentially, to that of her successor. In him the

Jacobean spirit, as opposed to the Elizabethan, is paramount. His were the first poems which protested, in their form alike and their tendency, against the pastoral sweetness of the Spenserians. Something new in English literature begins in Donne, something which proceeded, under his potent influence, to colour poetry for nearly a hundred years. The exact mode in which that influence was immediately distributed is unknown to us, or very dimly perceived. To know more about it is one of the great desiderata of literary history. The imitation of Donne's style begins so early, and becomes so general, that several critics have taken for granted that there must have been editions of his writings which have disappeared.

As a matter of fact, with the exception of two exceedingly slight appearances, that of ten sonnets contributed to Davison's *Poetical Rhapsody* in 1602, and of *An Anatomy of the World* in 1611, the poems of Donne are not known to have been printed until 1633, a year or two after his death. Yet the references to them in documents of twenty years earlier are frequent, and that they were widely distributed is certain. This was doubtless done by means of more or less complete transcripts, several of which have come down to our own day. These transcripts must have been passed from hand to hand at court, at the universities, in cultured country houses, and almost every poet of the Jacobean age must have been more or less familiar with their tenor. The style of Donne, like a very odd perfume, was found to cling to every one who touched it, and we observe the remarkable phenomenon of poems which had not passed through a printer's hands exercising the influence of a body of accepted classical work. In estimating the poetry of the Jacobean age, therefore, there is no writer who demands more careful study than this enigmatical and subterranean master, this veiled Isis whose utterances outweighed the oracles of all the visible gods.

For the secrecy with which the poems of Donne were produced no adequate reason is forthcoming. His conduct in other respects, though somewhat haughty, was neither cloistered nor mysterious. He was profuse in the publication of his prose writings, and denied his verse alone to his admirers. That the tenor of it clashed with his profession as a Churchman has been put forward as a reason, but it is not a very good one. Donne was not squeamish in his sermons, nor afraid of misconception in his *Pseudo-Martyr*. If he had had scruples of conscience about his secular poems he might have destroyed them, as George Herbert did his. It is idle to speculate on the cause of Donne's peculiar conduct. It suffices to record that having produced a quantity of poetry of extraordinary value, and intimately welcome to his generation, he would neither publish nor destroy it, but permitted, and perhaps preferred, that it should circulate among his most intelligent contemporaries in such a way as to excite the maximum of curiosity and mystery.

[He somewhat inaccurately outlines Donne's life and career, remarking that such an account does not touch the real interest of Donne's character.]

At the time of his death he was, beyond question, the most admired preacher in England. This brief sketch of the external circumstances of Donne's life may be sufficient for our purpose, but gives no idea of the mysterious discrepancies which existed in his character, of the singular constitution of his mind, or of his fiery eccentricity.

[He discusses the shortcomings of the early editions of Donne's poetry, and the danger of even conjecturing the dates of particular poems. He is nonetheless categorical in assigning the *Satires* – which 'are seven in number', he says – to the Elizabethan age and not the Jacobean.]

They are brilliant and picturesque beyond any of their particular compeers, even beyond the best of Hall's satires. But they have the terrible faults which marked all our Elizabethan satirists, a crabbed violence alike of manner and matter, a fierce voluble conventionality, a tortured and often absolutely licentious and erroneous conception of the use of language. The fourth is, doubtless, the best written, and may be taken as the best essay in this class of poetry existing in English literature before the middle-life of Dryden; its attraction for Pope is well known.

[He discusses the *Metempsychosis*, which he says 'is conjectured to have been written not earlier than 1610', and quotes De Quincey's praise of it.]

It is written in a variant of the Spenserian stanza, and is a hyperbolical history of the development of the human soul, extended to more than five hundred lines, and not ended, but abruptly closed. It is one of the most difficult of Donne's writings, and started a kind of psychological poetry of which, as the century progressed, many more examples were seen, none, perhaps, of a wholly felicitous character. It has the poet's characteristics, however, to the full. The verse marches with a virile tread, the epithets are daring, the thoughts always curious and occasionally sublime, the imagination odd and scholastic, with recurring gleams of passion.

Here is a fragment of this strange production . . .

[He quotes lines 301–20 and 331–40 of the *Metempsychosis*.]

Far less extraordinary are the Epistles, which form a large section of Donne's poetical works. All through life he was wont to address letters, chiefly in the heroic couplet, to the most intimate of his friends. These epistles are conceived in a lighter vein than his other writings, and have less of his characteristic vehemence. The earliest, however, 'The Storm', which he addressed from the Azores, possesses his Elizabethan mannerism; it is crudely picturesque and licentious, essentially un-poetical. 'The Calm', which is the parallel piece, is far better, and partly deserves Ben Jonson's high commendation of it to Drummond. The epistle to Sir Henry Goodyer is noticeable for the dignified and stately manner in which the four-line stanza, afterwards adopted by Gray for his *Elegy*, is employed; this poem is exceedingly like the early pieces written by Dryden some fifty years later. The school of the Restoration is plainly foreshadowed in it.

Many of these epistles are stuffed hard with thoughts, but poetry is rarely to be found in them; the style is not lucid, the construction is desperately parenthetical. It is not often that the weary reader is rewarded by such a polished piece of versification as is presented by this passage about love in the 'Letter to the Countess of Huntingdon',

[He quotes lines 57–76 of 'To the Countess of Huntingdon', 'That unripe side of earth'.]

Most of these epistles are New Year's greetings, and many are addressed to the noble and devout ladies with whom he held spiritual converse in advancing years. The poet superbly aggrandizes the moral qualities of these women, paying to their souls the court that younger and flightier cavaliers reserved for the physical beauty of their daughters.

The Epithalamia of Donne form that section of his work in which, alone, he seems to follow in due succession after Spenser. These marriage-songs are elegant and glowing, though not without the harshness which Donne could not for any length of time forego.

That composed for the wedding of Frederick Count Palatine and the Lady Elizabeth, in 1613, is perhaps the most popular of all Donne's writings, and opens with a delicious vivacity.

[He quotes the first stanza of the 'Epithalamion . . . on St Valentine's Day'.]

The ode within the rather stiff setting of the Allophanes and Idios eclogue is scarcely less felicitous.

The miscellaneous secular poems of Donne are generically classed under the heading of 'Elegies'. We have here some of the most extraordinary aberrations of fancy, some of the wildest contrasts of character and style, to be observed in literature. They are mainly Ovidian or Tibullan studies of the progress of the passion of love, written by one who proclaims himself an ardent, but no longer an illusioned lover, – hot, still, but violent and scandalous. The youth of the author is disclosed in them, but it is not the callous youth of first inexperience. He is already a past master in the subtle sophistry of love, and knows by rote 'the mystic language of the eye and hand'. Weary with the beauty of spring and summer, he has learned to find fascination in an autumnal face. The voluptuous character of these elegies has scandalized successive critics. Several of them, to be plain, were indeed too outstpoken for the poet's own, or for any decent age. Throughout it is seldom so much what the unbridled lover says, as his utter intemperance in saying it, that surprises, especially in one who, by the time the poems were given to the public, had come to be regarded as the holiest of men. Even saints, however, were coarse in the age of James, and the most beautiful of all Donne's elegies, the exquisite 'Refusal to allow his Young Wife to accompany him abroad as a Page', which belongs to his mature life and treats of a very creditable passion, is marred by almost inconceivable offences against good taste.

Another section of Donne's poems is composed of funeral elegies or requiems, in which he allowed the sombre part of his fancy to run riot. In these curious entombments we read nothing that seems personal or pathetic, but much about 'the magnetic force' of the deceased, her spiritual anatomy, and her soul's 'meridians and parallels'. Amid these pedantries, we light now and then upon extraordinary bursts of poetic observation, as when the eminence of the spirit of Mistress Drury reminds the poet of a vision, seen years before in sailing past the Canaries, and he cries out –

> Doth not a Teneriffe or higher hill,
> Rise so high like a rock, that one might think
> The floating moon would shipwreck there, and sink,

or as when one of his trances comes upon him, and he sighs –

> when thou know'st this,
> Thou know'st how wan a ghost this our world is.

These lovely sudden bursts of pure poetry are more frequent in the 'Funeral Elegies' than in any section of Donne's poetry which we have mentioned, and approach those, to be presently noted, in the Lyrics. The spirit of this strange writer loved to dwell on the majestic and gorgeous aspects of death, to wave his torch within the charnel-house and to show that its walls are set with jewels.

This may be taken as an example of his obscure mortuary imagination . . .

[He quotes lines 21–34 of the 'Elegy on the Lady Markham'.]

The presence of the emblems of mortality rouses Donne to an unusual intellectual ecstasy. The latest of these elegies is dated 1625, and shows that the poet retained his art in this kind of writing to the very close of his career, adding polish to his style, without any perceptible falling off in power.

A large number of 'Holy Sonnets', which Izaak Walton thought had perished, were published in 1669, and several remain still unprinted. They are more properly quatorzains than sonnets, more correct in form than the usual English sonnet of the age – for the octett is properly arranged and rhymed – but closing in the sestett with a couplet. These sonnets are very interesting from the light they throw on Donne's prolonged sympathy with the Roman Church, over which his biographers have been wont to slur. All these 'Holy Sonnets' probably belong to 1617, or the period immediately following the death of Donne's wife. In the light of certain examples in the possession of the present writer, which have not yet appeared in print, they seem to confirm Walton's remark that though Donne inquired early in life into the differences between Protestantism and Catholicism, yet that he lived until the death of his wife without religion.

A pathetic sonnet from the Westmoreland manuscript, here printed for the first time, shows the effect of that bereavement upon him . . .

[He gives the whole of the hitherto unknown *Holy Sonnet* 17, 'Since She Whom I Loved'.]

The sonnet on the Blessed Virgin Mary, however, has probably been attributed to Donne by error; the more likely name of Constable has been suggested as that of its author.

In his other divine poems, also, the Roman element is often very strong, and the theology of a cast which is far removed from that of Puritanism. In the very curious piece called 'The Cross', he seems to confess to the use of a material crucifix, and in 'A Litany' he distinctly recommends prayer to the Virgin Mary,

> That she-cherubim which unlocked Paradise.

All these are matters which must be left to the future biographers of Donne, but which are worthy of their closest attention in developing the intricate anomalies of his character.

We have now, by a process of exhaustion, arrived at what is the most interesting of the sections of Donne's poetry, his amatory lyrics. These are about seventy in number, and so far as the scanty evidence can be depended upon, belong to various periods from his twentieth to his thirty-fifth year. The series, as we now hold it, begins with the gross and offensive piece of extravagance called, 'The Flea', but is followed by 'The Good Morrow', which strikes a very different note. As a rule, these poems are extremely personal, confidential, and vivid; the stamp of life is on them. None the less, while confessing with extraordinary frankness and clearness the passion of the writer, they are so reserved in detail, so immersed and engulphed in secrecy, that no definite conjecture can be hazarded as to the person, or persons, or the class of persons, to whom they were addressed. One or two were evidently inspired by Donne's wife, others most emphatically were not, and in their lawless, though not gross, sensuality, remind us of the still more outstpoken 'Elegies'. In spite of the alembicated verbiage, the tortuousness and artificiality of the thought, sincerity burns in every stanza, and the most exquisite images lie side by side with monstrous conceits and ugly pedantries.

A peculiarity of the lyrics is that scarcely two of the seventy are written in the same verse-form. Donne evidently laid himself out to invent elaborate and far-fetched metres. He was imitated in this down to the Restoration, when all metrical effects tended to merge in the heroic couplet. But of the innumerable form-inventions of Donne and of his disciples scarcely one has been adopted into the language, although more than one, by their elegance and melody, deserve to be resumed.

This exemplifies one of the prettiest of his stanza-forms ...

[He quotes the second and third stanzas of the *Song* 'Go, and Catch a Falling Star'. Then he repeats, over some three pages, the account of Donne's prosody which he had given in his essay in the *New Revue* in the previous year. Finally he seeks to justify the attention he has paid to Donne.]

The prominence here given to Donne will be challenged by no one who considers what his influence was on the poetical taste of the time. It is true that among his immediate contemporaries the following of Spenser did not absolutely cease at once. But if a study on the poets of Charles I were to succeed the present volume, the name of Donne would have to be constantly prominent. On almost everything non-dramatic published in the succeeding generation, from Crashaw to Davenant, from Carew to Cowley, the stamp of Donne is set. Dryden owed not a little to him, although, as time went on, he purged himself more and more fully of the taint of metaphysical conceit. So late as 1692, in the preface to *Eleanora*, Dryden still held up Donne as 'the greatest wit, though not the best poet of our nation'. His poems were among the few non-dramatic works of the Jacobean period which continued to be read and reprinted in the age of Anne, and Pope both borrowed from and imitated Donne.

So far as we trace this far-sweeping influence exercised on the poets of a hundred years, we have difficulty in applauding its effects. The empassioned sincerity, the intuitions, the clarion note of Donne were individual to himself and could not be transmitted. It was far otherwise with the jargon of 'metaphysical' wit, the trick of strained and inappropriate imagery. These could be adopted by almost any clever person, and were, in fact, employed with fluent effect by people in whom the poetical quality was of the slightest. Writers like Mildmay Fane, Earl of Westmoreland, or like Owen Feltham (in his verse), show what it was that Donne's seed produced when it fell upon stony ground.

21. Sir Edmund Kerchever Chambers

1895

Explaining why Donne and his associates seem ill at ease with pastoral poetry, the Shakespearean scholar Sir Edmund Kerchever Chambers (1866–1954) developed a distinction, touched on by Edward Dowden and by Gosse, between the manner of Spenser and the manner of Donne, which became the orthodox view thereafter (*English Pastorals*, 1895, pp. xvii–xix).

Rightly to judge of the pastoral impulse in English verse we must look not to the eighteenth century, and not to the nineteenth, but strictly to the period between the coming of Elizabeth and that inauspicious moment, nearly a hundred years later, when Puritanism for a while snuffed out literature. Outside the drama, with only the fringes of which we are concerned, the poetry, and in a measure the prose, of that hundred years, is the outcome of two distinct and partly-opposed waves of tendency. One does not like the expression, 'a school of poetry'; but it is difficult to dissociate the tendencies or tempers in question from the influence of two representative and dominant personalities, those of Spenser the musical, and of Donne the imaginative. On the one hand there is a body of poetry, transparent, sensuous, melodious, dealing with all the fresh and simple elements of life, fond of the picture and the story, rejoicing in love and youth, in the morning and the spring; on the other, a more complex note, a deeper thrill of passion, an affection for the sombre, the obscure, the intricate, alike in rhythm and in thought, a verse frequent with reflections on birth and death, and their philosophies, a humour often cynical or pessimistic, always making its appeal rather to the intellect than to the senses. The manner of Spenser and the manner of Donne, the Elizabethan style and the Jacobean, if you will; the two have to be carefully distinguished in any adequate treatment of the age. Yet either nomenclature is misleading; we have not to deal with two rival masters and two coteries of imitators, nor with two styles, whereof one at some moment of crisis or upheaval succeeded and replaced the other, as, for instance, the literature of the romantic revival succeeded and replaced the literature of the age of Pope. Rather we have to deal with two habits of thinking and writing, which belong to different and alternating tendencies in the one full life of a complex age, but which, throughout that age, co-existed and interpenetrated each other in a hundred ways. Certainly Spenser and Donne are the typical exponents of their respective groups; certainly the personal influence of either would be hard to overestimate; certainly of imagination; for in national as in individual life, the simple invariably comes before the complex, feeling precedes thought; but though the one temper grows and the other diminishes, still to the last they appear side by side, often directing in this mood and in that the harmonies of the same pen.

There can be no question that pastoral poetry is the proper province of those writers whom we have associated with the name of Spenser. Amongst them alone it reaches the complete and characteristic development. Donne and his fellows write pastorals, but the shepherd's smock sits awkwardly upon them. They twist the bucolic theme and imagery to the expression of alien emotions and alien ideas. The convention becomes too obvious. It is the philosopher in the hay-field; the hands are the hands of Esau, but the voice is the voice of Jacob. But to the Spenserian manner, with its simple attitudes and ideals, its simple delight in natural and spiritual beauty, the pastoral lends itself admirably.

22. Charles Eliot Norton

1895

Professor C. E. Norton (1827–1908) was an American who spent a lot of time in Europe as a businessman. He co-edited the *North American Review* from 1864 to 1868 and founded the *Nation* magazine. He was a Dante scholar who became Professor of Art History at Harvard 1875–97 and wrote books on a wide range of subjects, from architecture and travel to literary figures such as Kipling and Longfellow. He edited collections of hymns, fairy-tales, the *Complete Writings of James Russell Lowell*, an edition of Donne's poems for the Grolier Club with J. Lowell, and, in 1905, the *Love Poems of John Donne*. In 1895 Norton drew on 'many hundreds' of J. R. Lowell's marginal emendations of the text and punctuation of the Boston edition of 1855, an edition which Lowell himself had sponsored.[1] In his introduction Norton paid tribute to Lowell's lifelong championship of Donne, observing: 'Donne's Poems were, from an early period of his life, among Mr Lowell's favourite books.' He went on to give an account of Donne's poetry, quoting some of Ben Jonson's remarks about Donne in the *Conversations* with Drummond (*The Poems of John Donne*, 1895, pp. xvii–xxxii).[2]

In some things Donne was indeed the first poet of his time, Shakespeare alone excepted, and yet this place is not generally accorded to him, because, if he do not wholly perish, he does suffer neglect for not being understood, and is hard to read for not keeping of accent. More than this, few poets are so unequal as Donne; few, capable of such high reaches as he, sink lower than he at times descends. His verse must be sifted with a coarse sieve; much of it will run through the meshes, but when all that is worthless or worse has been sifted out, there remains a residue of the pure grain of poetry, of poetry rich in imagination, fancy, wit, passion, and reflection, and in strong and often not unmusical verse.

[He observes that Donne did not see his own poems through the press, and was probably indifferent to the fate of the greater part of them.]

Moreover, he never was a poet by profession. Poetry was, for him, but an occasional resource, and for the greater part of his life he was much more scholar than poet. His zeal for acquisition was unbounded, and his stores of learning were immense.

It is mainly as poet, however, and not as scholar, preacher, or controversialist, that Donne holds his place in English literature. His better poetry is the revelation of a curiously interesting and complex nature, of a soul with rare capacity of intense feeling, of an intelligence at once deep and subtle, and of a varied experience of life.

His nature was essentially a product of the Elizabethan age.

[He gives an account of the various impulses which 'had quickened the imagination' of the English people, and of the evolution of the English language into 'the most serviceable instrument of expression which man has ever had at his command'.]

Another influence also was deeply affecting the intellectual life of England, that of the spirit of the Italian Renaissance. Donne was a child of this spirit. He shared in its exaltations and debasements, in its confusion of the sensual and the supersensual, in its love of physical and its adoration of spiritual beauty, in its poetic fervor, its ardor for experience and for learning, its rapid changes of mood, its subjection to the things of the flesh, its ascetic aspiration for the things of the spirit. The keen, penetrating breath which had blown westward from Italy was a mingling of the purest and most vivifying air with a poisonous malaria. All Western Europe had felt it. It had refined manners, it had corrupted the moral sense; it had quickened life, it had spread mortal contagion. A nature so susceptible as Donne's was subject to its full effect. He and Lord Herbert of Cherbury are among the striking illustrations which the England of 1600 affords of the force which this Italian spirit still exerted after its native source had run almost dry. In the next generation Milton, though directly exposed to the influence of the Italy of his own day, shows the recovery from its control and the revival of the healthier genius of England.

The moods and conditions of this period are displayed in Donne's poetry in such degree as to make it a sort of epitome and school of them all. Putting Shakespeare out of the question, as forming a class by himself, there is no poet of the time who surpasses Donne in the occasional power of his imagination, in easy flight of fancy, in sincerity of passionate utterance, in sweetness and purity of sentiment, in depth and substance of reflection, in terse expression of thought. But, on the other hand, his poems equally reflect the poetic age in its gross sensuality and coarse obscenity; in studied obscurity, fantasticality of conceit, exaggeration of affected feeling, harshness of diction, and cumbrousness of construction. The mingling of good and bad is often intricate. The sensualism of the verses of his youth is now and then lifted by a stroke of the wing of imagination out of the lower into the higher regions of life. The dreariness of a long stretch of labored and intricate conceits is not seldom lighted up by a flash of wit, or the illumination of an original and impressive thought. The extravagance of eulogy is here and there atoned for by a passage full of natural feeling, expressed with penetrating simplicity.

Much of his poetry seems to have been rapidly composed, and never subjected to considerate revisal. To this no doubt are due something of its obscurity, as well as those grave faults of art in his verse which show not so much a defect of poetic capacity, as carelessness, and indifference to perfection of rhythmical form.

[He quotes J. R. Lowell's view that Donne's occasional felicities have not saved him from 'the limbo of the formless and fragmentary', and adds that 'if he be adjudged to this limbo, he is one "of the people of great worth who are suspended there"'.]

The result of all his poetic faults has not been, as Jonson prophesied, that Donne has perished, but that his merits have been largely overlooked or falsely measured.

[He quotes Dryden's comments on Donne in the dedication of *Eleonora*, and in the *Discourse concerning Satire*, and remarks:]

Pope tried what Dryden here suggested, and 'versified', as he called it, two of Donne's Satires. But though his lines flow more smoothly than those of Donne, they lack the conciseness and sincerity of his original. 'Sense passed through him no longer is the same', and he often adds coarseness to what was gross enough before. The opening verses of the second Satire afford a good example of what Donne suffers in being translated into Pope's numbers and English. Donne begins:

> Sir, though (I thank God for it) I do hate
> Perfectly all this town, yet there's one state
> In all ill things so excellently best
> That hate towards it breeds pity toward the rest;

and Pope, transmuting this into more flowing lines, vulgarizes it as follows:

> Yes, thank my stars! As early as I knew
> This town, I had the sense to hate it too.
> Yet here, as e'en in Hell, there must be still
> One giant-vice so excellently ill
> That all beside one pities not abhors,
> As who knows Sappho smiles at other whores.

74

Parnell, whose name as a poet survives, rather than his verses, did for Donne's third Satire what Pope had done for the second and fourth; and in his hands this Satire, one of the most direct, serious, and masculine of Donne's poems, full of real emotion and the expression of sincere conviction, becomes a piece of artificial diction, feeble in substance and poor in form. For instance, Donne says, with fine, characteristic compression,

> Though Truth and Falsehood be
> Near twins, yet Truth a little elder is.
> Be busy to seek her, –

a passage which Parnell accommodates to the taste of his times by rendering thus:

> Though Truth and Falsehood seem as twins allied,
> There's eldership on Truth's delightful side.
> Her seek with heed,

One more sample of this transmuting of gold to clay will answer. Donne says:

> On a huge hill,
> Cragged and steep, Truth stands, and he that will
> Reach her, about must and about must go,
> And what the hill's suddenness resists win so.

This is rough, but strong and imaginative. It suggested to Mr Parnell that

> On a large mountain, at the basis wide,
> Steep to the top, and craggy at the side,
> Sits sacred Truth enthron'd; and he who means
> To reach the summit mounts with weary pains,
> Winds round and round and every turn essays,
> Where sudden breaks resist the shorter ways.

Obviously the genius of Parnell had a horror of these 'shorter ways'. But he is not to blame for sharing in the incapacity of appreciation which was common in his own and the next generation.

[He quotes Hume and Johnson on the metrical uncouthness of Donne's *Satires*, and remarks that even Coleridge does 'imperfect justice' to the quality of Donne's versifying. Southey's gibe that only a transformation of the internal structure of his ears could have made Donne a poet simply shows 'a somewhat characteristic want of taste and appreciation of poetic excellence'.]

Surely it could only be the ears of Midas himself that would not find music and poetry in [the first stanza of 'The Blossom']. And in *The Relic* there is a metrical felicity which corresponds with the intimate poetic sentiment and gives perfect express to it.

[He quotes the first stanza, and comments:]

I have omitted two verses of this stanza in which Donne's fondness for quips and his lack of refinement are characteristically displayed, but the number of single stanzas fine as this which might be chosen from his earlier poems is very large, and it is surprising that any lover of poetry should fail to take delight in the audacious, picturesque fancy of such a poem as *The Sun-rising*, the brilliant wit of *The Will*, the depth of sentiment in *Love's Growth*, *The Ecstasy*, *The Anniversary*, and *The Shadow*, the subtle delicacy of *The Undertaking*, and the exquisite imagery and true feeling of *A Valediction forbidding Mourning*, in all of which, as well as in many others, there is no defect of measure to interfere with the poetic charm.

I do not impugn Ben Jonson's opinion that Donne deserved hanging for not keeping of accent. His sins in this respect are, indeed, unpardonable and unaccountable. He puts accent where he likes, forcing it from one syllable to another as if it had no settled place of its own. Some of the transpositions are astounding, as, for instance:

> Blasted with sighs and súrrounded with tears.

> As fresh and sweet their ápparels be, as be
> The fields they sold to buy them.

> At their best
> Sweetness and wit, they're but mummý possest.

Accent seems as indifferent to him as spelling, and he writes cómplaint, éxtreme, úsurpers, tortúre, pictúre, answér, papér, giánt, prisón, kingdóm, presénce, and more than fifty other words, with similar disregard of English usage. I say English usage, for it is obvious that in many of these words Donne was following the French accentuation.

Even when the accent is correct his lines are often harsh, and he employs slurs and elisions to a degree that makes his verse difficult to a reader whose eyes and ears are not accustomed to the freedom in this respect which the poets of Donne's time allowed themselves, and who thus lies open to the charge which Holophernes brings against Sir Nathaniel's reading of Biron's sonnet: 'You find not the apostrophes and so miss the accent.'

It is hardly worth while to cite examples. The instances are so numerous that the reader soon gains skill by practice, and learns (to alter a phrase of Donne's own) to 'redress rough lines and make verse song'. In fine, Coleridge says truly: 'To read Dryden, Pope, etc., you need only count syllables; but to read Donne you must measure *time*, and discover the time of each word by the sense of passion.'

In Donne's longer poems there are few passages of many continuous verses of sustained excellence, but single verses or couplets are frequent which express a striking thought or a profound reflection with epigrammatic terseness. Some few of them have become familiar quotations, as, for example . . .

[He quotes *The Second Anniversary*, lines 244–6; *Elegy* 9, 'The Autumnal', lines 1–2; 'To the Countess of Bedford', 'Honour is so sublime perfection', lines 14–15; and adds that there are many other passages, 'less commonly known, which are not less memorable'. He quotes *The Second Anniversary*, lines 281–5 and 463–4; the 'Obsequies to the Lord Harington', lines 225–6; the 'Letter to the Lady Carey, and Mistress Essex Rich', line 33; 'To the Countess of Bedford', 'To have written then', lines 29–30; *The First Anniversary*, lines 144, 169–70, 446; 'A Funeral Elegy', line 76; 'Elegy on the Lady Markham', line 11; 'To the Countess of Huntingdon', 'That unripe side of earth', lines 129–30; and the 'Elegy upon . . . Prince Henry', lines 43–4. Then he apologizes for attempting to represent Donne in mere snippets.]

But it is, perhaps, doing the poet wrong thus to choose out these verses. For, as Donne himself said, 'Sentences in authors, like hairs in horsetails, concur in one root of beauty and strength; but being plucked out one by one, serve only for springes and snares.' Donne's better poems deserve to be read not only complete, but over and over again. They allure and hold the lover of poetry with an abiding charm. They have secure place in the small volume of immortal verse.

NOTES

1 See *John Donne: The Critical Heritage*, vol. I, ed. A. J. Smith (London: Routledge and Kegan Paul, 1975), pp. 425–6.
2 Ibid., pp. 65–70.

23. Felix E. Schelling

1895

Professor Felix E. Schelling (1858–1945) of the University of Pennsylvania, where he founded the Department of English Language and Literature, mentioned Donne in his introduction to an anthology of Elizabethan lyrics. The account occurs in a discussion of Elizabethan sonnets and sonnet-sequences. Schelling was a prolific writer on Elizabethan literature and at the time the foremost scholar in America on Elizabethan drama (*A Book of Elizabethan Lyrics*, 1895, pp. xxi–xxiii).

But, as in the case of the pastoral fashion, there were other currents of lyrical production, less directed by the conventionalities of the moment. Spenser aside, whose elaborated state does not lend itself readily to the shorter lyric, and whose singing robes are stiff with tissue of gold, wrought work, and gems inlaid, and Shakespeare, also, whose non-dramatic Muse is dedicated to thoughtful sonnet and mournful threnody, as well as to the sprightlier melodies of love, wine, and merriment, the most important poetical influence of this decade is that of that grave and marvelous man, Dr John Donne. I would respectfully invite the attention of those who still persist with Dr Johnson in regarding this great poet as the founder of a certain 'Metaphysical School of Poetry', a man all but contemporary with Cowley, and a writer harsh, obscure, and incomprehensible in his diction, first to an examination of facts

78

which are within the reach of all, and, secondly, to an honest study of his works. Ben Jonson told Drummond that 'Donne's best poems were written before he was twenty-five years old', *i.e.*, before 1598, and Francis Davison, apparently when collecting material for his *Poetical Rhapsody* in 1600, includes in a memorandum of 'MSS to get', certain poems of Donne. The Carews, Crashaws, and Cowleys begin at least thirty years later, and, be their imitations of Donne's characteristics what they may, Donne himself is an Elizabethan in the strictest possible acceptation of that term, and far in fact as in time from the representative of a degenerate and false taste. It is somewhat disconcerting to find an author whom, like Savage Landor in our own century, the critic cannot glibly classify as the founder of a school or the product of a perfectly obvious series of literary influences. Donne is a man of this difficult type. For, just as Shakespeare touched life and man at all points, and, absorbing the light of his time, gave it forth a hundredfold, so Donne, withdrawn almost wholly from the influences affecting his contemporaries, shone and glowed with a strange light all his own.

Few lyrical poets have ever rivaled Donne in contemporary popularity. Mr Edmund Gosse has recently given a reason for this, which seems worthy of attention, while by no means explaining everything. 'Donne was, I would venture to suggest, by far the most modern and contemporaneous of the writers of his time. . . . He arrived at an excess of actuality of style, and it was because he struck them as so novel, and so completely in touch with his age, that his immediate coevals were so much fascinated with him.' A much bequoted passage of the *Conversations with Drummond* informs us that Ben Jonson 'esteemeth Donne the first poet in the world in some things'. An analysis of these 'some things', which space here forbids, will, I think, show them to depend, to a large degree, upon that deeper element of the modern lyric, poetic insight; the power which, proceeding by means of the clash of ideas familiar with ideas remote, flashes light and meaning into what has hitherto appeared mere commonplace. This, mainly, though with much else, is the positive originality of Donne. A quality no less remarkable is to be found in what may be called his negative originality, by which I mean that trait which caused Donne absolutely to give over the current mannerisms of his time; to write neither in the usual Italian manner, nor in borrowed lyrical forms; indeed, to be at times wantonly careless of mere expression, and, above all, to throw away every trace of the conventional classic imagery and mannerisms which infected and conventionalized the poetry of so many of his contemporaries. It seems to me that no one, excepting Shakespeare, with Sidney, Greville, and Jonson in lesser measure, has done so much to develop intellectualized emotion in the Elizabethan lyric as John Donne. But Donne is the last poet to demand a proselyting zeal of his devotees, and all those who have learned to love his witching personality will agree to the charming sentiment of his faithful adorer, Izaak Walton, when he says: 'Though I must omit to mention divers persons, . . . friends of Sir Henry Wotton; yet I must not omit to mention of a love that was there begun betwixt him and Dr Donne, sometime Dean of Saint Paul's; a man of whose abilities I shall forbear to say anything, because he who is of this nation, and pretends to learning or ingenuity, and is ignorant of Dr Donne, deserves not to know him.'

24. Clyde Bowman Furst

1896/9

The American educational administrator C. B. Furst (1873–1931) opened a set of studies of old authors with a general account of Donne and his writings (*A Group of Old Authors*, 1899, pp. 14–57; the chapter on Donne from which the following extracts are taken first appeared in the *Citizen* (Philadelphia), September 1896).

[Furst reviews the various opinions which have been passed upon Donne, quoting Jonson, Carew, and Coleridge.]

Many, truly, will follow critics beyond appreciating his thought as quaint, ingenious, and elaborate, so far as to consider it unnatural, fantastic, and trifling. Some, imputing to the author lack of sympathy and designed ruggedness, call his work essentially unpoetic. Fortunately, but a few persons, although some there are, go so far as terming both poet and his work tasteless, unfeeling, violent, execrable, and disgusting.

His very staunchest friends of to-day can scarcely echo Ben Jonson's tribute to Donne as one, –

> Whose every work of thy most early wit
> Came forth example, and remains so yet.

This was, however, the expressed opinion of Carew, Cowley, Crashaw, Walton, Lord Herbert of Cherbury, Cleveland, Davidson, Bishop Corbet, Bishop King, Edmund Bolton, Endymion Porter, Heyde, Chudleigh, Dornelly, Mayne, and a number of others, whose opinions are no less entitled to respect.

The position which will do most credit to critical acumen, and will also bear a true meed of honest praise to Donne, is a medium one.

It must be acknowledged that his verses, on a superficial reading, seem like riddles made to conceal the thought instead of expressing it; but it is none the less true that a more careful study will always show wit, fancy, tenderness, and deep feeling. Although his lines will not allow themsleves to be read in the liquid way which modern criticism insists upon for model verse, they have, in compensation, a deep and subtle music which adds true feeling to the thought, and a dignity and movement which, like that of Milton's verse, does much to replace the wanting smoothness.

[He quotes praises of Donne by Jonson, Dryden and Lowell, then qualifies them with the remarks of the anonymous reviewer in the *Dial* of 1 May 1896, adding a word of his own on the growing appreciation of Donne's poetry.]

While a great many persons who have known Donne but slightly have not cared for him, and while to yet more he has been altogether unknown, the number of those who have been true, loving, and appreciative friends has continually increased from the time of Sir Henry Wotton and Izaak Walton down to the present day.

[He reviews Donne's career, attempting to place the writings chronologically and taking the *Holy Sonnets* first, as the supposed product of Donne's early 'Romanistic' period.]

The first of a series of 'Holy Sonnets' strongly recalls, both in matter and in expression, Michael Angelo's 'Prayer for Purification'. Another sonnet, which has been called by Archbishop Trench, 'The genuine cry of one engaged in that most terrible of all struggles', suggests that 'There is much in Donne ... which ... reminds us of St Augustine ... there was the same tumultuous youth, the same entanglement in youthful lusts, the same final deliverance from them; and then the same passionate and personal grasp of the central truths of Christianity, linking itself as this did with all that he had suffered and all that he had sinned, and all through which, by God's grace, he had victoriously struggled.'

[A comment on the *Elegies* oddly follows.]

Of all of Donne's elegies, – the term is used not in its original sense of a song of mourning, but in the wider meaning of a light essay on an intellectual or moral subject – of all of Donne's elegies, but two or three are unsullied by grossness and, if the leading of the larger number is accepted, one must leave the confines of pure, honest, and decorous society to follow to the unclean haunts of the immodest, loose, and shameless. To crowd out from remembrance these evil years and their records, there is needed all the noble, exalted, and truly magnificent work of the poet's later life. While the very fact that he had been evil and later became noble creates a greater personal sympathy for Donne, the wish is yet strong that the dark years had been other than they were.

[His account of the *Satires* is more sympathetic than was common.]

They rank among the best of the period in their freedom from the common servility in following originals in the classic languages.
These satires, – there are seven of them – treat of morality and religion and the poor rewards of literary life, but especially of royal evils, court follies, and public corruption. A reading between the lines suggests that the author must have been, at this period, a vigorous, fearless, mildly cynical, yet usually good humored, man of the world. Sometimes the touches are clever and humorous, abounding in light raillery, in puns, and in witty allusions; at other times, when the subject seems to require it, there is shown a force of idea which is powerful and even majestic in its crushing invective. The results of wide and exact observation and of unusual modes of thought are expressed with such accurate figures and such finished

word-fitting that the work abounds in passages remarkable in their aptness for quotation. This aptness for quotation is limited only by the unexpectedness of the thought and the extraordinary compactness of expression, making it often necessary to read and re-read a passage many times before its content is wholly understood and appreciated.

Dryden may have had in mind this difficulty of understanding Donne at a first reading, together with his unevenness of versification, when he remarked that the satires, if 'translated into numbers and English', might be much admired. Pope and Parnell so fully agreed with this opinion that they attempted the revision, but the result they attained by putting Donne's thought into smoothly flowing lines was not a happy one. Dr Samuel Brown, of Edinburgh, can be almost justified in thinking that Pope 'improved' Donne, as the sailor who had obtained a curiosity in the form of the weapon of a sword fish, 'improved' it by scraping and smoothing away all the protuberances which distinguished it from any other bone.

Together with the satires may be classed the epigrams, where the same characteristics of unusual thought and condensed expression are to be noted.

[He quotes 'Antiquary', 'Disinherited', and 'A Burnt Ship', remarking that the last of these 'shows the love of the antithesis at its height'.]

All along through the poet's life the lyric poems were written, and a number of them must have grown from these early London days. These lyrics, in more than fifty different metres, light, dainty, gay, and joyous, smooth and liquid, too, when he chose to make them so, whether working out original conceits or ringing the variations upon familiar themes, deserve all the epithets of charming, delightful, and admirable, which they have received.

Justly famous is the 'Song', in lighter vein, with the verses . . .

[He quotes stanzas 2 and 3 of *Song*, 'Go, and Catch a Falling Star'.]

There is much lightness as graceful and as heartless as this, but there is still more constancy and earnestness, as in the 'Song' which contains the stanzas . . .

[He quotes stanzas 1 and 2 of *Song*, 'Sweetest Love, I Do Not Go'.]

We do not wonder that such verses as these should captivate all who knew them, and that John Donne should have become the poet of his circle, and this, too, in spite of the fact that his poems circulated in manuscript alone, being first printed in a collection only after his death.

Among the 'Verse Letters' there are a number to various persons of prominence, all written in the adulatory vein considered proper for such addresses. Those, indeed, to the Countess of Bedford, the Countess of Huntingdon, the Countess of Salisbury, Lady Carey, and Mistress Rich, are stilted in thought and phrase. Similarly formal and studied is the letter to Sir Edward Herbert; but Donne's verses to his friends the Brookes, to Sir Henry Wotton, to the Woodwards, Sir Thomas Roe, and some friends whose names are indicated only by initials, abound in true friendliness as well as in sparkling wit.

The high grade of literary excellence maintained throughout all these letters stamps them as real poems, very far removed from the rhymed prose in some of the familiar letters of Cowper. These certainly were not written with the facility of ordinary corres-pondence, for they evince frequent references to the commonplace book, and such care in composition that a reading convinces one of the truth of the surmise that Donne was not a rapid, but a careful and painstaking writer.

There is always danger of discussing the 'Verse Letters' at greater length than their proportional importance deserves, but some such admirable passages occur that quotations may be taken from them rather than from some of Donne's more ambitious literary perform-ances. And these letters show in a manner different from that of any of his other works, the individuality of the author.

There is a Coleridge-like bit of description in 'The Calm', when all the world was so still that, –

> in one place lay
> Feathers and dust, to-day and yesterday.

Wit is frequent, –

> I have been told that virtue in courtiers' hearts
> Suffers an ostracism and departs.

There are many lines which combine epigrammatic terseness with philosophic depth, –

> Who prayerless labors, or without this prayes
> Doth but one-half, that's none.

Donne's adroit originality of thought is nowhere better shown than by his mode of excusing himself for having praised so many ladies. The lines read . . .

[He quotes lines 37–50 of the verse letter 'To the Countess of Salisbury'.]

In extricating himself from even so serious a predicament, it seems that Donne must be given the additional credit of being sufficiently sly not to exhaust his happy figure, but to preserve it for use in some future escape, when the creations of the first days might be made to pale beside the lovely Eve. One almost imagines him deliberately involving himself in a complication that he might employ so clever an explanation. . . .

He seems to have been, as became every good courtier of his day, an ardent lover, and the somewhat unsafe practice of constructing from a poet's work cycles of poems illustrative of his life, may be indulged in, in the case of Donne's love lyrics, with comparative safety.

Such a cycle might begin with 'The Ecstacie', treating of overwhelming love; with 'Love's Infiniteness', of love more than the poet's heart can contain; or with 'Negative Love', of affection which beggars description. In 'The Expiration', a cruel separation occurs, the lover being obliged to go upon a journey. In 'The Paradox', he is dying of love; and in 'The Legacy', he wishes to send the lady his heart, but, upon opening his bosom, her own heart is found in its stead.

So far as the lady is concerned, out of sight seems, indeed, out of mind, and in 'Love's Deitie', the poet bewails the sadness of unreturned affection and ventures a present. In 'A Jeate Ringe Sente', he is still disconsolate, lamenting her lack of faith and exhorting the artist to complete 'The Portrait', – begun in happier days as a present for her – in shadow and dark tints.

In sadness is written 'Twit'nam Garden', where the beauties of nature only increase sorrow to an agony of remembrance. The lover exhorts his lady, in 'A Valediction of My Name in the Window', to allow the sun, as it shadows his name into the room, to remind her of his love, or prays that, as she opens the casement to converse with another, the sight of his name may recall her to constancy.

In 'The Token', no ribbon, ring, bracelet, no picture, nor even letter is desired; the lady is asked merely to say she thinks the lover constant. All, however, is in vain as the poet had known it would be. He accepts, in 'The Prohibition', her hate, as he had done her love, yet laments that she should so have requited his deep affection.

The mood now seems to change into a Browning-like feeling that it is better so to be, and that, while she is forever lost to him, he has been made nobler by having nobly loved even one so unworthy of his constant affection. This is evidenced in 'A Dialogue between Sir Henry Wotton and Mr Donne', where love is praised for love's own sake. The lover still keeps his lady's hair bracelet as a token, he will wear it, in 'The Funeral', into his grave, and until, in 'The Relique', his bones are exhumed.

One reason why Donne's love poems were so full of feeling was discovered when it was learned that, shortly before Christmas of the year 1601, he had secretly married the daughter of Sir George Moore, Lord Lieutenant of the Tower, who, as the niece and companion of Lady Egerton, had seen much of the young secretary.

[He gives an account of the misfortunes which fell upon Donne after his marriage.]

That the shadows of the picture were somewhat compensated for by a brighter side, may be seen from the true love in the many lyrics addressed to his wife during this time of unhappiness.

[He turns to the funeral poems, and first considers the two *Anniversaries*.]

An outline of the first of the four sections into which, with a conclusion, the 'Anatomy' is divided, will show the peculiar and, at times, fantastic course of the thought.

In the poem there are crowded, sometimes most incongruously, remarkable observation of the beautiful and humorous, bits of satire, references to the absorbing discoveries of the new science, side by side with figures decidedly unhappy because of their lack of taste. The very vigor of the imaginative, daring, and fantastic figures frequently deflects, from its main theme, the train of speculative thought which runs through the development of the whole. Yet, paradoxical as it is, – Donne is full of paradoxes – one

of the striking characteristics of the work is the restraint by which
the poet vividly suggests, in a few words, what another man would
have made weak and ineffective by telling in many sentences.

Quotable passages await one on every side, but there is time to
pause an instant only, and that instant because it is impossible to
pass unnoticed such phrases as, –

> We're scarce our father's shadowes cast at noone.

> Onely death ads t'our length; nor are we growne
> In stature to be men, 'till we are none.

> Be more than man, or thou'rt lesse than an ant.

Beside the frequently quoted description of the lady, –

> her pure and eloquent blood
> Spoke in her cheeks, and so distinctly wrought,
> That one might almost say her body thought;

may be placed, –

> She, whose faire body no such prison was,
> But that a soule might well be pleased to passe
> An age in her;

and, –

> One whose deare body was so pure and thin,
> Because it need disguise no thought within,
> 'Twas but a through-light scarfe, her mind t'enroule.

Somewhat similar to these poems are the several 'Funeral
Elegies', which comprehend more strong passages, in proportion
to their extent, than any other of Donne's poems. Extreme extravagance of thought and expression is largely absent. The thought
is peculiar and the manner of expressing it quaint, yet there is a
reflective and philosophical depth and a reverential solemnity,
which is powerful and uplifting, as it manifests itself in the treatment of God, Providence, life and death, faith, trust, hope, knowledge, wisdom, peace, and the future life.

The honor, purity, goodness, courage, grace, and sweetness of
the dead are praised, while the tone of real honest feeling which
seems to underlie these tributes, as it does not underlie all of
Donne's work, both stimulates our sympathy for the loss and

our friendly feeling for the author. The 'Obsequies of Ye Lord Harrington' is the best of these elegies.

The 'Progress of the Soul', to some minds, is the best of all Donne's poems. The thought is fresh, original, and delightfully strange; while the fulness of apt expression and happy characterization, and the many passages of deeply earnest thought and of lightly playful humor, make the poem indeed an excellent one. The poet, according to the Pythagorean doctrine of metempsychosis, in following the soul of his lady from its creation in the forbidden fruit in the Garden of Eden, by his wonderful imagination, takes us into animal and vegetable, fish and fowl, monkey and man, tracing the soul until it comes into a woman.

Not least in the interest of the poem is the frequent working up of facts of folk-lore, of popular and ecclesiastical tradition. . . .

The quaintness of the ideas stimulates the imagination, the masterly manner in which they are presented arouses the admiration, and the abundance of quietly amused interest in the philosophic humor appeals to good nature; all of these elements unite to make 'The Progress of the Soul' most pleasant reading and stimulate a desire to know more of the life and work of its author.

[He throws in a comment on the *Epithalamions*.]

These marriage songs, although quite conventional in thought, are thoroughly artistic and have a light and airy beauty which is quite striking.

In drawing to its close a study of Donne, a poet who was yet more a man, whose kindly heart was and is felt through his poetry, one can appreciate the frame of mind in which those who have presented to his memory elegies and tributes have, practically without exception, concluded not with attempts at a critical summary of his literary methods or productions, but with words of deep personal feeling. We may then have countenance in concluding the present study by quoting, as a final illustration, the 'Hymn to God the Father', one of Donne's latest pieces of work. In its recounting of sin, repentance, forgiveness, struggle toward the ideal, longing cry for help, faith, and consequent peace, it sums up the life of Donne and of many another man.

[He gives the whole of 'A Hymn to God the Father'.]

25. George Edward Bateman Saintsbury

1896

Saintsbury introduced an edition of Donne's poems in two small volumes for the Muses' Library (*Poems of John Donne*, ed. E. K. Chambers, 1896, vol. I, pp. xi–xxxiii).

[Saintsbury notes how Donne's poetry evokes extreme responses for and against, making clear his own enthusiasm for Donne.]

There is hardly any, perhaps indeed there is not any, English author on whom it is so hard to keep the just mixture of personal appreciation and critical measure as it is on John Donne. It is almost necessary that those who do not like him should not like him at all; should be scarcely able to see how any decent and intelligent human creature can like him. It is almost as necessary that those who do like him should either like him so much as to speak unadvisedly with their lips, or else curb and restrain the expression of their love for fear that it should seem on that side idolatry. But these are not the only dangers. Donne is eminently of that kind which lends itself to sham liking, to coterie worship, to a false enthusiasm; and here is another weapon in the hands of the infidels, and another stumbling-block for the feet of the true believers. Yet there is always something stimulating in a subject of this kind, and a sort of temptation to attempt it.

To write anything about Donne's life, after Walton, is an attempt which should make even hardened *écrivailleurs* and *écrivassiers* nervous. That the good Izaak knew his subject and its atmosphere thoroughly; that he wrote but a very few years after Donne's own death; and that he was a writer of distinct charm, are discouraging things, but not the most discouraging. It is perhaps only those who after being familiar for years with Donne's poems, of which Walton says very little, make subsequent acquaintance with Walton's presentment of the man, who can appreciate the full awkwardness of the situation. It is the worst possible case of *pereant qui ante nos*. The human Donne whom Walton depicts is so exactly the poetical Donne whom we knew, that the effect is uncanny. Generally, or at least very frequently, we find the poet other than his form of verse; here we find him quite astoundingly akin to it. . . .

89

[He gives an account of Donne's life and career, commenting on the effect of Donne's circumstances upon his writing.]

Broken health, the loss of his wife, the bitterness to a man who must have known himself to be one of the greatest intellects of the age, of hopes delayed till long past middle life, and no doubt also sincere repentance for and reaction from youthful follies, will account for much of the almost unparalleled melancholy which appears in his later works, and seems to have characterized his later life. But a considerable residue remains for natural idiosyncrasy, and for the influence of the Renaissance, the peculiar pessimism of which was perfectly different from that of classical times, and from that of our own day, and can only be paralleled by the spirit of *Ecclesiastes*.

The circumstances of his life however do not greatly concern us here; nor does that part – an eminent and admirable part – of his work which is not in verse. But it does concern us that there is a strange, though by no means unexampled, division between the two periods of his life and the two classes of his work. Roughly speaking, almost the whole of at least the secular verse belongs to the first division of the life, almost the whole of the prose to the second. Again, by far the greater part of the verse is animated by what may be called a spiritualized worldliness and sensuality, the whole of the prose by a spiritualism which has left worldliness far behind. The conjunction is, I say, not unknown: it was specially prevalent in the age of Donne's birth and early life. It has even passed into something of a commonplace in reference to that Renaissance of which, as it slowly passed from south to north, Donne was one of the latest and yet one of the most perfect exponents. The strange story which Brantôme tells of Margaret of Navarre summoning a lover to the church under whose flags his mistress lay buried, and talking with him of her, shows, a generation before Donne's birth, the influence which in his day had made its way across the narrow seas as it had earlier across the Alps, and had at each crossing gathered gloom and force if it had lost lightness and colour. Always in him are the two conflicting forces of intense enjoyment of the present, and intense feeling of the contrast of that present with the future. He has at once the transcendentalism which saves sensuality and the passion which saves mysticism. Indeed the two currents run so full and strong in him, they clash and churn their waves so boisterously, that this is of itself sufficient to account for the obscurity, the extravagance, the undue quaintness which have been charged against him. He was 'of the first order of poets'; but he was not of the first amongst the first. Only Dante perhaps among these greatest of all had such a conflict and ebullition of feeling to express. For, so far as we can judge, in Shakespeare, even in the Sonnets, the poetical power mastered to some extent at the very first the rough material of the poetic instinct, and prepared before expression the things to be expressed. In Dante we can trace something of the presence of slag and dross in the ore; and even in Dante we can perhaps trace faintly also the difficulty of smelting it. Donne, being a lesser poet than Dante, shows it everywhere. It is seldom that even for a few lines, seldomer that for a few stanzas, the power of the furnace is equal to the volumes of ore and fuel that are thrust into it. But the fire is always there – over-tasked, over-mastered for a time, but never choked or extinguished; and ever and anon from gaps in the smouldering mass there breaks forth such a sudden flow of pure molten metal, such a flower of incandescence, as not even in the very greatest of poets of all can be ever surpassed or often rivalled.

For critical, and indeed for general purposes, the poetical works of Donne may be divided into three parts, separated from each other by a considerable difference of character and, in one case at least, of time. These are the Satires, which are beyond all doubt very early; and Elegies and other amatory poems, most of which are certainly, and all probably, early likewise; and the Divine and Miscellaneous Poems, some of which may not be late, but most of which certainly are. All three divisions have certain characteristics in common; but the best of these characteristics, and some which are not common to the three, belong to the second and third only.

It was the opinion of the late seventeenth and of the whole of the eighteenth century that Donne, though a clever man, had no ear. Chalmers, a very industrious student, and not such a bad critic, says so in so many words; Johnson undoubtedly thought so; Pope demonstrated his belief by his fresh 'tagging' of the Satires. They all to some extent no doubt really believed what they said; their ears had fallen deaf to that particular concord. But they all also no doubt founded their belief to a certain extent on certain words of Dryden's which did not exactly import or comport what Mr Pope and the rest took them to mean. Dryden had the knack, a knack of great value to a critic, but sometimes productive of sore misguiding to a critic's readers – of adjusting his comments solely to one point of view, to a single scheme in metric and other things. Now, from the point of view of the scheme which both his authority and his example made popular, Donne *was* rather formless. But nearly all the eighteenth-century critics and criticasters concentrated their attention on the Satires; and in the Satires Donne certainly takes singular liberties, no matter what scheme be preferred. It is now, I believe, pretty well admitted by all competent judges that the astonishing roughness of the Satirists of the late sixteenth century was not due to any general ignoring of the principles of melodious English verse, but to a deliberate intention arising from the same sort of imperfect erudition which had in other ways so much effect on the men of the Renaissance generally. Satiric verse among the ancients allowed itself, and even went out of its way to take, licences which no poet in other styles would have dreamt of taking. The Horace of the impeccable odes writes such a hideous hexameter as –

Non ego, namque parabilem amo Venerem facilemque,

and one of the Roman satirists who was then very popular, Persius, though he could rise to splendid style on occasion, is habitually as harsh, as obscure, and as wooden as a Latin poet well can be. It is not probable, it is certain, that Donne and the rest imitated these licences of malice prepense.

But it must be remembered that at the time when they assumed this greater licence, the normal structure of English verse was anything but fixed. Horace had in his contemporaries, Persius and Juvenal had still more in their forerunners, examples of versification than which Mr Pope himself could do nothing more 'correct'; and their licences could therefore be kept within measure, and still be licentious enough to suit any preconceived idea of the ungirt character of the Satiric muse. In Donne's time the very precisians took a good deal of licence: the very Virgils and even Ovids were not apt to concern themselves very greatly about a short vowel before *s* with a consonant, or a trisyllable at the end of a pentameter. If therefore you meant to show that you were *sans gêne*, you had to make demonstrations of the most unequivocal character. Even with all this explanation and allowance it may still seem probable that Donne's Satires never received any formal preparation for the press, and are in the state of rough copy. Without this allowance, which the eighteenth century either did not care or did not know how to give, it is not surprising that they should have seemed mere monstrosities.

The satiric pieces in which these peculiarities are chiefly shown, which attracted the attention of Pope, and which, through his recension, became known to a much larger number of persons than the work of any other Elizabethan Satirist, have the least share of Donne's poetical interest. But they display to the full his manly strength and shrewd sense, and they are especially noticeable in one point. They exhibit much less of that extravagant exaggeration of contemporary vice and folly which makes one of their chief contemporaries, Marston's *Scourge of Villany*, almost an absurd thing, while it is by no means absent from Hall's *Virgidemiarum*. We cannot indeed suppose that Donne's satire was wholly and entirely sincere, but a good deal in it clearly was. Thus his handling of the perennial subjects of satire is far more fresh, serious, and direct than is usual with Satirists, and it was no doubt this judicious and direct quality which commended it to Pope. Moreover, these poems abound in fine touches. The Captain in the first Satire –

> Bright parcel-gilt with forty dead men's pay –

the ingenious evildoers in the second –

> for whose sinful sake
> Schoolmen new tenements in hell must make –

the charming touch at once so literary and so natural in the fifth –

> so controverted lands
> 'Scape, like Angelica, the striver's hands,

are only a few of the jewels five words long that might be produced as specimens. But it is not here that we find the true Donne: it was not this province of the universal monarchy of wit that he ruled with the most unshackled sway. The provinces that he did so rule were quite other: strange frontier regions, uttermost isles where sensuality, philosophy, and devotion meet, or where separately dwelling they rejoice or mourn over the conquests of each other. I am not so sure of the *Progress of the Soul* as some writers have been – interesting as it is, and curious as is the comparison with Prior's *Alma*, which it of necessity suggests, and probably suggested. As a whole it seems to me uncertain in aim, unaccomplished in execution. But what things there are in it! What a line is –

> Great Destiny, the Commissary of God!

What a lift and sweep in the fifth stanza –

> To my six lustres almost now outwore!

What a thought that –

> This soul, to whom Luther and Mahomet were
> Prisons of flesh!

And the same miraculous pregnancy of thought and expression runs through the whole, even though it seems never to have found full and complete delivery in artistic form. How far this curious piece is connected with the still more famous 'Anniversaries', in which so different a stage of 'progress' is reached, and which ostensibly connect themselves with the life and death of Mrs Elizabeth Drury, is a question which it would be tedious to argue out here. But the successive stages of the 'Anatomy of the World' present us with the most marvellous poetical exposition of a certain kind of devotional thought yet given. It is indeed possible that the union of the sensual, intellectual, poetical, and religious temperaments is not so very rare; but it is very rarely voiceful. That it existed in Donne's pre-eminently, and that it found voice in him as it never has done before or since, no one who knows his life and works can doubt. That the greatest of this singular group of poems is the 'Second Anniversary,' will hardly, I think, be contested. Here is the famous passage –

> Her pure and eloquent blood
> Spoke in her cheeks and so distinctly wrought
> That one might almost say her body thought –

which has been constantly quoted, praised, and imitated. Here, earlier, is what I should choose if I undertook the perilous task of singling out the finest line in English sacred poetry –

> so long
> As till God's great *Venite* change the song –

a *Dies Iræ* and a *Venite* itself combined in ten English syllables.

Here is that most vivid and original of Donne's many prose and verse meditations on death, as –

> A groom
> That brings a taper to the outward room.

Here too is the singular undernote of 'she' repeated constantly in different places of the verse, with the effect of a sort of musical accompaniment or refrain, which Dryden (a great student of Donne) afterwards imitated on the note 'you' in *Astræa Redux*, and the *Coronation*. But these, and many other separate verbal or musical beauties, perhaps yield to the wonder of the strange, dreamy atmosphere of moonlight thought and feeling which is shed over the whole piece. Nowhere is Donne, one of the most full-blooded and yet one of the least earthly of English poets, quite so unearthly.

The Elegies, perhaps better known than any of his poems, contain the least of this unearthliness. The famous 'Refusal to allow his young wife to accompany him as his page', though a very charming poem, is, I think, one of the few pieces of his which have been praised enough, if not even a little overpraised. As a matter of taste it seems to me indeed more open to exception than the equally famous and much 'fie-fied' 'To his mistress going to bed', a piece of frank naturalism redeemed from coarseness by passion and poetic completeness. The Elegies again are the most varied of the divisions of Donne's works, and contain next to the Satires his liveliest touches, such as –

> The grim, eight-foot-high, iron-bound, serving-man,
> That oft names God in oaths, and only than [*i.e.* then] –

or as the stroke –

> Lank as an unthrift's purse.

In Epithalamia Donne was good, but not consummate, falling far short of his master, Spenser, in this branch. No part of his work was more famous in his own day than his 'Epistles' which are headed by the 'Storm' and 'Calm,' that so did please Ben Jonson. But in these and other pieces of the same division, the misplaced ingenuity which is the staple of the general indictment against Donne, appears, to my taste, less excusably than anywhere else. Great passion of love, of grief, of philosophic meditation, of religious awe, had the power to master the fantastic hippogriff of Donne's imagination, and make it wholly serviceable; but in his less intense

95

works it was rather unmanageable. Yet there are very fine things here also; especially in the Epistle to Sir Henry Goodyere, and those to Lucy Countess of Bedford, and Elizabeth Countess of Huntingdon. The best of the 'Funeral Elegies' are those of Mrs Boulstred. In the Divine Poems there is nothing so really divine as the astonishing verse from the 'Second Anniversary' quoted above. It must always however seem odd that such a poet as Donne should have taken the trouble to tag the Lamentations of Jeremiah into verse, which is sometimes much more lamentable in form than even in matter. The epigram as to Le Franc de Pompignan's French version, and its connection, by dint of Jeremiah's prophetic power, with the fact of his having lamented, might almost, if any Englishman had had the wit to think of it, have been applied a century earlier to parts of this of Donne. The 'Litany' is far better, though it naturally suggests Herrick's masterpiece in divine song-writing; and even the 'Jeremiah' ought not perhaps to be indiscriminately disapproved. The opening stanzas especially have a fine melancholy clang not unknown, I think, as a model to Mr Swinburne.

But to my fancy no division of Donne's poems, – the 'Second Anniversary' always excepted – shows him in his quiddity and essence as do the Lyrics. Some of these are to a certain extent doubtful. One of the very finest of the whole, 'Absence, hear thou my protestation', with its unapproached fourth stanza, appeared first in Davison's *Poetical Rhapsody* unsigned. But all the best authorities agree (and for my part I would almost go to the stake on it) that the piece is Donne's. In those which are undoubtedly genuine the peculiar quality of Donne flames through and perfumes the dusky air which is his native atmosphere in a way which, though I do not suppose that the French poet had ever heard of Donne, has always seemed to me the true antitype and fulfilment by anticipation of Baudelaire's

> Encensoir oublié qui fume
> En silence à travers la nuit.

Everybody knows the

> Bracelet of bright hair about the bone

of the late discovered skeleton, identifying the lover: everybody the perfect fancy and phrase of the exordium –

> I long to talk with some old lover's ghost,
> Who died before the god of Love was born.

But similar touches are almost everywhere. The enshrining once for all in the simplest words of a universal thought –

> I wonder by my troth what thou and I
> Did till we loved?

The selection of single adjectives to do the duty of a whole train of surplusage –

> Where can we find two better hemispheres
> Without *sharp* north, without *declining* west? –

meet us, and tell us what we have to expect in all but the earliest. In comparison with these things, such a poem as 'Go and catch a falling star', delightful as it is, is perhaps only a delightful quaintness, and 'The Indifferent' only a pleasant quip consummately turned. In these perversities Donne is but playing *tours de force*. His natural and genuine work re-appears in such poems as 'Canonization', or as 'The Legacy'. It is the fashion sometimes, and that not always with the worst critics, to dismiss this kind of heroic rapture as an agreeable but conscious exaggeration, partly betrayed and partly condoned by flouting-pieces like those just mentioned. The gloss does not do the critic's knowledge of human nature or his honesty in acknowledging his knowledge much credit. Both moods and both expressions are true; but the rapture is the truer. No one who sees in these mere literary or fashionable exercises, can ever appreciate such an *aubade* as 'Stay, O Sweet, and do not rise', or such a midnight piece as 'The Dream', with its never-to-be-forgotten couplet –

> I must confess, it could not choose but be
> Profane to think thee anything but thee.

If there is less quintessence in 'The Message', for all its beauty, it is only because no one can stay long at the point of rapture which characterizes Donne at his most characteristic, and the relaxation is natural – as natural as is the pretty fancy about St Lucy –

> Who but seven hours herself unmasks –

the day under her invocation being in the depths of December. But the passionate mood, or that of mystical reflection, soon returns, and in the one Donne shall sing with another of the wondrous phrases where simplicity and perfection meet –

> So to engraft our hands as yet
> Was all our means to make us one,
> And pictures in our eyes to get
> Was all our propagation.

Or in the other dwell on the hope of buried lovers –

> To make their souls at the last busy day,
> Meet at this grave, and make a little stay.

I am not without some apprehension that I shall be judged to have fallen a victim to my own distinction, drawn at the beginning of this paper, and shown myself an unreasonable lover of this astonishing poet. Yet I think I could make good my appeal in any competent critical court. For in Donne's case the yea-nay fashion of censorship which is necessary and desirable in the case of others is quite superfluous. His faults are so gross, so open, so palpable, that they hardly require the usual amount of critical comment and con-demnation. But this very peculiarity of theirs constantly obscures his beauties even to not unfit readers. They open him; they are shocked, or bored, or irritated, or puzzled by his occasional nastiness (for he is now and then simply and inexcusably nasty), his frequent involution and eccentricity, his not quite rare indulgence in extravagances which go near to silliness; and so they lose the extraordinary beauties which lie beyond or among these faults. It is true that, as was said above, there are those, and many of them, who can never and will never like Donne. No one who thinks *Don Quixote* a merely funny book, no one who sees in Aristophanes a dirty-minded fellow with a knack of Greek versification, no one who thinks it impossible not to wish that Shakespeare had not written the Sonnets, no one who wonders what on earth Giordano Bruno meant by *Gli eroici Furori*, need trouble himself even to attempt to like Donne. 'He will never *have done* with that attempt', as our Dean himself would have unblushingly observed, for he was never weary of punning on his name.

But for those who have experienced, or who at least understand, the ups-and-downs, the ins-and-outs of human temperament, the alternations not merely of passion and satiety, but of passion and melancholy reflection, of passion earthly enough and spiritual rapture almost heavenly, there is no poet and hardly any writer like Donne. They may even be tempted to see in the strangely mixed and flawed character of his style, an index and reflection of the variety and the rapid changes of his thought and feeling. To the praise of the highest poetical art he cannot indeed lay claim. He is of course entitled to the benefit of the pleas that it is uncertain whether he ever prepared definitely for the press a single poetical work of his; that it is certain that his age regarded his youth with too much disapproval to bestow any critical care on his youthful poems. But it may be retorted that no one with the finest sense of poetry as an art, could have left things so formless as he has left, that it would have been intolerable pain and grief to any such till he had got them, even in MS, into shape. The retort is valid. But if Donne cannot receive the praise due to the accomplished poetical artist, he has that not perhaps higher but certainly rarer, of the inspired poetical creator. No study could have bettered – I hardly know whether any study could have produced – such touches as the best of those which have been quoted, and as many which perforce have been left out. And no study could have given him the idiosyncrasy which he has. *Nos passions*, says Bossuet, *ont quelque chose d'infini*. To express infinity no doubt is a contradiction in terms. But no poet has gone nearer to the hinting and adumbration of this infinite quality of passion, and of the relapses and reactions from passion, than the author of 'The Second Anniversary' and 'The Dream', of 'The Relique' and 'The Ecstasy'.

26. Oswald Crawfurd

1896

Oswald Crawfurd (1834–1909) was the son of a diplomat and made his career in the Foreign Office, specializing in Portuguese affairs. In 1891, while British Consul, he witnessed the anti-British riots in Oporto and took early retirement. He wrote a number of novels, edited the *New Quarterly* and *Chapman's Magazine of Fiction* and became a director of the publishing house Chapman and Hall. In an anthology of lyric poetry he included Donne's poem 'The Will', on which he made the folowing note (*Lyrical Verse from Elizabeth to Victoria,* 1896, pp. 79–80 and 426).

'The Will of John Donne' is probably the wittiest and bitterest lyric in our language. Donne's love passages and their record in verse were over before the author was of age. His wit then turned into metaphysical sermon-writing and theological polemics, and his bitterness into a despairing austerity.

27. Anon., *Dial*

1896

An anonymous American reviewer of E. K. Chambers's *Poems of John Donne* proclaimed the inadequacy of existing accounts of Donne ('Briefs on New Books', *Dial* (Chicago), 1 May 1896, p. 280).

Whoever can write anything which shall give a true and sufficient idea of John Donne, such an idea as will make the general reader of poetry understand why he is regarded as a poet of surpassing genius, may deem himself no longer an apprentice in the art of criticism. Donne is the most baffling of the minor poets; Whipple and Lowell, Gosse and Dowden, and a number of lesser men, have tried their hands, and yet no lover of Donne feels that anything adequate has been said, and those who know the poet still remain an elect number.

　. . . taken all in all no sufficient word is said of the real man, the intense, the fascinating, the inscrutable poet. True to his own nature, as to the inevitable secrecy of youth, Donne drew around him a cloudy something which keeps him forever to himself. And whoever may have penetrated within has been unable, on coming forth, to render a good account of what he has experienced. The reader must still depend upon himself.

28. Lionel Johnson
1896

The poet and critic Lionel Johnson (1867–1902), a Catholic convert, contributed to a literary journal an unsigned essay on religious poetry ('The Soul of Sacred Poetry', *Academy*, 26 December 1896; the essay was reprinted after Johnson's death in a gathering of his literary papers called *Post Liminium*, ed. T. Whittemore, 1911, pp. 112–20).

[Johnson argues that a sacred poet must be devoted to his creed, as a lover to his mistress. He claims that only such a passion may overcome the timidity of the imagination which reduces sublime aspiration to 'a Sunday-school jog-trot'; and he cites examples of true 'ecstasies of imagination' in Dante, Vaughan, Donne, Michelangelo, Crashaw and Newman. Johnson takes the boldness of these effects for a mark of highest faith.]

. . . listen to the divine audacity of Donne:

> At the round earth's imagined corners, blow
> Your trumpets, angels, and arise, arise
> From death, you numberless infinities
> Of souls, and to your scattered bodies go.

It is as colossal in conception as the 'Last Judgment' of Michael Angelo: or the lines of the *Dies Irae* thus passionately rendered by Crashaw.

29. Thomas Bird Mosher

1897

The American publisher T. B. Mosher (1852–1923) gave eighteen of Donne's love-lyrics and 'A Hymn to God the Father' in the literary journal he edited. He introduced the poems with some appreciative passages from recent studies by Gosse and Saintsbury, and added a warm commendation of his own (*Bibelot*, 3 (1897), 106).

We may concede at once that Donne's poetry appeals to a narrow circle, the saving remnant whose judgments are something other than mere obiter dicta. Fortunately it is a widening circle. There is an inspired breath of the Renaissance in his verse, flashes of supreme insight as in the world of tragic art Webster only knew; single lines of beauty unsurpassed discoverable in this man's work and nowhere else. Let us consider the lyrics here chosen: they represent this great poet not unworthily.

30. Frederick Ives Carpenter

1897

F. I. Carpenter (1861–1925) was an American who wrote several guides to Edmund Spenser and edited a number of poetry anthologies. In the lengthy introduction to his much-reprinted *English Lyric Poetry 1500–1700*, he discussed the distinctiveness of Donne's lyrics (*English Lyric Poetry 1500–1700*, 1897, pp. lvi–lix).

The lyric manner of Donne certainly is in marked contrast with that of all preceding poets and of most of his early contemporaries, and the note of reaction in it is unmistakable. It was immediately recognized as a novelty, and, in that age of catholic tastes, it was very generally admired. Protests, however, were not wanting. Drummond, in a passage in a letter which seems to be directed against the new movement which starts from Donne, writes: '[Poesy] subsisteth by herself, and after one demeanour and continuance her beauty appeareth to all ages. In vain have some men of late, transformers of everything, consulted upon her reformation, and endeavoured to abstract her to metaphysical ideas and scholastical quiddities, denuding her of her own habits and those ornaments with which she hath amused the world some thousand years.' Donne's poetry, it cannot be denied, is denuded of most of the habits and ornaments which up till then had been considered *de rigueur* for polite verse. Whether the occasional ingenuity and remoteness of his imaginative turns deserve the appellation of 'metaphysical ideas and scholastical quiddities' might to-day be made a matter of question. Dr Johnson, indeed, using what appears to have been the traditional epithet – it is used also by Dryden in the same connection – calls the manner 'metaphysical'; and, by a heroical exercise of the time-fallacy (for the lyrical work of Donne and of Cowley was separated by a full quarter-century), ranks the poetry of Cowley under the same head. As a matter of fact Cowley's verse is, loosely speaking, 'metaphysical'; that is to say, it is far-fetched, abstract, and intellectualized. Cowley represents both the culmination and the incipient degeneracy of the school of wit and ingenuity in poetry. He is the reputed father of the bastard Pindarique ode, a species which represents the galvanic extravagance of individualism, already potential in Donne, and also the dissolution of organic poetic form, just as the conceits and the abstract manner of his thought represent a similar extravagance and decay in poetic substance. Donne's quality, however, is quite different from that of Cowley. His thought and his fancies indeed are often strange and fantastic; but his imagery is only too concrete and intense. It is primarily in this respect that his conceits represent an advance over the purely conventional and Italianate conceits of the early lyric school, or over the more elaborate and conscious prettiness of Marinists like Drummond. What marks the new poetic style is an intensification of conceit, weighting it with symbolism. Applied to more serious conceptions the tendency

103

results in the religious symbolism of Crashaw and Herbert. Donne is a thoroughly original spirit and a great innovator; he is thoughtful, indirect, and strange; he nurses his fancies, lives with them, and broods over them so much that they are still modern in all their distinction and ardour, in spite of the strangeness of their apparel – a strangeness no greater perhaps than that of some modern poets, like Browning, as the apparel of their verse will appear two hundred years hence. Ingenuity, allusiveness, the evocation of remote images and of analogies that startle the mind into a more than half acquiescence, phantoms of deep thoughts, and emotions half-sophisticated and wholly intense: these things mark the poetry of original and taking, but it lacks simple thoughts; it does not sing. It is ascetic and sometimes austere; the sense of sin, the staple of contemporary tragedy, enters the lyric with Donne. He is all for terseness and meaning; and his versification accords with his thought and is equally elliptical.

But as Donne's spirit is all for individualization, so his influence is rather masculine and genetic than formal. His influence is widely diffused, but he does not form a school. Indeed, some of those who show the attraction of his genius most are themselves in partial reaction against what is bizarre and extravagant in the rhythms and in the art of Donne. It is thus, for example, with Waller and Carew, who derive from Jonson in part and in part from Donne, and with the growing band of those who practised the heroic couplet and the formal graces of the new classical manner, which was destined so soon to supersede Elizabethan lyricism. With the cavalier and courtier lyricists of the Carolan age, however, the new lyric treatment of love and of the lighter concerns of life which was begun by Donne is carried to its inevitable if not its natural development. The note of serious artistic effort is lost; the man of the world supplants the poet. Cynicism, persiflage, badinage, gallantry, and rococo conceits mark the verses of Carew, Suckling, Lovelace, and Randolph; when they succeed it is by a happy lyric accident, but the result then is seen in little masterpieces of inimitable charm.

31. Augustus Jessopp

1897

Dr A. Jessopp (1823–1914), headmaster, parish priest and local historian, had a lifelong interest in Donne. He published the first modern edition of Donne's *Essays in Divinity* in 1855, and at Cambridge he was mentor to the future editor of Donne's sermons Evelyn M. Spearing. He had intended to write a full scholarly life of Donne, but resigned the task to Gosse in the end. In his life of Donne in the Leaders of Religion series he used Donne's letters to substantiate the narrative, as Gosse would do later (*John Donne: Sometime Dean of St Paul's*, 1897, pp. 18–19, 76–77, 83–4, 89, 171, 206 and 215).

[Jessopp ventures occasional comments on Donne's poetry.]

In the later years of Elizabeth's reign there was a great deal of literary activity, which was rather in danger of degenerating into frivolity and affectation than rising to seriousness. People were happy and gay, and their gaiety expressed itself in playfulness of style – in songs and epigrams, in eccentricities of manner, in far-fetched metaphors and odd fancies. There was a continual striving for effect – a taste for the fantastic, which by no means discouraged obscurity in diction, when the substance was often subordinated to the form, and the thought wrapped up in verbiage, which sometimes rather concealed than expressed it in harmonious language. Donne, in his earlier writings, may be said to have fallen into the sins of his time. He wrote much in verse – sonnets, lyrics, love-songs, elegies, and satires. In prose he threw off what he called his 'paradoxes' and problems – short essays, each containing some odd fancy of whimsical theory; as, 'That Nature is our worst Guide', 'That all things kill Themselves', 'Why doth not Gold soil the Fingers?' or 'Why do Women delight much in Feathers?' Ben Jonson, though he admitted his cleverness, was more than ordinarily severe upon him for his ruggedness. Why should subtlety of thought excuse neglect of rhythm? Nevertheless, the young poet became the rage, and his writings were widely circulated. It was not the fashion to print such trifles; they were handed about in manuscript, discussed at the ordinaries, read out in clubs and coteries – the writers looking for their reward in the shape of favours from those to whom they were presented or addressed, and not infrequently in the shape of actual pecuniary honorarium. Very few of Donne's poems of this period were published during his lifetime, and many which are attributed to him and were issued under his name never came from his hand. The carelessness with which they were tossed into the lap of the public by his unworthy son has rendered it almost a hopeless task to distinguish between what is spurious and what is genuine. Taking them, however, as we find them, – if we except some few exquisite passages, which will be remembered and quoted as long as our language and literature live, – it is difficult to believe that these earlier poems were not loved for the poet's sake rather than the poet for the sake of his verse.

[He comments on *The First Anniversary*:]

The poem is written in a style of extravagant panegyric, but it evidently gave unqualified pleasure to those for whom it was intended.

[He follows Walton's account of Donne's parting from his wife in 1611, and comments:]

It was then that Donne wrote the exquisite stanzas which he entitled 'The Valediction', perhaps the best known of all his poems.

[He gives the whole of 'A Valediction: Forbidding Mourning'. He speaks of Donne's dilemma immediately before his ordination.]

And yet even now he found it impossible to break away from his surroundings. In spite of himself he was compelled to play the part of courtier, and to do the work of a court poet at the bidding of his patrons. From the moment when he had made up his mind to give himself up to the higher life and the service of the Church of Christ in the sanctuary, the hollowness of this wretched routine of amusement, and ceremony, and pomps, and vanities must have fretted his soul with a continual sense of emptiness. What a purposeless life he was leading! The world was just using him for its own ends, and what was he gaining by it all? God schools some men in one way, and some in another. Donne had to endure a very, very hard schooling. The closer we follow his career at this time, the sadder and more pitiful does it appear to a thoughtful reader.

[He comments on the 'Elegy upon Prince Henry'.]

It is not a successful performance, and among the least readable of his poems that have been preserved.

[He quotes stanza 1 of 'An Epithalamion on St Valentine's Day', with the comment:]

The beautiful opening stanza sounds like an echo of Chaucer.

[He describes Donne's turn from secular to religious writing in the years before his ordination:]

I incline to believe that many of Donne's religious poems were written during this period. . . . For several years past his name had been associated with verses more or less frivolous; he had written Satires, Elegies, Songs and Sonnets, which had passed from hand to hand among the courtiers and men of letters – and some few of them were not such as he would wish to be read and dwelt on by the pure and innocent. . . .

Poetry in those days was not generally accepted as the legitimate language in which the soul might pour forth its nobler thoughts – its longings, its holier sorrows and regrets. George Herbert was now little more than at the beginning of his university career, and for many years after Donne's ordination was going through a very similar experience to that which had kept the elder man so long hanging about the court. A poet was under some suspicion of being a 'worldling', just as in our own days a clergyman with any reputation for culture or learning outside the domain of homiletics or theology is too generally assumed to be at best half-hearted in his ministerial life. Be it as it may, Donne thought it became him now to break with the old life and all its lighter pursuits and amusements, and from this time he allowed himself none of that joyous relaxation which the writing of poetry might have afforded him.

[He quotes lines 30–1 and 37–42 of 'An Hymn to the Saints, and to Marquis Hamilton', and comments:]

One would have thought that the beautiful conclusion of the poem might have protected the writer from any word of disparagement.

[He quotes the whole of 'the magnificent hymn which he calls "An Hymn to God the Father"', then speaks of Donne's last days of life, quoting the first and last stanzas of the 'Hymn to God my God, in my Sickness' as a poem Donne wrote on his deathbed.]

32. Anon., *Academy*

1897

In a review of Augustus Jessopp's biography of John Donne (1897), a reviewer claims that both Donne's sermons and his poetry are 'too demanding for the intellectual laziness of the present day' (*Academy*, 4 December 1897, pp. 474–5).

The typical modern, who wants to lie and let the plums of poetry fall into his mouth, had better hold aloof from Donne. He throws out teeming suggestions of ideas, and expects the reader to pursue, amplify, and make them his own. . . .

Poets, especially, can receive from Donne's poetry abundant fertilisation. This was the case in his own day; he was the cause of indefinitely more poetry in others than he wrote himself. Crashaw, and Cowley, and the whole of the 'Cavalier lyrists', drew directly or indirectly from Donne. It was he who sowed, it was they who reaped. We doubt whether he ever wrote a completely fine poem. Let him be on fire with emotion, his intellectual subtilising in small matters choked the fiery current with icy blocks.

Here, for instance, is the opening of a two-stanza poem which probably refers to one of his enforced separations from the girl he eventually married. He must have been fervid with feeling; and the opening is worthy to be ranked with the great sonnet of Drayton, if not with the great sonnets of Shakespeare:

> So, go, break off this last lamenting kiss,
> Which sucks two souls, and vapours both away.
> Turn, thou ghost, that way, and let me turn this;
> And let ourselves benight our happiest day.

But this beautiful passionate commencement incontinently subsides into an arrangement of coldly ingenious conceits. When he felt deepest, Donne's intellect was an overpowering barrier against the impetuous current of feeling. Most happy lines and stanzas are to be cited from him; he is a poet to be read, and loved, and judiciously imitated; none can study without learning from him; he is, in our opinion (Milton, of course, excluded), the poet fullest of primal genius in his time, except Crashaw. Yet this admirable and many-sided genius is only for the judicious. He has, we must iterate, left not one completely happy poem behind him. But read him, read all he wrote, for he is a mine of rough but priceless ore.

33. Anon., *Quarterly Review*
1897

An anonymous historian of taste placed Donne with Sterne and Keats as an initiator of literary impressionism ('Fathers of Literary Impressionism in England', *Quarterly Review*, 185 (1897) 175–81).

[The writer argues that in sixteenth-century England, Renaissance Hellenism was leavened and tempered by Reformation Hebraism, so that the classical sense of objective finality yielded to a subjective indulgence in the personal and plaintive. The outcome was a 'sentimental impressionism'.]

Both the Old and the New Testaments are pervaded by a sense of the infinite environing the individual, while the emphasis of the classical accent is, as we have said, *finality* objectively sublimed. In the personal and plaintive is to be found the method of what he style 'Impressionism'. It is just this quality, and not his acquaintance with the mythology of Lemprière, that makes Keats an impressionist; just this, and not his whimsical irregularities, that so causes us to regard Sterne; just this, and not his euphuisms and conceits, that places Donne in the same category.

It follows from what we have urged that impressionist writing is a department of sentimental literature eminently adapted for lyrical poetry, or for such prose as lends itself to vivid glimpses of life or nature through the medium of awakened associations.

None the less, however, it is unsuitable for prolonged or sustained employment; it is only truthful, and, by consequence, valuable, where the incompleteness, so to speak, of its statement is counterbalanced by the completeness of its suggestion. The tests, then, of how and when it is used must be applied, and we should never allow ourselves to believe that impressionism is *per se* a royal road to imaginative interpretation or is to be admired as an end in itself.

[He quotes Saintsbury's account of the conflicting forces in Donne's nature.]

It is just from such a nature that we should expect impressionism; and, when we add that he was a profound pessimist, the personal, the plaintive, the restive *timbre* is only natural. Mr Saintsbury himself bears out, though he has not attempted to explain, what we have adduced as to the temper of the Renaissance by saying that 'its peculiar pessimism was perfectly different from that of classical times, and can only be paralleled by the spirit of Ecclesiastes'.

By turns erotic and devotional, always morbid and fantastic, of considerable culture and attainments, his fervid originality stands out irregular and unrestrained among the brilliant galaxies of his age. His power of suggesting ideas was extraordinary; to employ his own phrase, he was wont to 'ideate', and, although one cannot say of him, as he said of Sidney, that

> 'Twas a double power by which he sung
> The highest matter in the noblest form;

still, no one, not even Keats, has conveyed subtler grades of feeling by the sound and significance of irresistible cadences. Indeed, he is often far nearer to Keats than he is to his contemporaries, as witness the following fragments: –

[He quotes some lines from *Elegy* 3, *The First Anniversary* and *The Second Anniversary*, remarking that Saintsbury justly considers *The Second Anniversary* to be the most striking and original of Donne's many prose and verse meditations on death.]

Nor can we, lastly, refrain from citing *in extenso* one of the songs, that it seems to us might almost have been indited by Keats himself. It is called 'The Goodmorrow' . . .

[He quotes the whole of 'The Good Morrow'.]

'Have you never,' ejaculates Keats in one of his letters, 'by being surprised with an old melody in a delicious place by a delicious voice, *felt* over again your very speculations and surmises at the time it first operated on your soul?' Here in truth is the secret of the method that links the sixteenth-century 'Anatomist of the World' with the eighteenth-century singer of 'Endymion' – the method of sensuous suggestion, the method of the true impressionist. With this difference, however, in its results, that the former charmed his contemporaries with it into enthusiasm, the latter surprised them into rebuff. Ben Jonson generously applauded Donne; there was no reviewer to chill the fantasies of the Jacobean who succeeded to a tumult of thought, language, and sensation that may aptly be termed the French Revolution of literature.

Donne's poems are divided into 'Divine' and 'Profane'; the latter mainly the products of his wilder youth, the former of his more spiritual maturity. Both are conspicuous for 'the amorousness of an harmonious soul', to borrow his own description. As Walton wrote beneath the frontispiece to the edition of 1635: –

> Witness this book, thy Emblem which begins
> With Love; but ends with sighs and tears for sins.

But the remarkable feature of them all is that none of them are addressed to the romantic themes, classic or chivalrous, which engrossed his brother bards. The praise of friends by 'verse letters', the praise of women through songs and sonnets, the praise of both by 'Elegies', 'Epicedes', and 'Obsequies', the praise of God through the so-called 'Divine Poems' – these, if we except the 'Satires,' for the most part nugatory, and the 'Anatomy of the World,' by far his finest series, exhaust the subjects of his muse. We find no poet of his period with so limited a range. The workings of his own heart and soul are indeed his only theme, nor does he, like Keats, attempt to transfer them to the nature around or the centuries behind him. He never treats humanity in combination; he is the mere diarist of his own feelings, detached and rarefied, as it were, from his own experiences. Such a phenomenon is unique in English literature. But in proportion to the narrowness of its focus is the intensity of his impressionism. That portion of the 'Anatomy' which is based on 'The Religious Death of Mistress Elizabeth Drury', and styled by him 'Of the progress of the soul', exhibits to the full magnificence of emotion, echoed, so to say, through associative sound. It is here that we light upon –

> No soul – whiles with the luggage of this clay
> It clogged is – can follow thee half-way.

Here, that unapproached and celebrated couplet –

> These hymns thy issue may increase so long
> As till God's great Venite change the song.

Here, two of the most significant passages already quoted; here, that epitome of the body –

> Think, when 'twas grown to most, 'twas a poor inn,
> A province pack'd up in two yards of skin.

Nor are the beauties of his 'verse-letters' less fine, if less frequent. How perfect is the emphatic picture of rustic squiredom in–

> You do not duties of societies,
> If from th'embrace of a loved wife you rise,
> View your fat beasts, stretch'd barns, and labour'd fields,
> Eat, play, ride, take all joys which all day yields.

How large in tone and type –

> But though she [*i.e.* the sea] part us, to hear my oft prayers
> For your increase, God is as near me here;
> And to send you what I shall beg, His stairs
> In length and ease are alike everywhere.

How Shakespearean in ring and rhythm –

> Love that imparts in everything delight
> Is fancied in the soul, not in the sight.

The same may be said of

> Alas,
> How little poison cracks a crystal glass!

in his elegy on the Lady Markham; of 'Great Destiny the Commissary of God', and of 'To the brain, the soul's bedchamber, went', in the 'Metempsychosis'. His songs and sonnets are no less characteristic, though often more rugged and unequal. We will transcribe two of the most tuneful: –

[He gives the first stanza of 'The Sun Rising', and the first stanza of Dowland's song 'Break of Day'.]

And, lastly, the 'Divine Poems' are in some respects the most extraordinary of all. We doubt if the impressionist method has ever since been applied to sacred lyrics. In the 'Hymn to Christ, at the author's last going into Germany,' occurs a remarkable passage: –

> I sacrifice this island unto Thee,
> And all whom I love there, and who love me;
> When I have put our seas 'twixt them and me,
> Put Thou Thy seas betwixt my sins and Thee.

Here the style is sincere and successful. Beautiful also are numbers 23 and 24, which we shall quote in full, as a final testimony to this first father of English literary impressionism.

[He quotes lines 199–216 of 'A Litany'.]

Surely the 'Thou in us dost pray' is what modern critics would term an 'epoch-making' thought, and yet it is through emotion that we realize it, and despite a crabbed and involved form of metre. We have, we imagine, discoursed enough to show that, if our definition of impressionism be just, Donne is an impressionist, and cited enough to give a fair notion of his quality; for, as might be guessed, he is inapt for prolonged effort, and therefore as well exemplified by brilliant facets as by a closer examination of the whole jewel. On his grossnesses and disfigurements we have not dwelt, as they are beside our present purpose.

[He then turns to Sterne as a curious example of 'sustained instead of spasmodic impressionism'.]

34. Francis Thompson

1897–9

Francis Thompson (1859–1907), Catholic poet and critic, frequently cited Donne in essays on other writers (*Literary Criticisms by Francis Thompson*, ed. T. L. Connolly, 1948, pp. 65, 68, 149, 251, 263; Thompson's essays first appeared in the *Academy* for 8 May 1897, 19 August 1899 and 28 October 1899).

[Thompson counts 'Donne at his best' as one of the supreme seventeenth-century poets with Crashaw, Dryden 'and a small number of others'; and, speaking of English sonnets, he remarks that 'Donne's are well known and ruggedly strong'. In a portrait of Robert Browning he couples Donne with Browning as a true poet who nonetheless 'lacks something of the quality of a singer'.]

. . . it sometimes happens that a singer with a rough voice commands attention in despite of its roughness. And so, we think, it is with Browning. Donne is another example. Criticism has come round to the recognition of Donne, in spite of the roughest utterance ever employed by a poet of like gifts. Upon this precedent we rest our recognition of Browning as a poet. He went out of his way to be rough, apparently for roughness' sake, and without any large scale of harmonies to justify it. But his intrinsic qualities, far more than in the case of Donne, make him a poet in the teeth of this defect of execution; such is our opinion.

[In a later essay on Daniel and Drayton, Thompson finds that Drayton belongs to the class of clumsy workmen who do have something to say, and he instances Donne as another such.]

. . . inexpert craftsmen who are full of matter almost invariably try to bring their matter within metrical compass by the omission of connecting words – what is technically called ellipsis. It takes a great artist to use ellipsis well. Shakespeare is a master of it; yet even Shakespeare sometimes faults by excessive and crabbed ellipsis. Donne, a very pregnant writer, who, like Drayton, is not a good craftsman, is full of violent and knotty ellipses. But he has at least the palliation that his ellipses are scholarly, and result from an indiscreet imitation of the Latin, where the inflected character of the language permits bold ellipsis inadmissible to an uninflected language like the English.

[In an essay on English satirists Thompson discusses the effect of libel laws upon satire.]

What a forest of flourishing trees would be thinned out from English literature had the Parliamentary Vulcan earlier furnished the Law with its awful libel thunderbolts! Chaucer and Langland might stand; so might Hall (no very biting satirist), and Donne (pungent, clever, with metre like a rope all hanks and knots); but from Butler downwards they are all inveterate libellists.

35. Henry Augustin Beers

1898

Beers (1847–1926) was an American author and poet, and Professor of English at Yale. As a scholar Beers was primarily interested in Romanticism, publishing the *History of English Romanticism in the Eighteenth Century* (1899; see No. 45) and the *History of English Romanticism in the Nineteenth Century* (1901). In *From Chaucer to Tennyson* (1898), he spoke of a new style in poetry at the end of the seventeenth century which was variously known as the Metaphysical school, the fantastic or conceited school, or 'English Marinists or Gongorists after the poets Marino and Gongora, who brought this fashion to its extreme in Italy and in Spain' (*From Chaucer to Tennyson*, 1898, pp. 105–7).

The one who set the fashion was Dr John Donne, Dean of St Paul's, whom Dryden pronounced a great wit, but not a great poet, and whom Ben Jonson esteemed the best poet in the world for some things, but likely to be forgotten for want of being understood. Besides satires and epistles in verse, he composed amatory poems in his youth, and divine poems in his age, both kinds distinguished by such subtle obscurity, and far-fetched ingenuities, that they read like a series of puzzles. When this poet has occasion to write a valediction to his mistress upon going into France, he compares their temporary separation to that of a pair of compasses:

> Such wilt thou be to me, who must,
> Like the other foot obliquely run;
> Thy firmness makes my circle just,
> And makes me end where I begun.

If he would persuade her to marriage he calls her attention to a flea –

> Me it sucked first and now sucks thee,
> And in this flea our two bloods mingled be.

He says that the flea is their marriage-temple, and bids her forbear to kill it lest she thereby commit murder, suicide and sacrilege all in one. Donne's figures are scholastic and smell of the lamp. He ransacked cosmography, astrology, alchemy, optics, the canon law, and the divinity of the school-men for ink-horn terms and similes. He was in verse what Browne was in prose. He loved to play with distinctions, hyperboles, paradoxes, the very casuistry and dialectics of love or devotion.

> Thou canst not every day give me thy heart:
> If thou canst give it then thou never gav'st it:
> Love's riddles are that though thy heart depart
> It stays at home, and thou with losing sav'st it.

Donne's verse is usually as uncouth as his thought. But there is a real passion slumbering under these ashy heaps of conceit, and occasionally a pure flame darts up, as in the justly admired lines:

> Her pure and eloquent blood
> Spoke in her cheek, and so divinely wrought
> That one might almost say her body thought.

This description of Donne is true, with modifications, of all the metaphysical poets. They had the same forced and unnatural style. The ordinary laws of the association of ideas were reversed with them. It was not the nearest, but the remotest, association that was called up. The finest spirit among them was 'holy George Herbert'.

36. David Hannay

1898

David Hannay (1853–1934) wrote a number of books on various aspects of the Navy and Merchant Navy, as well as several biographies, including one of Frederick Marryat and one of Tobias Smollett. His cultural history *The Later Renaissance* covered not only England but Spain, France and Italy too; it went through several impressions. Donne was given a passing mention (*The Later Renaissance*, 1898, p. 220).

[The author reports opinions of Donne with scrupulous neutrality.]

One of the most enigmatical and debated, alternately one of the most attractive and most repellent, figures in English literature.

37. George Edward Bateman Saintsbury

1898

Donne makes several star appearances in George Saintsbury's critical survey of English literature, figuring among the greatest English writers of prose as well as of poetry (*A Short History of English Literature*, 1898, pp. 365–8, 385–6 and 411–12).

[Saintsbury gives three pages to Donne's poetry in a chapter on 'The Schools of Jacobean Poetry', emphasizing its extraordinarily high standing in its day, and Donne's own status as a master who ranked at least equal with Spenser and Jonson. Donne's example was more powerful even than Jonson's in the turn against the fantastically embellished but intellectually low-powered manner of the followers of Spenser. For Jonson did not soar imaginatively, and his love poems are not 'metaphysically passionate'; whereas Donne]

seems to have been born to combine all elements of the Renaissance spirit – the haunting meditation on death, the passionate attention to love, the blend of classical and romantic form. And he added a peculiar mystical charm, the result of the taste for the conceit spiritualised, refined, and made to transcend.

[Saintsbury puzzles over Donne's formal idiosyncrasies, and offers several explanations of his seemingly deliberate roughness. He remarks that in the poetry other than the *Satires*]

the mere metre is as a rule correct enough. It is only that the intensity and fulness of the thought does not lend itself to actually smooth expression, without more labour than the writer seems to have cared to expend upon it.

[Then he goes on to show how this intensity and fulness appear in the several kinds of Donne's verse even though some of these kinds, such as the *Satires*, *Elegies* and *Verse Letters*, have the manner of routine performances. The *Satires* may be the best known, 'in consequence of Pope's rather blundering patronage', but are actually the least interesting part of Donne's work. Donne's full poetic power emerges elsewhere.

Saintsbury shows where it emerges at the conclusion of his chapter, in an outburst of personal reverence which he evidently felt the need to justify.]

We are thus left with the *Songs and Sonnets* and *The Anatomy of the World*, which yet complete each other in the most remarkable fashion. The *Songs* exhibit Donne's quintessential, melancholy, passionate imagination as applied, chiefly in youth, to Love; the *Anniversaries*, the same imagination as applied later to Death, the ostensible text being the untimely death of mistress Elizabeth Drury, but the real subject being the riddle of the painful earth as embodied in the death of the body. The *Songs* are, of course, in different lyrical forms, and the *Anniversaries* are in couplets. But both agree in the unique *clangour* of their poetic sound, and in the extraordinary character of the thoughts which find utterance in verse, now exquisitely melodious, now complicated and contorted almost beyond ready comprehension in rhyme or sense, but never really harsh, and always possessing, in actual presence or near suggestion, a poetical quality which no English poet has ever surpassed. It is from these poems that the famous epithet 'metaphysical' (which Johnson not too happily, and with great confusion between Donne and Cowley, applied to the whole school) is derived; and as applied to Donne it is not inappropriate. For behind every image, every ostensible thought of his, there are vistas and backgrounds of other thoughts dimly vanishing, with glimmers in them here and there, into the depths of the final enigmas of life and soul. Passion and meditation, the two avenues into this region of doubt and dread, are tried by Donne in the two sections respectively, and of each he has the key. Nor, as he walks in them with eager or solemn tread, are light and music wanting, the light the most unearthly that ever played round a poet's head, the music not the least heavenly that he ever caught and transmitted to his readers. If this language seems more highflown than is generally used in this book or than is appropriate to it, the excuse must be that every reader of Donne is either an adept or an outsider born, and that it is impossible for the former to speak in words understanded of the latter.

[In a later chapter Saintsbury makes Donne his 'last and greatest exemplar' of Jacobean prose. He rates Donne as highly for his prose as for his poetry; but then 'Few are more of a piece in poetry and prose than Donne.' All Donne's work is 'strikingly like itself and strikingly unlike anything else'; and the distinction of his prose appears no less in the tracts and letters than in his sermons. Saintsbury seeks the reason for Donne's power.]

... he has the three great characteristics of Jacobean writing – the learning, the profundity, and the fantastic imagination. And the profundity is here not merely real, but of a depth rarely surpassed in English, while the fantastic imagination becomes something more than merely fantastic. The 'kingship which Carew ascribed to Donne is at least as noticeable in his prose as in his verse, and though the realm over which he rules is rather a Kingdom of Night than of Day, a place of strangely-lit gloom rather than of mere sunlight, it is a kingdom of wonderful richness and variety. It may be questioned whether Donne's very best passages are exceeded, whether they are equalled, by any English prose-writer in the combination of fulness and rarity of meaning with exquisite perfection of sound and charm of style. In these latter points he is at least the equal of Jeremy Taylor at his best, and though Jeremy Taylor is no shallow thinker, his thought is a mere pool in the oceanic depth and breadth of Donne's. There is a certain quality of magnificence, too, in Donne beside which the best things of Taylor are apt to suggest the merely pretty. Unlike most of his contemporaries, Donne knew when to let a great thing alone; and few of them, for instance, would have been content to let such a phrase as the likening of the coming of God to the soul 'as the sun at noon to illustrate all shadows, as the sheaves in harvest to fill all penuries', without frittering away its massive and complete effect into subdivisions and added epithets, into appendices and fringes of thought and expression.

[Donne shares with Hooker but scarcely with any other writer 'the sense of the paragraph – of the crescendo and diminuendo of

119

cadence required to wind it safely and melodiously from start to finish'. His sentences are too often made to do the work of the paragraph.]

But whether they be called sentences or be called paragraphs, there linger round each of them the glimmer of an unearthly light and the notes of a more than earthly music.

[Saintsbury's account of the Metaphysical poets who succeeded Donne seeks to redress a false view of them. He speaks of the grotesque blunders which followed Johnson's lumping-together of Cowley with Donne, such as mar Wordsworth's comments on Donne. Cowley was only half a Metaphysical in any case. As for the term 'metaphysical' itself, it is 'not inappropriately used for the habit, common to this school of poets, of always seeming to express something after, something behind, the simple, obvious first sense and suggestion of a subject'. Johnson used the term to attribute to these poets qualities which Elizabethan writers also exhibit. Yet almost all the poets writing between 1630 and 1660 show a distinctive 'metaphysical tendency'.]

All, no doubt, owed much to that mighty influence of Donne, which was so strangely disconnected from any publication of his work. But Donne himself is metaphysical in the greatest and widest sense. His thoughts, even his conceits, are never far-fetched, because his immense and brooding imagination reaches to them all without the trouble of fetching. The others have to fetch them; they could in some cases hardly go farther, they could in many hardly fare worse.

38. Felix Schelling

1898

In an essay on Jonson and his followers, Schelling attempted to show that Spenser, Jonson and Donne sought different poetic ends and stood for distinct artistic principles ('Ben Jonson and the Classical School', *PMLA*, 13: 2 (1898), 227).

It is a commonplace of the history of literature that Jonson literally dominated the age in which he lived. . . . There was only one poet who shared even in part this literary supremacy of Jonson, and that poet was John Donne. To Donne, especially to the Marinist in him, must be granted the credit – if credit it be – of delaying for more than a generation the natural revulsion of English literature back to classicism and restraint. This is not the place in which to discuss the interesting relations of Jonson and Donne. Except for a certain rhetorical and dialectical address, which might be referred to a study of the ancients, the poetry of Donne is marked by its disregard of conventions, by its extraordinary originality of thought and expression, by that rare quality of poetic insight that justifies Jonson's enthusiastic claim that 'John Donne [was] the first poet in the world in some things.' Not less significant on the other hand are Jonson's contrasted remarks to Drummond on the same topic: 'That Donne's *Anniversary* [in which true womanhood is idealized if not deified] was profane and full of blasphemies', and 'that Donne, for not keeping of accent, deserved hanging'. The classicist has always regarded the romanticist thus, nor have the retorts been more courteous, as witness the well known lines of Keats' *Sleep and Poetry* in which the age of classicism is described as 'a schism nurtured by foppery and barbarism'.

Thus we find Spenser and Jonson standing as exponents respectively of the expansive or romantic movement and the repressive or classical spirit. In a different line of distinction Donne is equally in contrast with Spenser, as the intensive, or subjective artist. Both of these latter are romanticists in that each seeks to produce the effect demanded of art by means of an appeal to the sense of novelty; but Spenser's romanticism is that of selection, which chooses from the outer world the fitting and the pleasing, and constructs it into a permanent artistic joy. Donne's is the romanticism of insight, which, looking inward, descries the subtle relations of things and transmutes them into poetry with a sudden and unexpected flood of light. Between Jonson and Donne there is the kinship of intellectuality; between Spenser and Donne the kinship of romanticism; between Spenser and Jonson the kinship of the poet's joy in beauty. Spenser is the most objective and therefore allegorical and mystical; Donne is the most subjective and the most spiritual; Jonson, the most artistic and therefore the most logical.

But not only did Jonson dominate his age and stand for the classical ideal in the midst of current Spenserianism, Marinism, and other popular modes, it was this position of Jonson, defended as it was in theory as well as exemplified in his work, that directed the course which English literature was to take for a century and a half after his death.

[Schelling goes on to argue that the strong influence of Donne's subtle novelty of treatment was one of the forces that delayed the incoming tide of classicism in the seventeenth century.]

39. Edmund Gosse

1899

Gosse published his life of Donne in two volumes, which he had worked on for nearly twenty years. This was the most intimate biography of Donne since Izaac Walton's, and the first editing since 1851 of all Donne's extant letters. Two *Holy Sonnets* from the Westmoreland Manuscript (no. 18, 'Show Me Dear Christ', and 19, 'Oh, To Vex Me') now appeared in print for the first time ever.

Gosse's account of Donne's life, though inaccurate as to fact and dangerously distorted by his persistent invention of circumstances to fit the poems, remained standard until R. C. Bald's *John Donne: A Life* in 1970. His editing of Donne's letters is no less cavalier, but the text must still be consulted (*The Life and Letters of John Donne*, 1899, vol. I, pp. 36, 48–50, 64–5, 74–6, 117, 138–9, 263–9, 274–8, 317; vol. II, pp. 13, 44–5, 106–9, 279–80, 290–1, 330–1 and 370–1).

[Gosse made a strenuous and imaginative attempt to place Donne's poems in the context of his life and career. Speaking of Donne's youthful poems he compares the satires with satires by Marston and Hall.]

Neither of these satirists, however, displays so bold an originality as Donne. Hall in particular keeps so close to the ancients, that his text is sometimes little more than a cento of paraphrased passages from Juvenal. From the very first Donne was independent. His isolation from the accepted models of style – that feature on which we shall have incessantly to insist – is apparent from the opening of his poetical career. The earliest verses from his pen which we know that we possess are those with which the First Satire opens –

> Away, thou changing motley humourist,
> Leave me, and in this standing wooden chest,
> Consorted with these few books, let me lie
> In prison, and here be coffin'd when I die.

Thus, in 1593, with the verse of Spenser, Sidney, Peele, and Watson murmured around him, soft and voluptuous measures Italianating the rude tongues of the preceding generation – thus, with an accent not yet formed yet already his own, a native and individual accent founded on no English or foreign predecessor, the boy of twenty speaks to us.

The Satires of Donne are not general invectives as those of Hall are, nor fantastic libels against individuals like those of Marston, but a series of humorous and sardonic portraits of types. The edition of Theophrastus, which Casaubon was to revolutionise European *belles-lettres* by publishing in 1598, was still unknown, but Scaliger had more vaguely drawn attention to this class of ironic portraiture. Each of Donne's satires is woven about some such type as the Theophrastians a little later loved to define and describe.

[He gives an account of each of Donne's five *Satires*, with occasional critical comments, as when he describes *Satire* 3.]

Donne proceeds, with one of those grand and virile images for which his style was to be prominent –

> On a huge hill,
> Cragged and steep, Truth stands, and he that will
> Reach her, about must and about must go,
> And what the hill's suddenness resists, win so,
> Yet strive so, that before age, death's twilight,
> Thy soul rest, for none can work in that night.

This very remarkable poem is conducted in a darkness unusual even in the writings of Donne, but those who will adventure in it, and bring to it no more than they find – for glib conjecture is here all out of place – will be rewarded by a strange passion of intellectual poetry.

[He comments on *Satire* 4 and *Satire* 5.]

This Fourth Satire is furbished forth with an extraordinary array of learned allusions. The young poet is not averse to letting us remark how wide and curious his reading has been, nor to dazzling us with references to Calepine the lexicographer, and Surius the German historian. . . .

One of the features which was to distinguish Donne from most of his illustrious contemporaries was to be his aggressive realism, his determination to substitute for classical and romantic metaphors images drawn from the life, science, and speculation of his own day. If we compare the texture of one of Spenser's *Complaints* or a romance of Greene's with any of these early satires of Donne, we shall be astonished at their unlikeness in this respect. The Fourth Satire is particularly rich in details of this realistic order. . . .

The Fifth Satire is a very bad poem, much of it spoiled to the ear by the terrible rattle of redundant feet in verse which it is hard to explain and impossible to justify. Every now and then, however, the laborious reader meets with a splendid phrase, which illuminates the dark mass, as when the poet, in the course of a metaphor indeed most strained and obscure, speaks of 'the vast ravishing seas'.

[He moves on to the early *Verse Letters*.]

'The Storm' and 'The Calm' have a considerable resemblance in style to the *Satires*, and are written in the same harshly cadenced heroic measure. They are exercises in deliberate description, pure *tours de force* of artisan's work in poetry. They exemplify some of the worst features which the literary production of Donne was to develop – its aridity and roughness. That these were wilfully introduced, in direct opposition to and appeal against the rosy Elizabethan sweetness, we cannot allow ourselves to doubt. These were attempts, without any reference to antique examples or far-fetched illustrations, to paint what the poet saw or thought he saw. Here is an example from 'The Storm' –

> Then, like two mighty kings which, dwelling far
> Asunder, meet against a third to war,
> The south and west winds joined, and, as they blew,

> Waves like a rolling trench before them threw.
> Sooner than you read this line, did the gale,
> Like shot not feared till felt, our sails assail,
> And what at first was called a gust, the same
> Hath now a storm's, anon a tempest's name.

In this strained verse there is little melody and a deliberate abeyance of fancy, but the effort to obtain a realistic effect is most curious. Here is the result of the wind's action on the maimed and shattered flotilla –

> Then note they the ship's sickness, the mast
> Shaked with an ague, and the hold and waist
> With a salt dropsy clogged; all our tacklings
> Snapping like too-high stretchèd treble-strings;
> And from our tattered sails rags drop down so
> As from one hanged in chains a year ago.

Here, at all events, is observation – the eye is upon the object. 'The Calm', which was greatly admired by contemporaries, and won the difficult suffrages of Ben Jonson, is in the same manner, but displays a greater extravagance. The intense heat of the Tropics in August offers the poet a theme with which he plays like a conjurer with a set of balls. The sailors go mad with the 'calenture' or mirage-fever of nostalgia; and every extravagant phenomenon of great heat is dwelt upon –

> On the hatches, as on altars, lies
> Each one, his own priest, and own sacrifice.
> Who live, that miracle do multiply
> Where walkers in hot ovens do not die;
> If in despite of these we swim, that hath
> No more refreshing than a brimstone-bath;
> Back from the sea into the ship we turn
> Like parboiled wretches on the coals to burn.

These ingenuities were in an entirely new fashion, and those who were not repelled by their novelty were attracted by their 'wit'. Long afterwards, when visiting Drummond at Hawthornden, Jonson recited with strong commendation the lines from 'The Calm' –

> In one place lay
> Feathers and dust, to-day and yesterday;
> Earth's hollownesses, which the world's lungs are,
> Have no more wind than th' upper vault of air.

Here we find ourselves at the very start-point of a new spirit in literature, the love of precise notation of prosaic fact in the forms and languages of poetry. The exquisite Elizabethan idealism was undermined at last; here was the beginning of decadence; here opened the invasion of the Visigoths.

[Then he turns to the *Songs and Sonnets*, which he takes for a direct outcome of Donne's youthful philandering.]

In this earliest series of his poems we find him a mere butterfly of the court, ostentatiously flitting from flower to flower, indulging his curiosity and his sensuousness wherever satisfaction is offered to him. 'Woman's Constancy' is the complete expression of his unattached condition of mind and body. In 'Love's Usury', with the impertinence of the successful gallant, he promises to turn monogamous when he is old. In these early days his experiences are all of sensation and superficial emotion. He wanders wherever his desires attract him, rifles all blossoms for their honey, boasts – in the manner of impudent youth – his detachment from all chains of duty or reflection. He is the ideal light o' love; he will pluck the rose wherever he finds it, and he is confident that for the wise youth who knows how to nip the flower discreetly there can be no thorns. The tone of these earliest lyrics is one of sceptical, even contemptuous, arrogance. In 'A Fever' the mistress of the moment is ill, but it only amuses the lover. The malady is an excuse for a *feu de joie* of conceits; she may die of it, for all he really cares. In these foppish, heartless lyrics Donne is most interesting when most frankly sensual. 'The Good Morrow' is the perfectly contented and serene record of an illicit, and doubtless of an ephemeral, adventure. 'The Sun Rising', perhaps the strongest of the early lyrics, gives no evidence of soul, but is a fine hymn of sturdy, virile satisfaction. What could be more spirited, in its boyish way, than the opening stanza –

> Busy old fool, unruly Sun,
>   Why dost thou thus,
> Thro' windows and thro' curtains, call on us?
> Must to thy motions lovers' seasons run?
>   Saucy pedantic wretch, go chide
>   Late schoolboys and sour prentices;
> Go tell court-huntsmen that the king will ride,
>   Call country ants to harvest offices;
> Love, all alike, no season knows nor clime,
> Nor hours, days, months, which are the rags of time.

From a young lover in this mood we need not be scandalised to receive such a poem as 'The Flea', that extremely clever piece of impudent ribaldry, nor expect a deeper sense of the dignity of womanhood than is found in 'The Indifferent', that uproarious claim to absolute freedom in love. Here Donne reminds us of a very different poet, of the nomadic Verlaine, with his 'Es tu brune ou es tu blonde? – Je ne sais!' In 'The Legacy', more seriously, and with an intuition of deeper feeling, Donne playfully upbraids his heart for its own too-flagrant infidelities.

[He groups some of the *Songs and Sonnets* and *Elegies* together, as the record of an illicit passion which turned to raging jealousy and then disillusionment and hatred.]

But all these poems of hatred and enforced resignation pale before 'The Apparition', in which, as he tosses between sleep and waking, the horror of his situation, the vileness of the woman he has loved, and the whole squalor of the outworn liaison come upon him and overwhelm him. The fierce passion in this brief lyric, a 'hate-poem' of the very first class, is closely akin to those flashes of lurid light in which the contemporary tragedians excelled, 'steeping us', as Charles Lamb says, 'in agonies infernal'. Such error, however, as Donne had indulged in could be washed out in no less bitter waters. 'The Apparition' is brief, and must be read complete to produce the terrific effect of its reluctant malediction.

[He gives the entire poem.]

This is the culmination of the incident, the flames of hatred now quickly subsiding into a heap of the ashes of indifference and satiety. This exhausted cynicism is interpreted by 'Love's Alchemy', where the poet protests that all women are alike vile, and the elixir of happiness an imposture not to be discovered by any alchemist who 'glorifies his pregnant pot', only to be fooled and disenchanted. So, also, in a most curious ode, the 'Nocturnal upon St Lucy's Day', amid fireworks of conceit, he calls his mistress dead, and protests that his hatred has grown calm at last. So this volcanic passion sinks back into its crater at length, leaving this series of astonishing poems to illustrate it, poems which, as Donne himself says, are 'as all-confessing and through-shine' as glass itself. When he grew supine once more, he reflected, rather splenetically, on his want of common prudence in this revelation of the adventures of the soul. As he said to Rowland Woodward, he had shown these 'love-song weeds and satiric thorns' to too many of his friends to be able to quench the incident in oblivion, and too many copies of them had been made by his private admirers to preclude their circulation.

Donne, in his own words, had 'stained' his soul's 'first white', but his conduct from this time forth seems to have given no scandal. One or two love-passages appear to have ruffled the tenour of the wave of life which was carrying him towards the bourne of matrimony. He sees and is the sudden victim of beauty again and again.

His sensitive heart is ingenious in self-torture, and to what extremities it still can fling him we read in 'The Blossom'. The lady of the moment has left him a week ago, and in three weeks more he is to meet her in London. In subtle, modulated verse his heart taunts and plagues him, for he no longer knows what he desires nor what he is. His previous adventures have made him cautious, even sceptical, and he will not frankly give way to this sweet, insidious hope. He apostrophises his own trembling heart, which knows not whether to bide with him or to follow the new and desired mistress –

> Well then, stay here; but know,
> When thou has stay'd and done thy most,
> *A naked thinking heart, that makes no show,*
> *Is to a woman but a kind of ghost;*
> How shall she know my heart?

To the same vague category of emotions which faintly stirred the poet between his great criminal liaison and his ultimate betrothal, I am inclined also to attribute, on internal and structural evidence, the Tenth Elegy, as well as, perhaps, the extremely fantastic lyric called 'The Ecstasy', with its obsession on the word 'violet'; this had, unquestionably, at the time of its composition an illuminating meaning which time has completely obscured.

[In a fresh section Gosse gives an account of the circumstances of Donne's marriage, and comments on the poems which he assumes that it inspired.]

It was about this time that Donne wrote his noble poem, 'The Canonization', which affords us an index to the feelings of indignant and irritated impatience with which he regarded the obstacles set in the way of his happiness. It is marked by some of the most characteristic features of his genius, and shows that he had regained to the full the lyric fire which had for some years been dormant.

[He quotes several stanzas of the poem and gives an account of the rest. Gosse now tackles the *Metempsychosis* as an unclassifiable oddity, describing it in detail and drawing out some general impressions of Donne's art and aims.]

The Progress of the Soul may help us to understand why, with gifts of intellectual appreciation and keen refinement perhaps unsurpassed even in that consummate age, Donne never contrived to reach the first rank among men of letters. The puerility of the central idea is extraordinary; the Soul flits from body to body, without growth, without change, as a parasite leaps from one harbouring object to another. In this notion of the undeveloping restlessness of the Soul, if there is any thought at all, it is the bare satiric one, too cheap to be so magnificently extended and embroidered. It is probable that Donne's intention was to irradiate the dark places of ignorance and brutality as his narrative descended the ages, but, as we have seen, he could not induce the hare to start. He had little dramatic and positively no epic talent; and this is implicitly admitted even by De Quincey, who is the solitary uncompromising admirer of *The Progress of the Soul* whom three centuries have produced.

But when all this is conceded, the poem remains one of the most extraordinary in a majestic age. De Quincey, to quote him at the height of his argument, declares that 'massy diamonds compose the very substance of this poem on the Metempsychosis, thoughts and descriptions which have the fervent and gloomy sublimity of Ezechiel or Æschylus'. If a sober criticism may hesitate to admit the 'massy diamonds', there is yet no question that diamond dust is sprinkled broadcast over the stanzas of this grotesque poem. The effort after a complete novelty of style is apparent, and the result of this is occasionally, although not invariably, happy. What we notice in it first is resistance to the accepted Spenserian glow and amenity. The author is absolutely in revolt against the tendency and mode of Spenser. He is not less opposed to a dry and even manner of writing intellectual poetry, which was a revival, in measure, of what Spenser had cast forth, and which had been exemplified in the graceful and highly popular miscellanies of Samuel Daniel, first collected in this very year 1601; in the *Nosce Teipsum* of Sir John Davys, in 1599; and in the historical verse of Drayton (1597 and onwards). My own conviction is that it was the even flow of versification of these academic writers which, more than anything else, goaded Donne to the cultivation of that violently varied tonality in verse of which *The Progress of the Soul* gives innumerable examples. We have an exact parallel in the exacerbation of Wagner's genius through his impatience with the smoothness of Donizetti.

If we look around for any contemporary poetry which shall in measure remind us of Donne, we are confined to one or two works of pure eccentricity, such as Chapman's *Amorous Zodiac*, published in 1595, and Cyril Tourneur's *Transform'd Metamorphosis* of 1600.

[After surveying some of Donne's shorter prose writings Gosse turns to the religious poetry.]

The Divine Poems of Donne offer considerable difficulty to his biographer. A few of them already are, or can approximately be, dated, but the majority are subject to conjecture founded upon internal evidence. They are of two orders; there are hymns and spiritual poems of Donne's which, however rugged their form, breathe a fervid spirit of faith and a genuine humility. In others the intellectual element outweighs the religious. These verses are rather extremely ingenious exercises in metrical theology than bursts of impulsive piety. It may be broadly suggested that the latter belong to the second, and the former to the third or final, division of Donne's career. That is to say, the more metaphysical pieces are the outcome of the years when religious inquiry formed one of his prominent studies, but when no exclusive call had summoned him to the ministry. In form all the sacred poetry of Donne suffers from his determination to introduce Spanish effects into English prosody, and Spanish ingenuities into the expression of English thought. If Donne's early hymns and litanies do not move us, it is largely due to the fact that they did not move himself. They are frigid, they are stiffened with legal and medical phraseology, the heart of a sinner saved does not beat beneath their 'cross and correct concupiscence of wit'.

An excess of ingenuity is peculiarly fatal to the unction of religious poetry. Unless it is spontaneous, unless it palpitates with ecstasy or moans with aspiration, unless it is the outpouring of a contrite spirit, it leaves upon the listener a sense of painful artificiality. The dogmatic verses of Donne do not escape from this disability. We admit their cleverness, and are sure that it is misplaced. The solemn mystery of Christ's three days' sojourn in the tomb is not, for instance, illuminated when Donne speaks of Him as one

> Whose body, having walk'd on earth, and now
> Hasting to heaven, would – that He might allow
> Himself unto all stations and fill all –
> For those three days become a mineral.
> He was all gold when He lay down, but rose
> All tincture, and doth not alone dispose
> Leaden and iron wills to good, but is
> Of power to make e'en sinful flesh like His.

Here Donne's intellectual arrogance stood him in evil stead. He would not continue and intensify the tradition of such gentle Catholic singers of the Elizabethan age as Southwell and Constable; the hymns of Wither he had probably never seen, and would have despised; he shows not the slightest sign of having read the noblest religious poem written between the *Vision of Piers Plowman* and *Paradise Lost*, that *Christ's Victory and Triumph* which Giles Fletcher published just when Donne was moving to Drury House in 1610. He had doubtless read, without advantage to his style, Sylvester's popular version of the *Divine Weeks and Works*. But he disdained all that was purely English. His sympathy with Elizabethan verse, good or bad, was a negative quantity, and we can scarcely trace that he allowed himself to be even conscious of the existence of Spenser or Shakespeare. Among his English contemporaries he admired but one poet, Ben Jonson, and to him he was attracted by the very qualities which we now recognise as being anti-Elizabethan. Hence, in the history of literature, the sacred poetry of Donne is interesting mainly for its resolute independence of all existing English types, and for its effect in starting a new and efficient school of religious verse in which many of the disciples far exceeded the master. Donne prophesied, while those poets were not born or were but children, of George Herbert, of Crashaw, of the Vaughans, of Herrick in the *Noble Numbers*, of Cowley in the *Davideis*; and when we come to consider his posthumous glory we shall have to return to his crabbed and litigious early sacred poetry.

Of Donne's spiritual poems the most important, if we omit the two cycles of 'Holy Sonnets', which belong to a later period, is that which he called 'A Litany'. He composed it in his bed, during his tedious illness at Mitcham in 1609, and he sent it to Sir Henry Goodyer with a learned note on the Litaneia, or public form of chanted prayer to God, and on its use in the Primitive Church. His own specimen is composed in a curious measure of his invention, in grave lines with an odd singing break in the middle of each stanza, an artifice from which, it is only fair to say, he rarely extracts so much charm as we might reasonably expect. The 'Litany' is burdened with ingenuity. From a dogmatic point of view it shows Donne still imperfectly divorced from the tenets of Rome. He still proclaims the efficacy of the Virgin Mary's prayers to God the Father for souls on earth. Donne, who was much occupied at this time with the principle of martyrdom, dedicates these stanzas to the martyrs and confessors.

[He quotes stanzas 10 and 11 of 'A Litany'.]

The ingenious darkness of Donne's poetical expression never went further or achieved a richer gloom than it does in some of his Sacred Poems. The 'Litany' is certainly not for use by the poor of the flock. The intellectual dangers so strangely petitioned against in the following stanza do not certainly afflict many humble-minded Christians, although they were real enough to Donne.

[He quotes stanza 27 of 'A Litany'.]

One more stanza may be given from this highly metaphysical poem, in which a considerable flower of beauty is choked by the weeds of pedantry and misplaced intelligence.

[He quotes stanza 15 of 'A Litany'.]

A poem which we can exactly date is that written for Good Friday 1613. Donne had been staying at Polesworth, in Warwickshire, with Sir Henry Goodyer, and he set forth on horseback to visit Magdalen Herbert and her son, Sir Edward, at Montgomery Castle. Six years earlier he had sent to this beloved lady 'holy hymns and sonnets', of which but one survives, the quatorzain beginning –

> Her of your name, whose fair inheritance
> Bethina was, and jointure Magdalo.

He now, looking forward to the joys of high spiritual converse with these elected friends, sends to him whom he leaves at Polesworth a meditation on the day. He is more direct and less tortured than usual.

[He quotes lines 9–18 of 'Good Friday, 1613: Riding Westward'.]

That is impressive, and comparatively simple; but a spasm of his disease of style catches him, and he proceeds –

> It made His own lieutenant, Nature, shrink,
> It made His footstool crack, and the sun wink.
> Could I behold those hands, which span the poles
> And tune all spheres at once, pierced with those holes?
> Could I behold that endless height, which is
> Zenith to us and our antipodes,
> Humbled below us?

Nothing could be more odious; yet such was the taste of the day that, no doubt, when he read these verses that evening in Montgomery Castle, the noble Herberts were not merely astonished, but charmed and edified.

We may confidently attribute 'The Cross' to the Mitcham period. It shows Donne still more indignant at the obstinacy of political recusants than convinced with regard to the dogmas which separate Rome from the Reformed Churches. He writes here precisely as any fervent Italian or Spanish monk might do –

> From me no pulpit, nor misgrounded law,
> Nor scandal taken, shall this cross withdraw,

and he rejoices to see its emblem in every manifestation of natural force –

> Look down, thou spiest out crosses in small things;
> Look up, thou seest birds rais'd on cross'd wings;
> All the globe's frame, and spheres, is nothing else
> But the meridian's crossing parallels.

In composing these early sacred poems, although he was at the very time fighting with Morton for the Anglicans, he could not but look back to Rome as the real arbiter, and had no warmer excuse to make for his odes and litanies than that the Roman Church herself need not call them defective.

It is to be observed that the early and amatory writings of Donne contain no single example of the sonnet, and that with the exception of one or two unimportant epistles in the quatorzain form, all his work in this class is to be found among his divine poems. He disdained the softness and vagueness of the Petrarchists, and had no ambition to compete with Drayton or Daniel in their addresses to a dimly-outlined Idea or Delia. The form he ultimately adopted for his sonnets is neither purely Italian, nor purely Elizabethan. He had not Milton's courage in recurring to the splendid fulness of the sonnet of Petrarch, but he eschewed the laxity of the English writers of his age; and though we have to regret that he adopted the final couplet, his octett is of perfect arrangement, and boasts but two rhymes. It is strange that he did not perceive how much his sonnets lose in grandeur by this concession to triviality in the sestett. It is part, however, of Donne's irremediable imperfection as an artist, that he has produced much noble poetry in his divine sonnets, and yet not one sonnet that can be considered faultless.

The style of this section of his poetry is extremely characteristic of himself and of certain exotic influences of his time. When he was in Italy, he must have been familiar with Tansillo and Molza, the polished Petrarchists of the age, who celebrated love and religion with an equal refinement. But he is not more touched by their manner of writing than by that of Spenser. Underneath the graceful accomplishment of the Cinque Cento, however, there ran hidden the vehement stream of speculative philosophic style, rugged and bold, and it was this which attracted Donne. With Galileo we know that he had a close sympathy. Did he dip with curiosity into the forbidden writings of Galileo's fellow-martyr, Giordano Bruno? We know not; yet here at least was an Italian with whom Donne had not a little fellowship in the construction of his mind. He had still more with that of a Dominican monk who was more exactly his contemporary, and of whose misfortunes he cannot fail to have heard. The Sonnets of Campanella have more kinship with 'La Corona' and the Ecclesiastical Sonnets of Donne than with any other English writings. Yet neither poet can well have read the work of the other, and it is even a stretch of probability to hope that Donne may have seen the obscure volume of Campanella's poems which the German, Tobias Adami, published in 1622. The similarity is accidental, and is founded upon a certain double sympathy with the obscurity and with the heterodoxy of the strange Italian pantheists of the age. Had Donne been born south of the Alps, his work might probably have taken a less tormented form than it actually adopted, but his body would almost certainly have been tortured with Campanella's, if by a happy fate it escaped the stake with Vanini's.

[He now speaks of the two *Anniversary* poems for Elizabeth Drury.]

When a year had elapsed since the death of Elizabeth Drury, Donne gratified his patron by the composition of the very curious and fantastical gnomic poem called *An Anatomy of the World*. . . . In *An Anatomy of the World*, the extravagance of hyperbole, which the taste of the age permitted to such compositions, reaches a height unparalleled elsewhere. It is difficult to understand how the desire to please and the intoxication of his own ingenuity can have so blinded Donne to the claims of self-respect, as to permit him to use language which is positively preposterous. The death of Elizabeth Drury has so wounded and tamed 'the sick world' that it has thrown the globe into a lethargy. Her life was so precious that we might

> have better spared the Sun, or Man.

All light has left the earth except a ghostly glimmer, 'the twilight of her memory'. But a longer extract from this catalogue of superlatives will give a juster impression both of the reckless absurdity of Donne's extravagance, and of the technical beauty of the verse which he dedicated to such servile ends –

> She whose rich eyes and breast
> Gilt the West Indies, and perfumed the East;
> Whose having breathed in this world did bestow
> Spice on those isles, and bade them still smell so;
> And that rich India, which doth gold inter,
> Is but as single money coin'd from her;
> She to whom this world must itself refer,
> As suburbs, or the microcosm of her;
> She, she is dead; she's dead; when thou know'st this,
> Thou know'st how lame a cripple this world is.

The *Anatomy of the World* is an astonishing constellation of absurdities and beauties, of profound thoughts and maddening conceits. Nothing could be lovelier than some of its incidental passages, as, for instance, this reminiscence of the Expedition –

> Doth not a Teneriffe or higher hill
> Rise so high like a rock, *that one might think*
> *The floating moon would shipwreck there, and sink?*

or than this transcendental glorification of the delicate beauty of girlhood –

> she, in whom all white and red and blue,
> Beauty's ingredients, voluntary grew,
> As in an unvex'd paradise; from whom
> Did all things' verdure, and their lustre come;
> Whose composition was miraculous,
> Being all colour, all diaphanous,
> For air and fire but thick gross bodies were,
> And liveliest stones but drowsy and pale to her;
> She, she is dead; she's dead; when thou know'st this,
> Thou know'st how wan a ghost this our world is.

These beauties, however, are rare and transitory; they are soon eclipsed by the scholastic obscurity of the cold, extravagant eulogy. At the end Donne is almost cynical, for, addressing the 'blessed Maid', he begs her to

> Accept this tribute, and his first year's rent,
> Who till his dark short taper's end be spent,
> As oft as thy feast sees this widow'd earth,
> Will yearly celebrate thy second birth.

Accordingly, early in 1612 Donne paid 'rent' again in a 'second Anniversary', called *Of the Progress of the Soul*. This was a still longer metaphysical celebration of poor little Elizabeth Drury, whom the barest decency might by this time have left to sleep under her monument in Hawsted Church. In this Donne announces that his Muse's

> chaste ambition is
> Yearly to bring forth such a child as this.

This threat filled his friends with justifiable alarm, for even in the age of James I the *Second Anniversary* was not a poem to be generally appreciated, in spite of the sustained learning and cleverness of its reflections upon man's mortality. . . .

We can but regard this elaborate and repeated celebration of Elizabeth Druty as an eccentric and, on the whole, unfortunate episode in Donne's career as a poet. It is plain that he undertook and conducted it as a perfectly straightforward piece of business; he saw no reason why he should not expend his art on the eulogy of a young lady whom he had never seen, but whose father was generously expending upon him all the evidences of a princely hospitality. In return for house and home, for comforts to Donne's wife and food to his children, Sir Robert Drury asked a small expenditure of extravagantly laudatory verse, and Donne, no doubt, saw no shame in supplying what was asked for. He would probably have seemed to himself niggardly and ungrateful if he had refused to give it. But poetry composed under such conditions must needs be void and frigid, and if Donne thought to escape these faults by a strenuous exercise of intellect and fancy, he was disappointed. The expressions in his letters show that he was conscious of failure, and vexed at the sacrifice of his own dignity. At all events, we may be thankful that he did not carry out his dreadful threat of inditing a long poem upon each anniversary of Elizabeth Drury's death. He, like Sir Robert and Lady Drury, was presently to find distraction elsewhere.

[He speaks of the verse letter Donne wrote from Amiens to Lady Carey and Essex Rich.]

This is a composition in Donne's harshest and most scholastic manner, and was evidently intended to flatter the charming young ladies by the assumption that they could rapidly comprehend such subtleties as –

> Spiritual choleric critics, which in all
> Religions find faults, and forgive no fall,
> Have through their zeal virtue but in their gall.

> We're thus but parcel-gilt; to gold we're grown
> When virtue is our soul's complexion;
> Who knows his virtue's name or place, hath none.

> Virtue's but aguish, when 'tis several,
> By occasion wak'd, and circumstantial;
> True virtue's soul, always in all deeds all.

This is Donne in his very quiddity, and it would be difficult to find a more uncompromising specimen of the peculiar eccentricity of his style. An epistle to Lady Bedford, begun in France but never finished, is sweeter and more personal.

[He quotes lines 11–15 of the verse letter 'To the Countess of Bedford', 'Though I be dead, and buried'. He writes of the poems of Donne's 'Last Years as a Layman':]

His Marriage Song for St Valentine's Day is, indeed, one of his happiest productions, as fresh and gay as if a youth had written it, instead of a staid, melancholy paterfamilias of forty; and it is a poem singularly little troubled by the prevailing faults of Donne's style. It has all the characteristics required for an epithalamium; and a certain levity or faint fescennine quality, which is disconcerting, perhaps, to the refined taste of to-day, detracted in no wise from its merits in the judgment of the gravest or the most exalted personages in the reign of James I. Thus it opens, in a melodious burst of garrulity.

[He quotes lines 1–14 of the 'Epithalamion on St Valentine's Day'.]

The bird-analogy is preserved by telling the Bishop that his duty to-day is to unite two phoenixes,

> Whose love and courage never shall decline,
> But make the whole year through, thy day, O Valentine.

And in the address to the Bride, Donne rises to a great dignity and a rare music.

[He quotes lines 43–50. Then he goes on to give an account of the 'Obsequies to the Lord Harington'.]

The 'Obsequies' is the longest of Donne's minor funeral poems, and it is one of the best. The tone of panegyric is not so strained as to give us any doubt of the poet's sincerity of feeling. For Lord Harington, whom he had known from that nobleman's boyhood, he had a great esteem and affection. . . . The opening address is in Donne's gravest and weightiest metaphysical manner.

[He quotes lines 1–14.]

This is as full of ingenuity as of music, both indeed in a class more popular in the seventeenth than in the nineteenth century. But it is easy to see how directly Cowley was influenced by this movement of verse and of fancy when he came to write his immortal elegy on Crashaw. Donne proceeds, with a cleverness sometimes forced to the peril of his imagination, for 260 nervous lines, and closes with a rash vow to write poetry no more –

> Do not, fair soul, this sacrifice refuse
> That in thy grave I do inter my Muse,
> Which, by my grief, great as thy worth, being cast
> Behindhand, yet hath spoke, and spoke her last.

But poets' vows are like those of lovers. He was now over forty years of age, and doubtless the desire to write poetry invaded him less and less often. But he had no real intention of burying his Muse in Lord Harington's tomb, although he might in future choose to dedicate it to graver and graver uses.

[Coming to the poetry of Donne's later years, Gosse writes of the *Holy Sonnets*, which he supposes that Donne composed several years after his ordination.]

We know from Walton that Donne's life at this time was as a shining light among his old friends. This radiance beams from the *Holy Sonnets*, where the voice of personal emotion is more clearly audible than anywhere else in the religious poetry of Donne. The accent is that of a man who has discovered the truth so late, and has such a sense of the passage of time and of the nearness of his dissolution, that he hardly dares to hope that he may yet work for God. But he pours himself out in prayer to be preserved a little longer to serve his Lord and Master. Rarely was the natural language of the heart sustained so long by Donne in his verse as in this noble sonnet, which opens the series as it is now usually printed, but which was not published until 1635.

[He quotes the whole of *Holy Sonnet* 1, 'Thou Hast Made Me'.]

He attributes his condition of mind, softened and crushed so as to receive the impress of God's signet, to the agony caused by his bereavement. But he fears lest this natural affection may have taken an excessive fleshly form, may have been 'idolatry'. Yet this temporal sorrow has wrought in him a 'holy discontent', which is obviously salutary. Thrown out of the comfortable security of domestic life, he falls, he is bruised, but only to be lifted tenderly by the Divine hands. Nor is 'vehement grief' the only cause of the helpless physical condition in which he finds himself. Not bereavement only, but 'sickness, death's herald and champion', has assailed him. As he reflects upon his frailty, his old intellectual ingenuity comes back to him; we are startled at the sudden cry –

> I am a little world made cunningly
>> Of elements, and an angelic sprite;
>> But black sin hath betray'd to endless night
> My world's both parts, and oh! both parts must die.

He calls on the discoverers of America to lend him their new seas to add to the old, and make a flood deep enough to quench the fires of lust and envy before they have consumed his soul away, since he wishes to save as much of that soul as possible to be the prey of a very different conflagration, the zeal of the Lord and of His house burning him up.

With strenuous abhorrence he repudiates the World, the Flesh, and the Devil, and for the future his life shall be dedicated wholly to God. But, he reflects again, how little of that wasted life is left! This is his 'play's last scene', his 'pilgrimage's last mile', his 'span's last inch'. He conceives that death is absolutely upon him, and he breaks forth into a burst of almost Miltonic magnificence.

[He gives the octave of *Holy Sonnet* 7, 'At the Round Earth's Imagined Corners'.]

But he has no sooner summoned this cloud of witnesses that he considers again how unready he is, with no day's work done, to join the cohorts. In the course of the argument, we reach another phrase, which it is difficult indeed to believe that Milton did not read and recollect –

> that tree
> Whose fruit threw death on else-immortal us.

From this he passes to one of those invocations of Death himself, which were peculiarly in the spirit of the age –

> Death, be not proud, though some have callèd thee
> Mighty and dreadful, for thou art not so.

In this there seems to be more than an accidental resemblance to the famous appeal to 'eloquent, just, and mighty Death', which Sir Walter Raleigh had published in 1614. If so – and I feel it difficult to question the reminiscence– then this has its interest as an almost solitary example in which the work of an English contemporary is found exercising an influence on the style of Donne.

One of the most remarkable of the *Holy Sonnets* is the ninth of 1633 (thirteenth in 1635). In it we have a memorable instance of the clairvoyance with which Donne, from the vantage-ground of his conversion, looked back upon his profane past. Donne's reference here to his old erotic poetry is, to my mind, a singularly characteristic one, and helps to explain why he preserved so carefully, to the very last, though he never would publish, the evidences of his early enslavement to the flesh. This sonnet is a dialogue with his soul, whom he bids – as the approach of nightfall suggests the thought, 'What if the present were the world's last night?' – to turn through the gathering twilight and see whether it quails to watch, whitening on the wall, the picture of Christ crucified. Can that sweet face mean to doom the soul to hell?

> No! No! but as in my idolatry
>   I said to all my profane mistresses,
>   Beauty of pity, foulness only is
> A sign of rigour; so I say to thee,
> To wicked spirits are horrid shapes assign'd;
> This beauteous form assumes a piteous mind.

In another mood he conceives himself a helpless, beleaguered city held by a hateful and tyrannic foe. The city, unarmed, cannot resist, cannot even make a sign, but with all its heart it yearns after its besieger; and so the soul, bound and betrothed to Satan, and occupied by his armed forces, dearly loves God, and would fain see His victorious army enter its gates and drive out the abhorred usurper.

[He refers to three *Holy Sonnets* from the Westmoreland Manuscript: no. 17, 'Since She Whom I Loved'; no. 18, 'Show Me Dear Christ'; and no. 19, 'Oh, To Vex Me'; two of which he printed here for the first time.]

The three sonnets which are now added to the series have a peculiar importance. It is evident that they were suppressed by the editors of 1633 and 1635 because of the leaning which they betrayed to certain Romish doctrines. In this they offer to us a remarkable contribution to our knowledge of the inner mind of Donne.

[He quotes the whole of the 'Hymn to God My God, in My Sickness', which he dates 23 March 1631, supposing that Donne wrote it just eight days before his death.]

The evidence of the vigour of Donne's dying brain supplied by these verses is amazing. He had never, in the hey-day of his youth and genius, expressed himself with a more complete originality or more fully in accordance with the peculiarities of his intellectual temperament than in this his farewell to mortality.

[He sums up Donne's character, as the writing betrays it.]

We see, in his letters, indications of a certain personal timidity, a fluttering dread of results and future conditions, such as often accompanies an abnormal development of the imagination. Passion, with him, was a matter of extraordinary and exhausting intensity; we are always conscious of the leap and the throb of 'the naked thinking heart' which he presses beneath his trembling fingers. He seems to have betrayed his emotions in the colours of his face, flushing and paling with the violence of feeling, a characteristic to which Arthur Wilson may refer in his hideous couplet –

> Thy flesh, whose channels left their crimson hue,
> And whey-like ran at last in a pale blue.

And so we leave him, surely the most undulating, the most diverse of human beings, as Montaigne would say. Splendid and obscure he was, in the extreme versatility and passion, the profundity, the saintliness, the mystery of his inscrutable character. No one, in the history of English literature, as it seems to me, is so difficult to realise, so impossible to measure, in the vast curves of his extraordinary and contradictory features. Of his life, of his experiences, of his opinions, we know more now than it has been vouchsafed to us to know of any other of the great Elizabethan and Jacobean galaxy of writers, and yet how little we fathom his contradictions, how little we can account for his impulses and his limitations. Even those of us who have for years made his least adventures the subject of close and eager investigation must admit at last that he eludes us. He was not the crystal-hearted saint that Walton adored and exalted. He was not the crafty and redoubtable courtier whom the recusants suspected. He was not the prophet of the intricacies of fleshly feeling whom the young poets looked up to and worshipped. He was none of these, or all of these, or more. What was he? It is impossible to say, for, with all his superficial expansion, his secret died with him. We are tempted to declare that of all great men he is the one of whom least is essentially known. Is not this, perhaps, the secret of his perennial fascination?

[Gosse now goes on to consider the standing of Donne's poetry in its own day and later. He first refers to what he sees as Donne's contemptuous indifference to almost all the other poets of his time.]

One is left with the impression that Donne would not have turned to see Edmund Spenser go by, nor have passed into an inner room at the Mermaid to listen to the talk of Shakespeare. His was the scornful indifference of the innovator, the temperament of the man born to inaugurate a new order of taste.

[He instances Drayton and Daniel as poets whom Donne might be expected to mention, but does not.]

Donne's arrogant silence is unbroken. Daniel, with his smooth measures and his classic imagery, belonged to the old Elizabethan school, with which Donne, as a metrical iconoclast, would have neither part nor lot. It seems as though the poetry inspired by the Renaissance passion for beauty, the poetry written by Spenser and Shakespeare, and continued by a hundred tuneful spirits down to Shirley and Herrick, was to Donne a meat offered to idols. He carried his fierce nonconformity in his heart, and he would not sit at table with the heathen Spenserian and Petrarchist.

To this separatism there was one exception. To a solitary writer in verse of the age of Elizabeth, Donne is civil; one such writer afforded Donne so much attention as the veriest poetaster readily received from his masters and betters. Ben Jonson was not isolated in the sense that Donne was; but he too was out of sympathy with the age into which he was born; he fretted in its silken and tinselled fetters, and desired to break away from the melody and the pastoral sweetness. With the sturdy, rugged genius of Ben Jonson there is no question but that Donne enjoyed a certain imperfect sympathy. . . .

No doubt Donne shows little vital interest in Jonson's poetical experiments, but yet his slight references to the Masques and his compliment to *Volpone* vastly outweigh all that can be brought together from every source to prove his interest in the remainder of his contemporaries.

Ben Jonson, on the other hand, was cordially drawn to the severe and repellant Donne, who could be so charming in the world, and was so cold and scornful to all his brother-poets. In the austerity of Donne, Jonson recognised a quality sympathetic to his own roughness. He recognised too, no doubt, a superior strength of contumely in Donne.

143

[Gosse considers the common charge that Donne's early verse is rough because he just did not know how to scan.]

... what there was to know about prosody was, we may be sure, perfectly known to Donne. But it is evident that he intentionally essayed to introduce a revolution into English versification. One of the main objections he took to the verse of his youth was that it was so mellifluous, sinuous, and soft. A five-syllabled iambic line of Spenser or of Daniel trots along with the gentlest amble of inevitable shorts and longs. Donne thought that the line should be broken up into successive quick and slow beats. The conventional line vexed his ear with its insipidity, and it doubtless appeared to him that his great predecessors had never completely shaken off a timidity and monotony which had come down to them from Surrey and Gascoigne. It is possible that he wished to improve on the rhymed verse of Spenser, as Shakespeare had improved on the blank verse of Sackville.

The curious ruggedness of the *Satires* and *Elegies* becomes comprehensible only when we adopt some such theory I have suggested. Part of Donne's iconoclasm consisted in his scorn of the flaccid beat of the verse of the sonneteers. He desired greatly to develop the orchestral possibilities of English verse, and I have remarked that the irregular lyrics of Mr Robert Bridges and the endless experiments of the Symbolists in France are likely to be far more fruitful to us in trying to understand Donne's object, than any conventional repetition of the accepted rules of prosody. The iambic rhymed line of Donne has audacities such as are permitted to his blank verse by Milton; and although the felicities are rare in the older poet, instead of being almost incessant as in the younger, Donne at his best is not less melodious than Milton. One of his most famous traps for the ear, is the opening line of 'Twickenham Garden', which the ordinary reader is ever tempted to dismiss as not being iambic verse at all. We have to recognise in it the poet's attempt to identify the beat of his verse with his bewildered and dejected state, reading it somewhat in this notation: –

Blásted I with sighs II and I surroúnded I with teárs.

It is almost certain that this intrepid shifting about at will of the accent is a symptom of youth in the poem, that we can almost, that is to say, approximately, date any given piece of his by the degree in which this prosodical violence is sustained. After middle-life, Donne dropped the experiment more and more completely, having found, no doubt, that his closest friends were by no means certain to comprehend what he meant by the rapid changes of the instrument; nor, in reading to themselves, could produce the effect which he had intended. These variations of cadence, then, must be looked upon as a peculiarity not essential to Donne's style, nor persistent in it, but as a studied eccentricity of his youth. At his very best, as in

> I long to talk with some old lover's ghost,
> Who died before the God of Love was born,

or as in

> A naked, thinking heart, that makes no show,
> Is to a woman but a kind of ghost,

there is not trace of this 'not keeping of accent', which puzzled and enraged Ben Jonson.

His conscious isolation, no doubt, made Donne hesitate to press his poetry upon his own generation. He found its flavour, the strong herbal perfume of it, not agreeable in the nostrils of the latest Elizabethans. Neither the verse, nor the imagination, nor the attitude of soul were what people in 1600 were ready to welcome, or even to apprehend.

Among the contemporary impressions of Donne's mission as a poet, by far the most valuable which has come down to us is that contributed by the poet, Thomas Carew. As poetry and as criticism alike, his elegy on Donne is of high merit, and vastly outbalances all the rest of the more or less perfunctory pieces with which it is presented. We might not otherwise have been made aware of the acute attention paid by Carew to the reforms of Donne, nor of the influence which the latter exercised on a writer of genuine independent impulse and high talent.

[He gives an account of Carew's early career up to his return from the continent about 1619.]

It is not to be questioned that at this juncture one of the MS copies of his poems, which Donne had caused to be multiplied, fell into Carew's hands. Hitherto, Ben Jonson, in his lyrics, had been his model; it would not be true, perhaps, to say that those of Donne now or ever became Carew's model, but they excited his amazement and his curiosity. For a moment, the existing poetry of this country, from the Renaissance to the scholars of Spenser, seemed to be blotted out in a mist of admiring wonder. England had 'no voice, no tune' but what Donne supplied. So, about the year 1865, to young men then just leaving college, the melodies and ardours of Mr Swinburne seemed, for the time being, to drown and out-dazzle the rest of poetical literature. Carew endeavours to define the extraordinary effect of the first reading of Donne's verses. He describes, rapturously,

> the fire
> That filled with spirit and heat the Delphic choir,

at the approach of this new voice, and he proceeds, with the calmness gained by some twelve years of familiarity with this extraordinary and bewildering genius, to distinguish what it was which produced on the minds of himself and others this impression of Donne's novelty and unchallenged supremacy. In the first place, there was in Donne the note of revolt against the conventional imagery, diction, and order of ideas which had belonged to the Renaissance. This new poetry was a 'fire' which 'purged the Muses' garden of its pedantic weeds' – that is to say, of the time-honoured classical conventions. For servile imitation of the ancients, seen through the Italian atmosphere, Donne substituted 'fresh invention'. He 'paid the debts' of 'the penurious bankrupt age' by exchanging for mere loans upon antiquity a new, rich, realistic poetry of endless possibilities of resource. (The reader must be most careful to observe that these are not the sentiments of comparative criticism to-day, but the convictions of the young men, of whom Carew was the clairvoyant forerunner, who marshalled themselves under Donne's banner from 1620 to 1650.)

What these young poets saw in Donne, and what attracted them so passionately to him, was the concentration of his intellectual personality. He broke through the tradition; he began as if poetry had never been written before; he, as Carew says –

> open'd us a mine
> Of rich and pregnant fancy.

He banished the gods and goddesses from his verse, not a Round-head fiercer than he in his scorn of 'those old idols'. He wiped away 'the wrong' which the English language in its neo-pagan raptures had 'done the Greek or Latin tongue'. His gigantic fancy put such a strain upon the resources of the English language, that its 'tough, thick-ribb'd hoops' almost burst beneath the pressure. The earlier Elizabethan writers had been 'libertines in poetry'; Donne recalled them to law and order. This is how Carew describes the extra-ordinary emotion caused by the first reading of Donne's poems –

> the flame
> Of thy brave soul, that shot such heat and light
> As burned our earth and made our darkness bright,
> Committed holy rapes upon the will,
> Did through the eye the melting heart distil,
> And the deep knowledge of dark truths did teach.

Once again, Donne has

> opened us a mine
> Of rich and pregnant fancy, drawn a line
> Of masculine expression . . .
> Thou shalt yield no precedence, but of time, –

that is to say, the ancient poets have no advantage of originality over thee, save the purely accidental one of having been born in an earlier age.

When we return to Donne's poems, but in particular to his lyrics, and endeavour to find out what it was which excited these raptures of appreciation, we are at first unable to accept the seventeenth-century point of vision. Nothing is more difficult than to be certain that we value in the old poets what their contemporaries valued. . . .

. . . we have the greatest difficulty in constraining ourselves to regard Donne's verse from the point of view and in the light of its early, enthusiastic readers of 1620.

Perhaps we cannot do better than read over again an entirely typical poem, written towards the middle of his career, and illustrat-ing, without extravagance, the very peculiarities which Donne's disciples admired. For this purpose, 'Twickenham Garden' may serve as well as any.

[He gives the entire poem.]

If we compare this with an analogous piece of ordinary Elizabethan or early Jacobean poetry, we observe, first of all, that it is tightly packed with thought. As to the value of the thought, opinions may differ, but of the subtlety, the variety, and the abundance of mental movement in this piece there can be no question. The Elizabethan poet had held a mirror up to nature: Donne (the illustration is almost his own) shivered the glass, and preserved a reflection from every several fragment. This redundancy of intellectual suggestion was one of Donne's principal innovations.

In the second place, we notice an absence of all conventional or historical ornament. There is no mention here of 'cruel Amaryllis', or 'great Pan', or 'the wanton shears of Destiny'. A rigid adherence to topics and to objects familiar to the non-poetical reader of the moment is strictly observed. This, as I suppose, was another of the main sources of Donne's fascination; he was, in a totally new and unprecedented sense, a realist. In this he revolted with success against all the procedure of the Renaissance, and is, in his turbid and unskilful way, the forerunner of modern Naturalism in English poetry. This is an aspect of his influence which has been strangely overlooked, and, no doubt, for this reason, that what was realistic in the reign of James I seems utterly old-fangled and antiquarian in that of Victoria; so that the poetry of Donne, instead of striking us – as it did his contemporaries – as amazingly fresh and new in its illustrations, strikes us as unspeakably moth-eaten and decrepid. In this poem of 'Twickenham Hill' there is even an innovation in naming, topographically, a place by its existing, modern name; and this prepares us for all the allusions to habits, superstitions, rites, occasions of the moment which occur to the rapid brain of the author.

If the poems of Donne are examined, we shall find that it is only on the rarest occasions that he draws his imagery from mythology or romantic history. He has no interest in Greek or Latin legend. He neither translates nor paraphrases the poets of antiquity. For the conventional elements of beauty, as it was understood in that age, for roses, that is to say, and shepherds, lutes, zephyrs, 'Thetis' crystal floods', and 'flower-enamelled meadows', Donne has a perfect contempt. He endeavours to extract intellectual beauty from purely subjective sources, by the concentration of intensity and passion upon modern thought. Accordingly, he draws his illustrations, not from asphodel or from the moon, but from the humdrum professional employments of his own age, from chemistry, medicine, law, mechanics, astrology, religious ritual, daily human business of every sort. The decency of reticence between lovers reminds him of a sacerdotal mystery, and he cries –

> 'Twere profanation of our joys
> To tell the laity our love.

Love is a spider dropped into the luscious chalice of life and 'transubstantiating' it to poison. The sun is no more Phoebus, or the golden-haired son of Hyperion, but a pedantic lackey, whose duty is to 'tell court-huntsmen that the king will ride'. If the poet abuses his mistress for her want of faith, he does it in the language of an attorney, and his curses are 'annexed in schedules' to the document. A woman's tear, on which her lover's tear falls, is like a round ball, on which a skilled workman paints the countries of the world.

From the days of Dr Johnson downwards, the nature of these images has been not a little misunderstood. They have two characteristics, which have been unduly identified – they are sometimes realistic, and they are sometimes inappropriate. To us to-day they are almost all grotesque, because they are fetched from a scheme of things now utterly obsolete; but we must endeavour to recollect that such phrases as –

> no chemic yet the elixir got
> But glorifies his pregnant pot,
> If by the way to him befall
> Some odoriferous thing, or medicinal,

or,

> As he that sees a star fall, runs apace,
> And finds a jelly in the place,

phrases which now call for a commentary, and disturb our appreciation of the poet's fancy, were references to the science or half-science of the Jacobean age as modern and 'topical' as allusions to the Röntgen rays would be to-day. In less than the three hundred years which divide us from Donne's youth, the poems of Mr Rudyard Kipling will require a commentary five times as bulky as the text. Such is the inevitable result of indulging in the technical phraseology of the moment, and quitting the traditional basis of language.

But if many of Donne's illustrations were appropriate enough

149

and pointed enough in his own age, there were many which deserved from the very first the condemnation of good judges. Here it would be difficult to find better criticism than is supplied by Dr Johnson, in his vivacious *Life of Cowley*. What he says there of the whole school is peculiarly true of Donne, and may be specially adapted to his use.

[He quotes Johnson's account of Donne's extravagance of hyperbole, and determination to dazzle and excite his contemporaries by novelty.]

The age was perfectly ready to be thus excited and dazzled. It only asked to be conducted as promptly as possible into new and extravagant paths of fancy. Nor was this tendency to imaginative extravagance confined to England; it invaded all parts of Europe at the same moment, and in a manner so simultaneous as to baffle the critical historian. Three remarkable writers – Marini, Góngora, Donne – started this analytic and hyperbolic style at the same time, and it is very difficult to say whether either of the three was affected by the practices of the others.

[He describes the writings of Góngora and Marini, arguing that Donne is unlikely to have been influenced by either poet, though he is like both in some ways.]

... while it is certain that between Donne and Góngora there existed a very curious intellectual parallelism – which led each to create a school of *culteranismo* the results of which, in either country, had a remarkable resemblance – the likeness between Donne and Marini is, on the other hand, very superficial, and grows less and less definite the more narrowly we examine it. We must, at length, give to Donne such credit as is due to complete originality in working out and forcing upon English taste a style in which affectation and wilful obscurity took a part so prominent that by ordinary readers no other qualities are nowadays perceived. This style was gradually accepted, and it may now be interesting to trace with some precision the stages of the school of Donne in the seventeenth century.

There can be no doubt, I think, that the earliest of Donne's disciples in poetry was Henry King, his well-beloved friend and executor. . . .

The mild verse of Henry King does not lend itself very easily to quotation. Here, however, is a typical passage from 'The Exequy', one of the longest of King's pieces, and one of which, as of most of his poetry, it may be said that not a line would be what it now is if Donne had never lived. The poet urges Death to be careful of his mistress.

[He quotes lines 69–78 of King's 'Exequy'.]

Every image, every illustration here is taken from the pedestrian business of the hour, and follows only too closely the realistic law which Donne had invented.

A later but a more celebrated disciple of Donne's is George Herbert, who in his poetical work bears to the Dean very much the relation of Pope to Dryden. Herbert is more polished, more adroit, in fuller command of the medium; but we miss from his evenly attractive verse the strength and concentration, the high originality and the splendid flashes of intuition which light up the dark landscapes of Donne. The early poetry of George Herbert, courtly and amatory, was all destroyed when, about 1627, he passed through 'such spiritual conflicts, as none can think, but only those that have endured them'. It was just at this time, during the incursion of the plague, that he was so closely brought under the influence of Donne at Chelsea. The precious volume of sacred poems and private ejaculations, called *The Temple*, mirrors, as we have his own authority for saying, the ardours and tremors of this critical time. We need not be surprised, therefore, to find the very aura of Donne exhaled, like a spice, from this exquisite casket of divine verse. . . .

The same characteristics, in very unattractive form, are found in the verses of George Herbert's elder brother Edward, afterwards Lord Herbert of Cherbury, a very brilliant man who was a remarkably dull poetaster.

[He goes on to speak of the poets who wrote funeral elegies on Donne's death, and then of other admirers of Donne such as Habington, Davenant and Suckling.]

It is a reflection very melancholy to the admirer of the Dean of St Paul's that, as a rule, his work either attracted young men of an essentially unpoetic type to the study of verse, or else, which may be more disastrous, it encouraged in the genuinely poetic a cultivation of the most prosaic qualities of their minds. Even the great Cowley, who was the most illustrious of all Donne's direct disciples, is no exception to this rule. The following of Donne seems to have desiccated his imagination, and to have encouraged in him, at the expense of passion, a wearisome intellectual volubility.

The most illustrious of Donne's indirect disciples was Crashaw, the greatest of English mystics. Without the example of Donne, Crashaw would have written in a totally different manner, but the influences at work in the modelling of his genius are largely exotic also. He was seduced by the gorgeous and sensuous conceits of Marini, the worst of masters, but was saved from destruction by the Spanish neo-platonists. Donne wrote his chief poetry too early to be disturbed by the *Spiritual Works* of St John of the Cross, which were posthumously published in 1616, but these entered into the very blood of Crashaw, while to the great St Teresa he owed as much, nay, probably more, than Donne himself had done. The intensity of Donne's style at its best, and the mental concentration which he had taught, lent themselves peculiarly well to the expression of transcendental spiritual emotion. Indeed, in England, mysticism has always since the reign of Elizabeth spoken in the voice of Donne. The Spanish illuminates combined with the English master to impress upon the burning heart of Crashaw an ecstasy which found speech in some of the most exquisite utterances of the seventeenth century, and it is only fair, while we deplore the dulness of much of the verse which claimed descent from Donne, to remember that he was at least equally the forerunner and 'only begetter' of those 'large draughts of intellectual day', those throbbing and flaming phrases of divine hyperbole, which place the name of Crashaw, an Englishman, beside, or a very little way below, that of the Mother of all mystics, the incomparable Carmelite of Avila.

During the transitional period, when poetry, in its extreme decay, was hesitating to accept the reformed versification offered to it by Waller and Denham, the only influences to be observed were those of Ben Jonson on dramatic and of Donne on non-dramatic verse. The latter, in some cases, such as those of the Matchless Orinda, Flatman, and Nahum Tate, achieved positive popularity, although to our ears and eyes to-day almost entirely unreadable. The direct model of these poets, however, was not Donne, but Cowley, whose style was more directly imitable, and who did not offer the stumbling-block of profound imagination and daring flights of style. The corruption of the genius of Donne may be seen to great effect in Thomas Flatman, who was born about the time that Donne died. The *Poems and Songs* of this man, now fallen into absolute neglect, was a favourite book with readers of the Restoration period, and ran through many editions. This is an example of his manner –

> By immaterial defecated love,
> Your soul its heavenly origin doth prove,
> And in least dangerous raptures soars above.
> Our modish rhymes, like culinary fire,
> Unctuous and earthy, shall in smoke expire;
> In odorous clouds your incense shall aspire.

In such lines as these, Flatman contrives with astonishing precision to reproduce the fume, if not indeed what he calls 'the flame', of 'reverend Donne'.

No one who studies that remarkable and now neglected poem, the *Annus Mirabilis*, can fail to notice the paramount prestige which Donne exercised over the youthful mind of Dryden. The genius of the Dean of St Paul's was thus present at the inauguration of the new order of style, and although the preface says much of Lucan and of Ovid, and nothing of the English poet, yet it is Donne far more than the Latins who is really active in Dryden's memory. The weight of the lines, the intensity which the writer endeavours to press into them, the violence and startling nature of the illustrations, and, above all, the constant reference to images essentially modern and realistic, all this is due to no other model than Donne. The sound of the Dean's strong verse echoes in such stanzas as –

> Plied thick and close as when the fight begun,
>   Their huge unwieldy navy wastes away;
> So sicken waning moons too near the sun,
>   And blunt their crescents on the edge of day,

and the movement of his fancy is seen in such as this, so closely criticised both by Johnson and Scott –

> With roomy decks, her guns of mighty strength,
>   Whose low-laid mouths each mounting billow laves,
> Deep in her draught, and warlike in her length,
>   She seems a sea-wasp flying on the waves,

while the perilous agility of Donne's wit is felt in the description of
the heavy rains which checked the Great Fire –

> An hollow crystal pyramid He takes
>   In firmamental waters dipped above,
> Of it a broad extinguisher He makes,
>   And hoods the flames that to their quarry strove.

After 1667, the direct traces of the imitation of Donne disappear,
or at least become faint and general, in the verse of Dryden. He did
not, however, neglect his great predecessor, and in several of his
essays he made some critical remarks of great value.

[He quotes Dryden's comments on Donne in the preface to
Eleonora, and the *Discourse concerning Satire*.]

This is tantamount to saying that, especially in the department of
'wit', Dryden admired Donne more than he admired any other
British poet. And this more than sixty years after Donne's death,
and across more than one complete revolution in taste and literary
fashion! For those who were sagacious enough to read between the
lines, and discount the flattery of Dorset, this was praise for Donne
of an extraordinary quality. He has never since found an admirer
so strenuous among critics of a like authority with Dryden.

The words 'wit' and 'poet' have changed their meaning again in
two hundred years. With what was witty Dryden identified the
exercise of the intellect; it was the incessant mental preoccupation
which he came, in his old age, to blame in Donne. As poetry, he
now distinguished, not imagination, or even fancy, but a technical
uniformity and smoothness, and a close adherence to the supposed
Aristotelian laws. For Dryden's advanced taste, even Donne was now
too raw and spontaneous, and preserved too much of the barbaric
note of Elizabeth. English poetry, in its redeemed and corrected
forms, was to look no further back for models than to Cowley,
Waller, and Denham. But, after all, these had in their day been the
disciples and imitators of Donne, and had used his vogue with the
young as a lever to dislodge the romantic supremacy of Spenser and
the Petrarchists. So that in his very depreciation of Donne, and his
defence of the polite numbers of Waller and Denham, Dryden is
really asserting the permanent impress made by the Dean of St
Paul's on English poetry.

When the eighteenth century has fairly commenced, it grows

difficult to trace the influence of Donne. His *Poems*, as we have seen, were reprinted in 1719, and before that time his Satires were modernised by Pope in two paraphrases, of which that called *The Impertinent* is the more successful. It is easy to see that Pope, while far too acute not to perceive the masculine force of Donne, was completely out of sympathy with his style. He was even more conscious than Dryden had been of the rugosities of Donne's metre, and he was incapable of appreciating any method in satire except that of polished and pointed antithesis. The central quality of Donne, his mystical passion, was beyond the comprehension of Pope, who, nevertheless, has more than a touch of Donne's intellectual stress and fervour. Where the diction of Pope is richest and most idiomatic we see, or may think we see, the suffused influence of the Dean of St Paul's. If, for instance, we read the last lines of the *Dunciad,* where Chaos reasserts its sway, 'and universal darkness buries all', we must confess that if any Elizabethan poet can be imagined writing those verses, or any of them, it can only be Donne –

> Physic of metaphysic begs defence,
> And metaphysic calls for aid on sense!
> See mystery to mathematics fly!
> In vain! They gaze, turn giddy, rave and die!

These are lines which it is absolutely inconceivable should have proceeded from the pen of Spenser or Sir Philip Sidney or Drayton. It is, we feel, by no means so incredible that Donne might have included them in a 'metamorphosis' or an 'anniversary'. That kind of writing, at all events, may be traced backward to Donne, and no further. From him the descent of it is unbroken, and in that sense the direct influence of Donne may be discovered in the writings of Pope, although the two men were in most essentials so diametrically opposed.

In the minor figures around and below Pope, it seems entirely unrecognisable, except in the dissolved form in which all far-fetched conceits and arid sports of fancy may be traced back to the original heresies of the Dean of St Paul's. The funereal poets of the middle of the eighteenth century revived a species of gloomy passion which was far more in sympathy with the better part of Donne. It is difficult to believe that Young had not read the pieces in which the great Dean a hundred years earlier extolled the majesty of Death. The conceits of *Night Thoughts*, Young's laborious rhetorical affections, such as

> Amid such mighty plunder, why exhaust
> Thy partial quiver on a mark so mean,

or as –

> O had he, mounted on his wing of fire,
> Soar'd where I sink, and sung immortal man,
> How had it blest mankind – and rescu'd me!

are instances of forced poetic wit differentiated in nothing but changed phraseology from similar extravagances in the less fortunate passages of Donne.

The modern appreciation of Donne seems to begin with Robert Browning, who met with the poems when he was still a boy (about 1827), and was greatly influenced by them. He put the Mandrake song to music. He quoted and praised the Dean so constantly in later years that Miss Barrett noticed it early in their acquaintance; 'your Donne', she says on several occasions. The stamp of the Dean's peculiar intensity of feeling can be traced in many of Browning's lyrics; his famous 'obscurity' is closely analogous to Donne's.

40. Anon., *Athenaeum*

1899

An anonymous reviewer of Gosse's *Life and Letters of Donne* approved Jessopp's resigning to Gosse the task of writing Donne's life in view of Jessopp's admitted lack of enthusiasm for Donne's poetry. The reviewer judged that Gosse's study of Donne will take rank 'amongst the all too few masterly biographies of subjects worthy to receive masterly treatment'. He largely accepted Gosse's account of Donne, and threw in some observations of his own on Donne's character, career and writing.

This review started a three-weeks controversy in the *Athenaeum* between H. C. Beeching and the reviewer, which Gosse somewhat intemperately joined in, only to be caught in some factual howlers by another correspondent, Arthur Vincent. The argument turned on the dating of certain letters which might be taken to show Donne's spiritual temper at the time of his ordination (*Athenaeum*, 11 November 1899, pp. 645–6; 25 November 1899, p. 723; 2 December 1899, p. 760; 9 December 1899, p. 802; 16 December 1899, p. 836).

[The reviewer claims that Gosse shows himself capable of appreciating Donne's nature as Walton was not.]

Donne was wanton and imaginative in his youth; was imaginative and spiritual in his graver years; but throughout it was the exercise of the imaginative faculty on the material supplied now by amorous, now by religious experience, that dominated wantonness and spirituality alike. A capacity to follow with sympathy every manifestation of Donne's imagination is the first necessary qualification of his biographer.

[Then again a biographer of Donne must refuse to idealize his subject.]

If he is to paint Donne at all, he must paint him as he was, with the frailties, the worldliness, the morbidities, that not for the first or the last time accompanied his rare gifts of genius and character. Frankly, in reading Mr Gosse one has to forgive Donne much, and perhaps less even the full-blooded licence of his early years than the undeniable streak of ignobility in his middle age. The Victorian is not the Jacobean conception of the social hierarchy; yet it goes against the grain to find Donne writing really fine verse to countesses in the hope that they will pay his debts, and still more to find him doing dirty work for so poor a wretch as the Earl of Somerset.

[The reviewer regrets that no letters or documentary sources of information are available for the earlier part of Donne's life.]

Yet this is just the period during which his most individual and pregnant poetry, the amorous lyrics and elegies, was written. That poetry is, on the face of it, poetry which has been lived. It is only natural to scan it closely and curiously in the hope that it, too, may yield up its biographical secret. There can be little difficulty, we think, in distinguishing two well-marked groups of these love poems. The earlier consists of poems of extreme youth, poems which betray the boy cast loose upon the stream of the senses and the sentiments with little rudder or anchor of the conscience, and which are shot through with a cynicism perilously near the borders of insolence: –

> I can love her, and her, and you and you,
> I can love any, so she be not true.

The latter is of a chastened mood – tender, delicate, sincere. One connects it inevitably with the long romance of Donne's married life, beginning with the 'strange and fatal interview' already referred to, and ending only with those desperate weeks of mourning that proved so critical a turning-point in his spiritual history.

[Nonetheless he questions Gosse's account of Donne's affair with a married woman about 1596.]

With remarkable ingenuity the biographer traces the progress, the rise, and fall of this supposed passion, and it is only after a hard rub of the eyes that the reader realizes on how very little, after all, the conjecture is based. It depends, it would seem, upon an entirely arbitrary putting together of poems which are not linked by any external signs of position or local colour, and which, although they may all refer to one amour, may just as well, for anything that is known, refer to half a dozen. It is to be feared that, for once in a way, the passion to reconstruct has tempted Mr Gosse from his usual discretion.

[He gives the whole of *Holy Sonnet* 19, 'Oh, To Vex Me', amending Gosse's punctuation of line 8, and comments that the poem presents 'a not uncharacteristic example of Donne's love for tearing an analogy to shreds'. Then he offers a further qualification of Gosse's account of Donne, before summing up the entire enterprise.]

We should like to qualify his assertion of Donne's practical independence of all the poetical influences existing in England when he began to write by the suggestion that his elegies and epigrams must owe some inspiration to the joint volume of epigrams and translations from Ovid's 'Amores' published by Marlowe and Sir John Davies, and that if any English master influenced him it was probably Marlowe, whose famous pastoral he certainly imitated, or, if you will, parodied. . . . We can only conclude by once more expressing our sense of debt which English letters owes to Mr Gosse for his faithful presentment of one of its most unparalleled and fascinating personalities.

41. Richard Garnett
1899

Richard Garnett (1835–1906) was an influential man of letters, poet and bibliographer, and Keeper of Printed Books at the British Museum from 1890 to 1899. He wrote biographies of Percy Bysshe Shelley (1862) and Thomas Carlyle (1883), a study of *The Age of Dryden* (1895), and numerous articles. He warmly approved of Gosse's *Life and Letters of John Donne*, not least because it counterbalanced Izaak Walton's portrait of a saintly Donne ('Mr Gosse's Life of Donne', *Bookman*, 10 (1899), 582–4).

A biographer of Izaak Walton observes: '*Perhaps* the satires and the sermons of Donne might have kept his name alive amongst a small company of literary men; but Walton has made Donne familiar to the majority of English churchmen.' Donne's literary immortality is no matter of mere conjecture; but it is true that he has been in general better known as the exemplar of sanctity depicted by Walton than either as preacher or poet. He must have seemed to most a seventeenth-century John Sterling, mainly owing his vitality to his biographer. Students of his period must nevertheless have been aware that he was neither a saint nor a nonentity.

[Garnett discusses the contradictions which Gosse finds in Donne's character, and attempts to explain them.]

Such a character cannot be comprehended in a formula; and Donne will remain perpetually an object of interest, inasmuch as, to quote Goethe again, he is not merely a problematic but a daemonic man; one whom, once taken up, you cannot lay down until you have arrived at some conclusion respecting him. . . .

Donne was before all things a highly impressionable man. He lived entirely in the circumstance of the hour. This is sufficiently proved by the fact that, when called upon for a tribute to a friend, he could produce hundreds of lines not merely of verse, which others could have done, but of excellent verse. He could be many things alternately and successively, but only one thing at a time. When in love, the vehemence of his passion overwhelmed prudential or conventional or ethical considerations. Under the influence of mortification or jealousy, he could write what would have been very unworthy of him had he not been a man possessed. When engaged in Somerset's service, he could think of nothing but the obligations which he owed him. When at length placed in a dignified position, it was his one study to realise the ideal which his ardent imagination had formed of it. Had he been an ambassador, as he at one time seemed likely to be, he would have striven to realise an ideal of that office, and taken leaves from the book of Macchiavelli. Such is the temperament of a poet and an orator. As a poet Donne spoiled himself by his erroneous conception of poetry, which he confounded with *esprit*. As an orator he was entirely at home; and his great store of erudition, surprising when the agitation of his life is considered, combined with his impressionability and his fervour to qualify him for the pulpit. It is creditable to the much underrated James the First to have discerned what Donne was fit for better than Donne himself. . . .

Although the abiding charm of Donne consists rather in his personality than in his writings, he undoubtedly occupies a considerable place as theologian, speculator in morals, sacred orator and poet. We could wish that it had been possible to have given more copious examples of his pulpit eloquence. As a poet, we must agree with Mr Gosse in deeming his influence 'malign'. Instead of setting the thing or the thought clearly before the reader, he studies to discover of what ingenious variations the one may be capable, or what witty remarks may be made about the other. It is impossible not to admire the frequent brilliancy of these fireworks, but their coruscations are a poor substitute for the light of heaven. The example was most pernicious, and led through the extravagances of the Caroline era to the negation of imaginative poetry in the eighteenth century. Mr Gosse's chapter on the influences which affected Donne, and that which he himself exerted upon his successors, is among the most interesting in his book. It may be said in Donne's excuse that he did but transfer to poetry a fashion which he found flourishing in prose, particularly in epistolary prose. There he was no innovator; yet he would no more think of beginning a letter without a conceit than would an Eastern courtier of appearing before the Sultan without a gift. The very defects which gave him contemporary influence render him on that ground historically important.

42. Sir Leslie Stephen

1899

Sir Leslie Stephen (1832–1904) was ordained in 1864 but became an agnostic in 1870, founder of the *Pall Mall Gazette*, and editor of the *Cornhill Magazine* 1871–82. He was the first editor of the *Dictionary of National Biography* and initiated the English Men of Letters series with a life of Samuel Johnson (1878), followed by lives of Alexander Pope (1880), Jonathan Swift (1882), George Eliot (1902) and Thomas Hobbes (1904). He also wrote on philosophy and his great hobby, mountaineering. He was the father of Virginia Woolf and Vanessa Bell. He developed his own account of Donne in an extended review of Gosse's *Life and Letters of John Donne* ('John Donne', *National Review*, 34 (1899), 595–613).

There is something curiously and yet intermittently fascinating about Donne. His fame has been fitful. After the obscuration of the eighteenth century Coleridge and Lamb felt a charm which has been potent with some later critics. Browning was drawn to him by a congenial subtlety of intellect, and Lowell, an equally ardent lover of all that is quaint and witty, read and annotated him carefully. But his poetry seems to be for the select few. Not one of his lyrics appears in *The Golden Treasury*, whether because Palgrave disliked a style which is the antithesis of Tennyson's, or because he thought it unfit for the ordinary reader. To read Donne's verses is, indeed, for most people, to crack very hard nuts on a doubtful chance of finding a sweet kernel. Mr Gosse, in the 'Life' which has just appeared, professes his belief that Donne contains the quint-essence of poetry; but even Dr Jessopp – an enthusiastic admirer of the prose – honestly confesses that the poems are not to his taste. I may, therefore, take courage to confess that I too find them rather indigestible. They contain, I do not doubt, the true spirit; but I rarely get to the end, even of the shortest, without being repelled by some strange discord in form or in substance which sets my teeth on edge. Yet I am attracted as much as repelled. The man himself excites my curiosity. What was the character and the mind that could utter itself in so unique a fashion? Nothing less could have been required than extraordinary talents at the service of a most peculiar idiosyncracy and exposed to some trying combination of circumstance. For explanation one has hitherto been referred to the admirable Izaak Walton. His life of Donne is said to be the masterpiece of English biography. Critic after critic labours to show a genial appreciation of that performance. If, indeed, the book is to be read as we read *The Vicar of Wakefield* – as a prose idyll – a charming narrative in which we have as little to do with the reality of Donne as with the reality of Dr Primrose, I can only subscribe to the judgment of my betters. But there are two objections to the life if taken as a record of facts. The first is that the facts are all wrong; and the second that the portraiture is palpably false. As we read we imagine Walton gazing reverently from his seat at the dean in the pulpit, dazzled by a vast learning and a majestic flow of elaborate rhetoric, which seemed to the worthy tradesman to come as from an 'angel in the clouds', and offering a posthumous homage as sincere and touching as that which no doubt engaged the con-descending kindness of the great man in life. The book illustrates the most attractive aspect of the Anglicanism of those days. It recalls *John Inglesant* and the holy Mr Ferrar of Little Gidding. But the real

Donne – the strange complex human being, with his weaknesses, his passions, his remorse, his strange twists of thought and character – has disappeared, and just enough is revealed to make us ask for more. Our petition has been heard. For fifty years Dr Jessopp has been collecting materials. He has made them over to Mr Gosse, who cordially acknowledges the generosity of his ally. Mr Gosse, already an independent enquirer and an accomplished historian of literature, has given us all that can now be discoverable. There are still gaps – gaps which suggest regrets that we cannot cross-examine Donne himself, and doubts whether, if we could, he would be a satisfactory witness. Mr Gosse modestly avows that, to some extent, Donne 'eludes' him. The last secret of that singular character remains impenetrable or to be guessed from imperfect glimpses. If Mr Gosse hesitates after so much study and such familiarity with details, it is not for one who depends chiefly upon Mr Gosse himself to speak with confidence. Biography, alas! Even the biography of intimate friends, involves, as soon as one tries to penetrate the inner life, a great deal of guesswork. Donne, with his strange facility for seeing things in unexpected lights, was so ingenious in discovering reasons that he probably misunderstood his own motives. How are we, judging from fragmentary records and indigenous utterances and rose-coloured sophistications at a distance of some three centuries, to speak with any confidence?

Without over-confidence, however, one may point out some elements of this curious psychological problem. From the outset events conspired to make life one long problem in casuistry for Donne himself.

[He speaks of Donne's family history, his involvement in the religious controversies of the time, and his career as an eager student about town.]

It is plain, too, that he laid up causes for future remorse. The 'satires', 'elegies', and many early poems are left to indicate his state of mind; but the indication itself requires an interpreter. The 'satires' represent one natural outcome of the time. By a curious coincidence three or four contemporaries, especially Joseph Hall – whose career was closely parallel to Donne's – and the dramatist Marston, were independently writing similar satires. Brilliant young men, at once scornful of the world and yet proud of a premature interest in its ways, were inevitably satirists. Their position was analogous to that of the young Edinburgh reviewers, showing their superiority by contempt for the world around. The precedent of the Roman satirists, who had not as yet been imitated, occurred to them all as a happy thought to determine the best form of utterance. They all, moreover, made the curious blunder of assuming that satire must be rough and uncouth and obscure. A satirist must be a thorough cynic, a snarling foul-mouthed Diogenes, carrying his lantern into the slums and using coarse and indecent language to describe ugly sights. They had not made the simple discovery that the better our manners the more easily we can rub in a good caustic phrase. The movement was therefore a failure; but, meanwhile, Donne's attitude is no doubt significant both of his own character and of the time. Mr Gosse insists upon the contrast between his poetry and the exquisite 'rose-coloured Elizabethan idealism'. Donne represents a change of sentiment in the rising generation symptomatic of the domestic discords which were to supersede the patriotic enthusiasm of the Armada period. It may perhaps be doubtful whether Mr Gosse does not attribute to Donne too much of deliberate and conscious literary revolt. Donne was not, like Wordsworth, the deliberate prophet of a literary 'reaction'. But no doubt he was sitting in the seat of the scornful, and despised what we now take to be the glories of the ages. The friendship with Jonson, who represented learning, and a critical superiority to people who had 'small Latin and less Greek', is significant. Donne was the thoroughly trained scholar and gentleman, who belonged therefore to the aristocracy of the literary world, and despised the rabble of unlearned scribblers and playwrights with hands subdued to what they worked in.

Donne's poems, however, raise a far more interesting personal problem. Some of them show, to put it gently, a remarkable frankness. It is altogether surprising that he thought of printing, if not publishing, them at a period when he was aspiring to preferment in the Church. Certainly, as Mr Gosse points out, they were calculated to make Archbishop Abbot's hair stand on end, and would be only too much to the taste of the courtiers of James I. It is strange, though characteristic, that Donne, even in his saintly days, could not find it in his heart to destroy, though he could not make up his mind to publish. The question arises, how far they represent genuine autobiography? Mr Gosse holds that they tell a true story of an intrigue with a married woman, which, after a year, ended with a bitter quarrel and curses upon the now hated mistress. I will not dispute Mr Gosse's opinion, though I can also imagine that if Donne were as interesting as Shakespeare his poems might be interpreted as variously as the sonnets. One reserve must be made. The frank disregard of decency is but too intelligible. What is strange is Donne's insistence upon the ugly and repulsive collateral consequences. The lady's husband had to be injured, and the objections of her father and mother to the suspected intimacy were inevitable. Donne's passion might blind him to their wrongs; but to insist upon that aspect of the question triumphantly and emphasize disgusting details is, to speak mildly, not pretty. If the poems were to be taken in their 'first intention' as deliberate utterances of his sentiments we should have to call him not simply immoral, but unequivocally brutal. To me it seems that we merely have an illustration of a morbid tendency, not peculiar to Donne. In one of the 'elegies' Donne gives a description of another woman, only exceeded in offensiveness by some of Swift's worst performances. Swift's friends tell us that he was personally cleanly even to scrupulosity, and that he contemplated filthy images because they had a perverse fascination for him. He was a self-torturer by nature, and dwelt upon disgusting things precisely because they disgusted him. Donne, I fancy, had in this respect a real affinity to the later dean. Carried away by his passions, he does not blind himself to the brutality involved, but rather emphasizes and insists upon it. For the moment his audacity in facing and minutely analysing consequences gives zest to his love or is a proof of the strength of passion which makes even this ingredient tolerable. But, when the passion declines the feeling will turn into remorse, and perhaps is already, though half-consciously, remorse in disguise.

The interpretation may seem over subtle, but subtlety was the essence of Donne's nature. Both the student and the wild gallant appear in the poems of this date, and they are strangely combined in the qualities which led Johnson to describe Donne and his followers as the 'metaphysical' school. Literary critics have dwelt sufficiently upon the far-fetched conceits which gained currency at the same time in other countries. They are, it would seem, the natural utterances of the schoolman coming to court. Donne was all this time plunged in his omnivorous studies of divinity and philosophy. The philosophy in which he had been initiated at the Universities meant, of course, the still dominant scholastic philosophy. To reason was to 'syllogize'; to suppose that all truth was attainable by constructing vast piles of syllogism, defining, distinguishing, spinning whole webs of argumentation, and becoming an accomplished master of the art of logical fencing. He had studied the application of the art to casuistry; had a special familiarity with the Spanish Jesuits of his time; and was steeped in whole masses of scholastic controversy. The training was calculated to produce abnormal skill in dialectics; to sharpen the purely logical perceptions, but also to encourage more quibbling and ingenious evasions of difficulties for real solutions. Now, the sophistries and tricks of intellectual wrestling correspond exactly to the conceits of the 'metaphysical poets'. A commentator upon Donne's poems would have occasionally to illustrate his author from the schoolmen. Other poets, for example, have compared young women to angels; but to Donne, thoroughly acquainted with the natural history of angels, the comparison suggests new and strange points of resemblance. The schoolmen had taught him by syllogism that angels make temporary bodies out of air; and Donne makes poetical capital of this in the lyric called 'Air and Angels'. So his 'obsequies' to Lord Harrington raise the old problem whether angels in moving from one place to another pass through all the intermediate spaces. In the 'Hymn to the Saints and to Marquis Hamilton' he turns to account the scholastic doctrine that every angel is itself a 'separate species'. He several times expounds in verse the theory of three souls, vegetative, sensitive, and rational; and he knows at what precise moment the soul takes in 'the poisonous tincture of original sin'. Fuller information upon all these 'fickle points of niceness' may be found in the *Summa* of Aquinas, where they are carefully argued out. What strike us as unaccountable conceits are simply applications of the current philosophy. His mind is obviously full of such delicate enquiries, and he applies the same method to other topics. A characteristic poem is 'The Will'. He supposes himself to be dying, and bequeathes his moral and intellectual possessions. Then he works out a problem. A gift has not the proper virtue when the receiver is not benefited either (1) because he has a superfluity of the thing, or (2) because he does not know the use of it, or (3) because it is unpleasant to him, or (4) because it is really his own already, or (5) because accidents make it useless. His mistress has exemplified all these cases in her reception of him, and he concludes logically that

166

he will die intestate. This ingenious scheme might be stated as a theory of the ethics of giving – When is a present not a present? With Donne it becomes rhymed casuistry, or a brilliant little poem in six stanzas. Mr Gosse quotes it as illustrating the phase in which his passion is turning to bitterness. Mr Gosse is perfectly justified; but it is the more characteristic that an outburst of passionate bitterness should be thus crammed into a close logical framework, which must, one supposes, have taken as much hard thinking as strong feeling. It is, in fact, this odd combination of syllogism and sentiment which gives one peculiar flavour to Donne's poetry, and makes him, as Coleridge put it, 'wreathe iron pokers into true-love knots'. Sometimes he seems to be merely a schoolman trying in spite of nature to be a poet; and at times reveals himself as a genuine poet, cramped and distorted by the training of the schools.

[He tells of Donne's search for a career, his service with Sir Thomas Egerton, and the 'famous catastrophe' of his marriage; and he takes it for granted that such poems as *Elegy* 16, 'On His Mistress', were addressed to Ann More.]

His love is shown in a striking poem, which, in spite of some strange incongruities, made Lamb's voice tremble as he read it.

[Then he suggests that Donne's marriage obliged him to write eulogistic poems for a living.]

His prospects depended entirely upon his power of attracting patrons: and (taking for granted all proper apologies about the manners of the times) the story is not altogether attractive. Donne flattered with a will. The great Duchess of Bedford was praised by other poets, such as Jonson and Daniel, and, we will hope, deserved it. Donne was certainly not last in the race for adequate hyperboles. To commend oneself to the successful courtiers in the days of James I was a process which involved some trial of self-respect.

[He instances Donne's poetic flattery of the earls of Carlisle and Somerset, and also of the dead Elizabeth Drury.]

Donne carried on his hyperboles in two successive poems, commemorating anniversaries of the child's death, and rashly promised an annual celebration. His friends were scandalised by his outrageous compliments.

[He quotes Ben Jonson's observations to Drummond, and draws a lesson which he himself notoriously failed to observe.]

The poems may be a warning that we must not infer genuine autobiography from his utterances, for, if the truth had been unknown, injudicious critics might have constituted a romance out of lines intended simply to attract a patron. They hardly suggest, indeed, real feeling, although they are very curious iilustrations of Donne's 'metaphysical' subtleties, and contain some of his most striking phrases.

[He turns to discuss some of Donne's prose writings, and first considers the argument in favour of suicide in *Biathanatos*.]

There was a strong dash of the Hamlet in Donne, and Hamlet would have been still more puzzled whether to be or not to be if he had been as well crammed as Donne with whole bodies of casuistical divinity.

This, I fancy, gives us a significant glimpse into this most complex and perplexing character. His early errors of morality suggest at once defiance and remorse. His romantic love suggests gratitude for the blessings and repentance for the blunder. His poetical impulses are confused and distorted by his philosophy. His intellect, amazingly nimble and discursive rather than powerful, stimulates a boundless curiosity which tends to overwhelm his reason under vast masses of learning. He reminds us of Bacon by his fertility of illustration, and oddly enough seems, as Mr Gosse points out, to have been more receptive than Bacon of the new astronomy of Kepler and Galileo. And yet he remains hopelessly buried in the scholastic system upon which Bacon was pronouncing sentence. He wanders in a vast labyrinth of speculation instead of striking at once to the heart of the problem. Though his early prejudices drop off he only sidles and shifts by slow degrees and with infinite complications into the Anglican position, always holding to its continuity with Catholicism. His life is as distracted and dependent as his thought. He cannot fairly decide to be the divine, and apologizes for his want of learning while he is displaying learning enough for a whole bench of bishops. The Court still charms and fascinates the strong accomplished flatterer, and he cannot help hoping that one of the great favourites to whom he can make himself so acceptable will, at last, lift him out of his troubles. All the time the poor man is 'neurotic', troubled by ill-health, weighed down by family cares, and driven to speculate upon the ethics of suicide.

[He traces Donne's development as a preacher, and argues that the sermons gave freer scope to his genius than the poems.]

Donne's learning is, after all, subsidiary to a marvellous intellectual activity. In his poems the dialectical subtlety seems to fetter him. The fancy is condensed as well as constrained. He seems to labour till he can squeeze the imaginative impulse into a logical formula at the price of crabbed obscurity. But in the prose the two faculties play freely into each other's hands. There is a crowd and rush of thoughts and illustrations. His subtle intellect evolves endless distinctions and startling paradoxes and quaint analogies so abundantly, that he might apparently have preached for a week as easily as for an hour. He takes up one fancy after another, and revels in various applications till the display becomes astonishing.

[He quotes the peroration of the sermon Donne preached at St Paul's on 25 January 1629.]

This passage must be enough to illustrate the vigour with which Donne can often throw aside his 'mouse and elephant', and his elaborate refinements on grammatical and logical niceties, and glow with genuine fire, though frequently we have to exclude so much uncongenial matter that our appreciation ceases to be spontaneous. And there is perhaps the final interest of Donne. In one way he has partly became obsolete because he belonged so completely to the dying epoch. The scholasticism in which his mind was steeped was to become hateful and then contemptible to the rising philosophy; the literature which he had assimilated went to the dust-heaps; preachers condescended to drop their doctorial robes; downright common-sense came in with Tillotson and South in the next generation; and not only the learning but the congenial habit of thought became unintelligible. Donne's poetical creed went the same way, and if Pope and Parnell perceived that there was some genuine ore in his verses and tried to beat it into the coinage of their own day, they only spoilt it in trying to polish it. But on the other side, Donne's depth of feeling, whether tortured into short lyrics or expanding into voluble rhetoric, has a charm which perhaps gains a new charm from modern sentimentalists. His morbid or 'neurotic' constitution has a real affinity for latter-day

169

pessimists. If they talk philosophy where he had to be content with scholastic theology the substance is pretty much the same. He has the characteristic love for getting pungency at any price; for dwelling upon the horrible till we cannot say whether it attracts or repels him; and can love the 'intense' and super-sublimated as much as if he were skilled in all the latest æsthetic canons. But whether Mr Gosse and Dr Jessopp will be able to persuade the ordinary reader to feel the power hidden under such a mass of heterogeneous matter, is more than I can venture to prophesy.

43. Arthur Symons
1899/1916

Gosse's *Life and Letters of John Donne* called forth extended comment in literary journals, but centred attention chiefly on Donne's personality. Some essayists do attempt to relate the man to the poems in a critical way, and a few show a wider acquaintance with Donne's writings.

The symbolist critic Arthur Symons (1865–1945) finds that Gosse's account of Donne's character is summed up in two well-known representations of Donne, the one as a youth of 18, and the other the engraving of the dying man in his shroud ('John Donne', *Fortnightly Review,* n.s. 66 (1899), 734–45; Symons republished the essay as it stood in his *Figures of Several Centuries,* 1916, pp 80–108).

[Symons comments on the two engravings.]

Between them these portraits tell much, and Mr Gosse, in his narrative, tells us everything else that there is to tell, much of it for the first time; and the distinguished and saintly person of Walton's narrative, so simple, so easily explicable, becomes more complex at every moment, as fresh light makes the darkness more and more visible. At the end we seem to have become singularly intimate with a fascinating and puzzling creature, whom each of us may try to understand after his fashion, as we try to understand the real secrets of the character of our friends.

Donne's mind, then, if I may make my own attempt to understand him, was the mind of the dialectician, of the intellectual adventurer; he is a poet almost by accident, or at least for reasons with which art in the abstract has but little to do. He writes verse, first of all, because he has observed keenly, and because it pleases the pride of his intellect to satirise the pretensions of humanity. Then it is the flesh which speaks in his verse, the curiosity of woman, which he has explored in the same spirit of adventure; then passion, making a slave of him for love's sake, and turning at last to the slave's hatred; finally, religion, taken up with the same intellectual interest, the same subtle indifference, and, in its turn, passing also into passionate reality. A few poems are inspired in him by what he has seen in remote countries; some are marriage songs and funeral elegies, written for friendship or for money. But he writes nothing 'out of his own head', as we say; nothing lightly, or, it would seem, easily; nothing for the song's sake. He speaks, in a letter, of 'descending to print anything in verse'; and it is certain that he was never completely absorbed by his own poetry, or at all careful to measure his achievements against those of others. He took his own poems very seriously, he worked upon them with the whole force of his intellect; but to himself, even before he became a divine, he was something more than a poet. Poetry was but one means of expressing the many-sided activity of his mind and temperament. Prose was another, preaching another; travel and contact with great events and persons scarcely less important to him in the building up of himself.

[Symons describes Donne's indiscriminate interests and studies, familiarly calling upon the entire range of Donne's prose writings, as well as the circumstances of his career. He takes Donne's restless play of intelligence for a symptom of a feverish excitement of mind which also racked the physical organism.]

Scientific and technical terms are constantly found in his verse, where we should least expect them, where, indeed, they are least welcome. . . . This preying upon itself of the brain is but one significant indication of a temperament, neurotic enough indeed, but in which the neurosis is still that of the curious observer, the intellectual casuist, rather than of the artist. . . . It is this brain, turned inward upon itself, and darting out on every side in purely random excursions, that was responsible, I cannot doubt, for all the contradictions of a career in which the inner logic is not at first apparent.

Donne's career divides itself sharply into three parts: his youth, when we see him as a soldier, a traveller, a lover, a poet, un-restrained in all the passionate adventures of youth; then a middle period, in which he is a lawyer and a theologian, seeking knowledge and worldly advancement, without any too restraining scruple as to the means which come to his hand; and then a last stage of saintly living and dying. What then is the link between these successive periods, the principle of development, the real Donne, in short? 'He was none of these, or all of these, or more,' says Mr Gosse. But, surely, he was indeed all of these, and his individuality precisely the growth from one stage to another, the subtle intelligence being always there, working vividly, but in each period working in a different direction. 'I would fain do something, but that I cannot tell what is no wonder.' Everything in Donne seems to me to explain itself in that fundamental uncertainty of aim, and his uncertainty of aim partly by a morbid physical condition. He searches, nothing satisfies him, tries everything, in vain; finding satisfaction in the Church, as in a haven of rest. Always, it is the curious, insatiable brain searching. And he is always wretchedly aware that he 'can do nothing constantly'.

His three periods, then, are three stages in the search after a way to walk in, something worthy of himself to do.

[Symons quotes from the letters to bring out Donne's ambiguous attitude to his secular career and writing.]

So speculative a brain, able to prove, and proving for its own uneasy satisfaction, that even suicide is 'not so naturally a sin, that it may never be otherwise', could allow itself to be guided by no fixed rules; and to a brain so abstract, conduct must always have seemed of less importance than it does to most other people, and especially conduct which is argument, like the demonstrations on behalf of what seems, on the face of it, a somewhat inquitous divorce and re-marriage, or like those unmeasured eulogies both of this 'blest pair of swans', and of the dead child of a rich father.

[He cites Donne's defence of his claims for Elizabeth Drury, and admission that he had done best when he had least truth for his subject.]

He is always the casuist, always mentally impartial in the face of a moral problem, reserving judgment on matters which, after all, seem to him remote from an unimpassioned contemplation of things; until that moment of crisis comes, long after he has become a clergyman, when the death of his wife changed the world for him, and he became, in the words of Walton, 'crucified to the world. . . . From that time to the end of his life, he had found what he had all the while been seeking: rest for the restlessness of his mind, in a meditation upon the divine nature; occupation, in being 'ambassador of God', through the pulpit; himself, as it seemed to him, at his fullest and noblest. It was himself, really, that he had been seeking all the time, conscious at least of that in all the deviations of the way; himself, the ultimate of his curiosities.

[In the second section of his essay Symons turns to try his account of Donne against Donne's poetry itself.]

And yet what remains to us out of this life of many purposes, which had found an end so satisfying to itself in the Deanery of St Paul's, is simply a bundle of manuscript verses, which the writer could bring himself neither to print nor to destroy. His first satire speaks contemptuously of 'giddy fantastic poets', and, when he allowed himself to write poetry, he was resolved to do something different from what anybody had ever done before, not so much from the artist's instinctive desire of originality, as from a kind of haughty, yet really bourgeois, desire to be indebted to nobody. With what care he wrote is confessed in a passage of one of his letters.

[Symons quotes from Donne's letter to Sir Robert Carr, April 1627.]

But he thought there were other things more important than being a poet, and this very labour of his was partly a sign of it. 'He began', says Mr Gosse with truth, 'as if poetry had never been written before.' To the people of his time, to those who came immediately after him, he was the restorer of English poetry.

> The Muses' garden, with pedantic weeds
> O'erspread, was purged by thee,

says Carew, in those memorial verses in which the famous lines occur: –

> Here lies a king that ruled as he thought fit
> The universal monarchy of wit.

Shakespeare was living, remember, and it was Elizabethan poetry that Donne set himself to correct. He began with metre, and invented a system of prosody which has many merits, and would have had more in less arbitrary hands. 'Donne, for not keeping of accent, deserved hanging', said Ben Jonson, who was nevertheless his friend and admirer. And yet, if one will but read him always for the sense, for the natural emphasis of what he has to say, there are few lines which will not come out in at all events the way that he meant them to be delivered. The way he meant them to be delivered is not always as beautiful as it is expressive. Donne would be original at all costs, preferring himself to his art. He treated poetry as Aesop's master treated his slave, and broke what he could not bend.

But Donne's novelty of metre is only a part of his too deliberate novelty as a poet. As Mr Gosse has pointed out, with a self-evident truth which has apparently waited for him to say it, Donne's real position in regard to the poetry of his time was that of a realistic writer, who makes a clean sweep of tradition, and puts everything down in the most modern words and with the help of the most trivially actual images.

> To what a cumbersome unwieldiness,
> And burdensome corpulence my love hath grown,

he will begin a poem on 'Love's Diet'. Of love, as the master of hearts, he declares seriously: –

> He swallows us and never chaws;
> By him, as by chain'd shot, whole ranks do die;
> He is the tyrant pike, our hearts the fry.

And, in his unwise insistence that every metaphor shall be absolutely new, he drags medical and alchemical and legal properties into verse really full of personal passion, producing at times poetry which is a kind of disease of the intellect, a sick offshoot of science. Like most poets of powerful individuality, Donne lost precisely where he gained. That cumulative and crowding and sweeping intellect which builds up his greatest poems into miniature Escurials of poetry, mountainous and four-square to all the winds of the world, 'purges' too often the flowers as well as the weeds out of 'the

Muses' garden'. To write poetry as if it had never been written before is to attempt what the greatest poets never attempted. There are only two poets in English literature who thus stand out of the tradition, who are without ancestors, Donne and Browning. Each seems to have certain qualities almost greater than the qualities of the greatest; and yet in each some precipitation of arrogant egoism remains in the crucible, in which the draught has all but run immortally clear.

Donne's quality of passion is unique in English poetry. It is a rapture in which the mind is supreme, a reasonable rapture, and yet carried to a pitch of actual violence. The words themselves rarely count for much, as they do in Crashaw, for instance, where words turn giddy at the height of their ascension. The words mean things, and it is the things that matter. They can be brutal: 'For God's sake, hold your tongue, and let me love!' as if a long pre-supposed self-repression gave way suddenly, in an outburst. 'Love, any devil else but you', he begins, in his abrupt leap to the heart of the matter. Or else his exaltation will be grave, tranquil, measureless in assurance.

[He quotes the first stanza of *The Anniversary*.]

This lover loves with his whole nature, and so collectedly because reason, in him, is not in conflict with passion, but passion's ally. His senses speak with unparalleled directness, as in those elegies which must remain the model in English of masculine sensual sobriety. He distinguishes the true end of such loving in a forcible character-istically prosaic image: –

> Whoever loves, if he do not propose
> The right true end of love, he's one that goes
> To sea for nothing but to make him sick.

And he exemplifies every motion and the whole pilgrim's progress of physical love, with a deliberate, triumphant, unluxurious explicit-ness which 'leaves no doubt', as we say, 'of his intentions', and can be no more than referred to passingly in modern pages. In a series of hate poems, of which I will quote the finest, he gives expression to a whole region of profound human sentiment which has never been expressed, out of Catullus, with such intolerable truth.

[He quotes the whole of 'The Apparition'.]

Yet it is the same lover, and very evidently the same, who winnows all this earthly passion to a fine, fruitful dust, fit to make bread for angels. Ecstatic reason, passion justifying its intoxication by revealing the mysteries that it has come thus to apprehend, speak in the quintessence of Donne's verse with an exalted simplicity which seems to make a new language for love. It is the simplicity of a perfectly abstract geometrical problem, solved by one to whom the rapture of solution is the blossoming of pure reason. Read the poem called 'The Ecstasy', which seems to anticipate a metaphysical Blake; it is all close reasoning, step by step, and yet is what its title claims for it.

It may be, though I doubt it, that other poets who have written personal verse in English, have known as much of women's hearts and the senses of men, and the interchanges of passionate intercourse between man and woman; but, partly by reason of this very method of saying things, no one has ever rendered so exactly, and with such elaborate subtlety, every mood of the actual passion. It has been done in prose; may one not think of Stendhal, for a certain way he has of turning the whole forces of the mind upon those emotions and sensations which are mostly left to the heat of an unreflective excitement? Donne, as he suffers all the colds and fevers of love, is as much the sufferer and the physician of his disease as we have seen him to be in cases of actual physical sickness. Always detached from himself, even when he is most helplessly the slave of circumstances, he has that frightful faculty of seeing through his own illusions; of having no illusions to the mind, only to the senses. Other poets, with more wisdom towards poetry, give us the beautiful or pathetic results of no matter what creeping or soaring passions. Donne, making a new thing certainly, if not always a thing of beauty, tells us exactly what a man really feels as he makes love to a woman, as he sits beside her husband at table, as he dreams of her in absence, as he scorns himself for loving her, as he hates or despises her for loving him, as he realises all that is stupid in her devotion, and all that is animal in his. 'Nature's lay idiot, I taught thee to love', he tells her, in a burst of angry contempt, priding himself on his superior craft in the art. And his devotions to her are exquisite, appealing to what is most responsive in woman, beyond those of tenderer poets. A woman cares most for the lover who understands her best, and is least taken in by what it is the

method of her tradition to feign. So wearily conscious that she is
not the abstract angel of her pretence and of her adorers, she will
go far in sheer thankfulness to the man who can see so straight into
her heart as to have

> Found something like a heart,
> But colours it and corners had;
> It was not good, it was not bad,
> It was entire to none, and few had part.

Donne shows women themselves, in delight, anger, or despair; they
know that he finds nothing in the world more interesting, and they
much more than forgive him for all the ill he says of them. If women
most conscious of their sex were ever to read Donne, they would
say, He was a great lover; he understood.

And, in the poems of divine love, there is the same quality of
mental emotion as in the poems of human love. Donne adores God
reasonably, knowing why he adores him. He renders thanks point
by point, celebrates the heavenly perfections with metaphysical
precision, and is no vaguer with God than with woman. Donne
knew what he believed and why he believed, and is carried into no
heat of mist as he tells over the recording rosary of his devotions.
His 'Holy Sonnets' are a kind of argument with God; they tell over,
and discuss and resolve, such perplexities of faith and reason as
would really occur to a speculative brain like his. Thought crowds
in upon thought, in these tightly-packed lines, which but rarely
admit a splendour of this kind: –

> At the round earth's imagined corners blow
> Your trumpets, angels, and arise, arise
> From death, you numberless infinities
> Of souls, and to your scattered bodies go.

More typical is this too knotted beginning of another sonnet: –

> Batter my heart, three person'd God; for you
> As yet but knock; breathe, shine, and seek to mend;
> That I may rise, and stand, o'erthrow me, and bend
> Your force, to break, blow, burn, and make me new.

Having something very minute and very exact to say, he hates to
leave anything out; dreading diffuseness, as he dreads the tame
sweetness of an easy melody, he will use only the smallest possible

number of words to render his thought; and so, as here, he is too often ingenious rather than felicitous, forgetting that to the poet poetry comes first, and all the rest afterwards.

For the writing of great poetry something more is needed than to be a poet and to have great occasions. Donne was a poet, and he had the passions and the passionate adventures, in body and mind, which make the material for poetry; he was sincere to himself in expressing what he really felt under the burden of strong emotion and sharp sensation. Almost every poem that he wrote is written on a genuine inspiration, a genuine personal inspiration, but most of his poems seem to have been written before that personal inspiration has had time to fuse itself with the poetic inspiration. It is always useful to remember Wordsworth's phrase of 'emotion recollected in tranquility', for nothing so well defines that moment of crystallisation in which direct emotion or sensation deviates exquisitely into art. Donne is intent on the passion itself, the thought, the reality; so intent that he is not at the same time, in that half conscious way which is the way of the really great poet, equally intent on the form, that both may come to ripeness together. Again it is the heresy of the realist. Just as he drags into his verse words that have had no time to take colour from men's association of them with beauty, so he puts his 'naked thinking heart' into verse as if he were setting forth an argument. He gives us the real thing, as he would have been proud to assure us. But poetry will have nothing to do with real things, until it has translated them into a diviner world. That world may be as closely the pattern of ours as the worlds which Dante saw in hell and purgatory; the language of the poet may be as close to the language of daily speech as the supreme poetic language of Dante. But the personal or human reality and the imaginative or divine reality must be perfectly interfused, or the art will be at fault. Donne is too proud to abandon himself to his own inspiration, to his inspiration as a poet; he would make poetry speak straight. Well, poetry will not speak straight, in the way Donne wished it to, and under the goading that his restless intellect gave it.

He forgot beauty, preferring to it every form of truth, and beauty has revenged itself upon him, glittering miraculously out of many lines in which he wrote humbly, and leaving the darkness of a retreating shadow upon great spaces in which a confident intellect was conscious of shining.

> For though mind be the heaven, where love may sit,
> Beauty a convenient type may be to figure it.

he writes, in the 'Valediction to his Book', thus giving formal expression to his heresy. 'The greatest wit, though not the best poet of our nation', Dryden called him; the greatest intellect, that is, which had expressed itself in poetry. Dryden himself was not always careful to distinguish between what material was fit and what unfit for verse; so that we can now enjoy his masterly prose with more equable pleasure than his verse. But he saw clearly enough the distinction in Donne between intellect and the poetical spirit; that fatal division of two forces, which, had they pulled together instead of apart, might have achieved a result wholly splendid. Without a great intellect no man was ever a great poet; but to possess a great intellect is not even a first step in the direction of becoming a poet at all.

Compare Donne, for instance, with Herrick. Herrick has little enough of the intellect, the passion, the weight and the magnificence of Donne; but, setting out with so much less to carry, he certainly gets first to the goal, and partly by running always in the right direction. The most limited poet in the language, he is the surest. He knows the airs that weave themselves into songs, as he knows the flowers that twine best into garlands. Words come to him in an order which no one will ever alter, and no one will ever forget. Whether they come easily or not is no matter; he knows when they have come right, and they always come right before he lets them go. But Donne is only occasionally sure of his words as airs; he sets them doggedly to the work of saying something, whether or no they step to the beat of the music. Conscious writer though he was, I suppose he was more or less unconscious of his extraordinary felicities, more conscious probably of how they came than of what they were doing. And they come chiefly through a sudden heightening of mood, which brings with it a clearer and a more exalted mode of speech, in its merely accurate expression of itself. Even then I cannot imagine him quite reconciled to beauty, at least actually doing homage to it, but rather as one who receives a gift by the way.

44. Francis Thompson

1899

Thompson anonymously reviewed Gosse's *Life and Letters of John Donne* ('Mr Gosse's Life of Donne', *Academy*, 4 November 1899, pp. 505–6; given in *The Real Robert Louis Stevenson, and Other Critical Essays*, ed. T. L. Connolly, 1959, pp. 70–4).

[Thompson judges Gosse well qualified in various ways to be the biographer of Donne.]

In particular, his wide range of literary sympathy peculiarly fits him to point out both the derivations and the originality of Donne, most learned yet independent of writers.

A brilliant and unique figure is Donne. A Protestant Bishop, of stubborn Catholic stock; an amatory poet, full of mysticism and scholasticism; a wit, a courtier, a man of the world; to the last shrinking from the ecclesiastical state with the reluctant avoidance of a Thomas à Becket, yet ultimately the most famous of preachers and a voluminous theological writer; beginning with verse not doubtfully licentious, and ending with a death of ascetic piety.

[He speaks of Donne's family and upbringing, then goes on to discuss the early verse.]

Yet Donne's first poems were the reverse of what such influences might beget – they were satires, and among the very earliest of English satires, in the formal sense of the word. It was 1593, and he was then twenty; yet he was a satirist before Hall, and after the languid attempt of Lodge. Already he was himself, and utterly unlike the Spensers, Daniels, and the rest who furnished models for the young Shakespeare about this date. Mr Gosse's investigation as to the derivation of the satires therefore becomes of extreme interest. He shows that, probably owing to the authority exerted by the lectures of Casaubon at Geneva, Persius was the special model of the earlier English satirists. Moreover, it was Persius peculiarly understood. Crabbedness both of style and metre were supposed to be leading features of the old Roman poet, and therefore essential features of satire itself. It was accordingly of deliberate endeavour that Donne darkened his language and knotted his versification. The point is valuable, for these characters more or less clung to Donne ever afterwards. If you examine their extreme form in the satires, they depend on two things: violent ellipsis as regards sentence-structure; violent elision and wilful accentuation as regards metre. The unusual accentuation is sometimes found to be highly expressive, when you consider it; sometimes is purely wanton and defiant. The like traits disturb the reader, in less persistent measure, throughout Donne's best work; yet when he is not bent on being too clever, he can show verse as sinewily knit, as harmonious, or as melodious as anything in his great predecessors or contemporaries. Mr Gosse has done good service in pointing out what, apart from temperament, is probably the source of this mannerism, and that it was deliberately introduced as a protest against 'the rosy Elizabethan sweetness'. To this he soon added the use of imagery drawn from familiar, technical, or scholastic sources. The result is a style quite personal to himself, which his brilliant vogue at Court was powerless to alter. On the contrary, he became himself the leader of a school destined to overrun the whole field of seventeenth-century poetry.

Donne's verse, as Mr Gosse truly says, differs from most Elizabethan verse in being strongly personal. He anticipated the modern habit of making his poetry a record of his own feelings and experience. We have in it the express image of a lawless, curious, headstrong youth, trying all life, searching all knowledge, experimenting in all pleasure. He was a rake, if you can call a man a rake who is a master of law, a proficient in theology. He was a student, if you can call a man a student when he is a kind of strong and self-contained Sydney Carton who combined hard living and high thinking. You have the forcible turbulent mind in the strongly knit turbid verse, with its restless activity of fancy, its directness of feeling contrasting with the strangeness of expression. But with all its intellectual brilliancy, Donne's poetry was hard, until a legitimate love affair came to inform it with depth and height of feeling.

Of course, he fell in love in a forbidden quarter; and yet more of course he pursued the affair to marriage through every obstacle. It was at once the making and marring of Donne. Morally and poetically it was the best thing which could have happened to him; but it was the ruin of his fortune.

[He describes the frustration of Donne's hopes, and the decision to take holy orders.]

181

Thenceforth we have a new Donne. Not only does there arise Donne the great preacher, which might be a merely outward change. His life grows steadily more ascetic; his prose gives curious and brilliant testimony to his new preoccupations; and, above all, his poetry – with Donne ever the sincere index of the soul – becomes surcharged with profound religiousness. The sermons and prose-writings of this later period are little read nowadays; even Mr Gosse finds their admixture of scholasticism intolerable, and that you must disencumber them from it to enjoy them. But minds which love intellectual subtlety will find them a delightful exercise, and may even swallow the scholasticism. His mind retained its power to the very last. On his death-bed, emaciated by wearing sickness, he wrote a poem as strong and characteristic as ever he wrote. Those closing days remind one of the mystics whom he loved, with a touch of fantastic personality which is his own, and not altogether pleasing.

[He tells 'The story of his memorial in St Paul's', quoting Walton's account of how Donne posed for the portrait and had it set by his bedside thereafter. Then he returns to Donne's poetry.]

So Donne was Donne to the last.

His poetry, long forgotten, has in our days again become an influence with poets and students, if not with general readers. In spite of the faults already noted, in spite of its perverse ingenuities, it has at its best a strength of expression, a close-knit structure, a felicity of balance, a subtle perception of analogy, and a personal sincerity, which appeal irresistibly to strong minds. And now and again he breaks into a directness of powerfully-felt utterance which reminds one of the very greatest Elizabethans. How Shakespearean is this opening of one little poem:

> So, go, break off this last lamenting kiss,
>   Which sucks two souls, and vapours both away;
> Turn, thou ghost, that way, and let me turn this,
>   And let ourselves benight our happiest day.

Once, in the Epithalamium on the marriage of Princess Elizabeth with the Elector Palatine, he has an outburst of such fresh and open song as shows he might have been great in a more natural style than he adopted.

182

[He quotes the whole of stanza 1 of the 'Epithalamion on St Valentine's Day'.]

That is exquisite, and might have been written yesterday. One can well understand that Browning was attracted by so kindred a mind; though personally we do not see the resemblance in style which Mr Gosse detects between the two.

45. Henry Augustin Beers

1899

Beers (see No. 35) traces the changes from Donne to Augustanism in his *History of English Romanticism in the Eighteenth Century*, 1899, pp. 28 and 37–8.

[In a passage distinguishing between mediaeval and romantic style, Beers comments on the naivety and garrulity of the mediaeval as opposed to the quaintness and grotesquerie 'which are held to be marks of romantic speech'.]

Not archaic speech, but a certain mental twist constitutes quaintness. Herbert and Fuller are quaint; Blake is grotesque; Donne and Charles Lamb are wilfully quaint, subtle, and paradoxical. But Chaucer is always straight-grained, broad, and natural.

... by the middle of the seventeenth century the renaissance schools of poetry had become effete in all European countries. They had run into extravagances of style, into a vicious manner known in Spain as Gongorism, in Italy as Marinism, and in England best exhibited in the verse of Donne and Cowley and the rest of the group whom Dr Johnson called the metaphysical poets, and whose Gothicism of taste Addison ridiculed in his *Spectator* papers on true and false wit. It was France that led the reform against this fashion.

183

46. Anon., *Academy*

1900

An anonymous article, characteristic of attitudes at the time, was published in the *Academy* in 1900. Donne's poetry was summarized in a literary context and biographically in the usual three periods: early manhood, marriage 1601 to taking orders 1615, and 'the Dean of St Paul's' ('The Poetry of John Donne', *Academy*, 15 December 1900, pp. 608–9.)

Broadly speaking, Jacobean lyric, and still more Caroline lyric, is less of temperament than of convention. Felicities of expression, of music, of courtesy, it has in good measure; it charms and delights. But it lacks the intimate interest of personality. It is built upon common forms, and is everything rather than immediate and human. From this condemnation, if you think it a condemnation, you will exempt John Donne. It would be almost true to say that John Donne's temperament became the Jacobean convention. Nothing can be more misleading than to remember that his poems were first printed in 1633. For half a century they had been potent in MS. There is Walton's word for it, and Ben Jonson's, that they were written, so far as secular, by his twentieth or twenty-fifth year. This must not be pressed too literally, but it is clear that his style was already formed in the great 'nineties, the spacious days between the coming of the Armada and the coming of the Stuarts. And then it was unique. Among the contemporaries of his early manhood, Donne's sole affinities are with Marlowe. Metaphysical, rugged, and obscure, dowered with a *macabre* imagination and a white-heat of passion, he was an entirely new note in a literature dominated, outside the drama, by the distant influence of Spenser. The pretty fancies of sonnetteers, song-writers, and pastoralists he passed on one side, and witched *les jeunes* with a new and poignant lyric, imperfect in technique and full of extravagant conceits, lending itself as all strongly marked styles lend themselves, to formal imitation, but in his hands, at least, the fascinating reflex of an undeniable personality. He did not print, for his ambitions were in the world of state, not that of letters; but his precious verses filled innumerable common-place books, and that they set the poetic model for the first half of the seventeenth century there can be no manner of doubt. . . .

Since then Donne's poems are of temperament; they bear study as human documents; they are a record of that fiery enigmatic 'soul's progress' which was the life of Donne. Chronologically they fall into three groups. The first includes the poems of early manhood, the satires, the 'idylls' modelled on Ovid's *Amores*, and the lyrics of love. And here, in the lyrics in particular, you may trace two somewhat contradictory moods. Sometimes Donne writes as the man of pleasure, of *bonnes fortunes*, with a cynical laxity of ethics which goes to explain the almost morbid remorsefulness of the sermons of his later years, and with a strong sense of the vanity of things which makes pleasure and *bonnes fortunes* but as Dead Sea ashes in the mouth. Man delights him not, nor, save for the intoxication of an hour, women either. And both the intoxication and its reaction are realised and expressed with an almost modern subtlety of psychological insight. On Donne in this mood we do not love to linger. Here is, we suspect, the poetry of a young man, the typical travelled Italianate Englishman, whose precocious experience has been throughout of the senses rather than of the heart. And we turn gladly to other poems in which Donne writes more worthily of love, with no less psychology, and with an imaginative rapture which subordinates all time and all existence to the emotional fact. Here he gives you, by fits and starts – for, alas! his inspiration rarely extends throughout a whole poem – some of the finest love poetry in the world.

[The first eleven lines of *The Anniversary*, 'All kings, and all their favourites', lines 15–20 of 'Love's Growth'; and the first stanza of 'The Funeral' are quoted.]

The second group of Donne's poems, those of mature life, between his marriage in 1601 and his taking orders in 1615, are mostly verse letters to his friends, and to certain great ladies, such as Lucy Lady Bedford, who held a court of poets at Twickenham Park, through whom Donne probably hoped to obtain State employment. They include also some remarkable funeral elegies, of which the best are those on a somewhat enigmatic Mrs Cecilia Boulstred, a friend of Lady Bedford's, and on Elizabeth Drury, the child daughter of Sir Robert Drury of Drury Lane. As a flatterer, Donne is magnificent.

You may not like the use of his pen, but certainly neither dead nor living were ever celebrated with more splendid hyperbole of praise.

[Lines 43–72 of 'To the Countess of Bedford', 'Madam/ You have refined me' are chosen as an example.]

Finally, as Donne came more and more to occupy himself with theology, and especially in his latter years as a divine and Dean of St Paul's, he also came to regret some, at least, of his earlier verse. . . .

. . . Donne's divine poems have the same intensity of imagination, the same fine *exordia* which are characteristic of his secular verse. Space does not, unfortunately, permit of more than one brief example:

[The article ends with the sonnet 'Death Be Not Proud'.]

47. Reuben Post Halleck

1900

Halleck (1859–1936) was Principal of Male High School, Kentucky, an unusual institution granted 'all the rights and privileges of a university'. He resigned in 1915 to spend more time in writing textbooks, producing histories of American and English literature, books on psychology and physiology, and a number of patriotic studies. He dismissed Donne with a patter derived from Johnson (*A History of English Literature*, 1900, p. 186).

John Donne is of interest to the student of literature chiefly because of the influence which he exerted on the poetry of the age. His verse teems with forced comparisons and analogies between things remarkable for their dissimilarity. An obscure likeness and a worthless conceit were as important to him as was the problem of existence to Hamlet.

186

48. Anon., *Nation*

1900

A scathing (but anonymous) reviewer of Gosse's *Life and Letters of John Donne* claimed that Gosse misrepresents Donne's life because he does not know how to read Donne's poems ('Gosse's Life of Donne. i.', *Nation*, 8 February 1900, pp. 112–13; and 'Gosse's Life of Donne. ii.', *Nation*, 15 February 1900, p. 133).

Another large part of the volumes is occupied with an account and analysis of Donne's poems and other writings, and the student or lover of the poet is likely to turn to this portion of Mr Gosse's work with especial interest, because much of Donne's poetry, while it serves to illustrate his strange career and stranger character, presents such difficulties as to require intelligent and appreciative exposition in order that its true merits may be understood – merits which led Ben Jonson, one of the most capable of critics, 'to esteem John Donne the first poet in the world in some things'.

In his second chapter Mr Gosse deals with the earliest of Donne's poems, his Satires, of which the first four were probably written when Donne, born in 1573, was hardly more than twenty years old. They are extraordinary performances for a youth. Though rugged in versification, they show as a whole remarkable breadth and keenness of observation and maturity of thought. . . .

There is no one of Donne's earlier poems which is of more interest as an illustration of his character than his third Satire. It is an impassioned discourse, addressed to an unknown person, on the need of getting and holding to religion. . . .

The whole satire is the utterance of intimate personal conviction; it is full of vigor of thought, no less than of expression, and it is of the more interest because its main conception, that religious truth was not to be found complete in the creed of any one church, was one of Donne's abiding convictions, as appears alike in certain of his letters and of his sermons.

The best known poems of Donne are the Lyrics. Like his Satires, they mostly belong to his earlier years – years before his marriage in 1601, when he was twenty-eight years old. They are full of the buoyancy, the fancy, the passionateness, the recklessness and insolence of youth. They have a general autobiographical worth, exhibiting Donne as an inconstant but ardent lover of more than one mistress, leading a life in which religion and morality had little share; cynical, of poetic temperament capable of high exaltations and deep depressions, of exquisite delicacy of sentiment and extreme coarseness of mind, according as the spiritual or the sensual elements of his passionate and unbalanced nature had temporary supremacy in the mood of the moment. A few of these lyrics are among the most admirable in the language. No other poet has surpassed Donne in giving exquisite expression to refined and, at the instant, sincere sentiment; but also, no other poet of rank has surpassed him in preference for conceits to simplicity, and of obscure subtilties to limpid clearness of expression and none has sunk lower in grossness. At his best, Donne is one of the most delightful of poets; at his worst he is detestable.

[He gives an account of some of the *Songs and Sonnets* to show how Gosse's biographical reading falsifies them, and quotes Gosse's interpretation of 'The Blossom' with a comment:]

From this version of the poem let us turn to the poem itself. It begins with one of Donne's loveliest stanzas, in which, addressing the flower, he sets forth its ignorance of its own brief life, and says . . .

[He gives the first stanza, and then comes back upon Gosse's account of Donne's amorous career.]

Mr Gosse has framed out of some of Donne's lyrics and elegies an ugly elaborate story of what he calls 'a deplorable but eventful liaison' with a married woman of some social position. He declares that 'we can reconstruct the story almost without danger of a mistake'. But the reader will now not be surprised to learn that the narrative, as woven by Mr Gosse, is a pure chimera, the result simply of his method of misreading the contents of the poems. The poems justify any ill conclusion in regard to Donne's illicit loves, but afford no material for a connected narrative of the course of any one of his love adventures.

[The reviewer returned to the demolition of Gosse a week later.]

Mr Gosse devotes a chapter to that extraordinary fragment, 'The

Progress of the Soul', in which the vivacity of Donne's genius, the abundance of his fancy, and the vigor of his verse are displayed in a series of picturesque, often strikingly imaginative, and sometimes extravagant descriptions of the experience of a soul in its transmigrations from one body to another. Mr Gosse calls it 'a metaphysical narrative', which it is not, and his account of it shows his habitual misreading and misunderstanding of the poems before him. The value of his attempt at critical appreciation of this special poem, a poem characteristic alike of the eccentricities and of the genuine power of Donne's poetic faculty, may be inferred from this extract:

[He quotes from Gosse's account of the poem:]

The reader gradually ceases to be astonished at Mr Gosse's apparent incapacity to interpret correctly Donne's plainest writing, but the incapacity becomes more and more unintelligible. A brilliant little poem of the lyrical period, known to all the lovers of Donne's verse, is an expostulation addressed to his mistress against her proposal to accompany him, dressed as a page, on a journey to the Continent.

[He describes Donne's *Elegy* 16, 'On his Mistress', and shows the absurdity of Gosse's assumption that it was addressed to Donne's wife in 1606.]

49. Anon., *Church Quarterly Review*

1900

An anonymous reviewer of Gosse's *Life and Letters of John Donne* compared Gosse's account of Donne's life with the accounts given by Walton, Johnson and Jessopp, and questioned Gosse's reading of the poems. ('John Donne', *The Church Quarterly Review* 1, April 1900, pp. 97–8).

Mr Gosse assumes that the lyrics in stanzaic form, and the amatory poems in heroic measure, which he assigns to this period, are autobiographical. There are some grounds for thinking so, no doubt, but the case is not proved, and it is one in which we should be glad to give Donne the benefit of the doubt, and take the alternative possibility. For under Mr Gosse's ingenious treatment the poems are so woven into the history of Donne's life as to give a very definite picture to the 'irregularities' of his lay life, of which he naturally thinks when he is about to enter upon his ministerial life.

[The reviewer remarks that Gosse unnecessarily takes 'some of the finest hate-poems in the language' for a mere record of Donne's shabby conduct of an illicit affair. Yet his enthusiasm does not extend beyond the *Songs and Sonnets.*]

To these lyrical poems, for the complete estimate of Donne as a poet, must be added the 'metaphysical narrative' of 'The Progress of the Soul', a weird composition belonging to the poet's period of religious inquiry, and the 'Divine Poems', in some of which the intellectual and in others the religious element predominates.

[He concludes that Gosse's account of Donne will help readers of Donne's poems nonetheless.]

they will find much upon Donne's poetry which will enable them to understand the unique marks of his genius.

50. H. M. Sanders

1900

Gosse's *Life and Letters of John Donne* prompted Sanders to develop his own account of Donne's poetry ('Dr Donne', *Temple Bar*, 121 (1900), 614–28).

John Donne is one of the most fascinating and one of the most elusive of the Elizabethans. His name continually occurs in literary history, but not often revives any very definite memories. Seldom realized as a man, rarely read as a poet, Donne has had less than justice – the charm of the obscure and the mysterious being a poor compensation for neglect.

Donne was a popular poet who would not publish. But this was not his only contradiction. He was a scholar and a soldier, a cynic and a lover, a satirist and a writer of passionate love-songs, a man of the world, a burrower in folios, and a great preacher. He was both prosaic and poetic; deeply religious, with a frank enjoyment of outward pleasures. As Mr Henley has said of Stevenson, there was in Donne

> Much Antony, of Hamlet most of all,
> And something of the Shorter Catechist.

And not only is he a contradiction himself; he is also a cause of contradiction in others. From continuous praise up to the middle of the seventeenth century, he passed to something worse than oblivion in the eighteenth, and now that his work receives further study there is a tendency on the part of his new admirers 'to like him so much as to speak unadvisedly with their lips', as Professor Saintsbury puts it, while those who cannot appreciate him are equally positive in their dislike, and cannot see 'how any decent and intelligent human creature can like him'. Mr Gosse is of course a fervent and faithful admirer, but he does not let his zeal overbear his discretion or spoil his judicial attitude.

[He speaks of the poetry Donne wrote before his marriage.]

His sacred verses, his verse-letters, his deeper, more craggy, more subtle poems were for the most part unwritten, but most of his lyrics had been already sung, and they are worth all the rest of his works. They probably reflect his life faithfully enough, and his mingled chequered character. Devotion and cynicism, true love and un-abashed earthliness, vehement rapture and careless trifling, run through his songs and sonnets as they ran through his heart, and as they have run through the life of many a man since who has not had the wit to coin his heart into undying poetry. Perhaps if we knew the order in which the songs were written we could trace definite development, but without dogmatizing it is not difficult to believe that the genesis of his love for Anne More was responsible for the higher and nobler flights of his pen.

Of his early and flippant manner 'Go and catch a falling star' is a good example. 'The Indifferent' boasts the catholicity of his affections, and his affected superiority to serious love appears in the lines on 'Woman's Constancy', which begin

> Now thou has loved me one whole day.

These careless light o' love verses are often desperately ingenious, and have not the naturalness nor the conviction of truth that are to be found in what are most likely the later poems. They are rather the affected production of a young unbridled poet, full of the power of verse, flushed with the spirit of youth, and yet aping the very experienced man of the world. There is an air of bravado about them, and in spite of their frequent beauty they savour greatly of the *tour de force*. Rather more pleasing is the half-playful poem 'The Legacy'.

[He gives an account of the poem, quoting lines 1–6 and the last stanza.]

But there are many poems which do not owe their charm to playful ingenuity, poems which we believe show the true Donne better than the others. It would be easy to quote to the extreme limit of this paper, but we must be content with little more than the mention of such a characteristic poem as 'Love's Growth' (which may be ascribed to a date subsequent to Donne's marriage)–

[He quotes lines 1–6 and 15–20 of 'Love's Growth'.]

Or 'The Dream', with its musical opening –

> Dear love, for nothing less than thee
> Would I have broke this happy dream.

There is no juvenile flippancy here; nothing but rapture. So is it with 'The Canonization', with 'The Anniversary', 'The Ecstasy', and many more.

. . . with greater age and seriousness his poems became gradually less passionate, less emotional, more thoughtful, graver, more religious, until at last he began to regard with something like horror the lighter and more frivolous, though not more fantastic, outpourings of his youth. His 'Divine Poems' vary from what is perilously near doggerel to good examples of his second-best manner, but nowhere in them does he reach the pitch of some of his earlier work. His 'Hymn to God the Father', written in 1623 during a severe illness, is one of the best: it has more sense of form than many of them: it is short, and breathes sincerity. In most of his sacred poems, however, there is nothing good except the intention.

The want of the Art-Spirit, which is so conspicuous in his life, is perhaps one of the causes why his poems are so unequal and so full of irregularities and eccentricities and absurdities. Donne is not more remarkable for splendour of thought and imagery than for the inartistic lapses that disfigure many of his poems. Genius is there. The poet as creator, as thinker, is everywhere seen: not so often the poet as workman. In this respect he suggests a comparison with Browning. Both have been plentifully charged with obscurity and with artistic defects; and Browning, it is interesting to note, was clearly a student of the elder poet, for E. B. B. writing to R. B. quotes from 'The Dean', and calls him 'your Dr Donne'. Some of his poems are conspicuously beautiful and well wrought through-out; others, and these the majority, have their completeness spoilt by carelessness or wilful eccentricity. It is extraordinary that the man who could write such lines as –

> I long to talk with some old lover's ghost
> Who died before the God of Love was born,

could also send to Ben Jonson these verses –

> Poor I, whom every petty care doth trouble,
> And apprehend each hurt that's done me double,
> Am of this, though it should sink me, careless;
> It would but force me to a stricter goodness.

We may fancy the expression on Ben's face when he came to these last two lines. No wonder he told Drummond that Donne, 'for not keeping of accent, deserved hanging'.

Nor is it sufficient to ascribe these flagrant metrical defects to the well-abused printer. Coleridge distinguished between Donne's purely lyrical poems and poems not purely lyrical,

[He quotes Coleridge's marginal note on the relation of sense to metre in Donne.]

He referred to the song beginning –

> Sweetest Love, I do not go
> For weariness of thee,
> Nor in hopes the world can show
> A fitter love for me

as proof of his first contention (namely, that in songs Donne can be absolutely musical), and no one will venture to dispute with him on that point. His second contention is that with poems that are not lyrical it is necessary to read them through first to see what they mean, then afterwards, and only then, is it easy to read them metrically. This is as much as to say that such poems are only disguised prose, and for our own part we are willing to admit that such is sometimes the case.

Donne himself was not unconscious of his failing, for addressing I. W. – whom it is tempting but unsafe to identify with Izaak Walton – he says –

> Now, if this song be too harsh for rhyme, yet, as
> The painter's bad god made a good devil,
> 'Twill be good prose, although the verse be evil,
> If thou forget the rhyme as thou dost pass.

And true it is that not a few of his stanzas, especially in the epistles, would read better if read as prose. For example: –

> But, though she part us, to hear my oft prayers
> For your increase, God is as near me here;
> And to send you what I shall beg, His stairs
> In length and ease are alike everywhere.

The eighteenth century was disposed to regard these appalling infelicities as due to absolute ignorance of metrical laws on the part of the poet; it is safer to believe that Donne knew his prosody as well as anyone else, that his peculiarities are due in a large measure to design, and that he was an intentional innovator upon the smoothness of some of the writers of his time, though his iconoclastic impulse often led him wofully astray. But we are inclined to think that some of his worst offences are due, not so much to his reforming zeal as to the want of that Art-Spirit which should animate every worker in every art, and to the half-contemptuous carelessness which the absence of that Spirit produced. No one with a true sense of art would have left work so absolutely unlovely, so deficient in all beauty of form or colour, side by side with productions of genuine inspiration.

What loss has been ours by Donne's prosodical experiments and negligence, those know best who have most knowledge of the poet. At his best his phrases are unsurpassed, and though it is rather unfair to judge a writer by his best lines and grudge when any fall below that standard, yet against the poet who, in an oft-quoted line, could picture the reopening of his grave, and the discovery, with his skeleton, of the lock of his lady's hair which he had had buried wtih him –

> A bracelet of bright hair about the bone –

against the poet of the beautifully simple phrase –

> I wonder, by my troth, what thou and I
> Did till we loved –

against the poet whose words have so often an indefinable magic we cannot but nourish a feeling of resentment that he should ever fall from pure unalloyed beauty of thought and word to the obscure and crabbed depths to which his carelessness or his innovations led him.

Even Donne's lyrics are full of thought. His difficulty in writing was not to spin out a slender fancy to the requisite number of lines, but (task harder, but how much more enviable!) to crush into poetic form the ideas and the emotions that thronged for utterance. In the lighter poems this is noticeable, and his skill is often unable or unwilling to take the trouble to subdue his materials to artistic repose; in poems avowedly addressed to the intellect, the defect is striking, deterrent, sometimes grotesque, as in the extraordinary unfinished 'Progress of the Soul', and in the 'Anatomy of the World' – poems whose history and contents deserve more attention than we have space to give them. This constant rush of fancies and arguments, combined with an imperfect artistic equipment, makes even the best poems unequal, and the verbal inspiration that coins a perfect phrase is rarely maintained for many consecutive lines. As an example of his lyrical poems we may quote 'Lovers' Infiniteness', which, though it does not contain any of his best-known lines, is fairly equal throughout.

[He gives the whole of the poem.]

The dainty argument running all through this love-poem is very characteristic of Donne. There is quite as much argument in it as

195

the verse will carry, indeed the second verse is inclined to be suggestive of Coleridge's phrase about iron pokers and true-love knots, but the whole poem is well wrought, and expresses a very definite and subtle mood of the poet. It has, moreover, this merit, that a second and third reading will disclose only new excellencies.

The same wealth of thought, and the same want of power properly to arrange and marshal and clothe and present it artistically, are the causes of Donne's much-talked-of obscurity. It is not the obscurity of meaninglessness, but of too much meaning. He is obscure as Browning is obscure, with an opacity not absolutely impenetrable, but none the less daunting. And as if his natural tendency were not sufficient, he must needs stuff out his vocabulary with the scientific phraseology of his day, a day whose science is as dead as the terms it employed. This may have gained him applause in his own time on account of a certain vividness gained, but the habit of using technical terms in poetry is a dangerous one. . . .

That it is not this technical habit only which obscures Donne from the modern reader is emphasised by the statement of a far-sighted contemporary critic – that Donne 'for not being understood would perish'. Drummond was very likely surprised when Jonson confided this opinion to him, especially as at another time he declared Donne to be 'the first poet in the world in some things', but the two dicta are not incompatible. 'In some things', is a considerable qualification; there are several poets who might be said to be first in some things. But if Ben praised a little too generously, his prophecy of death erred on the side of severity. Donne has not perished yet, nor will perish. Yet will he be remembered rather for the unfathered and despised productions of the youthful Templar, than for the more dignified and learned efforts of the courtier or the dean; while the surprising influence he exercised on other poets – an influence which was chiefly based on his defects – we must now admit to have been an influence for evil rather than for good.

Donne's failings can always be studied in Dr Johnson's 'Life of Cowley', where he falls heavily on those poets who 'endeavoured to be singular in their thoughts and were careless of their diction', and whose 'wish was only to say what they hoped had been never said before'. The words that Landor in 'Pericles and Aspasia' uses concerning certain Greek poets, might almost be applied to these writers. Cleone writes to Aspasia: 'We really have at present in our city more good poets than we ever had; and the *queer* might be among the best if they pleased. But whenever an obvious or natural thought presents itself they either reject it for coming without imagination, or they Phrygianize it with such biting and hot curling irons, that it rolls itself up impenetrably.' But here is no occasion to trace the evil influence of Donne, rather to be thankful for the good that remains.

Undoubtedly Donne's was an essentially complex character, and consequently not one easy to catalogue or describe. He possessed most but not all of the attributes of what is inadequately described as the poetic temperament. Proud, self-conscious, sensitive, imaginative, reserved, passionate, melancholy – he was all this and more. He alternated between joy and dejection, between happiness and gloom. As we say, he was either up or down in his mood. His melancholy was not morose or bitter, but 'dwelt with beauty, beauty that must die'; and the lifted cloud made his company, as Walton informs us, one of the delights of mankind. He was a man not of many friends, but of strong friendships. With Ben Jonson he would say –

> True happiness
> Consists not in the multitude of friends
> But in the worth and choice.

There were few to whom he could open his heart, but, as is often the case with such temperaments, his friends were for life. His pride and his fastidiousness kept him from indiscriminate cordiality. He was none of your boon companions, none of your facile men who shine in casual intercourse (fortunate gift!), but among his intimates he was the best of company. 'I can allow myself', he writes in one of his letters, 'to be *animal sociale*, appliable to my company, but not *gregale*, to herd myself in every troop.'

Between Herrick and Donne a not uninteresting comparison might be made. Both are best known, and rightly so, by their amatory and lyrical poetry; both had a keen delight in beauty and its appeal to the senses. Both took orders late in life. Ben Jonson is the only poet Donne condescends to notice, and Herrick was proud to call himself a son of Ben, yet barely mentions any other contemporary writer. Both wrote a considerable quantity of religious poetry, though Donne never equals Herrick's best; both in their widely separated parsonages were true and pious clergymen.

Donne was incomparably deeper than Herrick, infinitely more learned, was undoubtedly the greater mind: Herrick was the more tuneful. Donne has occasional flashes of poetry of the first order; but his note is not sustained. On a much finer instrument he played fewer melodies. He has momentary bursts of the most suggestive music, but the harmonies are too often lost in obscurities and quaintnesses, and carelessness or eccentricity of execution. If Donne was the greater genius, Herrick was undeniably the better artist. The phrase recalls Donne's great defect as poet. Herrick gave his life to his book and is having his reward. Donne despised, or affected to despise, his own art. He had all the qualities that go to make a great poet – except one.

51. J. W. Chadwick

1900

Chadwick gave his own account of Donne in the course of reviewing together Gosse's *Life and Letters of John Donne*, and the editions of Donne's poems by C. E. Norton and E. K. Chambers. ('John Donne, Poet and Preacher', *New World*, 9 (1900), 33–48).

As for his poetry, if Donne has admirers who, like Browning's make virtues of his worst defects, they will not be satisfied with Mr Gosse's criticism. This, while it does not fail in appreciation of Donne's occasional music, the beauty and the splendor of certain lines and phrases, his intellectual vigor and abundance, and the penetrating spiritual suggestion of some parts in contrast with the daring sensuousness and sensuality of others, is, nevertheless, severe upon the roughness of his metre, the extravagance and absurdity of his conceits, the gross exaggerations whereby he aimed at the sublime and fell miserably short, and the misplaced and sickening adulation which he lavished on unworthy men and women who had done nothing that deserved such monstrous praise. At the same time certain of Donne's faults in poetry are explained in a satisfactory manner, and even for his faults of character there is pleaded in extenuation that they were such as were so common in Donne's England, that to judge him by our modern standards would be most unfair.

[He follows out Gosse's observation that Donne never shows any knowledge of Shakespeare's writing.]

This silence is significant of the impassable gulf between their poetical ideals. That Donne could be so undramatic in a period of intense dramatic realization, that he could be so rough in a period of 'sugared sonnets' and mellifluous verse, is eloquent of his stiff-necked individuality, and affords an interesting comment on Taine's method of explaining a man by his environment. If there were standards that he respected, they were not those of his own England, but those of Italy and Spain, – preëminently of Spain.

[He reviews Donne's early writings.]

Nothing could be more unlike the characteristic Elizabethan verse than the 'Satires'. The impulse to satiric writing seems to have come from certain lectures of Casaubon upon Persius, the Latin satirist. Heretofore there had been few attempts to naturalize in England the biting invective of the Latin satire, but from 1593 to 1599 there was quite a vigorous outburst in this kind, Donne's contribution being more than all the rest. It was of the essence of his opinion that satire should be not only full of 'inbred bitterness and tartness of particulars', but also 'hard of conceit and harsh of style', and in practice he made good his theory. His fourth satire afforded ample illustration of that stupendous learning which was the wonder of his time, and may well be of ours, with its 'resultance of 1400 authors, most of them abridged and analyzed with his own hand', but the third satire, with less learning, had more of Donne's 'strange fire'. Its subject was the extravagance and hypocrisy of the formally religious. Here will be found some of those things which have attracted quite as many to Donne's poetry as its riot of the senses and its sexual daring, as of a Whitman born in Shakespeare's time.

[He quotes lines 72–9 of *Satire* 3.]

In the same satire we have one of those splendid figures which illuminate the tortuous darkness of Donne's most serious and difficult verse.

[He quotes lines 79–84, 'On a huge hill . . .'.]

Certainly the metre does not necessitate the proper reading in such lines as these, and if Donne, knowing what he meant, and preferring quantity to accent, could read them musically, the secret of his art is hidden from us, and Mr Gosse has done little to make it opener than it has been heretofore. But, as in Emerson, there are passages of perfect music to make us wonder that he could ever be willingly so harsh. And, as in Emerson, we frequently condone the metrical offense through gratitude for the informing thought.

Donne, like Shakspere, was attached to the fortunes of the Earl of Essex, but more closely, sailing with him on the brilliant Cadiz expedition of 1596 and the next year on the ill-fated voyage to the Azores. Two remarkable poems, 'The Storm' and 'The Calm', came of this experience. The manner harks back to the Satires, and some of the conceits are as fanciful and as abominable as Donne's ingenuity devised at any time. Here as elsewhere Donne presents the contradiction of realism and romanticism, each running wild. We find the romanticism in the extravagant hyperbole, the realism in the abandoning of classical imagery and the adoption of the homeliest and most trenchant possible, as where, –

> From our tattered sails, rags drop down so
> As from one hanged in chains a year ago.

[He speaks generally of Donne's life and writings from 1592 to 1602.]

Corresponding to this period of wild excess we have reports of Donne's studies in law and medicine, and his hunger for encyclopaedic knowledge, yet to this period belong those 'Songs' and 'Elegies' in which his secular genius reached a high, if not its highest, mark. The arbiters of taste were as indifferent to him as he to them. His poems were widely circulated among his friends, but none of them found its way into 'England's Helicon' or any other contemporary anthology. It is a nice business to set his lyrics and amatory elegies in order and relate them to the successive stages of his experience, but Mr Gosse enters on it bravely, pursues it cautiously, and works out a system far more rational than the manner in which they have heretofore been jumbled together. In such poems as 'Woman's Constancy', 'Love's Usury', 'The Good Morrow', 'The Sun Rising', he finds Donne most interesting when most frankly sensual. He becomes yet more so when he calls his wandering fancies home, and concentrates on one foolish woman, a grand passion rescuing him from heartless promiscuity. 'His ethical ambition had risen a grade, from the pursuit of woman as a species to the selection of one who should present herself to his imagination as a symbol of the Feminine.' Hence some of the most sensual poetry written by any English poet of eminence. The stages of this miserable liaison can be traced by poem after poem through all their melancholy course from ardor to disgust and weariness. To the last stage belong 'The Curse', 'The Message', 'Love's Deity', 'The Prohibition', 'The Funeral'. 'There are no hate-poems in the language finer of their kind, filled with a stronger wind of vindictive passion, than those which now close this incident.' The series from beginning to end is such an amplification of Shakspere's One Hundred and Twenty-ninth Sonnet as literature does not afford elsewhere.

These poems and others of their period and their sensual inclination remained unprinted until 1633, two years after Donne's death; strangely enough we find him contemplating their publication after his determination to take holy orders and before entering upon priestly functions. It was as if he meant to purify himself by public confession and so wash his hands of them. But in fact he had a great affection for these naughty children of his early Muse. He could not find it in his heart to lay violent hands upon them, even when he had become the conscious saint as the great preacher of St Paul's. Mingled with them – no editor having yet attempted to make his ideal arrangement of the poems practical – are others that reflect an honest passion for the girl who in 1601 became Donne's wife by a clandestine marriage.

[He describes the consequences of the marriage.]

The bitter root of Donne's misery in 1602 bore that inestimable flower, 'The Canonization', with its justification of the sonnet anticipating Wordsworth's 'Nuns fret not' some two hundred years.

[He quotes lines 28–36.]

We are not permitted to doubt that 'Love's Growth' is a sincere report of Donne's increasing love for his poor wife from year to year, or that the quaint 'Valediction forbidding Mourning' is another. It is a pretty story that once, when he was going to the continent, she fain would go with him, disguised as a page. We have an elegy dissuading her, which contains some of those lines which reward us for much toiling through immeasurable sand. All will spy in her face

> A blushing womanly discovering grace.

She will suffer much from the French chameleons, the indifferent Italians and the 'spongy hydroptic Dutch'. Therefore,

> O stay here, for to thee
> England is only a worthy gallery
> To walk in expectation, till from thence
> Our greatest King call thee to his presénce.

It was during Donne's courtship at York House that he wrote that most fantastical of all his poems, 'The Progress of the Soul'. Mr Gosse elucidates it with all possible devotion, but is obliged to confess that the solitary uncompromising admiration of De Quincey is as much as it deserves. . . . Its resistance to the Spenserian glow and amenity is one of its noticeable traits. . . . The Iliad would have been, for length, a sonnet in comparison, had Donne carried out his plan.

[He surveys Donne's 'earlier' *Divine Poems*.]

'A Litany' is the most important. Its dull stream drags along a good deal of soil from Donne's inherited belief. The worship of the Virgin never lost its hold on his imagination and his heart.

> As her deeds were
> Our helps, so are her prayers; nor can she sue
> In vain, who hath such titles unto you.

With rare exceptions, these earlier 'Divine Poems' impress us as exercises in pious ingenuity, rather than as the spontaneous expressions of a religious soul. They read as if Donne were trying to work himself into a frame of mind that would justify him in taking a religious office. Nowhere do we find more of that execrable taste which disfigured some of his most beautiful and noble verse. Mr

Gosse's example from 'The Resurrection' is as good as any. The subject is Christ's three days' burial: –

> Whose body, having walk'd on earth, and now
> Hasting to heaven, would – that He might allow
> Himself unto all stations and fill all –
> For those three days become a mineral.
> He was all gold when He lay down, but rose
> All tincture, and doth not alone dispose
> Leaden and iron wills to good, but is
> Of power to make e'en sinful flesh like His.

It is quite posible that Donne would have found his way into the church a few years before 1615 if one of his most daring ventures in the art of flattery had not relieved the stress of his necessities. This was an elegy on Miss Elizabeth Drury, who died in 1610 in her fifteenth year. It was so extravagant that it seemed impossible for anything to be more so, but those who thought it so did not understand how hyperbolical and tasteless Donne could be. For the elegy he got from the fond father, one of the richest men in England, as Donne knew well enough, apartments rent free at Drury House in Drury Lane and much additional for his personal comfort and the encouragement of his studies. Grateful for these favors, Donne wrote 'An Anatomy of the World' for the first anniversary of Miss Drury's death, and for the second 'Of the Progress of the Soul', another long poem, but not to be confounded with 'The Progress of the Soul', already named and known. Flattery so gross was too much for the stomach of a time hard to nauseate, Ben Jonson telling Donne that 'if he had written it of the Virgin Mary it had been something'. The poor little lady was apostrophized as so precious that the earth could 'have better spared the Sun or Man'. Yet, for all the hyperbole and curious infelicity, there is quintessential poetry in these elaborate bids for princely patronage. Mr Gosse disdains to mention the best known: –

> Her pure and eloquent blood
> Spoke in her cheeks and so distinctly wrought
> That one might almost say her body thought.

Mr Saintsbury finds in the second of the following two the finest line in English sacred poetry: –

> These hymns thy issue may increase so long
> As till God's great *Venite* change the song.

Could Donne's awful threat of writing a new elegy on each successive anniversary have been realized, the dust heap would have been worth searching for such gems as these. How daintily this ponderous elephant could dance is shown by the 'Song' he wrote when he was going over to Paris in 1612.

[He deprecates Donne's flattery of his patrons, as in the poem for the scandalous marriage of the earl of Somerset to the countess of Essex in December 1613.]

He set about to write an epithalamium for the 'blest pair of swans' while the woman's divorce had not yet been decreed. And still his condition was that of the countryman who mistook some lesser light for Whitefield, and 'rolled himself in the dirt for nothing'. The death of Prince Henry evoked from him an elegy which would have been better than it was if his conscious sycophancy had not chilled the genial current of his proper admiration. He did better when writing an epithalamium for the Princess Elizabeth, with whom his relations were always those of mutual and sincere regard. It is one of the most spontaneous of Donne's products in this kind, and I am sorry for those persons whose prurient prudishness forbids them to enjoy its frank sincerity. They should go join them to some sect which is contemptuous of the body as a mere clog upon the spirit's unshared solipotence.

[He compares Donne's writing after his ordination (as he supposes) with the earlier work.]

. . . certainly the sermons and the prayers of 1617 and after, also the 'Holy Sonnets', import a different temper than he had manifested heretofore. The sonnets of this time are very different from the hard and gritty 'Divine Poems' of an earlier date; they are touched with emotion, and give an impression of profound reality. The first of all strikes the high note which is sustained throughout. We do not entirely escape the extravagant conceits which to the last were his besetting sin, but they are less conspicuous than formerly, and Donne is less the conscious rebel that he was against melodious verse. In one of these sonnets there is a stately music as if Milton were being heralded: –

[He gives the whole of *Holy Sonnet* 7 'At the Round Earth's Imagined Corners', then quotes stanzas 1 and 2 of 'A Hymn to God the Father', commenting that they have 'an inherent music which is sufficiently impressive.]

There is another stanza, but it does not keep the level of these two. A more dreadful falling-off is that of 'A Hymn to God, My God, in My Sickness', that sickness which was his last. It begins most perfectly.

[He quotes stanza 1.]

Having begun so well, it falls away into a geographical fancy that is singularly devoid of beauty though compact of vigorous imagination.

[Such a conceit reminds him of the effigy of Donne in his winding-sheet.]

It was rescued at the time of the great fire, the final proof of that intolerably bad taste which Donne shared with many Jacobeans, but which few illustrated so painfully as he.

[Then he sums up Donne's character and writing.]

His intellectual vigor was immense. For much of his obscurity we are asked to find an explanation in his endeavor to dispense with threadbare material and use such as was new. . . .

Donne's life was stranger than his verse, and the wonder is that Robert Browning, with whom Donne's modern praise began, did not find in the vicissitudes of his career more than one subject made to his hand. That 'wholeness of tissue' which Matthew Arnold missed in Emerson, is missing almost everywhere in Donne. Nevertheless, and though frequently as unsavory as he is crabbed and obscure, there are embedded in his poems passages and sentences, and phrases of such wondrous beauty and imperishable significance that those who love best the best things in poetry will oftenest return to him, and these will gratefully appreciate what Mr Gosse has done to make more plain the quality of Donne's genius and the course of his astonishing career.

52. Anon., *Quarterly Review*

1900

An anonymous reviewer of Gosse's *Life and Letters of John Donne* and Jessopp's *John Donne* sought to assess Donne's style and influence by demonstrating the intellectual degeneracy of the age ('John Donne and his Contemporaries', *Quarterly Review,* 192 (1900), 220–35).

[The reviewer does not take a high view of Donne and his contemporaries and followers.]

We have here to deal with poets whose station as poets is not of the first rank, who had perhaps not a great deal to say, but who said it exquisitely. We do not like their manner? Then we had better not read them; but if we do, we shall be well advised in accepting their manner, and not wishing that they had written differently. How bad their exquisiteness could be is easily seen. Take such lines as these, describing a pair of weeping eyes: –

> Two walking baths, two weeping motions;
> Portable and compendious oceans.

Or George Herbert's –

> Sweet rose, whose hue, angry and brave,
> Bids the rash gazer wipe his eye;
> Thy root is ever in its grave,
>   And thou must die.

Or Donne's –

> For when through tasteless flat humidity
> In dough-baked men some harmlessness we see,
> 'Tis but his phlegm that's virtuous, and not he.

Or Carew's –

> Ask me no more whither do stray
> The golden atoms of the day,
> For in pure love, Heav'n did prepare
> Those powders to enrich your hair.

206

What can be worse than the last two lines? – and in such a lovely poem, too.

A conceit, it would seem, is its own justification. Whether proper to the subject or not, a chance resemblance, a contrast or a paradox, has no sooner occurred to the subtle mind of the author than it demands to be enshrined in verse. Taste, when tortured in this way, cries outrage; and a later and calmer age refuses consent. But this exquisiteness has its reward in many a sparkling epigram and tender madrigal. Diamonds and pearls make up for toads and snakes. 'Thus it should have been said, and no otherwise', we cry when we read: –

> Some asked me where the rubies grew;
> And nothing did I say,
> But with my finger pointed to
> The lips of Julia.
> Some asked me how pearls did grow, and where?
> Then spoke I to my girl
> To part her lips, and shew them there
> The quarrelets of pearl.

Yet Hazlitt called this poem a 'petrifaction both of love and poetry'.

The merits of the Jacobean style are nicety of thought, clearness and conciseness of diction, apt illustration, the just use of conceits, learned allusions not too far-fetched, whether images or verbal felicities, 'jewels five words long', lines and short passages which could not be bettered. The faults of the style are obvious; and the most serious of them is an affectation which runs into insincerity. The thought is often subordinate to the manner; and, when too much attention is given to manner and expression, prettiness takes the place of solidity.

But the Jacobean writers do not fully enter into the succession of poets. They lie in a quiet back-water out of the main river, receiving and retaining its water, but not setting the current.

[He agrees with Gosse that a malign influence changed the direction of English literature for a time in the seventeenth century, but questions whether Donne was responsible for the change.]

It was 'malign' because Euphuism and its Jacobean development brought in the exaggerated pursuit of words, phrases, and conceits beyond their true value, established a new and affected criterion of

207

taste, and in general displayed a preference of matter to manner. 'Great thoughts', says Johnson, 'are always general.' It was the fault of the Euphuistic or, as Johnson styles it, the 'metaphysical' school that it is always occupied with particulars. The poets of this school left the great general thoughts to the Elizabethans. They had had enough of them, and wanted something new – sauces, not meats, they might have said; but human nature goes back with relish to the meats.

Towards the end of the sixteenth century a double influence is observable in European literature. Pedantry was taking the place of learning. The fresh springs of the Renaissance movement had dried up. The soil of ancient Rome had yielded its first crop of statues: Greek manuscripts were no longer to be found in the libraries of East or West. The living world had learnt as much as it wanted to know about the ancients, and left the study of antiquity to the dead world of pedants, those who think knowledge to be the end of knowledge. The scholars now became a class apart from the dilettante circles; from Bembo to Casaubon is as great a social decline as it is an ascent in learning; and where there was one Casaubon there were a hundred professional scholars, doing good and useful work, but work rather scientific than literary – slaves of the lamp of truth, not servants of beauty. The active and speculative intellect of the world took a new line of enquiry, which was marked out by the triumphs of Galileo, Bacon, and Harvey. Speculative philosophy and astronomical and anatomical discovery now held the field, and experimental science impugned authority. The tendency of the age was to investigate rarities and novelties in a scientific spirit; and this habit found its way into literature. Authority, however, had not said its last word, either in theology or in science: the scholastic method was dying, not dead. Real scientific enquiry was strangely mixed up with the study of the Cabbalists, the Schoolmen, Aristotle, Pliny, and Galen – authority and experiment forced into harmony. Occult speculations were confounded with observation of realities: nothing was improbable if it fitted in with a paradox or a parallel. Analogy was now pushed to its extreme; a mystical sense was perceived in natural phenomena; it became the fashion to seek out resemblances and to argue from them. In particular, anatomical facts and theories were adduced as analogies and made the groundwork of argument. The attention of writers was withdrawn from the contemplation of beauty, and diverted to the novelties of science, from large conceptions of nature to minute observations of detail.

This was in itself a declension from the proper objects of poetry; and along with it came in one of the common characteristics of a decadence, an exaggerated attention to form and diction, and the sentimentality which naturally accompanies the search for novelty. The great writers have always been artists in words, and have never thought lightly of the technique of their business; but it is one of the surest signs of a decadence to set the word above the thing signified, and to heighten effect by strangeness. . . .

Imitation – and not of the best authors – was another characteristic of this age. The moderns copied from each other, and the Latin which they all admired and imitated was that of Petronius and Apuleius, not the Ciceronian. There is no fault to be found with Barclay's 'Argenis' and 'Euphormio' in point of Latinity; his popularity is witnessed by edition after edition from the Elzevir press; but what we look for in an author is something from himself, and here is nothing but an echo. Another characteristic was parade of learning.

In the reign of James I to be learned was the first thing; to be original without reflection of antiquity was out of taste. It is impossible to say who set the fashion: it was in the air. It has been attributed to Góngora and the Gongorists, Marini and the Marinists, Ronsard and the Pleiad, Du Bartas, Lyly; but Hallam's characterisation of it as 'an unintelligible refinement, which every nation in Europe seems in succession to have admitted into its poetry', may serve both as a description of the phenomenon and as a note of its date, though not of its cause. The vice which corrupted the literature of this age is, in a word, pedantry, literary, classical, and scientific: the dragging of incongruous qualities and mannerisms into the service of poetry. The pedantry of conceits affected even the great Elizabethan poets, but it was not raised into a principal merit till the latter years of the reign. England was always backward in the race: France, Italy, and Spain were far gone in pedantry before the reign of conceits began in England. Elizabeth's personal influence was not without effect in setting the fashion; her own style – always affected – became later more involved and Euphuistic; and the court language, following the fashion, blossomed into conceits richer and rarer, from the sobriety of Burleigh's times to the

exuberance of Speaker Phelips under James I, who was himself one
of the most tedious of Euphuists.

Mr Gosse sets down the 'malign' influence of the new fashion
almost entirely to Donne. We should rather have said that Donne
followed the fashion already introduced, and gave it the weight of
his authority. So great a change is rarely brought about by one
writer, especially a writer whose works became known to his
contemporaries chiefly as manuscripts passed from hand to hand
around a circle of friends. Shakespeare shows how genius can turn
the current style to its own uses; Donne, with all his gravity,
learning, and passion, imagines nothing beyond the current style.
Shakespeare wrote many lines which Donne might have written,
and now and then Donne writes like Shakespeare himself. For
instance, in the well-known lines –

> her pure and eloquent blood
> Spoke in her cheeks, and so distinctly wrought,
> That one might almost say, her body thought –

he uses the symbolical method in perfection, and enriches a true
thought by a beautiful image. Donne's influence no doubt was
great; that it was not irresistible we may conclude from the fact that
when he set himself to break up smooth versification by new rules
of accent, and to depart from the natural iambic of his predecessors, he was not able to effect a revolution; nor was he
successful in using the instrument which he had invented.

Other poets of his day, and Shakespeare among them, adopted
the suggestion, and Milton's versification owes much to the boldness with which he trusted to balance and weight of syllables rather
than to the orderly sequence of accents. But the next generation
returned to smoothness, and Donne's experiment was not developed so as to become the character of a school. Donne founded
no school; he did not invent conceits; he did not establish a new
school of versification. He remains alone; a writer of originality, not
the pioneer of poets to be.

If it is true that Donne, as Mr Gosse thinks, felt no admiration or
even curiosity in the presence of his great contemporaries, so much
the worse for Donne. We will not do his memory the injustice to
believe that he had no ears for Spenser and Shakespeare. We can
see nothing in his poetry to justify Mr Gosse's theory that Donne,
'as a metrical iconoclast, would have neither part nor lot' with the

old Elizabethan school of Petrarchical poets. The liberties which Donne took with the English language and traditional prosody occur, for the most part, in the satires, in which he was imitating the roughness of the Latin satirists; and, as Mr Gosse allows, this 'experiment' was dropped by Donne after middle life. It was an experiment; it was not copied by his admirers; perhaps we should never have heard of it if Milton had not admitted something of Donne's principles of rhythm into the structure of his unmatched blank verse, stateliest of all measures next to Virgil's.

As for Donne's use of metaphors, the realism which made him (as Mr Gosse says) 'draw his illustrations, not from asphodel or from the moon', like the Petrarchists, 'but from the humdrum professional employments of his own age, from chemistry, medicine, law, mechanics, astrology, religious ritual, daily human business of every sort', in this again Donne was not original. He did but use the style of his time, a time which liked parade of learning. It is all in Burton (who was senior to Donne), in ceremonial and Parliamentary speeches, in the diaries of Sir Symonds d'Ewes, and in pamphlets, letters, and sermons by the dozen. It was neither invented nor brought into currency by Donne or any other single authority. It is the later Euphuism; the Euphuism not of Euphues, but of the Piercie Shaftons and Armados who buzzed round the king of pedants, the English Solomon himself.

The 'metaphysical poets' have never been so finely criticised as by Johnson, who invented the phrase; not a very happy phrase, perhaps, for their skill lay rather in exciting wonder than in stimulating or expressing thought. Any of our readers who will take the trouble to turn to the 'Lives of the Poets' will find in the biography of Cowley all that can be said on the subject.

[He cites Johnson's account of wit as a *discordia concors*.]

The vices of the school are oppressive learning, excessive particularity, and the combination of incongruous ideas by false analogy. Now and then they flash out a ray of splendid wit. Such lines as those of Donne on the 'twin compasses' cannot be surpassed; it would be hard if the labour of much rocking never brought to light a nugget of pure gold. The workmanship, if always laboured, is often successful; 'limæ labor et mora' deserves and sometimes receives its reward; and no poets have ever filed more industriously than these. It is a literature of art and erudition, not of nature: natural graces may be found there, because nature will out; but the poet values tricks of art more than the thoughts which his art expresses. Jacobean poetry in this resembles Provençal poetry, though, unlike that, it does not care for smoothness and perfection; it should have studied perfection of form, not only neatness of wit. The Jacobean poets might have learnt of Martial, who combined the perfection of wit with elegiac sweetness equal if not superior to the versification of Ovid himself. Martial among the ancients and La Fontaine among the moderns possess the secret beyond all others. . . .

Like the Jacobean architecture, Jacobean literature charms by delicacy and originality of detail, but cannot rise to large conceptions. A Jacobean monument, a row of cathedral stalls, such a gem as the Gate of Honour at Cambridge, is delightful in its small way, but ineffective if compared with a Palladian building or a church designed by Michael Angelo or Sansovino. A lengthy poem like Donne's 'Progress of the Soul' is unreadable; but little poems such as Carew's 'Boldness of Love' are perfection itself. Perhaps Donne never achieved a higher flight of poetry than in his 'Testament'. It is as good as that grand poem 'The Lye', which has claimed as many authors as Homer had birthplaces. It is dignified, bitter, almost sublime, and yet witty too. When we read this, we understand how Carew could say of him –

> Here lies a King, that ruled as he thought fit
> The universal Monarchy of wit.

When we remember that Shakespeare was living at the same time, how slight appears the account of contemporary fame!

The personality of Donne is quite as interesting as his literary position.

By his position, his character, and his peculiar genius Donne whilst living occupied a larger place among men of letters than later times have given him. Mr Gosse labours to restore this place to him but the verdict is given, and will hardly be reversed on appeal. . . .

Donne will be studied by a few, and remain an interesting figure to many who do not study him; but for our pleasure we shall read Herrick.

We have given most of the space at our disposal to Donne, partly because Mr Gosse's estimate of him appears to us somewhat overstrained, and his critical judgment biassed by the strong personal interest which is inseparable from the study of so original a character; and also because in him subtlety of thought, wit, learning, and piety are combined with fertility of expression in a rare degree. But what we demand from a poet is poetry, and here Donne, in our opinion, comes short of Herrick on one side and George Herbert on the other. After all, he was more a rhetorician than a poet. He could no more have imagined 'Corinna's Maying', 'Cherry Ripe', and a dozen more of Herrick's felicities, than he could have written Herbert's sonnet: –

[He quotes Herbert's *Prayer* (*i*).]

Here are conceits enough, and some roughnesses. One may perhaps trace the influence of Donne, but the thought, not the expression, is what attracts; and Herbert's poems, however they may bend to the popular demand for quaintness and learning, have a spontaneity which is not found in Donne.

53. Clarence Griffin Child

1900

Clarence Child (1864–1948) of the University of Pennsylvania published a number of editions and studies of Old English literature, and the syllabus of a course of six lectures on seventeenth-century works. Reviewing C. B. Furst's *A Group of Old Authors*, he applauded Furst's discretion in his treatment of Donne's character ('A Group of Old Authors', *Modern Language Notes*, 15 (1900), 61–3).

[Child points out that we miss in Furst's account of Donne 'those picturesque details with regard to Donne's personal peculiarities, which make so much of one's impression of him as derived from Walton's inimitable biography'. But he agrees that an undue concern with some aspects of Donne's life and character may hinder an appreciation of the true qualities of his verse.]

It is wise to make little of these, perhaps, for they might serve only to accentuate that first (and erroneous) impression the reader is apt to receive from his verse, that it is curiously bizarre, eccentric, and obscure, and that only. It is much better, no doubt, to emphasize, as Mr Furst does, the sterling traits of Donne's character and the real virtues of his verse, – its depth of thought, sincerity, emotional intensity, and its noble, though broken and irregular, music.

54. Thomas Hardy

1900

Hardy had evidently read Donne attentively, for he gave line 44 of *Elegy* 12, 'His Parting From Her', as the ironic epigraph to a section in a short story. ('Enter A Dragoon', *Harper's Monthly Magazine*, December 1900, p. 29a).

Section III has as epigraph: 'Yet went we not still on in constancy?'

55. Anon., *Chambers' Cyclopaedia of English Literature*

1901

Donne was allowed some three and a half double-column pages in an encyclopaedia of English literature, as part of a series of essays on sixteenth- and seventeenth-century poets. The preface to the volume ascribes to Edmund Gosse the revision of the articles on Jonson, Donne and Wither from an earlier edition of the work. ('John Donne', newly ed. David

Patrick, 1901, *Chambers' Cyclopaedia of English Literature*, vol. I, pp. 413b–417a).

[The writer deferentially follows Gosse's reading of Donne's poems and many of Gosse's judgements. He offers a scatter of critical comments, and observations on Donne's influence and reputation.

He finds that many of Donne's early poems 'are outspokenly sensual and at times cruelly cynical'. We are told that there are three anniversary poems for Elizabeth Drury, 'all containing beautiful and even splendid passages, but marred by overmultiplied and overstrained conceits and utterly preposterous hyperboles'. Donne consciously revolted against the manners of the earlier and contemporary Elizabethans, 'their mellifluous monotones, their pseudo-classical nomenclature, their pastoral and other conventions'. He deliberately adopted a 'hard and crabbed style'; and he stands curiously apart from 'the master influences in poetry at home', being 'markedly influenced by Spanish literature' yet remaining 'original to a fault'.]

In virtue of his studied carelessness, his avoidance of smoothness of form, his pedantry, his infectious harshness, the 'foremost of the metaphysical poets' opens a new era, if he does not found a school.

[Even in private circulation his poems 'had a great vogue, and powerful – evidently too powerful – influence on the next generation, who could more easily imitate his eccentricities than rival his soaring flights and exquisite beauties'. The long lapse of esteem for Donne's verse was repaired by Browning.]

Now it is agreed that, amidst roughness and obscurity, far-fetched allusions, contorted imagery and allegory, and unrhythmical wit, Donne often presents us with poetry of a high order, in expression as in thought.

[The writer attempts a general characterization of Donne as a metaphysical poet.]

His swift transitions from voluptuous ecstasies to meditation on the mystery of life and death, and his profound but at times not a little fantastic speculations, no doubt contributed to securing for Donne the epithet – seldom precisely used – of 'metaphysical'. His intellect was active and keen, his fancy vivid and picturesque, his wit playful and yet caustic. His too great terseness and prodigality of ideas breeds obscurity; the uneven and crabbed versification, with superfluous syllables to be slurred over, and accents that must be thrown on the wrong syllables – however much a part of his conscious design – is puzzling; you have to understand the poem before you can scan his verse. The conceits are often not merely striking but suggestive and beautiful, lightly and gracefully handled. . . . On the other hand Donne constantly piles up Ossas upon Pelions of metaphors, prefers such as are puerile or grotesque – defying the good taste of his own time as well as ours – and overelaborates them to wearisomeness. Thus treating of a broken heart, he runs off into a play on the expression 'broken heart'. . . . Then insisting on the idea of a heart broken to pieces, he goes on to exhaust the conceit and make it tedious.

[A scatter of supposedly confirmatory quotations follows from the *Songs and Sonnets, Epithalamions* and *Satires,* and from the *Metempsychosis.*

The account of Donne's writing also takes in some of the polemical prose and the sermons, which are represented by a passage from 'the second of Donne's five "Prebend Sermons", preached at St Paul's in 1625'. The writer calls this sermon 'a long poem of victory over death . . . one of the most magnificent pieces of religious writing in English literature', and considers that it 'closes with a majestic sentence of incomparable pomp and melody'. He adds a note on the merits of the successive editions of Donne's poems down to that of E. K. Chambers, and on the lives of Donne from Walton's *Life* on.]

56. Anon., *Quarterly Review*

1902

An anonymous expositor of the Elizabethan lyric brought in Donne and Jonson as poets who rejected the manners of their predecessors ('The Elizabethan Lyric', *Quarterly Review*, 196 (1902), 460–1).

Of Ben Jonson and of Donne it may seem unpardonable not to have spoken earlier in any account of the Elizabethan lyrical poets, but the fact is that both Donne and Jonson fall outside the true Elizabethan tradition. Both were rebels as much against the pastoral vogue, with its smooth, long-winded Italian stanzas, as against the supposed artlessness of the Shakespearian song; and they sought their effects, the one by a Horatian brevity and choiceness of phrase, the other in the utmost realism of poetic imagery. . . .

Donne is represented in Davison's 'Poetical Rhapsody' by a single poem, that by which he has at last taken his place in the 'Golden Treasury'; and it is a characteristic poem, being an address to 'Absence'. Donne's best lyrics are about his absences and partings from his wife; and the startling directness of his style gives them a poignancy of pathos above all other poems on the same theme in the language. The famous comparison of the souls of the two lovers to the limbs of a compass, at once joined and divided, in itself grotesque enough, takes under his handling a sincerity that brings tears to the eyes.

[He quotes the last two stanzas of 'A Valediction: Forbidding Mourning'.]

In such writing as this we are far enough from the pastoral Arcadia, far enough also from such romantic songs as 'Who is Silvia?' or 'Come away, death', or 'It was a lover and his lass'. Donne is, in fact, a changeling among Elizabethans.

57. Henry Charles Beeching

1902

Canon H. C. Beeching (1859–1919), churchman and man of letters, in a collection of essays on Anglican themes, offered a commonsense counter to the view of Donne's career and ministry then being promoted by anticlerical commentators (*Religio Laici: A Series of Studies Addressed to Laymen*, 1902, pp. 63–72 and 89–123).

[As Donne's distant successor in the chaplaincy of Lincoln's Inn, Beeching offered a sympathetic understanding of Donne's conduct of his religious life which rebuffed some common ideas about it. Two essays in the series concern Donne's writings. A study of *The Anglican Spirit* allows some ten pages to Donne's sermons, bringing out the moderation and sheer holiness which some lengthy extracts display. Then a long essay on *Izaak Walton's Life of Donne* effectively vindicates Walton's account of Donne against the recent onslaughts of Gosse and Leslie Stephen. Beeching scouts altogether 'the love story that Mr Gosse has concocted out of Donne's elegies and lyrics', pointing out the misreadings and wholesale inconsistencies on which Gosse's account depends: 'Mr Gosse has elected to go further by treating the "loose" poems of Donne's youth as biographical material, and has fared worse by discovering a mare's nest.' He claims that the *Elegies* stand entirely independent of each other, as we see by the presence among them of *The Autumnal*, 'addressed to George Herbert's mother'.

Beeching finds no substance in Leslie Stephen's account of a timeserving and self-seeking Donne, who stooped to some pretty dirty work in his dependence upon patronage in the middle part of his career, and then did not hesitate to feather his own nest in his management of office at St Paul's. All that can be held against him is that he wrote the two *Anniversaries* to order, and did not curb his praises of a young girl he had never even seen.]

That is true; they are hyperbole run mad, so mad that they cease to be panegyrics of any human being; but though Donne's eccentric taste in writing them may be censured, no moral blame can be imputed. They were his rent to the girl's father for house and home; and they contain some of the finest lines in the English language.

[As for the alleged self-interest at St Paul's, Beeching brings the records of the transaction in question to show that Donne was moved by just the opposite impulse in fact.

218

Beeching justifies Walton's account of the effect of Donne's sermons upon their audiences, which Stephen had sceptically called in question. He commends Stephen's analytic account of Donne's artistic merits as a real advance in the study of Donne's prose. Yet detached analysis cannot bring the critic to the true source of Donne's power.]

. . . though he refers to the famous peroration of the seventy-sixth sermon, he does not recognise that the amazing force of that passage does not lie in its rhetoric, or even in its emotion, but in the imaginative intensity with which it realises the being of God.

The secret of Donne's effect is 'a faith in God that is hardly removed from sight', a fire which is 'always smouldering' beneath the driest metaphysical matter or the slightest turn of style, 'and will sooner or later break out'. That is why 'the crabbed Donne' had 'tears' and 'raptures' at his command, such as 'were not at the command of the rich eloquence and graceful fancy of Jeremy Taylor'.

58. William Vaughn Moody and Robert Morss Lovett

1902

W. V. Moody (1869–1910) was a poet and playwright, and assistant professor at the University of Chicago from 1901 to 1907, after which he devoted his time to writing. His most successful play, *The Great Divide*, was produced in New York and London and made into a motion picture. His textbook *A History of English Literature*, written with Robert Lovett, was still in print, in an eighth edition, in the 1960s. In it Donne was taken to typify the spirit of seventeenth-century literature (*A History of English Literature*, 1902, pp. 143–5).

219

Bacon holds a commanding place in seventeenth century thought, but he can hardly be called typical of the century. He did not share its characteristic melancholy; his imagination is always subordinated to thought, whereas the characteristic mood of the century is one of dreamy or mystical contemplation, in which imagination always takes the lead of abstract thinking; and finally he does not pass, as the typical seventeenth century writers so frequently do, from moods of earthly passion to moods of religious ecstasy. In all these respects the spirit of the time is better represented by a man whose youth fell, like Bacon's, in the high tide of the Elizabethan era, but who, from the first, stood apart, prophesying, both in his matter and his manner, of the age of James and Charles, – John Donne (1573–1631).

Donne spent a wild and irregular youth at Oxford and Cambridge, in the London Inns of Court, and in the south of Europe. Before the end of the sixteenth century he produced a body of lyric poetry of the utmost singularity. It is full of strange, interrupted music, and of vivid passion which breaks in jets and flashes through a veil of obscure thought and tortured imagery. In these moments of illumination, it becomes wonderfully poignant and direct, heart-searching in its simple human accents, with an originality and force for which we look in vain among the clear and fluent melodies of Elizabethan lyrists. Unfortunately these moments are comparatively rare. What is more immediately apparent in Donne's poetry, and what fascinated his disciples, is his use of 'conceits', *i.e.*, far-fetched analogies and over-ingenious metaphors, which are so odd that we lose sight of the thing to be illustrated, in the startling nature of the illustration. With him, love is a spider, which, dropped into the wine of life, turns it to poison; night is an 'ebon box', into which weary mortals are put as 'disordered clocks' until the sun gives them 'new works'. This 'conceitful' form of writing was practised by Marini in Italy, and by Gongora in Spain, simultaneously with Donne in England, and during the first half of the seventeenth century it spread over Europe like an epidemic. It had a great and very baleful influence upon English poetry before the Restoration, affecting even Milton in his earlier work.

[They add a final comment on Donne himself.]

In the poetry of his youth he had seemed to feel the unrest and feverish intensity of a later generation.

59. Rudolf Richter

1902

In a collection of essays honouring Professor J. Schipper, Rudolf Richter of Elbogen followed out Schipper's work on Donne's metrics ('Der Vers Bei Dr John Donne', in *Beiträge zur neueren Philologie: Jakob Schipper*, 1902, pp. 391–415).

[Richter starts from the categorical assumption that Donne's poetic career falls into three distinct periods, separated by his marriage and then his taking holy orders; and he lists the poems which must consequently be assigned to each period. This scheme leads him to date some of the *Songs and Sonnets* and *Elegies* between 1609 and 1613, and to space out along the years from 1618 to 1631 the *Holy Sonnets*, the 'Autumnal' and the *Hymns*, among others. The supposed pattern of Donne's development then becomes the basis of an analysis of Donne's shifting metrical uses which shows in percentages, period by period, the relative occurrence of such technical features as end-stopped lines, run-on lines, mid-line caesuras, feminine line-endings, and so on. Richter generally agrees with Schipper that Donne was a conscious artist who could be harsh when the mode required it but also wrote love-lyrics of harmonious beauty.]

60. Thomas Seccombe and John W. Allen

1903

Seccombe (1866–1923) wrote collaboratively two books that were very popular – *The Age of Shakespeare* and *The Age of Johnson*. He also wrote introductions to a wide range of literary and historical works. In the first line of these literary histories,

Seccombe and Allen singled out Shakespeare and Donne from the run of Elizabethan love-poets (*The Age of Shakespeare*, 1903, pp. 29 and 65–85).

Two poets – and only two – of the Elizabethan age produced love poetry in which the true note of absolute passion is struck – Shakespeare and Donne. But comparison of the two reveals the fact that, while Donne seems sometimes to set down his impressions hot and crude, in Shakespeare the passion is always mastered by the artist.

[The commentators follow the progress of Donne's impassioned intellectualism.]

Gradually he worked out his sensuality: the intense intellectuality of his temperament gained the mastery. . . .

To turn from the love lyrics of Drayton or Spenser or Greene to the love lyrics of Donne is to receive a shock, pleasant or unpleasant. Almost all Elizabethan love poetry is impersonal, ideal. Compared with Donne's it may be called cold. Fantastic as he is, Donne writes of his own experience. Not that his lyrics are poems of pure passion. It is improbable that he ever loved simply. He had a passion for passionate experience, and at bottom is always more intellectual than emotional. His lyrics are poems of transcendental sensuality, highly intellectualized.

To demand of love poetry that it shall be pretty and graceful is to demand that it shall not be personal and passionate. Shakespeare's sonnets, though in them all passion is mastered, are not pretty or graceful: they are splendid and melancholy. Passion is neither graceful nor pretty: it is tender at one moment, cruel at another; it may be brutal and ugly; it is egotistic always. If it weeps there is rage in the weeping; if it pleads it is with an undertone of fierceness. It may go with scorn or bitterness, or even with hatred; but it is not pretty and it knows nothing of taste. So with Donne. His love poetry is sometimes positively ugly. It is abrupt, scandalous, ecstatic, fantastic, mocking, actual.

> Love's not so pure and abstract as they use
> To say, who have no Mistress but their Muse!

Drayton and Lodge and the rest keep saying the same things over and over again: Donne runs through mood after mood. Sometimes, but rarely, he expresses a universal feeling:

> I wonder, by my troth, what thou and I
> Did till we loved.

Ordinarily he is more intimate. He declares boldly his passion for experience. He will not be held; he appeals to Nature, to birds and beasts, against the claim to constancy.

> Now thou has loved me one whole day;

but even to-morrow we two shall not be 'just those persons which we were'. He can love any woman 'so she be not true'; and the worst torture of love, he finds, is to love 'one that loves me'.

> Rob me but bind me not and let me go.
> Must I, who came to travel thorough you,
> Grow your fixed subject because you are true?

He expresses contempt for the women he loves.

[They quote lines 19–24 of 'Community'.]

Yet he knows the idolatry of love, and would have passion perfect and eternal if he might. He insists on the idea that lovers make their own world, a very fragile world, but the only real one while it lasts. Sometimes he rails against his love for a woman who cannot understand him.

[They quote lines 25–32 of 'The Blossom'.]

All through he knows that he is seeking for something he does not know.

[They quote lines 1–9 of 'Negative Love'.]

The following poem (*The Relique*), which the blending of irony, sadness, worship and aspiration makes one of the most extraordinary in English, is highly characteristic of Donne.

[They quote an expurgated version of 'The Relic', replacing lines 3–4 with dots – 'For graves have learned that woman-head/ To be to more than one a bed').]

This perhaps represents, among other things, what was possibly the last stage of an exhausted and intellectual sensualism: the desire for a love essentially sexual, in which sex should be almost forgotten.

That Donne plays with words to excruciation, that he rejoices in the mere ingenuity of conceit, that he tortures his fancies to death and delights in the display of his curious lore, does not affect the originality or the essential sincerity of his love poems. In these respects he seems deliberately to exaggerate the mannerisms and affectations of Elizabethan literature. Yet it is in his later rather than in his love poetry that frigid conceits, learned flourishes, and the 'monstrous and disgusting hyperboles' which roused the wrath of Dr Johnson especially abound.[1]

In his later phase Donne's poetry was for the most part religious in character. He was certainly not insincere, but there is no sign that his religious sentiment was ever very profound. To compare him with George Herbert as a religious poet seems absurd: they are poles apart. Herbert indulged in vapid conceits, and even wrote shaped verses; but at his worst he is always tender and spiritual. Donne's religious poetry is, as a rule, cold, tortured, and artificial. He became more and more 'metaphysical': more and more he intellectualized among abstractions. Sometimes the thought of his 'divine poems' is deep and striking: far more often it is merely ingenious. Of these poems perhaps the best is *The Litany*, composed in 1609.

[They quote lines 129–44, 199–207, 235–43 of 'A Litany'.]

Putting the love poems aside, this is Donne at his best. But the emotional fire has almost gone out, and little but the subtle intelligence remains. The crowding of the thought would remind us of Shakespeare but for the almost complete absence of imagery. Strange as it may seem in a writer so fond of verbal quip and fantastical conceit, this absence of imagery is characteristic.

[They speak of the two *Anniversaries*.]

These extraordinary poems look almost like a caricature of Elizabethan extravagance: it is as if Donne had deliberately set himself to outdo the world in hyperbole. . . .

The truth seems to be that the Elizabethans enjoyed the extravagant, and that Donne set his ingenuity to work to produce something sublimely and preposterously extravagant. Yet these outrageous poems are full of weighty and subtle reflection, and in parts – esepcially of the *Second Anniversary* – are splendidly written. There are passages of intense imagination and profound philosophy.

[They quote lines 43–54 and 389–96 of *The Second Anniversary*.]

In this *Second Anniversary* Donne is at his best and at his worst.

Donne founded no school, though he of course had imitators. That which was valuable in him was quite inimitable. He certainly did not found the school of religious poetry which produced Herbert, Crashaw, and Vaughan. Elizabethan religious poetry did not begin with Donne, nor did he give it anything permanent save his own poems, though his popularity no doubt stimulated this kind of poetic expression. As to his versification, it is hard to say whether he was the more careless or perverse. He has a fine ear, as he shows constantly, yet he is capable of verse so harsh and crabbed as to be a positive offence. He deliberately breaks up the natural sequence of accent and trust to his ear to restore the broken cadence by a nice balance of emphasis. No poet's cadence depends more absolutely on his meaning, and therefore it is, indeed, that his cadence is often tortured and crabbed. Yet at his best his verse has a depth of often broken music rarely equalled by more regular craftsmen.

In his later years Donne was immensely admired and praised alike as preacher and saint, controversialist and poet.

[They quote Jonson, Drummond, Walton and Carew on Donne, with a comment in passing.]

'The first poet in the world in some things' Jonson declared him, and added acutely that 'Donne, for not being understood, would perish'. This prophecy concerning the most perverse and the most intellectual of all Elizabethan lyrists has almost been fulfilled.

[They invoke Donne in occasional critical judgements.]

[On William Drummond as a religious poet.]

He has not the subtlety or the strange strength of Donne, but he has far more religious feeling.

[On George Wither:]

No one writes more spontaneously. . . . His 'native wood-notes' offer an extreme contrast with the scholarly sweetness of Drummond or the subtleties and perversities of Donne.

[On Elizabethan satire:]

The only Elizabethan poets of remarkable talent who wrote formal satire were Lodge, Drayton, Wither, and Donne; and all these failed with it completely.

NOTE

1 It is significant that he wrote very few love sonnets. [Seccombe and Allen's note.]

61. A. H. Garstang

1903

In an essay on the love-poetry of the sixteenth and seventeenth centuries, Donne and Jonson are singled out for their influence upon their successors, and Donne is exhibited as a perturber of English verse ('The Love Songs of a Bygone Day', *Fortnightly Review*, 1 December 1903, pp. 976–7).

John Donne, erstwhile wit of the *Mermaid*, and finally Dean of St Paul's, infused a new element into English verse – the element of imagination. The craze for extraordinary metaphysical conceits, which Donne introduced, became so general and so deep-rooted that few poets before the Restoration were able to free themselves from it.

A wild and adventurous life found its counterpart in a turbulent imagination, and it is Donne's imaginative qualities which are the prevailing characteristics and at once the charm and the bane of his poetry. It is to this peculiarity we owe such fantastic nonsense as *The Paradox* and such gems of fancy as *Present in Absence*.

[He quotes two stanzas of a poem sometimes ascribed to Donne, 'Absence, hear thou this protestation'.]

226

Donne, moreover, introduces the fashion of elaborate and fanciful metres, and of his seventy lyrical poems scarcely two are written in the same verse form, a peculiarity which he transmitted directly to Herrick. Donne, however, entirely ignored quantity and regularity, and was one of the most untidy versifiers of the Elizabethan age, while Herrick's unfailing neatness is one of his most characteristic charms. He found the limited range to which the Elizabethan poets confined themselves irksome. His adventurous spirit demanded a larger license than that which had satisfied his immediate predecessors, and throwing to the wind every bond and convention, both of thought and form, he broke out into lawless revolt. Campion, whose work was most probably of much earlier date than Donne's, showed in his verse-construction an invention of almost equal fertility, but whereas the great variety of verse forms shown by Campion may be partly due to the object their author had in view when composing them, Donne's metrical inventiveness owes nothing to any other incentive than that supplied by his native wit, and is simply the reflection of his own restless and intrepid fancy.

Donne is a singularly enticing study, and those who would become better acquainted with this remarkable poet are recommended to read Mr Edmund Gosse's admirable essay; they will find it both a fascinating and exhaustive comprehensive introduction. Indeed, no poet could be said more truthfully to be 'of imagination all compact', or resemble more strikingly the picture of the poet, as Theseus portrays him, than John Donne.

62. Richard Garnett

1903

In the four-volume 'record' of English literature he compiled with Edmund Gosse, Garnett represented Donne as the scourge of the Spenserian poets and a disrupter of classical order (*English Literature: An Illustrated Record*, vol. II, 1903, pp. 290–7).

But a poet was in the field who was to sweep the pleasant flowers of the disciples of Spenser before him as ruthlessly as a mower cuts down the daisies with his scythe. In this age of mighty wits and luminous imaginations, the most robust and the most elaborately trained intellect was surely that of JOHN DONNE. Born as early as 1573, and associated with many of the purely Elizabethan poets, we have yet the habit of thinking of him as wholly Jacobean, and the instinct is not an erroneous one, for he begins a new age. His poems were kept in manuscript until two years after his death in 1631, but they were widely circulated, and they exercised an extraordinary effect. Long before any edition of Donne was published, the majority of living English verse-writers had been influenced by the main peculiarities of his style. He wrote satires, epistles, elegies, sonnets, and lyrics, and although it is in the last mentioned that his beauties are most frequent, the essence of Donne, the strange personal characteristic which made him so unlike every one else, is redolent in all. He rejected whatever had pleased the Elizabethan age; he threw the fashionable humanism to the winds; he broke up the accepted prosody; he aimed at a totally new method in diction, in illustration, in attitude. He was a realist, who studded his writings with images drawn from contemporary life. For grace and mellifluous floridity he substituted audacity, intensity, a proud and fulgurant darkness, as of an intellectual thunder-cloud. He thought to redeem poetry from triviality by a transcendental exercise of mental force, applied with violence to the most unpromising subjects, chosen sometimes merely because they were unpromising, in an insolent rejection of the traditions of plastic beauty. He conceived nothing less daring than a complete revolution of style, and the dethronement of the whole dynasty of modern verse, in favour of a new naturalism dependent solely on a blaze of intellect.

Unfortunately, the genius of Donne was not equal to his ambition and his force. He lacked the element needed to fuse his brilliant intuitions into a classical shape. He aimed at becoming a great creative reformer, but he succeeded only in disturbing and dislocating literature. He was the blind Samson in the Elizabethan gate, strong enough to pull the beautiful temple of Spenserian fancy about the ears of the worshippers, but powerless to offer them a substitute. What he gave to poetry in exchange for what he destroyed was almost wholly deplorable. For sixty years the evil taint of Donne rested on us, and our tradition is not free from it yet. To him – almost to him alone – we owe the tortured irregularities, the monstrous pedantries, the alembicated verbiage of the decline. 'Rhyme's sturdy cripple', as Coleridge called him, Donne is the father of all that is exasperating, affected, and 'metaphysical' in English poetry. He represented, with Marino in Italy, Gongora in Spain, and Du Bartas and D'Aubigné in France, that mania for an inflamed and eccentric extravagance of fancy which was racing over Europe like a hideous new disease; and the ease and rapidity with which the infection was caught shows how ready the world of letters was to succumb to such a plague. That Donne, in flashes, and especially in certain of his lyrics, is still able to afford us imaginative ecstasy of the very highest order – he has written a few single lines almost comparable with the best of Shakespeare's – must not blind us, in a general survey, to the maleficence of his genius. No one has injured English writing more than Donne, not even Carlyle.

[Garnett allows some of Donne's poems a qualified commendation. Thus the first two stanzas of 'The Canonization' 'exemplify the fiery violence of his early muse'. The *Metempsychosis* is 'one of the most brilliant and reckless of his writings'. In the *Holy Sonnets* 'the majesty of his sombre imagination is finely exemplified'.

63. William John Courthope

1903

In his six-volume survey of English poetry W. J. Courthope (1842–1917), erstwhile Professor of Poetry at Oxford, sought to place Donne's poetry in an elaborate scheme of wit (*A History of English Poetry*, vol. III, 1903, pp. 147–68).

[Courthope attempts to trace the 'Nature and Origin of Poetical "Wit"', and to discriminate the several kinds of witty poetry written in the late sixteenth and the seventeenth centuries. He accepts Johnson's definition of wit in the *Life of Cowley*,[1] and notes that witty writing of various kinds was fashionable throughout Europe from about the time of the Council of Trent. He finds 'the general causes of these phenomena' in conflicting cultural impulses:]

. . . the decay of the scholastic philosophy and of the feudal system, common to the whole of Europe, and in the revival, the same time, of the civic standards of antiquity operating on the genius of many rising nations and languages. Such a collision of forces is plainly sufficient to account for that *discordia concors* which Johnson describes as the essence of 'Wit'; and further analysis will enable us to trace to the same origin what are generally recognised to be the leading features of 'Wit', namely, 1) Paradox, 2) Hyperbole 3) Excess of Metaphor. All these qualities, which flourish exuberantly in the poetry of the seventeenth century, appear germinally in the poetry of the fourteenth; it is therefore not an unfair conclusion that they belong to a single system of thought, and that their predominance in the later age signifies the efflorescence of decay.

[He then considers separately these 'leading features of "Wit"'.]

1) The habit of startling the imagination with paradoxical reasoning about the order of the universe, physical and moral, which is so striking a characteristic of the metaphysical school of Donne, is, I think, the final result of the exaggerated importance attached by the schoolmen to the study of logic. . . .

2) With the habit of reasoning paradoxically was intimately associated the habit of writing hyperbolically. The spirit of the logician penetrated not only the poetry which derived its inspiration from theology, but also that which had its source in chivalrous action and sentiment. In the first volume of this History I showed that the poetry of the troubadours was based upon an instinct prompting the feudal aristocracy to separate their caste from the vulgar by all the refinements of art and imagination. In order to establish the necessary social distinctions, they added to the subtlety of the theologian the casuistry of the lawyer, and invented a Code of Love which prescribed the rules of chivalrous manners. . . .

3) If the metaphysical turn of thought in the poets of the seventeenth century has its origin in the mixture of theology, chivalrous sentiment, and logic in mediaeval education, their excessive use of metaphor is to be explained by the decay of allegory as a natural mode of poetic expression. . . .

[Courthope characterizes under three heads the several 'schools of English "wit"' which came into being in the reign of James I. He speaks of a school of theological wit, a school of metaphysical wit, and a school of court or classical wit. In the school of theological wit he places Southwell, Davies of Hereford, and Phineas and Giles Fletcher. In the school of metaphysical wit he places Donne. In the school of court wit he places Campion, Wotton, Jonson, Drummond and Beaumont. He then moves on to the reign of Charles I and puts Quarles, Herbert, Crashaw and Vaughan in a school of theological wit, and Carew, Suckling, Herrick and Waller among others in a school of court wit.

His attempt to account for metaphysical wit entails a substantial appraisal of Donne's poetry.]

Beyond the sphere of theological allegory, in which the traditions of the schools were still preserved, lay the region of pure thought; and here the contradiction between mediaeval and modern ideas furnished ample materials for the exercise of 'wit'. Assailed at once by the forces of the new faith, the new science, and the growing spirit of civic liberty, the ancient fabric of Catholicism and Feudalism fell more and more into ruin, but the innovating philosophy was yet far from having established a system of order and authority. The reasoning of Copernicus and Galileo shook men's belief in the truth of the Ptolemaic astronomy: the discoveries of Columbus extended their ideas of the terrestrial globe: the study of Greek and Hebrew literature in the original disturbed the symmetrical methods of scholastic logic: the investigations of the Arabian chemists produced havoc in the realm of encyclopaedic science. Still, the old learning had rooted itself too firmly in the convictions of society to be easily abandoned, and the first effect of the collision between the opposing principles was to propagate a feeling of philosophic doubt. In the sphere of reason a new kind of Pyrrhonism sprang up, which expressed itself in Montaigne's motto, *Que sçay je?* and this disposition of mind naturally exerted another kind of influence on the men of creative imagination. In active life the confusion of the times was the opportunity of the buccaneer and the soldier of fortune, who hoped to advance themselves by their swords; and like these, many poets, in their ideal representations of Nature, seized upon the rich materials of the old and ruined philosophy to decorate the structures which they built out of their lawless fancy. On such foundations rose the school of metaphysical wit, of which the earliest and most remarkable example is furnished in the poetry of John Donne.

[Courthope summarizes the 'external facts in the life of this poet', which offer 'useful landmarks for the interpretations of his genius', moving freely between the poetry and the circumstances. He judges that the character of Donne's poetry reflects very exactly the changes in his life and opinions.]

His love-poems are those of a man who has assimilated, with thorough appreciation, all the learning and intellectual methods of the schoolmen – their fine distinctions, their subtle refinement, their metaphysical renderings of the text of Scripture. We know that, at some uncertain date, he abandoned the Roman Catholic faith, but his scholastic education had grounded in his mind a doctrine which, to the close of his life, continued to lie at the root of all his convictions, and to give form and colour to his poetical style, namely, the belief in the indestructible character of the soul. He constantly alludes to the old theory of the schoolmen respecting the triple nature of the soul, as in the lines: –

> We first have souls of growth and sense; and those,
> When our last soul, our soul immortal, came,
> Were swallowed into it, and have no name.

In the middle period of his life, when his opinions were becoming more settled and religious, he writes of this individual soul: –

> Our soul, whose country's heaven, and God her father,
> Into this world, corruption's sink, is sent;
> Yet so much in her travel she doth gather,
> That she returns home wiser than she went.

This mixture of strong religous instinct and philosophic scepticism appears in its simplest form in his third *Satire*, which we know to have been among the earliest of his works. . . .

Certain it is that, in his poem called *The Progress of the Soul*, he had reached a stage of contemplative scepticism. . . . The subtle and searching analysis of the poet's imagination may be illustrated by the following stanza.

[He quotes stanza 7 of the *Metempsychosis*, and goes on to give an account of the poem with more quotations. Then he quotes the last lines.]

Here we have plainly the utterance of a sceptic in religion, who, having thrown off the forms of authoritative belief, indulges his imagination with a reconstruction of the ruins of Pythagorean and Rabbinical philosophy. Many allusions to natural history and theological dogma are scattered through Donne's *Songs and Sonnets*, and all are couched in the same reckless spirit.

And as Donne was at this stage a sceptic in religion, so was he a revolutionist in love. We have seen that, for many centuries, the law of chivalrous love had been rigorously defined. The Provençal poets and the female presidents of the *Cours d'Amours* had revised and extended the ancient canons of the art as expounded by Ovid; and, while they tacitly recognised the physical basis of the passion, they disguised it by the elaborate character of the imaginative superstructure they raised upon it. In the delicacy of their observation, the nicety of their distinction, and the keenness of their logic, they rivalled the theological science of the schoolmen; and by allying the phenomena of love with the loftier virtues of constancy, patience, loyalty, and self-surrender, they so spiritualised the former that, under the *régime* of chivalry – to use the words of Burke, – 'vice itself lost half its evil by losing all its grossness'.

This fine Platonic edifice is ruthlessly demolished in the poetry of Donne. To him love, in its infinite variety and inconsistency, represented the principle of perpetual flux in Nature. At the same time, his imagination was stimulated by the multitude of paradoxes and metaphors which were suggested to him by the varying aspects of the passion. He pushed to extremes the scholastic analysis and conventional symbolism of the Provençals; but he applied them within the sphere of vulgar *bourgeois* intrigue, as may be inferred from the following characteristic lines:

[He quotes lines 1–19 of *Elegy* 7, 'Nature's Lay Idiot'.]

The law of love in the *Cours d'Amours* required unfailing constancy in both lovers: in the philosophy of Donne this law is contrary to Nature, and is therefore heresy.

[He quotes lines 19–27 of 'The Indifferent'.]

Over and over again he insists on the essential falsehood and

233

fickleness of women. He asks, for instance, 'where lives a woman true and fair', and proceeds . . .

[He quotes lines 19–27 of *Song*, 'Go, and Catch a Falling Star'.]

This is the spirit of Ariosto's story of Gioconda. But Donne goes further, and cynically erects this observed habit of fickleness into a rule for constant, but discriminating, change.

[He quotes lines 19–36 of *Elegy* 3, 'Change'.]

From this spirit of cynical lawlessness he was perhaps reclaimed by genuine love. To his wife he seems to have been devotedly attached, and in the poems written after his marriage in 1601 we find a complete change of sentiment and style. The old underlying conviction of the indestructible nature of the soul and of the corruption of the material world remains, but it is now made the starting-point for a graver philosophy of conduct. The *Verse Letters* written to the Countesses of Bedford, Huntingdon, and Salisbury, though all are couched in a vein of metaphysical compliment, are decorous in tone; in *The Anatomy of the World* Donne seems to have intended to embody his serious thoughts about the meaning and duties of human life. . . .

Viewed literally *The Anatomy of the World* fully deserves the sentence passed upon it by Jonson. . . . It is no wonder that such absurdities should have provoked matter-of-fact criticism. They are, however, not of the essence of the composition. . . .

The true character of *The Anatomy of the World* is indicated in the respective titles of the two *Anniversaries*. . . .

In other words, the early death and religious character of Elizabeth Drury are merely the text justifying an elaborate exposition of Donne's philosophy of life. The girl stood to Donne, for his poetical purpose, in the same relation as Beatrice stood to Dante in the *Vita Nuova* and the *Divine Comedy*, being the incarnate symbol of the spiritual perfection – the Idea of Woman, as he put it to Ben Jonson – which he sought to express. When he says that her death was the cause of all the imperfections of the material world, he intended, in the first place, to pay a hyperbolical compliment to the daughter of his patron, and in the second, to express the theological doctrine of the corruption of Nature after the fall of man from his original state of perfection.

234

On the whole, it seems to me probable that the publication of *The Anatomy of the World* was part of a deliberate literary design on Donne's part. His affected depreciation of verse-writing is not to be taken seriously. His views of life were changing with his years: he was anxious for either secular or sacred employment: he regretted the evidences of a dissipated past which existed in his youthful poems: he hoped to attain the object of his ambition by giving public proof of the present gravity of his mind, and by securing the special favour of the most influential patrons of literature, such as the famous ladies of the Court, to whom so many of his *Verse Letters* are addressed.

[He quotes lines 13–18 of John Chudleigh's funeral elegy on Donne, which speak of Donne's transplanting his wit from love to piety.]

How just this criticism is may be seen from Donne's 'Hymn to Christ at the Author's Last Going into Germany'.

[He quotes lines 17–32 of the poem.]

Here we have precisely the same kind of paradoxical logic, the same subtlety of thought and imagery, as we find in the *Elegy on Change*, and though the imagination is now fixed on an unchangeable object, it plays round it precisely in the same way. The essence of Donne's wit is abstraction. Whether he is writing on the theme of sacred or profane love, his method lies in separating the perceptions of the soul from the entanglements of sense, and after isolating a thought, a passion, or a quality, in the world of pure ideas, to make it visible to the fancy by means of metaphorical images and scholastic allusions. The most characteristic specimens of his wit are to be found in his *Songs and Sonnets*, where he is dealing with the metaphysics of love, for here his imagination is at liberty to move whithersoever it chooses; and the extraordinary ingenuity with which he masters and reduces to epigrammatic form the most minute distinctions of thought, as well as the facility with which he combines contrary ideas and images, are well exemplified in a poem called *The Primrose Hill.*

[He gives the whole of 'The Primrose'.]

But for the purposes of great and true art the flight of metaphysical wit soon reveals the limitations of its powers. Sceptic as he was,

Donne never formed any organic idea of Nature as a whole, and his sole aim, as a poet, was to associate the isolated details of his accumulations of learning with paradoxes and conceits, which are of no permanent value. For example, he was acquainted with the Copernican theory, but he is only interested in it as far as it helps to supply him with a poetical illustration: –

> As new philosophy arrests the sun,
> And bids the passive earth about it run,
> So we have dulled our mind; it hath no ends,
> Only the body's busy, and pretends.

The theory that the earth was gradually approaching the sun suggests to him the following reflection: –

> If the world's age and death be argued well
>   By the sun's fall, which now towards earth doth bend,
> Then we might fear that virtue, since she fell
>   So low as woman, should be near her end.

But he at once corrects this conclusion into an extravagant compliment: –

> But she's not stooped but raised; exiled by men,
>   She fled to heaven, that's heavenly things, that's you.

The general scepticism, produced in his mind by the collision between the new philosophy and the old theology, is forcibly expressed in his first 'Anniversary'.

[He quotes lines 205–18 of *The First Anniversary*.]

The conclusion at which he finally arrived was the one to which all such souls, who have in them the element of religion, must be brought:

[He quotes lines 290–300 of *The Second Anniversary*.]

But before he arrives at this intelligible goal, his soul, wandering through an infinite maze of metaphysical ideas, has made shift to embody its transitory perceptions in the forms of poetical art; and, while he is engaged in a business which he acknowledges to be vain, he delights in involving himself and his readers in inextricable labyrinths of paradox. One of his favourite ideas is that Love is Death, and this thought he divides and subdivides by means of an endless variety of images. Thus he finds an opportunity of associ-

ating it with the reflections aroused by the shortest day, sacred to
St Lucy. . . .

In a poem called *The Paradox* he indulges in still more intricate
logic on the same subject.

[He gives the whole of 'The Paradox'.]

This perpetual endeavour to push poetical conception beyond the
limits of sense and Nature produced its necessary effect on the
character of Donne's metrical expression. When he seeks to embody
a comparatively simple and natural thought, he can write with
admirable harmony, as in the following lines, describing love in the
Golden Age:

[He quotes lines 47–60 of the verse letter 'To the Countess of
Huntingdon', 'That unripe side of earth'.]

Here, too, is an excellent compliment in a *Verse Letter* to the
Countess of Salisbury, grounded on the idea that chivalrous love is
a liberal education:

[He quotes lines 79–84 of 'To the Countess of Salisbury'.]

His whole philosophy of life, in his early days, is condensed in the
following couplet: –

> Be then thine own home, and in thyself dwell;
> Inn anywhere: continuance maketh hell.

And he is most vivid in the presentation of abstract ideas, as in the
famous lines:

> Her pure and eloquent blood
> Spoke in her cheeks, and so distinctly wrought
> That one might almost say her body thought.

The abrupt and forcible openings of his poems often strike a keynote of thought which promises completeness of treatment, but his
metaphysical wit and his love of endless distinctions generally cause
the composition to end nowhere. He begins a poem called *Love's
Deity* thus: –

> I long to talk with some old lover's ghost,
> Who died before the God of Love was born.

The object of the discourse is to be the mystery why love should be
forced from one lover where there is no return from the other. This

is a subject of universal interest, and the poet, on the assumption that Love, after being made into a deity, has abused his power, conducts a striking thought, by means of an appropriate image, to an intelligible conclusion: –

> O were we wakened by this tyranny
> To ungod this child again, it could not be
> I should love her who loves not me.

But such straightforward logic would not have suited the super-subtle character of Donne's intellect; and he proceeds to invert his reasoning, and to close his poem with a stanza of pure paradox, leaving the mind without that sense of repose which art requires: –

> Rebel and atheist, why murmur I,
> As though I felt the worst that love could do?
> Love may make me leave loving, or might try
> A deeper plague, to make her love me too;
> Which, since she loves before, I'm loth to see.
> Falsehood is worse than hate; and that must be,
> If she whom I love should love me.

Where he thinks simply the reader perceives that his thoughts are really common enough. He begins a *Verse Letter* to Sir H. Goodyere on his favourite subject of the necessity of change: –

> Who makes the last a pattern for next year,
> Turns no new leaf, but still the same thing reads;
> Seen things he sees again, heard things doth hear,
> And makes his life but like a pair of beads.

This has the simplicity and directness of Sir John Davies in his *Nosce Teipsum*. But we soon come to a quatrain in which the poet is anxious to show his wit: –

> To be a stranger hath that benefit,
> We can beginnings, but not habits choke.
> Go – whither? hence. You get, if you forget;
> New faults, till they prescribe to us, are smoke.

We certainly do *not* get anything by the mere negative act of forgetting; and nobody could gather from the last line that the meaning was, 'new faults, till they become our masters, are *merely* smoke'. Eagerness for novelty and paradox leads the poet to obscurity of expression; and the reader is justly incensed when he finds that the labour required to arrive at the meaning, hidden behind involved syntax and unmeasured verse, has been expended in vain. Ben Jonson does not express this feeling too strongly when he says, 'That Donne for not keeping of accent deserves hanging.' It is superfluous to justify this verdict by examples. The reader, in the numerous extracts I have given from Donne's poems, will have observed for himself how deliberately he seeks to attract attention to the extravagance of his thought, by the difficulty of his grammatical constructions, and by the dislocation of his accents.

All these things must be taken into account in deciding the place to be assigned to this acute and powerful intellect in the history of English poetry. Donne's qualities were essentially those of his age. His influence on his contemporaries and on the generation that succeeded him was great. They had all been educated under the same scholastic conditions as himself; they were all in touch with his theological starting-point, and set a value on the subtlety of his metaphysical distinctions. In Dryden's time, when the prestige of 'wit', still represented by the genius of Cowley, was weakening before the poetical school which aimed first at correctness of expression, men continued to speak with reverence of Donne's genius. But as the philosophy of Bacon, Newton, and Locke gradually established itself, the traditions of the schoolmen fell into discredit, so that, in the days of Johnson and Burke, the practice of the metaphysical wits had come to be regarded in the light of an obsolete curiosity. The revival of mediaeval sentiment, which has coloured English taste during the last three generations, has naturally awakened fresh interest in the poems of Donne, and there is perhaps in our own day a tendency to exaggerate his merits. 'If Donne', writes a learned and judicious critic, 'cannot receive the praise due to the accomplished poetical artist, he has that not perhaps higher, but certainly rarer, of the inspired poetical creator'.[2] Poetical creation implies that organic conception of Nature, and that insight into universal human emotions, which make the classical poets of the world – Homer and Dante, and Chaucer and Milton; and to this universality of thought, as I have endeavoured to show, Donne has no claim. Nor can he be reckoned among the poets who, by their sense of harmony and proportion, have helped to carry forward the refinement of our language from one social stage to another. The praise which Johnson bestows upon his learning adds little to his fame, for the science contained in his verse is mostly derived from those encyclopaedic sources of knowledge which, even in his own time, were being recognised as the fountains of 'Vulgar Error'. On the other hand, to those who see in poetry a mirror of the national life, and who desire to amplify and enrich their own imagination by a sympathetic study of the spiritual existence of their ancestors, the work of Donne will always be profoundly interesting. No more lively or character-istic representative can be found of the thought of an age when the traditions of the ancient faith met in full encounter with the forces of the new philosophy. The shock of that collision is far from having spent its effect, even in our own day; and he who examines historically the movements of imagination will find in Donne's subtle analysis and refined paradoxes much that helps to throw light on the contradictions of human nature.

NOTES

1 See *John Donne: The Critical Heritage*, vol. I, ed. A. J. Smith (London: Routledge and Kegan Paul, 1975), pp. 217–18.
2 Professor Saintsbury, Preface to *Poems of John Donne*. Edited by E. K. Chambers. [Courthope's note.]

64. John Smith Harrison

1903

In a published dissertation for Columbia University, J. S. Harrison sought to demonstrate that English poets of the sixteenth and seventeenth centuries held a Platonic con-ception of love, which they display in their constant endeavour to refine passion into a pursuit of pure idea or spirit (*Platonism in English Poetry of the Sixteenth and Seventeenth Centuries* (1903), 1915, pp. 93–4, 141–3, 144–6, 149–54 and 162–5).

[Harrison quotes very selectively from Donne's sermons and poems to bear out his claim that Donne aspired to a love of pure souls beyond the affections of the body, drawing on 'The Ecstasy', 'A Valediction: Forbidding Mourning', 'To the Countess of Huntingdon', 'That unripe side of earth', 'Love's Growth', 'The Dream'.

Harrison supposes that Donne takes from Plotinus his notion of a love which can be defined only by negatives, quoting 'Negative Love' in confirmation; and he discovers in Donne's reported reply to Ben Jonson's criticisms of the *Anniversaries* 'the secret of Donne's treatment of woman'. The secret is that Donne]

was interested in her not as a personality, but as an idea. In solving the nature of this idea he recurred to certain Platonic conceptions by which he thought to explain the source of her power.

[One such conception is the identification of woman with virtue, such as we may glimpse behind the 'torture of conceits' in 'To the Countess of Huntingdon', 'Man to God's image'. Another is the projection of an idealized woman's nature into a universal animating soul, as occurs in 'A Fever' and the two *Anniversaries*.

Harrison concludes that Donne is effectively a kind of riddling Platonist.]

Holding thus to this idea of woman, and striving to differentiate love from passion, Donne was able to confine his notion of love to the soul; and through the metaphysical manner of his poetic art he was able to express this notion in the most perplexing intricacies of thought.

65. August Wilhelm Trost

1904

W. Trost submitted to the University of Marburg a doctoral dissertation on Donne's style, with the modest title *Beiträge sur Kenntnis des Stils von John Donne* (reported in W. F. Melton, *The Rhetoric of John Donne's Verse*, 1906, p. 54).

[Trost's approach to Donne is descriptive; and his chapter headings indicate the scope of his work: 'Donne's Themes and Their Variations'; 'His Style in General'; 'Words'; 'Plays on Words'; 'Syntax'; 'Conceits'; 'Images'; 'Personifications'; 'Similes'; 'Climax'; 'Oxymoron'; 'Epizeuxis'; 'Alliteration'.]

66. Barrett Wendell

1904

Professor B. Wendell (1855–1921) of Harvard spent several periods lecturing abroad – at the Sorbonne (prompting him to establish an exchange programme between staff of French institutions and of Harvard) and at the University of Cambridge (where he gave Trinity College's Clark Lectures in 1902–3). He wrote several books on Elizabethan literature, on American literature (for which he was best known) and on politics. He also published two novels. His Clark Lectures were published as *The Temper of the Seventeenth Century in English Literature*, and in them Wendell discussed Donne's effect upon seventeenth-century writing (*The Temper of the Seventeenth Century in English Literature*, 1904, pp. 120–7).

At all events, though many of Donne's poems were long unpublished, his works were familiar in manuscript to his literary contemporaries; and, whatever else, they were recognized as the most individual of his time. Spenser frankly set forth in English poetry the influence of classical Italian. Jonson sturdily expounded and practised the permanent poetic principles of the enduring classics of antiquity. Donne wrote with utter disregard of both these influences; and, although he was manifestly influenced by the decadent ingenuities which had become fashionable in Italy and in Spain, his English manner was, almost rudely, his own.

[Wendell argues that our proper concern is not with the Doctor of Divinity, who sought to destroy his own poems.]

The Donne who touches us is the poet, whose verses have been collected, and persist in spite of him. To us they cannot have the sort of surprising quality which, in their own day, attracted instant attention. So far as I can discover, their approach to popularity came not so much from their aggressive peculiarity of form as from the fact that, in contrast to the literature about them, they must have appeared amazingly veracious. Their lack of conventional grace, when other men were so apt to be conventionally graceful, makes them seem astonishingly genuine: they seem to express not fancy, but fact, and in a temper very like that of the art which modern cant calls realistic.

In their own day, this spirit of realism was almost unprecedented; yet if this were all which made Donne memorable, he would be of hardly more than historical interest. And his fame, whether we care for him or not, is proving permanent. We must look a little closer; facing and trying to penetrate the surface of his obscurity. Sometimes, as in that epitaph on Prince Henry, this obscurity was mischievously deliberate:

> Look to me, faith, and look to my faith, God;
> For both my centres feel this period.
> Of weight one centre, one of greatness is;
> And reason is that centre, faith is this.

Yet even here one can feel the man's lasting power. Thoughtful to the degree of an over-ingenuity which here he frankly parodies – Herbert, and Greville, to name no more, had already been more ingenious still – he always manages to express himself also with a surgent, yet repressed, emotional power which makes him, among the poets of his time, the most intense. His obscurity is not a matter of language; his vocabulary is almost as pure as Jonson's own. The difficulties of him spring rather from this pervasive intensity, which strives, deliberately or instinctively, to charge his lines with a heavier burden of thought and feeling than any lines could unbendingly carry. Accordingly he seems, once for all, to disdain the oddities into which the lines distort themselves under the strain.

You can feel this peculiarity almost everywhere. Among his earlier poems are the 'Satires', in every sense the least palpably conventional, and so apparently the most genuine, of his time and perhaps of our language. Here is a bit from one of them, which chances still to be repeatable.

[He quotes lines 65–73 of *Satire* 3.]

For not keeping of accent, no doubt Donne deserved hanging; but he could plead in confession and avoidance this intensity which was all his own.

He never lost it, furthermore; rather he developed it. In his graver years, for example, just when Webster was publishing that preface to the 'White Devil', Donne's intensity produced such lines as these:

> The world is but a carcass; thou art fed
> By it, but as a worm that carcass bred;
> And why shouldst thou, poor worm, consider more
> When this world will grow better than before,
> Than those thy fellow-worms do think upon
> That carcass's last resurrection?

You cannot but feel the intense genuineness of this comparison. At the same time, its exasperating over-ingenuity is just of the kind which Dr Johnson so stoutly belabored in his comments on the figure of the compass, to which, long before, Donne had likened the souls of two lovers.

[He quotes the last three stanzas of 'A Valediction: Forbidding Mourning'.]

In both of these passages, over-ingenious though they be, you can feel the power of Donne. In neither, nor in anything we have glanced at yet, can you feel the vividness or the beauty which now and again consecrates this power. For an example of his vividness, take those lines from the 'Calm', which Jonson had by heart:

> No use of lanthorns; and in one place lay
> Feathers and dust, to-day and yesterday.

For an example of his beauty, take stray lines from the love-lyrics, generally so far from austerity that there need be no wonder why Donne regretted them in his reverend days. Yet, even at his sternest, he need not have cast away such stanzas as this:

> O, do not die, for I shall hate
>   All women so, when thou art gone,
> That thee I shall not celebrate,
>   When I remember thou wast one.

Better, still, take the haunting melody of those two lines of Donne which are most familiar – so familiar, indeed, as to be almost hackneyed:

> I long to talk with some old lover's ghost,
> Who died before the god of love was born.

Already we have dwelt on him more than enough to feel that intensity of individuality which made his work in his own time seem real beyond the rest, and which, with all its disdain of amenity, makes his verse in these days of ours reveal more and more to those who ponder it most.

Intense individuality, the while, is of all artistic influences the most destructive. . . .

Crescent art anywhere is that which is rooted in immemorial convention. Art which deliberately contradicts tradition is bound, however genuine, to be a noble heresy. The heresiarchs have something delusively like the virtue of the saints. It is only when we trace the extinction of their followers that we can feel the tragedy of their faithful and honest aberrations. The influence of Spenser could never quite lose the amenity of his Italianate grace; that of Jonson could never quite lose the civility of his classical poise; that of Donne was bound to fall into the affectations of a mannerism which grew lifeless the moment the master who vitalized it fell asleep.

Analogies are doubtless misleading, and those critics are right who have objected to the commonplace which has asserted that Donne was an Elizabethan Browning. Yet there is a suggestion of truth in the extended analogy – whose very imperfections help to correct its errors – which would liken in their mutual relations the three divergent Elizabethans on whom we have now touched to three eminent poets of the nineteenth century. Spenser was less like Wordsworth than Jonson was like Tennyson; and Jonson was less like Tennyson than Donne was like Browning; and Donne was, on the whole, so little like Browning that the comparison by itself is rather misleading than helpful. Yet when Spenser died, in 1599, Jonson and Donne were already pointing the ways in which

Elizabethan poetry must disintegrate, very much as, when Words-worth died, in 1850, Tennyson and Browning were already pointing the divergent ways in which the English poetry of the nineteenth century has begun to lose what integrity it ever had. If we liken Spenser to Wordsworth, accordingly, and Jonson to Tennyson, and Donne to Browning, we may feel – for all the dissimilarities which must often obscure all trace of similarity – what those mean who believe, in our day, that human expression must yield to natural law as surely as the stars in their courses.

For, though it would be foolish to say that Spenser, and Jonson, and Donne caused the disintegration of Elizabethan poetry, there can be no doubt, I think, that the three distinct tendencies, or influences, embodied in the work of these three divergent masters portend, with precision, the courses which that poetical disintegration was to take.

67. Stephen Lucius Gwynn

1904

Stephen Gwynn was an Irish biographer and literary historian who, after being a schoolmaster, became a journalist in London from 1896 to 1904, and then MP for Galway 1905–18. He referred to Donne in passing in his best-selling *Masters of English Literature* as a poet who had deservedly been forgotten (*The Masters of English Literature*, 1904, pp. 78, 127 and 400).

[Gwynn mentions Donne by way of placing other writings and writers. On Herrick's poem 'His Winding Sheet' he comments:]

the fantastic and grim conceits of the opening recall Donne, the 'metaphysical' poet whose fame then rivalled Jonson's.

[On Cowley:]

Cowley had succeeded Donne as chief of what has been called the 'metaphysical school' – poets who revelled in strange conceits drawn from unlikely sources of knowledge.

[On Browning:]

no one denies the vices of style which make his principal work, *The Ring and the Book*, so difficult of reading. He may vanish from general view, as Donne, a man of very similar qualities and defects, has vanished or as Cowley vanished half a century later.

68. Frank Lusk Babbott

1905

Babbott (1854–1933) was a collector of fine books and art. He edited *Classic English Odes from Spenser to Tennyson* and introduced a selected edition of Donne's poems with an assurance that Donne's work is best represented in selection, since so much of it is unfit for general reading. He presumed that Donne must have had some such self-censorship in mind when he thought to publish his poems in 1614 (*The Poems of John Donne . . .*, 1905, pp. vi–ix).

If he had edited his poems, as he proposed to do, he would have relieved some of his admirers from the embarrassment of becoming also his apologists, and have saved his own reputation from severe and at times not unjust criticism on the part of those who wished to be his friends.

Such collections of his poems as the Muses' Library and the edition of the Grolier Club are complete, but those are not volumes which one would leave carelessly on his library table. Some of the daintiest lyrics reflect the life of the seventeenth century in so gross a manner that it seems incredible in this age that an eminent Dean of St Paul's could be made out of such a poet.

It is because the weeds and flowers have been allowed to grow in such a luxuriant tangle in Donne's garden of verse that this separation has been undertaken. No one will find here all of Donne's poetry that is beautiful, or only the beautiful. Such a selection is an impossibility where the most perfect verses often form an inseparable part of stanzas that cannot be reproduced or too small a part of poems that are otherwise uninteresting. This volume is therefore intentionally incomplete, and in that respect differs from other collections in order that it may give greater pleasure by giving less offense.

There are few poems in the English language that have a purer lyrical ring than Donne's best. Keats and Milton and even Shakespeare flash through their lines on the reader's mind and reflect the same heavenly source. One can go back to them again and again without losing any of their inimitable witchery.

Nothing could be more charming than some of the passages of that extravagant and inexplicable eulogy, 'An Anatomy of the World – The First Anniversary'.

[He quotes lines 361–70 and 446 of *The First Anniversary*.]

While the 'Second Anniversary', here printed, is of uneven quality, many of its passages possess a supreme radiance that is seldom surpassed; and if it had been sustained by a nobler theme it might have made Donne's name conspicuous in a period when English poetry was at its apogee. . . .

This volume is printed as an expression of gratitude to John Donne the poet. It is a pleasure to reflect that there was a period in English history when great men kept in manuscript, for the delight of their friends, songs that have since charmed the race for three centuries. A few of them have been brought together here with what his biographer Izaak Walton would call 'sweet trouble'. If, now and again, this volume rests in a friend's hand with a pleasure somewhat akin to the joy that was had in its making, it may be said of its compilation that 'idle time was not idly spent'.

69. Charles Eliot Norton

1905

Norton introduced an edition of Donne's love-poems with an explanation of his editorial method, which derived from some questionable assumptions about the poems. Norton handled Donne's love-poetry cavalierly. He excluded major poems altogether, omitted whole sections of others, and took liberties with the texts of the poems he included (*The Love Poems of John Donne*, 1905, pp. vi–viii and 84).

Donne never made poetry his profession, and for the greater part of his life he was far more scholar and preacher than poet. His nature was extraordinarily complex. Heaven and Earth contended in it with a force that made his life a succession of alternating exaltation and depression, loftiness and baseness, rapture and despair. His work, whether in prose or verse, is the expression of a powerful intelligence, a passionate temperament and a vivid imagination irregularly subject to the check of a keen, practical understanding. As Jonson could justly hold him for some things the first poet in the world, so Dryden, with equal justice, could speak of him as 'the greatest wit, though not the greatest poet of our nation'.

The reader who has been unacquainted with Donne's poetry will be struck by the difference of the poems in this volume from the common love poetry of his sonneteering contemporaries. They show an individuality of sentiment, no less than of expression, which distinguishes them sharply from other poetry of the class to which they belong. Donne is essentially English, – a characteristically Elizabethan Englishman. There is no soft familiar Italian echo in his verse. He has often, indeed, been criticised for the harshness of his versification, and Ben Jonson (to cite another of his sayings concerning the poet) went so far as to assert that he 'deserved hanging for not keeping of accent'. His sins in this respect are frequent, but are committed more often in his other poems than in his love verse, and some of the faults of rhythm attributed to him are due to the reader rather than to the poet. He employs slurs and elisions to a degree that sometimes makes a faultless verse seem rough and difficult to a reader who may lie open to the charge which Holophernes brings against Sir Nathaniel in regard to his reading of Biron's sonnets, – 'You find not the apostrophes, and so miss the accent.' Donne sometimes moulded his verse more by the sense than by the sound, and used a license in versification strange to less eager and impassioned poets, and there is truth in the saying of Coleridge that 'to read Dryden, Pope, etc., you need only count syllables, but to read Donne you must measure time, and discover the time of each word by the sense of passion'.

In this little collection I have attempted to arrange the poems in a more natural order than that in which they have hitherto appeared. They fall for the most part into two divisions, the first being of those written when one mistress after another enthralled the youthful poet's susceptible fancy in a transient bondage, the second of those when his affections were fixed and his heart devoted to the woman who became his wife. Two or three poems lie outside either division.

[The edition does not include 'Love's Alchemy', 'Farewell to Love', 'The Flea', 'The Apparition', 'The Sun Rising', 'The Curse', 'The Dissolution', 'The Computation'. It is typical of Norton's treatment of the poems he includes that 'A Valediction: Of the Book' is retitled *Love's Records* and cut down by more than half, albeit with an explanatory comment.]

This little poem with its superb climax consists of the first three stanzas of the poem entitled in previous editions: *Valediction to her Book*. The omitted four stanzas are of little worth.

70. Anon., *Dial*

1905

An appreciative, business-like review of Charles Eliot Norton's selection of Donne's *Love Poems* limits his popularity to a few likely to appreciate difficult poetry and finely printed books (*Dial*, 16 November 1905, p. 299).

The little volume of 'Love Poems of John Donne', recently issued in a limited edition by the Riverside Press, is of unusual interest on several accounts. In the first place, its outward appearance is such that no lover of fine bookmaking could fail to rejoice in its possession. Then it gives us in convenient form perhaps the best work of a poet not easily accessible to the casual present-day reader. Finally, the name of Charles Eliot Norton on the title-page, as editor, would insure permanent value to a much less interesting publication than this. Professor Norton is the fortunate owner of some Donne manuscripts, and he has utilized these so far as they go in collating the present text. He contributes also a short but illuminating introduction, and a few necessary notes. It is not to be supposed that Donne will ever be very widely read or appreciated, but this little book should do much to make his work better known among poetry lovers. The volume is a slender duodecimo in form, printed from Caslon type on antique handmade paper, and bound in paper-covered boards with parchment back.

71. Geoffrey Langdon Keynes

1906

Sir Geoffrey Keynes (1877–1982), surgeon, bibliographer and literary scholar, was the brother of Lord John Maynard Keynes the economist. He was a man of diverse talents: pioneer in blood-transfusion, helping to found the London blood-transfusion service, Chairman of the National Portrait Gallery from 1958 to 1966, and author of a ballet, *Job*, with music by Ralph Vaughan Williams. He compiled bibliographies and editions of a number of authors, including Donne, John Evelyn, Sir Thomas Browne, William Blake, Jane Austen and William Hazlitt, and wrote biographies of his friends Rupert Brooke and Siegfried Sassoon, and one of Sir William Harvey.

He recalled the impact upon forward-looking young readers of E. K. Chambers's edition of Donne's poems, and of Gosse's *Life and Letters of John Donne* ('The Donne Revival', in *A City Tribute to John Donne*, 1972, p. 5).

As a schoolboy at Rugby I became aware of him through my more advanced friend, Rupert Brooke, and by the time we came up to Cambridge University in 1906 we had agreed that Donne was among the greatest of poets, whose works we both read in the Muses' Library edition. I had no talents or ambition as a literary critic, but was guided and influenced by Brooke's enthusiasm for Donne. I was attracted not only by his brilliant and astringent wit, but became fascinated by his personality and by the strange course of his life with its metamorphosis from a courtier and almost professional 'lover' into an imposing Dean of St Paul's, who became the greatest preacher of his age. He had written 'The Extasie', and was, as Brooke wrote in 1913, 'the one great lover-poet who was not afraid to acknowledge that he was composed of body, soul and mind, and one who faithfully recorded all the pitched battles, alarms, treaties, sieges and fanfares of that extraordinary triangular warfare'.

72. Henry Marvin Belden

1906

The American H. M. Belden, after completing a dissertation on prepositions in Anglo-Saxon prose, developed diverse literary interests, ranging from the Elizabethans to Samuel Taylor Coleridge and Edgar Allan Poe. He was also active in promoting American folksong, especially that of Missouri. He read a paper on Donne's prosody to the Central Branch of the Modern Language Association of America at the University of Wisconsin (reported in W. F. Melton, *The Rhetoric of John Donne's Verse*, 1906, pp. 56, 108–9 and 127).

[Belden addressed himself to the issue Coleridge had raised, the relation of rhythm and form to meaning.]

[Donne's] verse is possibly mad ... but there was method in his madness, and a definite purpose which he very effectually accomplished. ... The verse-rhythm of Donne's poetry is the natural outward and visible form of his mental temper. He writes so because he can best express his thoughts and his feeling. This I take it is the meaning of Coleridge's rather mysterious dictum that in Donne 'the sense, including the passion, leads to the metre'. But I should rather say that in Donne the meaning, straining against the rhythm of the fore-established metre in the reader's mind, reproduces there the slow, tense emphasis of Donne's thought. The melodists, from Greene and Marlowe to Swinburne, are always in danger (if it is a danger) of lulling the mind to sleep with the music of the sense. The verse pattern is caught at once; we get the tune; and the melodist never ventures far from it, however much he may adorn it with alliteration, assonance, and vowel-series. Such things we say sing themselves, – which can seldom if ever be said of Donne's poetry. It is the test of lyric as distinguished from other poetry that it does so sing itself. Donne's verse (with possibly one or two exceptions) is never lyric in this sense. Instead, he leaves you, line after line and phrase after phrase in doubt of the pattern, or of how the line is to be fitted to the pattern, producing thereby a searching pause on almost every syllable, – a sort of perpetual 'hovering accent'. This is the real idiosyncrasy of Donne's verses, and in it consists, no doubt, much of the peculiar charm of Donne's poetry for certain minds. ...

Donne is never, I think, difficult through carelessness or obscure through vagueness or indefiniteness of thought. What he thinks is concrete; and the reader who will follow him in his wrestlings with the language will generally be rewarded, as even Dr Johnson acknowledged, by 'genuine wit and useful knowledge'.

[Belden disputes Gosse's contention that Donne purposed innovation.]

... the verse-rhythm of Donne's poetry is the natural outward and visible form of his mental temper. He writes so because he can best express his thoughts and feelings.

73. Martin Grove Brumbaugh

1906

M. G. Brumbaugh (1862–1930) was a highly energetic and innovative educationalist in Philadelphia and Puerto Rico; he became Governor of Pennsylvania 1915–19 and was nominated as a presidential candidate in 1916. He wrote books on religion, geography and history and was editor of Lippincott schoolbooks. His doctoral thesis at the University of Pennsylvania was 'A Study of the Poetry of John Donne' (reported in W. F. Melton, *The Rhetoric of John Donne's Verse*, 1906, p. 130).

[Brumbaugh reviews the entire body of criticism which is concerned with Donne's style and thought. Yet he himself is at pains to point out Donne's absolute originality within his own restricted range.]

Donne . . . is . . . unlike all others in the range and limitations of his thinking, and in the marvellous power of condensation . . . contrary to most of his critics . . . he has . . . a very narrow range of thought. But in this limited field he holds absolute sway.

[Brumbaugh notes that Dryden, Johnson, Gray and Saintsbury had each sought a different antecedent for Donne's style, respectively deriving it from Horace, St Bernard, the conceited Italian writers, and the French Renaissance poets.]

It is remarkable that these four eminent critics should find Donne imitating the writers of four different and widely divergent national types. Nobody would scorn such an imputation with greater vehemence than Donne himself. He did not imitate anybody. . . . Had his method been such as to allow of what he would call zany efforts, he would in all probability have put himself in touch with some of the many poetic influences of his own times and of his own associates.

74. Charles Crawford

1906

Charles Crawford, who compiled concordances to Thomas Kyd and to Christopher Marlowe, set out in an article to show John Webster's borrowings from Florio's Montaigne, from John Marston and from Donne ('Montaigne, Webster and Marston: Dr Donne and Webster', 10:6 (1906), 122–4 and 242–4; reprinted in Crawford's *Collectanea*, 2nd series, 1907, pp. 38, 49 and 54–63).

[Crawford gives parallel passages from Donne's *Anniversaries* and from two works by Webster, which show how liberally Webster helped himself to Donne's conceits, images and diction. One of the works Crawford exhibits, Webster's elegy for Prince Henry called *A Monumental Column*, must have been written late in 1612 shortly after the publication of Donne's *Second Anniversary*. Crawford argues that the other work which draws freely on Donne, *The Duchess of Malfi*, is likely to have been written not long after that time.]

75. Wightman Fletcher Melton

1906

W. F. Melton (1867–1944), best known as a poet, submitted to the Johns Hopkins University, Baltimore, a doctoral dissertation on Donne's verse which was afterwards published. He went on to write a biographical sketch of Donne, and a book on Sidney Lanier, and prepared an edition of John Ruskin's *Crown of Wild Olive* and *The Queen of the Air* (*The Rhetoric of John Donne's Verse*, 1906, pp. 2, 8, 107–9, 148, 167–8, 193 and 206).

[Melton undertook two arduous tasks. He brought together a comprehensive collection of critical comment on Donne's versification from the poet's own day to 1906, including some unpublished work of the first years of the present century which might otherwise have been forgotten. Then he set himself to champion Donne's poetic idiom, offering page after page of analysed examples to justify Donne's rhythms in every particular.

Melton avows a long devotion to Donne, fostered and informed by mentors in America, which had brought him at last to the discovery of Donne's secret, the peculiar rhetorical principles on which Donne's verse is organized. In his view, Donne's reputation fluctuated as critics sensed this principle or failed to grasp it.]

The third chapter deals with a yet practically untouched aspect of the criticism of English verse. The revelation of Donne's 'secret' came to me suddenly after three years of daily, almost hourly, entreating, caressing, and wheedling of each line of his poetry. At first the thing seemed improbable; but, at the same time, it was so real and so plain as to give one that uncanny feeling experienced by those who dare to meddle with the affairs of 'some old lover's ghost'.

In this connection, I wish to say that this discovery came to me as a result of the 'secondary word-accent' theory taught by Professor Bright, and while I was actually engaged in applying it to Donne's verse. Were this theory in need of a final, clinching argument, it may be said that the man whose ear is too dull to catch the music of the ripples, and even the eddies, of rhythm, and who insists upon white-capped wave after wave, the inevitable long, (just so long and no longer), . . . and the inevitable short, (just so short and no shorter), can never, till he has been redeemed, appreciate the delicacy of Donne's lighter verse, or the straight thrust of his satire. . . .

To the close student of Donne it becomes more and more apparent that the charge of 'ruggedness' and 'harshness', which has been made against his verse for nearly three centuries, is due, (barring misprints), either to the influence of Ben Jonson's remark to Drummond (1618), or to the fact that critics have failed to compare the word-accents employed by him and by his contemporaries and successors. . . .

Professor Brumbaugh comes thrillingly near to our subject: 'The frequent repetition of the same monosyllable, generally at the

caesural pause, the repeated word having often a different meaning, and giving his verse by this change of accent a peculiar "swing"
that is at the same time characteristic and melodious, is very
common in Donne's verse. It is indeed so frequent (I have noted
about fifty instances) that illustration is necessary.'

Seventeen examples are cited of which these three are representative:

> *Up, up,* my drowsy soul, where they.
>> *An Anatomy. Second Anniv.,* 339
>
> Carrying his own house *still, still* is at home.
>> *To Sir Henry Wotton* (1) 50.
>
> *She, she* is dead, she's dead; when thou know'st this.
>> *An Anatomy. First Anniv.,* 183, 237, 325, 369, 427.

When, in person, I called Professor Brumbaugh's attention to
the fact that Donne, some four thousand times makes use of this
arsis-thesis variation of the same syllable or syllables, word or words
in the same line, or group of lines, and when I had read to him
more than a hundred of the most striking examples, he replied, 'I
am prepared to believe it'; and showed me the MS page from which
the above quotation is taken. Had he gone one step further he
would have discovered the peculiar characteristic, which, as unmistakable as the red strand of the rope of the English Navy, runs
through the entire body of Donne's verse. For example, had he
considered the very next line he would have found this variation,
not only at 'the caesural pause', but everywhere else in the couplet,
on similar words as: *shĕ, shé; thóu, thŏu;* and on similar sounds as: *ĭs,
thís, thĭs, ís;* and *knŏw'st, knów'st, ghŏst.*

> Shĕ, shé ĭs dead; shĕ's dead; when thóu knŏw'st thís
> Thŏu knów'st how wan a ghóst thĭs our world ís. . . .

That critics have not been able to understand Donne's peculiarity is
evidenced by the fact that Johnson describes him as 'Metaphysical';
DeQuincy, as 'Rhetorical'; Masson, as 'Metrical'. . . .

Observing how haltingly these great critics walk around the
poetry of Donne, one cannot get away from the impression that he
eluded their grasp. Some of them will not venture to view him
singly, but place him in a class to which he does not belong; and,
then, with one omniscient sweep of the hand, leave us in the dark.

Enough of Donne's characteristic peculiarity has appeared in his verse-references to poetry, and in the other examples quoted, to make a statement of his 'secret' seem more believable now than it would have been in the beginning of this chapter; furthermore, it can better be understood, now, what he means, in part at least, by 'excuse not my *excess*', in *A Litany*.

The 'rule' by which Donne seems to have worked, was: When a word, a syllable, or a sound, appears in arsis, get it into thesis as quickly as possible, and *vice versa*; having twisted, pressed, or screwed (Coleridge uses all three of these words in his quatrain) all the meaning out of that word, take up another and carry it through the same process. Better still, instead of pressing one word at a time, whenever convenient, take a whole handful of words and twist them so that men will not find out for centuries what it all means.

Coupling Donne's frequent rather mysterious remarks on his verse, – in which he uses such terms as 'measure', 'secret', 'excess', 'feet', and 'rule', and at the same time showing his characteristic accentuation in the most bewildering extravagance in some of the poems in which these references are made, – with the fact that whenever a word receives unusual accent, the same word, almost always, as has been seen from examples, stands near by accented as we expect it to be, – convinces me, unalterably, that his art was carefully mastered and executed with diligence and delight.

Fortunately the service to which a knowledge of Donne's peculiarity in verse may be put does not depend upon whether or not it was intentional. The field is inviting for psychological investigation. . . .

Having gone over the verse of the so-called Metaphysical School of poets, I find only sporadic instances of the thing which stands out boldly on every page of Donne. . . .

I am firmly convinced that Donne is a mine whose depths I have scarcely touched; that he possesses a richness which is not half apparent on the surface; and that, while the verses of other poets rime in the middle, or at the end, Donne's rime everywhere. Lest I be regarded as a victim of the 'editorial passion', I agree unreservedly with Dyce: '[Donne] was a man of great learning and extraordinary wit, and was not a bad poet.[1]

NOTE

1 *Early English Poems*, London, 1863, p. 124. [Melton's note.]

76. Herbert John Clifford Grierson

1906

Professor H. J. C. Grierson (1866–1960) of the University of Aberdeen, who would become Donne's greatest editor, embarked upon his study of Donne with an attempt to place Donne's poetry in relation to other writing of the time (*The First Half of the Seventeenth Century*, 1906, pp. 139–64).

Chapman comes at the head of a chapter on seventeenth-century poetry as a useful reminder that 'fantastic' is not a very distinctive title to apply to the poetry of Donne and his followers, – that if conceit and far-fetched similitudes are a sign of decadence, then Elizabethan poetry was born decadent, for from first to last it is, in Arnold's phrase, 'steeped in humours and fantasticality up to its very lips'.

It is difficult, in the absence of such contemporary evidence as is afforded to-day by critical reviews, to date exactly the changes in poetical taste. It seems clear, however, that in the closing years of the sixteenth century there was a reaction against the diffuse, flamboyant, Italianate poetry which Spenser, Sidney, and Lodge had made fashionable, – a reaction which showed itself in the satires of Hall and Marston, but found its fullest expression in the poetry – much of which is satirical – of Donne and of Jonson, who took the place in courtly circles which had been held earlier by Spenser and Sidney.

. . . it was the endeavour to give a denser intellectual texture to poetry which gave both harshness and obscurity to the verse of the two poets who began the movement that ended with Dryden.

These two poets, the chief shaping influences of Jacobean and Caroline poetry – John Donne (1573–1631) and Ben Jonson (1573? –1637) – were not only almost exactly contemporary, but were knit together by many common sympathies. They were both impatient of the diffuse and flamboyant style of the Spenserian and Italianate poets, and willing for the sake of pregnancy and vigour to overlook harshness and obscurity. Both were certainly admirers and imitators of Latin poetry, especially satirical and elegiac, and both cultivated a vein of frank, even cynical and brutal, satire. They

259

were courtly poets, and wrote abundance of high-flown eulogies and occasional verses, very often addressed to the same patrons. Donne's wit was not less courtly than Jonson's, if we remember that the court for which both wrote was James's.

Despite these resemblances, however, Donne and Jonson represent with startling distinctness the two discordant streams of tendency in the first half of the seventeenth century – the mediaeval or scholastic reaction on the one hand, the movement towards the rationalism and classicism of the closing century on the other. Jonson is, as the study of his drama has shown, the first of our classical poets. In his poetry we see the elegancies and extravagances of Petrarchian – what Mr Courthope calls Euphuist – wit meeting with and yielding to the simpler and more appropriate sentiments of classical poetry, the dignified and vigorous commonsense which was to be Dryden's ideal of wit. In Donne's poetry revives all that was most subtle and metaphysical in the thought and fancy of the Middle Ages.

[Grierson now gives an account of Donne's life and career, interspersing it with comments on the poetry.]

His strange, virile, powerful, often repellant, *Elegies* may record details of actual intrigues, as Mr Gosse supposes. I am more inclined to believe that, while Donne's stormy career doubtless supplied experiences enough from which to draw generally, the *Elegies* are his very characteristic contribution to the frankly pagan and sensuous poetry of the Nineties, represented otherwise by *Hero and Leander* and *Venus and Adonis*. . . .

Donne's poems – with the exception of his elegies on Mistress Elizabeth Drury, *The Anatomy of the World* – were not printed until after his death, and it is accordingly difficult to determine their order with accuracy. His *Satires* – the most interesting and, metrically, the most irregular of the late sixteenth-century work of this kind – may date from 1593, but the earliest unmistakable reference is to 1597. To his first years in town belong probably the more frankly sensuous and cynical of the *Elegies* and *Songs and Sonnets*. Those which strike a higher and more Platonic note may have been written after his engagement to Anne More. The satirical *Progress of the Soul* dates from 1601. The courtly and adulatory *Epithalamia, Verse-Letters, Epicedes and Obsequies*, as well as the *Divine Poems*, were the product of his later and more regular years.

Amorous and satirical, courtly, pious, these are the successive phases of Donne's life and poetry, – poetry in which the imaginative, emancipated spirit of the Renaissance came into abrupt contact, and blended in the strangest way with the scholastic pedantry and subtlety of the controversial court of James. The temper of Donne's poetry is that of Marlowe's and Shakespeare's. It has the same emancipated ardour and exaltation. Whatever his theme – love, eulogy, or devotion – his imagination, like theirs, takes wing, so soon as it is thrown off, to the highest pitch of hyperbole. What distinguishes him from the great Elizabethans is the prevailing character of his conceits, his 'metaphysical wit'. To the imaginative temper of Marlowe Donne superadded the subtlety and erudition of a schoolman, and brought to the expression of his intense, audacious passions imagery drawn from an intimate knowledge of mediaeval theology and of the science mediaeval, but beginning to grow modern, of the seventeenth century.

Johnson's term 'metaphysical' – which he derived from Dryden, and by which it is clear from what he says of Waller's 'wit' as well as Cowley's he meant simply learned or technical conceits, drawn not from 'the superficies of nature' but from the recondite stores of learning – is both more distinctive than any other name which has been suggested – 'fantastic' is very far from distinctive – and is historically interesting and accurate. 'Concetti metafisici ed ideali' are, according to Fulvio Testi, the distinctive feature of Italian as opposed to classical poetry. The ultimate source of the conceits and artificialities of Renaissance love-poetry is to be found, as Mr Courthope has indicated, in the poetry of the Middle Ages, from the Troubadours onwards. But it was in Italy, in the 'dolce stil nuovo' of Guido Guinicelli and Dante, that the 'metaphysical' element first appeared in love-poetry. 'Learning', says Adolf Gaspary, 'is the distinctive feature of the new school.' Writing first in the Troubadour fashion of the Sicilians, it was with the famous canzone 'Al cor gentil ripara sempre amore' that Guinicelli began to write in the metaphysical manner. 'The change in his poetry took place under the influence of science. Philosophy, which in that age when Thomas Aquinas and Bonaventura were teaching had again come to be regarded with favour, penetrated even into poetry, which drew from it its subject-matter, and even the manner of its exposition.' The high-priest of this ideal, metaphysical, abstract love-poetry was Dante. Petrarch brought love-poetry back to closer touch with ordinary human nature. His finer psychology made Petrarch 'the first of the moderns'; on the other hand, his subtle and refined compliments contained the germ, and more than the germ, of what in subsequent sonneteers took the place of Dante's philosophy and Petrarch's psychology – a kind of pseudo-metaphysics which elaborated in abstract and hyperbolical fashion every metaphor, natural or traditional to the theme of love. But the sonnet never lost the cast which it acquired from its origin in this combination of high passion and scholastic philosophy – a strain of subtle thought, a readiness to admit erudite and technical imagery – even though it be only occasionally that one finds again passionate and profound reflection upon the nature and mystery of love. A sonnet like 'Let me not to the marriage of true minds Admit impediment', is not less intense or philosophic in its own way than a canzone of the *Vita Nuova*.

It is this metaphysical, erudite, scholastic strain which Donne, under conditions similar to that in which it first appeared, renewed and heightened. He is hardly less concerned than Dante with the abstract nature of love. The 'concetti metafisici ed ideali' of the *Anatomy of the World* are not more metaphysical and hyperbolical – blasphemous, as Jonson bluntly put it – than those of the canzone in the *Vita Nuova*, which tells how the saints in heaven beseech God for the presence of Beatrice –

My lady is desired in the high heaven.

The central idea of the *Anatomy of the World*, the all-pervading influence of the loved one, is an expansion of one of the conventions of the school of Dante.

But after all there is a vast difference between Donne and Dante. Donne has no consistent metaphysic of love and its place in the upward movement of the soul to God. He elaborates in many of the *Songs and Sonnets* two radically inconsistent ideas, one the inherent fickleness of woman, the other the mystical identity of the souls of lovers. But often he simply ransacks his multifarious knowledge to discover new and startling conceits in which to express his bizarre and subtle moods. For it is a mistake – towards which I venture to think Mr Courthope tends – to let the intellectual and abstract element in Donne's poetry blind one to the passionate feeling it expresses. No love-poetry of the closing sixteenth century has more of the sting of real feeling in it except

262

Shakespeare's. There is nothing quite like Donne's love-poems in the language, except, perhaps, some of Browning's. Passion seems to affect both poets in the same way, not evoking the usual images, voluptuous and tender, but quickening the intellect to intense and rapid trains of thought, and finding utterance in images, bizarre sometimes and even repellent, often of penetrating vividness and power. The opening of one of Donne's songs affects us like an electric shock, jarring and arresting –

> For God's sake hold your tongue and let me love,

or –

> I long to talk with some old lover's ghost
> Who died before the God of Love was born,

or –

> Twice or thrice had I loved thee
> Before I knew thy face or name,
> So in a voice, so in a shapeless flame,
> Angels affect us oft and worshipped be;

and many of the best, as 'The Anniversary', the wonderful 'Ecstasy', 'The Funeral', 'The Relic', 'The Prohibition', preserve throughout this potent and unique impressiveness. Donne's *Songs and Sonnets* cannot take a place beside the great love-poetry of Dante, Petrarch, and Shakespeare. There is too large an element in them of mere intellectual subtlety, even freakishness. But his poetry is not to be dismissed as the result of conflicting conceptions of nature clashing in a subtle and bizarre intellect. It has a real imaginative as well as historical value, because it is the unique expression of a unique temperament.

The difference between Donne and Jonson comes out very distinctly if we compare their eulogistic verses. The non-dramatic poetry of Jonson is contained in the *Epigrams* and *Forest*, which he published in 1616, and the posthumous *Underwoods* (1640). A large proportion of it, including the best of the epigrams, consists of eulogistic addresses to patrons and friends. Donne's *Verse-Letters* are of the same kind, and there is abundance of eulogy in his *Epithalamia* and *Epicedes*. It is when he is paying compliments that Donne's mind works most abstractly, and that his subtleties are most purely intellectual. In the verses *To the Countess of Salisbury, August 1614,* beginning 'Fair, great and good', he elaborates with the utmost ingenuity the statement that the Countess is super-excellent in a world which has grown utterly corrupt, but he gives no indication of the qualities in which her excellence is shown. He tells the Lady Carey that while others are virtuous in this or that humour – phlegm, blood, melancholy, or choler – she has virtue so entire that it has made even her beauty virtuous, exciting not to passion but to goodness. Jonson's eulogies are in a different strain. He can be fancifully complimentary, but it is in a more Humanist and elegant, a less pedantic style. . . .

What was best done was in lyrical poetry, in which the influence of Donne and Jonson appears both blended and distinct. Donne's closest followers are the devout Anglican poets. They strike the same deep personal note; and the wide range of metaphysical imagery gratified their taste for quaint analogies, for symbols, and for points rhetorically effective rather than purely poetic. The courtiers, too, could turn metaphysical images to their service in compliment and badinage –

> Ask me no more whither do stray
> The golden atoms of the day,
> For in pure love heaven did prepare
> Those powders to enrich your hair.

But Jonson is their leader in courtly eulogy; a great deal of their imagery is, like his, a blend of Petrarchian and classical.

77. Caroline Spurgeon

1907/13

Professor C. F. E. Spurgeon (1869–1942) was the first woman to hold a chair in an English university. She was Professor of English Literature at the University of London from 1913 to 1929, and one of the founders and first President (1920–4) of the International Federation of University Women. In an essay on mysticism in English poetry, Spurgeon sought to show that Donne's poetry expresses mystical attitudes but falls short of true mysticism. She repeated her account of Donne's mysticism, with minor rephrasing and some telling amplifications, in her full-length study of mysticism in English literature, published six years after the essay. Amplifications made in this later version are given here in { } below ('Mysticism in English Poetry', *Quarterly Review*, 207 (1907), 450–2; *Mysticism in English Literature* (1913), 1922, pp. 72–6).

In Donne, Henry More, and Tennyson the mystical sense may be called philosophical in that it reaches them by way of the intellect, and that they present their convictions in a philosophical form {calculated to appeal to the intellect as well as to the emotions. These writers, as a rule, though not always, are themselves markedly intellectual, and their primary concern therefore is with truth or wisdom. Thus Donne, William Law, Burke, Coleridge, and Carlyle are all predominantly intellectual, while Traherne, Emily Brontë, and Tennyson clothe their thoughts to some extent in the language of philosophy.}

The dominating characteristic of Donne is intellectuality; and this may partly account for the lack in him of some essentially mystical qualities, more especially reverence, and that ascension of thought so characteristic of Plato and Browning. But these shortcomings are more strongly felt in his poetry than in his prose. They are very well illustrated in that extraordinary poem 'The Progress of the Soul'. The idea is a mystical one, derived from Pythagorean philosophy, and has great possibilities, which Donne entirely fails to utilise; for, instead of following the soul upwards on its way, he depicts it as merely jumping about from body to body, and we are conscious of an entire lack of any lift or grandeur of thought. This poem helps us to understand how it was that Donne, though so richly endowed with intellectual gifts, yet failed to reach the highest rank as a poet.

[She argues that Donne was brilliant in particulars but lacked the epic qualities of breadth, unity and proportion, characteristics which were destined to be the distinctive marks of the school of which he is looked upon as the founder.]

Apart from this somewhat important defect, Donne's attitude of mind is essentially mystical. This is especially marked of his feeling about the body and natural law, in his treatment of love, and in his conception of woman. The mystic's postulate – if we could know ourselves, we should know all – is very often on Donne's lips, as, for instance, in that curious poem written in memory of Elizabeth Drury on the second anniversary of her death. It is perhaps best expressed in the following verse:

> But we know ourselves least: mere outward shows
> > Our minds so store,
> That our souls, no more than our eyes, disclose
> But form and colour. Only he who knows
> > Himself, knows more.

One of the marked characteristics of Donne's poetry is his continual comparison of mental and spiritual with physical processes. This sense of analogy prevailing throughout nature is with him very strong; and as we have seen, it lies at the very centre of mystical symbolism. The mystery of continual flux and change particularly attracts him, as it did the early Greek thinkers; and Nettleship's remarks about the nature of bread and unselfishness are akin to the following comparison:

> > Dost thou love
> Beauty – and beauty worthiest is to move –
> Poor cozened cozener, that she and that thou,
> Which did begin to love, are neither now.
> Next day repairs – but ill – last day's decay.
> Nor are – although the river keep the name –
> Yesterday's waters and to-day's the same!
> > ('An Anatomy of the World,' 389–96)

[She maintains that Donne believed firmly in man's potential greatness and the power within his soul, quoting in confirmation lines 19–24 of the verse letter 'To Mr Rowland Woodward'.]

Although in the *Progress of the Soul* he failed to give expression to it, yet his belief in progress is unquenchable. He fully shares the mystic's belief that 'man, to get towards Him that's infinite, must first be great' (Letter to the Countess of Salisbury).

In his treatment of love Donne's mystical attitude is most clearly seen. He holds the Platonic conception that love concerns the soul only, and is independent of the body or bodily presence; and he is the poet who, at his best, expresses this idea in the most dignified and refined way. The reader feels not only that Donne believes it, but that he has in some measure experienced it; whereas with his imitators it degenerated into little more than a fashionable 'conceit'. The 'Undertaking' expresses the discovery he has made of this higher and deeper kind of love; and in the 'Ecstasy' he describes the union of the souls of two lovers.

[She claims that the language of 'The Ecstasy' proves Donne's familiarity with the description of ecstasy given by Plotinus, *Enn.* VI.9, §11.]

The great value of this spiritual love is that it is unaffected by time and space. . . .

In one of his verse-letters to the Countess of Huntingdon he explains how true love cannot be desire. He goes still further in the poem entitled 'Negative Love', where he says that love is such a passion as can only be defined by negatives; and his language here reminds us of Plato's 'Parmenides' and Plotinus' 'Enneads' (VI, vii, 41) when speaking respectively of the One and the Good.

78. George Edward Bateman Saintsbury

1908

In his exhaustive study of English prosody Saintsbury continued his engagement with Donne's metrical idiosyncrasies (*A History of English Prosody*, vol. II, 1908, pp. 159–66).

[Saintsbury finds that Donne's poetry sets 'one of the few well-known prosodic problems'.]

He has left us, speaking roughly, three classes of poetry – satires; miscellaneous poems chiefly in couplet; and lyrics. Now the puzzle of his prosody consists, not merely in the fact that the satires do not, as Ben calls it, and as some would still call it, 'keep accent', though that is a most inadequate description of their eccentricities. It lies in the fact that his peculiarity is very much less noticeable in the miscellaneous poems, and hardly noticeable at all in the lyrics.

That Donne takes the benefit of the general law, elsewhere often stated, in regard to satire hardly needs emphasising. But that general law, while it may cover the eccentricities of Lodge or Marston, Hall or Guilpin, will hardly find a lappet of its amplest gown that can protect such a passage as this

[He quotes a passage from a poem sometimes attributed to Donne as one of the *Satires*, 'Sleep, Next Society', and points out that some of its lines 'are absolutely *unrhythmical*, not merely unmetrical'.]

And yet the man who wrote them certainly wrote such a line as –

> A bracelet of bright hair about the bone,

such a couplet as –

> I must confess it could not choose but be
> Profane to think thee anything but thee,

with hundreds of other lines and couplets equally harmonious.

The mere Persian licence of satiric roughness will not, I say, cover this enormous difference. Sometimes I have been tempted to think that Donne and others thought themselves entitled to *scazontics* – that is to say, iambic lines with spondaic or trochaic endings, such as the ancient satirists who used the metre often preferred. But I am by no means sure that a bolder explanation, and one thoroughly in harmony with the general results of the inquiry on which this book is based, may not be applicable – to wit, that Donne, recognising the classic practice of equivalence and substitution, used it in experiment more freely than wisely, as upon the *corpus*, admittedly *vile*, of satire.

The poems which come between satire and lyric in him, whether in couplet or stanza, are still rough; though less so. The *Elegies*, which are nearest both in matter and time to the *Satires*, and the *Verse Letters*, some of which are in the same neighbourhood, are the roughest; the *Divine Poems*, which are the latest, are the smoothest. The wonderful *Anatomy of the World*, which appears to represent the tuning-point, though it has a certain ruggedness, resembling that of Chapman somewhat, is not exactly rough. If, however, we need any single thing to show that Donne was a great experimenter in prosody, and that he never took the trouble to criticise, polish, or cancel his experiment, we have it in that rather unlovely though not unpowerful the *Progress of the Soul.* The immense success of Spenser's stanza had naturally set his contemporaries and successors on seeing what they could do. The result, as in the Fletchers' case, was generally a conjugation of the untranslatable French verb *estropier* – untranslatable unless we use a hybrid paraphrase and say 'apply the strappado'. But I do not know that an uglier deformation was ever reached than in this ten-line stanza[1] of Donne's, which ruins itself from the outset by starting with a couplet, the very worst preparation of the ear for the distinctive rhyming which is to follow. As no one who glances at the edition I have used here for citation will doubt my enthusiasm for Donne as a poet, I do not fear to speak plainly on this part of his prosody. Indeed, it is well that he did not lick his early poems into prosodic shape; for then we should have lacked the most instructive prosodic figure between Spenser and Milton – a 'first poet of the world in some things', both poetically and otherwise, who, exploring further in a half-explored country, stumbled in many waste places. There is, however, no doubt that Donne's eccentricities had not a little to do with the severe syllabic and accentual reaction, which Milton fortunately did not share, and against which he remained a standing and impregnable protest. No one will suspect me of prosodic 'Popery'; but even the wooden shoes of the strict couplet were as seven-leagued boots to get us away from the possibility of such a line as –

His passions and the world's troubles rock me;

or, if anybody takes refuge there in 'woruld', from –

Here Sleep's house by famoùs Ariòs-tòw.

'What? What? *Barclay* come again?'

The utter and antinomian transformation of the prosody between Donne's other poems (especially his satires) and his lyrics can hardly be exaggerated. One experiences the shock of it afresh every time one reads this, more than Browning of the seventeenth century; and I confess that if I were to edit Donne, I should, without much fear of the charge of topsyturviness, put his lyrics last of the poems that are in any way certain, in order that this transformation might work the right way. Even here there are, of course, a few lapses. In the absence of the slightest revision on the author's part – in the absence even of any evidence that he so much as saw the copy from which our prints and MSS were taken – it was impossible that this should not happen. But these lapses are very slight, and in hardly a single case are they of the essence of the versification, as those in the *Satires* and elsewhere are. Here also, Donne is an experimenter; and there may not be universal agreement about the felicity of his experiments. For instance, beautiful as is the song –

Sweetest love, I do not go,

even among its author's, I am not sure that some may not think the bold reversal of the usual order – giving trochaic cadence first, and iambic second – a thing more bold than wise. I do not think so myself; but I should not hold any one reasonless who did. Perhaps the most inexhaustible delight is to be found in those pieces which are actually decasyllabic, such as 'The Good-morrow'. The 'nubbly' ruggedness of the satire-lines here melts honey-like into even sweetness. Nowhere shall we find a happier combination than that in 'Go and catch a falling star', from the rocking trochees of the sestet to the sudden spondees of the 'bob' and the iambic close. It is with the trochee that Donne does most of his feats here, and unless he wrote –

Thou sent'st me late a heart was crowned,

(of which I think far higher than some seem to do) I do not know that he has any of the greatest triumph of iambic 'C.M.' But his eights, as in 'O! Do not die, for I shall hate', are wonderful past all whooping. He has a marvellously sustained six-line stanza (6, 10, 8, 8, 10, 6 *ababcc*), where, though the rhyme order is the same as in the most usual sixain, the difference of line-lengths creates an entirely new music; lighter things like 'The Message', much twisted and 'bobbed', and that astounding 'Ecstasy', also in eights or long measure, where, perhaps, the boldest line with which poet ever dared fools –

And we said nothing all the day,

occurs, and justifies itself.

But one returns, somehow, to the pieces where most of the lines are decasyllabic, such as 'The Dream' and 'Love's Deity', so odd is the effect of contrast with the others, as if the poet were doing it on purpose, and saying to Ben, 'Oh! You think I deserve hanging, do you? Keep accent in this way, if even *you* can!' As for the famous 'Funeral', it even ventures the fourteener, and vindicates its audacity in a wreath of verse as 'subtle' as that which it celebrates. While if he wrote 'Absence', as I feel pretty certain that he did, he has made an almost unique special mould for this thought. We often say to ourselves how admirably the sense and sound suit each other in this or that poem. But here I could almost say that no other sound could possibly suit *this* sense – that we should not 'enjoy but miss' it, if a foot were changed.

But I must recall the reader and myself from enjoyment – it was very hard to leave off tapping this nectar – to the sober prosodic fact that the author of most of these things certainly, of all possibly, was also the author of the jolting monstrosities above cited. Many theories – my own of a rather irresponsible experiment, Mr Melton's of 'arsis–thesis variations', a dozen others – may be brought in to account for the contrast. One thing, however, is not theory but fact, that the contrast is *there*. In other words, it was possible for the same man to produce perfect harmony in one set of metres, almost perfect cacophony in others. In yet other words, Spenser's work was not quite done. And before Donne died, the fact that it was not quite done was shown, not merely in the older form of the couplet, but in the newer of blank verse.

NOTE

1 The beauty of the actual opening couplet in the following example will only emphasise its misplacement: –

> Prince of the orchard, fair as dawning morn,
> Fenced with the law and ripe as soon as born,
> That apple grew, which this soul did enlive.

[Saintsbury's note.]

271

79. Alfred Horatio Upham

1908

A. H. Upham (1877–1945) of the University of Miami wrote
a doctoral dissertation for Columbia University on 'The
French Influence in English Literature', later published. In
it, he sought a prototype of Donne's wit among European
writers (*The French Influence in English Literature* (1908), 1911,
pp. 177–85).

[Upham argues that Donne drew more from Du Bartas than from
witty poets in Italy or Spain.]

The various forms of wit, which characterize so much of the poetry
of the early seventeenth century, may of course have grown up
without outside impulse, finding sufficient cause in the somewhat
mechanical struggle of a decadent period to find new figurative
conceptions that would attract readers by surprise or sweep of
imagination. Yet it is unlikely that this problem can be completely
solved without reckoning with the encouragement given by numerous foreign or native compositions, already turning more or less in
these directions. The Italian lyric poets at the end of the *quattrocento*
had prepared the way for such activity. The work of Du Bartas,
either in its original form or in translation, opens a promising field
of further investigation in the matter of these outside impulses.
Even in the case of John Donne, the great leader in the use of
daring figures drawn from the material things of life, there seems
ample reason to consider the possible influence of the *Semaines.*
Foreign source-hunting for Donne has not proved especially satisfying. Marino came into the field too late, and his style is less like
Donne's, the more one studies it. The Spanish Gongora grew to
resemble Donne in extravagant metaphor and torturing obscurity,
but these features of his style likewise came too late. Donne carries
power and intensity of imagination far beyond that of Serafino and
his group. There is a degree of satisfaction in the notion that Donne
was Donne, and that his bold and virile imagination seized upon
startling conceptions which other men did not dream of. When one
considers, however, that practically all the peculiarities of Donne
had already appeared in Du Bartas, lacking there only the mastery

of genius to make them vital and impressive instead of vapid and commonplace, the element of French suggestion seems to some extent to find its place in the explanation of this English work. The poetry of Du Bartas was before him; he had every reason to know it. Even as he experimented and composed, Sylvester's translations were coming into circulation. Elaborate figures, complicated figures, comparisons drawn from all the minutiae of contemporary science and hardly pausing at the threshold of men's sense of taste and proportion: all these were spread out before him, and he had only to approve them and give them power.

The minor tricks of style concerned him but little. His use of compounds is not excessive, but they appear occasionally. Thus: –

1 'But truly keeps his first-last-everlasting day.'
2 ''Tis much that glass should be
As all confessing and through-shine as I.'
3 'Or like to full on-both-sides-written rolls.'
4 'Batter my heart, three-person'd God.'

Donne's use of verbal echoes and conceits is also moderate. A few examples appear: –

1 'As to a stomach starv'd, whose insides meet,
Meat comes, it came';
2 All things are one; and that one none can be,
Since all forms uniform deformity
Doth cover . . .'
3 'Verse, that draws Nature's works from Nature's law,
Thee, her best work, to her work cannot draw.'
4 'That all, which always was all, every where;
Which could not sin, and yet all sins did bear.
Which could not die, yet could not choose but die.'

This particular expression must have been especially pleasing to Donne, as it is repeated almost verbatim in the second of his *Holy Sonnets*: –

> That all, which always is all everywhere,
> Which cannot sin, and yet all sins must bear,
> Which cannot die, yet cannot choose but die.

In the use of complicated comparisons drawn from the material

273

details of human knowledge, Donne finds his distinguishing characteristic. Numerous entire poems of his are little else than meshes
of this sort, either playing upon a few elaborately wrought figures
or trying one daring notion after another. Examples of this are
found in such poems as 'The Flea', 'A Valediction of My Name in
the Window', 'Love's Alchymy', 'Elegy VIII (The Comparison)',
and the verses to Mr T. W. and Mr B. B. Masses of whimsical
conceits of this sort occur also in 'The Anatomy of the World – First
and Second Anniversaries', as well as in 'The Progress of the Soul'
and in 'The Cross'. Various valuable examples may be quoted from
other poems. Thus from 'Love's Growth'. . . .

[He quotes stanza 2 of the poem.]

An elaborate clock figure occurs in the Funeral Elegy 'To the Lord
Harrington's Brother'.

[He quotes lines 131–42 of the 'Obsequies to the Lord Harington'.]

A somewhat startling effect is obtained by Donne's way of stating
surprise that the world has gone on in its course, despite the fact
that Mrs Elizabeth Drury is dead.

[He quotes lines 9–22 of *The Second Anniversary.*]

Indeed, the two elegies, from the second of which this is drawn,
seem in a number of ways subject to the direct influence of Du
Bartas. They are both in honor of Mrs Elizabeth Drury, the 'First
Anniversary' being entitled 'The Anatomy of the World', and the
second, 'Of the Progress of the Soul'. They belong to the years 1611
and 1612, and are in the ten-syllable couplets of the *Satires* and of
Sylvester's translations. As already noted, they abound in Donne's
characteristics of style. References to the creation are frequent.

[He quotes lines 347–52 of *The First Anniversary*; lines 23–6 of *The
Second Anniversary*, and lines 37–50 of the verse letter 'To the
Countess of Huntingdon', 'That unripe side of earth'.]

Much is made in Donne's *Funeral Elegies* of the superior strength
and more extensive life of man soon after creation; in fact, the
poems are constantly reverting to the times described in the two
Semaines. The Microcosmos notion, which, though by no means
limited to Du Bartas, had been developed at length in his Sixth Day
of the *First Week*, finds many opportunities for mention in Donne's

poems, sometimes in a manner closely resembling the treatment in Du Bartas. A characteristically elaborated specimen of the type occurs in the 'Elegy on Lady Markham', and in several ways suggests Du Bartas.

[He quotes lines 1–12 of the 'Elegy on the Lady Markham'.]

One of Donne's poems, 'The Progress of the Soul', dated 1601, is a daring narrative development of the idea of metempsychosis, looking remarkably like a parody of such sacred epic as that of Du Bartas. The introduction is perhaps most significant.

[He quotes stanza 1 of the *Metempsychosis*.]

The recognized imitators of Donne – John Cleveland, Harry King, and Lord Herbert of Cherbury – carry on the same peculiarities of style seen in their master. Whether or not they went back of him to Du Bartas would be difficult to decide and of no great importance.

80. George Charles Moore Smith

1908

Professor Moore Smith (1858–1940) of the University of Sheffield dismissively reviewed W. F. Melton's *The Rhetoric of John Donne's Verse* (*Modern Language Review*, 3 (1908), 81–2).

The whole treatment is a case of 'petitio principii'. When it is said that Donne's verse is often rough, what is meant is that in reading it one often finds that to give the natural stress to the poet's words is to obscure the rhythm of his verse. But if we once allow that in poetry, it is not necessary to give a word its natural stress, but that one may remove the stress at will from the root-syllable to the suffix, the roughest verse becomes at once perfectly regular. This is the process which is here adopted, with a rare degree of self-satisfaction on the part of the writer.

Mr Melton's method tends to close his eyes to the real phenomena of Donne's verse. When verse is rough, the cause often lies in the fact that two or more feet of abnormal construction (e.g. with weak stress or inverted stress) occur together. There would only be a sense of pleasing variety if one such foot had stood alone, but the collocation of two or three causes the reader to lose the rhythm of the line. Mr Melton takes the case of a stress laid on a preposition such as 'of', and has no difficulty in showing that even in Shakespeare and other poets, 'of' may bear a secondary stress. But he does not point out that whereas in Shakespeare an irregular foot is generally isolated, in Donne such feet occur in juxtaposition to one another. There is an enormous waste of labour in finding parallels for lines which present no metrical difficulty, and no discrimination is made between such lines and lines that do.

[He gives some examples of Melton's accenting of Donne, which he condemns as mechanical.]

But enough. We can only say that we regard this as one of the most laboriously worthless dissertations we have ever seen.

81. Thomas Hardy

1908

Edmund Gosse sent Hardy a copy of a limited edition of Donne's poems (New York, 1905) as a present for his birthday, 2 June 1908. Hardy acknowledged the gift in a brief letter dated 24 July 1908 (*The Collected Letters of Thomas Hardy*, ed. R. L. Purdy and M. Millgate, vol. III, 1982, p. 326).

[In offering Gosse '1000 thanks' for the gift, Hardy observed that the copy is 'just the type for my eyes'. But he offered no response to Donne's poetry itself, claiming pressure of correspondence which had accumulated in his absence from home.

Evelyn Hardy examined a copy of Donne's poems in Hardy's library, which she took to be Gosse's gift; though she said that it was published in 1896. She found passages marked in several poems: 'The Indifferent', 'The Expiration', *Elegy* 2, *Song*, 'Sweetest Love', some of the *Divine Poems*. She comments: 'Hardy must have known Donne long since in an earlier, lost volume, but he did not quote and re-quote him in his novels as he did other favourite poets' (*Thomas Hardy: A Critical Biography*, 1954, p. 308).]

82. Herbert John Clifford Grierson
1909

Grierson contributed a chapter on Donne to the *Cambridge History of English Literature*. In it his work towards establishing the canon and more reliable texts than previously published (for which his edition of 1912 was to be known) is already evident. As with his 1906 article, he places Donne's work within its literary and biographical context but gives summaries of each of the categories of poetry and prose within which Donne worked that show the detailed attention he had been paying to his writing (*Cambridge History of English Literature*, vol. IV, 1909, pp. 196–223).

From the time of Wyatt, Surrey and their contemporaries of the court of Henry VIII, English lyrical and amatory poetry flowed continuously in the Petrarchian channel. . . .

The poet who challenged and broke the supremacy of the Petrarchian tradition was John Donne. Occasionally, when writing a purely complimentary lyric to Mrs Herbert or lady Bedford, Donne can adopt the Petrarchian pose; but the tone and temper, the imagery and rhythm, the texture and colour, of the bulk of his love songs and love elegies are altogether different from those of the fashionable love poetry of the sixteenth century, from Wyatt

and Surrey to Shakespeare and Drummond. With Donne, begins a
new era in the history of the English love lyric, the full importance
of which is not exhausted when one recognises in Donne the source
of the 'metaphysical' lyric as it flourished from Carew to Rochester.
Nor was this Donne's only contribution to the history of English
poetry. The spirit of his best love poetry passed into the most
interesting of his elegies and his religious verses, the influence of
which was not less, in the earlier seventeenth century perhaps even
greater, than that of his songs. Of our regular, classically inspired
satirists, he is, whether actually the first in time or not, the first who
deserves attention, the first whose work is in the line of later
development, the only one of the sixteenth century satirists whose
influence is still traceable in Dryden and Pope. *Religio Laici* is
indebted for some of its most characteristic arguments to Donne's
'Kind pity checks my spleen'; and Pope found in Donne a satirist
whose style and temper were closer in essential respects to his own
than those of the suave and urbane Horace.

For evil and for good, Donne is the most shaping and determin-
ing influence that meets us in passing from the sixteenth to the
seventeenth centuries. In certain aspects of mind and training the
most medieval, in temper the most modern, of his contemporaries,
he is, with the radically more pedantic and neo-classical Jonson, at
once the chief inspirer of his younger contemporaries and successors, and the most potent herald and pioneer of the school of
poetic argument and eloquence.

[Grierson gives a summary of Donne's life, in which he asserts that
despite his conversion and later polemical writing and preaching,
his most intimate religious poems indicate very clearly that he never
ceased to feel the influence of his Catholic upbringing. However,
'when he entered the service of Sir Thomas Egerton, in 1597, he
cannot have been a professed Romanist, and, in 1601, he dis-
claimed indignantly "love of a corrupt religion"'.

Disagreeing with Walton's claim in his *Life of Donne* that the
time he had spent in Italy and Spain had occurred late in the 1590s,
Grierson speculates that it is more likely to have been 'in the last
years of his earlier education, when he was still a Catholic and
under Catholic direction [*c.* 1590]', possibly 'with the intention
on the part of his guardians that he should enter a seminary . . .
or take service under a foreign ruler'.]

With more light on this point, we might be able to see in the singularly emancipated moral tone of Donne's mind and its complete openness on religious questions during the early years in London something of a reaction in his nature against a bent which others would have imposed upon it. Lastly, an early date fits best the evidence in the poems of foreign influence, which is not to be found specially in Donne's 'wit', but in the spirit of Italian literature and life reflected in the frank sensuality of some, the virulent satire of others, of his elegies and songs. The spirit of the renascence in Latin countries, and a wide acquaintance with Spanish casuists and other religious writers, are the most palpable indications of foreign influence in Donne's work. His direct indebtedness to any particular poet, Italian or Spanish, has not been established. Of all Elizabethan poets, he is, for good or evil, the most independent.

[Grierson turns to the establishing of the text of the poems.]

The history of his poems is involved in the difficulties and obscurities of his biography. Only three were published in his life time, *The Anatomy of the World* (1611, 1612); the satirical lines *Upon Mr Thomas Coryat's Crudities* (1611); and the *Elegie on Prince Henry* (1613). In 1614, when about to cross the Rubicon, Donne thought of hurriedly collecting and publishing his poems before the doing so could be deemed an actual scandal to his office. He had, apparently, no autograph copies, at least of many of them, but was driven to apply to his friends, and especially to Sir Henry Goodere, the Warwickshire friend to whom the larger number of his letters are addressed. 'This made me ask to borrow that old book of you.' The edition in question never appeared, but when, in 1633, the first collection was issued posthumously, the source was very probably this same 'old book' (though Goodere had died before Donne), for, along with the poems, were printed eight letters addressed to Goodere and one to the common friend of Goodere and Donne, the countess of Bedford. In this edition, the poems were arranged in a rather chaotic sequence of groups. The volume opened with *The Progresse of the Soule* and closed with the paraphrased *Lamentations of Jeremy* and the *Satyres*, the latter edited with a good many cautious dashes. There are obvious errors in the printing, but the text of such poems as this edition contains is more correct than in any subsequent one. In 1635, a second edition was issued, in which many fresh poems were added, and the grouping of the poems was carried out more

279

systematically, the arrangement being adopted which has been generally adhered to since, and is useful for reference – *Songs and Sonets, Epigrams, Elegies, Epithalamiums, Satyres, Letters to Severall Personages, Funerall Elegies, The Progresse of the Soule, Divine Poems.* The editions which followed that of 1635 added individual poems from various sources, sometimes rightly, sometimes wrongly; and made alterations from time to time in the text, conjecturally, or with the help of MS copies, which are sometimes emendations, more often further corruptions. Modern editors have followed in their wake, printing more carefully, correcting many errors, but creating not a few fresh ones. The canon of Donne's poems is far from being settled. Modern editions contain poems which are demonstrably not his, while there are genuine poems still unpublished. The text of many of his finest poems is disfigured by errors and misprints.

The order of the groups in the edition of 1635 corresponds, roughly, to the order of composition. Donne's earliest works were love songs or sonnets (using the word in the wider, freer sense of the Elizabethans) and elegies (after the manner of the Latin poets), through many of which runs a vein of pungent and personal satire, and regular verse satires. Of these last, the editions since 1669 contain seven. We have, however, the explicit testimony of Sir William Drummond that Donne wrote only five. It is clear from MSS such as Harleian 5110 and others which have survived in whole or in part, that the first five, or some of them, were copied and circulated by themselves. These alone were included in the edition of 1633. The so-called sixth, which was added in 1635, if it be Donne's, is much more in the manner of the satirical elegies than of the regular satires; while the seventh, addressed *To Sir Nicholas Smith,* which was first inserted in the edition of 1669, an edition the text of which abounds in conjectural emendations, differs radically in style and tone from all the others, and there can be little doubt that it is the work of Sir John Roe, to whom it is assigned in more than one MS.

Donne's satires have features in common with the other imitations of Juvenal, Persius and Horace which were produced in the last decade of the sixteenth century, notably a heightened emphasis of style and a corresponding vehemence and harshness of versification. But, in verse and style and thought, Donne's satires are superior to either Hall's 'dashing, smirking, fluent imitations of the ancients' or Marston's tedious and tumid absurdities. The verse of

these poets is much less irregular than Donne's. It approximates
more closely to the balanced couplet movement of Drayton's
Heroicall Epistles. Hall's couplets are neat and pointed, Marston's
more irregular and *enjambed*. But Donne's satiric verse shows
something like a consistent effort to eschew a couplet structure,
and to give to his verse the freedom and swiftness of movement to
which, when he wrote, even dramatic blank verse had hardly yet
attained. He uses all the devices – the main pause in the middle of
the line, weak and light endings (he even divides one word between
two lines) – by which Shakespeare secured the abrupt, rapid effects
of the verse of *Macbeth* and the later plays:

> Gracchus loves all (*i.e.* religions) as one, and thinks that so
> As women do in divers countries go
> So doth, so is Religion; and this blind-
> Ness too much light breeds; but unmoved thou
> Of force must one, and forc'd but one allow;
> And the right? ask thy father which is she,
> Let him ask his; though truth and falsehood be
> Near twins yet truth a little elder is;
> Be busy to seek her. Believe me this,
> He's not of none, nor worst, that seeks the best.

Such verse is certainly not smooth or melodious. Yet the effect is
studied and is not inappropriate to the theme and spirit of the
poem. Donne's verse resembles Jonson's much more closely than
either Hall's or Marston's. He had certainly classical models in view
– Martial and Persius and Horace. But imitation alone will not
account for Donne's peculiarities. Of the minor καλλωπίσματα
[embellishments] of verse, he is always a little careless; but if there
is one thing more distinctive than another of Donne's best work it
is the closeness with which the verse echoes the sense and soul of
the poem. And so it is in the satires. Their abrupt, harsh verse
reflects the spirit in which they are written. Horace, quite as much
as Persius, is Donne's teacher in satire; and it is Horace he believes
himself to be following in adopting a verse in harmony with the
unpoetic temper of his work:

> And this unpolish'd rugged verse I chose,
> As fittest for discourse and nearest prose.

The urbane spirit of Horace was not caught at once by those who, like Donne and Jonson, believed themselves to be following in his footsteps.

The style of Donne's satires has neither the intentional obscurity of Hall's more ambitious imitations of Juvenal, nor the vague bluster of Marston's onslaughts upon vice. If we allow for corruptions of the text, one might say that Donne is never obscure. His wit is a succession of disconcerting surprises; his thought original and often profound; his expression, though condensed and harsh, is always perfectly precise. His out-of-the-way learning, too, which supplies puzzles for modern readers, is used with a pedantic precision, even when fantastically applied, to which his editors have not always done justice.

In substance, Donne's satires are not only wittier than those of his contemporaries, but weightier in their serious criticism of life, and happier in their portrayal of manners and types. In this respect, some of them are an interesting pendant to Jonson's comedies. The first describes a walk through London with a giddy ape of fashion, who is limned with a lightness and vivacity wanting to Jonson's more laboured studies of Fastidious Brisk and his fellows. The second, opening with a skit on the lawyer turned poet, passes into a trenchant onslaught – obscured by some corruptions of the text – upon the greedy and unprincipled exacter of fines from recusant Catholics, and 'purchasour' of men's lands:

> Shortly (as the sea) he'll compass all the land;
> From Scots to Wight; from Mount to Dover strand.

He is the lineal descendant of Chaucer's Man of Law, to whom all was fee-simple in effect, drawn in more angry colours. The third stands by itself, being a grave and eloquent plea for the serious pursuit of religious truth, as opposed to capricious or indolent acquiescence, on the one hand, and contemptuous indifference on the other. The lines which are quoted above in illustration of Donne's verse, and, indeed, the whole poem, were probably in Dryden's mind when he wrote his first plea for the careful quest of religious truth, and concluded that,

> 'tis the safest way
> To learn what unsuspected ancients say.

These three satires are ascribed in a note on one manuscript collection to the year 1593. Whether this be strictly correct or not, they seem to reflect what we may take to have been the mind of Donne during his early years in London, at the inns of court, when he was familiar with the life of the town, but not yet an *habitué* of the court, and in a state of intellectual detachment as regards religion, with a lingering prejudice in favour of the faith of his fathers. The last two satires were written in 1597, or the years immediately following, when Donne was in the service of the lord keeper, and they bear the mark of the budding statesman. The first is a long and somewhat over-elaborated satire on the fashions and follies of court-life at the end of queen Elizabeth's reign. The picture of the bore was doubtless suggested by Horace's *Ibam forte via sacra*,[1] but, like all Donne's types, is drawn from the life, and with the same amplification of detail and satiric point which are to be found in Pope's renderings from Horace. The last of Donne's genuine satires is a descant on the familiar theme of Spenser's laments, the miseries of suitors.

Donne's satires were very popular, and, to judge from the extant copies or fragments of copies, as well as from contemporary allusions, appear to have circulated more freely than the songs and elegies, which were doubtless confined so far as possible, like the Paradoxes and ΒΙΑΘΑΝΑΤΟΣ [*Biathanatos*], to the circle of the poet's private friends. A Roman Catholic controversialist, replying to *Pseudo-Martyr*, expresses his regret that Donne has 'passed beyond his old occupation of making Satires, wherein he hath some talent and may play the fool without controll'. Such a writer, had he known them, could hardly have failed to make polemical use of the more daring and outrageous *Elegies* and those songs which strike a similar note. But, though less widely known, the *Songs and Sonets* and the *Elegies* contain the most intimate and vivid record of his inner soul in these ardent years, as the religious sonnets and hymns do of his later life. And the influence of these on English poetry was deeper, and, despite the temporary eclipse of metaphysical poetry, more enduring, than that of his pungent satires, or of his witty but often laboured and extravagant eulogies in verse letter and funeral elegy.

Of the *Songs and Sonets*, not one is a sonnet in the regular sense of the word. Neither in form nor spirit was Donne a Petrarchian poet. Some were written to previously existing airs; all, probably, with a more or less definite musical intention. The greater number of them would seem to have been preserved and may be found in the first section of Chambers's edition. He has rightly excluded the song, 'Dear Love, continue nice and chaste', which was included in the edition of 1635, but was written by Sir John Roe. A fresh editor would have to exclude, also, the song 'Soul's joy now I am gone' and the *Dialogue* beginning 'If her disdain least change in you can move', which, if the collective evidence of MSS be worth anything, were written by the earl of Pembroke, collaborating, in the last, with Sir Benjamin Ruddier. The Burley MS contains a few songs, as well as longer pieces which, from their accompanying indubitable poems and letters of Donne, are, presumably, given as his. None of them is specially characteristic or adds anything of great intrinsic value. It has been not unusual, since its first publication as by Donne in *The Grove* (1721), to ascribe to him the charming song 'Absence, hear thou my protestation'. But, in Drummond's copy of a collection of verses made by Donne himself, of which only a few are his own composition, this particular song is ascribed to J. H., *i.e.* (as another MS proves), John Hoskins. The touch is a shade lighter, the feeling a shade less intense, than in Donne's most characteristic work.

Of the *Elegies*, the canon is more difficult to ascertain exactly. Some of the most audacious, but not least characteristic, were excluded by the first editor, but crept into subsequent issues. Of the twenty given in Chambers's edition, all are Donne's, with the possible exception of the twelfth, 'Come, Fates, I fear you not'; and to these should be added that entitled *Love's War*, in the appendix, which was the first printed by Sir John Simeon. But the sixteenth, 'To make the doubt clear that no woman's true', was included in Ben Jonson's posthumous *Underwoods*, and it is not impossible that the three which there accompany it are also Donne's. As Swinburne has pointed out, they are more in his style than in that of Jonson. On the other hand, no MS collection of Donne's poems includes them, whereas their companion appears in more than one.

It is not difficult to distinguish three strains in Donne's love poetry, including both the powerful and enigmatical elegies and the strange and fascinating songs. The one prevails in all the elegies (except the famous *Autumnal* dedicated to Mrs Herbert, and the seventeenth, the subject of which may have been his wife) and in the larger number of the lyrical pieces, in songs like 'Go and catch a falling star', 'Send home my long stray'd eyes to me', or such lyrics as *Woman's Constancy, The Indifferent, Aire and Angels, The Dreame, The Apparition*, and many others. This is the most distinctive strain in

Donne's early poetry, and that which contrasts it markedly with the love poetry of his contemporaries, the sonneteers. There is no echo of Petrarch's woes in Donne's passionate and insolent, rapturous and angry, songs and elegies. The love which he portrays is not the impassioned yet intellectual idealism of Dante, nor the refined and adoring sentiment of Petrarch, nor the epicurean but courtly love of Ronsard, nor the passionate, chivalrous gallantry of Sidney. It is the love of the Latin lyrists and elegiasts, a feeling which is half rapture and half rage, for one who is never conceived of for a moment as standing to the poet in the ideal relationship of Beatrice to Dante or of Laura to Petrarch. *Das ewig Weibliche zieht uns hinan*[2] is not Donne's sentiment in these poems, but rather

> Hope not for mind in women; at their best
> Sweetness and wit, they're but mummy possest.

But if Donne's sentiment is derived rather from Latin than from Italian and courtly poetry, it was reinforced by his experience, and it is expressed with a wit and erudition that are all his own. And, in reading some, both of the elegies and the songs, one must not forget to make full allowance for the poet's inexhaustible and astounding wit and fancy. 'I did best', he said later, 'when I had least truth for my subject.' Realistic, Donne's love poetry may be; it is not safe to accept it as a history of his experiences.

The *Elegies* are the fullest record of Donne's more cynical frame of mind and the conflicting moods which it generated. Some, and not the least brilliant in wit and execution, are frankly sensual, the model of poems such as Carew's *The Rapture*; others, fiercely, almost brutally, cynical and satirical; others, as *The Chain* and *The Perfume*, more simply witty; a few, as *The Picture*, strike a purer note. A strain of impassioned paradox runs through them; they are charged with wit; the verse, though harsh at times, has more of the couplet cadence than the satires; the phrasing is full of startling felicities:

> I taught my silks their rustlings to forbear,
> Even my oppress'd shoes dumb and silent were;

and there are not wanting passages of pure and beautiful poetry:

> I will not look upon the quickening sun
> But straight her beauty to my sense shall run;
> The air shall note her soft, the fire most pure,
> Waters suggest her clear, and the earth sure.

This turbid, passionate yet cynical, vein is not the only one in Donne's love poetry. Two others are readily distinguishable, and include some of his finest lyrics. In one, which is probably the latest, as that described is the earliest, Donne returns a little towards the sonneteers, especially the more Platonising among them. Poems like *Twickenham Garden*, *The Funeral*, *The Blossom*, *The Primrose*, were probably addressed neither to the mistresses of his youth, nor to the wife of his later years, but to the high-born lady friends, Mrs Herbert and the countess of Bedford, for whom he composed the ingenious and erudite compliments of his verse letters. Towards them, he adopts the hopeless and adoring pose of Petrarchian flirtation (of Spenser towards lady Carew or Drayton towards mistress Anne Goodere) and, in high Platonic vein, boasts that,

> Difference of sex no more we knew
> Than our guardian angels do;
> Coming and going we
> Perchance might kiss, but not between those meals;
> Our hands ne'er touched the seals
> Which nature, injured by late law, sets free;
> These miracles we did; but now alas!
> All measure and all language I should pass,
> Should I tell what a miracle she was.

Less artificial than this last strain, purer than the first, and simpler, though not less intense, than either, is the feeling of those lyrics which, in all probability, were addressed to his wife. To this class belongs the exquisite song:

> Sweetest Love, I do not go
> For weariness of thee,
> Nor in the hope the world can show
> A fitter love for me.

In the same vein, and on the same theme, are the *Valediction of Weeping*:

> O more than moon,
> Draw not up seas to drown me in thy sphere;
> Weep me not dead in thine arms, but forbear
> To teach the sea what it may do too soon;

and the more famous *Valediction: forbidding Mourning*, with its characteristic, fantastical yet felicitous, conceit of the compasses:

286

> Such wilt thou be to me who must,
>   Like the other foot, obliquely run;
> Thy firmness makes my circle just,
>   And makes me end where I begun.

The seventeenth elegy, 'By our first strange and fatal interview', may belong to the same group, and so, one would conjecture, do *The Canonization*, 'For Godsake hold your tongue and let me love' and *The Anniversary*. In these, at any rate, Donne expresses a purer and more elevated strain of the same feeling as animates *The Dream, The Sun-Rising* and *The Break of Day*; and one not a whit less remote from the tenor of Petrarchian poetry. At first sight, there is not much in common between the erudite, dialectical Donne and the peasant-poet Burns, yet it is of Burns one is reminded rather than of the average Elizabethan by the truth and intensity with which Donne sings, in a more ingenious and closely woven strain than the Scottish poet's, the joy of mutual and contented love;

> All other things to their destruction draw,
>   Only our love hath no decay;
> This no to-morrow hath nor yesterday,
> Running it never runs from us away,
> But truly keeps his first, last, everlasting day.

Of the shadow of this joy, the pain of parting, Donne writes also with the intensity, if never with the simplicity, of Burns. The piercing simplicity of

> Had we never loved sae kindly

was impossible to Donne's temperament, in which feeling and intellect were inextricably blended, but the passion of *The Expiration* is the same in kind and in degree, however elaborately and quaintly it may be phrased:

> So, so, break off this last lamenting kiss,
> Which sucks two souls, and vapours both away.
> Turn thou ghost that way, and let me turn this,
> And let ourselves benight our happiest day;
> We ask'd none leave to love, nor will we owe
> Any so cheap a death as saying 'Go'.

The Ecstacy blends, and strives to reconcile, the material and the spiritual elements of his realistic and his Platonic strains. But, subtly and highly wrought as that poem is, its reconciliation is more metaphysical than satisfying. It is in the simpler poems from which quotations have been given that the diverse elements find their most natural and perfect union.

If Donne's sincere and intense, though sometimes perverse and petulant, moods are a protest against the languid conventionality of Petrarchian sentiment, his celebrated 'wit' is no less a corrective to the lazy thinking of the sonneteers, their fashioning and re-fashioning of the same outworn conceits.

> The Muses' garden, with pedantic weeds
> O'er-spread, was purged by thee: the lazy seeds
> Of servile imitation thrown away,
> And fresh invention planted.

This is Carew's estimate of what Donne achieved for English poetry. He would say what he felt and would say it in imagery of his own fashioning. He owes, probably, no more to Marino or Gongora than to Petrarch. 'Metaphysical wit', like *secentismo* or 'Gongorism' is, doubtless, a symptom of the decadence of renascence poetry which, with all its beauty and freshness, carried seeds of decay in its bosom from the beginning. But the form which this dissolution took in the poetry of Donne is the expression of a unique and intense indi-viduality; a complex, imaginative temperament; a swift and subtle intellect; a mind stored with the minutiae of medieval theology, science and jurisprudence. The result is often bizarre, at times even repulsive. When the fashion in wit had changed, Addison and Johnson could not see anything in Donne's poetry but far-sought ingenuity and extravagant hyperbole. His poetry has never, or never for long, the harmonious simplicity of perfect beauty; but, at its best, it has both sincerity and strength, and these are also constituents of beauty. . . .

If we owe to the influence of Donne in English poetry some deplorable aberrations of taste, we owe to it, also, both the splendid cadences, the *élan*, of the finest seventeenth century lyrics from Jonson and Carew to Marvell and Rochester and, at a lower imaginative level, the blend of passion and argument in Dryden's ringing verse rhetoric. . . .

During the last year of his residence in the household of Sir Thomas Egerton, Donne began the composition of a longer and more elaborate satirical poem than anything he had yet attempted,

288

a poem the personal and historical significance of which has received somewhat scant attention from his biographers. *The Progresse of the Soule. Infinitati Sacrum. 16 Augusti 1601. Metempsycosis [sic]. Poema Satyricon* was published for the first time in 1633, but manuscript copies of the poem, by itself and in collections of Donne's poems, are extant. That he never contemplated publication is clear from the fact that he adopted the same title, *The Progresse of the Soule,* for the very different *Anniversaries* on the death of Elizabeth Drury.

Starting from the Pythagorean doctrine of metempsychosis, it was Donne's intention, in this poem, to trace the migrations of the soul of that apple which Eve plucked, conducting it, when it reached the human plane, through the bodies of all the great heretics. . . .

It would have been interesting to read Donne's history of heresy, and characters of Mahomet and Luther, great, bad men as he apparently intended to delineate them; but the poem never got so far. After tracing through some tedious, not to say disgusting, episodes of the life of the soul in vegetable and animal form, Donne leaves it just arrived in Themech,

> Sister and wife to Cain, Cain that first did plough.

The mood in which the poem was conceived had passed, or the poet felt his inventive power unequal to the task, and he closed the second canto abruptly with a stanza of more than Byronic scepticism and scorn:

> Whoe're thou beest that readest this sullen writ,
> Which just so much courts thee as thou dost it,
> Let me arrest thy thoughts; wonder with me
> Why ploughing, building, ruling and the rest,
> Or most of those arts whence our lives are blest,
> By cursed Cains race invented be,
> And bless'd Seth vex'd us with astronomy.
> There's nothing simply good nor ill alone;
> Of every quality comparison
>   The only measure is, and judge opinion.

The more normal and courtly moods of Donne's mind in these central years of his life are reflected in the *Letters* and *Funerall Elegies.* Of the former, the earliest, probably, were *The Storm* and *The Calm,* whose vivid and witty realism first set Donne's 'name afloat'. . . .

The moral reflections in the ... letters are elevated, and are developed with characteristic ingenuity. The brilliance with which a train of metaphysical compliments is elaborated in such a letter as that to the countess of Bedford beginning 'Madam – you have refined me' is dazzling. But neither Donne's art nor taste – to say nothing of his character – is seen to best advantage in the abstract, extravagant and frigid conceits of these epistles and of such elegies as those on prince Henry and lord Harington. The strain of eulogy to which Donne suffers himself to rise in these last passes all limits of decency and reverence. To two feelings, Donne was profoundly susceptible, and he has expressed both with wonderful eloquence in verse and prose. He has all the renascence sense of the pomp and the horror of death, the leveller of all earthy distinctions; and he can rise, like Sir Thomas Browne, to a rapt appreciation of the Christian vision of death as the portal to a better life. But his expression of both moods, when he is writing to order, is apt to degenerate into an accumulation of 'gross and disgusting hyperboles'. In an elegy on Mrs Bulstred, which is divided into two separately printed poems, *Death I recant* and *Death be not proud*, these moods are combined in a sonorous and dignified strain.

But the finest of Donne's funeral elegies is the second of the *Anniversaries*, which he composed on the death of Elizabeth Drury. The extravagance of his praise, indeed, offended even Jacobean readers, and the poem was declared by Jonson to be 'profane and full of blasphemies'. It is clear, however, that Donne intended Elizabeth Drury to be taken as a symbol of Christian and womanly virtue. He may have known something of the Tuscan poets' metaphysic of love, for Donne is one of the few poets of the day who had read 'Dant'. It cannot be said that he succeeded in investing his subject with the ideal atmosphere in which Beatrice moves. *The First Anniversary* is little more than a tissue of frigid, metaphysical hyperboles, relieved by occasional felicities, as the famous

> Doth not a Teneriffe or higher hill
> Rise so high like a rock, that one might think
> The floating moon would shipwreck there and sink?

The *Second*, however, is not only richer in such occasional jewels but is a finer poem. With the eulogy, which is itself managed with no small art, if in a vein of extravagance jarring to our taste, the poet has interwoven a *meditatio mortis*, developed with the serried eloquence, the intense, dull glow of feeling and the sonorous cadences which we find again in the prose of the sermons.

Of Donne's religious verses other than the funeral elegies, the earliest, *On the Annunciation and Passion falling in the same year*, was written, according to the title given in more than one manuscript, in 1608. *The Litany* was composed in the same year as *Pseudo-Martyr*; and it is interesting to note that, though the Trinity is followed, in Catholic sequence, by the Virgin, the Angels, the patriarchs and so forth, there is no invocation of any of these, but only commemoration. The two sequences of sonnets, *La Corona* and *Holy Sonnets*, belong, the first to 1608–9, the second to the years of his ministry. One of the latter, first published by Gosse from the Westminster MS, refers to the recent death of his wife in 1617; and *The Lamentations of Jeremy* would appear to be a task which he set himself at the same juncture. The hymns *To Christ, at the Authors last going into Germany*, *To God, my God in my Sickness* and *To God the Father* were written in 1619, 1623–4 and either the same date or 1631.

There is a striking difference of theme and spirit between the 'love-song weeds and satiric thorns' of Donne's brilliant and daring youth and the hymns and sonnets of his closing years; but the fundamental resemblance is closer. All that Donne wrote, whether in verse or prose, is of a piece. The same intense and subtle spirit which, in the songs and elegies, analysed the experiences of passion is at work in the latter on a different experience. To be didactic is never the first intention of Donne's religious poems, but, rather, to express himself, to analyse and lay bare his own moods of agitation, of aspiration and of humiliation in the quest of God, and the surrender of his soul to Him. The same erudite and surprising imagery, the same passionate, reasoning strain, meets us in both.

> Is the Pacific sea my home? Or are
>   The Eastern riches? Is Jerusalem?
> Anyan, and Magellan, and Gibraltar,
>   All straits (and none but straits) are ways to them,
> Whether where Japhet dwelt, or Ham, or Shem.

The poet who, in the sincerities of a sick bed confession, can spin such ingenious webs for his thought is one of those who, like Baudelaire, are 'naturally artificial; for them simplicity would be affectation'. And as Donne is the first of the 'metaphysical' love poets, he is, likewise, the first of the introspective, Anglican, religious poets of the seventeenth century. Elizabethan, and a good deal of Jacobean, religious poetry is didactic in tone and intention, and, when not, like Southwell's, Romanist, is protestant and Calvinist but not distinctively Anglican. With Donne, appears for the first time in poetry a passionate attachment to those Catholic elements in Anglicanism which, repressed and neglected, had never entirely disappeared; and, from Donne, Herbert and his disciples inherited the intensely personal and introspective tone to which the didactic is subordinated, which makes a lyric in *The Temple*, even if it be a sermon, also, and primarily, a confession or a prayer; a tone which reached its highest level in the ecstatic outpourings of Crashaw.

Donne's earliest prose writings were, probably, the *Paradoxes* and *Problems* which he circulated privately among his friends. . . . Like everything that Donne wrote, they are brilliant, witty and daring, but, on the whole, represent the more perverse and unpleasant side of his genius. His other prose works are: a tract on the Jesuits, very similar in tone and temper to *Paradoxes*, entitled *Ignatius his Conclave: or, His Inthronisation in a late Election in Hell*, which was published anonymously, the Latin version about 1610, the English in 1611; the serious and business like *Pseudo-Martyr*, issued with the author's name in 1610; ΒΙΑΘΑΝΑΤΟΣ [*Biathanatos*] *A Declaration of that Paradoxe or Thesis that Self-Homicide is not so Naturally Sinne that it may never be otherwise*; the *Devotions upon Emergent Occasions, and Several Steps in my Sickness, digested into Meditations, Expostulations and Prayers*, published in 1624; the *Essays in Divinity*, printed by his son in 1651; and the sermons.

All Donne's minor or occasional writings, except the rather perfunctory *Essays in Divinity*, partake of the nature of paradoxes more or less elaborately developed. Even *Pseudo-Martyr* irritated the Roman Catholic controversialist who replied to it by its 'fantastic conceits'. Of them all, the most interesting, because bearing the deepest impress of the author's individuality, his strange moods, his subtle reasoning, his clear good sense, is ΒΙΑΘΑΝΑΤΟΣ [*Biathanatos*]. It is not rightly described as a defence of suicide, but is what the title indicates, a serious and thoughtful discussion of a fine point in casuistry. Seeing that a man may rightly, commendably, even as a duty, do many things which promote or hasten his death, may he ever rightly, and as his bounden duty, consummate that process – may he ever, as Christ did upon the cross (to this Donne recurs more than once in the sermons), of his own free will render up his life to God?

But Donne's fame as a prose writer rests not on these occasional and paradoxical pieces, but on his sermons. His reputation as a preacher was, probably, wider than as a poet, and both contributed to his most distinctive and generally admitted title to fame as the greatest wit of his age, in the fullest sense of the word. . . .

In Donne's sermons, all the qualities of his poems are present in a different medium; the swift and subtle reasoning; the powerful yet often quaint imagery; the intense feeling; and, lastly, the wonderful music of the style, which is inseparable from the music of the thought. The general character of the sermon in the seventeenth century was such as to evoke all Donne's strength, and to intensify some of his weaknesses. The minute analysis of the text with a view to educing from it what the preacher believed to be the doctrine it taught or the practical lessons it inculcated, by legitimate inference, by far-fetched analogy, or by quaint metaphor, was a task for which Donne's intellect, imagination and wide range of multifarious learning were well adapted. The fathers, the schoolmen and 'our greatest protestant divines' (notably Calvin, to whom, in subtlety of exposition, he reckons even Augustine second) are his guides in the interpretation and application of his text; and, for purposes of illustration, his range is much wider – classical poets, history sacred and secular, saints' legendaries, popular Spanish devotional writers, Jesuit controversialists and casuists, natural science, the discoveries of voyagers and, of course, the whole range of Scripture, canonical and apocryphal. It is strange to find, at times, a conceit or allusion which had done service in the love poems reappearing in the texture of a pious and exalted meditation. In the sermons, as in the poems (where it has led to occasional corruptions of the text), he uses words that, if not obsolete, were growing rare – 'bezar', 'defaulk', 'triacle', 'lation' – but, more often, he coins or adopts already coined 'inkhorn' terms – 'omnisufficiency', 'nullifidians', 'longanimity', 'exinanition'. . . .

The relation of Donne to Elizabethan poetry might, with some justice, be compared with that of Michael Angelo to earlier Florentine sculpture, admitting that, both as man and artist, he falls far short of the great Italian. . . .

293

And ... just as Michael Angelo was a bad model for those who came after him and had not his strength and originality, Donne, more than any other single individual, is responsible for the worst aberrations of seventeenth century poetry, especially in eulogy and elegy. . . .

And yet it would be a mistaken estimate of the history of English poetry which either ignored the unique quality of Donne's poetry or regarded its influence as purely maleficent. The influence of both Donne and Jonson acted beneficially in counteracting the tendency of Elizabethan poetry towards fluency and facility. If Donne somewhat lowered the ethical and ideal tone of love poetry, and blighted the delicate bloom of Elizabethan song, he gave it a sincerer and more passionate quality. He made love poetry less of a musical echo of Desportes. In his hands, English poetry became less Italianate, more sincere, more condensed and pregnant in thought and feeling. The greatest of seventeenth century poets, despite his contempt for 'our late fantastics', and his affinities with the moral Spenserians and the classical Jonson, has all Donne's intense individuality, his complete independence, in the handling of his subjects, of the forms he adopts, even of his borrowings. He has all his 'frequency and fulness' of thought. He is not much less averse to the display of erudition, though he managed it more artfully, or to the interweaving of argument with poetry. But Milton had a far less keen and restless intellect than Donne; his central convictions were more firmly held; he was less conscious of the elements of contradiction which they contained; his life moved forward on simpler and more consistent lines. With powers thus better harmonised; with a more controlling sense of beauty; with a fuller comprehension of 'the science of his art', Milton, rather than Donne, is, in achievement, the Michael Angelo of English poetry. Yet there are subtle qualities of vision, rare intensities of feeling, surprising felicities of expression, in the troubled poetry of Donne that one would not part with altogether even for the majestic strain of his great successor.

NOTES

1 See No. 11, n. 1.
2 'The eternal Female draws us upwards.'

83. Janet Spens

1909

The Oxford scholar Janet Spens discovered a disquieting likeness between her own age and the early seventeenth century (*Two Periods of Disillusion*, 1909, pp. 3–41).

[Spens argues that the similar spirit of the two eras accounts for Donne's likeness to some late nineteenth-century poets.]

The fundamental grief alike of the late nineteenth century and of the early seventeenth century is that we are not truly living, and it is taken for granted that emotion is life.

The idea is expressed most directly by Donne, 'who casts', says Mr Gosse, 'his shadow over the whole century'. Donne is the epitome of what is most characteristic of his time, and his extraordinary resemblance to Browning on the one hand and to Arnold on the other is highly significant. A certain allowance must be made, of course, for the method of expression, but if this is done he appears at times amazingly modern and intimate. Donne is full of the idea of man's corruptness and littleness, and his explanation is that the men of the day are of the Afterborn. His cry is almost exactly the same as Arnold's, that we are pigmies, miserable shadows of our forefathers. Like Arnold he is inconclusive, for though for himself his quest ended in conscious and perfect satisfaction, his final vision was not uttered in poetry, and even taking his prose there is a chasm of thought and feeling over which no bridge is thrown. For us therefore he remains an 'imperfect speaker', but all the nearer to us, perhaps, because of his uncertainty.

The key to Donne's nature is an insatiable thirst for intense spiritual existence. He scarcely sees the external world at all. One of the few passages in which inanimate nature is mentioned is the description in the 'Anatomy' of the new made Earth, and its beauty for the poet depends entirely on shimmering and changeful colour.

> When Nature was most busy, the first week
> Swaddling the new-born earth, God seemed to like

295

> That she should sport herself sometimes, and play,
> To mingle and vary colours every day;
> And then, as though she could not make enow,
> Himself his various rainbow did allow.

It is the weaving and unweaving of clouds and waters that attracts him. He thinks of the Earth as still unfixed in form and pulsating with emotion, like his lady:

> her pure and eloquent blood
> Spoke in her cheeks, and so distinctly wrought
> That one might almost say her body thought.

And he feels himself degraded by the necessities of his material nature by the processes of thought and perception, that he must needs 'see through lattices of eyes and hear through labyrinths of ears'. He hates his body because of the helplessness and humiliation it subjects him to in birth and in death. It is against this humiliation that he tries to arm himself in the 'Anatomy'. Death is a groom to wait upon him, he tries to fancy, not a force which takes possession of him, and men violate his person because they

> Dare not trust a dead man's eye with that
> Which they from God and angels cover not.

This intense sense of life and emotion was, of course, only possible for moments, and at times he felt that he had never touched it, that at the heart of life there was mere nothingness.

> Some that have deeper digg'd love's mine than I
> Say, where his centric happiness doth lie,

he says half beseeching, half mocking, and we know that it is not merely the centric bliss of love he means but of all joy.

> Oh! 'tis imposture all,
> And as no chemic yet th' elixir got
> But glorifies his pregnant pot,
> If by the way to him befall
> Some odoriferous thing or medicinal,

so we are pitifully content with the little unessential joys that come to us.

It is the feeling of the age. Such happiness and beauty as we attain to and conceive of are accidental, not what we had asked. The poets turn from it like disappointed children. 'It is got', Vaughan thinks, 'by mere despair of wings.' Donne's own lyrics seem the very incarnation of this evanescent loveliness rejected alike by Heaven and earth. One can but describe them by his own phrase for a mass of sun-lit hair – they are 'scattering bright' with marvellous single lines which by their dazzling points of light disembody the whole poem. Many of these magic lines owe their charm to their intensity. They tend to come at the beginning of a poem or verse, and probably Donne gave the hint of that clash into music, as of emotion suddenly vocal through intensity, which is the peculiarity of the best lyrics of the time. But the momentariness of this vitality, so 'like the lightning which doth cease to be ere one can say "it lightens"', leaves a sense of the unearthly, of a joy that can never be captured. Very often there is a direct suggestion of strange worlds of which the poet knows, and the accent of whose tongue he has caught. It is a world where 'past years' lie buried, and where wander ghosts of lovers dead before passion had become a secular thing. It is an abstract world, a negation:

> I am re-begot
> Of absence, darkness, death, – things which are not

and as such it brings after a time a sense of aridity. It is as if one had been walking in a desert. Life is not a little thing, but it is gaunt, abstract, like a skeleton.

> O'er our thoughts there hangs a darkness, call it solitude or blank desertion,
> No familiar shapes remain, no pleasant images of trees, of sea or sky,
> No colours of green fields.

Donne himself certainly felt this. There came in the end a sickness or a terror of the abstract, and the frightened soul plunged for a time into a materialism whose appalling coarseness is some measure of the revulsion.

In the seventeenth century Vaughan alone of the poets seems conscious of the connection between the transcendentalism of their passions and the recurrent loathing of all emotion at all. Nowhere in his work do you find the utter weariness of life and thought which forms an undertone in all Donne's life. And it seems to be his tolerance of the material and his love of nature which saved him. For instance, he has none of Donne's fierce rebellion against the fact of corruption. . . . Himself, one feels, a man of no sensual passions, he sees a value, a poetic quality in the body with its frailties and desires, a quality which had quite escaped Donne, who felt these desires so infinitely more intense. . . .

The perception, however, of the consolation that may lie in the 'meanest flower that blows' is almost peculiar to Vaughan in the seventeenth century. The keynote of the time is the infinite aspiration, the magnificent sickness for infinity, the insatiate thirst after righteousness which has in it no touch of the yearning for love, for response. It soars to lyric rapture in 'Comus' when Milton dreams that the pure soul may rise on earth to hear the converse of the habitants of Heaven, so that a beam is cast on the outward shape and gradually the mortal body is transmuted into eternal essence. Milton does not desire absorption into the infinite. His god is himself risen to his own ideal. That is why he does not really understand any of his characters except Satan.

Now Donne is extremely like Milton. His religion is of the same intensely intellectual type. It is alleged that he had led a very dissipated life as a young man, and when we find him hesitating as to his worthiness to enter the Church we are reassured as to his honesty. But if we look closer we find no indications at all of repentance for this sort of sin. His misgiving is all concerning intellectual errors, – 'an immoderate hydroptic desire of human learning' – the perverting, as he thinks, of his intellect to tracing out eagerly 'by and forbidden ways' for the mind's wanderings. He does not feel the need of forgiveness, perhaps, at bottom, he scarcely believed in its possibility. He prefers, he tells us, 'God's justice to his mercy'. To Donne as to Browning, the preserving of the soul's capacity for intensity, for 'adventure new', was the great duty, and however the theology which he had embraced might preach the beauty of repentance and forgiveness, his whole soul rebelled at the personality and sentimentality of such a relationship. What is worshipful to him is the Justice that is impersonal and divinely unconscious. . . .

The idea that there is another ruling power in life, whose logical anatomy, so to speak, we do not understand, is most definitely expressed by Donne. He speaks of 'Great Destiny, the commissary of God', and in another place of 'Fate whom God made, but doth not control', which is simply equivalent to saying that it is divine and independent. Now both these expressions occur in that fragment 'The Progress of the Soul', which is entitled, one is not sure whether by the author or not, a satiric poem, and which seems to conceal within it the key to all that Donne might have told us if there had not been laid on him some mysterious barrier of silence. On the surface it is coarse and cynical in the extreme for the most part, and yet its title connects it with what Professor Saintsbury calls 'the most unearthly' of all Donne's work – the 'Anatomy of the World'. There can be very little doubt that the two formed in some way a connected whole in the poet's mind. It is true that Donne very frequently repeats his phrases in different poems, in a way which suggests unconscious self-plagiarism, and which would have been impossible if he had published his poems. But even if that is the case here, there must have been at least an inarticulate link between the two poems, and since he apparently regarded both as very important, they should give us the hint of his undeveloped philosophy. The 'Anatomy' is ostensibly an elegy, the essential idea of which is that Mrs Elizabeth Drury was the soul of the world, and now that she is dead the whole creation has 'vapoured with her breath' and is a grey phantom. The theory is very much the same as Shelley's in 'Adonais'. She is not dead, 'tis we decay like corpses in the charnel. Eternity was to Donne, as to Shelley, a white radiance, and life at times a coloured evil mist. The poem is on one side the culminating expression of Donne's weariness of life, and on the other anticipates in places the magnificent passage in the great sermon on death. We understand the impression he produced on his contemporaries as of an 'angel speaking from a cloud, but in none'.

He is like Shelley's skylark. . . .

[She quotes several stanzas of Shelley's 'To a Skylark'.]

Just so Donne's voice and his spirit with it seems to soar up till we lose sight of him in a blue immensity of shining ether.

[She quotes a long passage from one of Donne's sermons describing the flight of the soul to heaven, pointing out that it closely parallels lines 181–218 of *The Second Anniversary*.]

The slight sense of artificiality and unreality in the ecstasy of the 'Anatomy' vanishes when we place it beside the prose, as is often the case with Donne. Expressions which seem the vapid hyperbole of compliment in some of the poems reappear in the letters with a personality which takes from them all sense of hypocrisy, and so here the sermon supplies, as it were, links of feeling in the chain up which the elegist climbs to his poetic Heaven.

The question there remains, what has this transcendental 'Progress of the Soul' to do with the other?

[She turns to discuss the *Metempsychosis*.]

... not only the fine opening, 'I sing the progress of a deathless soul', but nearly the whole of the first twelve stanzas is poetry of a deep and often splendid seriousness. Moreover the 4th, 5th, and 6th verses are intensely personal. ...

The nearest analogy to Donne's conception seems to be that of Euripides in the 'Bacchae'. You have the novelty of the religious creed, the horror of heresy combined with inexplicable power with nature, and a strain of brutal cruelty in the god. There is a force in the world, he admits, at last, not the sophisticated world which we build for ourselves, but the real cosmos against which we come when thrown out among inanimate things, a force which is of the essence of physical law, yet intellectual; evil, yet on which all beauty depends. It is always new, always an innovation, and has the shallowness of crudity about it.

Donne had had the mountain sickness of Eternity. The rapturous spiritual life left certain sides even of his intellect unsatisfied, his ideal philosophy did not account for all the variety and incident of life. Whence did that variety arise? He asked himself, and the answer that came was that it was somehow the product of what we are accustomed to call evil. 'Wonder with me why ploughing, building, ruling and the rest, Or most of these arts whence our lives are blest, By cursed Cain's race invented be And blest Seth vex'd us with astronomy.' Cain's race are the great heretics, and they are linked closely with the material in life and governed by the impersonal Destiny whom Donne apostrophises almost in the words of Euripides as:

> Knot of all causes, thou whose changeless brow
> Ne'er smiles nor frowns.

Perhaps it might be more correct to say that they are incarnations of this force. The poem in one mood was probably intended to be a half satirical apology for his own sensuality, in another it is a serious attempt to bring this secular force into relation with the spiritual one. The soul of the apple passes eventually into Mrs Drury, we can hardly doubt, and she is in some sense the whole meaning of life.

A good deal has been made of the resemblance between Donne and Browning, and there seems some reason to think that Browning's intense subjectivity owes its origin to Donne. To both poets the universe is in flux round man. Donne says 'our business is to rectify nature to what she was', and Browning tells us that all landscapes are equally beautiful, since all are but material for imagination to amend. Following on from this he tells us that the truth is within us and to discover it we must not seek in outward things but open up a way whence the imprisoned glory may escape 'that inmost . . . glory which is truth'.

But Browning links the objective world with the subjective by means of what Donne would have called Destiny. 'How the world is made for each of us, how all we perceive and know in it, tends to some moment's product thus – the hate or love of a man.' And this world thus infinite in variety, lying in wait for man, with a prescience of all that he can be or do, having implicit in it the reaction for all his unpredestined activity, of a majestic and incommensurable patience and impersonality is for Browning the one half of the Divine.

> Why where's the need of Temple, when the walls
> O' the world are that. . . .
>
> That one Face, far from vanish, rather grows
> Or decomposes but to recompose,
> Become my universe that feels and knows.

The other half is in men. To some such conception Donne seems to have tended at one time and his difficulty perhaps lay in this, that he was not content with such divided Deity. Worship was only possible of an objective Unity, and yet he rebelled against the tyranny of such external determination. The ideal woman of the 'Anatomy' looks like an attempt to get over this difficulty, to image the unimaginable, to give phenomenal life to a metaphysical abstraction, to combine the personal with the impersonal.

84. Phoebe Anne Beale Sheavyn

1909

Phoebe Sheavyn wrote her D.Litt. dissertation for the University of London on 'Economic Aspects of the Life of the Professional Writer under Elizabeth and James I'. Five chapters of this formed *The Literary Profession in the Elizabethan Age*, in which she argued that Elizabethan poets were obliged by the lack of a natural patron for their work to attract patronage by artificial means – 'Hence extravagance in eulogy; hence servile humility in the writer' (*The Literary Profession in the Elizabethan Age*, 1909, pp. 22–3 and 195).

[Sheavyn takes Donne's memorial eulogies of Elizabeth Drury for prime specimens of forced endeavours, which show us]

to what lengths of exaggerated praise a man of genius could be carried in his desire to earn the good will of a possible patron. . . . Transfigured though they are by imaginative power they yet betray unmistakeable signs of the effort to bid high. The verses reached their mark, and Donne became for many years the intimate friend and dependant of the wealthy Sir Robert Drury.

[Donne's verses, like those of Spenser's *Daphnaida*, lack 'a sense of reality and sincerity' such as we recognize in Chaucer's lament for his patron's wife Blanche. Donne's work also exemplifies the 'decline in the literary taste of authors' which followed the decline of manners in the court of James I.]

Donne's writing, though full of genius, shows a reckless disregard of beauty and good taste.

85. William Macdonald Sinclair

1909

The Venerable W. M. Sinclair (1850–1917), Archdeacon of
London, wrote books on religious subjects and church architecture and gave lectures to the Royal Society of Literature on
the religious poetry of Tennyson and of Donne. His lecture
on Donne, read to the Society on 26 January 1910, he had
previously published as a general appreciation of the 'poet
and preacher' (*Transactions of the Royal Society of Literature*,
29:2 (1909), 179–202).

[Much of Sinclair's account of Donne is strung together from
standard sources, drawing on Walton and Gosse for Donne's life
and career, and Carew and Saintsbury for Donne's literary genius.
But he does undertake to demonstrate the harsh injustice of
Hallam's dismissal of Donne.[1]

Sinclair's way of countering the familiar detractions of Donne is
to quote copiously from Donne's poems, with commendatory
linking comments. He gives stanza 1 of 'The Good Morrow',
remarking that it is 'very characteristic of Donne's originality'. The
Song, 'Go, and Catch a Falling Star', given entire, 'shows him in his
lightest mood'. Stanza 4 of 'The Canonisation' is one of 'several
charming verses' in this poem. Lines 15–28 of 'Love's Growth' make
up 'two exquisite stanzas'. Stanzas 1–3 and 7 of 'The Bait' contain
'a pretty conceit'. Lines 1–8 of 'The Primrose' present a 'picture
from Nature' which 'could hardly be surpassed'; and the first stanza
of the Epithalamion 'Hail Bishop Valentine' is likewise 'full of vivid
observations of Nature'. *Holy Sonnet* 1, 'Thou Hast Made Me', given
entire, is 'one of a great number [of sonnets] of remarkable beauty'.
Stanza 23 of 'A Litany' affords a taste of this 'noble poem'. Two
passages from *The Second Anniversary* (lines 33–44 and 65–81)
present 'a fine example of one of his finest poems'. Lines 1–24 of
Satire 1 exemplify the vigour of Donne's *Satires*.

Sinclair follows up these quotations with a series of brief snippets
to show that 'Noble lines stud every page'. He gives lines 31 and
66–7 of the *Metempsychosis*; lines 85–6 of *The Second Anniversary*;
lines 1–2 of 'Love's Deity', and lines 19–20 of 'The Dream'.

He rounds off his recital with appraisals of Donne's personal and literary character, drawn from Walton, Saintsbury and Gosse. But then he adds an impression of his own.]

Personally, I should be inclined to describe him as a man of immense genius, unlimited human sympathies, great poetic gifts, an imagination undaunted by the highest flights, a magnetic personal fascination, and indefatigable energy. To whatever influence he surrendered himself it absorbed him for the time. In his youth it was singing the delights of love, in manhood the pursuit of knowledge and imagination, in later years the worship of God and the teaching of religious truth; in each field alike he, in his day, had few rivals.

NOTE

1 See *John Donne: The Critical Heritage*, vol. I, ed. A. J. Smith (London: Routledge and Kegan Paul), 1975, pp. 379–81.

86. Felix E. Schelling

1910

Schelling devoted to 'Donne and His Place among Lyrical Poets' an entire chapter of a book on Elizabethan and Jacobean literature (*English Literature during the Lifetime of Shakespeare*, 1910, pp. 364–71).

[Schelling introduces his account of Donne's poetry with an inaccurate summary of Donne's career, which advances Donne's election to the Deanship of St Paul's by four years, and his death by five years. These errors point Schelling's own assertion that 'there are more mistakes prevalent about Donne as a poet than about any one of even approximately equal rank'. Nonetheless, he shrewdly notes Gosse's shortcomings as the biographer of Donne, and seeks to amend them in his own appraisal of Donne's poems.]

We know more of the outward events of the life of John Donne than of any poet or writer of his age, and yet he remains a personage strange and enigmatic, and a poet more often misjudged than appreciated. Donne's was a twofold greatness. A biographer, not long since, wrote a *Life of Donne* in which he confesses to little sympathy with his poetry. He was writing of the famous Dean of St Paul's, amongst the most learned divines in an age of deep theological learning, the most brilliant and persuasive preacher of his day. Of Donne as a divine we have already heard in this book. But Donne would remain great in the history of literature with the Dean of St Paul's neglected, in that he is the most original, the most independent, the most perverse, yet in some respects among the most illuminated of the poets of the latter days of Elizabeth. Nor is it possible to separate wholly these two aspects of Donne's career; for although there is little of the future divine in those strange and cynical erotic poems which formed so interesting a part of the exercises of his youth, still his poetry would be far from what it is to us were the spirituality of his later poems not to enter into account. On the other hand, it is the power of poetry in the divine as well as the beauty and sanctity of his life that endeared him to those whose privilege it was to know him, and made him a power for good in his day. . . .

There is no better illustration of Donne's uncompromising realism matched with his characteristic remoteness of thought than this which follows. He is speaking of the storm and its effects upon his shipmates.

[He quotes lines 45–58 of 'The Storm'.]

Indeed, nothing could be more discordant to the general acceptation of poetry than these harsh, vivid, and ingenuous lines. We are concerned neither with their place in literature nor their qualities as poetry, but with their marked characteristics and divergences from the prevailing type of the moment. And as to this, there can be no two opinions.

The lyrical poetry of a secular character which Donne has left us lies in point of date of writing between 1592 and 1602. It contains that fascinating, yet forbidding, group of poems which add to all his other traits of idiosyncrasy the new note of a frank and daring cynicism. The audacious outspokenness of several of these erotic poems has blinded readers to their possible autobiographical significance. And yet these poems give us really very little definite biographical information. They are often as cryptic as the Sonnets of Shakespeare themselves. Indeed, it is possible that we may make too much of all these throes, and agonies, and intensities of fleshly love. There is such a thing as the libertine in thought as well as the roué in practice. Of the latter we hear very little subjectively in literature. He wallows in his sty, and even Circe takes little note of him save to feed him. It is otherwise with the libertine in thought. It is the adventure, the danger, the imaginativeness of the pursuit of unlawful love – dare we call it the sporting instinct? – which interests him. The very cynicism of Donne's earlier erotic poetry confirms this opinion. It was the same active insatiable curiosity and interest in the fulness of life which caused Donne on the one hand to dip into forbidden volumes of heresy, alchemy, and pseudo-science, and on the other to court and dally imaginatively with experiences which come not to those that tread the beaten paths of virtue. Take, for example, the famous song, 'Go and catch a falling star', wherein one who has journeyed far to see 'strange sights' is compelled to 'swear'

> Nowhere
> Lives a woman true, and fair.

The concluding stanza of the lyric is even more outrageously cynical.

[He quotes it.]

The poems of Donne came much into fashion from their absolute originality, and it may be affirmed that he exerted a powerful influence on the course of English poetry before he was aware of it himself. Indeed, Donne's attitude towards his poetry throughout his life was that of the gentleman and courtier of his day, except that he was sincere in his regard of poetry as a trifle: others often affected this attitude.

There are more mistakes prevalent about Donne as a poet than about any one of even approximately equal rank. The first is the notion that Donne was a late Jacobean or Caroline writer, contemporary as a poet with Cowley. This error arises from the accident that the earliest extant edition of Donne's poetry is posthumous and dates 1633. Cowley's *Poetical Blossoms*, the appropriately named budding poetry of a precocious boy of thirteen, appeared in the same year. Donne would have been sixty, if alive. Without entering into the clear evidences which are at hand for all to use, Donne is an Elizabethan in his poetry in the strictest acceptation of that term, the forerunner of a remarkable movement, not soon assimilated or even imitated by his immediate contemporaries.

A more serious error is that which has arisen out of the term 'metaphysical school of poetry'. The word 'metaphysics' was first associated with the poetry of Donne by Dryden in his *Discourse on Satire*; and Cowley is there charged with imitating Donne, which it is not to be questioned that he did. Although the mention of Donne is purely incidental, he is praised for 'variety, multiplicity and choiceness of thought'. Now this passage fell under the eye of the great Dr Samuel Johnson when he was writing his 'Life of Cowley' in *The Lives of the English Poets*. He expanded it into a sonorous critical dictum in which the word 'metaphysical' was extended from an incidental trait of Donne and his late imitator, Cowley, to the distinguishing characteristic of a whole 'school' of poetry; in which this 'school' was thrown into violent contrast as 'wits' with real poets, and in which only one thing was omitted concerning Donne, and that was the 'variety, multiplicity and choiceness of thought' with which the judicious Dryden had credited him. This famous deliverance of Dr Johnson's is a glaring example of the species of criticism which is worked up out of the critical dicta of others, a mystery unhappily not confined to the age of the Georges. We may give over expectation of a time when popular histories of literature will not discuss 'the metaphysical poets' in eloquent passages expanded from Dr Johnson's 'Life of Cowley', as Dr Johnson expanded the incidental words of Dryden. The instinct that bids each critic follow his predecessor has determined once and for all that the poetical indiscretions of the saintly Dean of St Paul's, perpetrated thirty-five years before, shall be linked to all eternity to the clever imitations of a school-boy fifty years his junior. But let us turn from the discouraging negative function of criticism, the detection of error, to its positive mission, the affirmation – if we may be so fortunate as to find it – of truth.

The salient qualities of the poetry of Donne are, foremost, a contempt for mere form, shown in his disregard for the graces of diction as such, alliteration, choice of words for sound or smoothness, and other like tricks of the trade. Neither harshness of sound nor violence to meter deter him; and he repeats and uses the plain word where necessary to the force and rhetoric of thought.

> Some man unworthy to be possessor
>> Of old or new love, himself being false or weak
> Thought his pain and shame would be the lesser,
>> If on womankind he might his anger wreak,
>>> And thence the law did grow,
>>> One might but one man know;
>>> But are other creatures so?

It was with reference to such a line as the fourth that Jonson observed to Drummond that Donne 'deserved hanging for not keeping accent'. And yet there will be found a rhetorical value in even the roughness of Donne. His stanzas are often elaborate and always original, they are fitting to the subject in hand. Moreover, the roughness of Donne has been exaggerated. Secondly, Donne's contempt of form carried with it an absolute discarding of the poetical apparatus of the past. The gods of Greece and Rome dwell not with him, and though abundantly learned he scorns allusion or imitation, representing in this the very antithesis of Jonson. Donne's illustrations are powerful for their homeliness, vividness, and originality. He bids a lover ride 'till age snow white hairs on thee'. He craves 'to talk with some old lover's ghost that died before the god of love was born'; Christ is addressed as the 'strong ram that battered heaven for me'. Once more, Donne is not a nature poet, his work discloses no love of animals or of flowers. The forms of this world were nothing to him; he neither painted nature nor sought nature for his model. There is, for example, a strange absence of the sense of colour in the poetry of Donne. When he uses colour words at all, they are crude and perfunctory. On the other hand the abstractions of light and darkness are always before him. The relations of men to each other were likewise matters sealed. There is a completer absence of dramatic instinct in Donne than in any poet of his age. The concrete was nothing to him except as illustrative of the abstract. The reason for this, as for his want of an appreciation of nature, is to be found in the intense subjectivity of his poetry. It is related of him that he never saw, much less knew personally, the young maiden, Elizabeth Drury, whose untimely death he has immortalized in that strange and fascinating poem, 'The Anatomy of the World'. To him she is a beautiful abstraction, the symbol of all that is spiritual, divine, and permanent in this passing world. The symbol is not the real thing; the real is here the ideal. We must cross into the kindred sphere of speculative thought for the glow, the white passion, the power and subtlety of this remarkable work; and yet it remains poetry, for, however speculative its thought and eloquently rhetorical the expression, its real traffic is with the divine illusions and phantasmagoria of this world. The personality of Donne is ever present in his works; but it is not his bodily self but the spiritual part of him in these poems, sublimed, if it may be so put, into a universal meaning. Donne is himself the spiritual microcosm of the world. With him the one is all; and hence to such a man the body is but a veil for the soul. He speaks of the body of Elizabeth Drury as

> so pure and thin
> Because it need disguise no thought within,
> 'Twas but a through-light scarf her mind to enrol
> Or exhalation breathed out of her soul.

So that

> We understand her sight; her pure and eloquent blood
> Spoke in her cheeks, and so distinctly wrought
> That one might almost say her body thought.

To Donne the soul alone is worthy of contemplation whose inner harmony is broken by too close a contact with the objective world. What seems a confusion of visual ideas really has this inner contemplative harmony to one to whom time and space are nought. By a natural step Donne 'entertains a universal, almost Pantheistic faith in the unity and totality of his soul with all souls'. In Donne will be found a romanticism of soul. His lyrics and satires are to be regarded as his struggle with sense. The sonnets, epistles, and 'Anatomy of the World', these are the real Donne, though not alone the most poetical of his work.

Returning, Donne's originality shows itself in his themes which are of life, death, everything, and all; whatever he touches he treats as an abstraction. Take for example such lines as these, apostrophizing 'Strong and long lived Death'.

[He quotes lines 5–6 and 12–20 of the 'Elegy on Mistress Boulstred'.]

His originality is likewise in his style, which in addition to the negative qualities already noted displays a totally new range of imagery derived from science, medicine, law, mathematics, astronomy, alchemy, and the chemistry of the day. Not 'learned eccentric' as some one described the vocabulary of Robert Browning at times, nor crammed for the nonce as in Jonson's *Alchemist*, but the natural utterance of a mind accustomed to think in technical terms. In Donne's vocabulary there are many peculiar words, not technicalities, and many words repeatedly used with a kind of fondness. His must have been one of those minds that form strong associations about certain symbols, and use words with a deeper significance than can ever reach him who runs as he reads.

When all has been said, there remains however that quality by which Donne is chiefly known, namely, his use of conceit. Of the conceit, its origin among the imitators of Petrarch, and of Sidney's position as the popularizer of extravagant metaphors among the lyrists, we have already heard in this book. That the conceit originated with Donne is no longer maintained by those who have knowledge on the subject; but it is still held by some that Donne is responsible for its prevalence in Jacobean poetry: a position equally untenable. The mistake in this whole matter is the general confusion of Donne with the 'concettists' who preceded him, and who, affected more or less by him, followed him. What may be true of English concettists in general may not be true of Donne in particular and vice versa. The confusion of Donne with Gongora is as bad as the confusion of Donne with Lyly. That Donne is a concettist is unquestionable. He often employs a thought which is far-fetched and ingenious rather than of natural and obvious meaning. Moreover, it is true of the Donnian conceit (in contrast with the hyperbolical conceit of Sidney, the ingenuities of Cowley, and the antithetical wit of the next, the 'classical', age), that the twist with Donne, if it may be so called, is in the thought rather than in the words. Let us take a typical passage of Donne from a poem entitled 'The Ecstasy'. The theme is of the spiritual nature of the ecstasy of love.

[He quotes lines 41–60 of 'The Ecstasy'.]

This passage is subtle, as is the whole poem, almost dialectic. A

310

keen, sinuous, reasoning mind is playing with its powers. Except for the implied personification of the body regarded apart from the soul, the language is free from figure; there is no confusion of thought. The new soul, the able soul, is that which, uniting the strength in the soul of each lover, 'controls' loneliness in that union. This new soul is indestructible, because composed of the atomies (atoms we should say) which, being indivisible and the primal material of all things, are incapable of destruction. There is the distinctively Donnian employment of ideas derived from physical and speculative science: the 'atomies' with their indivisibility, a term of the physics of the day; the body is the 'sphere' or superficies which includes within it the soul, a term of the old astro-philosophy; the body is not 'dross' but an 'allay', alchemical terms; the 'influence' of heaven is the use of that word in an astrological sense, meaning 'the radiation of power from the stars in certain positions or collocations affecting human actions and destinies'; and lastly, the phrase 'imprints the air' involves an idea of the old philosophy, by which 'sensuous perception is explained by effluxes of atoms from the things perceived whereby images are produced ("imprinted") which strike our senses'. Donne subtly transfers this purely physical conception to the transference of divine influence. How different all this is to the earlier hyperboles of the Sidneian school, the rhapsodical extravagance of Crashaw, or the persistently clever ingenuity of Cowley, need be pointed out only to be understood. In Donne, even where the conceit in all its ingenuity does exist, it is again and again raised out of its class by a certain fervor, sincerity, and applicability that not only condones its extravagance but justifies it. Such is the famous image of the compass, best known of the Donnian conceits, yet none the less worthy of quotation once more. It occurs in a poem entitled 'A Valediction Forbidding Mourning', written to his beloved wife, and runs thus:

[He quotes lines 21–36 of 'A Valediction: Forbidding Mourning', then goes on to consider Donne's effect upon other seventeenth-century writers.]

Herbert remains the most certain of the successors of Donne to be affected immediately by his influences in poetry; and Herbert, in his youth, as we have seen, was personally intimate with Donne. A recent editor claims for Herbert that 'he devised the religious love-lyric and he introduced structure into the short poem.'[1] With the long line of lyrists before us and the wealth of their stanzaic variety and invention, this last is obviously too large a claim, but in view of the inventiveness of Donne as to stanza and the intensity of the passion of his secular love-songs, it may well be surmised that the poetry of Donne was George Herbert's immediate poetical inspiration and model. To Herbert, even more certainly, Donne transmitted his own peculiar use of the conceit, though Herbert is often quaintly ingenious where Donne flashes unexpected illumination by the original bias of his mind. . . .

To return in conclusion to Donne, it is somewhat disconcerting to find an author whom, not unlike to Walter Savage Landor in our own late century, the critics can not glibly classify as the founder of a school or the product of a perfectly obvious series of literary influences. Donne is a poet of this difficult type. For, just as Shakespeare touched life and mankind at all points, and, absorbing the light of his time, gave it forth a hundred-fold, so Donne, withdrawn almost entirely from the influences affecting his contemporaries, shone and glowed with a strange light all his own. Orthodoxy – or rather a restoration of orthodoxy – as to John Donne demands that we recognize him in his poetry as an Elizabethan, as strictly such as Shakespeare, far more so than Jonson; that while we grant Donne to be a concettist he was such from the originality and natural bias of his mind, not from affected singularity or a striving after effect; that his strange and fascinating poetry, so caviare to the general, yields a true and rich reward to him who will seek with labour and true faith; and, lastly, that Donne, next to Spenser and Jonson, exercised the most potent influence of his time on English poetry. Donne's highest contribution to literature, like Shakespeare's in a very different way, depends on that deeper element of modern poetry which we call poetic insight, a power in his case which, proceeding by means of the clash of ideas familiar with ideas remote, flashes light and meaning into what has hitherto appeared mere commonplace. No one, in short, excepting Shakespeare, with Sidney, Greville, and Jonson in lesser degree, has done so much to develop intellectualised emotion in the Elizabethan lyric as Donne. In comparison with all this the notions about a metaphysical school, even a 'rhetorical school of poetry' and the fiction of a fantastical prince of concettists, leading a generation of poetlings deliberately astray, become vagaries of criticism com-

paratively unimportant. Donne deserves the verdict of his friend
Ben Jonson, who called him 'the first poet in the world in some
things'. But Donne is the last poet to demand a proselytizing zeal
of his devotees, and all those who have learned to love his witching
personality will agree to the charming sentiment of his faithful
adorer, Izaak Walton, when he says: 'Though I must omit to
mention divers persons ... friends of Sir Henry Wotton; yet I
must not omit to mention of a love that was there begun betwixt
him and Dr Donne, sometime Dean of St Paul's, a man of whose
abilities I shall forbear to say anything, because he who is of this
nation, and pretends to learning or ingenuity, and is ignorant of
Dr Donne, deserves not to know him.'

NOTE

1 G. H. Palmer, *The Life and Works of George Herbert*, i, p. 57. [Schelling's
note.]

87. Edward Thomas
1910/11

In his *Feminine Influences on the Poets* (1910), the critic
(though not yet poet) Edward Thomas (1878–1917) considered Donne's various relationships with women as the love-
poems represent them. Thomas gathered these observations
together in an essay on Donne in *The Tenth Muse*, published
in the following year. (*Feminine Influences on the Poets*, 1910,
pp. 107–8, 147, 286; *The Tenth Muse*, 1911, pp. 21–8, 68
and 107).

[Donne emerges in *The Tenth Muse* as one of some twenty-four
English poets whom Thomas distinguishes for their authentic
portrayal of women. The essay on Donne is largely made up of

313

illustrative quotations with a few appraising comments. It follows a short piece on Shakespeare's sonnets; and Thomas opens it with a parallel between Shakespeare's love-poems and Donne's in respect of the nature of the experience the two poets describe.]

If at all these sonnets are to be equalled by the love poems of Donne. . . . The feelings in many of the poems attributed to this period are not what most men would admit to be love. *The Sun Rising*, for example, with its opening [he quotes the first three lines] has none of the Provençal poet's misery 'that day should come so soon'. It is what Mr Gosse calls it, a 'hymn of virile satisfaction'. A little more passionate, perhaps, is another, *Break of Day*.

[He quotes it, and gives brief accounts of some other poems too – *Song*, 'Go, and Catch a Falling Star', 'Woman's Inconstancy' (*sic*), 'Love's Alchemy', *Elegy* 18 – making it clear that this aspect of Donne's poetry is of value not least because it calls for a drastic reappraisal of received expectations of love. He considers that *Elegy* 19]

is the finest expression of his enjoyment of the body, so intense here in fact that he is not so far removed as he appears from that lover who 'could not see her body for her soul'.

[Thomas assumes that all these are early poems, and comments on their manner, returning shrewdly upon Walton's approving account of Donne's later repudiation of them.]

If this were only the insolence of libertinism to a passive instrument, it would not be surprising that Donne should 'reluct at the excesses of it'; but mere libertinism, even if allied to genius, would be more likely to content itself with deeds not words, to be followed by the ferocity of repentance and by sackcloth upon the body, ashes on the head and in the mouth; and although Donne may have condescended to please Walton by flouting the early poems he never went back upon them in writing or action, but, whatever he did, did it to excess and to the astonishment and confusion of the many.

There is another class of love poems including those which were certainly written for his wife, but many more on which biographers can throw not even a marsh light. To this class belongs *The Ecstasy*.

[He quotes it, and then gives *Elegy* 5. Thomas attempts to sum up Donne's understanding of love.]

This love, it may be seen, has little to do with Petrarch, little to do with Cupid. If there is anything but subtlety in

> I never stoop'd so low, as they
> Which on an eye, cheek, lip, can prey,

it must be an expression of the inexpressibility of love, the craving for he knows not what, which is beyond sense and understanding.

[He quotes snippets of 'The Expostulation' and *The First Anniversary*, then line 6 of 'The Relic' and all the last stanza, still bringing out the unexampled sense of actual human relationships which Donne's writing about women projects.]

One of the rare qualities of this poetry is that the woman is apparently the man's equal. Her love is not sought; it has already been gained; yet it stands the test and the poet suggests her to us as a companion of perfect intimacy, and as far as can be imagined from the prostituted wife of his epithalamion.

[He quotes lines 88–90 of the *Epithalamion made at Lincoln's Inn.*]

Those which are or may be poems of marriage have to wait until our own day to find worthy companions in Browning's *One Word More* and William Morris's *Message of the March Wind*.

[He quotes the first stanza of *Song*, 'Sweetest Love, I Do Not Go'.]

It was Donne's distinction to be the first after Shakespeare, and almost at the same time as Shakespeare, to write love poems in English which bear the undeniable signs not only of love but one moment of love and for one particular woman. His poems to his wife are of the same kind. There is none of the old-fashioned generalisation in them at all.

[He speaks of Donne's love for his wife, and the hardships it brought them during seventeen years of marriage.]

... such a passion and such suffering produced from Donne's sensuous and sensual nature the holy flowers of the sermons and divine poems.

315

[He calls in John Clare's love-poems to dead or imaginary women, by way of caution against Gosse's confident extrapolations from Donne's poems to his life.]

In the face of these things it is bold to do more than smile at even so astonishing a conceit as Donne's *Flea*, where he bids his mistress spare the 'three lives' in the one flea who has sucked the blood of both and so become their 'marriage temple'; and it is unwise to dismiss as 'the perfectly contented and serene record of an illicit, doubtless of an ephemeral adventure', the same poet's *Good Morrow.*

[He quotes the first four lines of the poem. Thomas finds only a few love-poets who share Donne's power to convey a substantial sense of the woman's presence, and of a shared experience.]

Except Shakespeare's and Donne's there is hardly a woman of the lyric poets to be compared with Burns's, who will stand the sunlight and the breath of life like his.

[He finds that Keats's 'Unfelt, Unheard, Unseen' is 'a poem which is like Donne's *The Sun Rising*', presumably in that it evokes a mutual erotic bliss.

88. Edward Thomas

1912

In a study of Swinburne's writings, Thomas found that Swinburne's poems of love and sin lack the human voice of an authentic poet–lover (*Algernon Charles Swinburne: A Critical Study*, 1912, p. 84).

As his poems are seldom personal, so they are not as real as Donne's or Byron's or Browning's are, though often more 'realistic' at certain points. They are magnificent, but more than human.

316

89. Herbert John Clifford Grierson

1912

Grierson published his magisterial edition of Donne's poems in two volumes, being the first of Donne's editors to aim for an authentic text of the poems by an analytic comparison of all the early manuscripts and published versions which had then come to light. Grierson wrote later that he had realized in the 1890s the need for textual work on Donne such as commonly went into the editing of a classical text. He remarked that his interest in Donne had been aroused by the essays of Dowden and Minto, and the edition of Donne's poems by E. K. Chambers.[1]

The new edition of Donne made such an impact that Grierson is sometimes credited with the modern rediscovery of Donne, and the year 1912 spoken of as a turning-point in English literary studies. Beyond doubt Grierson's work massively confirmed Donne's stature and furthered the serious study of his poetry, as well as preparing the ground for all future work on the text of the poems.

In the second volume of his edition Grierson essayed a long introduction to the poems, and commentary upon them, whose tenor is markedly more conservative than his editorial approach. Yet he did initiate some ideas about Donne's poetry which would be developed in later criticism ('The Poetry of John Donne', *The Poems of John Donne*, 1912, vol. ii, pp. v–lv).

[Grierson begins by approving Courthope's account of 'Donne's position among English poets, regarded from the historical and what we like to call scientific point of view'.]

What we are shown is the connexion of 'metaphysical wit' with the complex and far-reaching changes in men's conception of Nature which make the seventeenth century perhaps the greatest epoch in human thought since human thinking began.

[He judges that Courthope 'has probably said the last word' on the subject of Donne's conceits. Then he goes on to trace the vicissitudes of Donne's reputation over three centuries, showing how early admiration cooled and turned to detraction when readers began to distinguish great wit from great poetry, as Dryden did. He cites Dryden's comparison of Donne to the earl of Dorset in *A Discourse concerning Satire.*]

Dryden's estimate of Donne, as well as his application to his poetry of the epithet 'metaphysical', was transmitted through the eighteenth century. Johnson's famous paragraphs in the *Life of Cowley* do little more than echo and expand Dryden's pronouncement, with a rather vaguer use of the word 'metaphysical'. In Dryden's application it means correctly 'philosophical'; in Johnson's, no more than 'learned'. . . .

What is to-day the value and interest of this wit which has arrested the attention of so many generations? How far does it seem to us compatible with poetry in the full and generally accepted sense of the word, with poetry which quickens the imagination and touches the heart, which satisfies and delights, which is the verbal and rhythmical medium whereby a gifted soul communicates to those who have ears to hear the content of impassioned moments?

Before coming to close quarters with this difficult and debated question one may in the first place insist that there is in Donne's verse a great deal which, whether it be poetry in the full sense of the word or not, is arresting and of worth both historically and intrinsically. Whatever we may think of Donne's poetry, it is impossible not to recognize the extraordinary interest of his mind and character. In an age of great and fascinating men he is not the least so. The immortal and transcendent genius of Shakespeare leaves Donne, as every other contemporary, lost in the shadows and cross-lights of an age that is no longer ours, but from which Shakespeare emerges into the clear sunlight. Of Bacon's mind, 'deep and slow, exhausting thought', and divining as none other the direction in which the road led through the débris of outworn learning to a renovated science and a new philosophy, Donne could not boast. Alike in his poetry and in his soberest prose, treatise or sermon, Donne's mind seems to want the high seriousness which comes from a conviction that truth is, and is to be found. A spirit of scepticism and paradox plays through and disturbs almost everything he wrote, except at moments when an intense mood of feeling, whether love or devotion, begets faith, and silences the

318

sceptical and destructive wit by the power of vision rather than of intellectual conviction. Poles apart as the two poets seem at a first glance to lie in feeling and in art, there is yet something of Tennyson in the conflict which wages perpetually in Donne's poetry between feeling and intellect. ,

But short of the highest gifts of serene imagination or serene wisdom Donne's mind has every power it well could, wit, insight, imagination; and these move in such a strange medium of feeling and learning, mediaeval, renaissance and modern, that every imprint becomes of interest. To do full justice to that interest one's study of Donne must include his prose as well as his verse, his paradoxical *Pseudomartyr,* and equally paradoxical, more strangely mooded *Biathanatos,* the intense and subtle eloquence of his sermons, the tormented passion and wit of his devotions, and the gaiety and melancholy, wit and wisdom, of his letters. But most of these qualities have left their mark on his poetry, and given it interests over and above its worth simply as poetry.

One quality of his verse, which has been somewhat overlooked by critics intent upon the definition and sources of metaphysical wit, is wit in our sense of the word, wit like the wit of Swift and Sheridan. The habit in which this wit masquerades is doubtless old-fashioned. It is not always the worse for that, for the wit of the Elizabethans is delightfully blended with fancy and feeling. There is a little of Jaques in all of them. But if fanciful and at times even boyish, Donne's wit is still amusing, the quickest and most fertile wit of the century till we come to the author of *Hudibras.*

It is not in the *Satyres* that this wit is to us most obvious. Nothing grows so soon out of date as contemporary satire. . . .

How then should we be interested in Elizabeth's fantastic 'Presence', the streets of sixteenth century London, and the knavery of pursuivants, presented with a satiric art which is wonderfully vivid and caustic but still tentative, – over-emphatic, rough in style and verse, though with a roughness which is obviously a studied and in a measure successful effect. The verses upon *Coryats Crudities* are in their way a masterpiece of insult veiled as compliment, but it is a rather boyish and barbarous way.

It is in the lighter of his love verses that Donne's laughable wit is most obvious and most agile. Whatever one may think of the choice of subject, and the flame of a young man's lust that burns undisguised in some of the *Elegies,* it is impossible to ignore the

319

dazzling wit which neither flags nor falters from the first line to the last. And in the more graceful and fanciful, the less heated *Songs and Sonets*, the same wit, gay and insolent, disports itself in a philosophy of love which must not be taken altogether seriously. Donne at least, as we shall see, outgrew it. His attitude is very much that of Shakespeare in the early comedies. But the Petrarchian love, which Shakespeare treats with light and charming irony, the vows and tears of Romeo and Proteus, Donne openly scoffs. He is one of Shakespeare's young men as these were in the flesh and the Inns of Court, and he tells us frankly what in their youthful cynicism (which is often even more of a pose than their idealism) they think of love, and constancy, and women.

[He gives an account of and quotes from *Song*, 'Go, and Catch a Falling Star', 'Woman's Constancy' and 'The Indifferent'.]

It is not often that the reckless and wilful gaiety of youth masking as cynicism has been expressed with such ebullient wit as in these and companion songs. And when he adopts for a time the pose of the faithful lover bewailing the cruelty of his mistress the sarcastic wit is no less fertile. It would be difficult to find in the language a more sustained succession of witty surprises than *The Will*. Others were to catch these notes from Donne, and Suckling later flutes them gaily in his lighter fashion, never with the same fullness of wit and fancy, never with the same ardour of passion divinable through the audacious extravagances.

But to amuse was by no means the sole aim of Donne's 'wit'; gay humour touched with fancy and feeling is not its only quality. Donne's 'wit' has many strands, his humour many moods, and before considering how these are woven together into an effect that is entirely poetical, we may note one or two of the soberer strands which run through his *Letters*, *Epicedes*, and similar poems – descriptive, reflective, and complimentary.

Not much of Donne's poetry is given to description. Of the feeling for nature of the Elizabethans, their pastoral and ideal pictures of meadow and wood and stream, which delighted the heart of Izaak Walton, there is nothing in Donne. A greater contrast than that between Marlowe's *Come live with me* and Donne's imitation *The Baite* it would be hard to conceive. But in *The Storme* and *The Calme* Donne used his wit to achieve an effect of realism which was something new in English poetry, and was not reproduced till

Swift wrote *The City Shower.* From the first lines, which describe how

> The South and West winds join'd, and as they blew,
> Waves like a rolling trench before them threw,

to the close of *The Storme* the noise of the contending elements is deafening:

> Thousands our noises were, yet we 'mongst all
> Could none by his right name, but thunder call:
> Lightning was all our light, and it rain'd more
> Than if the Sunne had drunke the sea before.
> . . . .
> Hearing hath deaf'd our sailors, and if they
> Knew how to hear, there's none knowes what to say:
> Compared to these stormes, death is but a qualme,
> Hell somewhat lightsome, and the Bermuda calme.

The sense of tropical heat and calm in the companion poem is hardly less oppressive, and, if the whole is not quite so happy as the first, it contains two lines whose vivid and unexpected felicity is as delightful to-day as when Ben Jonson recited them to Drummond at Hawthornden:

> No use of lanthorns; and in one place lay
> Feathers and dust, to-day and yesterday.

Donne's letters generally fall into two groups. The first comprises those addressed to his fellow-students at Cambridge and the Inns of Court, the Woodwards, Brookes, and others, or to his maturer and more fashionable companions in the quest of favour and employment at Court, Wotton, and Goodyere, and Lord Herbert of Cherbury. To the other belong the complimentary and elegant epistles in which he delighted and perhaps bewildered his noble lady friends and patronesses with erudite and transcendental flattery.

In the first class, and the same is true of some of the *Satyres*, notably the third, and of the satirical *Progresse of the Soule*, especially at the beginning and the end, the reflective, moralizing strain predominates. Donne's 'wit' becomes the instrument of a criticism of life, grave or satiric, melancholy or stoical.

[He speaks of 'verse talkers' in English.]

. . . Butler and Dryden, Pope and Swift, Cowper and Burns, Byron and Shelley, Browning and Landor. It did not come easy to the Elizabethans, whose natural accent was song. Donne's chief rivals were Daniel and Jonson, and I venture to think that he excels them both in the clear and pointed yet easy and conversational development of his thought, in the play of wit and wisdom, and, despite the pedantic cast of Elizabethan erudite moralizing, in the power to leave on the reader the impression of a potent and yet a winning personality. We seem to get nearer to the man himself in Donne's letters to Goodyere and Wotton than in Daniel's weighty, but also heavy, moralizing epistles to the Countess of Cumberland or Sir Thomas Egerton; and the personality whose voice sounds so distinct and human in our ear is a more attractive one than the harsh, censorious, burly but a little blustering Jonson of the epistles on country life and generous givers. Donne's style is less clumsy, his verse less stiff. His wit brings to a clear point whatever he has to say, while from his verse as from his prose letters there disengages itself a very distinct sense of what it was in the man, underlying his brilliant intellect, his almost superhuman cleverness, which won for him the devotion of friends like Wotton and Goodyere and Walton and King, the admiration of a stranger like Huyghens, who heard him talk as well as preach: – a serious and melancholy, a generous and chivalrous spirit.

> However, keepe the lively tast you hold
>   Of God, love him as now, but feare him more,
> And in your afternoones thinke what you told
>   And promis'd him, at morning prayer before.
>
> Let falshood like a discord anger you,
>   Else be not froward. But why doe I touch
> Things, of which none is in your practise new,
>   And Tables, or fruit-trenchers teach as much;
>
> But thus I make you keepe your promise Sir,
>   Riding I had you, though you still staid there,
> And in these thoughts, although you never stirre,
>   You came with mee to Micham, and are here.

So he writes to Goodyere, but the letter to Wotton going Ambassador to Venice is Donne's masterpiece in this simpler style, and it seems to me that neither Daniel nor Jonson nor Drayton ever catches this note at once sensitive and courtly. To find a like courtliness we must go to Wotton; witness the reply to Donne's earlier epistle which I have printed in the notes. But neither Wotton nor any other of the courtly poets in Hannah's collection adds to this dignity so poignant a personal accent.

This personal interest is very marked in the two satires which are connected by tone and temper with the letters, the third of the early, classical *Satyres* and the opening and closing stanzas of the *Progresse of the Soule*. Each is a vivid picture of the inner workings of Donne's soul at a critical period in his life. . . . Scepticism and melancholy, bitter and sardonic, are certainly the dominant notes in the sombre fragment of satire *The Progresse of the Soule*. . . .

The fragment has some of the sombre power which De Quincey attributes to it, but on the whole one must confess it is a failure. The 'wit' of Donne did not apparently include invention, for many of the episodes seem pointless as well as disgusting, and indeed in no poem is the least attractive side of Donne's mind so clearly revealed, that aspect of his wit which to some readers is more repellent, more fatal to his claim to be a poet, than too subtle ingenuity or misplaced erudition – the vein of sheer ugliness which runs through his work, presenting details that seem merely and wantonly repulsive. . . .

The reflective, philosophic, somewhat melancholy strain of the poems I have been touching on reappears in the letters addressed to noble ladies. Here, however, it is softened, less sardonic in tone, while it blends with or gives place to another strain, that of absurd and extravagant but fanciful and subtle compliment. Donne cannot write to a lady without his heart and fancy taking wing in their own passionate and erudite fashion. Scholastic theology is made the instrument of courtly compliment and pious flirtation. He blends in the same disturbing fashion as in some of the songs and elegies that depreciation of woman in general, which he owes less to classical poetry than to his over-acquaintance with the Fathers, with an adoration of her charms in the individual which passes into the transcendental.

[He instances the *Verse Letters* to Lady Bedford and Mrs Magdalen Herbert.]

Nothing could surpass the strain of intellectual and etherealized compliment in which he addresses the Countess. If lines like the following are not pure poetry, they haunt some quaint borderland of poetry to which the polished felicities of Pope's compliments are a stranger. If not pure fancy, they are not mere ingenuity, being too intellectual and argumentative for the one, too winged and ardent for the other:

> Should I say I liv'd darker then were true,
> Your radiation can all clouds subdue;
> But one, 'tis best light to contemplate you.
>
> You, for whose body God made better clay,
> Or tooke Soules stuffe such as shall late decay,
> Or such as needs small change at the last day.
>
> This, as an Amber drop enwraps a Bee,
> Covering discovers your quicke Soule; that we
> May in your through-shine front your hearts thoughts see.
>
> You teach (though wee learne not) a thing unknowne
> To our late times, the use of specular stone,
> Through which all things within without were shown.
>
> Of such were Temples; so and such you are;
> *Beeing* and *seeming* is your equall care,
> And *vertues* whole *summe* is but *know* and *dare.*

The long poem dedicated to the same lady's beauty,

> You have refin'd me

is in a like dazzling and subtle vein. Those addressed to Mrs Herbert, notably the letter

> Mad paper stay,

and the beautiful Elegie

> No Spring, nor Summer Beauty hath such grace
> As I have seen in one Autumnall face,

are less transcendental in tone but bespeak an even warmer admiration. Indeed it is clear to any careful reader that in the poems addressed to both these ladies there is blended with the respectful flattery of the dependant not a little of the tone of warmer feeling permitted to the 'servant' by Troubadour convention. And I suspect that some poems, the tone of which is still more frankly and ardently lover-like, were addressed to Lady Bedford and Mrs Herbert, though they have come to us without positive indication.

The title of the subtle, passionate, sonorous lyric *Twickenham Garden*,

> Blasted with sighs, and surrounded with teares,

points to the person addressed, for Twickenham Park was the residence of Lady Bedford from 1607 to 1618, and Donne's intimacy with her seems to have begun in or about 1608. There can, I think, be little doubt that it is to her, and neither to his wife nor the mistresses of his earlier, wandering fancy, that these lines, conventional in theme but given an amazing *timbre* by the impulse of Donne's subtle and passionate mind, were addressed. But if *Twickenham Garden* was written to Lady Bedford, so also, one is tempted to think, must have been *A Nocturnall upon S. Lucies Day*, for Lucy was the Countess's name, and the thought, feeling, and rhythm of the two poems are strikingly similar.

But the *Nocturnall* is a sincerer and profounder poem than *Twickenham Garden*, and it is more difficult to imagine it the expression of a conventional sentiment. . . .

I can find no note of bitterness, active or spent, in the song. It *might* have been written to Ann More. It is a highly metaphysical yet sombre and sincere description of the emptiness of life without love. The critics have, I think, failed somewhat to reckon with this stratum in Donne's songs, of poems Petrarchian in convention but with a Petrarchism coloured by Donne's realistic temper and impatient wit. . . .

[He ponders Lady Bedford's feeling for Donne, and his for her.]

Friendship between man and woman is love in some degree. There is no need to exaggerate the situation, or to reflect on either her loyalty or his to other claims, to recognize that their mutual feeling was of the kind for which the Petrarchian convention afforded a ready and recognized vehicle of expression.

[He considers Donne's relationship with Mrs Herbert.]

. . . to her also it would seem that at some period in the history of their friendship, the beginning of which is very difficult to date, he wrote songs in the tone of hopeless, impatient passion, of Petrarch writing to Laura, and others which celebrate their mutual affection as a love that rose superior to earthly and physical passion.

[He gives an account of and quotes from some poems supposedly written to Mrs Herbert: 'The Primrose', 'The Blossom', 'The Funeral', 'The Relic'.]

Such were the notes that a poet in the seventeenth century might still sing to a high-born lady his patroness and friend. No one who knows the fashion of the day will read into them more than they were intended to convey. No one who knows human nature will read them as merely frigid and conventional compliments. Any uncertainty one may feel about the subject arises not from their being love-poems, but from the difficulty which Donne has in adjusting himself to the Petrarchian convention, the tendency of his passionate heart and satiric wit to break through the prescribed tone of worship and complaint.

Without some touch of passion, some vibration of the heart, Donne is only too apt to accumulate 'monstrous and disgusting hyperboles'. This is very obvious in the *Epicedes* – his complimentary laments for the young Lord Harington, Miss Boulstred, Lady Markham, Elizabeth Drury and the Marquis of Hamilton, poems in which it is difficult to find a line that moves. . . .

In the metaphysical elegy as cultivated by Donne, Beaumont, and others there was no escape from extravagant eulogy and sorrow by way of pastoral convention and mythological embroidery, and this class of poetry includes some of the worst verses ever written. In Donne all three of the strains referred to are present, but only in the third does he achieve what can be truly called poetry. In the elegies on Lord Harington and Miss Boulstred and Lady Markham it is difficult to say which is more repellent – the images in which the poet sets forth the vanity of human life and the humiliations of death or the frigid and blasphemous hyperboles in which the virtues of the dead are eulogized.

Even the *Second Anniversary*, the greatest of Donne's epicedes, is marred throughout by these faults. There is no stranger poem in the English language in its combination of excellences and faults, splendid audacities and execrable extravagances. 'Fervour of inspiration, depth and force and glow of thought and emotion and expression' – it has something of all these high qualities which Swinburne claimed; but the fervour is in great part misdirected, the emotion only half sincere, the thought more subtle than profound, the expression heated indeed but with a heat which only in passages kindles to the glow of poetry.

Such are the passages in which the poet contemplates the joys of heaven. There is nothing more instinct with beautiful feeling in *Lycidas* than some of the lines of Apocalyptic imagery at the close:

> There entertain him all the Saints above,
> In solemn troops, and sweet Societies
> That sing, and singing in their glory move,
> And wipe the tears for ever from his eyes.

But in spiritual sense, in passionate awareness of the transcendent, there are lines in Donne's poem that seem to me superior to anything in Milton if not in purity of Christian feeling, yet in the passionate, mystical sense of the infinite as something other than the finite, something which no suggestion of illimitable extent and superhuman power can ever in any degree communicate.

> Think then my soule that death is but a Groome,
> Which brings a Taper to the outward roome,
> Whence thou spiest first a little glimmering light,
> And after brings it nearer to thy sight:
> For such approaches does heaven make in death.
> . . . .
> Up, up my drowsie Soule, where thy new care
> Shall in the Angels songs no discord heere, &c.

In passages like these there is an earnest of the highest note of spiritual eloquence that Donne was to attain to in his sermons and last hymns.

Another aspect of Donne's poetry in the *Anniversaries*, of his *contemptus mundi* and ecstatic vision, connects them more closely with Tennyson's *In Memoriam* than Milton's *Lycidas*. Like Tennyson, Donne is much concerned with the progress of science, the revolution which was going on in men's knowledge of the universe, and its disintegrating effect on accepted beliefs. To him the new astronomy is as bewildering in its displacement of the earth and disturbance of a concentric universe as the new geology was to be to Tennyson with the vistas which it opened into the infinities of time, the origin and the destiny of man:

[He quotes lines 205–12 of *The First Anniversary*, interestingly misrendering the first word of the quotation – '*The* new philosophy calls all in doubt'.]

327

On Tennyson the effect of a similar dislocation of thought, the revelation of a Nature which seemed to bring to death and bring to life through endless ages, careless alike of individual and type, was religious doubt tending to despair:

> O life as futile, then, as frail!
>
> . . . .
>
> What hope of answer, or redress?
> Behind the veil, behind the veil.

On Donne the effect was quite the opposite. It was not of religion he doubted but of science, of human knowledge with its uncertainties, its shifting theories, its concern about the unimportant:

[He quotes lines 254–6, 263–8 and 281–7 of *The Second Anniversary*.]

With this welter of shifting theories and worthless facts he contrasts the vision of which religious faith is the earnest here.

[He quotes lines 290–300 of *The Second Anniversary*.]

It will seem to some readers hardly fair to compare a poem like *In Memoriam*, which, if in places the staple of its feeling and thought wears a little thin, is entirely serious throughout, with poems which have so much the character of an intellectual *tour de force* as Donne's *Anniversaries*, but it is easy to be unjust to the sincerity of Donne in these poems. Their extravagant eulogy did not argue any insincerity to Sir Robert and Lady Drury. It was in the manner of the time, and doubtless seemed to them as natural an expression of grief as the elaborate marble and alabaster tomb which they erected to the memory of their daughter.

The spiritual sense in Donne was as real a thing as the restless and unruly wit, or the sensual, passionate temperament. The main thesis of the poem, the comparative worthlessness of this life, the transcendence of the spiritual, was as sincere in Donne's case as was in Tennyson the conviction of the futility of life if death closes all. It was to be the theme of the finest passages in his eloquent sermons, the burden of all that is most truly religious in the verse and prose of a passionate, intellectual, self-tormenting soul to whom the pure ecstasy of love of a Vondel, the tender raptures of a Crashaw, the chastened piety of a Herbert, the mystical perceptions of a Vaughan could never be quite congenial.

I have dwelt at some length on those aspects of Donne's 'wit'

328

which are of interest and value even to a reader who may feel doubtful as to the beauty and interest of his poetry as such, because they too have been obscured by the criticism which with Dr Johnson and Mr Courthope represents his wit as a monster of misapplied ingenuity, his interest as historical and historical only. Apart from poetry there is in Donne's 'wit' a great deal that is still fresh and vivid, wit as we understand wit; satire pungent and vivid; reflection on religion and on life, rugged at times in form but never really unmusical as Jonson's verse is unmusical, and, despite frequent carelessness, singularly lucid and felicitous in expression; elegant compliment, extravagant and grotesque at times but often subtle and piquant; and in the *Anniversaries*, amid much that is both puerile and extravagant, a loftier strain of impassioned reflection and vision. It is not of course that these things are not, or may not be constituents of poetry, made poetic by their handling. To me it seems that in Donne they generally are. It is the poet in Donne which flavours them all, touching his wit with fancy, his reflection with imagination, his vision with passion. But if we wish to estimate the poet simply in Donne, we must examine his love-poetry and his religious poetry. It is here that every one who cares for his unique and arresting genius will admit that he must stand or fall as a great poet.

For it is here that we find the full effect of what De Quincey points to as Donne's peculiarity, the combination of dialectical subtlety with weight and force of passion. Objections to admit the poetic worth and interest of Donne's love-poetry come from two sides – from those who are indisposed to admit that passion, and especially the passion of love, can ever speak so ingeniously (this was the eighteenth-century criticism); and from those, and these are his more modern critics, who deny that Donne is a great poet because with rare exceptions, exceptions rather of occasional lines and phrases than of whole poems, his songs and elegies lack beauty. Can poetry be at once passionate and ingenious, sincere in feeling and witty, – packed with thought, and that subtle and abstract thought, Scholastic dialectic? Can love-poetry speak a language which is impassioned and expressive but lacks beauty, is quite different from the language of Dante and Petrarch, the loveliest language that lovers ever spoke, or the picturesque hyperboles of *Romeo and Juliet*? Must not the imagery and the cadences of love poetry reflect 'l'infinita, ineffabile bellezza' which is its inspiration?

[He quotes the whole of Robert Bridges' lyric outpouring 'Awake, My Heart, To Be Loved, Awake, Awake!'.]

Donne has written nothing at once so subtle and so pure and lovely as this, nothing the end and aim of which is so entirely to leave an untroubled impression of beauty.

But it is not true either that the thought and imagery of love-poetry must be of the simple, obvious kind which Steele supposes, that any display of dialectical subtlety, any scintillation of wit, must be fatal to the impression of sincerity and feeling, or on the other hand that love is always a beautiful emotion naturally expressing itself in delicate and beautiful language. To some natures love comes as above all things a force quickening the mind, intensifying its purely intellectual energy, opening new vistas of thought abstract and subtle, making the soul 'intensely, wondrously alive'. Of such were Donne and Browning. A love-poem like 'Come into the garden, Maud' suspends thought and fills the mind with a succession of picturesque and voluptuous images in harmony with the dominant mood. A poem such as *The Anniversarie* or *The Extasie, The Last Ride Together* or *Too Late*, is a record of intense, rapid thinking, expressed in the simplest, most appropriate language – and it is a no whit less natural utterance of passion. Even the abstractness of the thought, on which Mr Courthope lays so much stress in speaking of Donne and the 'metaphysicals' generally, is no necessary implication of want of feeling. It has been said of St Augustine 'that his most profound thoughts regarding the first and last things arose out of prayer ... concentration of his whole being in prayer led to the most abstract observation'. So it may be with love-poetry – so it was with Dante in the *Vita Nuova*, and so, on a lower scale, and allowing for the time that the passion is a more earthly and sensual one, the thought more capricious and unruly, with Donne. *The Nocturnall upon S. Lucies Day* is not less passionate because that passion finds expression in abstract and subtle thought. Nor is it true that all love-poetry is beautiful. Of none of the four poems I have mentioned in the last paragraph is pure beauty, beauty such as is the note of Mr Bridges' song, the distinctive quality. It is rather vivid realism. ...

But this sacrifice of beauty to dramatic vividness is a characteristic of passionate poetry. ...

Beauty is the quality of poetry which records an ideal passion recollected in tranquillity, rather than of poetry either dramatic or lyric which utters the very movement and moment of passion itself.

Donne's love-poetry is a very complex phenomenon, but the two dominant strains in it are just these: the strain of dialectic, subtle play of argument and wit, erudite and fantastic; and the strain of vivid realism, the record of a passion which is not ideal nor conventional, neither recollected in tranquillity nor a pure product of literary fashion, but love as an actual, immediate experience in all its moods, gay and angry, scornful and rapturous with joy, touched with tenderness and darkened with sorrow – though these last two moods, the commonest in love-poetry, are with Donne the rarest. The first of these strains comes to Donne from the Middle Ages, the dialectic of the Schools, which passed into mediaeval love-poetry almost from its inception; the second is the expression of the new temper of the Renaissance as Donne had assimilated it in Latin countries. Donne uses the method, the dialectic of the mediaeval love-poets, the poets of the *dolce stil nuovo*, Guinicelli, Cavalcanti, Dante, and their successors, the intellectual, argu-mentative evolution of their *canzoni*, but he uses it to express a temper of mind and a conception of love which are at the opposite pole from their lofty idealism. The result, however, is not so entirely disintegrating as Mr Courthope seems to think: 'This fine Platonic edifice is ruthlessly demolished in the poetry of Donne. To him love, in its infinite variety and inconsistency, represented the principle of perpetual flux in nature.' The truth is rather that, owing to the fullness of Donne's experience as a lover, the accident that made of the earlier libertine a devoted lover and husband, and from the play of his restless and subtle mind on the phenomenon of love conceived and realized in this less ideal fashion, there emerged in his poetry the suggestion of a new philosophy of love which, if less transcendental than that of Dante, rests on a juster, because a less dualistic and ascetic, conception of the nature of the love of man and woman. . . . if we turn from Elizabethan love-poetry to the *Songs and Sonets* and the *Elegies* of Donne, we find at once two distinguishing features. In the first place his poetry is in one respect less classical than theirs. There is far less in it of the superficial evidence of classical learning with which the poetry of the 'University Wits' abounds, pastoral and mythological imagery. The texture of his poetry is more mediaeval than theirs in as far as it is more dialectical, though a dialectical evolution is not infrequent in the Elizabethan sonnet, and the imagery is less picturesque, more scientific, philosophic, realistic, and homely. The place of the

> goodly exiled train
> Of gods and goddesses

is taken by images drawn from all the sciences of the day, from the definitions and distinctions of the Schoolmen, from the travels and speculations of the new age, and (as in Shakespeare's tragedies or Browning's poems) from the experiences of everyday life. Maps and sea discoveries, latitude and longitude, the phoenix and the mandrake's root, the Scholastic theories of Angelic bodies and Angelic knowledge, Alchemy and Astrology, legal contracts and *non obstantes*, 'late schoolboys and sour prentices', 'the king's real and his stamped face' – these are the kind of images, erudite, fanciful, and homely, which give to Donne's poems a texture so different at a first glance from the florid and diffuse Elizabethan poetry, whether romantic epic, mythological idyll, sonnet, or song; while by their presence and their abundance they distinguish it equally (as Mr Gosse has justly insisted) from the studiously moderate and plain style of 'well-languaged Daniel'.

But if the imagery of Donne's poetry be less classical than that of Marlowe or the younger Shakespeare there is no poet the spirit of whose love-poetry is so classical, so penetrated with the sensual, realistic, scornful tone of the Latin lyric and elegaic poets. If one reads rapidly through the three books of Ovid's *Amores*, and then in the same continuous rapid fashion the *Songs* and the *Elegies* of Donne, one will note striking differences of style and treatment. Ovid develops his theme simply and concretely, Donne dialectically and abstractly. There is little of the ease and grace of Ovid's verses in the rough and vehement lines of Donne's *Elegies*. Compare the song,

> Busie old foole, unruly Sunne,

with the famous thirteenth Elegy of the first book,

> Iam super oceanum venit a seniore marito,
> Flava pruinoso quae vehit axe diem.[2]

Ovid passes from one natural and simple thought to another, from one aspect of dawn to another equally objective. Donne just touches one or two of the same features, borrowing them doubtless from Ovid, but the greater part of the song is devoted to the subtle and extravagant, if you like, but not the less passionate development of the thought that for him the woman he loves is the whole world.

But if the differences between Donne's metaphysical conceits and Ovid's naturalness and simplicity is palpable it is not less clear that the emotions which they express, with some important exceptions to which I shall recur, are identical. The love which is the main burden of their song is something very different from the ideal passion of Dante or of Petrarch, of Sidney or Spenser. It is a more sensual passion. The same tone of witty depravity runs through the work of the two poets. There is in Donne a purer strain which, we shall see directly, is of the greatest importance, but such a rapid reader as I am contemplating might be forgiven if for the moment he overlooked it, and declared that the modern poet was as sensual and depraved as the ancient, that there was little to choose between the social morality reflected in the Elizabethan and in the Augustan poet.

And yet even in these more cynical and sensual poems a careful reader will soon detect a difference between Donne and Ovid. He will begin to suspect that the English poet is imitating the Roman, and that the depravity is in part a reflected depravity. In revolt from one convention the young poet is cultivating another, a cynicism and sensuality which is just as little to be taken *au pied de la lettre* as the idealizing worship, the anguish and adoration of the sonneteers. There is, as has been said already, a gaiety in the poems elaborating the thesis that love is a perpetual flux, fickleness the law of its being, which warns us against taking them too seriously; and even those *Elegies* which seem to our taste most reprehensible are aerated by a wit which makes us almost forget their indecency. In the last resort there is all the difference in the world between the untroubled, heartless sensuality of the Roman poet and the gay wit, the paradoxical and passionate audacities and sensualities of the young Elizabethan law-student impatient of an unreal convention, and eager to startle and delight his fellow students by the fertility and audacity of his wit.

It is not of course my intention to represent Donne's love-poetry as purely an 'evaporation' of wit, to suggest that there is in it no reflection either of his own life as a young man or the moral atmosphere of Elizabethan London. It would be a much less interesting poetry if this were so. Donne has pleaded guilty to a careless and passionate youth:

> In mine Idolatry what showres of raine
> Mine eyes did waste? what griefs my heart did rent?
> That sufferance was my sinne; now I repent;
> Cause I did suffer I must suffer pain.

From what we know of the lives of Essex, Raleigh, Southampton, Pembroke, and others it is probable that Donne's *Elegies* come quite as close to the truth of life as Sidney's Petrarchianism or Spenser's Platonism. The later cantos of *The Faerie Queene* reflect vividly the unchaste loves and troubled friendships of Elizabeth's Court. Whether we can accept in its entirety the history of Donne's early amours which Mr Gosse has gathered from the poems or not, there can be no doubt that actual experiences do lie behind these poems as behind Shakespeare's sonnets. In the one case as in the other, to recognize a literary model is not to exclude the probability of a source in actual experience.

But however we may explain or palliate the tone of these poems it is impossible to deny their power, the vivid and packed force with which they portray a variously mooded passion working through a swift and subtle brain. If there is little of the elegant and accomplished art which Milton admired in the Latin Elegiasts while he 'deplored' their immorality, there is more strength and sincerity both of thought and imagination. The brutal cynicism of

> Fond woman which would have thy husband die,

the witty anger of *The Apparition*, the mordant and paradoxical wit of *The Perfume* and *The Bracelet*, the passionate dignity and strength of *His Picture*,

> My body a sack of bones broken within,
> And powders blew stains scatter'd on my skin,

the passion that rises superior to sensuality and wit, and takes wing into a more spiritual and ideal atmosphere, of *His parting from her,*

> I will not look upon the quick'ning Sun,
> But straight her beauty to my sense shall run;
> The ayre shall note her soft, the fire most pure;
> Water suggest her clear, and the earth sure –

compare these with Ovid and the difference is apparent between an artistic, witty voluptuary and a poet whose passionate force redeems many errors of taste and art. Compare them with the sonnets and mythological idylls and *Heroicall Epistles* of the Elizabethans and it is they, not Donne, who are revealed as witty and 'fantastic' poets content to adorn a conventional sentiment with mythological fancies and verbal conceits. Donne's interest is his theme, love and woman, and he uses words not for their own sake but to communicate his consciousness of these surprising phenomena in all their varying and conflicting aspects. The only contemporary poems that have the same dramatic quality are Shakespeare's sonnets and some of Drayton's later sonnets. In Shakespeare this dramatic intensity and variety is of course united with a rarer poetic charm. Charm is a quality which Donne's poetry possesses in a few single lines. But to the passion which animates these sensual, witty, troubled poems the closest parallel is to be sought in Shakespeare's sonnets to a dark lady and in some of the verses written by Catullus to or of Lesbia:

The expense of spirit in a waste of shame.

But neither sensual passion, nor gay and cynical wit, nor scorn and anger, is the dominant note in Donne's love-poetry. Of the last quality there is, despite the sardonic emphasis of some of the poems, less than in either Shakespeare or Catullus. There is nothing in his poetry which speaks so poignantly of an outraged heart, a love lavished upon one who was worthless, as some of Shakespeare's sonnets and of Catullus's poems. The finest note in Donne's love-poetry is the note of joy, the joy of mutual and contented passion. His heart might be subtle to plague itself; its capacity for joy is even more obvious. Other poets have done many things which Donne could not do. They have invested their feelings with a garb of richer and sweeter poetry. They have felt more deeply and finely the reverence which is in the heart of love. But it is only in the fragments of Sappho, the lyrics of Catullus, and the songs of Burns that one will find the sheer joy of loving and being loved expressed in the same direct and simple language as in some of Donne's songs, only in Browning that one will find the same simplicity of feeling combined with a like swift and subtle dialectic.

335

I wonder by my troth what thou and I
Did till we loved.

For God's sake hold your tongue and let me love.

If yet I have not all thy love,
Deare, I shall never have it all.

Lines like these have the same direct, passionate quality as . . .

O my love's like a red, red rose
That's newly sprung in June.

The joy is as intense though it is of a more spiritual and intellectual quality. And in the other notes of this simple passionate love-poetry, sorrow which is the shadow of joy, and tenderness, Donne does not fall far short of Burns in intensity of feeling and directness of expression. These notes are not so often heard in Donne, but

So, so break off this last lamenting kiss

is of the same quality as

Had we never lov'd sae kindly

or

Take, O take those lips away.

And strangest of all perhaps is the tenderness which came into Donne's poetry when a sincere passion quickened in his heart, for tenderness, the note of

O wert thou in the cauld blast,

is the last quality one would look for in the poetry of a nature at once so intellectual and with such a capacity for caustic satire. But the beautiful if not flawless *Elegy XVI*,

By our first strange and fatal interview,

and the *Valedictions* which he wrote on different occasions of parting from his wife, combine with the peculiar *élan* of all Donne's passionate poetry and its intellectual content a tenderness as perfect as anything in Burns or in Browning.

[He quotes lines 19–22 of 'A Valediction: Of Weeping'; lines 33–40 of the *Song*; 'Sweetest Love I Do Not Go'; and lines 33–6 of 'A Valediction: Forbidding Mourning'.]

The poet who wrote such verses as these did not believe any longer that 'love . . . represents the principle of perpetual flux in nature'.

But Donne's poetry is not so simple a thing of the heart and of the senses as that of Burns and Catullus. Even his purer poetry has more complex moods – consider *The Prohibition* – and it is metaphysical, not only in the sense of being erudite and witty, but in the proper sense of being reflective and philosophical. Donne is always conscious of the import of his moods; and so it is that there emerges from his poems a philosophy or a suggested philosophy of love to take the place of the idealism which he rejects. Set a song of the joy of love by Burns or by Catullus such as I have cited beside Donne's *Anniversarie*,

> All Kings, and all their favorites,
> All glory of honors, beauties, wits,
> The Sun itselfe, which makes times, as they passe,
> Is elder by a year, now, than it was
> When thou and I first one another saw,

and the difference is at once apparent. Burns gets no further than the experience, Catullus than the obvious and hedonistic reflection that time is flying, the moment of pleasure short. In Donne's poem one feels the quickening of the brain, the vision extending its range, the passion gathering sweep with the expanding rhythms, and from the mind thus heated and inspired emerges, not a cry that time might stay its course,

> Lente, lente currite noctis equi,[3]

but a clearer consciousness of the eternal significance of love, not the love that aspires after the unattainable, but the love that unites contented hearts. The method of the poet is, I suppose, too dialectical to be popular, for the poem is in few Anthologies. It may be that the Pagan and Christian strains which the poet unites are not perfectly blended – if it is possible to do so – but to me it seems that the joy of love has never been expressed at once with such intensity and such elevation.

And it is with sorrow as with joy. There is the same difference of manner in the expression between Donne and these poets, and the deepest thought is the same. The *Nocturnall on S. Lucies Day* is at the opposite pole of Donne's thought from the *Anniversarie*, and compared with

Had we never loved sae kindly

or

Take, O take those lips away,

both the feeling and its expression are metaphysical. But the passion is felt through the subtle and fantastic web of dialectic; and the thought from which the whole springs is the emptiness of life without love.

What, then, is the philosophy which disengages itself from Donne's love-poetry studied in its whole compass? It seems to me that it is more than a purely negative one, that consciously or unconsciously he sets over against the abstract idealism, the sharp dualism of the Middle Ages, a justification of love as a natural passion in the human heart the meaning and end of which is marriage. The sensuality and exaggerated cynicism of so much of the poetry of the Renaissance was a reaction from courtly idealism and mediaeval asceticism. But a mere reaction could lead no-whither. There are no steps which lead only backward in the history of human thought and feeling. Poems like Donne's *Elegies*, like Shakespeare's *Venus and Adonis*, like Marlowe's *Hero and Leander* could only end in penitent outcries like those of Sidney and Spenser and of Donne himself. The true escape from courtly or ascetic idealism was a poetry which should do justice to love as a passion in which body and soul alike have their part, and of which there is no reason to repent.

And this with all its imperfections Donne's love-poetry is. It was not for nothing that Sir Thomas Egerton's secretary made a runaway match for love. For Dante the poet, his wife did not exist. In love of his wife Donne found the meaning and the infinite value of love. In later days he might bewail his 'idolatry of profane mistresses'; he never repented of having loved. Between his most sensual and his most spiritual love-songs there is no cleavage such as separates natural love from Dante's love of Beatrice, who is in the end Theology. The passion that burns in Donne's most out-spoken elegies, and wantons in the *Epithalamia*, is not cast out in *The Anniversarie* or *The Canonization*, but absorbed. It is purified and enriched by being brought into harmony with his whole nature, spiritual as well as physical. It has lost the exclusive consciousness of itself which is lust, and become merged in an entire affection, as a turbid and discoloured stream is lost in the sea.

This justification of natural love as fullness of joy and life is the deepest thought in Donne's love-poems, far deeper and sincerer than the Platonic conceptions of the affinity and identity of souls with which he plays in some of the verses addressed to Mrs Herbert. The nearest approach that he makes to anything like a reasoned statement of the thought latent rather than expressed in *The Anniversarie* is in *The Extasie*, a poem which, like the *Nocturnall*, only Donne could have written. Here with the same intensity of feeling, and in the same abstract, dialectical, erudite strain he emphasizes interdependence of soul and body:

> As our blood labours to beget
>   Spirits, as like soules as it can,
> Because such fingers need to knit
>   That subtile knot, which makes us man:
> So must pure lovers soules descend
>   T'affections, and to faculties,
> Which sense may reach and apprehend,
>   *Else a great Prince in prison lies.*

It may be that Donne has not entirely succeeded in what he here attempts. There hangs about the poem just a suspicion of the conventional and unreal Platonism of the seventeenth century. In attempting to state and vindicate the relation of soul and body he falls perhaps inevitably into the appearance, at any rate, of the dualism which he is trying to transcend. He places them over against each other as separate entities and the lower bulks unduly. In love, says Pascal, the body disappears from sight in the intellectual and spiritual passion which it has kindled. That is what happens in *The Anniversarie*, not altogether in *The Extasie*. Yet no poem makes one realize more fully what Jonson meant by calling Donne 'the first poet in the world for some things'. 'I should never find any fault with the metaphysical poems', is Coleridge's judgement, 'if they were all like this or but half as excellent.'

It was only the force of Donne's personality that could achieve even an approximate harmony of elements so divergent as are united in his love-verses, that could master the lower-natured steed that drew the chariot of his troubled and passionate soul and make it subservient to his yoke-fellow of purer strain who is a lover of honour, and modesty, and temperance, and the follower of true glory. In the work of his followers, who were many, though they owed allegiance to Jonson also, the lower elements predominated.

[He speaks of the degeneration of the treatment of love during the later seventeenth century into 'sensual and cynical flippancy on the one hand, a passionless, mannered idealism on the other' and notes the limitation Milton's 'want of the experience' placed upon his art.]

Donne is not a Milton, but he sounded some notes which touch the soul and quicken the intellect in a way that Milton's magnificent and intense but somewhat hard and objective art fails to achieve.

That the simpler and purer, the more ideal and tender of Donne's love-poems were the expression of his love for Ann More cannot of course be proved in the case of each individual poem, for all Donne's verses have come to us (with a few unimportant exceptions) undated and unarranged. But the general thesis, that it was a great experience which purified and elevated Donne's poetry, receives a striking confirmation from the better-known history of his devotional poetry. Here too wit, often tortured wit, fancy, and the heat which Donne's wit was always able to generate, would have been all his verse had to show but for the great sorrow which struck him down in 1617 and gave to his subsequent sonnets and hymns a sincerer and profounder note, his imagery a more magnificent quality, his rhythms a more sonorous music.

Donne was not by nature a devotional poet in the same way and to the same degree as Giles Fletcher or Herbert or Crashaw. It was a sound enough instinct which, despite his theological questions, made him hesitate to cross the threshold of the ministry and induced him to seek rather for some such public service as fell to the lot of his friend Wotton.

... such a spirit will not easily produce great devotional poetry. There are qualities in the religious poetry of simpler and purer souls to which Donne seldom or never attains. The natural love of God which overflows the pages of the great mystics, which dilates the heart and the verses of a poet like the Dutchman Vondel, the ardour and tenderness of Crashaw, the chaste, pure piety and penitence of Herbert, the love from which devotion and ascetic self-denial come unbidden – to these Donne never attained. The high and passionate joy of *The Anniversary* is not heard in his sonnets or hymns. Effort is the note which predominates – the effort to realize the majesty of God, the heinousness of sin, the terrors of Hell, the mercy of Christ. Some of the very worst traits in Donne's mind are brought out in his religious writing. . . .

Some of the poems, and those the earliest written, before Donne had actually taken Orders, are not much more than exercises in these theological subleties, poems such as that *On the Annunciation and Passion falling in the same year* (1608), *The Litany* (1610), *Good-Friday* (1613), and *The Cross* (*c.* 1615) are characteristic examples of Donne's intense and imaginative wit employed on traditional topics of Catholic devotion to which no change of Church ever made him indifferent. . . .

But, as Mr Gosse has pointed out, the sincerest and profoundest of Donne's devotional poetry dates from the death of his wife. The loss of her who had purified and sweetened his earliest love songs lent a new and deeper *timbre* to the sonnets and lyrics in which he contemplates the great topics of personal religion, – sin, death, the Judgement, and throws himself on the mercy of God as revealed in Christ. The seven sonnets entitled *La Corona* have been generally attributed to this period, but it is probable that they were composed earlier, and their treatment of the subject of Christ's life and death is more intellectual and theological than spiritual and poetical. It is when the tone becomes personal, as in the *Holy Sonnets*, when he is alone with his own soul in the prospect of death and the Judgement, that Donne's religious poetry acquires something of the same unique character as his love songs and elegies by a similar combination of qualities, intensity of feeling, subtle turns of thought, and occasional Miltonic splendour of phrase. Here again we meet the magnificent openings of the *Songs and Sonets*.

[He quotes lines 1–4 of *Holy Sonnet* 6; lines 1–4 of *Holy Sonnet* 7 – misrendering the first line as 'At the round earth's imagined quarters'; and lines 1–6 of *Holy Sonnet* 13.]

This passionate penitence, this beating as it were against the bars of self in the desire to break through to a fuller apprehension of the mercy and love of God, is the intensely human note of these latest poems. Nothing came easily to his soul that knew so well how to be subtle to plague itself. The vision of divine wrath he can conjure up more easily than the beatific vision of the love that 'moves the sun in heaven and all the stars'. Nevertheless it was that vision which Donne sought. He could never have been content with

Milton's heaven of majesty and awe divorced from the quickening spirit of love. And there are moments when he comes as close to that beatific vision as perhaps a self-tormenting mind involved in the web of seventeenth-century theology ever could, – at moments love and ecstasy gain the upper hand of fear and penitence. . . .

The noble hymn, 'In what torn ship so ever I embark', is in somewhat the same anguished tone as the *Holy Sonnets*; but the highly characteristic

> Since I am coming to that Holy roome,
> Where with thy Quire of Saints for evermore,
> I shall be made thy Musique;

and the *Hymn to God the Father,* speak of final faith and hope in tones which recall – recall also by their sea-coloured imagery, and by their rhythm – the lines in which another sensitive and tormented poet-soul contemplated the last voyage.

[He quotes stanza 3 of 'A Hymn to God the Father'.]

Beside the passion of these lines even Tennyson's grow a little pale:

> Twilight and evening bell
> And after that the dark;
> And may there be no sadness of farewell
> When I embark:
> For though from out our bourne of Time and Place
> The flood may bear me far,
> I hope to see my Pilot face to face
> When I have crost the bar.

It has not been the aim of the present editor to attempt to pronounce a final judgement upon Donne. It seems to him idle to compare Donne's poetry with that of other poets or to endeavour to fix its relative worth. Its faults are great and manifest; its beauties *sui generis*, incommunicable and incomparable. My endeavour here has been by an analysis of some of the different elements in this composite work – poems composed at different times and in different moods; flung together at the end so carelessly that youthful extravagances of witty sensuality and pious aspirations jostle each other cheek by jowl; and presenting a texture so diverse from that of poetry as we usually think of it – to show how many are the strands which run through it, and that one of these is a poetry, not perfect in form, rugged of line and careless in rhyme, a poetry in which intellect and feeling are seldom or never perfectly fused in a work that is of imagination all compact, yet a poetry of an extraordinarily arresting and haunting quality, passionate, thoughtful, and with a deep melody of its own.

NOTES

1 *The Poems of John Donne*, ed. E. K. Chambers, 2 vols, The Muses' Library (London, 1896).
2 'She is coming already over the ocean from her too-ancient husband – she of the golden hair who with rimy axle brings the day' (Ovid, *Amores*, I. xiii. 1–2; Loeb translation).
3 'Run softly, softly, steeds of night' (cf. ibid., I. xiii. 40).

90. William Butler Yeats

1912

Grierson sent a copy of his edition of Donne's poems to W. B. Yeats, who wrote from Coole Park, Lady Gregory's home, where he was once again recuperating, to thank him in terms that suggest a felt affinity with Donne (*The Letters of W. B. Yeats*, ed. A. Wade, 1954, pp. 570–1).

Nov 14 [1912]   *Coole Park*
Dear Prof Grierson: I write to thank you for your edition of Donne. It was very generous of you to send it to me. I have been using it constantly and find that at last I can understand Donne. Your notes tell me exactly what I want to know. Poems that I could not understand or could but understand are now clear and I notice that the more precise and learned the thought the greater the beauty, the passion; the intricacy and subtleties of his imagination are the length and depths of the furrow made by his passion. His pedantry and his obscenity – the rock and the loam of his Eden – but make

me the more certain that one who is but a man like us all has seen God.

I would have written before but I have been ill – a combination of rheumatism and nervous indigestion – and am indeed still rather weak. I do not like however to delay longer about thanking you for work that has given me and shall give me I think more pleasure than any other book I can imagine. I came here a couple of days ago to get well in the quiet of the country. I shall fish for pike and plan out poems. Yours

W B YEATS

I find it difficult to believe from the evidence you give that Donne was not the lover of Lady Bedford. You I notice still doubt it but as George Moore would say 'I hope for the best.' The poem written on the supposition of her death, if it indeed refers to her, seems to me conclusive. No courtly compliment could go so far, no courtly beauty accept such compliments – and then he thinks her dead and so may well speak out.

91. Edward Bliss Reed

1912

E. B. Reed (1872–1940) graduated from Yale in 1894. He was known as a poet and published various books, including collections of carols, selections of Shakespeare's sonnets and of the works of Thomas Fairfax, of Alexander Pope and of Joseph Addison, and several books on artillery. In a book on lyric poetry he gave some prominence to Donne (*English Lyrical Poetry*, 1912, pp. 234–42).

[Reed follows Gosse in his account of Donne's literary career, but makes his own judgement of Donne's originality.]

One of the most fascinating characters in English literature, it is unfortunate that with the exception of his hymns, his lyrics do not represent the different stages of his development; they do not spring from years of thought and experience, for they are sparks struck out in youth by his vigorous nature.... They were first published a few months after his death, but they had long circulated in manuscript, working as great a change in English poetry as though they had gone through edition after edition.

The moment we open Donne's lyrics, we find ourselves in an unexplored realm. As a rule the young poet follows his models until he has attained the difficult art of self-expression. Chatterton imitates the ballads; Keats writes with his Spenser before him, but over Donne's pages we might place his own line, 'To all, which all love, I say no'. The age was fascinated not only by the emotional force and the unconventional thought of his poems, but by their new and strange style. In the case of Donne it is peculiarly unsatisfactory to consider the style apart from the content of his verse, but we shall attempt this and examine first his manner of expressing himself.

We have seen that Elizabethan verse was lyrical in the oldest sense of that term, for an astonishingly large number of poems were written for music and many that were never sung are perfectly adapted for instrumental accompaniment. Few of Donne's poems are actually songs; they are lyrics because they are short, subjective pieces, showing in every line the poet's dominating personality. If we do not find the lilt of song in most of his work, it is not because song was beyond him. He could write, Walton pointed out, verses 'soft and smooth when he thought them fit and worth his labour', as in his adaptation of Marlowe:

> Come live with me, and be my love,
> And we will some new pleasures prove
> Of golden sands, and crystal brooks,
> With silken lines and silver hooks.

If this meter seems too facile, we turn to 'Go and catch a falling star', with a tripping refrain in each stanza:

> And find
> What wind
> Serves to advance an honest mind,

or the better known, and far more sincere

> Sweetest love, I do not go,
>   For weariness of thee,
> Nor in hope the world can show
>   A fitter love for me.

If we could restrict ourselves in the selection, it would be possible to show that Donne's work had rare metrical beauty. His ear was not defective; he did not possess an imperfect sense of rhythm, for no man can write splendidly again and again by sheer accident. He deliberately put aside the popular manner of the day and going to the other extreme, wrote verses crabbed and unmusical in their movement and disconcerting, to say the least, in their rhymes:

> Whether abstract, spiritual love they like.

> For I am a very dead thing.

> Ends love in this, that my man
> Can be as happy as I can, if he can
> Endure?

These are typical examples of harsh rhythm; for slovenly rhymes take the triplet:

> When this book is made thus,
> Should again the ravenous
> Vandals and Goths invade us.

To select from Donne's poems lines that lack all metrical charm, verses as uncouth as Skelton's, is a simple task; the difficulty is to reconcile them with stanzas marked by a rare and haunting beauty.

[He quotes lines 1–4 of 'Air and Angels'; lines 1–4 of 'The Relic'; and lines 1–7 of 'The Good Morrow'.]

The simplest, most familiar meters acquire a new tone at his hands.

[He quotes stanzas 5–7 of 'The Undertaking'.]

Such work as this unfortunately comprises the smaller part of his verse, and taking his poems as a whole, we can readily understand Jonson's vigorous remark, that Donne, for not keeping accent, deserves hanging.

There are several reasons we may give to account for his unmusical moments. Undoubtedly many of the poems were struck off at white heat, and were never revised. All that he wished was to express the thought, the emotion of the hour. At times, his ideas found perfect expression; at others, language faltered, and instead of deliberating and searching painfully for the well-made phrase, he was content with the first imperfect utterance. Moreover, as we shall see, he flouted the ideas of the day, and what more natural than that he should dislike the sweetness of Spenser, the grace of the song writers, the refinement of Jonson? There was a morbid strain in Donne; the grotesque appealed strongly to him; and as it affected his thought, it made itself felt in his style. We can endure his worst dissonances because at his best his verse has a music which no other writer of his day could reach.

Turning to the poems, we find that many of them bear the marks of that irregular life he led when he left the university for the town, of wild days whose memories long troubled his mind. Several poems are frankly sensual in tone, but their cynicism is too much on parade; one detects in them the swagger of precocious youth delighting to shock old-fashioned morality. Donne declares for community in love; boasts of his inconstancy; and asserts that no true woman exists. It would be a mistake to refuse to see in such writing the marks of days ill spent, but it is equally a mistake to read too much into them or to construct from them, as Mr Gosse has done, a definite tale of dishonorable intrigue. To his own times, the boldness of these poems must have seemed amazing. The Petrarchian tradition still lingered; the poets of the age worshipped woman from afar; she was a goddess, a saint, or at the very least a shepherdess of surpassing virtue and beauty. Donne writes that women

> are ours as fruits are ours;
> He that but tastes, he that devours,
> And he that leaves all, doth as well;
> Changed loves are but changed sorts of meat;
> And when he hath the kernel eat,
> Who doth not fling away the shell?

So absurdly cynical are such poems as *The Indifferent, Community, Confined Love,* or *Love's Alchemy* with its ending

> Hope not for mind in women; at their best,
> Sweetness and wit they are, but mummy, possess'd,

that Donne loses the very effect he seeks to gain.

Had he written in this fashion only, he would never have made his impression upon the lyric. Side by side with these poems, which

347

explain in part the neglect of Donne to-day, are found a sharply contrasted group of lyrics expressing in tones of passionate sincerity the deepest affection and devotion. This sudden change in his mood may be attributed to his meeting with Ann More, whom he married in 1601 despite the opposition of her family. This runaway match cost him his secretary's position and reduced him to utter poverty, yet through years of ambitions unrealized and hopes deferred, his devotion to her never faltered; when she died in 1617, he grieved until his friends despaired for his own life. We know that 'Sweetest love, I do not go', was written for her; we may assume she inspired his finest work.

Donne was a romanticist at heart. He thought of love as a mystic power transcending all boundaries of time and space; it was a union of two spirits forming a new and controlling soul. To depict such a love he brought all the strength of his vigorous intellect, all the emotion of his sensitive nature; in celebrating it he departed as widely from Elizabethan tradition as when he mocked it. He wastes no words in praising a woman's beauty, in comparing her eyes to stars, her hair to golden wires:

> But he who loveliness within
>   Hath found, all outward loathes,
> For he who colour loves, and skin
>   Loves but their oldest clothes.

To the familiar situations of Elizabethan love poetry Donne brings his own, never the conventional point of view. The Elizabethans uttered bitter complaints on absence from their loves; for Donne there can be no such thing as real separation:

[He quotes stanzas 4 and 5 of 'A Valediction: Forbidding Mourning'.]

Nothing is commoner in the song books or the sonnet collections than pictures of a lady weeping; descriptions of beauty in distress with a comparison of tearful eyes to flowing springs. By his unusual and forceful similes, and by the rush of his final apostrophe, Donne completely transforms this stock theme:

> O! More than moon,
> Draw not up seas to drown me in thy sphere;
> Weep me not dead, in thine arms, but forbear
> To teach the sea, what it may do too soon.

Though many illustrations of Donne's avoidance of the beaten track could easily be given, one more must suffice. It was a custom for men of the sixteenth and seventeenth centuries to wear bracelets of their ladies' hair. Among the slain at Marston Moor, Sir Charles Lucas recognized 'one cavalier with a bracelet of hair round his wrist. He desired the bracelet to be taken off, saying that he knew an honourable lady who would give thanks for it.' Verses on these love tokens are common in all languages; Melin de Saint-Gelais has a poem, Alessandro Gatti a madrigal, both in the tone of gallantry, on such a gift. Donne writes of one, but disdaining the spirit of trifling compliment, his imagination pierces the tomb and sees there a mouldering skeleton with 'A bracelet of bright hair about the bone'.

Originality is not enough to establish a poet's fame; it may or may not lead to the finest work. With Donne's unconventionality went two rare qualities which our citations have illustrated: he stirred the feelings, he awoke the imagination by far-reaching suggestion. In *Canonization* he speaks of two lovers 'who did the whole world's soul contract' into their eyes, and Donne could put the heart of a poem – contract the soul – into a single phrase. The Elizabethans would express in a sonnet what he tells in a line. By sheer intellectual force, far removed from mere cleverness, he could transform a thought or feeling by expressing it in similes startlingly quaint yet apposite. The best of them were not sought out with care and calculation; his mind, deeply moved, found them instinctively. When Shelley compares the skylark, hidden in the cloud, to a poet, a maiden, a glow worm, a rose, we do not feel that he painfully seeks these comparisons, but that his mind naturally overflows in them. So with Donne; every stanza in his *Fever* embodies a new and strange thought:

> But yet thou canst not die, I know;
> To leave this world behind, is death;
> But when thou from this world wilt go,
> The whole world vapours with thy breath.
>
> . . . . .
>
> O wrangling schools, that search what fire
> Shall burn this world, had none the wit
> Unto this knowledge to aspire,
> That this her fever might be it?

This peculiar turn of mind persisted to the end. In the *Hymn to God, my God, in my sickness*, written on his death-bed, after a touching and beautiful opening stanza, he compares himself to a map which his doctors, 'grown cosmographers', are studying.

Attempting to discover the secret of Donne's power, the age thought it lay in this ability to detect curious analogies. This was called 'wit', but with our modern notions of the meaning of that word, it is strange to read of the 'witty Donne'. Dr Johnson was more misleading when he applied the term 'metaphysical' to this trait of Donne's mind. Moved by this poetry and desiring to imitate it, the men of the day seized upon 'wit' as the one thing needful. At times they partially caught Donne's manner; his spirit escaped them. Through all the ingenuity of Donne's thought, we feel the glow of emotion. The *Fever* ends with this passionate declaration:

> Yet 'twas of my mind, seizing thee,
> Though it in thee can not perséver;
> For I had rather owner be
> Of thee one hour, than all else ever.

It is small wonder that such writing changed the whole spirit of the lyric.

92. Andrew Lang

1912

Andrew Lang (1844–1912), Scottish man of letters, was a Fellow of Merton College, Oxford 1868–74, when he studied myth and ritual. He moved to London in 1875 to become a journalist, specializing in mythology, on which he published a number of books. He also published several popular collections of fairy-tales, critical studies of literary figures, a translation of Homer, a *History of Scotland* in three volumes, and *A History of English Literature*, in which he allowed five pages to Donne (*A History of English Literature from 'Beowulf' to Swinburne*, 1912, pp. 284–9).

[Lang's account of Donne's poetry amounts to a string of scattered impressions which largely repeat the received Johnsonian demurs. Thus the *Satires* are all but unreadably obscure and rough, while *The Storm* and *The Calm* are similarly 'rude in versification and exaggeration', redeemed only by some vivid 'pictures of Nature and the sea'. Again, the 'amorous conceits in *The Flea* are equally rich in ingenious fancies and in bad taste'.

Lang follows Gosse in taking the *Elegies* and *Songs and Sonnets* for direct confessions of youthful affairs and disapproves of the moral attitudes they express, comparing Donne with Byron. The *Elegies* 'address ladies of whose nature purity is no part', and 'win no admiration for Donne's taste, temper, or morals. *The Curse* on a woman, or a man who loves his mistress, far outdoes the Epodes of Horace in cold ferocity'. Chance felicities relieve the harshness. *Love's Deity* opens with a couple of charmed lines, 'thence descends into crabbed and difficult conceits'. *The Funeral* and *The Relic* are momentarily lifted by 'A bracelet of bright hair about the bone'. *Air and Angels* is a wholly 'charming song', but that is probably because it comes from 'a later period, when he met his future wife'. Lang concludes that this youthful libertine was too much at odds with himself and with his experience to attain true lyric ease.]

These verses of Donne's disturbed and adventurous youth, poems ingenious, conceited, passionate, mystical, or cynical, have not the music as of birds' songs which rings in the lyrists of that age: nor have the *Epithalamia* the charm of Spenser's. Donne in youth was not at ease with himself: he speculates too curiously. He may try to play the sensualist, but there is a dark backward in his genius; there are chords not in tune with mirth and pleasure. He is as unique as Browning, as little like other poets. If his *Elegies* contain, as has been supposed, the story of a love affair, it was of a nature to make him uneasy.

93. Evelyn Mary Simpson
(née Spearing)
1912

E. M. Simpson (1885–1963) was the first woman to take a D.Phil. at Oxford. After a spell as Assistant in English at Bedford College London 1909–11, she became tutor in English literature at St Hugh's College, Oxford 1918–21. She worked on Elizabethan translations of Seneca, on Ben Jonson and on Donne, where she is known for her editing of his sermons. She entered upon her lifelong engagement with Donne's prose by calling attention to its disregarded literary merits, as well as to the links between Donne's poems and his other writings ('Donne's Sermons, and Their Relations to his Poetry', *Modern Language Review*, 7 (1912), 40–53).

[Simpson reminds us that the distinctions of Donne's prose remained all but unrecognized long after his poems had returned to favour: 'The revival of interest in Donne's poetry which has occurred in recent years does not seem to have extended to his prose works.' She attributes this neglect to the lack of satisfactory modern editions of the writings themselves, and commends Donne's style by quoting some excerpts from the sermons which exhibit 'a dignity and beauty that have seldom been surpassed in English prose'.

The sermons also claim attention for the light they throw on the poetry; and she points out a number of passages which directly parallel effects in particular poems. She concludes with some high flights from the sermons which express Donne's yearning to transform his secular attachments into the joy of eternal love.]

94. Anon., *Nation*

1913

An anonymous reviewer of Grierson's edition of Donne's poems explained Donne's appeal to modern readers. He warmly commended Grierson's work on the text of the poems but thought the introductory appraisal superfluous because Grierson lacked sympathy with the spirit of Donne's poetry ('John Donne, the Elizabethan', *Nation*, 15 February 1913, pp. 825–6).

One of the most remarkable of the English pictures in the recent 'Post-Impressionist' exhibition depicts 'John Donne arriving in Heaven'. 'I don't know who John Donne is', a sturdy member of the public was lately heard to remark in front of it, 'but he seems to be getting there.' Unconsciously, he summed up Donne's recent history. Of all the great English poets, his name is least known beyond 'literary' circles; but he is certainly 'getting there'. If one has entered, any time these last years, a railway carriage, and found some studious vagabond deep in a little blue book, it generally turns out to be Mr Chambers's invaluable edition in the Muses' Library. And now Professor Grierson and the Delegates of the Clarendon Press have given us, clothed in the most attractive garb possible, a perfect text of the poems, and an immense body of elucidatory comment.

Such service is merited. It proceeds, perhaps, from our modern clearer perception of the true nature of that Elizabethan literature of which Donne was a chief glory. The writers, principally the dramatists, of that great period between 1580 and 1640 have been treated without discrimination. From Lamb and Swinburne, who revered almost all as gods, they have passed into the hands of scholars, who find each equally a subject for annotation and conjecture. At length we are beginning to discern their degrees and kinds, and to note the limits and nature of the short period when the Elizabethans found their highest expression – a period whose spirit is almost completely the spirit of Donne. For the drama, the crown of the time, was at its best for little more than a decade. Between, roughly, 1598 and 1613, all the dramatists were doing their best work. The spirit of power came upon them startlingly.

[He rehearses the glories of the drama of those fifteen years.]

One must understand this period, his background, to understand Donne. The soul of its art was the soul of his. Webster repeatedly steals from his published poems. His wit was essentially of that curious kind the austere Chapman somewhere praises: –

> Your wit is of the true Pierian spring
> That can make anything of anything.

Hamlet, with his bitter flashes, his humor, his metaphysical inquisitiveness, and his passion, continually has the very accent of the secular Donne; but that he is an avenger, not a lover. To Ophelia he must have been Donne himself. Indeed, Donne, the bulk of whose good poetry seems to have been written between 1595 and 1613, heralded, and in some part led, this age, when English literature climbed and balanced briefly on the difficult pinnacle of sincerity. Poetry is always a few years ahead of drama. But Donne applied the same spirit the dramatists applied to the whole world, almost solely to love. He is, for width and depth, incomparably the greatest love-poet in English. Every pain or pleasure contained in or relevant to that emotion comes under his notice. He can praise in lines where all the music of verse of the last three centuries seems to ring together:

> So may thy mighty, amazing beauty move
> Envy in all women, and in all men, love!

or harp on that external perplexity of human relationships:

> What hate could hurt our bodies like our love?

He belonged to an age when men were not afraid to mate their intellects with their emotions. In his own words, he 'loved to be subtle to plague himself'. He would startle the soul from her lair with unthinkable paradoxes, and pursue her, with laughter and tears, along all the difficult coasts between sense and madness. At one moment he knows the most unworldly ecstasy of the communion of two souls: –

> And whilst our souls negotiate there,
> We like sepulchral statues lay!
> All day the same our postures were,
> And we said nothing, all the day.

At another he contemplates the consummation of human love within the black, bright walls of a flea. He compares his lady to a primrose, an angel, the number five, Mary Magdalen, a gingerbread figure, Newfoundland, the stationary leg of a compass, God. And one can never doubt his sincerity.

[He acclaims Grierson's editorial judgement and elucidatory scholarship but thinks that Grierson does not fully appreciate the poems.]

Mr Grierson points out elsewhere how the superb 'Sappho to Philaenis' has influenced Swinburne's 'Anactoria'. As a matter of fact, it is even closer to 'Erotion'. Donne's metrical power is marvellous, and Swinburne learnt only some of his lessons. His passionate colloquialism of style has influenced even later poetry.

Mr Grierson's general remarks about the 'philosophy of Donne's love-poetry' are not sufficiently illuminating. Moreover, he is reprehensibly out of sympathy with some sides of that many-colored character. He misses the point of that superb and extraordinary satiric poem 'The Progress of the Soul'; and he undervalues 'The Second Anniversary', one of the greatest long poems in English. Worst of all, he is prudish about Donne; a serious handicap in an editor or critic of the Elizabethans. It is so easy to distinguish between obscenity and non-obscenity; so hard and so much more important to distinguish between cleanness and dirtiness. But, on the whole, this edition is one of those triumphs of industry, clear thinking, and literary knowledge, which occur only a few times in a generation, and establish the nobility of scholarship. To obtain a perfect text of the obscure Donne was one of the chief needs of literature.

[He expresses praise and gratitude to Grierson and the Clarendon Press, and declares that two things are now needed to complete this joint achievement, 'the extension of the edition to include Donne's prose works, and the issue of the text alone in a cheap, small volume'.]

Donne's glory is ever increasing. He was the one English love-poet who was not afraid to acknowledge that he was composed of body, soul, and mind; and who faithfully recorded all the pitched battles, alarms, treaties, sieges, and fanfares of that extraordinary triangular warfare.

95. Felix E. Schelling

1913

Schelling frequently cited Donne in a study of English lyric poetry (*The English Lyric*, 1913, pp. 55, 62–3, 67–70, 76, 80, 93, 96–7, 142, 275, 294).

[Schelling characterizes Donne's poetry by its eschewal of the furniture of Renaissance verse, the choice epithets and diction, mythic properties, similitudes drawn from nature.]

In place of all these things discarded, he enriched the lyrical poetry of his day with a new poetic style of surprising directness, with a vocabulary free from the accepted smoothness and over-indulgence in figure, and with a versification, abrupt and harsh at times, but always vigorous. Donne applied to the lyric the freedom, in a word, of the best dramatic verse of his day. Above all, he furnished lyrical poetry with a totally new order of metaphor, drawn from his study of the dialectics of divinity and especially from the technical nomenclature of contemporary science. In the difficult and often recondite allusions of Donne's poetry the literature of his successors found a new and undiscovered mine, and his influence became patent and widespread in the lyric almost before he could have been well aware of it himself. To Donne, his total break with the past, his mannerisms, ingenious similitudes, even, to some extent, his cynicism – however some of it may have been an affectation of his wit – were genuine and innate qualities of his genius; in his imitators they often degenerated into sheer mannerism and into a struggle after the ingenious and that which had never been said before. It was this that led, years after, to the indiscriminate dubbing of this whole poetical perversity by the title, 'the metaphysical school of poetry'. Donne is distinguishable from the Petrarchists that went before, as he is distinguishable from the 'metaphysicals' that came after. He is a notable poet whose lyrical art stands equally in contrast with the refined worship of beauty idealized that characterized Spenser, and with the sweeter music and more consummate artistry of the lyrical poetry of Shakespeare.

[In shedding his predecessors' superficialities of style Donne

356

'discarded their superficialities of thought, substituting the actual experiences and emotions of his strange personality, clothed in the stranger garb of illustration drawn from contemporary abstractions of scientific and philosophic thought'. Schelling oddly finds that Donne is more concerned with abstract conceptions than with human relationships, and he denies Donne's poetry the very quality which has so commended it to modern readers.]

As to man in relation to man, it may be affirmed that Donne is freer from any touch of the dramatic than any other poet of his time or perhaps any English poet of any other time.

[He has difficulty in accommodating Donne's poetry to received ideas of the lyric, puzzling over the image of the compasses in 'A Valediction: Forbidding Mourning', pointing out the contradictory attitudes to be found in the love-poetry, weighing 'the weird intensity and abandon' of Donne's sceptical lyrics, 'such as English poetry had not known before Donne's time', against the wholly different understanding Donne expresses elsewhere.]

But with respect to his cynicism and scepticism as to human passion, it is to be remembered that no lyrist has so glorified the constancy and devotion of pure love as Donne, whose own life exemplified alike its beauty and its glory.

[Schelling enlarges the scope of lyric poetry to take in the two *Anniversaries*, though he allows that their length might seem to disqualify them.]

None the less, it would be difficult to find a purer specimen of the lyric of intellectualized emotion, sublimed to the abstract.

[Schelling makes Donne's poetry a touchstone of some leading qualities of lyric poetry. Against the continuing misjudgement of precisians, he argues that Donne used his stanza forms felicitously and was prolific in the invention of new ones. Donne 'wrote some exquisitely fervent devotional poetry' which opened the way to Herbert, Crashaw, Vaughan. In fact Donne's conceited manner rings true just because he 'sees things oddly from the innate originality of his mind'; whereas Crashaw often lapses into tasteless extravagance in straining for rhetorical effect. Donne's disregard of human figures is quite unlike Blake's, marking a worldly man's rejection of the world, rather than an ardour for abstraction out of sheer unworldliness.]

Donne's wisdom is the wisdom of speculation and experience; Blake's the innocence of childhood.

[Francis Thompson stands comparison with Donne in that no other English poets have 'so poeticized metaphysical thought'.

Schelling's concluding survey gives pre-eminence to the late Elizabethan lyric poets in qualities of mind as well as grace. We cannot claim greater profundity for more recent song]

in view of the depth of thought, the wealth of imagination, and the fullness of significance that characterizes, now and again, the lyrical poetry of Greville, Shakespeare, Jonson, and Donne.

96. George Charles Moore Smith

1913

Moore Smith questioned a number of assertions in Gosse's *Life and Letters of John Donne* ('Donniana', *Modern Language Review*, 8 (1913), 47–52).

[None of Moore Smith's cavils affects the understanding of Donne's poems but he does point out Donne's several echoes of Shakespeare, correct some misreadings in Gosse's text of Donne's letters, and propose the likely date of the 'Hymn to God my God, in my Sickness'.]

97. Rupert Brooke

1913

Brooke (1887–1915), established critic as well as poet, had championed Donne's poetry from his schooldays.[1] He now reviewed Grierson's edition of Donne's poems ('John Donne', *Poetry and Drama*, 1 (1913), 185–8).

Donne is the one poet who demands a commentary, not for allusions, but, sometimes, for his entire train of thought. And in the same way he is the one poet who requires a perfect text, for (it is a minor merit) all his lines always 'mean something'. . . .

Donne was labelled, by Johnson, a 'metaphysical' poet; and the term has been repeated ever since, to the great confusion of critics. Mr Grierson attempts to believe that it means erudite, and that erudition is one of the remarkable and eponymous characteristics of Donne's poetry. It rested on erudition, no doubt, as Mr Grierson has valuably shown; but it was not so especially erudite – not so erudite as the writings of Ben Jonson, a far less 'metaphysical' poet. But the continual use of this phrase may have aimed vaguely at a most important feature there is in Donne's poetry. He is the most *intellectual* poet in English; and his intellectualism had, even, sometimes, a tendency to the abstract. But to be an intellectual poet does not mean that one writes about intellectual things. The pageant of the outer world of matter and the mid-region world of the passions came to Donne through the brain. The whole composition of the man was made up of brain, soul, and heart in a different proportion from the ordinary prescription. This does not mean that he felt less keenly than others; but when passion shook him, and his being ached for utterance, to relieve the stress, expression came through the intellect. Under the storm of emotion, it is common to seek for relief by twisting some strong stuff. Donne, as Coleridge said, turns intellectual pokers into love-knots. An ordinary poet, whose feelings find far stronger expression than a common man's, but an expression according to the same prescription, praises his mistress with some common idea, intensely felt:

> Oh, thou art fairer than the evening air,
> Clad in the beauty of a thousand stars!

Donne, equally moved and equally sincere, would compare her to a perfectly equilateral triangle, or to the solar system. His intellect must find satisfaction. If a normal poet – it is not very probable – in thinking of his mistress being ill with a fever, had had suggested to him the simile of these fevers soon passing and dying away in her, just as shooting stars consume and vanish in the vastness and purity of the sky, he would have tried to bring the force of his thought home by sharpening and beautifying the imagined vision. He might have approached it on the lines of:

> Through the serene wide dark of you
> They trail their transient gold, and die.

Donne feels only the idea. He does not try to visualise it. He never visualises, or suggests that he has any pleasure in looking at things. His poems might all have been written by a blind man in a world of blind men. In 'The Fever' he gives you the thought thus:

> These burning fits but meteors be,
> Whose matter in theee is soon spent.
> Thy beauty, and all parts, which are thee,
> Are unchangeable firmament.

The mediation of the senses is spurned. Brain does all.

And as Donne saw everything through his intellect, it follows, in some degree, that he could see everything humorously. He could see it the other way, too. But humour was always at his command. It was part of his realism; especially in the bulk of his work, his poems dealing with love. There is no true lover but has sometimes laughed at his mistress, and often at himself. But you would not guess that from the love-songs of many poets. Their poems run the risk of looking a little flat. They are unreal by the side of Donne. For while his passion enabled him to see the face of love, his humour allowed him to look at it from the other side. So we behold his affairs in the round.

But it must not appear that his humour, or his wit, and his passion, alternated. The other two are his passion's handmaids. It should not be forgotten that Donne was one of the first great English satirists, and the most typical and prominent figure of a satirical age. Satire comes with the Bible of truth in one hand and the sword of laughter in the other. Donne was true to the reality of his own heart. Sometimes you hear the confident laughter of lovers who have found their love:

> I wonder, by my troth, what thou and I
> Did, till we loved? were we not weaned till then?
> But sucked on country pleasures, childishly?
> Or snorted we in the Seven Sleepers' den?

And there is the bitterer mirth of the famous –

> For God's sake, hold your tongue, and let me love.

He could combine either the light or the grave aspects of love with this lack of solemnity that does but heighten the sharpness of the seriousness. His colloquialism helped him. It has been the repeated endeavour of half the great English poets to bring the language of poetry, and the accent and rhythm of poetry, nearer to those of the intensest moments of common speech. To attempt this was especially the mark of many of the greatest of the Elizabethans. Shakespeare's 'Prithee, undo this button!' finds its lyrical counterpart in several of Donne's poems. Yet he did not confine his effects to laughter and slang. He could curiously wed fantastic imagination with the most grave and lofty music of poetry; as in the great poem where he compares his wife to the stationary leg of a compass, himself to the voyaging one:

> And though it in the centre fit,
>   Yet when the other far doth roam,
> It leans, and hearkens after it,
>   And grows erect, as that comes home.
>
> Such wilt thou be to me, who must,
>   Like the other foot, obliquely run:
> Thy firmness makes my circle just,
>   And makes me end where I begun.

For indeed, while the quality of his imagination was unique and astonishing, he expressed it most normally as a great poet, with all the significance and beauty that English metre and poetry can give:

> O more than moon,
> Draw not up seas to drown me in thy sphere!

and –

> Thou art not soft, and clear, and straight, and fair,
> As down, as stars, cedars, and lilies are;
> But thy right hand, and cheek, and eye, only
> Are like thy other hand, and cheek, and eye –

contain as much inexplicable loveliness and strangeness as any of the writings of the Romantics. The mere technique of his poetry has been imitated and followed by many of all the poets who followed him and loved him, from Dryden to Swinburne. It is a good thing that he is slowly spreading from that select band of readers to a wider public. This edition has opportunely appeared at the time of the spreading of his fame. It is fitting he should be read in an age when poetry is beginning to go back from nature, romance, the great world, and the other fine hunting-places of the Romantics, by devious ways and long *ambages*, to that wider home which Donne knew better than any of the great English poets, the human heart. 'The heart's a wonder.'

NOTE

1 See No. 71.

98. Walter de la Mare

1913

Walter de la Mare (1873–1956), poet and novelist, reviewed together Grierson's edition of Donne's poems, and *Georgian Poetry 1911–12* ('An Elizabethan Poet and Modern Poetry', *Edinburgh Review*, 444 (1913), 372–85).

[De la Mare argues that the best and rarest things can never be really popular, and quotes Ben Jonson's epigram on Donne: 'A man should seek great glory, and not broad'.]

That will always, as things go, be Donne's fate as a poet – great glory, but not broad. He captures an ardent, almost impassioned, few; but has little share in the admiration of the many. He is too bare and direct, and he is too obscure and abstruse. He is at the same time

too little and too much a poet. Jonson, indeed, though he en-
thusiastically acknowledged him as 'the first poet in the world for
some things', also remarked in convivial confidence to Drummond,
that 'Donne himself, for not being understood, would perish.' It is
undeniable that the full appreciation of his work, even by his
devotees, needs not only all the research, scholarship, acute analysis,
and sustained and penetrating diligence and thought that Professor
Grierson has given to this new and surely definitive edition: it needs
also some temperamental affinity, a certain openness of mind, and
freedom from prejudice. To some extent, too, even in regard to the
work of Donne's headlong, hedonistic youth, such appreciation is
a question of age. Life, fortunately, does not empty her whole
cornucopia of delights on man's devoted head in one generous
gesture. She refuses to let him ever irretrievably 'come of age'. She
reserves joys for maturity, joys for antiquity. And Donne is among
those intended for life's meridian – when we look before and after
and are compelled to realise that thenceforth, though our wisdom
may ripen, it will ripen at the expense of the tree.

It is possible, of course, to read and delight in Donne, to blunder
on through the difficulties, putting one's own free interpretation
on his meaning, without seeking or desiring the aid of notes and
references. Most poetry should be so read. But even if Mr Grierson
were not concerned with textual corruptions and misreadings,
Donne's poetry is only enriched, much of it even is actually
retrieved, by the sagacity which such an editor can bring to bear
upon it.

[He speaks of Grierson's introductory account of Donne's poetry.]

He explains the by no means inexplicable extremes of sensuality
and spiritual exaltation revealed in his love poetry. But though Mr
Grierson expresses a warm and discerning appreciation, the general tone of his essay – to those readers at least who find it
impossible to keep their admiration of Donne on this side idolatry
– will suggest something in the nature of an apology. He seems to
be addressing an audience inclined to be hostile, or at least neutral,
rather than sympathetic. And his references, for comparison, to
Tennyson, Burns, and Mr Bridges are neither very apt nor happy.

[He goes on to develop his own view of Donne's poetry.]

The finest achievement of most lyrical poets – Keats, Coleridge,

Herrick, Blake, Shelley – seems to be something apart and aloof from their mere workaday selves. It is the outcome of rare, heightened moments, of an elusive and, to a certain degree, alien impulse. . . .

Existence is simplified in this intensified and isolated moment. Life is no longer a riddle but a dream.

Donne's poetry is different. He is the poet not of escape from, but into, the depths and mysteries of personality. It is his personality that enslaves us. 'By our first strange and fatall interview', we are once and for all made captive. He can be almost as intolerably coarse as Swift, as ecstatic as Shelley, as imaginative as Sir Thomas Browne, as nimble and insolent as Mercutio, as thought-ridden as Hamlet, as solemn as the *Dies Irae*, as paradoxical as a latter-day moralist. He may overwhelm a lyric with learning, juggle with the erudite ideas of 'wrangling schooles', be affectedly and fantastically intellectual, tediously labyrinthine. 'Subtile to plague himself' he was; but however straitened the view we catch of him, he is always in some indefinable and virtual fashion the man – John Donne. And it is from out of the midst of his obscurity, in the hugger-mugger, as it were, of his alembics and retorts, that we are suddenly dazzled and enthralled by a sheer incandescence of thought and feeling – the attar of his poetry. Donne 'perplexes the mind of the fair sex', said Dr Johnson. None the less, except it be Browning, far more of a sentimentalist, in spite of his philosophical gallantry, than Donne, to no other poet do women – apart from the 'fair sex' – owe a rarer debt for his insight, exquisite tenderness, and masculine understanding. No man ever 'deeper digg'd loves Myne' than Donne, nor retrieved from it a stranger treasure. Who that has really read him does not know 'by heart' 'The undertaking', 'Sweetest love, I do not goe', 'The Funeral', 'The Exstacie', 'A Nocturnall', 'A Valediction: of weeping', the Anniversaries, the best of the Elegies; the wonderful onset of 'Aire and Angels', of 'Loves Deitie', 'The Legacie', 'A Feaver', of 'The good-morrow'?

Throughout his life the same bare, emotional directness is apparent, from 'The Canonization' – 'For Godsake hold your tongue, and let me love', – to the 'Holy Sonnets'.

[He quotes the whole of *Holy Sonnet* 1, 'Thou Hast Made Me'.]

Reading him, we do not throw off the world; we are not, as by a miracle, made innocent and happy. 'Witty depravity', the sharpest

actuality, extremes of exultation and despair, passion and disillusionment, love, death, the grave, corruption – all this is the
material of his verse – a verse that breaks into beauty and music the
moment feeling and thought are clear and free. Everything that we
have – mind, body, soul – he invites to his intimacy.

A naked thinking heart, that makes no show,

is his demand; a reader 'mad with much heart', rather than 'ideott
with none'; but he exercises also all our mature, modern complexity, for 'man is a lumpe, where all beasts kneaded bee'. 'Made
one anothers hermitage', we share with him a tense, vigilant,
silence in some withdrawn chamber of our minds,

as men who through a Cipres see
The rising sun.

'Forget this rotten world!' he cries; what 'fragmentary rubbidge' it
all is!

And unto thee
Let thine own times as an old story be.

The house of life, darkened, haunted, is above and around us.
Brightest lover and friend, like clear-illumined ghosts, offer their
wordless company. Passionately realised, or dimmed in ecstatic
brooding, long they have been away,

long, long, yet none
Offers to tell us who it is that's gone.

For us in this solitude with him, at any moment a further door may
quietly open, and Death, like a groom, will bring a 'taper to the
outward room'. 'The last busie day' done, we shall 'ebbe out with
them, who homeward goe': and then, 'good morrow to our waking
soules'. Only the best of life is in most poets; all man's inward life
is in Donne – from his reckless, squandered youth, the youth of the
long sensual face, with its high, sloping forehead, wide, dreaming,
searching, interrogative eyes, to the shroud-swathed, 'ruinous
Anatomie' of the Droeshout engraving. And his poetry has con-
ferred upon him, so far as this world is concerned, life's only real
immortality.

[De la Mare now turns to discussion of *Georgian Poetry, 1911–1912*.]

There are many influences perceptible in this volume; but that of Donne – Donne in his headlong, rebellious youth – it traceable only in the work of Mr Rupert Brooke. He is more self-centred than the rest, more analytical and intellectual. He is also more impatient of tradition, defiant of the dictates of poetic Grundyism. His verse keeps unusually close to actual experience and is yet imaginatively in focus. He rails at dull sublunary 'fools', and, like Mr Abercrombie, cannot resist the fascination of what repels him. He is at once the youngest and the most promising of his contemporaries.

99. Anon., *Spectator*

1913

An anonymous reviewer of Grierson's edition of Donne's poems traced Donne's reputation as a poet, and then developed his own view of Donne ('The Poetry of John Donne', *Spectator*, 110 (1913), 102–3).

[The reviewer judges: 'The history of the poetical reputation of John Donne is one of the most curious in literature.' He attests Donne's reputation in his own day, then follows its rapid decline in Dryden's time, and its partial recovery in the late nineteenth century.]

In 1896 the admirable edition of Mr Chambers in the Muses' Library for the first time brought Donne within the reach of the average reader, and for the last fifteen years there has probably been more genuine interest taken in his poetry by lovers of English literature than during the whole preceding period since the days of Dryden. The full and scholarly edition which Professor Grierson has just published is at once a proof of this growing interest in Donne's work and an assurance of its increase in the future. . . .

Donne's work is peculiarly interesting, not only on account of its high intrinsic merits, but owing to the extraordinary strength and the no less extraordinary diversity of its influence upon subsequent writers. It is a curious paradox that a poet whose traces are to be found all over English literature should still be almost unknown to the majority of English readers. It would be difficult, for instance, to name two works more remote from each other in style, in subject, in feeling, in general conception, than Butler's *Hudibras* and Crashaw's *Hymn to Saint Teresa*; yet both the ingenious ribaldry of the one and the mystical frenzies of the other are the direct offspring of Donne's poetry. More important, because more far-reaching, was his influence on Dryden. Dryden, we know, was in his youth an enthusiastic disciple of Donne; and his early work shows the signs of his admiration plainly enough. There is nothing surprising in this. Apart from Chaucer, Donne was the first English writer to grasp to the full the importance of the realistic and intellectual elements in poetry. It was he who, by leading a revolt against the sugared and sensuous style of Spenser, opened the way to that great movement in our literature which culminated in the Satires of Pope. And it was through Dryden that the way lay. Dryden's eminently rationalistic and mundane mind recognized in Donne the master who could teach him how to use verse both as an instrument of argumentative exposition and as a brilliant mirror of actual life. Having learnt this, he went a step further, discarded what was *baroque* and unessential in Donne's manner, and introduced once for all the modern spirit into poetry. Thus, in a sense, he superseded Donne, but the magnificent original conception of the great Elizabethan lies at the root of Dryden's finest work, and of that of his numerous spiritual progeny. Just as *Endymion* is implicit in the *Faerie Queene*, so is *English Bards and Scotch Reviewers* implicit in the Satires of Donne.

But though the main importance of Donne's influence lay in this direction, the actual characteristics of his poetry itself are curiously complex, and the essential nature of his work differs entirely from that of any of his successors. The intellectuality of Dryden and Pope, the mysticism of Crashaw and Vaughan, the gallantry of Cowley, the bitter wit of Butler, all these elements are to be found in him, not side by side, but completely interfused and compounded together into a strange and unique whole. It is here that the peculiar interest of his poetry lies – in the amazing many-sidedness of the personality which it reveals. It shows us a man who was at once religious, sensual, erudite, passionate, and argumentative. 'He combined', says De Quincey, 'what no other man has ever done – the last sublimation of dialectical subtlety and address with the most impassioned majesty.' His love poems are probably the most extraordinary in the world. Loaded with complicated reasonings, learned allusions to obscure writers, abstruse references to philosophical systems, it seems almost impossible that they should be anything but frigid and absurd. And, of course, many critics – with Dr Johnson at the head of them – have failed to see more in Donne's poetry than a preposterous collection of 'conceits'. Dryden himself, with the blindness of a reformer, wrote of Donne that 'he affects the metaphysics, not only in his satires, but in his amorous verses, where nature only should reign; and perplexes the minds of the fair sex with nice speculations of philosophy when he should engage their hearts, and entertain them with the softnesses of love'. The criticism seems perfectly just until we turn to the poems themselves, and find that Donne really has achieved the impossible. The ardours of his passionate soul transfuse his antiquated mannerisms, his contorted and remote conceptions, and fill them with an intensely human significance. He has the art of endowing the strangest speculations with a personal thrill: –

> I long to talk with some old lover's ghost,
> Who died before the god of Love was born.

He can make a far-fetched, complicated simile the occasion for a lyrical outburst of astonishing beauty:–

> O more than moon!
> Draw not up tears to drown me in thy sphere,
> Weep me not dead in thine arms. . . .

Or he can turn an epigram into an intimate confession of adoration: –

> I must confess, it could not choose but be
> Profane, to think thee anything but thee.

Nor is it only in his love poems that the remarkable qualities of Donne's poignant and powerful nature are apparent. In his elegies, his satires, and his devotional verses the same bizarre and highly strung individuality makes itself felt. Perhaps the most characteristic of all his works are the two 'Anniversaries' written to commemorate the early death at the age of fifteen of Elizabeth Drury, the daughter of one of Donne's patrons. In these strange poems his genius seems to pour itself forth without restraint in a sort of intoxication. No one has a right to consider himself a true worshipper of Donne unless he can admire whole-heartedly these extraordinary productions. Whether Professor Grierson comes within the category is a little doubtful. He seems to apologize for the tremendous and elaborate structure of hyperboles which Donne has erected over the grave of this young girl. But here apologies are out of place; one must either reject wholly or accept wholly; Donne is either revolting or magnificent. Probably it is the very intensity of his seriousness that tends to mislead some of his modern readers. To him God and Heaven were blazing and palpitating realities, and the human soul was a miracle about which no exaggeration of statement was possible. He saw in Elizabeth Drury, not only the type, but the actual presence, of all that is most marvellous in the spirit of man.

> One, whose clear body was so pure and thin,
> Because it need disguise no thought within:
> 'Twas but a through-light scarf, her mind t'inroll;
> Or exhalation breathed out from her Soul.

And he meant not less, but more, than what he wrote of her: –

> She to whose person Paradise adhered
> As courts to Princes, she whose eyes ensphered
> Starlight enough to have made the South control
> (Had she been there) the star-full Northern Pole,
> She, she is gone; she is gone; when thou knowest this,
> What fragment rubbidge this world is
> Thou knowest, and that it is not worth a thought.

In such lines as these one recognizes the same spirit which led Donne, on his death-bed, to wrap himself in his shroud to have his portrait painted. For that strange nature rhetorical eccentricity seems to have been the sincerest expression of mystical ravishment, just as dialectical quibbling was the natural language of his most passionate love.

100. Ernest Percival Rhys

1913

E. P. Rhys (1859–1946), Anglo-Welsh editor and writer, was a mining-engineer who from 1886 devoted his time to writing. After working freelance, he joined the staff of Constable's as editor of the Camelot Classics series and the Everyman Library of Classics. He wrote two novels and some volumes of verse. In a chronological survey of English lyric poetry he gave three pages to Donne (*Lyric Poetry*, 1913, 195–9).

[Rhys developed a single idea, which is that Donne's verse unpredictably mingles 'intense melody' with dullness. He conventionally contrasts some passages from the *Songs and Sonnets* to bring out the disparity between Donne's 'ideal verse' and 'his forced note', playing off the opening of 'Love's Deity' against lines 11–13 of the same poem, and 'the curious imaginative passages' of stanzas 3–5 of 'A Valediction: Forbidding Mourning' against stanza 1 of 'The Broken Heart'.

Rhys supposes that Donne's extreme unevenness follows from his attempts to 'assimilate reflective ideas to the primary emotions', which failed partly because 'he was not able to perceive where the line between the song of passion confessed and the doctor's diagnosis should be drawn', but more because he tried to use in his verse 'not the philosophical results of thought . . . but the processes themselves'. Moreover Donne could not equate 'his own amorous superpropensities' with 'his struggling religious instincts'; Rhys quotes lines 61–72 of 'The Ecstasy' to prove it, albeit with due acknowledgement of a remarkable attempt: 'If the lyric could ever succeed in fusing subjective, introspective subject-matter, and yet keep true pitch, one would say that Donne of all men was the poet to accomplish it.' Then Donne was fatally impeded by his wit, which is 'quick of thought and subtle to a degree' and yet 'juggles with ideas and words, and surprises by its caracoles', in a way that must inhinit spontaneous inspiration. Nonetheless, 'At his best his achievement is surpassingly fine – finer than we perceive at once.'

Rhys particularly praises the *Holy Sonnets*, which are 'conceited in passages, and erratic in detail' yet 'vital in thought and style'. He

370

gives the first four lines of *Holy Sonnet* 8, 'Why Are Wee by All Creatures Waited On?', as 'characteristic of Donne's religious fantasy and introversion', and the whole of *Holy Sonnet* 10, 'Death, Be Not Proud', for the 'Sidneian ring of its lines' and the way it 'holds its eloquence like the trumpets heard at a state funeral in his own church of St Paul's. He adds that Donne's prose is quite as dignified and noble as this verse and 'can rise at times to the purest singing rhythms of oratory', as it does in a passage which he quotes from the second Prebend Sermon upon Psalm 63.7.]

101. Horace Ainsworth Eaton
1914

Professor H. A. Eaton wrote his doctoral dissertation for Harvard on the pastoral idea in English poetry in the six-teenth century. He became head of the English Department at the University of Syracuse, New York State, and published several books on Thomas De Quincey. He made a general evaluation of Donne's love-lyrics in an article published in the *Sewanee Revue* ('The Songs and Sonnets of John Donne', *Sewanee Revue*, 22 (1914), 51–72).

Among the most striking poets of this Elizabethan age so fertile in poets and yet, curiously, so blotted by the blinding brilliancy of Shakespeare, is a figure of extraordinary variety – a scholar of civil and canon law, a wit, a poet, a preacher. There is but one man who answers to all the names upon this list – John Donne; and scholars have learned to appreciate the impressiveness of his name. It required powerful attainments to give Donne a reputation for incomparable legal learning, for unmatched pulpit eloquence; to make Ben Jonson, the competent critic, tell Drummond that John Donne was 'the first poet in the world in some things'. Nor was his character less striking and wonderful. Of all the men in those rich days, we know most, perhaps, of Donne; and yet that fullness of knowledge merely means greater ignorance, such contrasts, antitheses, appear in him – sensuality and spirituality, worldliness and godliness, coarseness and refinement; characteristics which dwell together in society, but rarely in the individual. His nature and his attainments, all in their great variety, tax our imaginations to unify, to make alive.

This has been made clear by discussions and recent attempts at biographical composition: that, fascinating as his elusive character is from the psychological standpoint, valuable as it is from the literary and historical in giving a comment upon the time, interesting as are the prose works, devotional and legal, for the antiquarian and the lover of quaint and outworn forms of expression and learning – fascinating and interesting as Donne is from every approach, the real value of the man for us lies in his poetry. Careful reading will convince us, when the ear is alert for strange and beautiful melody, and the mind for pregnant turn, and the heart for sincere and tender feeling. But patience must be with us to sustain through arid wastes of quibble, conceit and ludicrous uncouthness. The strange man has written strange verse; in that, as in his attainments and his character, the antipodes sit together. His verse is the expression of his time, sincere, extravagant, wild and wonderful.

We have much verse of Donne preserved to us, almost miraculously one might think, since only after his death were the floating fragments of his youth gathered together and put forth in print, all claiming attention for some reason, illustrative or poetic. The admirer of Donne will find discrimination invidious, yet one must admit that the *Songs and Sonnets* carry heaviest freight of poetic value. They are as a body the love poems, if not the only poems dealing with love: and on them must hang the importance of Donne for these changed times, whatever varied notability was his three centuries ago. Donne was infinitely more than a lover and a poet in this world when he trod the old streets of London. His contemporaries thought of him primarily as the great scholar and divine; but his life work has been abraded by the slow wash of time until it has diminished, to almost pure lyric proportions. In spite of all the heavy books of sermon and the rest, John Donne remains a figure in English literature because of these fifty odd little poems labelled since 1635 'Songs and Sonnets'. So has our later age shifted the judgment of earlier days, so do the lesser often prove the greater against the touchstone of time.

II

The central quality in a poet invariably appears to the mind with full certainty only after one has read, and the particular facts and lines and melodies have become a bit blurred and dim. Memory, if not the surest discoverer of central principles, is the surest tester. This faculty dwelling upon constant re-reading of the *Songs and Sonnets* brings out with tangible distinctness the quality of sincerity as the very essence of the lyrics – passionate sincerity or earnestness, even in his lightest moods. The quality is no passive thing, but vigorous. It is the quality which to some extent pervades all Elizabethan literature, speaking most broadly – for there were flaccid singers then as always – and gives us so lively a sense of manly enterprise and indefatigable curiosity. The whole age is alive to the finger tips. It is what we should expect then in a man of original power, this energy and fullness of life. But what makes these songs unprecedently nervous is their almost exaggerated energy and vitality. Donne was, indeed, in these poems Elizabethan, but more, one cannot help feeling it, he was hyperbolically Elizabethan.

He had the sincere self-confidence, the fine self-assertion which held him from weak imitation. He was no follower; hardly a leader, for he struck out at too fast a pace; but a party unto himself. He said his say, sang his song, with no imitative thought; but rather, one imagines, abhorring even precedent as hampering the full expression of personality. His thought or his mood at the moment was his interest, and only that. One thinks of him as seized by a desire to write his lyric, expressive not of remembered, but of present mood; and unhappy, or incapacitated from any other thought or occupation, until he has obeyed the inner tyrannous impulse. His lyrics have the reality which, one feels, could come only from necessity, as if written for no one's pleasure, perhaps not even for his own, but because they had to be, before he could turn with easy mind to the next intense moment. We do not need to know the facts of his biography to be sure that life each day to him was as absorbing as only genius can know it. The songs glow with the heat of compressed energy, glitter with feverish eagerness to note the emotion which must have utterance, and almost ring with the triumph of mood caught or thought suggested.

The poems are pure lyric – lyric with the true spirit of lyric poetry, the sincere expression of personal emotion. In an age when dramatic literature and attitude claimed chief attention, it is notable to find in Donne a spirit distinctly undramatic. Outside of the satires where the dramatic element was imitative and experimental, there is hardly a trace in his work of this instinct. One imagines that he felt in such expression a certain indirection which seemed to him half insincerity. Or, perhaps, rather, this attitude even in lyric poetry did not interest him. The dramatic form must always – certainly the dramatic mood – appeal from inception through all stages of execution to an audience. The dramatic is, to be sure, the attitude of the greatest poets, but it was foreign to Donne's whole nature. Mindful of his own soul, he was more completely than any other of the minor poets the laureate of his own emotions.

If the poets of the spontaneous or intimate class be few and rare, they have a charm all their own. The listener may overhear, as it were, their most secret thoughts, and if, as is certainly the case, he is not completely an intruder, he is rather tolerated than invited. They are lovable for their rich nature and their full experience, if not admirable for finished art and sustained levels of poetic expression. It is indeed a fault of Donne, as of his fellow singers, – this imperfection of the art of which he is the exponent. Donne at least gives one, in the light of treatise and large sermon, the impression of being a poet by the way. Not art but matter was the end of his creed of life. He said what he must as he must. For him the moment produced and the moment obliterated. Was the mood fervent enough to flash forth in perfect word or line, the better; did it miss complete expression, the worse. But the moment of inspiration past, to try to recall it was vain. Such is the impression hardly detachable from these varied and uneven lyrics; such is the art of Donne, – a thing of necessity, or if you will, of accident, with all its inherent unevenness of result.

It is only fair, then, mindful of this irregularity of inspiration, to come to Donne prepared to rejoice at the fine moments, and to pass lightly over the lines which fail of poetic completeness. He does not demand toleration; he was not writing for us who read; and yet we may well be aware that were he a greater artist or more even singer we should lose the sudden flash which opens for us new treasures, perhaps reveals depths of nature or of life which we never

374

before suspected. So does irregularity of genius become in these poems a thing of interest in itself, as always holding in reserve a possible reward beyond all reckoning.

The very unevenness of these pieces has too a curious result upon the reader. The perfect poet, say Tennyson or Keats, guiding his genius with firm hand, impresses us in wholes – the mind feels and recalls the whole of a poem, in which every phrase is final in itself, in its harmony, and its relation to others. So that until the poem has become by actual study the reader's own for always, the single word or turn fails to become easily a part of the mental possession. In the case of Donne it is not so. We are constantly taken by surprise, by a happy phrase, a mere adjective, by a line of startling suggestiveness. Such pregnant phrases may not be thinly strewn, and yet, forced apart by obscure or ugly passages, they stand as unconnected units in separately memorable form. To read Donne carefully is to go away with a hundred such phrases and thoughts, whereas in reading much greater poets one has an impression, finer and nobler in its integrity and kind perhaps, but hardly more satisfactory.

Yet even though one harks back to Donne in one's memory as a poet of lines and phrases, he is more than that. Many of his pieces have a unity of form, a vigor of outline, which makes them far from things of shreds and patches. When the divine mood was on, it did not allow him to stop short of artistic unity. One could name twenty poems with real perfection of composition, rugged but balanced and developed with full rhythmic sense of lyric poetry. One hardly finds here, nor should one think to find, the chaste and perfect beauty of a Greek vase, but rather the beauty which comes from the infinite vitality of invention, of vigorous design, of, say, a goblet of Benvenuto Cellini.

But after all qualifications are made, Donne's inspiration rarely lasts long enough to result in wholes. Even where the design of the lyric has beautiful balance the execution within the design is uneven; like a hasty sketch in the open, which is in many a place left unfinished for retouching, except that Donne probably had no intention to stipple later the rough washes of the moment. The reader thus returns to the poem for a few lines, a happy word, or an awakening thought. It is not so much 'Love's Alchemy' which makes the impression upon one as the fine beginning, –

Some that have deeper digg'd love's mine than I; –

it is not so much 'The Good Morrow' as the lovely lines, –

> If ever any beauty I did see
> Which I desired and got, 'twas but a dream of thee.

Nor can one wonder; for thoughts, expressions, and music of the verse cling to one like salt of the sea breeze.

Like every man of profound nature and originality, Donne is full of fresh and illuminating thought. Often a poetic phrase comes like a revelation. The poet looks into himself and thinks with eyes as free from dead visions of the past as Adam in the garden of Eden. To him the world is transparent, opening up to his super-sensual sight essential meanings, even though his vision like his art is irregular and unsustained. The very passionate intensity of the man blinds him now and again where a calmer nature would have 'seen life steadily and seen it whole'. His character conditioned him and his work too. His uneven temper and art were as likely to chase the *ignis fatuus* of some far-fetched conceit or fantastic thought with all his intensity, as to pursue a worthier object. The very originality which gives him power when at his best, makes him doubly, nay trebly, liable to these divagations which leave these fatal marks upon his verse, to dim if not destroy the pure light of his truer and happier moments. The eyes which now and again could pierce the wrappings of life, could see what was not there and think to find beauty and poetic truth in wild unlikeness and grotesque paradox. He was too brilliant, too innately witty. The man of passionate intensity is almost certain, it seems, to be entirely, or almost entirely, devoid of all sense of humor. He lacks the requisite detachment from things of the moment. It is at least certain that nowhere in Donne's poems does one find evidence to contradict this generalization. But of wit Donne was the living embodiment, if wit is the keen play of mind upon ideas, delighting to find likeness in unlikeness and strange, unexpected relationships. Sermon and hymn and love-lyric are full of consequent paradox and conceit, far-fetched simile and metaphor; so full, indeed, that Donne's fame as poet has been blurred by this unhappier quality of his genius; and he has long stood in literature as a mere juggler with the ludicrous, a clown dancing with infinite cleverness upon the tight-rope of conceit. What is more, he has been held the laborious constructor of enigmas, as if the constant presence of the same fine-spun ingenuity even in his letters and sermons were not convincing evidence that he was spontaneously witty, from nature and from long training in subtle distinction of scholastic argument and learning. In this again he was merely going his age one better, and tossed off, we may believe, his involved lyrics with all the ready carelessness their spirit seems to show. They are still, with all their elaborate wit, the personal expression of a spontaneous poet.

The witticisms of the *Songs and Sonnets* certainly are the product of the worse side of Donne's genius. They are the sediment polluting 'the sacred well that from beneath the seat of Jove doth spring'. Yet so completely are the faults and virtues bound up in him, that one can even be thankful for extravagances – as if in Donne all poetic canons were broken, and his strange genius had the power to validate the most obvious vices. The wonder is not that with his nature and training he should use forced and extraordinary metaphors, but that he should be able to endow them with such spiritual meaning that they occasionally take on a beauty of their own. None but an extravagant wit could think of making so poetically ludicrous a comparison as that between parting lovers and the legs of a draughtsman's compass; but clothed upon with the deep feeling and tender love of the 'Valediction Forbidding Mourning' the figure becomes a thing of haunting suggestiveness and piquancy.

[He quotes the last three stanzas of the poem.]

Such is the power of complete honesty in phrasing thought and feeling – the strangest matter transmuted to gold by the white heat of sincerity.

It is the prerogative of the poet to speak a new language and create, as it were, a new aesthetic, not by theory, but by happy practice. And the *Songs and Sonnets* are full of examples, even if they are not themselves examples, of this fact. No verse but bears the hall-mark of John Donne. There is the splendid condensation of meaning in a single word, sign of the true poet, as in the full line, –

> Without sharp north, without declining west, –

a line which, like many more, gives endless joy, so alive with meaning is it, so alert. And then there are the lines with not less illuminating and vital music of rhythm, which sing, and speak, too, and speak in singing. Indeed, it seems almost as if there were in Elizabethan air a something which forced words in lyric measure to sing, so full are the song-books of the music of the spheres. Those were the days when songs were songs; and no one could write without catching, it would appear, some echoes of this all-pervasive music. Donne's verses are distinctly Elizabethan in this as in other respects, and in spite of their traditional ruggedness are full of rich harmonies. So instinct are they with rhythm that long after reading the poems, it is possible to hear ringing in the head measures of which one has lost the words.

Yet the poems are rugged; oftentimes are difficult to read with the lilt and flow that we expect to find in songs of this cast and size. They certainly have not the luscious quality of, say, the charming pieces of *England's Helicon*. In measure as in other things Donne stands alone. So individual is he that critics have wished to settle upon him conscious theories of metrical structure and attempted reforms of Elizabethan prosody. However this may be in the satires, where there is small doubt that Donne, like his contemporary imitative satirists, tried the rough metres of Persius and Juvenal, it is hardly justifiable to assume the same consistent purpose in the songs, where all characteristics seem emphatically to point away from steadily conscious artistic effort. It seems more likely, although it might be difficult to prove, that Donne was actually without keen ear for music, but that driven by his time and his own overpowering poetic instincts he wrote more or less unconsciously the gloriously melodious lines – a supposition not so impossible it would seem when one remembers the occasional melody of Emerson's verse, albeit his ear was notably unmusical. Perhaps, too, it might be added as a possible corollary, that Donne, unimpressionable to the melody which is presumably always present consciously or unconsciously in the mind of a poet writing lyrics musically conceived, attuned his verse not to sung rhythm but to spoken, and that thus conceived, his verse took on break in line and shift in accent, violent when read with an assumed singing melody in mind, but poetically justified when the poems are considered not as songs for music in any sense, but as pieces for rhythmic speech. This is no place to elaborate so involved a possibility, but it must be lightly suggested as offering an explanation which accords with the spontaneity of the poems themselves. But whatever the explanation of the haunting rhythms and melodies of the *Songs and Sonnets*, there are repeatedly splendid bursts of music, soft and low, or swelling into impressive grandeur – to use a word of Donne's own, into 'organic tones' – as in these lines from 'The Anniversary': –

> Only our love hath no decay;
> This no to-morrow hath, nor yesterday.

However the music comes, studied or unstudied, it is here and there, and yonder, – the poems rise and fall with it, and now and again, like Wordsworth's vale, are 'overflowing with the sound'.

It is indeed a point to be insisted upon even out of due proportion, considering the unfair judgment of Donne's verse, – the just beauty of his finest lines. Everyone knows the metallic glint of –

> A bracelet of bright hair about the bone, –

even though it is hardly more wonderful in its perfect service of sound to sense than others less strikingly brilliant. There is the sweet surprise which trembles in –

> I wonder by my troth what thou and I
> Did till we loved?; –

the ecstasy in –

> Some lovely glorious nothing did I see; –

the passionate devotion in –

> Thou art so true, that dreams of thee suffice
> To make dreams truths, and fables histories.

These have a suggestiveness of verse music so absolutely in harmony with the thought and mood beneath, that they take rank among the final lines in our rich lyric literature. But these are samples merely of many so subtly beautiful that they seem sometimes hid by pure perfection. Donne is no poet to read once, but a hundred times, and at each new reading new harmonies strike the ear, new meanings and suggestions appear in what one thinks to be familiar passages. So that one is constantly surprised by the exquisite ways in which Donne's genius has 'knit that subtle knot' between thought and expression which makes verse poetry.

So easy is it to forget in thinking of the splendid passages in the

Songs and Sonnets, that one has often to shake oneself to the realization of the limitations of his work. Unevenness of inspiration, ruggedness of verse, incompleteness of expression, all make his poetry a thing to be read with pencil in hand, – especially since many a passage which seems obscure upon reading and re-reading, flashes suddenly forth as a passage to be marked after all hope has been given up. For Donne is like all intimate poets, and far more than most, difficult. His art is casual; he writes for himself; and his writings become at times a sort of short-hand for his own reading. One feels that Leonardo da Vinci is a type of the whole school – illustrated by his notebooks written for himself from right to left. The same holds for this our most exacting of poets, difficult from carelessness and unacquired art. A crisp morning, untired mind, and perfect leisure in fact and feeling, these are the requisites for enjoying and understanding these lyrics. One must love them with full energy of being, for it is the reader who must do half the work in lifting the thoughts into the light. Donne had neither the time nor the inclination to make clear, he merely noted down with greatest conciseness what was surging within him for utterance. If this attitude of mind and its consequent lack of perfect workmanship keep him forever from the higher company of poets and from the greater public which he never sought, they add a charm to those who love stern exercise with its intellectual and emotional glow. His poems may be oftentimes – too often are, let us grant – strange and forbidden puzzles, taxing strength and patience; but they are, past peradventure, for those who know, puzzles with endlessly rich and rewarding answers.

III

Underneath the form and color of poetry lies the reality of thought and passion which gives substantial value to the verse – the great depths of living waters of which the swinging toss of waves is but the superficial play. And underneath these songs of Donne, dazzling, playful, cruel as the sea waves themselves, lie also depths of emotional life which sustain the lyrical expression as the chance winds of occasion and impulse stir. The *Songs and Sonnets* are one and all the love poems of a man profound beyond sounding, Protean in change.

[He speaks of the brilliance of Donne's early career in London.]

. . . for the gay circle in which he moved, he was not only reputed but proven to have extraordinary wit – capable as his work and his later life show of sallies as original, as spontaneous, as germane to the taste of Elizabethan youth as if Donne had really been, as he was in figurative sense, the embodiment of the spirit of the age. The strange, the startling, the unexpected – such sallies of word and act were native to him, albeit the company he kept in life and books must have sharpened and confirmed what was his by birthright.

But not alone in wit and brilliancy was he unlike other men; not least was he unusual in breadth of sensibility. He was extraordinarily awake to impressions. Through a delicate and nervous body he was capable of the intensest pleasures of sense; through a vigorous and curious mind he was open to the keenest intellectual and spiritual joys; through both he was constantly guided or driven by over-powering impulse. He was high-strung in his desires and his enjoyments, whole-souled in his surrender to the moment, whether it brought gaiety or desperation, cynicism or unquestioning devotion. Inapt in his longing for pleasure to restrain impelling passion or whim, he ran the full circle of life in that London of the alert nineties; and if he leaned long hours over the tomes with which he became so intimate, it was among men and women that he was most alive, a gallant in striking doublet and bright hose, we can imagine, extravagant of health and fortune, a man of the world in the heyday of youth with all its ups and downs, its longings and its disappointments.

In such a youth, richly endowed in body and mind, each capable of much, and each attracted in different ways towards pleasures compelling as the songs of sirens, there was, as might be expected, hot division. From the mere strength of forces, without common aim for self-forgetful consecration, there was bound to be a house divided against itself. As yet the great objects of his life, love and religion, had not taken command. The realities were merely interesting as problems to be played with by his intellectual curiosity, acutely, intensely; but not to be lived and felt. The world was to be tried and enjoyed, not grappled with and won. And yet to the immature student, those early days were not merely 'full of sound and fury signifying nothing', but pregnant with later dignity of character and splendid strength. Indeed this time of flux and change, pictured so vividly in the *Songs and Sonnets*, was a great battle-ground, or rather a scene of war, across which, with wavering fortunes, the body and the soul, not less really than in some mediaeval allegory, waged a prolonged strife. Now one side gained advantage, now the other, and again the struggle hung undecided, so evenly balanced were the powers; and only after the hurly-burly of adolescence and young manhood was past was the victory of his nobler nature finally and entirely won by aid of the devoted love which his future wife, Anne Moore, called up in him. And, to carry a suggestive figure still further, the poems which were the outcome of this struggle were the trophies set up by the contending hosts to mark their victories – the sensual and cynical lyrics the trophies of the body, those full of mystic fervor and sweet tenderness the trophies of the spirit. So was commemorated in fine poetic way this contest of vast moment for the life and character of Donne.

Unfortunately the songs are so disordered that we can never hope to trace the progress of the struggle, to know the right succession of elevation and abasement. As we have the pieces they are thrown together as carelessly as the toys of a child picked up at the end of a long tired day. There is no sequence that we have a right to subscribe to; we can only accept the collection as it stands as perhaps no untrue if vague symbol of the confusion in the mind and heart of Donne. For the poems are mostly due to the shifts and vagaries of mood of a young and ardent nature, untouched by the love that fires and holds unshakably, yet momentarily seized upon by deep if transient passions. In their waywardness they are the eddies of a stream fiercely or idly playing among rocks, before it gathers itself in unity of purpose for a steep plunge in powerfully sweeping rapids.

As youthful poems the *Songs and Sonnets* take on a certain regularity. Even the 'unpleasant' poems themselves, as the work of adolescence and young manhood, become records instead of mere blots, as they have long been considered, upon a fascinating group. They become actually significant when we recognize, though unwillingly, – since they must still shock our finer sensibilities, – the fact that they are the genuine expression of a universal mood. Unfettered license and endless change in love, the demand of the more physical poems, is the voice of the natural man unbound from convention, always heard more or less loud in adolescence, however civilization may bind tighter the elemental instincts and purer spoken ages may deny it utterance. And Donne with his strong animal impulses, living in that free time of renaissant exuberance

382

when every form of human experience and enjoyment was sought with unashamed and unrestrained vigor, gave himself up to his baser nature with the unmoral sense that such was life.

'Woman is made for man, – not him nor me', is the doctrine of his unfettered license, phrased conversely in 'Love's Usury', –

> For every hour that thou wilt spare me now,
>   I will allow,
> Usurious god of love, twenty to thee,
> When with my brown my gray hairs equal be,
> Till then, Love, let my body range, and let
> Me travel, sojourn, snatch, plot, have, forget,
> Resume my last year's relict; think that yet
> We'd never met.

It is the complete eager surrender to the passion of the moment, exaggerated in its contrast with to-morrow's deceptive voluntary self-renunciation. And these poems are the trophies which commemorate the surrender of the soul to the body, the victory of the untamed animal in man.

If in the *Songs and Sonnets* Donne never but once or twice strikes the note of entire sensuality, he is saved, one may think, by the fact that in his basest moods he finds easier expression in the *Elegies* – pieces heavier, longer, more frankly indecent – imitative, one may hope, as if that might palliate, of Ovidian *Amores*. In the songs there is a certain lightness of mood, a flitting gaiety of mind which saves him from brutal surrender to sense. The satisfaction of desire here is not an end, but an amusement by the way, an attitude hardly less ugly, except that it holds within itself the possibility of being outgrown, that it is the attitude of a man of potential loftiness astray. It is indeed a sort of light cynicism imposed by the very conditions of thoughtlessness and gay submission to the drifting desires of the flesh, – a submission certain to carry with it in a man who is above the brute, certain conscious or unconscious corollaries. Donne was merely young and passionate, not really heartless, and needed to postulate, at least to feel, that if he longed to 'travel, sojourn, snatch, plot, have, forget', his mistresses were not less fickle and shifting in their desires. Even he in headlong licentiousness would have found a better taste in such pleasures if he felt that woman's constancy were a reality. We may at least trace this attitude in the gay lyric, cynical at bottom: –

I can love both fair and brown,
Her whom abundance melts and her whom want betrays,
Her who loves loneness best, and her who masks and plays,
Her whom the country formed and whom the town . . .
I can love her, and her, and you, and you,
I can love any, so she be not true.

The assumption of the essential inconstancy of woman finds emphasis in songs as light-hearted and tripping as the well-known, 'Go and catch a falling star', and in pieces part tender, part quizzical, such as 'Woman's Constancy':–

Now thou has loved me one whole day.
To-morrow when thou leavest, what wilt thou say?
Wilt thou then ante-date some new-made vow? . . .
    Or your own end to justify,
For having purposed change and falsehood, you
Can have no way but falsehood to be true?

Such is the gay and easy recklessness which plays upon the surface of the undiscovered depths – undiscovered not least to himself – of his great nature. It is a tone that pervades a dozen of the pieces, fascinating in brilliant expression, in unexpected play of wit and imaginative fancy, running through many shades and half-shades of emotional doubt and cynicism. In all these is the proud swinging step of the young gallant, conscious of unknown powers, half-insolent in self-centred independence, given up in gay hours – whatever may have been his labor in his study – to the free enjoyment of the untrammeled life of an untrammeled time. Not flippancy nor shallowness was in these moods, but rather in the very lightness a paradoxical proof of depth. A shallow nature would have responded more readily to influences, as the shallow pool among rocks is warmed by the noon-day sun, when the deeper lies cool and unresponsive.

But it is impossible to suppose that all the poems reflecting this gaiety, stand together and apart, a group of unified experience and feeling. In the midst of them sprang intense if fleeting passions, which cried out with joy or pain in convincing phrase and rhythm. The deeper nature finds at least momentary victory to reassure that the power of feeling lies beneath, if in large measure dormant and ineffective.

Momentary the passions might be, but not for that less deep or true, nor less adequate in expression. For Donne through the power of these emotions, complete in that they struck into the very centre of human nature, though not lasting, was made clairvoyant and wise, singing as the poet does from intensive rather than extensive feeling. Here in these better moments was no doubting of the reality of love, of the constancy of woman; nor was there possible in one of Donne's essential loftiness of nature, sensuality. We catch in the finer verses the harmonies that live and make live.

> If yet I have not all thy love,
> Dear, I shall never have it all;
> I cannot breathe one other sigh, to move,
> Nor can intreat one other tear to fall;
> And all my treasure which should purchase thee,
> Sighs, tears, and oaths, and letters I have spent;
> Yet no more can be due to me,
> Than at the bargain made was meant.
> If then thy gift of love were partial,
> That some to me, some should to others fall,
> Dear, I shall never have thee all.

Here is unrivalled tenderness of sincere devotion, and whether the love that conceived was permanent or not, it produced imperishable beauty for all noble lovers. Here is a trophy, indeed, of a victory of soul.

This group of poems of the clearer moods is notable not less than those of the darker, for subtle variations in attitude and perception. Not only does Donne record faithfully the shifts of love, but also points of nicer observation, arguing delicacy of feeling and, what is perhaps rarer in a passion so absorbing, keenness of analysis. The words are weighted with original interpretation and insight, not only expressing but illuminating the universal passion. Thus he notes with charming precision in his 'Lecture upon the Shadow' –

> That love has not attained the highest degree,
> Which is still diligent lest other see; –

while on the other hand he discriminates –

> If our loves faint and westwardly decline
> To me thou, falsely thine,
> And I to thee mine actions shall disguise.

Again, he catches the lover's truth that love which was infinite before yet increases; and that love, however constant and devoted, varies with time and seasons. Only close reading and an understanding heart can appreciate this rare subtlety of touch – a touch which is, one must feel, instinctive rather than consciously analytic; for conscious analysis must chill deft fingers in such exquisite tasks. Nor is it possible to conceive of the young Donne sitting coldly introspective; one must think of him as seizing instinctively his facts with the clear sight of genius, proof again of the spontaneity of the poet who declares of himself, 'Whatever love would dictate, I writ that.' If he wrote variously and subtly, he felt even more variously and subtly, was more awake than others to life in all its fullness.

Perhaps, however, the most striking quality in this group of poems – most striking in its penetration and its loftiness of vision – is pervasive mysticism. Love is a strange paradox; it is the union of souls, a combination whence 'an abler soul . . . does flow'. And the mind of Donne plays endlessly about this conception, turning it and finding in it always new lights, new thoughts. It seems as if Donne were first perceiving here in this conception of love his religious emotions, and were, so to speak, making preliminary trial of his devotional wings. This emphasis of mystery, in fact, gives a certain religious solemnity to the moods, and makes the love of these pieces in their fine reach the eloquent speech of all lovers worthy of the name.

> Call's what you will, we are made such by love;
>   Call her one, me another fly,
>   We're tapers too, and at our own cost die,
> And we in us find th' eagle and the dove.
>   The phoenix riddle hath more wit
>   By us; we two being one, are it;
> So to one neutral thing both sexes fit.
>   We die and rise the same, and prove
>   Mysterious by this love.

This mystic paradox appears and reappears in phrase and figure, scattered up and down the collection, in lines which one keeps by one to ponder, they strike so deep and far; as if too in such phrases one had the spirit of the nobler poems in portable form.

> And we were mutual elements to us,
>   And made of one another.

So, again, –

> Our two souls, therefore, which are one,
>   Though I must go, endure not yet
> A breach, but an expansion,
>   Like gold to airy thinness beat.

Then in fine shifts we have the variation of love negating space – love which 'makes one little space an everywhere'; and transcending time, –

> Only our love hath no decay,
> This no to-morrow hath, nor yesterday.

So through and under all this group runs the mystic attitude of spiritual devotion and union.

Love thus potent transubstantiates in its religious fervor flesh to very spirit. The highest qualities, the passion itself, become symbolized in flesh, as if the world of the lover were but the concrete poetic phrasing, so to say, of glorious ideas and ideals. The beloved is but the beautiful made perfect in special manifestation.

> Twice or thrice had I loved thee,
> Before I knew thy face or name, –

he sings in that rarely diaphanous and delicate poem 'Air and Angels', – a thought elaborated in succeeding lines of difficult subtlety. In even finer phrasing he writes in 'The Good Morrow', lines already quoted, –

> If ever any beauty I did see,
> Which I desired and got, 'twas but a dream of thee.

Even from the lower standpoint of body, of the physical in love, we find the same spiritualizing imagination. In that strange poem, 'The Ecstasy', glowing incandescent with the heat of mystic love passion, we find its typical expression. After long ecstasy of the two souls in union, the poet and lover cries –

> We owe them [our bodies] thanks, because they thus
>   Did us, to us, at first convey,
> Yielded their senses' force to us,
>   Nor are dross to us, but allay. . . .
>
> So must pure lovers' souls descend
>   To affections and to faculties,
> Which sense may reach and apprehend,
>   Else a great prince in prison lies.

387

This attitude, not the transcendental dream of the poets who forget the body or despise, is one of splendid balance, in which we have the sensuous always present but beautified. It is the love of a complete man, not of an angel. And there in this brave facing of the realities of human love, and finding beauty in the realities, we have to be thankful, not indeed for the ugly sensual poems which hurt his literary name, but for the nature in him which, though too often escaping the guidance of his better self, was present to make his love poems manly and lofty too. The very feeling that here is one who through bitter experience knows the lowest and the highest, and that, so knowing, he cleaves unqualifiedly to the highest in the end – this feeling gives to the poems authority and to the poet a right to lead and to assure. The noble victory of the spirit is the result of hard conflict, and so the more worth winning.

And yet, we must remind ourselves, we cannot assume the easy grouping of the low together and of the high together. From the peaks we fall to ravine and valley; in the long run, however, approaching the summit towards which his nature was impelling him, even in the descents. The passions of the man, flashing now and then white light from pure intensity, burned red and dim. The purer moments revealed him to himself, and so to us; but whether it was his fault in being strangely fickle, or his misfortune to be tricked by unfaithful mistresses, bitter cynicism presses between and follows some at least of the truer pieces. One can measure by the very intensity of bitterness of these poems the height from which he had fallen. So can one certainly trace in the vigorous and terrible poem, 'The Apparition', not only power, the result of sad awakening, but a maturity of mind, the outgrowth of trial and failure. It is a poem unpleasant in its nature, in its very might; but is no longer the expression of immature youth, superabounding in gay wit and light love; it betrays the man suffering and aware. The emotions are deepening and lifting.

Among these pieces of Donne's early years there are a few of later date, emanating from the period when the love that knew no change or lessening had gained the final victory. Of these we are reasonably certain of two – two of the finest in the collection – 'The Valediction Forbidding Mourning', and the song, 'Sweetest love, I do not go' – both probably from 1611, Donne's thirty-eighth year. In these, restless passion has visibly given way to repose, to a mature, a rich, a lasting devotion, not less fervent than his wildest outbursts of earlier days, if, perhaps, less spontaneously expressive. The mood is not so tyrannous in impelling song, but the poems are 'full of ripeness to the core'. They possess the very essence of his qualities toned, as it were, by age, as one feels the calm maturity of Shakespeare in his later plays. Tenderness, devotion, the best in the man are there, singing the song of married love with the same authority and sureness with which he had sung the younger lover's love.

[He quotes the whole of the Song, 'Sweetest Love, I Do Not Go'.]

These two poems are the culmination of all the *Songs*, not trophies of conflict, but rather memorials of the war past and over, as if to declare the victory won for always. They are, we may consider them, the final word of Donne upon the great reality of love, the conclusions of a man wise through bitter and dear-bought experience, the final word of singular sweetness of one who had found in the love of man for woman, next to his religion, the most sustaining thing in the whole world.

The *Songs and Sonnets* are, then, the records of the struggles and visions of youth, imperfect because of the very unconsciousness of the age in which brooding introspection was unknown. Pervaded by the spirit of spontaneity, these lyrics possess amidst consequent irregularity of verse, a sincere and intimate quality. They lie, indeed, too close to intense emotions for perfect expression, but in that gain splendor of momentary effects. As a spontaneous poet Donne is in part explicable; as a young poet he becomes still more so. Controlled by fierce adolescent passions of body and soul, he wrote songs variously compounded – sensual, they are saved by a touch of higher feeling; mystic, they are kept human by the man in him. The final result is noble elevation of a spiritual devotion phrased in glorious flashes of deepest enduring significance. The lyrics are, indeed, irregular, but not chaotic. They have order, in that they all tend towards the heights, – are, as it were, a sort of rugged alpine country, difficult and broken, but affording from ascending crag and peak glimpses that reward for all toil of climbing, and impress the lover with the beauty of the world he lives in.

102. Sir Sidney Colvin

1914

Colvin (1845–1927), lately Keeper of Prints and Drawings at
the British Museum, characterized Donne's poetry in his
presidential address to the English Association (*On Concentration and Suggestion in Poetry*, 1915, pp. 16–19).

[Colvin makes Donne the arch-representative of the minority of
poets who aim at intellectual concentration rather than expansiveness.]

So much by way of instance and of indication, for what such
summary finger-pointing may be worth, concerning those poets,
and they are the majority, who use the method of intense and
suggestive concentration not continuously but by strokes and
flashes, as the occasion or their inspiration bids them. Now for the
minority who by principle or instinct pack and condense and
concentrate and compress habitually and all the time. They are for
the most part the same in whose poetry the element of intellect
plays the largest and most restless part along with the elements of
imagination and emotion. We have reminded ourselves how at a
certain stage of Shakespeare's work the purely intellectual element
thrust itself into a predominant place among his other tremendous
gifts and faculties, and how it put into the mouths of his characters
poetry of a more strenuous concentration, a denser imaginative
and intellectual tissue, so to speak, than before. Among some poets
of Shakespeare's generation and the next there existed both a
passion and a fashion, much stimulated by the study of certain
Spanish and Italian models, for intellectual athletics, sometimes of
a highly fantastical kind. The most consistent and indefatigable of
mental athletes in our Jacobean poetry was – it is needless to say to
such an audience as this – John Donne, the Dean of St Paul's. From
the range and depth both of his attainments and experiences, and
the mingled elements of sensuality, cynicism, and intense brooding
piety in his nature, the work of Donne derives a quality unique in
our literature. In his hands poetry turned away from many of the
pleasant conventions, pastoral, Petrarchan, and allegoric, beloved
by Spenser and his followers, to concern itself with the hot and

urgent realities both of earthly passion and spiritual travail and aspiration. At the same time he went beyond all his contemporaries in his love of acrobatic thought-play and of forcing together into strained imaginative relation ideas that naturally had none. No imagery was too rich or complicated for him, none too far-fetched and odd or too familiarly gross and common: no snag of thought was too stubbed or knotty, no clot of learning too stiff or insoluble: he grasped at all alike and flung them into the strong and chafing current of his verse, which runs turbid with all manner of substances and among them a high proportion of gold. Let us consider a passage in his characteristic though not at all in his extreme manner. He had written verses defying and belittling the power of death. Now, death having carried off a virtuous and excellent lady of his acquaintance, he recants and declares

> Spiritual treason, atheism 'tis to say
> That any can thy summons disobey.
> Th' earth's face is but thy table; there are set
> Plants, cattle, men, dishes for death to eat.
> In a rude hunger now he millions draws
> Into his bloody, or plaguy, or starved jaws.

(Note how that single rough line crams into itself all the victims of war, pestilence, or famine since the world began.)

> Now wantonly he spoils, and eats us not,
> But breaks off friends, and lets us piecemeal rot.
> Nor will this earth serve him; he sinks the deep
> Where harmless fish monastic silence keep;
> Who – were Death dead – by roes of living sand
> Might sponge that element, and make it land.

Those last four lines illustrate well the far-fetched learned queerness of the ideas which often moved Donne to poetry. The silence or voicelessness of fish had struck the ancient Greeks as something almost uncanny. Hesiod and the tragedians have a special word for it; the Pythagoreans attached a kind of sacredness to it. Donne has all this in his mind as well as the rule and custom of monks in the refectory, when he talks about fish keeping monastic silence: and then the grotesque fancy strikes him that if fish didn't die, their roes would gradually accumulate at the bottom and fill up the sea like sandbanks. Then he goes on with more beauty and less eccentricity:

He rounds the air, and breaks the hymnic notes
In birds', heaven's choristers, organic throats;

[He quotes lines 17–30 of the 'Elegy on Mistress Boulstred', 'Death
I recant'.]

The poetry of Donne, slighted as intractably harsh and crabbed
even by so illustrious a critic as Coleridge, is coming to its own again
– has indeed among lovers of poetry in the young generation come
into perhaps a little more than its own. Through the so-called
'metaphysical' group of seventeenth-century poets which followed
him – poets most of them men of 'wit' as well as of ardent Christian
devotion, and prone as such to weave into the fine tissue of their
religious rapture strands of glittering intellectual ingenuity, conceits no matter how far-fetched and discordant – through that
school Donne handed down a kind of poetic tradition to the
nineteenth century. The tradition is in various modes to be traced
in the *Unknown Eros* of Coventry Patmore; in the work of Mrs
Meynell, subtle beyond most of our time in the interfusion of
fastidiously distilled thought and feeling; above all in that of the
late Francis Thompson, with its continual confluent rush of religious passion and vehement figurative thinking. Other younger
writers not directly of the same lineage, as Mr Lascelles Abercrombie and the late, untimely lost Rupert Brooke, have under-
gone the same influence.

103. Sir Edmund Kercherver Chambers

1914

Sir Edmund Kercherver Chambers (1866–1954) was a historian of the English stage, first President of the Malone Society
(1906–39) and a civil servant, becoming Second Secretary in
the Department of Education 1921–6. He edited numerous

English classics, including *Early English Lyrics* (1907) and *The Oxford Book of Sixteenth-Century Verse* (1932), and wrote *The Medieval Stage* (2 vols, 1903), *The Elizabethan Stage* (4 vols, 1923) and *Shakespeare* (2 vols, 1930), as well as biographies of Samuel Taylor Coleridge and Matthew Arnold. He reviewed Grierson's edition of Donne's poems, applauding the recent recovery of Donne's reputation (*Modern Language Review,* 9 (1914), 269).

The reputation of Dr John Donne has sensibly advanced during the last decade. Possibly it now stands higher than ever it did since a new manner of writing first displaced his as a model for the versifiers of the Restoration. And this revaluation, for which men of letters, caught by the essential poetry in Donne, and literary historians, discerning his unique influence upon the fashioning of Caroline verse, are almost equally responsible, now receives its appropriate seal in Professor Grierson's elaborate and critical volumes.

104. Robert Seymour Bridges

1914

Robert Bridges (1844–1930), poet laureate and prosodist, notoriously 'couldn't abide' Donne's poetry. H. J. C. Grierson sent him a copy of the 1912 edition of Donne's poems, which he promised to study very carefully and apparently went on to annotate. But his immediate response to Grierson was to account for his dislike of Donne's verse (*The Selected Letters of Robert Bridges,* ed. D. E. Stanford, vol. II, 1984, pp. 650–1).

My attitude towards Donne has been unsympathetic because of (1) the ugliness which you admit, and (2) the school of versification – which I suppose came out of 15th Century Chaos by way of Ben Jonson, and was perfected by Dryden, while Milton was more ably working out a better tradition through Shakespeare from Chaucer (to Shelley). Now that I have your good edition I will observe him more carefully. Also (3) his psychology (especially of sensual love) seems to me bad as well as ugly and (4) I am antipathetic to his 'learning' which seems to me pestilential. I shelve him with Burton's Anatomy of Melancholy, and Sir Thomas Browne's lucubrations.

105. Geoffrey Langdon Keynes

1914

Geoffrey Keynes compiled the first bibliography of the writings of Donne, a work which continued to appear in revised and enlarged editions down to 1972 (*A Bibliography of Dr John Donne, Dean of St Paul's*, 1914).

[In the General Preface to the final edition, in 1972, Keynes himself wrote of the first edition that three hundred copies of it were printed]

as the second (and last) publication of the Baskerville Club. It was distributed to the thirty-seven members of the Club after the outbreak of the first World War and I received my copy while serving with the Royal Army Medical Corps in France.

106. David Macleane

1915

A reviewer of Geoffrey Keynes's *Bibliography of Donne* questioned whether Donne justifies Keynes's labour ('Donne', *Saturday Review,* 21 August 1915, pp. 178–9).

Is Donne sufficiently an immortal to have made [the bibliography] worth while? . . . Donne is not everybody's reading. Dryden pronounced him 'our greatest witt, though not our greatest poet', and Jacobean 'wit' – though the word must not be taken in its present narrow sense – had often too much preciosity for modern enjoyment, especially when fantastic conceit is conveyed in a gnarled and unmelodious medium. If one compares Donne with an epigrammatic poet of the nineteenth century, Coventry Patmore, the advantage is wholly with the latter in respect of a tender sweetness and charm of style, as well as elevation and gracefulness of thought, and though the older writer has more flame it is often a murky one, and not seldom a make-believe. . . .

Rough lines like the following are a frequent jar: –

> Thy beauty and all parts which are thee
> Are unchangeable firmament;

or,

> The taper's beamy eye
> Amorously twinkling beckons the giddy fly;

or,

> These rhymes too bad
> To be counted children of poetry,
> Except confirmed and bishoped by thee.

Donne rhymes 'danger', 'carpenter', and 'ambassador'. On the other hand, the modern reader has to allow for many archaisms of pronunciation. . . .

Donne is fond also of archaic words. . . .

Picturesque phrases abound in his verse. . . . And there are many alluring lines. . . . And especially in the 'Divine Poems' are found pregnant and happy expressions.

107. Ezra Pound

1916

Pound wrote to Iris Barry in May 1916, recounting his publisher's attempt at a last-minute censorship of his forthcoming *Lustra* (*The Letters of Ezra Pound*, ed. D. D. Paige, 1951, p. 130).

[Pound remarks that 'the Lawrence fuss' has put publishers in a panic, so that Elkin Mathews had *Lustra* set up and then marked twenty-five poems for deletion. He adds a postscript.]

P.S. Elkin Mathews ... called in Yeats to mediate and Yeats quoted Donne at him for his soul's good. I don't know what will come of it.

108. Philipp Aronstein

1916

Professor P. Aronstein (1862–1942) of the University of Berlin published studies of Ben Jonson, English Renaissance drama, Charles Dickens, Thomas Carlyle, Benjamin Disraeli and Oscar Wilde, as well as an English-language textbook for foreigners, and a history of the Jews in England and America in the seventeenth and eighteenth centuries. The first of his several essays on Donne, written in German, appeared in 1916 ('John Donne und Francis Bacon', *Englische Studien*, 49 (1916), 360–76).

[Aronstein gives an account of Donne's association with Francis Bacon in the circle of the earl of Essex, discusses the effect on both men of Essex's rising and downfall, and relates Donne's

Metempsychosis to that event and the sceptical attitudes it engendered. He sketches Bacon's train of thought in the *Novum Organum* and *Advancement of Learning*, and compares Donne's response to the New Philosophy in the two anniversary poems for Elizabeth Drury.]

109. Sir William Watson

1917

The conservative poet William Watson, heavily influenced by Alfred, Lord Tennyson in his own work, used Donne as a warning to modern writers who neglect traditional craftsmanship (*Pencraft: A Plea for the Older Ways*, 1917, pp. 64–5).

Consider the case of Donne. His best poems abound in meat and marrow. He had a temper as remarkable for emotional intensity as for intellectual subtlety. Until disease – perhaps the Nemesis of his torrid youth – had wasted his body he seems to have been in a very high degree what Tennyson said that John Richard Green was – 'a vivid man'. His thick, choked utterance cannot disguise the force and ardency of his nature. At their smokiest and sootiest his suffocated fires crackle and explode into sudden surprising flame. But scarcely anything had the luck to come shapen right out of that forge. His uncouthness really passes toleration, and, with a strange irony, has condemned this man, so 'vivid' in his life, to the driest and dustiest kind of embalmment – he is read by the literary student only! Professor Grierson, who not long ago rendered Donne the invaluable service of editing his poems with an enthusiasm only equalled by his erudition and acumen, has explored every nook of his poet's rugged and volcanic landscape, and has applied to some of its tangled thickets an ingenious system of metrical guide-posts, so that the wayfaring man, though a fool, shall not err there. They enable us to wrestle more successfully with a versification which in its supreme crabbedness must be the envy of one or two living practitioners; but even with those amenities of travel the region will never attract any but the hardier kind of tourist.

Such is the doom that overtakes whatever is flagrantly ill made.

110. Mary Paton Ramsay

1917

M. P. Ramsay, a patriotic Scot who wrote ón Calvin and art, spent five years carrying out research in Paris, where she completed a doctorate for the University of Paris. She followed the interests of her mentors Grierson and Picavet in Donne's debt to the mediaeval metaphysicians. Her published dissertation argues that, for all Donne's originality as a poet, his conception of the universe and manner of formulating it are 'essentially mediaeval' (*Les Doctrines médiévales chez Donne, le poète métaphysicien de l'Angleterre* (1917), 1924).

[Ramsay seeks to show that a complete metaphysical system and a profound mysticism underlie all Donne's work, even 'his light and satiric verse'.]

He expounds a mystical and Christian system which is strongly plotinean, and his plotinism comes to him from such Fathers of the Church as St Augustine and St Cyril of Alexandria, by way of St Thomas Aquinas and his predecessors – by the whole of the Middle Ages in sum.

[She systematically extracts Donne's 'doctrines' from his prose works, showing the provenance of his ideas in the several areas of scholastic metaphysics, the universe and being, God, the angels, man, ecstatic union with God, the sciences.

She claims that the study of Donne's doctrines brings us back to the poems 'with quite new interest', not least because Donne's

398

poems themselves 'everywhere reveal the depth of his knowledge in the domain of metaphysics and of the sciences'. Donne does not attain in his poetry the clear synoptic vision of a poet of the first order. His unevenness and inequalities preclude an overall coherence. Nonetheless Courthope (see No. 63) offers a 'fundamentally inexact' account of Donne's poetry when he takes it for evidence of intellectual conflict and the sceptical fragmentation of experience. Donne's prose works demonstrate his philosophical integrity.]

111. George Jackson

1917

The Reverend George Jackson (1864–1945) entered the Wesleyan Methodist ministry and became Professor of English Language, Literature and the Bible at Didsbury College, Manchester, as well as Governor of the John Rylands Library. He was a prolific and popular writer on religious subjects, who devoted to Donne the fifth of a series of fireside homilies about sacred writers ('The Bookshelf by the Fire. V: John Donne', *Expository Times*, 28 (1917), 216–20).

[Jackson does not find it easy to justify Donne's inclusion in the series, and offers several reasons for it: Donne was the friend and mentor of George Herbert and Isaac Walton; he had unequalled celebrity in his own day, as preacher no less than as poet; his writing remains highly prized, albeit by the few students who know and grasp more of it than a scatter of anthology pieces. Nonetheless, the true answer to the question is to be found]

not so much in anything that Donne wrote as in the man himself, in the strange fascination of his complex and mysterious personality. . . . There is about him a splendid obscurity as baffling as it is attractive.

[Jackson draws uncritically upon Gosse for his account of Donne's life and personality, which takes up most of his essay. But he quotes with approval the opening stanza of the 'Hymn to God my God, in My Sickness', and the opening of 'A Hymn to God the Father'. Then he qualifies his commendations at once in a lengthy passage which effectively writes off the rest of Donne's poetry as fatally flawed.]

I am not thinking so much of the obscurities, the roughnesses, the grotesque conceits, the studied eccentricities that mar so much of Donne's poetry. . . . In matter of this sort every age has its own standards, and it is useless to complain because those of the seventeenth century are not ours. But Donne's offence lies deeper. To speak plainly, there are extant poems of his which are fit only for the dunghill.

[He draws confirmation from Saintsbury of the sheer nastiness and licentiousness of some of Donne's poetry, and supposes that such 'literary indecencies' might have passed without comment in the days of James I.]

But when all is said the unhappy fact remains that across some of his poems Donne's shame is written in letters of fire.

112. François Joseph Picavet

1917

A group of historians of doctrine in the University of Paris sought to show the continuing debt of European thinkers to the scholastic theologians. The director of these studies was Professor Picavet. He had done his doctorate on the history of philosophic and scientific ideas in France since 1789; this was published, and subsequently reprinted in an extended form to include religious ideas. He wrote several studies of scholasticism and its origins in France and Germany, and a *History of Medieval Philosophy*, as well as translating Immanuel Kant's *Critique of Pure Reason*. His survey of the influence of scholasticism on English thinkers gave prominence to Donne ('The Medieval Doctrines in the Works of Donne and Locke', *Mind*, n.s. 104 (1917), 385–92).

[Picavet's account of work on Donne's mediaeval antecedents simply summarizes and commends the investigations of his research student Mary Paton Ramsay.[1] He singles out Miss Ramsay's identification of specific metaphysical doctrines in Donne, and supports her conclusion that Donne 'cannot pretend to originality as metaphysician and as theologian'. He adds a judgement of his own:]

It is as moralist, as mystic, and as poet, that his individuality reveals itself. He may thus be considered as an interpreter of his epoch. As a poet of real genius he is greater than his time; as priest he spoke a language and expressed a thought which must be understood by his contemporaries. And that thought is above all mediaeval and Plotinian.

NOTE

1 See No. 110.

113. Sir Arthur Quiller-Couch

1918/20

Professor Sir Arthur Quiller-Couch (1863–1944) lectured on Donne at Cambridge in a course of lectures on seventeenth-century poets. The published version of the lectures starts from the testimony of Donne's contemporaries that he was 'a very great man indeed' (*Studies in Literature*, 1920, pp. 96–117).

And truly he was a great man; yes, and is one of the greatest figures in English literature, albeit perhaps the worst understood: one of the tribe of strong generative giants . . . whose stature we recognise albeit we cannot measure it by their writings, which sometimes disappoint and not seldom fatigue us; giants of whom we still feel . . . that their worth is somehow known although their height be not taken. Donne . . . wrote some of the most magnificent and astounding pages in our literature, if we know where to look for them. We may not call them, though unparalleled, absolutely beautiful: there is nothing absolute in Donne but his greatness and his manhood.

[Quiller-Couch elaborates Coleridge's image of Donne as a smith who works language itself in his forge.]

This Demiourgos casts all kinds of costly stuff into the furnace in order to produce a paving stone, a primrose, or 'a whole length of celestial wall', yet remains too intent on his vision upon the anvil to offer any help to his onlookers.

[He offers some readings from the *Songs and Sonnets* to show how great beauties mingle with cruelly cynical attitudes in Donne. In such poems as 'Woman's Constancy' and 'Love's Diet' we may 'watch the fierce contempt withering down into worse cynicism . . . and there is worse – far worse – than that'. Donne could also lapse into flatness, as in his account of the storm which drove back the Islands expedition in 1596:]

described by him in a dull poem, praised by a modern critic as 'most vivid' in pictures of nature and the sea; actually as full of both, or of either, as this room.

[Quiller-Couch follows Donne's career as far as the advancement to St Paul's, and refers to Donne's contemporary fame as a preacher:]

There is where you shall seek for the great Donne, the real Donne: not in his verse, into which posterity is constantly betrayed, but in his *Sermons*, which contain (as I hold) the most magnificent prose ever uttered from an English pulpit, if not the most magnificent prose ever spoken in our tongue.

[Then he reads two short passages from Donne's sermons and weighs Donne's prose against his poetry:]

He had no architectonic gift in poetry: in poetry the skill that articulated, knit, compacted his *Sermons* and marched his arguments as warriors in battalion, completely forsook him. Through lack of it *The Progresse of the Soule* which might have been a triumph, is a wobbling fiasco. Of the art that constructs a *Divina Commedia*, an *Othello*, a *Samson Agonistes*, or even a *Beggar's Opera*, he had no inkling whatever. It was not that he strove for it and missed; it was that he either knew not or cared not a farthing about it.

He had (they say) a most peccable ear in verse. Critics so great as Dryden, Pope, Johnson, Coleridge, all agree on this point: so I suppose they must be right. They agree also in calling him difficult, crabbed, etc. Being so great men, therefore, let them be right.

I can only say that after trial, especially in reading him aloud to myself, I find him by nine-tenths less inharmonious, halting, crabbed, or difficult than these great critics take for granted that he is.

[He gives some examples of lines which may be wrecked by clumsy reading but are exquisite when properly accented, and reads the whole of 'The Blossom' without comment, just to 'test this alleged harshness'. Yet he allows that]

Donne's ear for the beat of verse is so wayward, its process often so recondite, that the most of his poetry is a struggle rather than a success.

[And he insists that Donne 'could not plan a poem'. In fact Donne's poetic shortcomings go deeper than this.]

For the present be it enough to say that he was an imperfect poet, and mainly for two reasons: (1) he had no constant vision of beauty, (2) he had too busy an intellect, which ever tempted him (as Touchstone would say) to be breaking his shins on his own wit: or as an American friend used to put it, he suffered from 'a rush of brains to the head'. In lines and short passages he could be exquisite. Witness this:

[He quotes the first two lines of 'Love's Deity', and lines 244–6 of *The Second Anniversary*.]

But more than half his time we see the man sweating and straining at the forge and bellows. Obviously half the time he himself cannot see what he is working at, hammering at 'that is as it may turn out', and then, suddenly, out of the smoke, shine verses like this, from *The Extasie*:

[He quotes lines 13–20 of 'The Ecstasy'.]

Quiller-Couch returns to the large questions posed by his own estimate of Donne's artistry.]

Why then does everyone insist on judging as a poet, and a faulty one, this man who had a superlatively fine ear for the rhythm of prose and could construct in prose? And why am I following the multitude?

[His first answer is that nobody reads sermons any more. But the main reason must be that Donne's poetry is important for what it made possible.]

... his verse *did* smash up an effete tradition of verse. It smashed up Petrarch-in-English, and it was high time.

[This destruction was not wanton. It was effected in the interest of a discovery which is not so much metaphysical as mystical. Yet Donne himself was no more than an imperfect mystic. Though he was 'always eloquent against the grave', as in 'Death be not proud', he fell prey to a preoccupation with death and physical horrors which sometimes ran to such 'horrible silly' devices as the full-length portrait in his shroud. Nonetheless his stature is the greater for his frailty.]

... a great man, indubitably a very great man: all the taller for standing in the mire of corruption and reaching up to grasp celestial doors.

114. Philipp Aronstein
1919

Aronstein essayed an independent appraisal of Donne's poetic character in an account of the *Songs and Sonnets*. ('John Donnes Liebeslyrik', *Germanisch-romanische Monatsschrift*, N. F. 7 (1919), 354–69).

[By way of preparing his ground, Aronstein reviews critical attitudes to Donne, from Jonson to Browning, briefly sketches Donne's career, and cites Donne's reputation in the seventeenth century as the frequent publication of his poems attests it. Then he sets out the contrasting categories of Donne's poetry overall.

He defends Donne's love-poetry against such detractors as Dryden and Johnson, who did not recognize its roots in actual experience. Yet he also rejects Gosse's assumption that the poems chronicle specific encounters with women. He believes that Donne was chiefly interested in his own feelings, and dispensed with the trappings of courtly convention just because he was more concerned to explore the nuances of his love than to celebrate a mistress. Against conventional expectation, Donne testified that impassioned love is naturally sensual, and brought out the complexity of love, showing how opposite impulses intermingle in the passion itself. The love-poems have great emotional power because their subject is feeling.

Donne exploited the formal properties of English verse to a wholly different end from Spenser's. He rejected mythological allusions and the pastoral mode in favour of an unidealized nature and the language of daily life. His attempt to accommodate the rhythms and diction of natural speech gives his writing a modern inflection, as does his free recourse to the idiom of current sciences. Aronstein quotes Coleridge's marginal observations on the relation of rhythm to meaning in Donne's verse,[1] illustrating Donne's rhythms and diction from the *Songs and Sonnets* and the *Holy Sonnets*.

Aronstein upholds the metaphysical mode of writing against Johnson on the ground that it reflects real life in the manner of Shakespeare, bringing reason to modulate feeling. Donne propounds no metaphysical system, yet his style is aptly called metaphysical because it catches the self-probing of a mind trained in scholastic and Neoplatonic thought.

The conclusion irresistibly follows that Donne is a poet for the few, whose style was bound to have a deleterious effect upon his formal imitators. His defiant assertion of his own subjectivity anticipates Romantic writers such as Coleridge and De Quincey, and gives his work a cast of modernity. Donne reminds this German commentator of Goethe and Byron, in that all his work amounts to 'a great confession'. Like those great poets he is an *Ich-Künstler* out and out.]

NOTE

1 See *John Donne: The Critical Heritage*, vol. I, ed. A. J. Smith (London: Routledge and Kegan Paul, 1975), pp. 265–6.

115. Aldous Huxley

1919

Reviewing Gregory Smith's *Ben Jonson* in the *London Mercury*, the novelist Aldous Huxley (1894–1963) wrote of Donne as Jonson's fellow in protest against the exaggerations of their age, not least the fantastic unrealities of late Elizabethan love-poetry ('Ben Jonson', *London Mercury*, 6 (1919), 184–91; reprinted in Huxley's *On the Margin*, 1923).

[Huxley judges that Donne called love-poetry back from unreality 'a little grossly perhaps, to facts with the dry remark': he quotes lines 11–12 of 'Love's Growth'.]

There have been poets who have written more lyrically than Donne, more fervently about certain amorous emotions, but no one who has formulated so rational a philosophy of love as a whole, who has seen all the facts so clearly and judged of them so soundly. Donne laid down no literary theory. His followers took from him all that was relatively unimportant – the harshness, itself a protest against Spenserian facility, the conceits, the sensuality tempered by mysticism – but the important and original quality of Donne's work, the psychological realism, they could not, through sheer incapacity, transfer into their own poetry. Donne's immediate influence was on the whole bad. Any influence for good he may have had has been on poets of a much later date.

[Huxley continues to praise Jonson by coupling him with Donne as a 'great literary Protestant of the time'. Like Donne, Jonson 'was a realist' who 'had no use for claptrap, or rant, or romanticism'. Like Donne, he reacted against the facility and floridity of those who wrote in the grand Elizabethan tradition, though his protest did not follow Donne's mode of 'conceited subtlety of thought combined with a harshness of metre'. Huxley's assumption throughout is that both poets deliberately turned their backs on 'the realm of romantic beauty' so as to occupy themselves with 'the ugly world of fact'.]

116. William Butler Yeats
1919

Yeats cited Donne in his short poem 'To a Young Beauty' (*The Wild Swans at Coole*, 1919). The 'young beauty' was Iseult Gonne.

[Yeats takes Landor and Donne to epitomize the artist who writes for and consorts with only the most discriminating circle of friends.]

> Dear fellow-artist, why so free
> With every sort of company,
> With every Jack and Jill?
> Choose your companions from the best;
> Who draws a bucket with the rest
> Soon topples down the hill.
>
> You may, that mirror for a school,
> Be passionate, not bountiful
> As common beauties may,
> Who were not born to keep in trim
> With old Ezekiel's cherubim
> But those of Beauvarlet.

I know what wages beauty gives,
How hard a life her servant lives,
Yet praise the winters gone:
There is not a fool can call me friend,
And I may dine at journey's end
With Landor and with Donne.

117. Percy Herbert Osmond

1919

P. H. Osmond published an anthology of Anglican devotion, biographies of Isaac Barrow and of John Cosin, bishop of Durham, a book on Paolo Veronese's art, and *The Mystical Poets of the English Church*, in which he used Donne as a contrary case, contending over some nine pages that Donne was not a mystical writer at all (*The Mystical Poets of the English Church*, 1919, pp. 46–54).

[Osmond finds in Donne's 'earlier poems' a 'curious amalgam of licence and seriousness' which mingles quite shameless expressions with a 'theoretic Platonism, which, however, hardly carries conviction'. Osmond takes these contrasting attitudes for so many arbitrary switches of mood. 'In one mood he wallows in sensualism; in the next he idealizes love, praising the spirit within and deprecating the appeal of sex'; and he quotes stanza 4 of 'The Undertaking', pointing out that the same thought occurs in other poems such as 'The Ecstasy', 'Negative Love', and 'A Valediction: Forbidding Mourning'. Another such switch resulted in the 'curiously misnamed *Progress of the Soul*' (that is, the *Metempsychosis*), which uses the doctrine of transmigration 'in the savagely satiric vein of Swift, apparently to vent the author's spleen against Protestantism'. Osmond inconsequentially assumes that Donne failed to

408

finish this poem because he lost his courage, being 'as yet un-convinced of the errors of Rome'.

The *Anatomy of the World* is taken to mark a second phase of Donne's poetic career, which shows just the waywardness of the earlier phase. *The First Anniversary* 'has all the faults, and few of the merits of the *Second Anniversary*'. *The Second Anniversary* 'is, perhaps, the greatest of all Donne's poems'. Osmond gives lines 81–120 and 433–70 of *The Second Anniversary*, though the quotation does not.seem to reassure him in his own evaluation of the poem: 'With another sixty lines of far-fetched analogy and hyperbolic flattery the poem drags laboriously to its close.'

Osmond owes too much to Dr Johnson's characterization of the metaphysical poets to take Donne's thought seriously. *The Second Anniversary* is a mere 'rhapsody', and Donne's poetry in general presents a 'surfeit of tortured ingenuity'. Remarkably, he thinks that if we get beyond the intellectual juggling and faking of passion we discover a kind of airy transcendentalist in Donne.]

When we have penetrated the layer of over-subtle thought which so seldom reaches real profundity, and of emotionalism which so rarely rings true, we find that the dominant notion in Donne is that of the Transcendence of the Infinite, conceived of as altogether external to, and even alien from this present life.

[He concludes that this is not a mystical attitude.

Donne's religious poetry gives Osmond the impression of 'an abject penitence and a faltering faith, struggling – with very imperfect success – to burst through its clouds to the light of GOD'S LOVE'. He cites in evidence the 'Hymn to God the Father', and gives the whole of the 'Hymn to Christ, at the Author's Last Going into Germany'. He finds that the *Devotions* do not live up to Walton's account of them, being 'morbid rather than ecstatic' in that they dwell on the less hopeful aspects of spiritual life. The deprecations of 'A Litany' are 'magnificent in their self-disclosing candour', but in nothing else. Osmond raps the knuckles of those who would admit to the order of Anglican mystics a writer whose work does not follow out a deep inner conviction at all.]

... the tendency to confuse mere theoretic Platonism and a tone of other-worldliness with mysticism is one against which it seems important to make a stand.

118. Logan Pearsall Smith

1919

Logan Pearsall Smith (1865–1946), man of letters, was born in New Jersey and had degrees from Harvard and Oxford. His publications included *Life and Letters of Sir Henry Wotton* and *Milton and His Modern Critics*. He became an acknowledged authority on Donne, publishing a selection of highlights from Donne's sermons designed to introduce Donne's prose to an audience already interested in his poetry. This was the first convenient exhibition of the artistry and power of Donne's prose, and it made a considerable impact, running to many reprints over the following decades (*Donne's Sermons: Selected Passages. With an Essay*, 1919, pp. xiii–lii).

[Smith introduced his selection with an essay of some forty pages, opening with a not particularly sympathetic account of the revival of interest in Donne's poetry.]

The remarkable and somewhat enigmatic figure of John Donne is one that has attracted a good deal of attention in recent years; his life has been studied, his poems and letters carefully edited, his character analysed, and his position as a poet acutely debated. His harshness, his crabbed and often frigid way of writing, his forced conceits, his cynicism and sensuality, are extremely repellent to some readers; while to others his subtlety, his realism, and a certain modern and intimate quality in his poems, illuminated as they are with splendid flashes of imaginative fire, possess an extraordinary interest and fascination. There are people who hate Donne; there are others who love him, but there are very few who have read his poems and remain quite indifferent to him. His character is still a puzzle, his reputation as a poet, eclipsed for a long time and only revived in our own day, is by no means yet the subject of final agreement.

[Nonetheless, the 'immense body' of Donne's theological writing has been neglected, not just as a consequence of its sheer weight but because 'there is much in the writing itself which renders it difficult and distasteful to the modern mind'. The obsolete modes of thought and expression which keep us from reading Jeremy Taylor and South will strike us still more forcibly in Donne's sermons.]

All that has ceased to interest, all that actually repels us in the old theology, the scholastic divinity, the patristic learning, the torturing of texts, the interpretation of old prophecies, the obsolete controversies and refutation of forgotten heresies, the insistence on moral commonplaces, the intolerance of human frailty, and the menaces of fearful judgment on it – with all these stock subjects, Donne, like his contemporaries, filled his sermons. But his case is even worse than theirs; not only as a theologian was he of an older breed, more remote and medieval than Jeremy Taylor or South, he had also, personal to himself, the unhappy faculty of developing to their utmost the faults of any form of literary expression he adopted; and when he abandoned verse for sermon-writing, every defect of this kind of composition, everything that most offends us in the old preachers and sound expositors, was carried by him to a pitch which gives him a bad eminence over the most unreadable of them all.

[He quotes Dean Milman's wonderment at the effect Donne's preaching is reported to have had upon his congregation,[1] and approves Milman's strictures: 'It is only necessary to open a volume of Donne's sermons to find a justification for his successor's criticisms.' Yet if Donne]

surpasses the preachers of that period in their faults and drawbacks, he shares also in their achievements, and indeed in many ways he overtops them all. Lost in the crabbed, unread, unreadable folios of his sermons, these 'volumes of religion and mountains of piety', there are pages and passages of surprising beauty, which are nevertheless entirely unknown to English readers.

[The growing recognition of Donne's merits as a poet has drawn attention away from 'the excellence of his prose'.]

Equal in power and beauty to that of Sir Thomas Browne or Jeremy Taylor, and in passionate intensity surpassing even these great writers, it is almost unrepresented in our prose anthologies; and, indeed, the best of these . . . includes no specimen of his writing.

[But then the fact is that his best prose is not easily accessible, since 'he put forth his full strength' only 'here and there in isolated passages of his sermons'.]

... few even of the most enthusiastic readers of Donne's verse are aware that however highly they estimate his merits as a poet, he is equally worthy of fame as a prose writer – that, indeed, his mastery of the means of expression was perhaps even greater in prose than in poetry, was less impeded by those defects of technique and temperament which kept him from reaching the highest level of poetic achievement.

[In all, Smith argues, Donne's prose is best recommended to 'modern and secular-minded readers' like himself in a series of selections from the sermons. Such readers may even find that the best of Donne's prose is better than his poetry.]

As a poet Donne seems to have adopted a certain harsh and crabbed way of writing, in revolt against the influence of the Elizabethan taste; his poems show here and there that he could, if he wished, touch those harp-strings of sweet music; but they also show, only too abundantly, that in this soft harmony he could not find the medium for the personal expression he desired. This crabbedness shows itself, too, in his letters and his earlier prose writing, and also in the uninspired portions of his sermons. But when he was most in earnest, when he came to treat with passionate seriousness some great theme of faith or morals, his wilfulness of language fell from him; and in his attempt to bring his message home to the hearts of his congregation he availed himself without stint of his own gifts as a poet, and all the music and splendour of the great contemporary speech.

[Indeed some passages in the sermons express the self-awareness we discover in the poems.]

... we find in them a curiously modern note or quality which we find almost nowhere else in the literature of that age. For in spite of his medieval cast of thought Donne was in some ways the most modern writer of his period; in his poems and in his strange, feverish *Meditations* there is a subtlety of self-analysis, an awareness of the workings of his own mind, which seems to belong to the nineteenth rather than to the seventeenth century.... Dr Donne was still Jack Donne, though sanctified and transformed, and those who have learned to know the secular poet will find in the writer of religious prose the same characteristics, the subtle, modern self-analytic mind moving in a world of medieval thought, the abstract,

412

frigid scholastic intellect and the quickest senses, the forced conceits and passionate sincerity, the harsh utterance and the snatches of angel's music – in fact all that has attracted or perhaps repelled them in the author of the 'love-songs and satiric weeds', the sensual elegies and rugged verse-letters of his earlier period.

[Smith reports some contemporary accounts of the effect of Donne's sermons upon their congregations, and then surveys Donne's preaching career altogether. He sets out the plan of his own selection, which is arranged by topics rather than chronologically. Thus the extracts take us from Donne's self-intimations to his portrayals of the world, from secular concerns to matters of faith and the heights of revelation; and they culminate in some pages from *Death's Duel.*]

NOTE

1 See *John Donne: The Critical Heritage*, vol. I, ed. A. J. Smith (London: Routledge and Kegan Paul, 1975), p. 454.

119. Robert Seymour Bridges

1919

Bridges wrote to his friend Logan Pearsall Smith to say how 'tremendously delighted' he found himself with Smith's prefatory essay to *Donne's Sermons: Selected Passages*, which he had just read hot from the press (*The Selected Letters of Robert Bridges*, ed. D. E. Stanford, vol. II, 1984, p, 761).

It is most delightful reading, and you have said many good things – and it seems to me that it could not have been better done – and it certainly disposes one to read your author. I read one or two of the extracts, and I will do my best to study him as you would wish. – He certainly has a greater power of rhetorical grammar than one would have expected from his poems. I took a volume of them down and opened on 'A funeral Elegy' beginning 'Tis lost, to trust a Tombe with such a guest' and from beginning to end of that poem I did not find a line that I could tolerate. I doubt if I can get over my dislike for a man whose mind has such a wretched twist but I will have a good try at his prose.

120. John Livingston Lowes

1919

John Livingston Lowes (1867–1945), Professor of English in Harvard University, best known for his work on sources in Coleridge published as *The Road to Xanadu*, delivered a series of lectures at the Lowell Institute in Boston in January 1918. In them he explored aspects of the conventions that make of poetry 'a fabric of truth based on reality, but not reproducing reality' (p. 46). He mentioned Donne sympathetically as an example of a poet rebelling against established poetic conventions (*Convention and Revolt in Poetry*, 1919, pp. 152–3).

And there is perhaps no more salient instance in English poetry of this revulsion from the conventional to an unchartered individuality of expression than the case of John Donne. For here was one of the most daring and penetrating imaginations, one of the most subtle and restless intellects that ever, before or since, expressed itself through the medium of verse. Yet for all his magnificent and lavish gifts, Donne is the preëminent example of the inability of genius itself to escape the inevitable, when a dominant individuality refuses to be subdued to what it works in, and rebels against the limitations imposed upon every one who would impart his thoughts. Donne imagines (or recalls) a flea, in which his own and his lady's 'two bloods mingled be'. 'Oh! Stay', he cries,

> three lives in one flea spare,
> Where we almost, yea, more than marry'd are.
> This flea is you and I, and this
> Our marriage bed and marriage temple is.
> Though parents grudge, and you, we're met,
> And cloister'd in these living walls of jet.
> > Though use make you apt to kill me,
> > Let not to that self-murder added be,
> > And sacrilege, three sins in killing three.

But ideas that essentially belong asunder cannot, even at the hands of genius, be permanently joined together, and the shock of surprise once over, we wonder at an amazing and perverse ingenuity, and pass on. And in Donne at his worst, the passion for singularity contorts, through its excess, both stuff and form into the fantastic. Yet he has also left, along with profoundly imaginative poems, imperishable lines: 'I long to talk with some old lover's ghost Who died before the god of love was born'; the famous characterization of 'her pure and eloquent blood', and that supremely characteristic interpenetration of Love and Death and Beauty in one haunting phrase: 'a bracelet of bright hair about the bone'. But those lines of his which live, survive by virtue of a transcendent and unique originality of another type, which works through perversion, not distortion, and which leaves what it touches strangely, it may be even eerily, luminous. The others coruscate like brilliant pyrotechnics – and go out.

121. Thomas Stearns Eliot
1919

T. S. Eliot (1888–1965) began to review for the *Athenaeum* in April 1919. His review of Pearsall Smith's selection from Donne's sermons was not reprinted in a subsequent collection. ('The Preacher as Artist', *Athenaeum*, 28 November 1919, pp. 1252–3).

The selection is well made, and should also convince the reader that it was worth making. To what Mr Pearsall Smith has said there are no objections to be raised; there are only one or two critical codicils to be added.

Donne's prose is worth reading both because it is a significant moment in the history of English prose, and because it has at its best uncommon dignity and beauty – a style which gives at times what is always uncommon in the sermon, a direct personal communication. Mr Pearsall Smith is quite aware of Donne's personality, and of the occasions on which it appears immediately in his prose with the same immediacy as in his verse. But we cannot appreciate the significance, the solitariness, of this personal expression in Donne's sermons unless we compare him with one or two of the great preachers of his time, the great preachers whose sermons were fine prose. The absence of such comparison is the single important defect of Mr Pearsall Smith's introduction. Without it, we are not in a position to criticize Donne's style at all analytically; the comparative study would educe what is doubtless well known to Mr Pearsall Smith, but not patent to the cultured reader: that a great deal in Donne's predicatory style is traditional, and that some of the most praised passages are produced by a method which is more than traditional, which is immemorial, almost imposed by the sermon form. Not until we see this can we understand the difference between certain passages: the difference between Donne as an artist doing the traditional better than any one else had done it, and Donne putting into the sermon here and there what no one else had put into it.

Merely the fact that these are extracts, that you can extract from the sermons of Donne, is indicative. It is possible to select sermons of Bishop Latimer or Bishop Andrewes, but it would probably be futile to attempt to select passages out of the sermons. From one point of view, it is a disadvantage to Donne that it is possible to make excerpts from his sermons. The excerpts are enough to show Donne's place in English prose; but the sermon is a form of prose, the form in which Donne's prose was written. It follows that we cannot wholly apprehend Donne's prose without seeing the structure. For the Sermon was a form of literary art – 'applied' art as the drama of Donne's day was applied art, applied poetry. And on the other hand, Donne had more in him than could be squeezed into the frame of this form: something which, if it does not crack the

416

frame, at least gives it, now and then, a perceptible outward bulge. We must know what the sermon was, to know what Donne accomplished; and finally, to know what it was in Donne to which the sermon did not give free play. And perhaps this knowledge will supply a clue as to why the sermon is difficult, perhaps the most difficult form of art; why compositions which were superlatively fine sermons possess none of the permanent qualities of the true work of art; and why Donne, who might have made a great prose art, failed to do so.

Hugh Latimer was a fine writer, and Lancelot Andrewes was a writer of genius. They both had gifts of style; in the style of Andrewes there are points which might very profitably be studied by any prose writer. They both wrote sermons which have beauty, though not the greatness of works of art; the gift of each of them was a gift for the sermon; they had nothing to say which could not be put into a very good sermon, no feelings which the sermon could not satisfy. And many of the passages of Donne given by Mr Pearsall Smith can be paralleled from Latimer or Andrewes; paralleled in such a way as to leave it open to us to think Donne better, but better only in the same kind. There are touches of poetry in Donne and in Andrewes. The following of Donne is pleasing:

If you be, when you are, remember that as in that good Custome in these Cities, you hear cheerful street musick in the winter mornings, but yet there was a sad and doleful bel-man, that wak'd you, and call'd upon you two or three hours before that musick came.

And also Andrewes:

Our fashion is to see and see again before we stir a foot, specially if it be to the worship of Christ. Come such a journey at such a time? No; but fairly have put it off to the spring of the year, till the days longer, and the ways fairer, and the weather warmer, till better travelling to Christ.

The odd syntax, the forceful phrase, must have been as effective spoken as they are read. This is positively Andrewes, as much as the other is positively Donne, and both are perfectly suited to the needs of the sermon.

But the selection No. 44 in Mr Pearsall Smith's book, the famous 'Mundus Mare', will illustrate, better than any other, Donne's execution of a usual sermon method. The method is a vivid figure of speech, an image developed at length with point by point reference to spiritual truth. The world is a sea, has ebbs and flows, storms and tempests, the greater fish devour the less; it is like the sea, no place of habitation, but a passage to our habitations. We fish in this sea for the souls of men; we fish with the Gospel of Christ Jesus. The net has leads, the denouncing of God's judgments, and corks, the power of absolution. It is easy to see the value of such analogy for the sermon. The sermon is not oratory: it aims not so much to persuade as to give a fresh emotional tone to what is accepted. Donne does this in a more masterly way than Latimer, but by the same method even in detail. The effect is obtained not only by the analogy, but by repetition of phrase like wave upon wave:

The world is a Sea, in many respects and assimilations. It is a Sea, as it is subject to stormes, and tempests. . . . So the world is a Sea. It is a Sea, as it is bottomlesse to any line. . . . So the world is a Sea. . . . All these wayes the world is a Sea, but especially it is a Sea in this respect, that the Sea is no place of habitation, but a passage to our habitations.

Compare Latimer in his Sermon on the Card:

Now turn up your trump, your heart (hearts is trump, as I said before), and cast your trump, your heart, on this card; and upon this card you shall learn what Christ requireth of a christian man.

The method – the analogy, and the repetition – is the same as that once used by a greater master of the sermon than either Donne or Andrewes or Latimer: it is the method of the Fire-Sermon preached by the Buddha.

As a writer of sermons, Donne is superior to Latimer, and more mature in style, if not more original or more important, than Andrewes. His style is nearer to Taylor or Browne than to either of these. He might be a little higher than any of these men, but in the same circle. But there are other passages, such as Mr Pearsall Smith has done well to put first, which carry him out of it:

I am not all here, I am here now preaching upon this text, and I am at home in my library considering whether S. Gregory, or S. Hierome, have said best of this text, before. I am here speaking to you, and yet I consider by the way, in the same instant, what it is likely you will say to one another, when I have done, you are not all here neither; you are here now, hearing me, and yet you are thinking that you have heard a better sermon somewhere else, of this text before . . . you are here, and you remember your selves that now ye think of it: This had been the fittest time, now, when every body else is at Church, to have made such and such a private visit; and because you would be there, you are there.

Things like this break, now and again, through the close convention of Elizabethan–Jacobean speech; they are rarer in the prose
than in the verse. You will find as gorgeous or as marmoreal prose
as Donne could write, in Andrewes or in Hooker: as terse and as
direct, here and there in Hakluyt or in Ralegh; but very seldom, in
the prose of Donne's age, but seldom, as in this passage, the sense
of the artist as an Eye curiously, patiently watching himself as a man.
'There is the Ego, the particular, the individuall, I.' Donne was an
Egoist, but not an egoist of the religious, the mystical type. Perhaps
he was something less important. At all events he was something
else; and it was an Ego which nowhere in his works finds complete
expression, and only furtively in his sermons. 'Amourous soule,
ambitious soule, covetous soule, voluptuous soule, what wouldest
thou have in heaven?' We should like to know that, but Donne
cannot tell us. The difficulty is not to be laid solely to the charge
of discerning, critical James I, who plucked Donne from the world
and pushed him into a pulpit. We feel that English prose was not
sufficiently developed, or developed in the right direction, for this
introspective faculty of Donne to tell its tale. Montaigne was all
right, but Donne did not find what he wanted; yet he had one of
the finest brains of his time, perhaps the finest for its possible
purpose. He does not fit: he is no Buddha, but certainly not an
Andrewes either. But it would be a great injustice to him, and
indeed to his editor as well, to regard him merely as the author of
a considerable number of purple paragraphs.

122. Raymond Macdonald Alden

1920

Professor R. M. Alden (1873–1924) of Stanford University was
known in America for his work on prosody and on Shakespeare. He published a number of general handbooks of
English verse, and *An Introduction to Poetry*, as well as studies
of Tennyson and of Shakespeare and a variorum edition of

Shakespeare's sonnets. In an article for *Studies in Philology*, he attempted to characterize the conceits of the Metaphysical poets ('The Lyrical Conceits of the "Metaphysical Poets"', *Studies in Philology*, 17 (1920), 183–98).

[Alden orders conceits from Donne, Carew and Cowley in three general categories, paraphrasing the argument of each poem so as to bring out the mode of the conceit. Thus conceits may be predominantly verbal, or imaginative, or logical; and since Donne's conceits hardly ever depend upon word-play, Alden's chief concern with him is to distinguish plays of images from plays of reasoning – metaphysical reasoning, as he terms it.

Alden links Donne with Cowley, and approves Johnson's account of metaphysical poetry. But his overall assumption is that the conceits of the seventeenth-century poets rework the conceits of the Petrarchan poets of the fifteenth and sixteenth centuries. In Donne's case, 'the individual play of mind upon them is conspicuous from first to last'. Donne gives the customary Petrarchan paradoxes a 'reflective complexity'. He brings to the theme of love 'transcendental considerations which seem to make the art of love a part of both science and philosophy'. The differences between the conceits of the earlier poets and those of the seventeenth-century poets have been exaggerated; yet the special development of the conceit in the seventeenth century is clearly traceable to the influence of the 'extraordinary personality of Donne'.]

He helped to change the emphasis from the imaginative to the metaphysical type, and showed how, even when the old types were used, they might be transformed to something quite different in intellectual tone. In the spirit of the new era, no doubt, there were elements which assisted his influence. The intellectual view of life may be said to have been increasing, as compared with what might be called the romantic–chivalric, and the theme of love, in particular, was now less a matter of social convention and more one for introspective analysis. Yet none of Donne's disciples really represents this intellectuality with at all the same seriousness as himself. For him the metaphysical conceit was much more than a plaything; it was an appropriate means to the expression of his philosophy of love.

[Alden cannot accept Johnson's judgement that Donne's writing lacked passion, and prefers De Quincey's account of it.[1] But he finds that Donne's poems lack unity, because they heap up conceits which have no necessary connection with each other so that the reader has to leap from thought to thought. Nonetheless, Donne does attain perfect unity]

in the beautiful 'Lecture Upon the Shadow', where a genuine and veracious symbolism is maintained from beginning to end. Still finer in its art, though less profound, is the astonishing 'Computation', where one marvels at Donne's restraint in stopping his hyperbolical paradox of the length of a lover's separation with the tenth pregnant line.

[Donne's unique contribution to the development of the lyrical conceit is to fuse intellectual processes with lyrical feeling.]

Donne, of all poets, that ever lived, perhaps most strikingly exemplifies this interpenetration of lyric feeling and intellectual activity.

Donne's followers merely imitate his feeling and his intellect. Yet the only followers whom Alden has in mind seem to be the Caroline poets, Cleveland, and Cowley. Herbert, Vaughan, Marvell simply do not figure as adepts of the metaphysical conceit, and are not so much as mentioned in this essay.

NOTE

1 See *John Donne: The Critical Heritage*, vol. I, ed. A. J. Smith (London: Routledge and Kegan Paul, 1975), p. 346.

123. John Cann Bailey

1920

J. C. Bailey (1864–1931), critic and essayist, wrote books on Dr Johnson and his circle, on Milton and Shakespeare. He was a regular contributor to the *Times Literary Supplement,* the *Quarterly Review*, the *Edinburgh Review*, the *Fortnightly Review* and other periodicals. Assessing Pearsall Smith's selection from Donne's sermons (see No. 118), he gave his own explanation of 'the revival of interest in Donne which has been very marked for the last twenty years or more, and still continues' ('The Sermons of a Poet', *Quarterly Review*, April 1920, pp. 317–28).

[Bailey argues that Donne attracts young readers in particular 'for the simple reason that he is the most self-willed individualist of all our older poets'. Though he was far from being an anarchist, 'Donne accepted no limitations. He used verse ... to invade the province of prose'.]

... there is nothing, not even the ugly and disgusting, which his verse will not say, no manner, not even the rudest, which it will not adopt to attain its almost impossible ends. Verse itself, and still more poetry, were reluctant to have anything to do either with the crude grossness, or with the prosaic literalness, or with the unbodied dialectic, one or other of which was what, at different times, Donne brought for their shaping. But over that reluctance his strong brain and violent will rode roughshod, compelling them to do his bidding. Or perhaps that was only what he thought they did. It is not easy to force poetry to obey alien laws; and those who try to do so usually pay the penalty. Donne's penalty is that, while he ranks among the greatest geniuses who have written English poetry, he does not quite rank among the greatest English poets.

[In fact Donne's 'all-including intellectual covetousness' found fitter scope in prose.]

Here that colloquial ease to which his poetry owes some moments of pure felicity, finds its natural home. Here his eloquence and subtlety, the immense range and fiery energy of his mind, were less likely to defeat their own purpose.

[Donne's best prose is to be found in his sermons, in which he displays 'an imagination of Time, Death, and Judgment as stupendous as that of Bossuet, and far more like a personal experience'. Bailey quotes an impassioned plea for God's forgiveness of his sins, and comments:]

Was there ever a printed sermon in which one heard the preacher's voice more plainly than we hear it in such a passage as this? It is the very genius of oratory, all the freedom of the speech of a voluble speaker, going on and on, as each new aspect of the subject comes into his head; and yet subtly and imperceptibly, perhaps unconsciously to the preacher himself, the freedom is controlled and form imposed upon the material, and the result is art, a masterpiece of English prose. And the art in no way hides the sincerity and directness. The words are so many arrows shot by Donne at his hearers and going straight to their hearts.

[Further excerpts from the sermons are taken to illustrate]

the extraordinary fullness of Donne's mind, quotation following upon quotation, fancy upon fancy, argument upon argument, and often, one must confess, conceit upon conceit ... his power of visual and physical imagination.

[Of one passage Bailey says that it displays the greatest of Donne's gifts, 'his sheer eloquence. There are few more splendid flights in any language.' Of another passage he remarks that it shows many of Donne's characteristics in small space.]

... the beauty of his thought and also its curiousness; his mingling of the life of his day with the life of eternity; his vivid directness and actuality; the Latin sentences which he scatters about his English with such surprising felicity; the ease and abundance of it all, which yet never affects its clarity, the note of sincerity and truth, of an individual and personal voice, which neither his art not his learning ever long conceal.

124. Robert Wilson Lynd

1920

R. W. Lynd (1879–1949), journalist and essayist, became literary editor of the *Daily News* and, as 'Y. Y.', essayist for the

New Statesman 1913–45. He published a book on Dr Johnson and, in an essay on Tennyson, took Donne as a familiar example of a poet whose work is suddenly rediscovered after long neglect ('Tennyson: A Contemporary Criticism', in *The Art of Letters*, 1920, p. 136).

If Donne is esteemed three hundred years after his death less as a great Christian than as a great poet this is because we now look for him in his writings rather than in his biography, in his poetry rather than in his prose, and in his *Songs and Sonets* and *Elegies* rather than in his *Divine Poems*. We find, in some of them, abundant evidence of the existence of a dark angel at odds with the good angel of Walton's raptures.

. . . we need not go beyond his poems for proof of the wilderness of learning that he had made his own. He was versed in medicine and the law as well as in theology. He subdued astronomy, physiology, and geography to the needs of poetry. Nine Muses were not enough for him, even though they included Urania. He called in to their aid Galen and Copernicus. He did not go to the hills and the springs for his images, but to the laboratory and the library, and in the library the books that he consulted to the greatest effect were the works of men of science and learning, not of the great poets with whom London may almost be said to have been peopled during his life-time. I do not think his verse or correspondence contains a single reference to Shakespeare, whose contemporary he was, being born only nine years later. The only great Elizabethan poet whom he seems to have regarded with interest and even friendship was Ben Jonson. Jonson's Catholicism may have been a link between them. But, more important than that, Jonson was, like Donne himself, an inflamed pedant. For each of them learning was the necessary robe of genius. Jonson, it is true, was a pedant of the classics, Donne of the speculative sciences; but both of them alike ate to a surfeit of the fruit of the tree of knowledge. It was, I think, because Donne was to so great a degree a pagan of the Renaissance, loving the proud things of the intellect more than the treasures of the humble, that he found it easy to abandon the Catholicism of his family for Protestantism. . . .

Few converts in those days of the wars of religion wrote with such wise reason of the creeds as did Donne in the lines:

> To adore or scorn an image, or protest,
> May all be bad; doubt wisely; in strange way
> To stand inquiring right, is not to stray;
> To sleep or run wrong is. On a huge hill,
> Cragged and steep, Truth stands, and he that will
> Reach her, about must and about must go;
> And what the hill's suddenness resists, win so.

This surely was the heresy of an inquisitive mind, not the mood of a theologian. It betrays a tolerance springing from ardent doubt, not from ardent faith.

[He quotes lines 39–42 of 'The Calm'.]

In these lines we get a glimpse of the Donne that has attracted most interest in recent years – the Donne who experienced more variously than any other poet of his time 'the queasy pain of being beloved and loving'. Donne was curious of adventures of many kinds, but in nothing more than in love. As a youth he leaves the impression of having been an Odysseus of love, a man of many wiles and many travels. He was a virile neurotic, comparable in some points to Baudelaire, who was a sensualist of the mind even more than of the body. His sensibilities were different as well as less of a piece, but he had something of Baudelaire's taste for hideous and shocking aspects of lust. One is not surprised to find among his poems that 'heroical epistle of Sappho to Philaenis', in which he makes himself the casuist of forbidden things. His studies of sensuality, however, are for the most part normal, even in their grossness. There was in him more of the Yahoo than of the decadent. There was an excremental element in his genius as in the genius of that other gloomy dean, Jonathan Swift. Donne and Swift were alike satirists born under Saturn. They laughed more frequently from disillusion than from happiness. Donne, it must be admitted, turned his disillusion to charming as well as hideous uses. *Go and Catch a Falling Star* is but one of a series of delightful lyrics in disparagement of women. In several of the *Elegies*, however, he throws away his lute and comes to the satirist's more prosaic business. He writes frankly as a man in search of bodily experiences:

> Whoever loves, if he do not propose
> The right true end of love, he's one that goes
> To sea for nothing but to make him sick.

In *Love's Progress* he lets his fancy dwell on the detailed geography of a woman's body, with the sick imagination of a schoolboy, till the beautiful seems almost beastly. In *The Anagram* and *The Comparison* he plays the Yahoo at the expense of all women by the similes he uses in insulting two of them. In *The Perfume* he relates the story of an intrigue with a girl whose father discovered his presence in the house as a result of his using scent. Donne's jest about it is suggestive of his uncontrollable passion for ugliness:

> Had it been some bad smell, he would have thought
> That his own feet, or breath, that smell had brought.

It may be contended that in *The Perfume* he was describing an imaginary experience, and indeed we have his own words on record: 'I did best when I had least truth for my subjects.' But even if we did not accept Mr Gosse's common-sense explanation of these words, we should feel that the details of the story have a vividness that springs straight from reality. It is difficult to believe that Donne had not actually lived in terror of the gigantic man-servant who was set to spy on the lovers.

But the most interesting of all the sensual intrigues of Donne, from the point of view of biography, especially since Mr Gosse gave it such commanding significance in that *Life of John Donne* in which he made a living man of a mummy, is that of which we have the story in *Jealousy* and *His Parting from Her*. It is another story of furtive and forbidden love. . . .

It is an extraordinary story, if it is true. It throws a scarcely less extraordinary light on the nature of Donne's mind, if he invented it. . . .

I confess that the oftener I read the poetry of Donne the more firmly I become convinced that, far from being primarily the poet of desire gratified and satiated, he is essentially the poet of frustrated love. He is often described by the historians of literature as the poet who finally broke down the tradition of Platonic love. I believe that, so far is this from being the case, he is the supreme example of a Platonic lover among the English poets. He was usually Platonic under protest, but at other times exultantly so. Whether he finally overcame the more consistent Platonism of his mistress by the impassioned logic of *The Ecstasy* we have no means of knowing. . . .

It is enough for us to feel, however, that these poems railing at or glorying in Platonic love are no mere goldsmith's compliments, like the rhymed letters to Mrs Herbert and Lady Bedford. Miracles of this sort are not wrought save by the heart. We do not find in them the underground and sardonic element that appears in so much of Donne's merely amorous work. We no longer picture him as a sort of Vulcan hammering out the poetry of base love, raucous, powerful, mocking. He becomes in them a child of Apollo, as far as his temperament will allow him. He makes music of so grave and stately a beauty that one begins to wonder at all the critics who have found fault with his rhythms – from Ben Jonson, who said that 'for not keeping accent, Donne deserved hanging', down to Coleridge, who delcared that his 'muse on dromedary trots', and described him as 'rhyme's sturdy cripple'. Coleridge's quatrain on Donne is, without doubt, an unequalled masterpiece of epigrammatic criticism. But Donne rode no dromedary. In his greatest poems he rides Pegasus like a master even if he does rather weigh the poor beast down by carrying an encyclopaedia in his saddle-bags.

Not only does Donne remain a learned man on his Pegasus, however: he also remains a humorist, a serious fantastic. Humour and passion pursue each other through the labyrinth of his being, as we find in those two beautiful poems, *The Relic* and *The Funeral*, addressed to the lady who had given him a bracelet of her hair.

[He gives some account of 'The Relic', 'The Funeral','The Blossom', 'The Primrose', and 'The Undertaking'.]

It seems to me, in view of this remarkable series of poems, that it is useless to look in Donne for a single consistent attitude to love. His poems take us round the entire compass of love, as the work of no other English poet – not even, perhaps, Browning's – does. He was by destiny the complete experimentalist in love in English literature. He passed through phase after phase of the love of the body only, phase after phase of the love of the soul only, and ended as the poet of the perfect marriage. In his youth he was a gay – but was he ever really gay? – free-lover, who sang jestingly:

> How happy were our sires in ancient times,
> Who held plurality of loves no crime!

By the time he writes *The Ecstasy* the victim of the body has become the protesting victim of the soul. He cries out against a love that is merely ecstatic friendship:

> But O alas, so long, so far,
> Our bodies why do we forbear?

He pleads for the recognition of the body, contending that it is not the enemy but the companion of the soul:

> Soul into the soul may flow
> Though it to body first repair.

The realistic philosophy of love has never been set forth with greater intellectual vehemence:

> So must pure lovers' souls descend
> T' affections and to faculties,
> Which sense may reach and apprehend,
> Else a great Prince in prison lies.
> To our bodies turn we then, that so
> Weak men on love reveal'd may look;
> Love's mysteries in souls do grow
> But yet the body is the book.

I, for one, find it impossible to believe that all this passionate verse – verse in which we find the quintessence of Donne's genius – was a mere utterance of abstract thoughts into the wind. Donne, as has been pointed out, was more than most writers a poet of personal experience. His greatest poetry was born of struggle and conflict in the obscure depths of the soul as surely as was the religion of St Paul. I doubt if, in the history of his genius, any event ever happened of equal importance to his meeting with the lady who first set going in his brain that fevered dialogue between the body and the soul. Had he been less of a frustrated lover, less of a martyr, in whom love's

> Art did express
> A quintessence even from nothingness,
> From dull privations and lean emptiness,

much of his greatest poetry, it seems to me, would never have been written.

[He refers to the *Anniversary*, the 'Nocturnal upon St Lucy's Day', 'The Canonisation', and the several *Valedictions*.]

Of many of the other love-poems, however, we can measure the intensity but not guess the occasion. All that we can say with confidence when we have read them is that, after we have followed one tributary or another leading down to the ultimate Thames of his genius, we know that his progress as a lover was a progress from infidelity to fidelity, from wandering amorousness to deep and enduring passion. The image that is finally stamped on his greatest work is not that of a roving adulterer, but of a monotheist of love. It is true that there is enough Don-Juanism in the poems to have led even Sir Thomas Browne to think of Donne's verse rather as a confession of his sins than as a golden book of love.

To the modern reader, on the contrary, it will seem that there is as much divinity in the best of the love-poems as in the best of the religious ones. Donne's last word as a secular poet may well be regarded as having been uttered in that great poem in celebration of lasting love, *The Anniversary*, which closes with so majestic a sweep.

[He quotes lines 23–30 of the poem.]

Donne's conversion as a lover was obviously as complete and revolutionary as his conversion in religion.

It is said, indeed, to have led to his conversion to passionate religion.

[He tells how Donne ruined his fortunes by his marriage.]

The truth is to be forty and a failure is an affliction that might sour even a healthy nature. The effect on a man of Donne's ambitious and melancholy temperament, together with the memory of his dissipated health and his dissipated fortunes, and the spectacle of a long family in constant process of increase, must have been disastrous. To such a man poverty and neglected merit are a prison as they were to Swift. One thinks of each of them as a lion in a cage, ever growing less and less patient of his bars. Shakespeare and Shelley had in them some volatile element that could, one feels, have escaped through the bars and sung above the ground. Donne and Swift were morbid men suffering from claustrophobia. They were pent and imprisoned spirits, hating the walls that seemed to threaten to close in on them and crush them. In his poems and letters Donne is haunted especially by three images – the hospital, the prison, and the grave. Disease, I think, preyed on his mind even more terrifyingly than warped ambition. . . .

As a preacher, no less than as a poet, he is inflamed by the creative heat. He shows the same vehemence of fancy in the presence of the divine and infernal universe – a vehemence that prevents even his most far-sought extravagances from disgusting us as do the lukewarm follies of the Euphuists. . . .

Nine out of ten readers of the *Sermons*, I imagine, will be first attracted to them through love of the poems. They need not be surprised if they do not immediately enjoy them. The dust of the pulpit lies on them thickly enough. As one goes on reading them, however, one becomes suddenly aware of their florid and exiled beauty. One sees beyond their local theology to the passion of a great suffering artist. Here are sentences that express the Paradise, the Purgatory, and the Hell of John Donne's soul. A noble imagination is at work – a grave-digging imagination, but also an imagination that is at home among the stars. One can open Mr Pearsall Smith's anthology almost at random and be sure of lighting on a passage which gives us a characteristic movement in the symphony of horror and hope that was Donne's contribution to the art of prose.

[If Donne had written much prose as good as his best 'his Sermons would be as famous as the writings of any of the saints since the days of the Apostles'.]

Even as it is, there is no other Elizabethan man of letters whose personality is an island with a crooked shore, inviting us into a thousand bays and creeks and rivermouths, to the same degree as the personality that expressed itself in the poems, sermons, and life of John Donne. It is a mysterious and at times repellent island. It lies only intermittently in the sun. A fog hangs around its coast, and at the base of its most radiant mountain-tops there is, as a rule, a miasma-infested swamp. There are jewels to be found scattered among its rocks and over its surface, and by miners in the dark. It is richer, indeed, in jewels and precious metals and curious ornaments than in flowers. The shepherd on the hillside seldom tells his tale uninterrupted. Strange rites in honour of ancient infernal deities that delight in death are practised in hidden places, and the echo of these reaches him on the sighs of the wind and makes him shudder even as he looks at his beloved. It is an island with a cemetery smell. The chief figure who haunts it is a living man in a winding-sheet.

[He tells how Donne posed for the portrait in his shroud and generally prepared for death.]

Among all his fantasies none remains in the imagination more despotically than this last fanciful game of dying. Donne, however, remained in all respects a fantastic to the last, and we may see in that hymn which he wrote eight days before the end, tricked out with queer geography, and so anciently egoistic amid its worship.

Donne was the poet-geographer of himself, his mistresses, and his God. Other poets of his time dived deeper and soared to greater altitudes, but none travelled so far, so curiously, and in such out-of-the-way places, now hurrying like a nervous fugitive, and now in the exultation of the first man in a new found land.

125. Philipp Aronstein
1920

In an extended survey of Donne's life and work, Aronstein introduced Donne to a German audience which he assumed to know little of the English literary context of Donne's poetry ('John Donne', *Anglia* 44 (1920), 113–213.

[Aronstein gives a full account of Donne's career and personality, drawn from Gosse. Then he parades Donne's poetry by categories, rehearsing the circumstances and describing the features of each kind. Finally he characterizes Donne's art in general. What emerges is a competent but featureless round-up of current orthodoxies. Aronstein does essay a critical judgement at last, in words very close to his 1919 article, which is that Donne ranks with Byron as an *Ich-Künstler* – presumably one who makes art out of his own ego.]

126. Louise Imogen Guiney

1920

Louise I. Guiney (1861–1920) was an American, who, after working as a postmistress and freelance writer for newspapers and magazines in America, emigrated to England at the turn of the century and settled in Oxford as a poet, researcher and writer. She wrote biographies and edition of Matthew Arnold, James Clarence Mangan and Henry Vaughan, poems on Edmund Campion, a book on Charles II, and a collection of recusant poetry published posthumously in 1938. She was a devout Catholic whose religious views were strongly evident in her writing. In 1919 she contributed an article to the *Month*, the journal of the Society of Jesus, on Gerard Manley Hopkins, whose poetry she had known before Robert Bridges' edition of 1918. The following year she wrote an article, again for the *Month*, with the explanatory title 'Donne as a Lost Catholic Poet' (*Month* 136 (July–December 1920), 13–19).

Guiney begins by suggesting that 'some one ... should write a ... scientific and authentic study of Dr John Donne as a Catholic: preferably should the author of it be of the same faith'. This in small compass she sets out to do, combining both general analysis of the Catholic and Protestant sentiment in Donne's verse and sermons and describing his family's connections with Catholicism. She states that

every Catholic who is an attentive reader, every psychologist brought in contact with the interesting and peccable characters of that English age, will agree that Donne, wherever his utterance is devotional, shows himself a child (and not a strayed child) of the old Church.

[While his prose]

both in the controversial works expected from one in his position, and in the sermons which entranced his sermon-loving generation with their sombre music, can hardly be called lacking in antagonism to Catholic doctrine, or innuendo against Catholic practice ... his poetry is never merely Anglican. Placed beside George

Herbert, Donne looks like a mediaeval scholiast. Should he utter in passing an Anglican sentiment, however, he shows no self-consciousness.

[Most of the rest of the article is on the Catholic faith of Donne's family especially his mother, Elizabeth Heywood.]

Donne's mother had to live on through the heart-break of his great change, and of his reception of orders and preferments in which she could take no pride. She passed the whole of her old age under his kind roof. She had been fifty-six years a widow when she drew her last breath in 1632, having survived by one year the genius she had brought into the world. By her deathbed may have stood her worthless grandson, John Donne, the younger. On him, the embodiment of her fine gold scattered, her priceless Catholic inheritance beaten down into the dust, her last glance in this world may have rested.

[To Guiney Donne is 'one of our greatest apostates' yet]

to all who try to study his uniquely difficult temperament, his pages of every mood between Hell and Heaven, he stands forth as essentially honest. Granted that his lapse from the faith of his fathers had something to do with early moral aberrations, or was even caused by them; granted that he listened lingeringly to the voice of ambition, never heard in Recusant thickets, but only on the new national highway of smooth pavements and easy ascents; granted that, sensitive in the supreme degree, he left like a coward the boding Gethsemane where his own family had knelt in the shadows for nearly a hundred years.

[She located her own attitude to the poet in the final paragraph.]

There are those who, in regard to Donne, will always be conscious chiefly of certain vile stuff, 'writ in his wild unhallowed times', which, to be his punishment before posterity, is in all his best editions preserved; though it should also be remembered that no verses of his were published until he was in his grave. There are those who perceive and resent his haughtily tempestuous mentality, creating its own laws, hurrying into words beautiful and turbid as any torrent pouring down the channelled hills, and moulding and colouring seventeenth-century England as they go. There are those who find merely horrible his lean, patient, ghost-like effigy. . . .

433

But other of us Catholics are only sorry for John Donne, and still miss him from the hearth, and are willing to leave him unsolved until the Day when our judgment of one another can be just.

[The article ends with a quotation of lines 8–14 and 22–8 from 'A Hymn to Christ, at the Author's Last Going into Germany', saying that they date from Donne's visit to Germany in 1519.]

But they might have come from a would-be Cistercian gliding happily and for ever into his cloister. Donne, at his best, is always like that, giving surprises and vistas and 'long, long thoughts' of the questing soul of man.

127. Thomas Stearns Eliot

1919/20

Eliot's first gathering of his essays, *The Sacred Wood*, had several well-known observations on the poetic language of Donne and his contemporaries which Eliot developed in his later essay on the metaphysical poets. The first passage that follows comes from an essay called 'Imperfect Critics: Swinburne as Critic', first published as a review in the *Athenaeum*, 19 September 1919, pp. 909–10. The second passage comes from the essay on Ben Jonson, which first appeared as reviews in the *Times Literary Supplement*, 13 November 1919, pp. 637–8, and the *Athenaeum*, 14 November 1919, pp. 1180–1. The third passage comes from the essay on Philip Massinger, first published as reviews in the *Times Literary Supplement*, 27 May 1920, pp. 325–6, and the *Athenaeum*, 11 June 1920, pp. 760–1. Eliot reprinted the essays on Jonson and Massinger in his *Selected Essays*, 1932 (*The Sacred Wood* (1920), 1934, pp. 22–3, 115, and 128–9).

1

Chapman is a difficult author, as Swinburne says; he is far more difficult than Jonson, to whom he bears only a superficial likeness. He is difficult beyond his obscurity. He is difficult partly through his possession of a quality comparatively deficient in Jonson, but which was nevertheless a quality of the age. It is strange that Swinburne should have hinted at a similarity to Jonson and not mentioned a far more striking affinity of Chapman's – that is, Donne. The man who wrote

> Guise, O my lord, how shall I cast from me
> The bands and coverts hindering me from thee?
> The garment or the cover of the mind
> The humane soul is; of the soul, the spirit
> The proper robe is; of the spirit, the blood;
> And of the blood, the body is the shroud:

and

> Nothing is made of nought, of all things made,
> Their abstract being a dream but of a shade.

is unquestionably kin to Donne. The quality in question is not peculiar to Donne and Chapman. In common with the greatest – Marlowe, Webster, Tourneur, and Shakespeare – they had a quality of sensuous thought, or of thinking through the senses, or of the senses thinking, of which the exact formula remains to be defined. If you look for it in Shelley or Beddoes, both of whom in very different ways recaptured something of the Elizabethan inspiration, you will not find it, though you may find other qualities instead. There is a trace of it only in Keats, and, derived from a different source, in Rossetti. You will not find it in the *Duke of Gandia*. . . .

2

If we look at the work of Jonson's great contemporaries, Shakespeare, and also Donne and Webster and Tourneur (and sometimes Middleton), have a depth, a third dimension, as Mr Gregory Smith rightly calls it, which Jonson's work has not. Their words have often a network of tentacular roots reaching down to the deepest terrors and desires. Jonson's most certainly have not. . . .

435

3

We may conclude directly from these quotations that Massinger's feeling for language had outstripped his feeling for things; that his eye and his vocabulary were not in co-operation. One of the greatest distinctions of several of his elder contemporaries – we name Middleton, Webster, Tourneur – is a gift for combining, for fusing into a single phrase, two or more diverse impressions.

> . . . in her strong toil of grace

of Shakespeare is such a fusion; the metaphor identifies itself with what suggests it; the resultant is one and is unique –

> Does the silk worm *expend* her *yellow labours?* . . .
> Why does yon fellow *falsify highways*
> And lays his life between the judge's lips
> To *refine* such a one? keeps horse and men
> To *beat their valours* for her?

> Let the common sewer take it from distinction . . .
> Lust and forgetfulness have been amongst us.

These lines of Tourneur and of Middleton exhibit that perpetual slight alteration of language, words perpetually juxtaposed in new and sudden combinations, meanings perpetually *eingeschachtelt* into meanings, which evidences a very high development of the senses, a development of the English language which we have perhaps never equalled. And, indeed, with the end of Chapman, Middleton, Webster, Tourneur, Donne we end a period when the intellect was immediately at the tips of the senses. Sensation became a word and word was sensation. The next period is the period of Milton (though still with a Marvell in it); and this period is initiated by Massinger.

128. Herbert John Clifford Grierson

1921

Grierson's anthology of metaphysical poems is remembered chiefly because it prompted T. S. Eliot's essay on the metaphysical poets. In fact Grierson's introductory appraisal raised just the issues which Eliot took up (*Metaphysical Lyrics and Poems of the Seventeenth Century: Donne to Butler,* 1921, pp. xiv–xli).

[Grierson makes no question of Donne's stature. He takes Donne for a poet of the highest order, one of the consummate masters of English writing whose strange effects are proper to great poetry when they express so vividly a temperament in which seemingly unlike impulses of our nature come together. He finds that Donne and his seventeenth-century heirs are metaphysical poets in a special way, and spends much of his introduction in pondering the distinction of their writing.

Grierson argues that the term 'metaphysical' is aptly used of the poems he presents.]

Donne is familiar with the definitions and distinctions of Mediaeval Scholasticism [and] is metaphysical not only in virtue of his scholasticism, but by his deep reflective interest in the experiences of which his poetry is the expression, the new psychological curiosity with which he writes of love and religion.

[The divine poets who followed Donne have each the inherited metaphysics of their Church. But none have for main theme a metaphysic like that of Epicurus or St Thomas.]

Donne, the most thoughtful and imaginative of them, is more aware of disintegration than of comprehensive harmony.

[He is acutely aware of the clash between the older physics and metaphysics and the new science of Copernicus, Galileo, Vesalius, Bacon.

Lucretius and Dante are metaphysical poets, Milton is a grand mythmaker. Grierson allows that Donne and his followers are not metaphysical in any such large way. But the word better describes the peculiar quality of their poetry than any other which has been proposed, such as 'fantastic'.]

It lays stress on the right things – the survival, one might say the reaccentuation, of the metaphysical strain, the *concetti metafisici ed ideali* as Tesi calls them in contrast to the simpler imagery of classical poetry, of mediaeval Italian poetry; the more intellectual, less verbal, character of their wit compared with the conceits of the Elizabethans; the finer psychology of which their conceits are often the expression; their learned imagery; the argumentative, subtle evolution of their lyrics; above all the peculiar blend of passion and thought, feeling and ratiocination which is their greatest achievement. Passionate thinking is always apt to become metaphysical, probing and investigating the experience from which it takes its rise. All these qualities are in the poetry of Donne, and Donne is the great master of English poetry in the seventeenth century. . . .

Donne's genius, temperament, and learning gave to his love poems certain qualities which immediately arrested attention and have given them ever since a power at once fascinating and disconcerting despite the faults of phrasing and harmony which, for a century after Dryden, obscured, and to some still outweigh, their poetic worth. The first of these is a depth and range of feeling unknown to the majority of Elizabethan sonneteers and song-writers. . . . Donne's treatment of love is entirely unconventional. . . . His songs are the expression in unconventional, witty language of all the moods of a lover that experience and imagination have taught him to understand – sensuality aerated by a brilliant wit; fascination and scornful anger inextricably blended.

[Grierson points out that a metaphysical strand had run through mediaeval love-poetry of which Elizabethan sonnets are descendants. This apprehension of love attained its fullest development in Dante and his school, became subordinated in Petrarch to rhetoric and subtleties of expression rather than thought, and then lost itself in the pseudo-metaphysical extravagances of Tebaldeo, Cariteo, Serafino. An old mode comes vividly back to life in a new age.]

Donne was no conscious reviver of the metaphysics of Dante, but to the game of elaborating fantastic conceits and hyperboles which was the fashion throughout Europe, be brought not only a full-blooded temperament and an acute mind, but a vast and growing store of the same scholastic learning, the same Catholic theology, as controlled Dante's thought, jostling already with the new learning of Copernicus and Paracelsus. The result is startling and disconcerting.

[He gives various examples of Donne's 'metaphysical' devices – the lovers as the legs of a pair of compasses, the definition of deity by negatives, the references to angels' knowledge, the quintessence of nothingness, the mixture of souls, the significance of numbers, the aerial bodies of angels, the phoenix, the mandrake root, alchemy, astronomy, the distinction between the king's real face and a stamped likeness of it. But the effect aimed for and secured is not entirely fantastic and erudite. The motive is the same as Shakespeare's in the metaphors of *Hamlet* and *Macbeth* – 'It is the same desire for vivid and dramatic expression.'

The final effect of every poem by Donne is bizarre and blended: 'yet very great poetry may be bizarre if it be the expression of a strangely blended temperament, an intense emotion, a vivid imagination'.

Then he goes on to justify Donne's 'harsh and rugged verse', which produces the effect of thought and feeling *breaking through* the prescribed pattern – as in the verse of Shakespeare's tragedies, 'bending and cracking the metrical pattern to the rhetoric of direct and vehement utterance'. The effect is]

not finally inharmonious. Donne's verse has a powerful and haunting harmony of its own. For Donne is not simply, no poet could be, willing to force his accent, to strain and crack a prescribed pattern; he is striving to find a rhythm that will express the passionate fullness of his mind, the fluxes and refluxes of his moods; and the felicities of verse are as frequent and startling as those of phrasing. He is one of the first masters, perhaps *the* first, of the elaborate stanza or paragraph in which the discords of individual lines or phrases are resolved in the complex and rhetorically effective harmony of the whole group of lines.

[Grierson claims that Donne's wrenching of accent 'has often both a rhetorical and a harmonious justification'. He refers to W. F. Melton's thesis,[1] and the devices by which Donne gets special effects of stress and assonance; and he concludes that Donne is our first great master of poetic rhetoric – poetry used for effects of oratory rather than of song, as Dryden and Pope would use it. The comparison with these smoother poets need not work to Donne's disadvantage.]

439

... the advance which Dryden achieved was secured by subordinating to oratory the more passionate and imaginative qualities which troubled the balance and movement of Donne's packed but imaginative rhetoric.

[Grierson allows that 'Donne's metaphysical eulogies and elegies and epistles are a hard nut to crack for his most sympathetic admirers'. Yet he finds that 'they have undeniable qualities' nonetheless.]

If some of the elegiac pieces are packed with tasteless and extravagant hyperboles, the Anniversaries (especially the second) remains, despite all its faults, one of the greatest poems on death in the language, the fullest record in our literature of the disintegrating collision in a sensitive mind of the old tradition and the new learning. Some of the invocational passages in *Of the Progresse of the Soule* are among the finest examples of his subtle and passionate thinking as well as of his most elaborate verse rhetoric.

[Donne's 'religious sonnets and songs' are 'the most intense and personal' of his poems after the love-songs and elegies. 'The two notes' of these poems 'are the Catholic and the personal.']

He is the first of our Anglo-Catholic poets, and he is our first intensely personal religious poet, expressing not the mind simply of the Christian as such, but the conflicts and longings of one troubled soul, one subtle and fantastic mind.

[He describes Donne's techniques in the *Holy Sonnets* and the rest, his individual phrasing and conceits, mediaeval Christian metaphysics, packed verse with bold irregular fingering, and echoing vowel sounds as in 'O might those *sighs* and tears return again'. Then he returns to distinguish Donne's poetic concerns.]

A metaphysical, a philosophical poet, to the degree to which even his contemporary Fulke Greville might be called such, Donne was not. The thought in his poetry is not his primary concern but the feeling. No scheme of thought, no interpretation of life became for him a complete and illuminating experience. The central theme of his poetry is ever his own intense personal moods, as a lover, a friend, an analyst of his own experiences worldly and religious. His philosophy cannot unify these experiences. It represents the re-

440

action of his restless and acute mind on the intense experience of the moment, a reading of it in the light now of one, now of another philosophical or theological dogma or thesis caught from his multifarious reading, developed with audacious paradox or more serious intention, as an expression, an illumination of that mood to himself and his reader. Whether one choose to call him a metaphysical or a fantastic poet, the stress must be laid on the word 'poet'. Whether verse or prose be his medium, Donne is always a poet, a creature of feeling and imagination, seeking expression in vivid phrase and complex harmonies, whose acute and subtle intellect was the servant, if sometimes the unruly servant, of passion and imagination.

[Grierson doubts if the Caroline court poets belong to a 'school of Donne', since they lack Donne's subtlety of mind, as well as 'what gives its interest to this subtle and fantastic misapplication of learning':]

the complexity of mood, the range of personal feeling which lends such fullness of life to Donne's strange and troubled poetry.

[He quotes lines 27–32 of Marvell's 'Coy Mistress', which are often taken for the very roof and crown of the metaphysical love-lyric, 'at once fantastic and passionate', and he comments:]

Donne is weightier, more complex, more suggestive of subtle and profound reaches of feeling, but he has not one single passage of the same length that combines all the distinctive qualities of the kind, in thought, in phrasing, in feeling, in music; and Rochester's most passionate lines are essentially simpler, less metaphysical. . . . The 'metaphysicals' of the seventeenth century combined two things, both soon to pass away, the fantastic dialectics of mediaeval love poetry and the 'simple, sensuous' strain which they caught from the classics – soul and body lightly yoked and glad to run and soar together in the winged chariot of Pegasus. Modern love poetry has too often sacrificed both to sentiment.

[Nonetheless, Donne's devout poetry goes deep, expressing a more agonized self-awareness than Herbert's.]

. . . there is no evidence in Herbert's most agitated verses of the deeper scars, the profounder remorse which gives such a passionate, anguished *timbre* to the harsh but resonant harmonies of his older friend's *Divine Poems.*

NOTE

1 See No. 75.

129. Thomas Stearns Eliot

1921

Anonymously reviewing H. J. C. Grierson's anthology of metaphysical poems, T. S. Eliot sought the qualities the Metaphysical poets have in common that distinguish them from later writers. Many passages of Eliot's essay refer to Donne or evidently have Donne in view ('The Metaphysical Poets', *Times Literary Supplement,* pp. 669–70. Eliot reprinted the review as an essay in his *Selected Essays,* 1932).

By collecting these poems from the work of a generation more often named than read, and more often read than profitably studied, Professor Grierson has rendered a service of some importance ... we think that he was right in including so many poems of Donne, elsewhere (though not in many editions) accessible, as documents in the case of 'metaphysical poetry'. The phrase has long done duty as a term of abuse, or as the label of a quaint and pleasant taste. . . .

Not only is it extremely difficult to define metaphysical poetry, but difficult to decide what poets practise it and in which of their verses. The poetry of Donne (to whom Marvell and Bishop King are sometimes nearer than any of the other authors) is late Elizabethan, its feeling often very close to that of Chapman. . . .

Donne, and often Cowley, employ a device which is sometimes

442

considered characteristically 'metaphysical'; the elaboration (contrasted with the condensation) of a figure of speech to the furthest stage to which ingenuity can carry it. Thus Cowley develops the commonplace comparison of the world to a chess-board through long stanzas (*To Destiny*), and Donne, with more grace, in *A Valediction*, the comparison of two lovers to a pair of compasses. But elsewhere we find, instead of the mere explication of the content of a comparison, a development by rapid association of thought which requires considerable agility on the part of the reader.

[He quotes the whole of the second stanza of 'A Valediction: Of Weeping'.]

Here we find at least two connexions which are not implicit in the first figure, but are forced upon it by the poet: from the geographer's globe to the tear, and the tear to the deluge. On the other hand, some of Donne's most successful and characteristic effects are secured by brief words and sudden contrasts:

A bracelet of bright hair about the bone,

where the most powerful effect is produced by the sudden contrast of associations of 'bright hair' and of 'bone'. This telescoping of images and multiplied associations is characteristic of the phrase of some of the dramatists of the period which Donne knew: not to mention Shakespeare, it is frequent in Middleton, Webster, and Tourneur, and is one of the sources of the vitality of their language.

Johnson, who employed the term 'metaphysical poets', apparently having Donne, Cleveland, and Cowley chiefly in mind, remarks of them that 'the most heterogeneous ideas are yoked by violence together'. The force of this impeachment lies in the failure of the conjunction, the fact that often the ideas are yoked but not united; and if we are to judge of styles of poetry by their abuse, enough examples may be found in Cleveland to justify Johnson's condemnation. But a degree of heterogeneity of material compelled into unity by the operation of the poet's mind is omnipresent in poetry.

[He gives examples from eighteenth- and nineteenth-century poetry, including some lines from Johnson's *The Vanity of Human Wishes*, then goes on to show that in some of the finest of 'metaphysical' poetry there is nothing that fits 'Johnson's general observations on the metaphysical poets in his essay on Cowley'.]

If so shrewd and sensitive (though so limited) a critic as Johnson failed to define metaphysical poetry by its faults, it is worth while to inquire whether we may not have more success by adopting the opposite method: by assuming that the poets of the seventeenth century (up to the Revolution) were the direct and normal development of the precedent age; and, without prejudicing their case by the adjective 'metaphysical', consider whether their virtue was not something permanently valuable, which subsequently disappeared, but ought not to have disappeared. Johnson has hit, perhaps by accident, on one of their peculiarities, when he observes that 'their attempts were always analytic'; he would not agree that, after the dissociation, they put the material together again in a new unity.

It is certain that the dramatic verse of the later Elizabethan and early Jacobean poets expresses a degree of development of sensibility which is not found in any of the prose, good as it often is. If we except Marlowe, a man of prodigious intelligence, these dramatists were directly or indirectly (it is at least a tenable theory) affected by Montaigne. Even if we except also Jonson and Chapman, these two were notably erudite, and were notably men who incorporated their erudition into their sensibility: their mode of feeling was directly and freshly altered by their reading and thought. In Chapman especially there is a direct sensuous apprehension of thought, or a recreation of thought into feeling, which is exactly what we find in Donne.

[He gives a passage from Chapman and compares it with passages from Browning and Tennyson.]

The difference is not a simple difference of degree between poets. It is something which had happened to the mind of England between the time of Donne or Lord Herbert of Cherbury and the time of Tennyson and Browning; it is the difference between the intellectual poet and the reflective poet. Tennyson and Browning are poets, and they think; but they do not feel their thought as immediately as the odour of a rose. A thought to Donne was an experience; it modified his sensibility. When a poet's mind is perfectly equipped for its work, it is constantly amalgamating disparate experience; the ordinary man's experience is chaotic, irregular, fragmentary. The latter falls in love, or reads Spinoza, and these two experiences have nothing to do with each other, or with the noise of the typewriter or the smell of cooking; in the mind of the poet these experiences are always forming new wholes.

We may express the difference by the following theory: The poets of the seventeenth century, the successors of the dramatists of the sixteenth, possessed a mechanism of sensibility which could devour any kind of experience. They are simple, artificial, difficult, or fantastic, as their predecessors were; no less nor more than Dante, Guido Cavalcanti, Guinicelli, or Cino. In the seventeenth century a dissociation of sensibility set in, from which we have never recovered; and this dissociation, as is natural, was aggravated by the influence of the two most powerful poets of the century, Milton and Dryden. Each of these men performed certain poetic functions so magnificently well that the magnitude of the effect concealed the absence of others. The language went on and in some respects improved; the best verse of Collins, Gray, Johnson, and even Goldsmith satisfies some of our fastidious demands better than that of Donne or Marvell or King. But while the language became more refined, the feeling became more crude. The feeling, the sensibility, expressed in the *Country Churchyard* (to say nothing of Tennyson and Browning) is cruder than that in the *Coy Mistress.*

The second effect of the influence of Milton and Dryden followed from the first, and was therefore slow in manifestation. The sentimental age began early in the eighteenth century, and continued. The poets revolted against the ratiocinative, the descriptive; they thought and felt by fits, unbalanced; they reflected. In one or two passages of Shelley's *Triumph of Life*, in the second *Hyperion*, there are traces of a struggle toward unification of sensibility. But Keats and Shelley died, and Tennyson and Browning ruminated.

After this brief exposition of a theory – too brief, perhaps, to carry conviction – we may ask, what would have been the fate of the 'metaphysical' had the current of poetry descended in a direct line from them, as it descended in a direct line to them? They would not, certainly, be classified as metaphysical. The possible interests of a poet are unlimited; the more intelligent he is the better; the more intelligent he is the more likely that he will have interests: our only condition is that he turn them into poetry, and not merely meditate on them poetically. A philosophical theory which has entered into poetry is established, for its truth or falsity in one sense ceases to matter, and its truth in another sense is proved. The poets in question have, like other poets, various faults. But they were, at best, engaged in the task of trying to find the verbal equivalent for states of mind and feeling. And this means both that they are more mature, and that they wear better, than later poets of certainly not less literary ability.

It is not a permanent necessity that poets should be interested in philosophy, or in any other subject. We can only say that it appears likely that poets in our civilization, as it exists at present, must be *difficult*. Our civilization comprehends great variety and complexity, playing upon a refined sensibility, must produce various and complex results. The poet must become more and more comprehensive, more allusive, more indirect, in order to force, to dislocate if necessary, language into his meaning. . . .

Jules Laforgue, and Tristan Corbière in many of his poems, are nearer to the 'school of Donne' than any modern English poet. But poets more classical than they have the same essential quality of transmuting ideas into sensations, of transforming an observation into a state of mind. . . .

In French literature the great master of the seventeenth century – Racine – and the great master of the nineteenth – Baudelaire – are in some ways more like each other than they are like anyone else. The greatest two masters of diction are also the greatest two psychologists, the most curious explorers of the soul. It is interesting to speculate whether it is not a misfortune that two of the greatest masters of diction in our language, Milton and Dryden, triumph with a dazzling disregard of the soul. If we continued to produce Miltons and Drydens it might not so much matter, but as things are it is a pity that English poetry has remained so incomplete. Those who object to the 'artificiality' of Milton or Dryden sometimes tell us to 'look into our hearts and write'. But that is not looking deep enough; Racine or Donne looked into a good deal more than the heart. One must look into the cerebral cortex, the nervous system, and the digestive tracts.

May we not conclude, then, that Donne, Crashaw, Vaughan, Herbert and Lord Herbert, Marvell, King, Cowley at his best, are in the direct current of English poetry, and that their faults should be reprimanded by this standard rather than coddled by antiquarian affection? They have been enough praised in terms which are implicit limitations because they are 'metaphysical' or 'witty', 'quaint' or 'obscure', though at their best they have not these attributes more than other serious poets. On the other hand, we must not reject the criticism of Johnson (a dangerous person to disagree with) without having mastered it, without having assimilated the Johnsonian canons of taste. In reading the celebrated passage in his essay on Cowley we must remember that by wit he clearly means something more serious than we usually mean to-day; in his criticism of their versification we must remember in what a narrow discipline he was trained, but also how well trained; we must remember that Johnson tortures chiefly the chief offenders, Cowley and Cleveland. It would be a fruitful work, and one requiring a substantial book, to break up the classification of Johnson (for there has been none since) and exhibit these poets in all their difference of kind and of degree, from the massive music of Donne to the faint, pleasing tinkle of Aurelian Townshend – whose *Dialogue between a Pilgrim and Time* is one of the few regrettable omissions from the excellent anthology of Professor Grierson.

130. George Edward Bateman Saintsbury/Thomas Stearns Eliot

1921

In a letter to the *Times Literary Supplement*, George Saintsbury replied to the anonymous reviewer of Grierson's *Metaphysical Poetry* (i.e. T. S. Eliot), taking up the reviewer's comments on Johnson's use of the term 'metaphysical'. A courteous exchange of views then ensued. (*Times Literary Supplement*, 27 October 1921, p. 698; 3 November 1921, p. 716; 10 November 1921, p. 734).

[Saintsbury remarks that there is no such word in Greek as 'metaphysical', which Dryden was well aware of when he applied the word to Donne and the rest.]

What Dryden directly opposes to 'the metaphysics' is 'nature'. Now, Dryden was a much better read man than some people have chosen to think; and he, no doubt, knew that there is no such word in Greek as μεταφυσικος, and that, traditionally, the title of Aristotle's treatise comes from a catalogue-entry by some one shirking a definition of the contents τὰ μετὰ τὰ φυσικά, 'that which comes after the physics'. Now he might very easily shift the last word from the title of a book about nature to its literal sense of 'natural things', and so use 'metaphysics' as equivalent to 'second thoughts', things that come *after* the natural first; and, once more, this definition would, I think, fit all the poetry commonly called 'metaphysical', whether it be amatory, religious, satirical, panegyric, or merely trifling; while 'philosophical', though of course not seldom suitable enough, sometimes has no relevance whatever.

No matter what they are dealing with, these poets always 'go behind' the first, simple, obvious, natural thought and expression of thought.

He offers an anecdote about an undergraduate friend of his who had argued scornfully that Swinburne first wrote his line 'Time with a gift of tears, Grief with a glass that ran', the other way round and then just turned it about 'to make fools like you admire'. Saintsbury argues that this was a general method in the short time of the flourishing of the metaphysical poets.

[T. S. Eliot replied in the following issue, signing himself *Contributor*.]

I only regret that the conclusion to be drawn from Mr Saintsbury's letter appears to contradict my own conclusions from the study of Caroline verse. Mr Saintsbury appears to believe that these poets represent not merely a generation, but almost a particular theory of poetry. The 'second thoughts' to which he alludes are, I think, and as I tried to point out, frequent in the work of many other poets besides, of other times and other languages. I have mentioned Chapman, and the contemporaries of Dante. I do not believe that the author of *Hamlet* and *Measure for Measure* was invariably satisfied with 'the first simple, obvious natural thought and expression of thought'; or that the author of the 'Phoenix and Turtle' whistled as he went for want of thought. Nor can I believe that Swinburne thought twice, or even *once*, before he wrote.

[Saintsbury replied a week later.]

May I suggest ... that there is no *real* contradiction between us? I fully agree with him that, in the great examples he quotes, and perhaps in all similar things, there *is* 'second thought'. I might even go so far as to say – indeed, I meant to hint this in my last sentence – that all true poetry must be in a way second thought, though much second thought is not in any way poetry. What I was endeavouring to point out was that *in this period*, the quest of the second thought became deliberate, a business, almost itself a *first* thought.

131. Edmund Gosse

1921

Gosse wrote a number of book reviews for the *Sunday Times*, a collection of which was republished as *Books on the Table* (London, 1921). Gosse's review of Logan Pearsall Smith's selection of Donne's *Sermons* is titled 'The Sepulchral Dean'. It occupies four pages, a brevity for which Gosse offers no apology: 'Books, very properly, have to be satisfied with what crumbs of space may fall from the platters of Football and the League of Nations' (*Books on the Table*, 1921, pp. 185–9).

Gosse sketches the growth of Donne's popularity since the eighteenth century, mentioning several landmarks in the understanding of Donne. Izaak Walton's memoir is, according to Gosse]

perhaps the most sparkling and the most picturesque life written in the seventeenth century, but ... though ... an English classic, is now discovered to have been seriously defective as to facts.

[Donne was ignored, or misrepresented, by the critics of the eighteenth century. By those of the beginning of the nineteenth he was consistently disregarded, except by Coleridge, who was 'alternately attracted and repelled by him', and whose series of disconnected notes 'illustrate the mind of Coleridge much more correctly than that of Donne'. The attention given to Donne's poems culminated in 'the two volumes published at the Clarendon Press by Professor Grierson in 1912', a model of 'elegant erudition'. Gosse suggests, however, that the recent steady growth of Donne's stature as a poet]

has not been founded so much upon pedantic curiosity ... as upon the extraordinary attraction which he offers to young readers of a serious and enthusiastic turn of mind. There is no other English writer so passionate, so sensual, so perversely sardonic as Donne. This violent emotion was combined with a 'scholastic, almost a mediaeval, temperament' producing 'a fascination which is particularly potent among youthful readers'.]

But while the verse of Donne has now become assured of a foremost place in all intelligent study of our literature, his prose has hitherto suffered from an almost complete indifference.... [But] the world ... is to be excused if, while clasping Donne to its heart as a poet, it has been content to take him for granted as a prose-writer.

[Gosse records that his own experience of reading Donne's correspondence left him]

often on the point of breaking down, not merely under the pressure of the obscure mass, but under the intense irritation caused by some features of Donne's character. Often, for pages after pages, the form is so tortured, the sentiment so remote, the emotion so pitiless and inquisitorial, that human nature, in its lax modern moods, seems unable to support the strain of all this crabbed and obsolete invective. He wrote most detestable prose in an age which had not yet strained the language of common life through the jelly-bag. All the torrent which poured from his lips ... was turbid with the refuse of scholastic Latin, and stained with the experiments of an English still unrefined. [Though] Donne is perhaps worse than the rest in certain qualities and relations ... he is better than almost all at certain moments of inspiration and glory.

[Of Smith's selection Gosse says:]

out of the howling wilderness of Donne's Sermons he has created an artificial paradise for us by extracting all the oases, and arranging them side by side.

450

132. Stuart Petre Brodie Mais
1921

S. P. B. Mais (1885–1975) worked for radio and television, was a schoolmaster, novelist and freelance journalist and became Professor of English at the RAF Cadet College. He was an amazingly prolific witer, on subjects from literature to travel and wildlife. In a collection of essays on English and European authors, he gave a brief account of Donne (*Why We Should Read*, 1921, pp. 51–7).

[The avowed aim of Mais's essays is to introduce these authors to new readers by communicating the pleasure of reading them. Mais scorns the idea of critical judgement; yet he rounds up opinions of Donne's writing, from Walton to the modern commentators such as Saintsbury, Pearsall Smith, Rupert Brooke, Robert Lynd. He quotes highlights of the sermons, culled from Pearsall Smith, and the customary beauties from the *Songs and Sonnets* and *Anniversaries*. He offers the view that Donne is important as a poet]

because he treats of the universal passion of love in more phases than any other poet. He was the complete experimentalist in love, both in actual life and in his work. He is frankly in search of bodily experience.

[Then follows a string of illustrations from the *Elegies* and *Songs and Sonnets*, with simple descriptive comments. Mais occasionally ventures an observation of his own: 'There is a good deal of frank naturalism in the elegy entitled 'To His Mistress Going to Bed', but it is healthily coarse, though scarcely quotable in these times, which is a pity. He offers his impression that all Donne's experimenting in love came together in the end in 'an abiding love for one person, Ann More, his wife'. He quotes bits of 'The Ecstasy', the *Anniversary*, 'Break of Day', and 'The Dream', supposedly to attest this love. Then he essays a balanced recommendation.]

There is enough nastiness, eccentricity, coarseness, roughness and extravagance in Donne to put off many fastidious readers: but his faults lie open to the sky: his beauties are frequently hidden, but they are worth searching for. . . . We read Donne, then, for his fiery imagination, for his deep and subtle analysis, for his humanity, for his passion, for his anti-sentimentalism, for his eager search 'to find a north-west passage of his own' in intellect and morals, for the richness and rarity of the gems with which all his work, both prose and poetry, is studded, for his modernity and freshness. We read Donne as a corrective of lazy thinking: he frees us from illusion.

133. John Sampson

1921

John Sampson (1862–1931) was a Romany scholar, a comparative philologist and the first Librarian of the University of Liverpool. He wrote an essay about laudatory annotations by one 'G. O.' which he found in the 1639 edition of Donne's poems[1] ('A Contemporary Light upon John Donne', *Essays and Studies by Members of the English Association*, 7 (1921), 82–107).

[Sampson finds in G.O.'s near-contemporary commentary a help to a true appraisal of Donne's poems.]

NOTE

1 See *John Donne: The Critical Heritage*, vol. I, ed. A. J. Smith (London: Routledge and Kegan Paul, 1975), pp. 127–9.

134. Elbert Nevius Sebring Thompson

1921

E. N. S. Thompson (1877–1948) was Professor of English
Literature at the State University of Iowa from 1921. He
published a number of books on Renaissance subjects, including *Controversy between the Puritans and the Stage*, *Literary
Bypaths of the Renaissance* and *The English Essay of the Seventeenth
Century*. He also compiled a *Topical Bibliography of Milton*. In
a lengthy survey of mysticism in seventeenth-century English
writing, largely about Thomas Traherne and the Vaughan
twins, he devoted several pages to Donne ('Mysticism in
Seventeenth-Century English Literature', *Studies in Philology*,
18 (1921), 170–231).

[Thompson takes mysticism to include any impulse which seeks an
order of reality beyond the physical order; and so Donne must be
allowed his mystical strivings despite the strong appearance to the
contrary.]

Of all the poets of the Jacobean age Donne would be least suspected
of a mystical turn of mind. His keen restless intellect, his constant
dependence on the external features of daily life for his illustrative
material, as well as his open cynicism and irreverence in the *Elegies*
and *Songs*, would isolate him, necessarily it appears, from the
spiritual forces of the day. This, however, was not the case. Cynicism,
impudent ribaldry, realism tingle in his early verse. Yet not even
Browning recognised more unqualifiedly than Donne that the life
of the spirit is the matter of sole moment to man. 'I wonder by my
troth, what thou and I / Did, till we loved?' he asks, forgetful of
all the soul-stirring episodes of his venturesome youth. This was not
because Donne scorned or despised our bodies [he quotes lines
53–6 of 'The Ecstasy']. But the spirit's welfare seemed of greater
importance than the body's.

[The writer argues that Donne's very conception of love has
something mystical about it when it posits that the passion of true
love can inseparably unite two lovers. He quotes 'The Ecstasy' and
'A Valediction: Of Weeping', and comments:]

453

Love . . . is a passion of the heart that raises man above the limiting conditions of physical existence into the freedom of the spiritual world. And by mental energy even God and man are united; for God is both the ultimate end of knowledge and the source of knowledge in man [he quotes from *The Second Anniversary*]. Therefore Donne could disregard material good fortune or ill fortune [he quotes from *The First Anniversary*]. If this conviction be one of the foundation stones of Donne's poetry, the transition after all is not hard from the secular poems of his youth to the finest of his sacred verse, 'At the round earth's imagined corners, blow' and 'Death be not proud'.

[He allows that in notable respects Donne's habits of thought and temperament are alien to the mystics. Donne believed that faith comes by reason, and mistrusted sudden conversions and illuminations. Yet his sermons show his fascination with St Paul's supernatural way to God (the sermons are quoted). Then a single line in 'A Valediction: Of the Book' conveys the whole essence of the mystic's faith – 'since all divinity/ Is love or wonder'.]

135. Arthur Hobart Nethercot

1922

A. H. Nethercot of Northwestern University made a sustained scholarly attempt to map the reputation of the Metaphysical poets, which included the writing of books on *Abraham Cowley* and *The Attitude toward Metaphysical Poetry in Neo-classical England*. In an essay published in *Modern Language Notes*, he traced the lineage of the designation itself ('The Term "Metaphysical Poets" before Johnson', *Modern Language Notes*, 37 (1922), 11–17).

[Nethercot finds uses of the term 'metaphysical' in Italian and English writings of the seventeenth and eighteenth centuries, in reference to the conceited manner of such poets as Petrarch, Marino, Donne, Davenant and Cowley. He shows that the term was well established by the time Johnson used it to characterize a school of seventeenth-century poets.]

136. Arthur Hobart Nethercot
1922

A. H. Nethercot sought to explain the reversal of attitudes towards Donne's versification which has come about in the present century, playing off recent high praise of Donne's haunting rhythms against traditional disparagements of his harshness ('The Reputation of John Donne as Metrist', *Sewanee Review,* 30 (1922), 463–74).

[Nethercot points out that the censurers from Dryden's time on tended to concentrate their attacks on Donne's satires, and gives a full account of the adverse commentaries down to 1900, also noting the few commentators who acknowledge that Donne can be perfectly harmonious in his lyric poems and in the *Metempsychosis.*

He traces the development of a true understanding of Donne's metrics from Carew through Coleridge and Browning down to W. F. Melton. Yet he is struck by the general advance in sympathy for Donne's idiom which has come about between 1906 and 1922. Without question, Donne's 'position is stronger than ever', just because he speaks directly to our times.]

For Donne was essentially a modern poet. One can imagine him in complete sympathy with the realists, imagists, and vers librists of the last decade and a half. 'Hardness', 'the exact word', 'intensity', 'no compromise with public taste', 'accommodation of metre to sense', 'the deeper, subtler rhythms of common speech', etc., etc., – these all seemed to be cardinal articles in Donne's poetical creed. The contemporary revival of interest in the whole group of 'Metaphysical' poets has concentrated on Donne and has not neglected his metrics. Readers of all classes have been attracted and piqued by him. Poets like J. C. Squire and T. S. Eliot have been called (sometimes, indeed, with overstatements of the case) 'Metaphysical' in both style and substance; and so have Hardy and Meredith. Richard Aldington, a true classicist among vers librists, often mentions Donne and Cowley in his criticisms; and even such American poets of the youngest generation as Glenway Westcott have been carried away by Donne's religious sonnets. A friend of mine – an amateur poet (for he 'has published nothing as yet'), who reads verse with the long, chanting cadence so popular today – was overjoyed to pick up Grierson's edition of Donne at half price, and I have already noticed the influence of Donne's metre in some of his more chameleon-like work. The literary critics of the newspapers – as, for instance, Llewellyn Jones of the *Chicago Post* – frequently refer to Donne and his metrical style. Nor, finally, have the schools overlooked him, for many college students and teachers of my acquaintance have shown themselves fascinated both by what he has to say and by the manner and form in which he says it.

[Nethercot points out that even the conversational rhythms of the satires offer a model for modern poets.]

Today it is not quite such a criminal offence as it was in the eighteenth century to draw upon the resources of less obvious prose rhythm for true poetical metrical effects. 'Free verse', having squandered its overflow of vitality in excess, is beginning to settle down and adjust and combine itself with the older metres; and this combination is exactly what we find in Donne. Is it any wonder, then, that Donne is becoming more and more widely read for his technique, just as he and the other 'Metaphysical' poets are also being read for their substance?

137. William Butler Yeats

1922

Speaking of the aims he shared with his fellow-artists in the 1890s, Yeats showed why he admired Donne ('The Tragic Generation', in *The Trembling of the Veil*, 1922; reprinted in *Autobiographies*, 1961, p. 326).

The critic might well reply that certain of my generation delighted in writing with an unscientific partiality for subjects long forbidden. Yet is it not most important to explore especially what has been long forbidden, and to do this not only 'with the highest moral purpose', like the followers of Ibsen, but gaily, out of sheer mischief, or sheer delight in that play of the mind? Donne could be as metaphysical as he pleased, and yet never seemed unhuman and hysterical as Shelley often does, because he could be as physical as he pleased; and besides, who will thirst for the metaphysical, who have a parched tongue, if we cannot recover the Vision of Evil?

I have felt in certain early works of my own which I have long abandoned, and here and there in the work of others of my generation, a slight, sentimental sensuality which is disagreeable, and does not exist in the work of Donne, let us say, because he, being permitted to say what he pleased, was never tempted to linger, or rather to pretend that we can linger, between spirit and sense. How often had I heard men of my time talk of the meeting of spirit and sense, yet there is no meeting but only change upon the instant, and it is by the perception of a change, like the sudden 'blacking out' of the lights of the stage, that passion creates its most violent sensation.

138. Robert Seymour Bridges

1922

Edward Thompson, a friend and neighbour of Robert Bridges, remarked that he knew no one who was so sensitive about human physical suffering. Bridges had trained and worked as a doctor in London hospitals; his comprehension of physical pain influenced his religious views, making him regard ideas of hell as abhorrent human inventions which should be disregarded in the formation of modern religious doctrines incorporating scientific understanding. Bridges referred privately to *The Testament of Beauty*, the long poem in which he set out his religious beliefs, as 'De Hominum Natura', in tribute to the *De rerum natura*, Lucretius' sceptical metaphysical picture using the science of his day. In a letter to H. J. C. Grierson, Bridges disparages puns in Shakespeare and Donne in the face of Grierson's attempts to justify them. He took the opportunity to explain why he found Donne himself so uncongenial (*The Selected Letters of Robert Bridges*, ed. D. E. Stanford, vol. II, 1984, p. 782).

I naturally very much dislike 'humans' who are afraid of Hell. I feel Lucretian on that topic, and I also dislike the Phallic tribe, wherefore I have little sympathy with Donne as a human: and am no doubt severe on him or towards him.

139. Thomas Stearns Eliot

1923

Eliot returned to ponder Donne's particular interest for modern readers in a review of the Nonesuch *Love Poems of John Donne* ('John Donne', *Nation and Athenaeum*, 9 June 1923, pp. 331–2).

The appearance of a very fine edition of Donne's love poems provokes an inquiry into the reasons for Donne's present popularity; for it is such an edition as only a poet highly esteemed by a prosperous public could receive. For the production, the Nonesuch Press deserves every compliment; for the compilation, there are only two reserves to be made. It is questionable whether the love poems should be published separately from the rest of Donne's poems; and it is questionable whether an editor ought to tamper with the sequence in which the poems are printed. If these two licences are allowed – that of selection and that of order – it may be admitted that the editor of this volume has shown excellent taste (though the present writer prefers to see 'The Relic' and 'The Funeral', the first verses of which are variations of the same theme, printed farther apart). But selection and order represent a criticism, the imposition of a critical taste upon the reader; it was by such means that Matthew Arnold, in a volume which still supplies to many readers their only knowledge of Wordsworth, imposed a criticism upon the nineteenth century. For Donne the danger is much less: he is less difficult and less voluminous than Wordsworth, and most of his admirers, we presume, already own the Muses' Library edition. But the arrangement made, and very neatly made, in this volume is a kind of pigeon-holing of Donne's sentiments.

First in order come the great love poems, expressing absolute, static and ecstatic love; then, the lighter ones on wooing and winning and the joy of the senses; then, those that deal with parting and grief; then, the more or less disillusioned and cynical analyses of love and lovers; and finally, the way in which earthly and heavenly love are contrasted – and compared.

So much for the order. As for the selection, the editor explains: –

The selection has been confined to Donne's subjective poetry and does not include any of the conventional complimentary Letters and Epithalamia, which were made to order after the fashion of his time.

Both these statements contain interesting critical judgments; and, as all critical judgments excite criticism, we may be allowed to hold these up to question. One of the characteristics of Donne which wins him, I fancy, his interest for the present age, is his fidelity to emotion as he finds it; his recognition of the complexity of feeling and its rapid alterations and antitheses. A change of feeling, with Donne, is rather the regrouping of the same elements under a mood which was previously subordinate: it is not the substitution of one mood for a wholly different one. As an example of the latter process, we may take 'Don Juan', turn to 'The Isles of Greece', and observe the shift of tone after that splendid piece of nationalist propaganda –

> Thus sung, or would or could or should have sung,
> The modern Greek, in tolerable verse.

Byron's 'effective' change here is not only a theatrical effect: it is callowness masquerading as maturity of cynicism; it represents an uninteresting mind, and a disorderly one. Compare it with those of Baudelaire, certainly a master of surprises: in the French poet every new mood is prepared by and implicit in the preceding mood – the mind has unity and order. And so with Donne. Impossible to isolate his ecstasy, his sensuality, and his cynicism.

Impossible, furthermore, to isolate what is 'conventional' in Donne from what is individual. If the 'Autumnal', which is included in this volume, be admitted to be a love poem, are we yet safe in separating it from 'conventional complimentary' poems? Such separation can only be made, at best, by appeal to biographical data, which are, for the literary value, irrelevant. The epithet 'conventional', like the epithet 'tour de force', is equally easy and dangerous to apply: it might be made a censor for some, if not all, of Shakespeare's sonnets. The editor would have been on safer ground, had he said bluntly that some of Donne's verse is insignificant. With sincerity in the practical sense, poetry has little to do; the poet is responsible to a much more difficult consciousness and honesty. And it is because he has this honesty, because he is so often expressing his genuine whole of tangled feelings, that Donne is, like the early Italians, like Heine, like Baudelaire, a poet of the world's literature.

There are two ways in which we may find a poet to be modern: he may have made a statement which is true everywhere and for all time (so far as 'everywhere' and 'for all time' have meaning), or there may be an accidental relationship between his mind and our own. The latter is fashion; we are all susceptible to fashion in literature as in everything else, and we all require some indulgence for it. The age of Donne, and the age of Marvell, are sympathetic to us, and it demands a considerable effort of dissociation to decide to what degree we are deflected toward him by local or temporary bias. The question is all the more puzzling because Donne's popularity is neither recent nor limited: he has been approved, for many years, by Mr Edmund Gosse and Professor Le Roy Barron Briggs; and he receives close attention from some of the most interesting younger poets. And again, it is impossible to say to what extent the interest in Jacobean and Caroline poetry is not due to Mr Saintsbury – whose catholicity of taste is beyond a doubt. It is difficult, and indeed irrelevant, to discover why any one critic admires Donne; one is content to believe that they all appreciate his excellence. But it is possible to conjecture why Donne should be fashionable, as well as appreciated, in the present age.

The age objects to the heroic and sublime, and it objects to the simplification and separation of the mental faculties. The objections are largely well grounded, and react against the nineteenth century; they are partly – how far I do not inquire – a product of the popularization of the study of mental phenomena. Ethics having been eclipsed by psychology, we accept the belief that any state of mind is extremely complex, and chiefly composed of odds and ends in constant flux manipulated by desire and fear. When, therefore, we find a poet who neither suppresses nor falsifies, and who expresses complicated states of mind, we give him welcome. And when we find his poetry containing everywhere potential or actual wit, our thirst has been relieved. To inquire why we now demand the presence of wit in poetry – or of something for which this seventeenth-century term has been revived.

The process which has carried us so far will carry us farther. The heroic and sublime, banished as reality, we take back as myth: Mr Bloom is Ulysses. The pursuit of mental states is likely to bring us to the farthest extreme from the realism of the later nineteenth century. But, meanwhile, those who take Donne as a contemporary will be taking him as a fashion only. Neither the fantastic (Cleveland-ism is becoming popular) nor the cynical nor the sensual occupies an excessive importance with Donne; the elements in his mind had an order and congruity. The range of his feeling was great, but no more remarkable than its unity. He was altogether present in every thought and in every feeling. It is the same kind of unity as pervades the work of Chapman, for whom thought is an intense feeling which is one with every other feeling. Compared with these men, almost every nineteenth-century English poet is in some way limited or deformed. It is this limitation which makes them seem to us in some way immature, and which, while it allows them to occupy an important place in English literature, deprives most of their work

461

of a place in the literature of the world. And when their poetry pretended the most licence it was – as Swinburne's or Dowson's – the most restricted.

Our appreciation of Donne must be an appreciation of what we lack, as well as of what we have in common with him. What is true of his mind is true, in different terms, of his language and versification. A style, a rhythm, to be significant, must embody a significant mind, must be produced by the necessity of a new form for a new content. For this reason the extraordinary virtuosity of Tennyson is of little use to us. And for this reason, I suspect, most contemporary verse is so uninteresting in rhythm and so poor or so extravagant in vocabulary. The labour of composition for a poet to-day is very great, and the amount of time that he must expend on experiment unlimited. Verse and language have not kept up with economic progress, and have halted behind the development of sensibility. The dogmatic slumbers of the last hundred years are broken, and the chaos must be faced: we cannot return to sleep and call it order, and we cannot have any order but our own, but from Donne and his contemporaries we can draw instruction and encouragement.

APPENDIX A. Publication of Donne's poems since 1922

Only complete editions and collections containing a substantial number of Donne's poems have been included. A fuller listing, with more bibliographical detail of many of the books before 1972, can be found in Geoffrey Keynes's *Bibliography* (Oxford, 1973).

1922   *Selection from John Donne.* London: Medici Society.
1923   *Selections from John Donne.* London: Medici Society.
       Love Poems of John Donne, with some account of his life taken from the writings in 1639 of Izaak Walton. London: Nonesuch Press; and a special edition in Fell types by Oxford University Press.
1926   *Selections from John Donne.* London [etc.]: Medici Society.
       Poems, ed. E. K. Chambers; introd. George Saintsbury. London: G. Routledge and Sons.
1927   *John Donne*, ed Humbert Wolfe, The Augustan Books of English Poetry, 2nd ser. 1. London: Ernest Benn.
1928   *John Donne: Selected Shorter Poems*, ed. G. D. H. and M. I. Cole, Ormond Poets 7. London: Noel Douglas.
1929   *John Donne Dean of St Paul's Complete Poetry and Selected Prose*, ed. John Hayward. London: Nonesuch Press.
       The Poems of John Donne, ed. H. J. C. Grierson, London: Oxford University Press (revised version of his 1912 edition; reprinted many times).
1930   *John Donne Dean of St Paul's Complete Poetry and Selected Prose*, ed. John Hayward. Bloomsbury: Nonesuch Press (revised version of his 1929 edition; frequently reprinted).
1931   *The Poems of John Donne*, ed. Hugh l'Anson Fausset, Everyman's Library 867. London and Toronto: J. M. Dent and Sons; New York: E. P. Dutton and Co.

1933   Reprint of *Poems,* ed. Sir Herbert Grierson, 1929.

1937   *The Love Poems of John Donne Dean of St Paul's,* Zodiac Books 3. London: Chatto and Windus (reprinted a number of times).

1938   *Holy Sonnets,* ed. Hugh l'Anson Fausset; engravings by Eric Gill. London: J. M. Dent and Sons for Hague and Gill Ltd (uses Grierson's 1929 text).

Poetry and Prose of John Donne, sel. and ed. A. Desmond Hawkins, Nelson Classics. London: Thomas Nelson and Sons.

1941   *The Complete Poetry and Selected Prose of John Donne & The Complete Poetry of William Blake,* with an Introduction by Robert Silliman Hillyer. New York: Random House. (The text of Donne is that of John Hayward's 1930 edition).

1942   *The Complete Poems of John Donne,* ed. Roger E. Bennett, University Classics. Chicago: Packard and Co.

1946   *John Donne: Selected Poetry and Prose, with Izaac Walton's Life and Appreciations by Ben Jonson, Dryden, Coleridge and others,* ed. H. W. Garrod. Oxford: Clarendon Press.

John Donne: Selected Poems, ed. Clara Eggink. Amsterdam: A. A. Balkema (uses John Hayward's 1930 text).

Love Poems of John Donne together with the Devotion 'For whom the Bell Tolls'. Mount Vernon, NY: Peter Pauper Press.

Selected Poetry and Prose of John Donne, ed. Walter Sydney Scott. London: John Westhouse.

1948   *The Love Poems of Robert Herrick and John Donne,* ed. Louis Untermeyer. New Brunswick, NJ: Rutgers University Press.

1950   *John Donne: A Selection of his Poetry,* ed. John Hayward. Harmondsworth: Penguin.

1951   *John Donne: Love Poems including Songs and Sonets and Elegies.* Mount Vernon, NY: Peter Pauper Press.

1952   *The Complete Poetry and Selected Prose of John Donne,* ed. Charles M. Coffin, Modern Library. New York: Random House (uses John Hayward's 1930 text).

John Donne: The Divine Poems, ed. Helen Gardner. Oxford: Clarendon Press (revised edition 1966).

John Donne: Selected Poems, ed. James Reeves. Melbourne, London and Toronto: William Heinemann.

1953   *John Donne: Divine Poems, Devotions, Prayers.* Mount Vernon, NY: Peter Pauper Press.

1956 *The Songs and Sonets of John Donne*, ed. Theodore Redpath. London: Methuen (2nd edn 1983).

1958 *John Donne: Poems of Love*, ed. Kingsley Hart. London: Folio Society (uses text of the Oxford Standard Authors).
Selected Poems, ed. Mathias A. Shaaber, Croft's Classics. New York: Appleton–Century–Crofts.

1959 *Seventeenth Century English Poetry*, ed. R. C. Bald, Harper's English Series. New York: Harper & Bros.

1961 *John Donne Love Poems*, Pocket Poets. London: Vista Books.
The Metaphysical Poets [selections], ed. Helen Gardner. London: Oxford University Press.

1962 *Donne* [selection], ed. Andrews Wanning, Laurel Poetry Series. New York: Dell Publishing (frequently reprinted).

1964 *Donne* [selection], *The English Poets: Chaucer to Yeats*. London: Oxford University Press in association with the British Council

1965 *John Donne: The Elegies and the Songs and Sonnets*, ed. Helen Gardner. Oxford: Clarendon Press.

1966 *John Donne: Selected Poetry*, ed. Marius Bewley, Signet Classic Poetry Series. New York, Toronto and London: Signet.
John Donne's Poetry [authoritative texts, criticism], ed. Arthur L. Clements. London and New York: Norton (2nd edn 1991).

1967 *The Complete Poetry of John Donne*, ed. John R. Shawcross, Anchor Books. New York: Doubleday and Co.
John Donne: The Satires, Epigrams and Verse Letters, ed. W. Milgate, Oxford English Texts. Oxford: Clarendon Press.
John Donne: Poetry and Selected Prose, ed. P. J. Warnke. New York: Modern Library

1969 *Poems by J. D. with Elegies on the Author's Death*. Menston, York. (Facsimile of the first edition of 1633).

1970 *The Selected Poems of John Donne*, ed. Frank Kermode. New York: Heritage Press.

1971 *John Donne: The Complete English Poems*, ed. A. J. Smith, Penguin Educational Poetry. Harmondsworth: Penguin (revised edition 1973; reprinted a number of times).
John Donne: Poetical Works, ed. Herbert J. C. Grierson. London: Oxford University Press (uses his 1933 text).
The Epithalamions, Anniversaries and Epicedes, ed. W. Milgate. Oxford: Clarendon Press.

1982   *The Love Poems of John Donne*, ed. Charles Fowkes. New York: St Martin's Press, 1982; London: Macmillan, 1983.

1983   *Selected Poems*, ed. Phillip Mallett. Harlow: Longman.

1985   *The Complete English Poems of John Donne*, ed. C. A. Patrides, Everyman's Library. London: J. M. Dent and Sons.

      Four Metaphysical Poets: An Anthology of Poetry by Donne, Herbert, Marvell and Vaughan, ed. Richard Willmott. Cambridge: Cambridge University Press.

1986   *Selected Poetry and Prose*, ed. T. W. and R. J. Craik, Methuen English Texts. London: Methuen.

      Holy Sonnets, introd. Clare Gaster. Winchester: Alembic.

1988   *The First and Second Dalhousie Manuscripts* [poems and prose selections, facsimile edn], ed. Ernest W. Sullivan. Columbia: University of Missouri Press.

      John Donne, ed. Peter Porter, Illustrated Poets. London: Aurum Press.

1990   *John Donne*, ed. John Carey, Oxford Authors. Oxford: Oxford University Press.

      John Donne: Selected Poems, ed. Richard Gill, Oxford: Oxford University Press.

      Selections from Divine Poems, Sermons, Devotions and Prayers, ed. John Booty. New York.

1992   *Variorum Edition of the Poetry of John Donne*, vol. VIII: *The Anniversaries and the Epicedes and Obsequies*, ed. G. A. Stringer. Columbia: University of Missouri Press.

1993   *Donne*, Bloomsbury Classics Poetry. London: Bloomsbury Publishers.

1994   *The Complete English Poems*, ed. C. A. Patrides; updated by Robin Hamilton. Everyman's Library. London: J. M. Dent and Sons.

Appendix B. Poems by Donne known to have been set to music since 1872

Anniversarie, The (All Kings and all their favourites) David Cox, *The Humours of Love: Three Songs for Tenor and Piano.* London: Mills Music, 1962.

At the round earths imagin'd corners (i) C. H. H. Parry, *Songs of Farewell,* motet. London, 1917.

(ii) William Brocklesby Wordsworth, *Four Sacred Sonnets* (1944). London: A. Lengnick and Co., 1946.

(iii) Benjamin Britten, *The Holy Sonnets of John Donne,* op. 35, high voice and piano. London and New York: Boosey and Hawkes (*c.* 1946; reprinted 1951).

(iv) Howard Boatwright, MS, voice and piano. New Haven, April 1954.

(v) Dorian LeGallienne, *Four Divine Poems of John Donne.* Melbourne: Allans, 1967.

(vi) Geoffrey Burgon, soprano (or tenor), trumpet and organ. London: J. and W. Chester, 1971.

(vii) B. Kelly, cantata, tenor solo, SATB, piano. London: Musical Times, 1977.

(viii) Francis Routh, unaccompanied voices, 1978.

(ix) Michael Berkeley, anthem for soprano and baritone soloists, chorus, organ and optional trumpet, 1982.

Baite, The (Come live with mee and bee my love) David Cox, *The Humours of Love: Three Songs for Tenor and Piano.* London: Mills Music, 1962.

Batter my heart (i) Douglas Stuart Moore, *Three Sonnets of John Donne Set to Music for High Voice and Piano.* New York: G. Schirmer Inc., 1944.

(ii) William Brocklesby Wordsworth, *Four Sacred Sonnets* (1944). London: A. Lengnick and Co., 1946.

(iii) Benjamin Britten, *The Holy Sonnets of John Donne*, op. 35, high voice and piano. London and New York, Boosey and Hawkes (*c.* 1946; reprinted 1951).

(iv) Dorian LeGallienne, *Four Divine Poems of John Donne*. Melbourne: Allans, 1967.

(v) Lennox Berkeley, soprano solo, choir, oboe, cellos, double-basses and organ. (*c.* 1962). London: J. And W. Chester, 1963.

(vi) Mervyn Burtch, *Three Sonnets of John Donne: for Four-Part Choir of Mixed Voices Unaccompanied*. Aylesbury: Roberton Publications, 1976.

Breake of Day (i) Peter Warlock (lost), 1918.

(ii) Vivian Fine, *Four Elizabethan Songs for Voice and Piano*. New York, 1938.

(ii) Harl McDonald, Philadelphia, Elkan-Vogel Co. Inc, 1939.

(iii) *Poèmes de Donne, Herbert et Crashaw mis en musique par leurs contemporains G. Coprario, A. Ferrabosco, J. Wilson, W. Corkine, J. Hilton,* transcription et réalisation par André Souris d'après des recherches effectuées sur les sources par John Cutts; introduction par Jean Jacquot, Editions du Centre National de la Recherche Scientifique 15, Quai Anatole-France Paris, 1961. (Seven settings for poems by Donne: 'Breake of Day' by William Corkine.)

Computation, The Hale Smith, *Two Love Songs for Soprano and Nine Instruments*. New York: Independent Music Publishers, 195?

Confined Love (i) Hale Smith, *Two Love Songs for Soprano and Nine Instruments*. New York, Independent Music Publishers, 195?

Crosse, The Sir Henry Walford Davies, *Noble Numbers: Poems by Robert Herrick, George Herbert, John Donne and an Anonymous Writer for Solo Voice, Chorus, Violin and Orchestra*, op. 28, written for the Hereford Festival 1909. London: Novello and Co., 1909.

Death be not proud (i) Douglas Stuart Moore, *Three Sonnets of John Donne Set to Music for High Voice and Piano*. New York: G. Schirmer Inc., 1944.

(ii) William Brocklesby Wordsworth, *Four Sacred Sonnets* (1944). London: A. Lengnick and Co., 1946.

(iii) Benjamin Britten, *The Holy Sonnets of John Donne*, op. 35, high voice and piano. London and New York: Boosey and Hawkes [*c.* 1946; reprinted 1951].

(iv) Dorian LeGallienne, *Four Divine Poems of John Donne*. Melbourne: Allans, 1967.

(v) Fenno Heath, four-part chorus of men's voices a cappella, 1963.

(vi) Donald Jenni, four-part chorus of mixed voices with chimes and piano accompaniment, 1975.

(vii) Mervyn Burtch, *Three Sonnets of John Donne: for Four-Part Choir of Mixed Voices Unaccompanied*. Aylesbury: Roberton, 1976.

Devotions (A statue of snowe) (A flowre at sun-rising) (Poor intricated soule) (The seasons of his mercies) Richard Rodney Bennett, London: Universal, 1975.

Elegies (i) Daniel Pinkham, Jr, *Four Elegies* [Herrick, Crashaw, Vaughan, Donne], soloists, mixed chorus, orchestra, 1975.

Expiration, The (So, so breake off this last lamenting Kisse) *Poèmes de Donne, Herbert et Crashaw mis en musique par leurs contemporains G. Coprario, A. Ferrabosco, J. Wilson, W. Corkine, J. Hilton*, transcription et réalisation par André Souris d'après des recherches effectuées sur les sources par John Cutts; introduction par Jean Jacquot, Editions du Centre National de la Recherche Scientifique 15, Quai Anatole-France Paris, 1961. (Seven settings for poems by Donne: 'The Expiration' by Alfonso Ferrabosco.)

Flea, The Ernst Krenek, high voices and piano (1960). London: British and Continental Music Agencies, 1964.

Good-morrow, The (i) Bernard George Stevens, *Three Songs: The Words by John Donne*. London: Oxford University Press, 1948.

(ii) Donald McWhinnie, voice and piano, 194?

(iii) Malcolm Arnold, *Two John Donne Songs*, op. 114. Aylesbury: Roberton Publications, 1977.

(iv) Giles Swayne, mezzo-soprano, piano, 1971; first performance London 1979.

Holy Sonnets (i) John Charles Eaton, *Holy Sonnets*, soprano, piano/orchestra, 1957.

(ii) John Tavener, *Three Holy Sonnets*, baritone, two horns, two trombones, strings, 1962.

Hymne to Christ, A Elizabeth Maconchy, tenor, piano, 1965, broadcast by the BBC 1966.

Hymne to God the Father, A (i) Edgar L. Bainton, chorus and orchestra, first performed at the Three Choirs Festival, Worcester, September 1926. London: Oxford University Press, 1926.

(ii) Pelham Humphrey [Humfrey, *Harmonia Sacra*, 1688], arranged from the figured base by Michael Tippet and Walter Bergmann. London: Schott; New York: Associated Music Publishers, 1947.

(iii) *Poèmes de Donne, Herbert et Crashaw mis en musique par leurs contemporains G. Coprario, A. Ferrabosco, J. Wilson, W. Corkine, J. Hilton,* transcription et réalisation par André Souris d'après des recherches effectuées sur les sources par John Cutts; introduction par Jean Jacquot, Editions du Centre National de la Recherche Scientifique 15, Quai Anatole-France Paris, 1961. (Seven settings for poems by Donne: 'A Hymne to God the Father' by John Hilton.)

(iv) Edmund Rubbra, motet for unaccompanied choir, 1964.

(v) Elizabeth Maconchy, tenor, piano, 1965, broadcast by the BBC 1966.

(vi) John McCabe, anthem for SATB choir, 1966.

(vii) Dorian LeGallienne, *Four Divine Poems of John Donne.* Melbourne, Allans, 1967.

(viii) Guy Henry Eldridge, anthem for four-part chorus of mixed voices, unaccompanied. Aylesbury: Roberton, 1974.

(ix) Alec Wyton. London: Novello, 1978.

(x) John Joubert, op. 114, mixed voices unaccompanied. London: Novello, 1989. (First performed by the Finzi singers in July 1987 at the Summer Festival of English Music, Radley College.)

La Corona (i) Henry Fusner, for tenor solo, mixed chorus, oboe, harp, and strings. Vocal score with organ accompaniments. Roselle Park, NJ, *c.* 1912.

(ii) A. Didier Graeffe, *Seven Sonnets,* mixed chorus a cappella, *Seventeenth Century News,* 10: 1 (1952), special supplement.

La Corona – Nativitie (i) Ernst Krenek, *La Corona,* cantata for mezzo-soprano, baritone, organ, percussion, 1941.

(ii) Barry O'Neal, mixed voices a cappella. Associated Music, 1974.

(iii) Arthur Wills, Oecumuse, 1986.

Litanie XV (From being anxious, or secure) (i) Ernst Krenek, *Five Prayers for Women's Voices over the Pater Noster as Cantus Firmus* (1944). London: Universal Edition, 1954.

Litanie XVI (From needing danger, to bee good) (i) Ernst Krenek, *Five Prayers for Women's Voices over the Pater Noster as Cantus Firmus* (1944). London: Universal Edition, 1954.

(ii) Richard Rodney Bennett, *Verses No. 1,* for chorus a cappella. London: Universal, 1965.

Litanie XX (Through thy submitting all) (i) Ernest Krenek, *Five*

Prayers for Women's Voices over the Pater Noster as Cantus Firmus (1944). London: Universal Edition, 1954.

(ii) Richard Rodney Bennett, *Verses No. 2*, for chorus a cappella. London: Universal, 1965.

Litanie XXIII (Heare us, O heare us Lord) (i) Ernst Krenek, *Five Prayers for Women's Voices over the Pater Noster as Cantus Firmus* (1944). London: Universal Edition, 1954.

(ii) Cecil Cope, Elkin, 1962.

(iii) Richard Rodney Bennett, *Verses No.3*, for chorus a cappella. London: Universal, 1965.

(iv) Lee Hoiby, anthem for mixed voices and organ. Broude: Breitkopf und Härtel, 1979.

(v) Anthony Piccolo, Royal School of Church Music, 1980.

Litanie XXVII (That learning, thine Ambassador) (i) Ernst Krenek, *Five Prayers for Women's Voices over the Pater Noster as Cantus Firmus* (1944). London: Universal Edition, 1954.

Love's Growth Ross Lee Finney, *Three Love Songs* (1948). South Hadley, MA: Valley Music Press, 1957.

Message, The (Send home my longe strayd eyes to mee) (i) William Flanagan, 1949.

(ii) *Poèmes de Donne, Herbert et Crashaw mis en musique par leurs contemporains G. Coprario, A. Ferrabosco, J. Wilson, W. Corkine, J. Hilton,* transcription et réalisation par André Souris d'après des recherches effectuées sur les sources par John Cutts; introduction par Jean Jacquot, Editions du Centre National de la Recherche Scientifique 15, Quai Anatole-France Paris, 1961. (Seven settings for poems by Donne: 'The Message' by Giovanni Coprario).

Nocturnal (i) Havergal Brian, *Three Songs*, op.6, for contralto or baritone c. 1901–6; performed ?1905; published 1913.

(ii) Richard Rodney Bennett, soprano, piano, 1954.

(iii) Iain Hamilton, for eleven solo voices (1959). London: Schott, 1963.

O my blacke soule! (i) Benjamin Britten, *The Holy Sonnets of John Donne*, op. 35, high voice and piano. London and New York: Boosey and Hawkes (*c.* 1946; reprinted 1951).

(ii) Mervyn Burtch, *Three Sonnets of John Donne: for Four-Part Choir of Mixed Voices Unaccompanied.* Aylesbury: Roberton, 1976.

O Holy Ghost Ernst Krenek, for four-part chorus a cappella. Berlin: Bärenreiter, 1965.

O might those sighes and teares Benjamin Britten, *The Holy Sonnets* *of John Donne*, op. 35, high voice and piano. London and New York: Boosey and Hawkes (*c.* 1946; reprinted 1951).

Oh, to vex me Benjamin Britten, *The Holy Sonnets of John Donne*, op. 35, high voice and piano. London and New York: Boosey and Hawkes (*c.* 1946; reprinted 1951).

Since she whom I loved Benjamin Britten, *The Holy Sonnets of John Donne*, op. 35, high voice and piano. London and New York: Boosey and Hawkes (*c.* 1946; reprinted 1951).

Songs (i) John Joubert, *Five Songs* [Chapman, Donne, anon.], op. 5, tenor, piano: 1951.

(ii) Elizabeth Maconchy, *Three Donne Songs*, tenor, piano, 1966.

(iii) Ezra Sims, *Five Songs* [Nashe, Herrick, Fletcher, Ford, Donne], alto, viola, 1979.

Song (Goe, and catche a falling starre) (i) Bernard George Stevens, *Three Songs: The Words by John Donne*. London: Oxford University Press, 1948.

(ii) William Flanagan, high voices and piano. New York: Peer International, 1949.

(iii) Lee Hoiby, tenor and piano. London and New York: Boosey and Hawkes.

(iv) *Poèmes de Donne, Herbert et Crashaw mis en musique par leurs contemporains G. Coprario, A. Ferrabosco, J. Wilson, W. Corkine, J. Hilton*, transcription et réalisation par André Souris d'après des recherches effectuées sur les sources par John Cutts; introduction par Jean Jacquot, Editions du Centre National de la Recherche Scientifique 15, Quai Anatole-France Paris, 1961. (Seven settings for poems by Donne: 'Goe and catch a falling star' by anon.).

(v) David Cox, *The Humours of Love: Three Songs for Tenor and Piano*. London: Mills Music, 1962.

(vi) Colin Brumby, *The English Songs*. Sydney, 1979.

Song: Sweetest love, I do not go (i) Bernard George Stevens, *Three Songs: The Words by John Donne*. London: Oxford University Press, 1948.

(ii) Bryan Kelly, baritone voice and piano. London: Novello, 1961.

(iii) and (iv) *Poèmes de Donne, Herbert et Crashaw mis en musique par leurs contemporains G. Coprario, A. Ferrabosco, J. Wilson, W. Corkine, J. Hilton*, transcription et réalisation par André Souris d'après des recherches effectuées sur les sources par John Cutts; introduction par Jean Jacquot, Editions du Centre National de la Recherche

Scientifique 15, Quai Anatole-France Paris, 1961. (Seven settings for poems by Donne: 'Sweetest love' by anon.).

Sonnets Geoffrey Burgon, *Five Sonnets of John Donne*, soprano, mezzo-soprano, flute, oboe, clarinet, horn, piano, timpani, cello, 1967.

Stay O Sweet (i) M. Davidson, med. voice and piano. London, 1923.

(ii) Geoffrey Bush, in *Three Elizabethan Songs*. London: Novello, 1948.

Sunne Rising, The Elizabeth Maconchy, 1966; broadcast by BBC 1966.

Thou hast made me (i) Douglas Stuart Moore, *Three Sonnets of John Donne Set to Music for High Voice and Piano*. New York: G. Schirmer Inc., 1944.

(ii) William Brocklesby Wordsworth, *Four Sacred Sonnets* (1944). London: A. Lengnick and Co., 1946.

(iii) Benjamin Britten, *The Holy Sonnets of John Donne*, op. 35, high voice and piano. London and New York: Boosey and Hawkes (*c.* 1946; reprinted 1951).

(iv) Lennox Berkeley, for mixed choir and organ. Chester, 1960.

Valedictions Vivian Fine, *Valedictions*, soprano, tenor, mixed chorus, ten instruments, 1959.

Valediction: Forbidding Mourning, A Ross Lee Finney, *Three Love Songs*. South Hadley, Mass: Valley Music Press, 1957.

Valediction: Of Weeping, A Ross Lee Finney, *Three Love Songs*, South Hadley, Mass: Valley Music Press, 1957.

What if this present Benjamin Britten, *The Holy Sonnets of John Donne*, op. 35, high voice and piano. London and New York: Boosey and Hawkes (*c.* 1946; reprinted 1951).

Woman's Constancy (Now thou hast lov'd me) Malcolm Arnold, *Two John Donne Songs*, op. 114, Aylesbury: Roberton, 1977.

Appendix C: Select Bibliography

Many of the sources listing references to Donne's poetry or tracing the currency of his poems in the twentieth century were included in A. J. Smith's Bibliography at the back of vol. 1. of the Critical Heritage series, *Donne*. There are three more recent volumes that in particular need to be added to the list:

John Donne: An Annotated Bibliography of Modern Criticism 1912–1967, ed. John R. Roberts, Columbia: University of Missouri Press, 1973.

John Donne: An Annotated Bibliography of Modern Criticism 1968–1978, ed. John R. Roberts, Columbia and London: University of Missouri Press, 1982.

Deborah Aldrich Larson, *John Donne and Twentieth-Century Criticism*, London and Toronto: Associated University Presses, 1989.

There is also the *John Donne Journal: Studies in the Age of Donne*, published twice a year since 1982 by the English Department of North Carolina State University, Raleigh.

Index

Bradford on 54–5; De la Mare on 363; Dowden on 34–5; Eaton on 371–2, 376; Garnett on 160; Gosse on xxix–x, 142–3; Grierson on 318, 339–40; Jackson on 399; Lynd on 430; Minto on 6–7; Norton on 249; Sanders on 197; Stephens on 162, 164
Petrarch xxxii; Grierson on 261–3, 277, 285, 288, 325, 329, 333, 438; Nethercot on 455; Quiller-Couch on 404; Reed on 347; Schelling on 310
Petronius 209
Phillpis, Catherine xli
'Physics of metaphysic' begs defence' see Pope, Gosse on
'Phoenix and Turtle' (Shakespeare) 448
Picavet, François Joseph **400–1**
Piccolo, Anthony 471
'Picture, The' xxiv, 41, 285
Pinkham, Daniel 469
Plato 265, 331, 339, 408, 409
platonic love: Collins on 21–2; Courthope on 233; Dowden on xxiv, 44–6; Grierson on 260, 286; Harrison on 240–1; Lynd on 426–8; Spurgeon on 266–7; see also friendship; love
Plotinus 241, 267
Poems and Songs (Flatman) 152
Poetical Blossoms (Cowley) 307
Pope, Alexander xxvi, xxx; Anon on 367; Bradford on 54; Gosse on 52, 64, 69, 155; Grierson on 278, 283, 439; Norton on 74, 75; Saintsbury on 91, 92, 93, 118; Stephen on 169
Porter, Endymion 81
Porter, Peter 466
'Portrait, The' 85
portrait of Donne in shroud 51, 182, 205, 431
Pound, Ezra **396**
Prayer (Herbert) 213
Preludes (Patmore) xxiv, 45

Present in Absence 226
'Primrose, The' 235, 286, 303, 326, 427
Prior, Matthew 93
Problems 8, 105, 292
'Progress of the Soul, Of the' see *Second Anniversary*
'Progress of the Soul, The' (unfinished fragment) see *Metempsychosis*
'Prohibition, The' 86, 201, 263, 337
prose works: Grierson on 292–3, 319; Saintsbury on 119; Stephen on 168–9; see also *Biathanatos*; *Essays*; *Pseudo-Martyr*; *Sermons*
Provence 212, 233
Pseudo-Martyr 63, 283, 291, 292, 319

Quarles, Francis 231
Quarterly Review xxx, 109–13, 206–13, 216–17, 422–3
Quiller-Couch, Sir Arthur **401–4**
Quiver (journal) 15

Racine, Jean 446
Raleigh, Sir Walter 140, 334, 419
Ramsay, Mary Paton **398–9**, 401
Randolph, Thomas 24
Rapture, The (Carew) 285
realism: Gosse on 148, 149, 151; Grierson on 320–1, 330–1; lack of, Morley on 1; Pearsall Smith on 410; Schelling on 305; Wendell on 243
Redpath, Theodore xv, 465
Reed, Edward Bliss **344–50**
Reeves, James 464
'Refusal to allow his Young Wife to accompany him abroad as a Page' *38, 66, 95, 189, 202*
Regnier, Mathurin 29
Relic, The: Bradford on 55–6; Dowden on *45–6*; Eaton on *379*; Eliot on 443, 459; Furst on 86; Grierson on 263, *286*; 326; Lang on 351; Lowes on *415*;

THE CRITICAL HERITAGE SERIES

GENERAL EDITOR: B.C. SOUTHAM

GEORGE GISSING	Pierre Coustillas and Colin Partridge
OLIVER GOLDSMITH	G.S. Rousseau
THOMAS HARDY	R.G. Cox
GEORGE HERBERT	C.A. Patrides
GERARD MANLEY HOPKINS	Gerald Roberts
BEN JONSON	D.H. Craig
SAMUEL JOHNSON	James T. Boulton
JOHN KEATS	G.M. Matthews
SIR THOMAS MALORY	Marylyn Parins
CHRISTOPHER MARLOWE	Millar MacLure
ANDREW MARVELL	Elizabeth Story Donno
GEORGE MEREDITH	Ioan Williams
JOHN MILTON 1628–1731	John T. Shawcross
JOHN MILTON 1732–1801	John T. Shawcross
WILLIAM MORRIS	Peter Faulkner
WALTER PATER	R.M. Seiler
ALEXANDER POPE	John Barnard
EARL OF ROCHESTER	David Farley-Hills
JOHN RUSKIN	J.L. Bradley
SIR WALTER SCOTT	John O. Hayden
WILLIAM SHAKESPEARE 1623–1692	Brian Vickers
WILLIAM SHAKESPEARE 1693–1733	Brian Vickers
WILLIAM SHAKESPEARE 1733–1752	Brian Vickers
WILLIAM SHAKESPEARE 1753–1765	Brian Vickers
WILLIAM SHAKESPEARE 1765–1774	Brian Vickers
WILLIAM SHAKESPEARE 1774–1801	Brian Vickers
PERCY BYSSHE SHELLEY	James E. Barcus
PHILIP SIDNEY	Martin Garrett
JOHN SKELTON	Anthony S.G. Edwards
TOBIAS SMOLLETT	Lionel Kelly
ROBERT SOUTHEY	Lionel Madden
EDMUND SPENSER	R.M. Cummings
LAWRENCE STERNE	Alan B. Howes
ROBERT LOUIS STEVENSON	Paul Maixner
JONATHAN SWIFT	Kathleen Williams
ALGERNON SWINBURNE	Clyde K. Hyder

PHILIP SIDNEY

Printed in the United States
by Baker & Taylor Publisher Services